W9-BGX-450

BASIC ECONOMETRICS

BASIC ECONOMETRICS

Damodar Gujarati
Bernard Baruch College
City University of New York

McGraw-Hill Book Company

New York St. Louis San Francisco Auckland Bogotá Düsseldorf
Johannesburg London Madrid Mexico Montreal New Delhi Panama
Paris São Paulo Singapore Sydney Tokyo Toronto

This book was set in Times Roman. The editors were J. S. Dietrich and Frances A. Neal; the cover was designed by John Hite; the production supervisor was Dominick Petrellese. The drawings were done by Fine Line Illustrations, Inc. Fairfield Graphics was printer and binder.

BASIC ECONOMETRICS

34567890 FGRFGR 7832109

Library of Congress Cataloging in Publication Data

Gujarati, Damodar.
    Basic econometrics.

    Bibliography: p.
    Includes indexes.
    1. Econometrics. I. Title.
HB139.G84   330′.01′82   77-11931
ISBN 0-07-025182-7

CONTENTS

* This is an optional chapter.

PART 2 Violations of the Assumptions of the Classical Model

9 Multicollinearity

10 Heteroscedasticity

11 Autocorrelation

PART 3 Topics in Econometrics

PART 4   Simultaneous-Equations Models

Appendixes 389

PREFACE

The primary objective of *Basic Econometrics* is to provide an elementary but comprehensive introduction to the art and science of econometrics, a field which is becoming increasingly an integral part of training in business and economics.

The book assumes no matrix algebra, calculus, or statistics beyond the elementary level, and it is directed to three classes of readers, namely, junior and senior level undergraduates, beginning graduate students in these disciplines who do not have much prior training in econometrics, and researchers in business, industry, and government who are looking for an informal yet systematic treatment of econometric methods.

Basic ideas of econometrics are presented as simply and as directly as possible without recourse to advanced mathematics and mathematical statistics. Mathematical derivations are kept to an absolute minimum and are usually relegated to the appendixes. This is done deliberately so that the beginner can get a feel for the subject without becoming bogged down in mathematical derivations. The basic philosophy of the book is that econometrics, although grounded in higher mathematics and mathematical statistics, can be taught to the beginner in such a manner that he or she can acquire a fairly good intuitive feeling about the field.

There are several distinguishing features of this book. It is written in very simple and understandable language: matrix algebra or calculus is not essential to follow the text. On the principle of "learning by doing," each econometric technique is illustrated by charts, tables, and real-life economic data. Thus, the reader is made aware of the situations in which a particular economic method is appropriate. The practitioner will find Parts II and III of the text especially appealing. These parts discuss what may be called the "bread-and-butter" aspects of econometrics. Topics such as multicollinearity, heteroscedasticity, and auto-correlation, which are frequently encountered in practice, are discussed logically in a standard format, namely: What is the nature of the problem, what are its consequences, how does one find out whether a problem exists, and what can be done to remedy the problem? This step-by-step approach will help the researcher to solve a problem systematically.

The extensive and varied exercises at the end of each chapter will distinguish this book from many others; most of the currently available textbooks have very few exercises which are based on real economic data. In all there are about 230 exercises. Detailed solutions to all these exercises are given in the *Instructor's Manual*. Answers and hints to solutions of some 60 exercises are given at the end of the text.

I have included a fairly extensive bibliography which lists several advanced books and articles in econometrics. It is hoped that my book will whet the appetite of the reader so that he or she can approach some of the mathematically advanced material given in the advanced textbooks with less apprehension.

This text can be used in several ways as follows:

Courses in Econometrics

A two-semester course: Chapters 1 to 18, Appendixes A and B. (If matrix algebra is not required, Chapter 8 and Appendix B can be omitted.)

A one-semester course: Chapters 1 to 11, Appendixes A and B. (Again Chapter 8 and Appendix B are optional if matrix approach is not used.)

Courses in Regression Analysis

A one-semester course: Chapters 1 to 11, Appendixes A and B. (Chapter 8 and Appendix B are optional if matrixes are not used.)

A short course of one quarter (about 7 to 8 weeks): Chapters 1 to 7 and Appendix A. (If matrix approach is included, add Chapter 8 and Appendix B.)

In writing this book I have received help from several people. My foremost thanks go to Professor Ann R. Horowitz of the University of Florida and my colleague Professor Albert Zucker. Ann Horowitz's searching and very constructive comments have substantially improved the organization and quality of the text. Al Zucker spent countless hours in the reading of the manuscript and making very valuable suggestions both as to the style and substance. My colleagues, Professors Peter Gutmann, Jay Lee, and Vincent Su, made some very useful suggestions on various chapters, and I am grateful to them. I am also indebted to Professor Giles Burgess of the Portland State University, Professor Ramu Ramanathan of the University of California at San Diego, and Professor Bernard J. Marks of Wichita State University, who read the book in manuscript form and made several constructive suggestions to improve the quality of the text. Needless to say, none of these people are responsible for any deficiencies that may remain. I would also like to acknowledge my debt to my students who read the book while it was in preparation and offered constructive suggestions to improve the substance and form of the topics covered in the text. I am much indebted to my research assistant Joan Rahav for all her help. Finally, my thanks are due to my editor J. Stephen Dietrich and his associate Diane DeLuca for all their behind-the-scene help and encouragement.

Damodar Gujarati

INTRODUCTION

1 WHAT IS ECONOMETRICS?

Literally interpreted, *econometrics* means "economic measurement." Although measurement is an important part of econometrics, the scope of econometrics is much broader, as can be seen from the following quotations.

Econometrics, the result of a certain outlook on the role of economics, consists of the application of mathematical statistics to economic data to lend empirical support to the models constructed by mathematical economics and to obtain numerical results.[1]

. . . econometrics may be defined as the quantitative analysis of actual economic phenomena based on the concurrent development of theory and observation, related by appropriate methods of inference.[2]

Econometrics may be defined as the social science in which the tools of economic theory, mathematics, and statistical inference are applied to the analysis of economic phenomena.[3]

Econometrics is concerned with the empirical determination of economic laws.[4]

---

[1] Gerhard Tintner, *Methodology of Mathematical Economics and Econometrics*, The University of Chicago Press, Chicago, 1968, p. 74.
[2] P. A. Samuelson, T. C. Koopmans, and J. R. N. Stone, "Report of the Evaluative Committee for *Econometrica*," *Econometrica*, vol. 22, no. 2, April 1954, pp. 141–146.
[3] Arthur S. Goldberger, *Econometric Theory*, John Wiley & Sons, Inc., New York, 1964, p. 1.
[4] H. Theil, *Principles of Econometrics*, John Wiley & Sons, Inc., New York, 1971, p. 1.

2 WHY A SEPARATE DISCIPLINE?

As the preceding definitions suggest, econometrics is an amalgam of economic theory, mathematical economics, economic statistics and mathematical statistics. Yet, it is a subject that deserves to be studied in its own right for the following reasons.

Economic theory makes statements or hypotheses that are mostly qualitative in nature. For example, microeconomic theory states that, other things remaining the same, a reduction in the price of a commodity is expected to increase the quantity demanded of that commodity. Thus, economic theory postulates a negative or inverse relationship between the price and quantity demanded of a commodity. But the theory itself does not provide any numerical measure of the relationship between the two; that is, it does not tell by how much the quantity will go up or down as a result of a certain change in the price of the commodity. It is the job of the econometrician to provide such numerical estimates. Stated differently, it is econometrics that gives empirical content to most economic theory.

The main concern of mathematical economics is to express economic theory in mathematical form (equations) without regard to measurability or empirical verification of the theory. Econometrics, as noted previously, is mainly interested in the empirical verification of economic theory. As we shall see, the econometrician often uses the mathematical equations proposed by the mathematical economist but puts these equations in such a form that they lend themselves to empirical testing. And this conversion of mathematical into econometric equations requires a great deal of ingenuity and practical skill.

Economic statistics is mainly concerned with collecting, processing, and presenting economic data in the form of charts and tables. This is the job of the economic statistician. It is he or she who is primarily responsible for collecting data on GNP, employment, unemployment, prices, etc. The data thus collected constitute the raw data for econometric work. But the economic statistician does not go any further, not being concerned with using the collected data to test economic theories. Of course, one who does that becomes an econometrician.

Although mathematical statistics provides many of the tools used in the trade, the econometrician often needs special methods in view of the unique nature of most economic data, namely, that the data are not generated as the result of a controlled experiment. The econometrician, like the meteorologist, generally depends on data that cannot be controlled directly. Thus, data on consumption, income, investment, savings, prices, etc., which are collected by public and private agencies, are nonexperimental data. The econometrician takes these data as given. This creates special problems not normally dealt with in mathematical statistics. Moreover, such data are likely to contain errors of measurement, and the econometrician may be called upon to develop special methods of analysis to deal with such errors of measurement.

3 METHODOLOGY OF ECONOMETRICS

To illustrate the methodology of econometrics, let us consider the keynesian theory of consumption. Keynes states:

> The fundamental psychological law ... is that men [women] are disposed, as a rule and on average, to increase their consumption as their income increases, but not by as much as the increase in their income.[5]

In short, Keynes postulates that the marginal propensity to consume (MPC), the rate of change of consumption for a unit (say, a dollar) change in income, is greater than 0 but less than 1. To test this theory, the econometrician may proceed as follows.

Specification of the Econometric Model

Although Keynes postulates a positive relationship between consumption and income, he does not specify the precise form of the functional relationship between the two. For simplicity, a mathematical economist may suggest the following form for Keynes' consumption function:

$$Y = \alpha + \beta X \tag{1}$$

where Y = consumption expenditure
  X = income
  α, β = constants or parameters

The slope coefficient β represents the MPC.

Equation (1), which states that consumption is linearly related to income, is an example of a mathematical model. A model is simply a set of mathematical equations. If the model has only one equation, as in the preceding example, it is called a *single-equation model*, whereas if it has more than one equation, it is known as a *multiequation* or *simultaneous-equation model*.

The purely mathematical model of the consumption function given in (1) is, however, of limited interest to the econometrician for it assumes that there is an exact or deterministic relationship between consumption and income. But relationships between economic variables are generally inexact. Thus, if we were to obtain data on consumption expenditure and disposable (after-tax) income of a sample of, say, 5000 American families and plot these data on a graph paper with consumption expenditure on the vertical axis and disposable income on the horizontal axis, we would not expect all 5000 observations to lie exactly on the straight line of equation (1). This is because in addition to income there are other variables which also affect consumption expenditure. For example, size of family, ages of the members in the family, family religion, etc., are likely to exert some influence on consumption.

---

[5] John Maynard Keynes, *The General Theory of Employment, Interest and Money*, Harcourt Brace Jovanovich, Inc., New York, 1936, p. 96.

To allow for the inexact relationships between economic variables, the econometrician would modify the deterministic consumption function (1) as follows:

$$Y = \alpha + \beta X + u \tag{2}$$

where u, known as the *disturbance*, or *error*, term, is a random (stochastic) variable which has well-defined probabilistic properties. The disturbance term u may represent all those forces that affect consumption but are not taken into account explicitly.

Equation (2) is an example of an econometric model. More technically, (2) is an example of a linear regression model, which is a major concern of this book. The econometric consumption function (2) hypothesizes that the dependent variable Y (consumption) is linearly related to the explanatory variable X (income), but the relationship between the two is not exact; it is subject to individual variation.

Estimation

Having specified the econometric model, the next task of the econometrician is to obtain estimates (numerical values) of the parameters of the model from the data available; these data may be provided by the economic statistician. These estimates give empirical content to economic theory. Thus, if in a study of the keynesian consumption function given previously it is found that $\beta = 0.8$, this value not only provides a numerical estimate of MPC, but also supports Keynes' hypothesis that MPC is less than 1.

How does one estimate the parameters, such as α and β? An answer to this question will be provided in the following chapters. Suffice it to note here that the statistical tool of regression analysis is the main technique used in this book to obtain the estimates.

Verification (Statistical Inference)

Having obtained estimates of the parameters, the next task of the econometrician is to develop suitable criteria to find out whether the estimates obtained are in conformity with the expectations of the theory that is being tested. As noted previously, Keynes expected the MPC to be positive but less than 1. Suppose in a study of the consumption function it is found that the MPC = 0.9. Although numerically this estimate is less than 1, one may enquire whether the estimate is sufficiently below unity to convince us that this is not an accidental outcome of sampling process. In other words, is this estimate statistically less than 1? If it is, it supports Keynes' contention; otherwise it may refute it.

Such confirmation or refutation of economic theories on the basis of empirical evidence is based on a branch of statistical theory known as *statistical inference* (hypothesis testing). Throughout this book we shall see how this inference process is actually conducted.

Forecasting or Prediction

A frequent usage of the estimated econometric model is the prediction of future value(s) of the dependent variable on the basis of known or expected future value(s) of the explanatory variable(s). For example, suppose that the government is contemplating a reduction in the personal income tax to stimulate the sagging economy. What will be the effect of this policy on consumption expenditure (and thereby on employment and income)?

As macroeconomic theory shows, the change in the consumption expenditure following, say, a dollar's worth of change in income is given by the *consumption multiplier M*, which is defined as $M = [1/(1 - \text{MPC})]$. If MPC = 0.8, M will be 5, meaning that if income increases by a dollar it will ultimately lead to a fivefold increase in the consumption expenditure. The critical value in this computation is the consumption multiplier, which depends on the (value of) MPC. Thus, a quantitative estimate of MPC provides valuable information for policy purposes. Knowing MPC, one can predict the future course of consumption following changes in the government's fiscal policies.

As the preceding example illustrates, an econometric inquiry generally proceeds along the following lines:

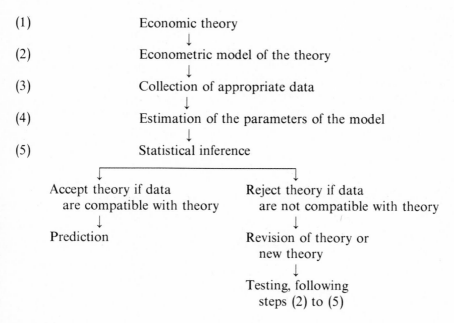

(1)   Economic theory
                             ↓

(2)   Econometric model of the theory
                             ↓

(3)   Collection of appropriate data
                             ↓

(4)   Estimation of the parameters of the model
                             ↓

(5)   Statistical inference

Accept theory if data   Reject theory if data
   are compatible with theory   are not compatible with theory
           ↓   ↓
     Prediction   Revision of theory or
                                   new theory
                                       ↓
                           Testing, following
                           steps (2) to (5)

4 TYPES OF ECONOMETRICS

Broadly speaking, econometrics may be divided into two categories: *theoretical econometrics* and *applied econometrics*. Theoretical econometrics is concerned with the development of appropriate methods for measuring economic relationships specified by econometric models. In this aspect, econometrics leans heavily on mathematical statistics. For example, one of the tools that is used extensively in this book is the method of least squares. It is the concern of theoretical econometrics to spell out the assumptions of this method, its properties, and what happens to these properties when one or more of the assumptions of the method are not fulfilled.

In applied econometrics we use the tools of theoretical econometrics to study some special field(s) of economics, such as the production function, consumption function, investment function, demand and supply functions, etc.

This book is concerned largely with the development of econometric methods, their assumptions, their uses, and their limitations. These methods are illustrated with suitable examples from various areas of economics and business. But this is not a book on applied econometrics in the sense that it delves deeply into any particular field of economic application. That job is best left to the books that are written specifically for this purpose.[6]

5 MATHEMATICAL AND STATISTICAL PREREQUISITES

Although this book is written at an elementary level, it is assumed that the reader is familiar with elementary statistics, especially with the basic concepts of statistical estimation and hypothesis testing. However, a broad overview of some of the statistical concepts used in this book is given in App. A for the benefit of those who want to freshen up their knowledge. Insofar as mathematics is concerned, a nodding acquaintance with the notions of differential calculus is desirable, although not essential. Matrix algebra is used in Chap. 8, which is optional. However, it is hoped that with the knowledge of matrix algebra given in App. B, the reader will not have great difficulty in following Chap. 8.

6 PLAN OF THIS BOOK

This book is divided into four parts. Parts I to III deal with single-equation regression models, i.e., models in which the behavior of a variable Y (the dependent variable) is explained by one or more variables, the X's (the explanatory variables). In Part I we present the classical linear regression model and develop the method of least squares and spell out its assumptions. In Part II we find out what happens to the properties of the method of least squares if one or more of its assumptions are not fulfilled and what alternative methods of estimation are available. Part III presents some special topics in econometrics which are designed to handle some of the problems that may be unique to economics. In

---

[6] See, for instance, J. S. Cramer, *Empirical Econometrics*, North-Holland Publishing Company, Amsterdam, 1969.

Part IV we consider the special features of simultaneous-equations models and discuss some of the methods specifically designed to estimate the parameters of such models.

In each part there are several chapters which develop various econometric techniques. Each new technique is illustrated with suitable examples from economics and business.

The exercises given at the end of each chapter are an integral part of the book. Some of the problems involve routine calculations, but some are theoretical in nature and shed additional light on the material discussed in the chapter. It is hoped that the reader will attempt most of the exercises for they will test his or her grasp of the theory. Answers to a few selected exercises are given at the end of the text.

A word on the notation used in this book is in order. Each chapter is divided into sections, which are numbered serially within each chapter. Thus, Sec. 5.3 means the third section of Chap. 5. Equations in each chapter are identified by the chapter number followed by the section and the equation number, all in parentheses. Thus, (3.5.8) means the eighth equation in Sec. 5 of Chap. 3.

Wherever an asterisk appears, it means the material is optional. The book is written so that there is no loss of continuity if the asterisked material is omitted.

ONE

SINGLE-EQUATION
REGRESSION MODELS

Part I of this text introduces single-equation regression models. In these models, one variable, called the *dependent variable*, is expressed as a linear function of one or more other variables, called the *explanatory variables*. In such models it is assumed implicitly that causal relationships, if any, between the dependent and explanatory variables flows in one direction only, namely, from the explanatory variables to the dependent variable.

In Chap. 1, we discuss the historical as well as the modern interpretation of the term *regression* and illustrate the difference between the two interpretations with several examples drawn from economics and other fields.

In Chap. 2, we introduce some fundamental concepts of regression analysis with the aid of the two-variable linear regression model, a model in which the dependent variable is expressed as a linear function of only a single explanatory variable.

In Chap. 3, we continue to deal with the two-variable model and introduce what is known as the *classical linear regression model*, a model that makes several simplifying assumptions. With these assumptions, we introduce the method of *ordinary least squares* (OLS) to estimate the parameters of the two-variable regression model. The method of OLS is simple to apply, and yet it has some very desirable statistical properties.

In Chap. 4, we intioduce the (two-variable) classical *normal* linear regression model, a model which assumes that the random dependent variable follows the normal probability distribution. With this assumption, the OLS estimators obtained in Chap. 3 possess some stronger statistical properties than the nonnormal classical linear regression model—properties which enable us to engage in statistical inference, namely, hypothesis testing.

Chapter 5 is devoted to the topic of hypothesis testing. In this chapter, we try to find out whether the estimated regression coefficients are compatible with the hypothesized values of such coefficients, the hypothesized values being suggested by theory and/or prior empirical work.

In Chap. 6, we consider the multiple regression model, a model in which there is more than one explanatory variable and show how the method of OLS can be extended to estimate the parameters of such models.

In Chap. 7, we extend the concepts introduced in Chap. 5 to the multiple regression model and point out some of the complications arising from the introduction of several explanatory variables.

Chapter 8, an optional chapter, summarizes the developments of the first seven chapters in terms of matrix algebra. Although matrix notation does not introduce any new concepts, it provides a very compact method of presenting regression theory involving any number of explanatory variables.

ONE

THE NATURE OF REGRESSION ANALYSIS

As mentioned in the Introduction, regression is a main tool of econometrics, and in this chapter we consider very briefly the nature of this tool.

1.1 HISTORICAL ORIGIN OF THE TERM "REGRESSION"

The term *regression* was introduced by Francis Galton. In a famous paper, Galton found that although there was a tendency for tall parents to have tall children and for short parents to have short children, the distribution of heights of a population did not change substantially from generation to generation.[1] His explanation was that there was a tendency for the *average* height of children with parents of a given height to move or *regress* toward the average height of the entire population. Galton's *law of universal regression* was confirmed by his friend Karl Pearson, who collected more than a thousand records of heights of members of family groups.[2] He found that the average height of sons of a group of tall fathers was less than their fathers' height and the average height of sons of a group of short fathers was greater than their fathers' height, thus "regressing" tall and short sons alike toward the average height of all men. In the words of Galton, this was "regression to mediocrity."

[1] Francis Galton, "Family Likeness in Stature," *Proceedings of Royal Society, London*, vol. 40, 1886, pp. 42–72.
[2] K. Pearson and A. Lee, *Biometrika*, vol. 2, 1903, p. 357.

1.2 THE MODERN INTERPRETATION OF REGRESSION

The modern interpretation of regression is, however, quite different. Broadly speaking,

> Regression analysis is concerned with the study of the dependence of one variable, the *dependent variable*, on one or more other variables, the *explanatory variables*, with a view to estimating and or predicting the (population) mean or average value of the former in terms of the known or fixed (in repeated sampling) values of the latter.

The full import of this view of regression analysis will become clearer as we progress, but a few simple examples will make the basic concept quite clear.

Examples

1. Reconsider Galton's law of universal regression. Galton was interested in finding out why there was a stability in the distribution of heights in a population. But in the modern view our concern is not with this explanation but rather to find out how the *average* height of sons changes, given the fathers' height. In other words, our concern is with predicting the average height of sons knowing the height of their fathers. To see how this can be done, consider Fig. 1.1 which is a *scatter diagram*, or *scattergram*.

   The figure shows the distribution of heights of sons in a hypothetical population corresponding to the given or fixed values of the fathers' height. Notice that corresponding to any given height of a father, there is a range (distribution) of the

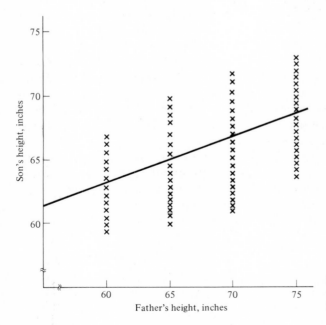

Figure 1.1 Hypothetical distribution of sons' heights corresponding to given heights of fathers.

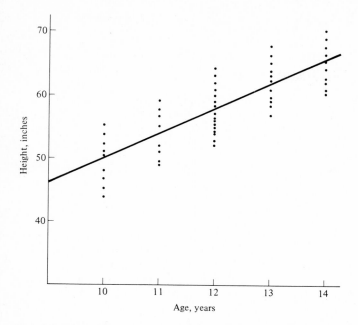

Figure 1.2 Hypothetical distribution of heights corresponding to selected ages.

heights of the sons. However, notice that the average height of sons increases as the height of the fathers increases. To see this clearly, we have sketched through the scatter points a straight line which shows how the average height of the sons increases with the fathers' height. This line, as we shall see, is known as the *regression line.*[3] Note that this line has a positive slope; but the slope is less than 1, which is in conformity with Galton's regression to mediocrity. (Why?)

2. Consider the scattergram in Fig. 1.2, which gives the distribution of heights of boys measured at fixed ages in a hypothetical population. Notice that corresponding to any given age we have a range of heights. Obviously not all boys of a given age are likely to have identical heights. But height on the average increases with age (of course up to a certain age). Thus, knowing the age, we may be able to predict the average height corresponding to that age.

3. Turning to economic examples, an economist may be interested in studying the dependence of personal consumption expenditure on after-tax or disposable real personal income. Such an analysis may be helpful in estimating the marginal propensity to consume (MPC), that is, average change in consumption expenditure for, say, a dollar's worth of change in real income.

---

[3] At this stage of the development of the subject matter we shall call this regression line simply the *line of average relationship between the dependent variable (son's height) and the explanatory variable (father's height).*

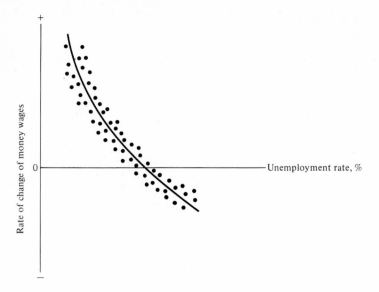

Figure 1.3 Hypothetical Phillips curve.

4. A monopolist who can fix the price or output (but not both) may want to find out the response of the demand for a product to changes in price. Such an experiment may enable the estimation of the price elasticity (i.e., price responsiveness) of the demand for the product and may help determine the most profitable price.

5. A labor economist may want to study the rate of change of money wages in relation to the unemployment rate. The historical data are shown in the scattergram given in Fig. 1.3. The curve shown in Fig. 1.3 is an example of the celebrated *Phillips curve* relating changes in the money wages to the unemployment rate. Such a scattergram may enable the labor economist to predict the average change in money wages given a certain unemployment rate. Such knowledge may be helpful in stating something about the inflationary process in an economy, for increases in money wages are likely to be reflected in increased prices.

6. An investment analyst, especially the technical analyst or chartist, may be interested in predicting the change in the price of a security knowing changes in some market index, such as the Dow-Jones index. If a predictable relationship between the two can be found, its advantages to the analyst and the investors are obvious.

7. The marketing director of a company may want to know how the demand for his product is related to, say, advertising expenditure. Such a study will be of considerable help in finding out the advertising expenditure elasticity of demand, that is, the average responsiveness of demand to, say, dollar's worth of increase in the advertising budget. This knowledge may be helpful in determining the "optimal" advertising budget.

8. Finally, an agronomist may be interested in studying the dependence of crop yield, say, of wheat, on temperature, rainfall, amount of sunshine, and fertility. Such a dependence analysis may enable the prediction or forecasting of the average crop yield, given information about the explanatory variables.

The reader can supply scores of such examples of the dependence of one variable on one or more other variables. And the techniques of regression analysis discussed in this text are specially designed to study such dependence among variables.

1.3 STATISTICAL VS. FUNCTIONAL DEPENDENCIES

From the examples cited in Sec. 1.2 the reader will notice that in regression analysis we are concerned with what is known as the *statistical*, not *functional or deterministic*, dependence among variables, such as those of classical physics. In statistical relationships among variables we essentially deal with *random* or *stochastic*[4] variables, that is, variables which have probability distributions. In functional or deterministic dependency, on the other hand, we also deal with variables, but these variables are not random or stochastic.

The dependency of crop yield on temperature, rainfall, sunshine, and fertility, for example, is statistical in nature in the sense that the explanatory variables, although certainly important, will not enable the agronomist to predict crop yield accurately because of errors involved in measuring these variables as well as a host of other factors (variables) which collectively affect the yield but may be difficult to identify individually. Thus there is bound to be some "intrinsic" or random variability in the dependent-variable crop yield, which cannot be fully explained no matter how many explanatory variables we consider.

In deterministic phenomena, on the other hand, we deal with relationships of the type, say, exhibited by Newton's law of gravity, which states: Every particle in the universe attracts every other particle with a force directly proportional to the product of their masses and inversely proportional to the square of the distance between them. Symbolically, $F = k(m_1 m_2 /r^2)$, where F = force, m_1 and m_2 are the masses of two particles, r = distance, and k = constant of proportionality. Another example is Ohm's law, which states: For metallic conductors over a limited range of temperature the current C is proportional to the voltage V; that is, $V/C = k$, where k is the constant of proportionality. Other examples of such deterministic relationships are Boyle's gas law, Kirchhoff's law of electricity, and Newton's law of motion.

In this text we are not concerned with such deterministic relationships. Of course, if there are errors of measurement, say, in the k of Newton's law of gravity, the otherwise deterministic relationship becomes a statistical relationship. For in

---

[4] The word "stochastic" comes from the Greek word *stokhos* meaning "a bull's eye." The outcome of throwing darts on a dart board is a stochastic process, that is, a process fraught with misses.

this situation force can be predicted only approximately from the given value of k (and m_1, m_2, and r) which contains errors. The variable F in this case becomes a random variable.

1.4 REGRESSION AND CAUSATION

Although regression analysis deals with the dependence of one variable on other variables, it does not necessarily imply causation. In the words of Kendall and Stuart: "A statistical relationship, however strong and however suggestive, can never establish causal connexion: our ideas of causation must come from outside statistics, ultimately from some theory or other."[5]

In the crop-yield example cited previously, there is no *statistical reason* to assume that rainfall does not depend on crop yield. The fact that we treat crop yield as dependent on rainfall (among other things) is due to nonstatistical considerations: Common sense suggests that the relationship cannot be reversed for we cannot control rainfall by varying crop yield.

In all the examples cited in Sec. 1.2 the point to note is that a statistical relationship per se cannot logically imply causation. To ascribe causality, appeal must be made to a priori or theoretical considerations. Thus, in the third example cited, one can invoke economic theory in saying that consumption expenditure depends on real income.

1.5 REGRESSION VS. CORRELATION

Closely related but conceptually very much different from regression analysis is *correlation analysis* where the primary objective is to measure the *strength* or *degree* of *linear association* between two variables. The *correlation coefficient*, which we shall study in detail in Chap. 3, measures this strength of (linear) association. For example, we may be interested in finding the correlation (coefficient) between smoking and lung cancer, between scores on statistics and mathematics examinations, between high school grades and college grades, and so on. In regression analysis, as already noted, we are not primarily interested in such a measure. Instead, we try to estimate or predict the average value of one variable on the basis of the fixed values of other variables. Thus we may want to know whether we can predict the average score on a statistics examination knowing a student's score on a mathematics examination.

The two techniques of regression and correlation have some fundamental differences which are worth mentioning. In regression analysis there is an asymmetry in the way the dependent and explanatory variables are treated. The depen-

[5] M. G. Kendall and A. Stuart, *The Advanced Theory of Statistics*, Charles Griffin Publishers, New York, 1961, vol. 2, chap. 26, p. 279.

dent variable is assumed to be statistical, random, or stochastic, that is, to have a probability distribution. The explanatory variables, on the other hand, are assumed to have fixed values (in repeated sampling),[6] which was made explicit in the definition of regression given in Sec. 1.2. Thus in Fig. 1.2 we assumed that the variable age was fixed at given levels and height measurements were obtained at these levels. In correlation analysis, on the other hand, we treat any (two) variables symmetrically; there is no distinction between the dependent and explanatory variables. After all, the correlation between scores on mathematics and statistics examinations is the same as that between scores on statistics and mathematics examinations. Moreover, both variables are assumed to be random. As we shall see, most of the correlation theory is based upon the assumption of randomness of variables, whereas most of the regression theory to be expounded in this book is conditional upon the assumption that the dependent variable is stochastic but the explanatory variables are fixed or nonstochastic.

1.6 TERMINOLOGY AND NOTATION

Before we proceed to a formal analysis of regression theory, let us dwell briefly on the matter of terminology and notation. In the literature the terms *dependent variable* and *explanatory variable* are described variously. A representative list is as follows:

Dependent variable   Explanatory variable

$\updownarrow$ $\updownarrow$

Explained variable   Independent variable

$\updownarrow$ $\updownarrow$

Predictand   Predictor

$\updownarrow$ $\updownarrow$

Regressand   Regressor

$\updownarrow$ $\updownarrow$

Response   Stimulus or control variable

Although it is a matter of personal taste and tradition, in this text we use the dependent-variable–explanatory-variable terminology.

If we are studying the dependence of a variable on only a single explanatory variable, such as that of consumption expenditure on real income, such a study is known as the *simple*, or *two-variable*, *regression analysis*. However, if we are studying the dependence of one variable on more than one explanatory variable, such

---

[6] It is crucial to note that the explanatory variables may be intrinsically stochastic, but for the purpose of regression analysis we assume that their values are fixed in repeated sampling (that is, X assumes the same values in various samples), thus rendering them in effect nonrandom or nonstochastic.

as the crop-yield, rainfall, temperature, sunshine, and fertilizer example, it is known as *multiple regression analysis*. In other words, in two-variable regression there is only one explanatory variable, whereas in multiple regression there is more than one explanatory variable.

The term *random* is a synonym for the term *stochastic*, which is itself a synonym for *probability*. As noted earlier, a random or stochastic variable is a variable which can take on any set of values, positive or negative, with a given probability.[7]

Unless stated to the contrary, the letter Y will denote the dependent variable and the X's $(X_1, X_2, \ldots, X_k)$ will denote the explanatory variables, X_k being the kth explanatory variable. The subscript i or t will denote the ith or tth observation or value. We shall generally use the subscript i for cross-section data, that is, data collected at one point in time, such as the census of population, survey of consumer expenditure periodically conducted by the University of Michigan, opinion polls such as those conducted by Gallup and Harris, etc. The subscript t will usually be used for time series data, that is, data collected over a period of time, such as Gross National Product, employment, unemployment, production, etc. X_{ki} (or X_{kt}) will denote the ith (or tth) observation on variable X_k. N will denote the total number of observations or values in the population or sample as the case may be.

1.7 THE ROLE OF THE COMPUTER IN REGRESSION ANALYSIS

In studying the dependence of one variable on one or more other variables, regression analysis often involves tedious and lengthy calculations. If the number of observations is very small, say, 10 to 15, these calculations can be done with a desk calculator or even with a pocket calculator thanks to the availability of pocket calculators that are well within the economic reach of the student. In most real problems involving a reasonably large number of observations and several explanatory variables, the modern electronic computer is almost a necessity. For speed, accuracy, flexibility, and versatility the desk or pocket calculator is no match for the computer. It is no exaggeration to say that in this day and age regression analysis is almost unthinkable without the computer; the two are inextricably wedded to each other.

Although with some training and practice one can write his or her own computer program (basically a set of instructions written in specialized machine readable language such as Fortran), in practice this is often not necessary, especially if the user is not interested in the mathematics of the programming per se. There are some excellent *packaged* or *canned* regression programs which can be used, depending upon the computing facilities at one's disposal. Appendix C gives

---

[7] See App. A for further details.

a list of some of the comprehensive canned regression programs, their sources, uses, limitations, etc. It is hoped that the reader will become familiar with some of these programs.

Most of the illustrative examples used in this book are solved with the aid of some of the packaged regression programs. To give the reader the flavor of what these programs do, we have reproduced the actual computer printouts of most of the illustrative examples given in Part I of this book. As the reader will soon see, it is usually not very difficult to read the computer printout even if he or she does not know all the details of the program used in the computations.

1.8 SUMMARY AND CONCLUSIONS

The purpose of this chapter was to introduce the basic nature of regression analysis as informally and as intuitively as possible. The key idea behind regression analysis is the statistical dependence of one variable, the dependent variable, on one or more other variables, the explanatory variables. The objective of such analysis is to estimate and/or predict the mean or average value of the dependent variables on the basis of the known or fixed values of the explanatory variables.

Although the theory and the mechanics of regression analysis will be discussed thoroughly in the following chapters, the reader is forewarned that regression analysis requires extensive use of the computer. Fortunately, readers need not worry about writing their own regression programs for some excellent packaged or canned regression programs are readily available and can be used with minimum efforts. Moreover, these packaged programs generally will handle most of the regression techniques discussed in this text.

TWO-VARIABLE REGRESSION ANALYSIS: SOME BASIC IDEAS

In Chap. 1 we discussed the concept of regression in more or less broad terms. In this chapter we approach the subject matter somewhat formally. Specifically, this and the following three chapters introduce the reader to the theory underlying the simplest possible regression analysis, namely, the two-variable case. This case is considered first, not necessarily because of its practical adequacy, but because it presents the fundamental ideas of regression analysis as simply as possible and some of these ideas can be illustrated with the aid of two-dimensional diagrams. Moreover, as we shall see, the more general multiple regression analysis is in many ways a logical extension of the two-variable case.

2.1 A HYPOTHETICAL EXAMPLE

As pointed out in Sec. 1.2, regression analysis is largely concerned with estimating and/or predicting the (population) mean or average value of the dependent variable on the basis of the known or fixed values of the explanatory variable(s). To understand how this is done, consider the following example.

Imagine a hypothetical country with a *total population* of 60 families. Suppose we are interested in studying the relationship between weekly family consumption expenditure Y and weekly after-tax or disposable family income X. More specifically, assume that we want to predict the (population) mean level of weekly consumption expenditure knowing the family's weekly income. To this end, suppose we divide these 60 families into 10 groups of approximately the same income and examine the consumption expenditures of families in each of these income

Table 2.1 Weekly family income X, \$

$Y \downarrow$ $X \rightarrow$	80	100	120	140	160	180	200	220	240	260
Weekly family	55	65	79	80	102	110	120	135	137	150
consumption	60	70	84	93	107	115	136	137	145	152
expenditure Y, \$	65	74	90	95	110	120	140	140	155	175
	70	80	94	103	116	130	144	152	165	178
	75	85	98	108	118	135	145	157	175	180
	$\cdots$	88	$\cdots$	113	125	140	$\cdots$	160	189	185
	$\cdots$	$\cdots$	$\cdots$	115	$\cdots$	$\cdots$	$\cdots$	162	$\cdots$	191
Total	325	462	445	707	678	750	685	1043	966	1211

groups. The hypothetical data are given in Table 2.1. (For the purpose of discussion, it is assumed that only the income levels given in Table 2.1 were actually observed.)

Table 2.1 is to be interpreted as follows: Corresponding to a weekly income of \$80, for example, there are five families whose weekly consumption expenditures range between \$55 and \$75. Similarly, given $X = \$240$, there are six families whose weekly consumption expenditures fall between \$137 and \$189. In other words, each column (vertical array) of Table 2.1 gives the distribution of consumption expenditure Y corresponding to a fixed level of income X; that is, it gives the *conditional distribution of Y* conditional upon the given values of X.

Noting that the data of Table 2.1 represent the population, we can easily compute the *conditional probabilities of Y $p(Y|X)$*, probability of Y given X, as follows. For $X = \$80$, for instance, there are five Y values: \$55, \$60, \$65, \$70, and \$75. Therefore, given $X = 80$, the probability of obtaining any one of these consumption expenditures is $\frac{1}{5}$. Symbolically, $p(Y = 55 | X = 80) = \frac{1}{5}$. Similarly, $p(Y = 150 | X = 260) = \frac{1}{7}$, and so on. The conditional probabilities for the data of Table 2.1 are given in Table 2.2.

Table 2.2 Conditional probabilities $p(Y|X_i)$ for the data of Table 2.1

$p(Y\|X_i) \downarrow$ $X \rightarrow$	80	100	120	140	160	180	200	220	240	260
Conditional	$\frac{1}{5}$	$\frac{1}{6}$	$\frac{1}{5}$	$\frac{1}{7}$	$\frac{1}{6}$	$\frac{1}{6}$	$\frac{1}{5}$	$\frac{1}{7}$	$\frac{1}{6}$	$\frac{1}{7}$
probabilities	$\frac{1}{5}$	$\frac{1}{6}$	$\frac{1}{5}$	$\frac{1}{7}$	$\frac{1}{6}$	$\frac{1}{6}$	$\frac{1}{5}$	$\frac{1}{7}$	$\frac{1}{6}$	$\frac{1}{7}$
$p(Y\|X_i)$	$\frac{1}{5}$	$\frac{1}{6}$	$\frac{1}{5}$	$\frac{1}{7}$	$\frac{1}{6}$	$\frac{1}{6}$	$\frac{1}{5}$	$\frac{1}{7}$	$\frac{1}{6}$	$\frac{1}{7}$
	$\frac{1}{5}$	$\frac{1}{6}$	$\frac{1}{5}$	$\frac{1}{7}$	$\frac{1}{6}$	$\frac{1}{6}$	$\frac{1}{5}$	$\frac{1}{7}$	$\frac{1}{6}$	$\frac{1}{7}$
	$\frac{1}{5}$	$\frac{1}{6}$	$\frac{1}{5}$	$\frac{1}{7}$	$\frac{1}{6}$	$\frac{1}{6}$	$\frac{1}{5}$	$\frac{1}{7}$	$\frac{1}{6}$	$\frac{1}{7}$
	$\cdots$	$\frac{1}{6}$	$\cdots$	$\frac{1}{7}$	$\frac{1}{6}$	$\frac{1}{6}$	$\cdots$	$\frac{1}{7}$	$\frac{1}{6}$	$\frac{1}{7}$
	$\cdots$	$\cdots$	$\cdots$	$\frac{1}{7}$	$\cdots$	$\cdots$	$\cdots$	$\frac{1}{7}$	$\cdots$	$\frac{1}{7}$
Conditional means of Y	65	77	89	101	113	125	137	149	161	173

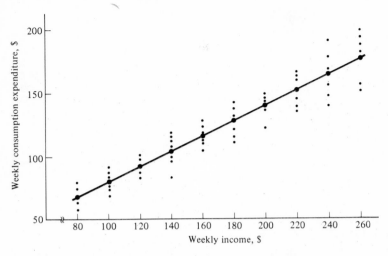

Figure 2.1 Conditional distribution of expenditure for various levels of income (data of Table 2.1).

Now for each of the conditional probability distributions of Y we can compute its mean or average value, known as the *conditional mean or conditional expectation*, denoted by $E(Y|X)$ and read as "the expected value of Y given X." (*Note:* An expected value is simply a population mean or average value.) For our hypothetical data, these conditional expectations can be easily computed by multiplying the relevant Y values given in Table 2.1 by their conditional probabilities given in Table 2.2 and summing up these products. As an illustration, the conditional mean or expectation of Y given $X = 80$ is $55(\frac{1}{5}) + 60(\frac{1}{5}) + 65(\frac{1}{5}) + 70(\frac{1}{5}) + 75(\frac{1}{5}) = 65$. The conditional means thus computed are given in the last row of Table 2.2.

Before proceeding further, it is instructive to see the data of Table 2.1 on a scattergram, as shown in Fig. 2.1. The scattergram shows the conditional distribution of Y corresponding to various X values. Although there are variations in individual family consumption expenditures, Fig. 2.1 shows very clearly that consumption expenditure *on the average* increases as income increases. Stated differently, the scattergram reveals that the (conditional) mean values of Y increase as X increases. This can be seen more vividly if we concentrate on the oversized points representing various conditional means of Y. The scattergram shows that these conditional means lie exactly on a straight line with a positive slope.[1] This line is known as a *regression line*, or, more generally, a *regression curve*. More precisely, it is the regression curve of Y on X.

Geometrically, then, a regression curve is simply a locus of the conditional means or expectations of the dependent variable for the fixed values of the explanatory variable(s). It can be depicted as in Fig. 2.2, which shows that for each X_i

---

[1] The reader should keep in mind the hypothetical nature of our data. It is not suggested here that the conditional means should always lie on a straight line; they may lie on a curve.

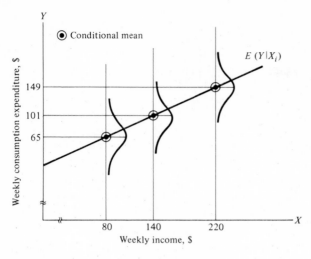

Figure 2.2 Regression line (data of Table 2.1).

there is a population of Y values (assumed to be normally distributed for reasons explained later) and a corresponding (conditional) mean. And the regression line or curve passes through these conditional means. With this interpretation of regression curve the reader might find it instructive to re-read the definition of regression given in Sec. 1.2.

2.2 THE CONCEPT OF POPULATION REGRESSION FUNCTION (PRF)

From the preceding discussion and especially Figs. 2.1 and 2.2, it is clear that each conditional mean $E(Y\mid X_i)$ is a function of X_i. Symbolically,

$$E(Y\mid X_i) = f(X_i) \tag{2.2.1}$$

where $f(X_i)$ denotes some function of the explanatory variable X_i. [In our hypothetical example, $E(Y\mid X_i)$ is a linear function of X_i.] Equation (2.2.1) is known as the (two-variable) *population regression function* (PRF), or *population regression* (PR) for short. It states merely that the (*population*) mean of the distribution of Y given X_i is functionally related to X_i. In other words, it tells how the (population) average value of Y varies with the X's.

What form does the function $f(X_i)$ assume? This question is important because in real situations we do not have the entire population available for examination. The functional form of the PRF is, therefore, an empirical question, although in specific cases theory may have something to say. For example, an economist might posit that consumption expenditure is linearly related to income. Therefore, as a first approximation or a working hypothesis, we may assume that the PRF $E(Y\mid X_i)$ is a linear function of X_i, say, of the type

$$E(Y\mid X_i) = \beta_0 + \beta_1 X_i \tag{2.2.2}$$

where β_0 and β_1 are unknown but fixed parameters known as the *regression coefficients*; β_0 and β_1 are also known as the *intercept* and *slope coefficient*, respectively. Equation (2.2.2) itself is known as the *linear population regression function*, or simply the *linear population regression*. Some alternative expressions used in the literature are linear population regression model or linear population regression equation. In the sequel, the terms *regression, regression equation,* and *regression model* will be used synonymously.

In regression analysis our interest is in estimating the PRFs like (2.2.2), that is, estimating the values of the unknowns β_0 and β_1 on the basis of observations on Y and X. This topic will be studied in detail in Chap. 3.

2.3 THE MEANING OF THE TERM "LINEAR"

Since this text is concerned primarily with linear models like (2.2.2), it is essential to know what the term *linear* really means for it can be interpreted in two different ways.

Linearity in the Variables

The first and perhaps more "natural" meaning of linearity is that the conditional expectation of Y is a linear function of X_i, such as, for example, (2.2.2).[2] Geometrically the regression curve in this case is a straight line. In this interpretation, a regression function such as $E(Y \mid X_i) = \beta_0 + \beta_1 X_i^2$ is not a linear function because the variable X appears with a power or index of 2.

Linearity in the Parameters

The second interpretation of linearity is that the conditional expectation of Y, $E(Y \mid X_i)$, is a linear function of the parameters, the β's; it may or may not be linear in the variable X.[3] In this interpretation, $E(Y \mid X_i) = \beta_0 + \beta_1 X_i^2$ is a linear regression model but $E(Y \mid X_i) = \beta_0 + \sqrt{\beta_1} X_i$ is not. [The latter is an example of nonlinear (in the parameters) regression model; we shall not deal with such models in this text.]

Of the two interpretations of linearity, linearity in the parameters is relevant for the development of the regression theory to be presented shortly. Therefore, *from now on the term "linear" regression will always mean a regression that is linear in the parameters, the β's; it may or may not be linear in the explanatory variables, the X's.* Schematically, we have Table 2.3. Thus, $E(Y \mid X_i) = \beta_0 + \beta_1 X_i$, which is linear both in the parameters and variable, is LRM, and so is $E(Y \mid X_i) = \beta_0 + \beta_1 X_i^2$, which is linear in the parameters but nonlinear in variable X.

---

[2] A function $Y = f(x)$ is said to be linear in X if X appears with a power or index of 1 only (that is, terms such as X^2, $\sqrt{X}$, and so on, are excluded) and is not multiplied or divided by any other variable (for example, $X \cdot Z$ or X/Z, where Z is another variable.)

[3] A function is said to be linear in the parameter, say, β_1, if β_1 appears with a power of 1 only and is not multiplied or divided by any other parameter (for example, $\beta_0 \beta_1$, β_1/β_0, and so on).

Table 2.3 Linear regression models

Model linear in parameters?	Model linear in variables?	
	Yes	No
Yes	LRM	LRM
No	NLRM	NLRM

Note: LRM = linear regression model
NLRM = nonlinear regression model

2.4 STOCHASTIC SPECIFICATION OF PRF

It is clear from Fig. 2.1 that as family income increases, family consumption expenditure on the average increases, too. But what about the consumption expenditure of an individual family in relation to its (fixed) level of income? It is obvious from Table 2.1 and Fig. 2.1 that an individual family's consumption expenditure does not necessarily increase as the income level increases. For example from Table 2.1 we observe that corresponding to the income level of $100 there is one family whose consumption expenditure of $65 is less than the consumption expenditures of two families whose weekly income is only $80. But notice that the *average* consumption expenditure of families with a weekly income of $100 is greater than the average consumption expenditure of families with a weekly income of $80 ($77 vs. $65).

What, then, can we say about the relationship between an individual family's consumption expenditure corresponding to a given level of income? We see from Fig. 2.1 that given the income level of X_i, an individual family's consumption expenditure is clustered around the average consumption of all families at that X_i, that is, around its conditional expectation. Therefore, we can express the *deviation* of an individual Y_i around its expected value as follows:

$$u_i = Y_i - E(Y \mid X_i)$$

or

$$Y_i = E(Y \mid X_i) + u_i \qquad (2.4.1)$$

where the deviation u_i is an unobservable random variable taking positive or negative values. Technically, u_i is known as the *stochastic disturbance*, or *stochastic error term*.

Equation (2.4.1) postulates that an individual family's expenditure, given its income level, is equal to the average consumption expenditure of all the families with that income level plus some amount, positive or negative, which is random. We shall examine shortly the nature of the disturbance term u_i, but for the moment assume that it is a surrogate or proxy for all the omitted or neglected variables which affect Y but are not (or for various reasons cannot) be included in the regression model.

If $E(Y | X_i)$ is assumed to be linear in X_i, as in (2.2.2), equation (2.4.1) may be written as

$$Y_i = E(Y | X_i) + u_i$$
$$= \beta_0 + \beta_1 X_i + u_i \tag{2.4.2}$$

Equation (2.4.2) posits that the conditional consumption expenditure of a family is linearly related to its income plus the disturbance term. Thus, the individual consumption expenditures given $X = \$80$ (see Table 2.1) can be expressed as

$$Y_1 = 55 = \beta_0 + \beta_1(80) + u_1$$
$$Y_2 = 60 = \beta_0 + \beta_1(80) + u_2$$
$$Y_3 = 65 = \beta_0 + \beta_1(80) + u_3 \tag{2.4.3}$$
$$Y_4 = 70 = \beta_0 + \beta_1(80) + u_4$$
$$Y_5 = 75 = \beta_0 + \beta_1(80) + u_5$$

Now if we take the expected value of (2.4.1) on both sides, we obtain

$$E(Y | X_i) = E[E(Y | X_i)] + E(u | X_i)$$
$$= E(Y | X_i) + E(u | X_i) \tag{2.4.4}$$

where use is made of the fact that the expected value of a constant is that constant itself.[4] Notice carefully that in (2.4.4) we have taken the conditional expectation, conditional upon the given X's.

Equation (2.4.4) implies that

$$E(u | X_i) = 0 \tag{2.4.5}$$

Thus the assumption that the regression line passes through the conditional means of Y (see Fig. 2.2) implies that the conditional mean values of u_i (conditional upon the given X's) are zero.

From the previous discussion it is clear (2.2.2) and (2.4.2) are equivalent forms if $E(u | X_i) = 0$.[5] But the stochastic specification (2.4.2) has the advantage that it clearly shows that besides income there are other variables which affect consumption expenditure and that an individual family's consumption expenditure cannot be fully explained only by the variable(s) included in the regression model.

---

[4] See App. A for a brief discussion of the properties of the expectation operator E. Note that $E(Y | X_i)$, X_i given, is a constant.

[5] As a matter of fact, in the method of least squares to be developed in Chap. 3 it is assumed explicitly that $E(u | X_i) = 0$.

2.5 THE NATURE OF THE STOCHASTIC DISTURBANCE TERM

As noted in Sec. 2.4, the disturbance term u_i is a surrogate for all those variables which are omitted from the model but which collectively affect Y. The obvious question is: Why not introduce these variables into the model explicitly? Stated otherwise: Why not develop a multiple regression model with as many variables as possible? The reasons are many.

1. The theory, if any, determining the behavior of Y may be, and often is, incomplete. We might know for certain that weekly income X influences weekly consumption expenditure Y, but we might be ignorant or unsure about the other variables affecting Y. Therefore, u_i may be used as a substitute for all the excluded or omitted variables from the model.

2. Even if we knew what some of the excluded variables are and therefore consider a multiple regression rather than a simple regression, we may not have quantitative information about these variables. It is a common experience in empirical analysis that the data we would ideally like to have often are not available. For example, in principle we could introduce family wealth as an explanatory variable in addition to the income variable to explain family consumption expenditure. But unfortunately, information on family wealth generally is not available. Therefore, we may be forced to omit the wealth variable from our model despite its great theoretical relevance in explaining consumption expenditure.

3. Assume in our consumption-income example that besides income X_1, the number of children per family X_2, sex X_3, religion X_4, education X_5, and geographical region X_6 also affect consumption expenditure. But it is quite possible that the joint influence of all or some of these variables may be so small and at best nonsystematic or random that as a practical matter and for cost considerations it does not pay to introduce them into the model explicitly. Hopefully, their combined effect can be treated as a random variable u_i.[6]

4. Even if we succeed in introducing all the relevant variables into the model, there is bound to be some "intrinsic" randomness in individual Y which cannot be explained no matter how hard we try. The disturbances, the u's, may very well reflect this intrinsic randomness.

5. Finally, following Occam's razor,[7] we would like to keep our regression model as simple as possible. If we can explain the behavior of Y "substantially" (in the sense of R^2 or the coefficient of determination to be considered in Chap. 3) with two or three explanatory variables and if our theory is not strong enough to suggest what other variables might be included, why introduce more variables? Let u_i represent all other variables. Needless to say, we should not exclude relevant and important variables just to keep the regression model simple.

---

[6] A further difficulty is that variables such as sex, education, religion, etc., are difficult to quantify.

[7] "That descriptions be kept as simple as possible until proved inadequate," *The World of Mathematics*, vol. 2, J. R. Newman (ed.), Simon & Schuster, Inc., New York, 1956, p. 1247.

For all the preceding reasons, the stochastic disturbances u_i assume an extremely critical role in regression analysis, which we shall see as we progress.

2.6 THE SAMPLE REGRESSION FUNCTION (SRF)

By confining our discussion so far to the population of Y values corresponding to the fixed X's, we have deliberately avoided sampling considerations (note that the data of Table 2.1 represent the population, not a sample). But it is about time to face up to the sampling problems. For most practical situations what we have is but a sample of Y values corresponding to some fixed X's. Therefore, our task now is to estimate the PRF on the basis of the sample information.

As an illustration, pretend that the population of Table 2.1 was not known to us and the only information we had was a randomly selected sample of Y values for the fixed X's as given in Table 2.4. Unlike Table 2.1, we now have only one Y value corresponding to the given X's; each Y (given X_i) in Table 2.4 is chosen randomly from similar Y's corresponding to the same X_i from the population of Table 2.1.

The question is: From the sample of Table 2.4 can we predict the average weekly consumption expenditure Y in the population as a whole corresponding to the chosen X's? In other words, can we estimate the PRF from the sample data? As the reader surely suspects, we may not be able to estimate the PRF "accurately" because of sampling fluctuations. To see this, suppose we draw another random sample from the population of Table 2.1, as presented in Table 2.5.

Plotting the data of Tables 2.4 and 2.5, we obtain the scattergram given in Fig. 2.3. In the scattergram two sample regression lines are drawn visually so as to "fit" the scatters reasonably well: SRF_1 is based on the first sample, and SRF_2 is based on the second sample. Which of the two regression lines represent the "true" population regression line? If we avoid the temptation of looking at Fig. 2.1, which purportedly represents the PR, there is no way we can be abso-

Table 2.4 A random sample from the population of Table 2.1

Y	X
70	80
65	100
90	120
95	140
110	160
115	180
120	200
140	220
155	240
150	260

Table 2.5 Another random sample from the population of Table 2.1

Y	X
55	80
88	100
90	120
80	140
118	160
120	180
145	200
135	220
145	240
175	260

lutely sure that either of the regression lines shown in Fig. 2.3 represents the true population regression line (or curve). The regression lines in Fig. 2.3 are known as the *sample regression lines*. Supposedly they represent the population regression line, but because of sampling fluctuations they are at best an approximation of the true PR.

Now, analogous to the PRF which underlies the population regression line, we can develop the concept of the *sample regression function* (SRF) to represent the sample regression line. The sample counterpart of (2.2.2) may be written as

$$\hat{Y}_i = \hat{\beta}_0 + \hat{\beta}_1 X_i \tag{2.6.1}$$

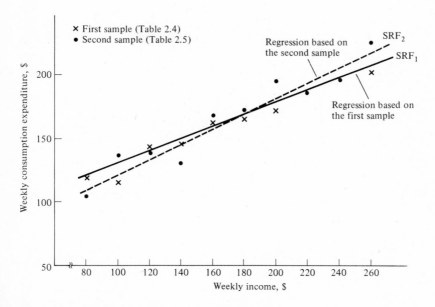

Figure 2.3 Regression lines based on two different samples

where $\wedge$ is read as "hat" or "cap"

$\hat{Y}_i$ = estimator of $E(Y \mid X_i)$

$\hat{\beta}_0$ = estimator of β_0

$\hat{\beta}_1$ = estimator of β_1

It may be noted that an estimator, also known as (sample) *statistic*, is simply a rule or formula or a method which tells how to estimate the population parameter from the information provided by the sample at hand. A particular numerical value obtained by the estimator in an application is known as an *estimate*.[8]

Now just as we expressed the PRF in two equivalent forms (2.2.2) and (2.4.2), we can express the SRF (2.6.1) in its stochastic form as follows:

$$Y_i = \hat{\beta}_0 + \hat{\beta}_1 X_i + e_i \qquad (2.6.2)$$

where, in addition to the symbols already defined, e_i denotes the (sample) *residual* term. Conceptually it is analogous to u_i and can be regarded as an *estimate* of u_i. It is introduced in the SRF for the same reasons as u_i was introduced in the PRF.

To sum up, then, our primary objective in regression analysis is to estimate the PRF

$$Y_i = \beta_0 + \beta_1 X_i + u_i \qquad (2.4.2)$$

on the basis of the SRF

$$Y_i = \hat{\beta}_0 + \hat{\beta}_1 X_i + e_i \qquad (2.6.2)$$

because more often than not our analysis is based upon a sample from some population. But because of sampling fluctuations our estimate of the PRF based on the SRF is at best an approximate one. This approximation is shown diagrammatically in Fig. 2.4.

For $X = X_i$, we have one (sample) observation $Y = Y_i$. In terms of the SRF, the observed Y_i can be expressed as

$$Y_i = \hat{Y}_i + e_i \qquad (2.6.3)$$

and in terms of the PRF, it can be expressed as

$$Y_i = E(Y \mid X_i) + u_i \qquad (2.6.4)$$

Now obviously in Fig. 2.4 $\hat{Y}_i$ *overestimates* the true $E(Y \mid X_i)$ for the X_i shown therein. By the same token, for any X_i to the left of the point A, the SRF will *underestimate* the true PRF. But the reader can readily see that such over- and underestimation is inevitable due to sampling fluctuations.

---

[8] Hereafter $\wedge$ above a variable will signify an estimator or estimate of the relevant population value.

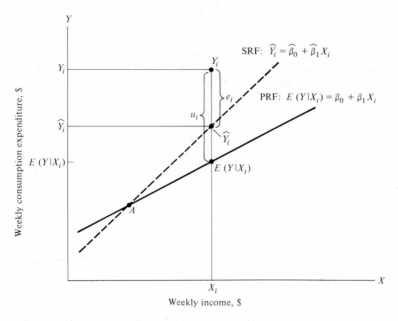

Figure 2.4 Sample and population regression lines

The critical question now is: Granted that the SRF is but an approximation of the PRF, can we devise a rule or a method which will make this approximation as "close" as possible? In other words, how should the SRF be constructed so that $\hat{\beta}_0$ is as "close" as possible to the true β_0 and $\hat{\beta}_1$ is as "close" as possible to the true β_1?

The answer to this question will occupy much of our attention in Chap. 3. Suffice it to note here that we can develop procedures which tell us how to construct the SRF to mirror the PRF as "faithfully" as possible. It is fascinating to consider that this can be done even though we never actually determine the PRF itself.

2.7 SUMMARY AND CONCLUSIONS

In this chapter we discussed some of the fundamental ideas of regression analysis. Starting with the key concept of the population regression function (PRF), we developed the concept of linear PRF. Most of this book is devoted to linear PRFs, that is, regressions which are linear in the unknown parameters regardless of whether they are linear in the variables. We then introduced the idea of stochastic PRF and discussed in detail the nature and the role of the stochastic disturbance term u_i. PRF is, of course, a theoretical or idealized construct because in practice all we have is only a sample(s) from some population. This necessitated the discussion of the sample regression function (SRF). It is the SRF which enables us to estimate the PRF. How this is accomplished is the subject matter of Chap. 3.

EXERCISES

2.1 The following table gives the joint probability distribution, $p(x, y)$, of variables X and Y.

Y \ X	1	2	3
1	0.06	0.06	0.06
2	0.02	0.04	0.04
3	0.09	0.18	0.18
4	0.06	0.12	0.12

Using the definitions given in App. A, determine the
  (a) Marginal or unconditional probability distributions of X and Y.
  (b) Conditional probability distributions $p(X \mid Y_i)$ and $p(Y \mid X_i)$.
  (c) Conditional expectations $E(X \mid Y_i)$ and $E(Y \mid X_i)$.

2.2 For 50 married couples the ages (in years) of wife X and husband Y are grouped in the following table with class intervals of 10 years for each, the frequencies for the different classes being shown in the body of the table. The values of X and Y shown are the midvalues in the classes.

Y \ X	20	30	40	50	60	70	Total
20	1						1
30	2	11	1				14
40		4	10	1			15
50			3	6	1		10
60				2	3	2	7
70					1	2	3
Total	3	15	14	9	5	4	50

Thus, for the class in which the age of the husband is between 35 and 45 and the age of the wife is between 25 to 35, the values of Y and X are taken (as centered on) 40 and 30, respectively, and the frequency is 4.
  (a) Determine the mean of each array, that is, of each row and each column.
  (b) Using the abscissa for the X variable and the ordinate for the Y variable, plot the array (or conditional) means obtained previously. You may use + symbol for the column means and 0 for the row means.
  (c) What can you say about the relationship between X and Y?
  (d) Do the conditional row and column means lie on straight lines approximately? Sketch the regression lines visually.

2.3 Consider the following data:

Median salaries of economists in selected age and experience groups, national register, 1966

Median salary (thousands of dollars)

Age	\multicolumn{10}{c}{Years of professional experience}
	0–2	2–4	5–9	10–14	15–19	20–24	25–29	30–34	35–39	40–44†
20–24	7.5									
25–29	9.0	9.1	10.0							
30–34	9.0	9.5	11.0	12.6						
35–39		10.0	11.7	13.2	15.0					
40–44		9.6	11.0	13.0	15.5	17.0				
45–49				12.0	15.0	17.0	20.0			
50–54				11.3	13.3	15.0	18.2	20.0		
55–59						13.8	16.0	18.0	19.0	
60–64							13.1	16.0	17.2	18.8
65–69									13.8	17.0
70–74‡										12.5

Note: Selected groups comprise all those represented by 25 or more respondents who reported the indicated combinations of age and experience.

† The actual category is 40 or more.

‡ The actual category is 70 and over.

Source: N. Arnold Tolles and Emanuel Melichar, "Studies of the Structure of Economists' Salaries and Income," *American Economic Review*, vol. 57, no. 5, pt. 2, Suppl., December 1968, table H, p. 119.

(*a*) What do the preceding data suggest?

(*b*) Is age or experience more closely related to salary level? How do you know?

(*c*) Draw two separate figures, one showing median salary in relation to age and another showing median salary in relation to professional experience (in years).

2.4 Examine the following data:

Economists with Ph.D. degrees: median salaries in three types of employment by years of professional experience, national register, 1966

\multicolumn{4}{l}{Median salary (thousands of dollars) per calendar year}
Years of experience	Educational institutions	Federal government	Industry or business
0–2	10	...	...
2–4	11	12	...
5–9	12	13	15.6
10–14	14	15.2	18.0

(*continued*)

(*continued*)

Median salary (thousands of dollars) per calendar year			
Years of experience	Educational institutions	Federal government	Industry or business
15–19	15	17.6	20.0
20–24	16.3	18.4	24.0
25–29	18.0	20.0	25.0
30–34	17.4	20.6	25.5
35–39	17.5	...	...
40–44†	18.0	...	...

† The actual category is 40 or more.

Source: N. Arnold Tolles and Emanuel Melichar, "Studies of the Structure of Economists' Salaries and Income," *American Economic Review*, vol. 57, no. 5, pt. 2, Suppl., December 1968, tables III B-13 and 14, p. 113.

(*a*) What general conclusions do you draw?

(*b*) Using the X axis for years of experience and the Y axis for the median salary, sketch visually regression curves relating median salary to years of experience for the three types of employment shown in the preceding table.

2.5 Examine the following table:

Median salaries of economists by academic degrees

Median salary, 1966 (thousands of dollars)			
Years of experience	Ph.D.	Masters	Bachelors
Under 2	9.8	8.0	9.0
2–4	10.0	8.8	8.9
5–9	11.5	10.5	10.6
10–14	13.0	12.3	13.0
15–19	15.0	15.0	15.6
20–24	16.2	15.6	17.0
25–29	18.0	17.0	20.0
30–34	17.9	17.7	20.0
35–39	16.9	16.2	20.5
40–44†	17.5	14.2	22.0

† The actual category is 40 or more.

Source: N. Arnold Tolles and Emanuel Melichar, "Studies of the Structure of Economists' Salaries and Income," *American Economic Review*, vol. 57, no. 5, pt. 2, Suppl., December 1968, table III-B-3, p. 92.

(*a*) Plot the median salaries for the three groups against the midvalues of the various years of experience intervals and visually sketch the regression lines.

(*b*) What factors account for the differences in the salaries of the three groups of economists? Especially, why is it that economists with bachelor's degrees earn more than their Ph.D. counterparts for 15 or more years of experience? Does this imply that it does not pay to hold a Ph.D. degree?

2.6 Consider the following table.

Number of economists by years of experience and age (full-time professionally employed economists only)

Age group (years)	Years of experience						
	2	2–4	5–9	10–14	15–19	20–24†	Total
20–24	24	13	1	⋯	⋯	⋯	38
25–29	121	405	184	⋯	⋯	⋯	710
30–34	77	407	825	197	3	⋯	1599
35–39	18	125	535	780	194	1	1653
40–44	6	36	161	652	761	235	1851
45–49	1	15	48	183	433	751	1431
50–54	1	5	19	52	119	784	980
55–59	1	2	10	18	27	612	670
60–64	1	⋯	3	6	8	382	400
65–69	⋯	1	1	2	4	206	214
70–74‡	⋯	⋯	⋯	⋯	1	27	28
Total	250	1099	1787	1890	1550	2998	9574

† The actual category is 20 or more.
‡ The actual category is 70 or over.
   Source: Adapted from "The Structure of Economists' Employment and Salaries, 1964," *American Economic Review*, vol. 55, no. 4, December 1965, table VII, p. 40.

The preceding table gives the joint absolute frequencies of the variables age and years of experience. Using relative frequencies (absolute frequencies divided by the total number) as measures of probabilities:

   (*a*) Obtain the joint probability distribution of age and years of experience.
   (*b*) Obtain the conditional probability distributions of age for various years of experience.
   (*c*) Obtain the conditional probability distribution of years of experience for various ages.
   (*d*) Using the midpoints of the various age and years of experience intervals, obtain the conditional means from the distributions derived in (*b*) and (*c*).
   (*e*) Draw appropriate scattergrams showing the various conditional means.
   (*f*) If you connect the conditional means shown in (*e*), what do you obtain?
   (*g*) What can you say about the relationship between years of experience and age?

2.7 Determine whether the following models are linear in the parameters, or the variables, or both. Which of these models are linear regression models?

(*a*) $Y_i = \beta_0 + \beta_1 \dfrac{1}{X_i} + u_i$
(*b*) $\ln Y_i = \beta_0 + \beta_1 X_i + u_i$
(*c*) $Y_i = \beta_0 + \beta_1 \ln X_i + u_i$
(*d*) $\ln Y_i = \ln \beta_0 + \beta_1 \ln X_i + u_i$
(*e*) $Y_i = \beta_0 X_i^{\beta_1} + u_i$
(*f*) $Y_i = \beta_0 + \beta^3 X_i + u_i$
(*g*) $Y_i = \beta_0 + (0.75 - \beta_0)e^{-\beta_1(X_i - 2)} + u_i$
Note: $\ln$ = natural log, (i.e., log to the base e); u_i is the stochastic disturbance term.

THREE

TWO-VARIABLE REGRESSION MODEL: THE PROBLEM OF ESTIMATION

As noted in Chap. 2, our first task is to estimate the population regression function (PRF) on the basis of the sample regression function (SRF) as accurately as possible. Now there are several methods of constructing the SRF, but insofar as regression analysis is concerned, the method that is used most extensively is the *method of ordinary least squares* (OLS).[1] In this chapter we shall discuss this method in terms of the two-variable regression model. The generalization of the method to multiple regression models is given in Chap. 6.

3.1 THE METHOD OF ORDINARY LEAST SQUARES

The method of ordinary least squares is due to Carl Friedrich Gauss, a German mathematician. Under certain assumptions, the method of OLS has some very attractive statistical properties which has made it one of the most powerful and popular methods of regression analysis.

To illustrate the gaussian approach, let us revert to the two-variable PRF:

$$Y_i = \beta_0 + \beta_1 X_i + u_i \qquad (2.4.2)$$

---

[1] Another method, known as the *method of maximum likelihood*, will be considered very briefly in Chap. 4.

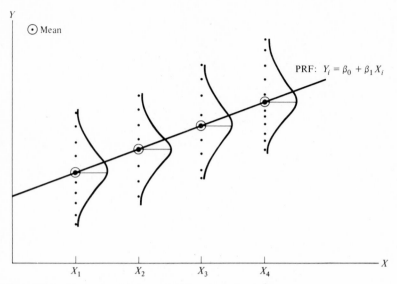

Figure 3.1 Conditional distribution of the disturbances u_i.

Gauss makes the following assumptions:

Assumption 1

$$E(u_i \mid X_i) = 0 \qquad (3.1.1)$$

In words, this assumption states that the conditional expected value of u_i, conditional upon the given X_i, is zero. Geometrically, this assumption can be pictured as in Fig. 3.1, which shows a few values of the variable X and the Y populations associated with each of the X's. As shown, each Y population corresponding to a given X is distributed around its mean value (shown by the circled point on the PRF) with some Y values above the mean value and some below it. The distances of these points above and below the mean values are nothing but the u_i, and what (3.1.1) requires is that the average or mean value of these deviations corresponding to any given X_i should be zero.[2]

Assumption 2

$$
\begin{aligned}
\text{cov}\,(u_i, u_j) &= E[u_i - E(u_i)][u_j - E(u_j)] \\
&= E(u_i u_j) \qquad \text{because of Assumption 1} \\
&= 0 \qquad\qquad i \neq j \qquad\qquad (3.1.2)
\end{aligned}
$$

where i and j are two different observations and where cov means the covariance.

---

[2] For illustration, we are assuming merely that the u's are distributed symmetrically as shown in Fig. 3.1. But in Chap. 4 we shall assume that the u's are distributed normally.

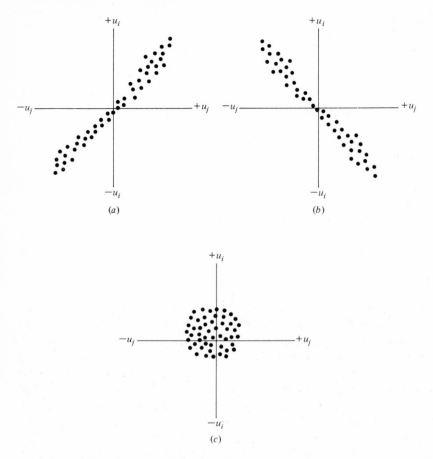

Figure 3.2 Patterns of correlation among the disturbances. (*a*) Positive serial correlation. (*b*) Negative serial correlation. (*c*) Zero correlation.

In words, (3.1.2) postulates that the disturbances u_i and u_j are uncorrelated. Technically, this assumption is known as the *assumption of no serial correlation*, or *no autocorrelation*. What this means is that, given X_i, the deviations of any two Y values from their mean value do not exhibit patterns such as those shown in Fig. 3.2*a* and *b*. In Fig. 3.2*a* we see that the u's are *positively correlated*, a positive u followed by a positive u or a negative u followed by a negative u. In Fig. 3.2*b* the u's are *negatively correlated*, a positive u followed by a negative u and vice versa.

If the disturbances (deviations) follow systematic patterns, such as those shown in Fig. 3.2*a* and *b*, there is auto- or serial correlation, and what Assumption 2 requires is that such correlation be absent. Figure 3.2*c* shows that there is no systematic pattern to the u's, thus indicating zero correlation.

Assumption 3

$$\text{var}\,(u_i\,|\,X_i) = E[u_i - E(u_i)]^2$$
$$= E(u_i^2) \qquad \text{because of Assumption 1}$$
$$= \sigma^2 \qquad\qquad\qquad\qquad (3.1.3)$$

where var stands for variance.

Equation (3.1.3) states that the variance of u_i for each X_i (that is, the conditional variance of u_i) is some positive constant number equal to σ^2. Technically, (3.1.3) represents the assumption of *homoscedasticity*, or *equal* (homo) *spread* (scedasticity), or *equal variance*. Stated differently, (3.1.3) means that the Y populations corresponding to various X values have the same variance. Diagramatically, the situation is shown in Fig. 3.3.

In contrast, consider Fig. 3.4, where the conditional variance of the Y population increases as X increases. This situation is known appropriately as *heteroscedasticity*, or *unequal spread*, or *variance*. Symbolically, in this situation (3.1.3) can be written as

$$\text{var}\,(u_i\,|\,X_i) = \sigma_i^2 \qquad\qquad\qquad (3.1.4)$$

Notice the subscript on σ^2 in equation (3.1.4), which indicates that the variance of the Y population is no longer constant.

To make the difference between the two situations clear, let Y represent weekly consumption expenditure and X weekly income. Figures 3.3 and 3.4 show that as income increases the average consumption expenditure also increases. But in Fig. 3.3 the variance of consumption expenditure remains the same at all levels of income while in Fig. 3.4 it increases with increase in income. So to speak, the richer families on the average consume more than the poorer families, but there is also more variability in the consumption expenditure of the former.

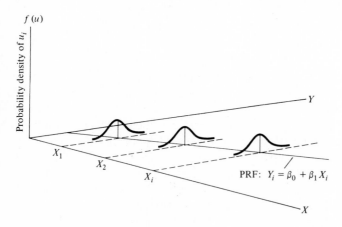

Figure 3.3 Homoscedasticity.

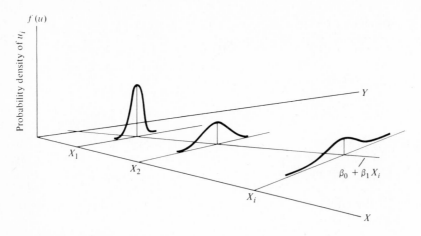

Figure 3.4 Heteroscedasticity.

Assumption 4

$$\text{cov}\,(u_i,\,X_i) = E[u_i - E(u_i)][X_i - E(X_i)]$$
$$= 0 \tag{3.1.5}$$

Assumption 4 states that the disturbance u and explanatory variable X are uncorrelated. The rationale for this assumption is as follows: When we expressed the PRF as in (2.4.2), we assumed that X and u (which may represent the influence of all the omitted variables) have separate (and additive) influence on Y. But if X and u are correlated, it is not possible to assess their individual effect on Y. Thus, if X and u are positively correlated, X increases when u increases and it decreases when u decreases. Similarly, if X and u are negatively correlated, X increases when u decreases and it decreases when u increases. In either case, it is difficult to isolate the influence of X and u on Y.

Assumption 4 is automatically fulfilled if the X variable is nonrandom or nonstochastic and Assumption 1 holds {in this case, $\text{cov}\,(u_i,\,X_i) = [X_i - E(X_i)]E[u_i - E(u_i)] = 0$}. Since most of the single-equation regression theory expounded in this text is based on the assumption that the X variable(s) is nonstochastic, Assumption 4 is not very critical for us; it is stated here merely to point out that the regression theory presented in the sequel holds true even if the X's are stochastic or random, provided they are independent or at least uncorrelated with the disturbances u_i. (We shall examine the consequences of relaxing Assumption 4 in Part II.)

A linear regression model satisfying the preceding four assumptions is known as the *classical, standard,* or *general linear* regression model. It is classical in the sense that it was developed first by Gauss in 1821 and since then has served as a norm or a standard against which may be compared the regression models that do not satisfy the gaussian assumptions.

Table 3.1 Assumption of the classical linear regression model

Assumption no.	In terms of u	In terms of Y
1	$E(u_i \mid X_i) = 0$	$E(Y_i \mid X_i) = \beta_0 + \beta_1 X_i$
2	$\text{cov}\,(u_i, u_j) = 0 \qquad i \neq j$	$\text{cov}\,(Y_i, Y_j) = 0 \qquad i \neq j$
3	$\text{var}\,(u_i \mid X_i) = \sigma^2$	$\text{var}\,(Y_i \mid X_i) = \sigma^2$

Some obvious questions are: Why these assumptions? How realistic are they? What happens if some or all the assumptions are relaxed? These weighty questions will be answered thoroughly in Part II. For the time being, it is sufficient to note that with the preceding assumptions Gauss has shown that the estimators of the regression parameters obtained by the method of least squares are "optimum" in the sense implied by the Gauss-Markov theorem, which will be discussed shortly.

In passing it may be noted that Assumptions 1 to 3 can be expressed alternatively as shown in Table 3.1. (In Exercise 3.1 the reader is asked to show the equivalence between assumptions expressed in terms of u and in terms of Y.)

The Least-Squares Principle

As noted in Chap. 2, the PRF is not directly observable. We estimate it from the SRF. But how is the SRF itself determined? Recalling the two-variable linear SRF, we write

$$Y_i = \hat{\beta}_0 + \hat{\beta}_1 X_i + e_i \qquad (2.6.2)$$

$$= \hat{Y}_i + e_i \qquad (2.6.3)$$

where $\hat{Y}_i$ is the estimated (conditional mean) value of Y_i. We can express (2.6.3) alternatively as

$$e_i = Y_i - \hat{Y}_i$$

$$= Y_i - \hat{\beta}_0 - \hat{\beta}_1 X_i \qquad (3.1.6)$$

which shows that the e_i (the residuals) are simply the differences between the actual and estimated Y values.

Now given N pairs of observations on Y and X, we would like to determine the SRF in such a manner that it is as close as possible to the actual Y. To this end, we may adopt the following criterion: Choose the SRF in such a way that the sum of the residuals $\sum e_i = \sum (Y_i - \hat{Y}_i)$ is as small as possible. Although intuitively appealing, this is not a very good criterion, as can be seen in the hypothetical scattergram shown in Fig. 3.5.

If we adopt the criterion of minimizing $\sum e_i$, Fig. 3.5 shows that the residuals e_2 and e_3 as well as the residuals e_1 and e_4 receive the same weight in the sum $(e_1 + e_2 + e_3 + e_4)$ although the first two residuals are much closer to the SRF than the latter two. In other words, all the residuals receive equal importance no

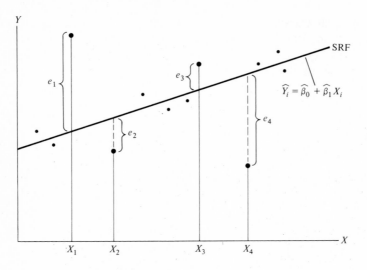

Figure 3.5 Least-squares criterion.

matter how close or how widely scattered the individual observations are from the SRF. A consequence of this is that it is quite possible that the algebraic sum of the e_i is small (even zero) although the e_i are widely scattered about the SRF. To see this, let e_1, e_2, e_3, and e_4 in Fig. 3.5 assume the values of 10, -2, $+2$, and -10, respectively. The algebraic sum of these residuals is zero although e_1 and e_4 are scattered more widely around the SRF than e_2 and e_3. We can avoid this problem if we adopt the *least-squares criterion*, which states that the SRF can be fixed in such a way that

$$\sum e_i^2 = \sum (Y_i - \hat{Y}_i)^2$$
$$= \sum (Y_i - \hat{\beta}_0 - \hat{\beta}_1 X_i)^2 \tag{3.1.7}$$

is as small as possible, where e_i^2 are the squared residuals. By squaring e_i, this method gives more weight to residuals such as e_1 and e_4 in Fig. 3.5 than the residuals e_2 and e_3. As noted previously, under the minimum $\sum e_i$ criterion, the sum can be small even though the e_i are widely spread about the SRF. But this is not possible under the least-squares procedure, for the larger the e_i (in absolute value), the larger the $\sum e_i^2$. A further justification for the least-squares method lies in the fact that the estimators obtained by it have some very desirable statistical properties, as we shall see shortly.

It is obvious from (3.1.7) that

$$\sum e_i^2 = f(\hat{\beta}_0, \hat{\beta}_1) \tag{3.1.8}$$

that is, the sum of the squared residuals is some function of the estimators $\hat{\beta}_0$ and $\hat{\beta}_1$: For any given set of data, choosing different values for $\hat{\beta}_0$ and $\hat{\beta}_1$ will give different e's and hence different values of $\sum e_i^2$. The principle of least squares chooses $\hat{\beta}_0$ and $\hat{\beta}_1$ in such a manner that for a given sample $\sum e_i^2$ is as small as possible. How is this done? This is a straightforward exercise in differential calculus. As shown in App. 3A, Sec. 3A.1, the process of differentiation yields the following formulas for estimating β_0 and β_1:

$$\sum Y_i = N\hat{\beta}_0 + \hat{\beta}_1 \sum X_i \tag{3.1.9}$$

$$\sum Y_i X_i = \hat{\beta}_0 \sum X_i + \hat{\beta}_1 \sum X_i^2 \tag{3.1.10}$$

where N is the sample size. These simultaneous equations are known as the *normal equations*.

Solving the normal equations simultaneously, we obtain

$$\hat{\beta}_1 = \frac{N \sum X_i Y_i - \sum X_i \sum Y_i}{N \sum X_i^2 - (\sum X_i)^2}$$

$$= \frac{\sum (X_i - \bar{X})(Y_i - \bar{Y})}{\sum (X_i - \bar{X})^2}$$

$$= \frac{\sum x_i y_i}{\sum x_i^2} \tag{3.1.11}$$

where $\bar{X}$ and $\bar{Y}$ are the sample means of X and Y and where we define $x_i = (X_i - \bar{X})$ and $y_i = (Y_i - \bar{Y})$. Henceforth we adopt the convention of letting the lowercase letters denote deviations from mean values:

$$\hat{\beta}_0 = \frac{\sum X_i^2 \sum Y_i - \sum X_i \sum X_i Y_i}{N \sum X_i^2 - (\sum X_i)^2}$$

$$= \bar{Y} - \hat{\beta}_1 \bar{X} \tag{3.1.12}$$

The last step in (3.1.12) can be obtained directly from (3.1.9) by simple algebraic manipulations.

The estimators obtained previously are known as the *least-squares estimators* for they are derived from the least-squares principle. Note the following features of these estimators:

1. They are expressed solely in terms of the observable (i.e., sample) quantities.
2. They are *point estimators*; that is, given the sample, each estimator will provide only a single (point) value of the relevant population parameter. (In Chap. 5 we shall consider the so-called interval estimators, which provide a range of possible values for the unknown population parameter.)

Once the least-squares estimates are obtained from the data at hand, the sample regression line (cf. Fig. 3.5) can be easily fitted. The regression line thus obtained has the following properties:

1. It passes through the sample means of Y and X. This is obvious from

(3.1.12), for the latter can be written as $\bar{Y} = \hat{\beta}_0 + \hat{\beta}_1 \bar{X}$, which is shown diagramatically in Fig. 3.6.

2. The mean value of the estimated $Y (= \hat{Y}_i)$ is equal to the mean value of the actual Y for

$$\hat{Y}_i = \hat{\beta}_0 + \hat{\beta}_1 X_i$$
$$= (\bar{Y} - \hat{\beta}_1 \bar{X}) + \hat{\beta}_1 X_i$$
$$= \bar{Y} + \hat{\beta}_1 (X_i - \bar{X}) \tag{3.1.13}$$

Summing both sides of this last equality over the sample values and dividing through by the sample size N gives

$$\bar{\hat{Y}} = \bar{Y} \tag{3.1.14}$$

where use is made of the fact that $\sum (X_i - \bar{X}) = 0$. (Why?)

3. The mean value of the residuals e_i is zero. From App. 3A, Sec. 3A.1, the first equation is

$$-2 \sum (Y_i - \hat{\beta}_0 - \hat{\beta}_1 X_i) = 0$$

But since $e_i = Y_i - \hat{\beta}_0 - \hat{\beta}_1 X_i$, the preceding equation reduces to $-2 \sum e_i = 0$ whence $\bar{e} = 0$.

As a result of the preceding property, the sample regression

$$Y_i = \hat{\beta}_0 + \hat{\beta}_1 X_i + e_i \tag{2.6.2}$$

can be expressed in an alternative form, known as the *deviation form*, where both Y and X are expressed as deviations from their mean values. To see this, sum (2.6.2) on both sides to give

$$\sum Y_i = N\hat{\beta}_0 + \hat{\beta}_1 \sum X_i + \sum e_i \tag{3.1.15}$$
$$= N\hat{\beta}_0 + \hat{\beta}_1 \sum X_i \quad \text{since } \sum e_i = 0 \qquad = \text{(3.1.9)}$$

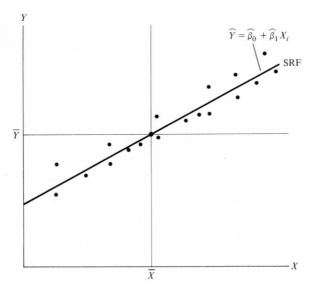

Figure 3.6 Diagram showing that the sample regression line passes through the sample mean values of Y and X.

Dividing equation (3.1.15) through by N, we obtain

$$\bar{Y} = \hat{\beta}_0 + \hat{\beta}_1 \bar{X}$$

$$\begin{aligned} &(3.1.16)\\ &= (3.1.12) \end{aligned}$$

Subtracting (3.1.16) from (2.6.2), we obtain

$$Y_i - \bar{Y} = \hat{\beta}_1(X_i - \bar{X}) + e_i$$

or

$$y_i = \hat{\beta}_1 x_i + e_i \tag{3.1.17}$$

where y_i and x_i, following our convention, are deviations from their respective (sample) mean values.

Equation (3.1.17) is known as the *deviation form*. Notice that the intercept term $\hat{\beta}_0$ is no longer present in it. But the intercept term can always be estimated by (3.1.12), that is, the fact that the sample regression line passes through the sample means of Y and X. An advantage of the deviation form is that it often simplifies arithmetical calculations while working on a desk calculator. But in this age of the computer, this advantage may be rather minor.

In passing note that in the deviation form, the estimated PRF can be written as

$$\hat{y}_i = \hat{\beta}_1 x_i \tag{3.1.18}$$

whereas in the original units of measurement it was $\hat{Y}_i = \hat{\beta}_0 + \hat{\beta}_1 X_i$, as shown in (2.6.1).

4. The residuals e_i are uncorrelated with the predicted Y_i. This can be verified as follows: Using the deviation form, we can write

$$\begin{aligned} \sum \hat{y}_i e_i &= \hat{\beta}_1 \sum x_i e_i \\ &= \hat{\beta}_1 \sum x_i(y_i - \hat{\beta}_1 x_i) \\ &= \hat{\beta}_1 \sum x_i y_i - \hat{\beta}_1^2 \sum x_i^2 \\ &= \hat{\beta}_1^2 \sum x_i^2 - \hat{\beta}_1^2 \sum x_i^2 \\ &= 0 \end{aligned} \tag{3.1.19}$$

where use is made of the fact that $\hat{\beta}_1 = \sum x_i y_i / \sum x_i^2$.

5. The residuals e_i are uncorrelated with X_i; that is $\sum e_i X_i = 0$. This follows from the equation (2) in App. 3A, Sec. 3A.1.

Precision or Standard Errors of Least-Squares Estimates

From equations (3.1.11) and (3.1.12) it is evident that the least-squares estimates are a function of the sample data. But since the data are likely to change from sample to sample, the estimates will change ipso facto. Therefore what is needed is some measure of "reliability" or precision of the estimates $\hat{\beta}_0$ and $\hat{\beta}_1$. Now in statistics the precision of an estimate is measured by its *standard error* (se).[3] Given the gaussian assumptions, it is shown in App. 3A, Sec. 3A.2, that the standard errors of the OLS estimates can be obtained as follows:

$$\text{var}\,(\hat{\beta}_1) = \frac{\sigma^2}{\sum x_i^2} \tag{3.1.20}$$

$$\text{se}\,(\hat{\beta}_1) = \frac{\sigma}{\sqrt{\sum x_i^2}} \tag{3.1.21}$$

$$\text{var}\,(\hat{\beta}_0) = \frac{\sum X_i^2}{N \sum x_i^2}\,\sigma^2 \tag{3.1.22}$$

$$\text{se}\,(\hat{\beta}_0) = \sqrt{\frac{\sum X_i^2}{N \sum x_i^2}}\,\sigma \tag{3.1.23}$$

where var = variance and se = standard error and where σ^2 is the constant or homoscedastic variance of u_i of Assumption 3.

All the quantities entering into the preceding equations except σ^2 can be estimated from the data. As shown in App. 3A, Sec. 3A.3, σ^2 itself is estimated by the following formula:

$$\hat{\sigma}^2 = \frac{\sum e_i^2}{N - 2} \tag{3.1.24}$$

where $\hat{\sigma}^2$ is the OLS estimator of the true but unknown σ^2 and where the expression $N - 2$ is known as the *number of degrees of freedom* (df), $\sum e_i^2$ being the sum of the residual squared or the residual sum of squares (RSS).[4]

Once $\sum e_i^2$ is known, $\hat{\sigma}^2$ can be easily computed. $\sum e_i^2$ itself can be computed either from (3.1.7) or from the following expression (see Sec. 3.3 for the proof):

$$\sum e_i^2 = \sum y_i^2 - \hat{\beta}_1^2 \sum x_i^2 \tag{3.1.25}$$

Compared with equation (3.1.7), equation (3.1.25) is easy to use for it does not require computing e_i for each observation although such a computation will be useful in its own right (as we shall see in Chap. 11).

---

[3] The *standard error* is nothing but the standard deviation of the sampling distribution of the estimator, and the sampling distribution of an estimator is simply a probability or frequency distribution of the estimator, that is, a distribution of the set of values of the estimator obtained from all possible samples of the same size from a given population. Sampling distributions are used to draw inferences about the values of the population parameters on the basis of the values of the estimators calculated from one or more samples.

[4] The term *the number of degrees of freedom* means the total number of observations in the sample $(= N)$ less the number of independent (linear) constraints or restrictions put on them. In other words, it is the number of independent observations out of a total of N observations. For example, before the RSS (3.1.7) can be computed, $\hat{\beta}_0$ and $\hat{\beta}_1$ must first be obtained. These two estimates therefore put two restrictions on the RSS. Therefore, there are $N - 2$, not N, independent observations to compute the RSS. Following this logic, in the three-variable regression RSS will have $N - 3$ df, and for the k variable model it will have $N - k$ df. The general rule is: df $= N -$ number of parameters estimated.

How does the standard error of an estimate enable one to judge the reliability of that estimate? This is a problem in statistical inference, and it will be pursued in Chaps. 4 and 5.

3.2 PROPERTIES OF LEAST-SQUARES ESTIMATORS: THE GAUSS-MARKOV THEOREM

The theoretical justification of the method of least squares rests on the *Gauss-Markov theorem*.[5] To understand this theorem, we need to consider the *best linear unbiasedness property of an estimator*. As stated in App. A, an estimator, say, $\hat{\theta}$ is said to be best linear unbiased estimator (BLUE) of θ if it is linear, unbiased, and has minimum variance in the class of all linear unbiased estimators of θ. In short, an estimator is BLUE if it is linear (i.e., linear function of a random variable such as the dependent variable Y in the regression model) and efficient (i.e., unbiased as well as minimum variance).

> **Gauss-Markov theorem:** Given the assumption of the classical linear regression model, the least-squares estimators, in the class of unbiased linear estimators, have minimum variance; that is, they are BLUE.

The proof of the theorem is sketched in App. 3A, Sec. 3A.4.

3.3 THE COEFFICIENT OF DETERMINATION r^2: A MEASURE OF "GOODNESS OF FIT"

Thus far we were concerned with the problem of estimating regression coefficients, their standard errors, and some of their properties. We now consider the *goodness of fit* of the fitted regression line to a set of data; that is, we shall find out how "well" the sample regression line fits the data. From Fig. 3.5 it is clear that if all the observations were to lie on the regression line, we would obtain a "perfect" fit, but this is rarely the case. Generally, there will be some positive e_i and some negative e_i. What we hope for is that these residuals around the regression line are as small as possible. Now the coefficient of determination r^2 (two-variable case) or R^2 (multiple regression) is a summary measure which tells how well the sample regression line fits the data.

To compute this r^2, we proceed as follows: Recall that

$$Y_i = \hat{Y}_i + e_i \qquad (2.6.3)$$

or in the deviation form

$$y_i = \hat{y}_i + e_i \qquad (3.3.1)$$

---

[5] Although known as the *Gauss-Markov theorem*, the least-squares approach of Gauss antedates (1821) the minimum-variance approach of Markov (1900).

where use is made of (3.1.17) and (3.1.18). Squaring (3.3.1) on both sides and summing over the sample, we obtain

$$\sum y_i^2 = \sum \hat{y}_i^2 + \sum e_i^2 + 2 \sum \hat{y}_i e_i$$
$$= \sum \hat{y}_i^2 + \sum e_i^2$$
$$= \hat{\beta}_1^2 \sum x_i^2 + \sum e_i^2 \tag{3.3.2}$$

since $\sum \hat{y}_i e_i = 0$ (why?) and $\hat{y}_i = \hat{\beta}_1 x_i$.

The various sums of squares appearing in (3.3.2) can be described as follows: $\sum y_i^2 = \sum (Y_i - \bar{Y})^2$ = total variation of the actual Y values about their sample mean,[6] which may be called the *total sum of squares* (TSS). $\sum \hat{y}_i^2 = \sum (\hat{Y}_i - \bar{\hat{Y}})^2 = \sum (\hat{Y}_i - \bar{Y})^2 = \hat{\beta}_1^2 \sum x_i^2$ = variation of the estimated Y values about their mean $(\bar{\hat{Y}} = \bar{Y})$, which appropriately may be called the sum of squares due to regression [i.e., due to the explanatory variable(s)], or explained by regression, or simply the *explained sum of squares* (ESS). $\sum e_i^2$ = residual or *unexplained* variation of the Y values about the regression line, or simply the *residual sum of squares* (RSS). Thus, (3.3.2) is

$$\text{TSS} = \text{ESS} + \text{RSS}$$

and shows that the total variation in the observed Y values about their mean value can be partitioned into two parts, one attributable to the regression line and the other to random forces because not all actual Y observations lie on the fitted line. Geometrically, we have Fig. 3.7.

---

[6] The terms *variation* and *variance* are different. Variation means the sum of squares of the deviations of a variable from its mean value. Variance is this sum of squares divided by the appropriate degrees of freedom. In short, variance = variation/df.

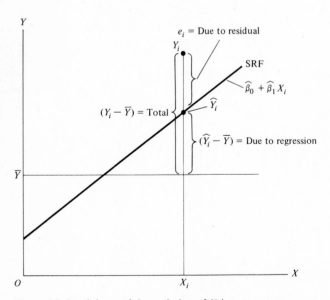

Figure 3.7 Breakdown of the variation of Y_i into two components.

Now dividing (3.3.2) by TSS on both sides, we obtain

$$1 = \frac{\text{ESS}}{\text{TSS}} + \frac{\text{RSS}}{\text{TSS}}$$

$$= \frac{\sum (\hat{Y}_i - \bar{Y})^2}{\sum (Y_i - \bar{Y})^2} + \frac{\sum e_i^2}{\sum (Y_i - \bar{Y})^2} \qquad (3.3.3)$$

We now define

$$r^2 = \frac{\sum (\hat{Y}_i - \bar{Y})^2}{\sum (Y_i - \bar{Y})^2} = \frac{\text{ESS}}{\text{TSS}} \qquad (3.3.4)$$

The quantity r^2 thus defined is known as the (sample) *coefficient of determination* and is the most commonly used measure of the goodness of fit of a regression line. Verbally, r^2 *measures the proportion or percentage of the total variation in Y explained by the regression model.*

Two properties of r^2 may be noted:

1. It is a nonnegative quantity. (Why?)
2. Its limits are $0 \leq r^2 \leq 1$. An r^2 of 1 means a perfect fit, whereas an r^2 of zero means no relationship between the dependent variable and the explanatory variable(s).

Although r^2 can be computed directly from its definition given in (3.3.4), it can be obtained more quickly from the following formula:

$$r^2 = \frac{\text{ESS}}{\text{TSS}}$$

$$= \frac{\sum \hat{y}_i^2}{\sum y_i^2}$$

$$= \frac{\hat{\beta}_1^2 \sum x_i^2}{\sum y_i^2}$$

$$= \hat{\beta}_1^2 \left(\frac{\sum x_i^2}{\sum y_i^2} \right) \qquad (3.3.5)$$

If we divide the numerator and the denominator of (3.3.5) by the sample size N (or $N - 1$ if the sample size is small), we obtain

$$r^2 = \hat{\beta}_1^2 \left(\frac{S_x^2}{S_y^2} \right) \qquad (3.3.6)$$

where S_y^2 and S_x^2 are the sample variances of Y and X, respectively.

A quantity closely related to but conceptually very much different from r^2 is the *coefficient of correlation*, which, as noted in Chap. 1, is a measure of the degree of association between two variables. It can be computed either from

$$r = \pm \sqrt{r^2} \qquad (3.3.7)$$

or from its definition

$$r = \frac{\sum x_i y_i}{\sqrt{(\sum x_i^2)(\sum y_i^2)}}$$

$$= \frac{N \sum X_i Y_i - (\sum X_i)(\sum Y_i)}{\sqrt{[N \sum X_i^2 - (\sum X_i)^2][N \sum Y_i^2 - (\sum Y_i)^2]}} \qquad (3.3.8)$$

which is known as the *sample correlation coefficient.*[7]

Some of the properties of r are as follows:

1. It can be positive or negative, the sign depending on the sign of the term in the numerator of (3.3.8), which measures the sample *covariation* of two variables.
2. It lies between the limits of -1 and $+1$; that is, $-1 \leq r \leq 1$.
3. It is symmetrical in nature; that is, the coefficient of correlation between X and Y (r_{XY}) is the same as that between Y and $X (r_{YX})$.
4. It is independent of the origin and scale; that is, if we define $X_i^* = aX_i + c$ and $Y_i^* = bY_i + d$, where $a > 0, b > 0$, and c and d are constants, then, r between X^* and Y^* is the same as that between the original variables X and Y.
5. If X and Y are statistically independent (see App. A for the definition), the correlation coefficient between them is zero; but if $r = 0$, it does not mean that two variables are independent. In other words, zero correlation does not necessarily imply independence.
6. It is a measure of *linear association* or *linear dependence* only; it has no meaning for describing nonlinear relations.
7. Although it is a measure of linear association between two variables, it does not necessarily imply any cause and effect relationship, as noted in Chap. 1.

In the regression context, r^2 is a more meaningful measure than r for the former tells us the proportion of variation in the dependent variable explained by the explanatory variable(s) and therefore provides an overall measure of the extent to which the variation in one variable determines the variation in the other, but r does not have such value. Moreover, as we shall see, the interpretation of r $(= R)$ in a multiple regression model is of dubious value.

3.4 AN ILLUSTRATIVE EXAMPLE

Assume that we have the sample data of Table 2.4, which is reproduced as Table 3.2 for convenience. Assume, further, that Y is linearly related to X as in (2.4.2). The raw data required to obtain the estimates of the regression coefficients, their

---

[7] The population correlation coefficient, denoted by ρ, is defined in App. A.

Table 3.2 Hypothetical data on weekly family consumption expenditure Y and weekly family income X

Y ($)	X ($)
70	80
65	100
90	120
95	140
110	160
115	180
120	200
140	220
155	240
150	260

standard errors, etc., are given in Table 3.3. Based on these raw data, the following calculations are obtained, and the reader is advised to check them. (The computer printout of the problem is given in App. 3A, Sec. 3A.5.)

$$\hat{\beta}_0 = 24.4545 \quad \text{var}(\hat{\beta}_0) = 41.1370 \quad \text{and} \quad \text{se}(\hat{\beta}_0) = 6.4138$$

$$\hat{\beta}_1 = 0.5091 \quad \text{var}(\hat{\beta}_1) = 0.0013 \quad \text{and} \quad \text{se}(\hat{\beta}_1) = 0.0357 \quad (3.4.1)$$

$$\hat{\sigma}^2 = 42.1591 \quad r^2 = 0.9621 \quad r = 0.9809 \quad df = 8$$

Table 3.3 Raw data based on Table 3.2

Y_i	X_i	Y_iX_i	X_i^2	$x_i = X_i - \bar{X}$	$y_i = Y_i - \bar{Y}$	x_i^2	x_iy_i	$\hat{Y}_i$	$e_i = Y_i - \hat{Y}_i$	$\hat{Y}_ie_i$
(1)	(2)	(3)	(4)	(5)	(6)	(7)	(8)	(9)	(10)	(11)
70	80	5600	6400	−90	−41	8100	3690	65.1818	4.8181	314.0524
65	100	6500	10000	−70	−46	4900	3220	75.3636	−10.3636	−781.0382
90	120	10800	14400	−50	−21	2500	1050	85.5454	4.4545	381.0620
95	140	13300	19600	−30	−16	900	480	95.7272	−0.7272	−69.6128
110	160	17600	25600	−10	−1	100	10	105.9090	4.0909	433.2631
115	180	20700	32400	10	4	100	40	116.0909	−1.0909	−126.6434
120	200	24000	40000	30	9	900	270	126.2727	−6.2727	−792.0708
140	220	30800	48400	50	29	2500	1450	136.4545	3.5454	483.7858
155	240	37200	57600	70	44	4900	3080	146.6363	8.3636	1226.4073
150	260	39000	67600	90	39	8100	3510	156.8181	−6.8181	−1069.2014
Sum 1110	1700	205500	322000	0	0	33000	16800	1109.9995 ≑ 1110.0	0	0.0040 ≑ 0.0
Mean 111	170	nc	nc	0	0	nc	nc	110	0	0

Notes: ≑ symbolizes "approximately equal to"; nc means "not computed."

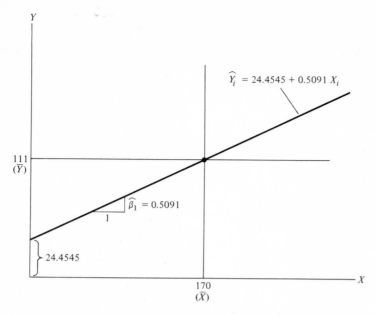

Figure 3.8 Sample regression line based on the data of Table 3.2.

The estimated regression line therefore is

$$\hat{Y}_i = 24.4545 + 0.5091X_i \qquad (3.4.2)$$

which is shown geometrically as Fig. 3.8.

Following Chap. 2, the SRF [equation (3.4.2)] and the associated regression line are interpreted as follows: Each point on the regression line gives an *estimate* of the expected or mean value of Y corresponding to the chosen X value; that is, $\hat{Y}_i$ is an estimate of $E(Y|X_i)$. The value of $\hat{\beta}_1 = 0.5091$, which measures the slope of the line, shows that within the sample range of X between \$80 and \$260 per week as X increases, say, by \$1, the estimated increase in the mean or average weekly consumption expenditure amounts to about 51 cents. The value of $\hat{\beta}_0 = 24.4545$, which is the intercept of the line, indicates the average level of weekly consumption expenditure when weekly income is zero. However, this is a mechanical interpretation of the intercept term. In regression analysis such literal interpretation of the intercept term may not be always meaningful, although in the present example it can be argued that a family without any income (because of unemployment, layoff, etc.) might maintain some minimum level of consumption expenditure either by borrowing or dissaving. But in general one has to use common sense in interpreting the intercept term for very often the sample range of X values may not include zero as one of the observed values.

Perhaps it is best to interpret the intercept term as the mean or average effect on Y of all the variables omitted from the regression model. The value of r^2 of 0.9621 means that about 96 percent of the variation in the weekly consumption expenditure is explained by income. Since r^2 can at most be 1, the observed r^2 suggests that the sample regression line fits the data very well.[8] The coefficient of correlation of 0.9809 shows that the two variables, consumption expenditure and income, are highly positively associated. The estimated standard errors of the regression coefficients will be interpreted in Chap. 5.

3.5 FUNCTIONAL FORMS OF REGRESSION MODELS

In our consumption-income example we used a model that was linear in the parameters as well as the variables. But as noted in Chap. 2, in this text we are concerned mainly with regression models which are linear in the parameters; they may or may not be linear in the variables. In this section we examine some of the commonly used regression models which are linear in the parameters (or which can be so made) but which are not necessarily linear in the variables and consider some of their special features.

Double-Log, Log-Linear, or Constant-Elasticity Models

Consider the following model:

$$Y_i = \beta_0 X_i^{\beta_1} e^{u_i} \tag{3.5.1}$$

which may be expressed alternatively as

$$\ln Y_i = \ln \beta_0 + \beta_1 \ln X_i + u_i \tag{3.5.2}$$

where $\ln$ = natural log (i.e., log to the base e, where $e = 2.718$).[9] If we write (3.5.2) as

$$\ln Y_i = \alpha + \beta_1 \ln X_i + u_i \tag{3.5.3}$$

where $\alpha = \ln \beta_0$, this model is linear in the parameters α and β_1 and linear in the logarithms of the variables Y and X, hence the name *double-log*, or *log-linear*, model.

If the assumptions of the classical linear regression model are fulfilled, the parameters of (3.5.3) can be estimated by the method of OLS by letting

$$Y_i^* = \alpha + \beta_1 X_i^* + u_i \tag{3.5.4}$$

where $Y_i^* = \ln Y_i$ and $X_i^* = \ln X_i$. The OLS estimators $\hat{\alpha}$ and $\hat{\beta}_1$ obtained will be best linear-unbiased estimators of α and β_1, respectively.

---

[8] A formal test of the goodness of fit will be presented in Chap. 7.

[9] In practice one may use the common logarithms, that is, log to the base 10. The relationship between the natural log and common log is $\ln_e X \doteq 2.3026 \log_{10} X$. By convention, ln means natural logarithm, and log means logarithm to the base 10; hence there is no need to write the subscripts e and 10.

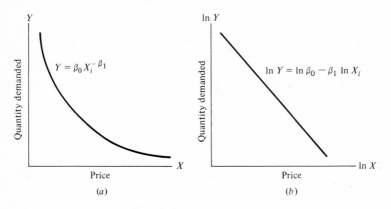

Figure 3.9 Constant-elasticity model.

One attractive feature of the double-log model is that the slope coefficient β_1 measures the elasticity of Y with respect to X, that is, the percentage change in Y for a given (small) percentage change in X.[10] Thus, if Y represents the quantity of a commodity demanded and X its unit price, β_1 measures the price elasticity of demand, a parameter of considerable economic interest. If the relationship between quantity demanded and price is as shown in Fig. 3.9a, the double-log transformation, as shown in Fig. 3.9b, will then give the estimate of the price elasticity $(-\beta_1)$.

Two special features of the log-linear model may be noted: The model assumes that the elasticity coefficient between Y and X, β_1, remains constant throughout (why?), hence the alternative name *constant-elasticity model*. Another feature of the model is that although $\hat{\alpha}$ and $\hat{\beta}_1$ are unbiased estimators of α and β_1, β_0 (the parameters entering the original model) when estimated as $\hat{\beta}_0 = $ antilog $(\hat{\alpha})$ is itself a biased estimator. In most practical problems, however, the intercept term is of secondary importance, and one need not worry about obtaining its unbiased estimate.[11]

In the two-variable model, the simplest way to decide whether the log-linear model fits the data is to plot the scattergram of $\ln Y_i$ against $\ln X_i$ and see if the scatter points lie approximately on a straight line, as in Fig. 3.9b.

Semilog Models

Models of the type

$$\ln Y_i = \alpha_0 + \alpha_1 X_i + u_i \tag{3.5.5}$$

and

$$Y_i = \beta_0 + \beta_1 \ln X_i + u_i \tag{3.5.6}$$

[10] The elasticity coefficient is defined as $(dY/Y)/(dX/X) = (dY/dX)(X/Y)$. Readers familiar with calculus will readily see that β_1 is, in fact, the elasticity coefficient.

[11] Concerning the nature of the bias and what can be done about it, see Arthur S. Goldberger, *Topics in Regression Analysis*, The Macmillan Company, New York, 1968, p. 120.

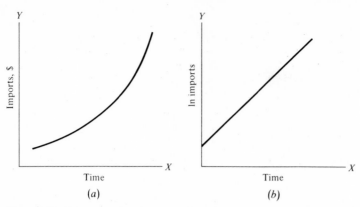

Figure 3.10 Constant-percentage growth model.

are called *semilog models* because only Y or X is expressed in the log form. In the model (3.5.5), it can be shown that the slope coefficient α_1 measures the constant relative or proportional change in Y for a given absolute change in X; that is,[12]

$$\alpha_1 = \frac{\text{Relative change in } Y}{\text{Absolute change in } X} \tag{3.5.7}$$

Therefore, in situations where it is observed that for a given absolute change in X, Y changes by a constant percentage amount, the model (3.5.5) is appropriate. Such a model is called a (constant) *growth model* and has been used to measure the (constant rate of) growth over time of the trend variables such as employment, consumer prices, import and export of goods, labor productivity, etc. (see Fig. 3.10).

In the model (3.5.6), it can be shown that the slope coefficient β_1 measures the absolute change in (the expected or mean value of) Y for a given relative or proportional change in X; that is,[13]

$$\beta_1 = \frac{\text{Absolute change in } Y}{\text{Relative change in } X} \tag{3.5.8}$$

The model (3.5.6) is therefore appropriate in situations where a given proportional change in X leads to a constant absolute change in Y.

Reciprocal Transformations

Models of the following type are known as *reciprocal transformation models:*

$$Y_i = \beta_0 + \beta_1\left(\frac{1}{X_i}\right) + u_i \tag{3.5.9}$$

---

[12] Using differential calculus, it can be shown that $\alpha_1 = d(\ln Y)/dX = (1/Y)(dY/dX) = (dY/Y) \times (1/dX)$, which is nothing but (3.5.7). In passing, note that a relative change multiplied by 100 becomes a percentage change.

[13] Again using differential calculus, $dY/dX = \beta_1(1/X)$. Therefore $\beta_1 = dY/(dX/X) = (3.5.8)$.

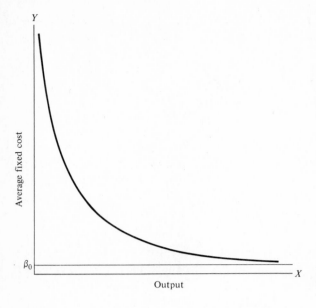

Figure 3.11 Reciprocal-transformation model.

If β_0 and β_1 are positive, this model shows that Y decreases nonlinearly as X increases. This model may therefore be used to study, for example, the behavior of the average fixed cost (AFC) of production. Thus, if we let Y = average fixed cost of production and X = output, then the average fixed cost curve is shown in Fig. 3.11.

Notice a special feature of the model (3.5.9). As Fig. 3.11 shows, the AFC of production declines continuously as X increases (because the fixed cost is spread over a large number of units) and eventually becomes asymptotic with the output axis. Therefore, models like (3.5.9) have built in them an asymptotic or limit value which the dependent variable will take when the value of the X variable increases indefinitely. An estimate of the asymptotic or limit value is provided by $\hat{\beta}_0$. [This can be seen readily from (3.5.9): When X_i increases indefinitely, the term $\beta_1(1/X_i)$ approaches zero.][14]

3.6 SUMMARY AND CONCLUSIONS

In this chapter we introduced the least-squares approach to regression analysis. Carl Friedrich Gauss, the originator of the approach, has shown that under certain assumptions the method of least squares produces estimators which are linear, unbiased, and in the class of all the linear and unbiased estimators have

---

[14] For the purpose of estimation, model (3.5.9) may be written as $Y_i = \beta_0 + \beta_1 X_i^* + u_i$, where $X_i^* = (1/X_i)$. Expressed in this form, the model becomes linear in the parameters as well as the variables Y and X_i^*.

minimum variance. In short, they are BLUE. This is the gist of the famous Gauss-Markov theorem, which provides the theoretical foundation of the method of least squares.

After discussing the problem of point estimation of the regression coefficients, we considered the question of their precision. The precision of the estimates is measured by their standard errors. It is these standard errors which enable us to draw inferences about the (population) parameters, a topic which will be discussed in Chap. 4.

A problem closely related to that of estimation of the regression coefficients is the overall goodness of fit of the sample regression. The goodness of fit is measured by the coefficient of determination r^2, which tells what proportion of the variation in the dependent variable is explained by the explanatory variable(s). This r^2 ranges between 0 and 1; the closer it is to 1, the better the fit.

Although conceptually very much different from regression analysis, we considered the related concept of the coefficient of correlation r, which is a measure of the degree of association between two variables and ranges between -1 and $+1$. In discussing the properties of r we pointed out some of its limitations, especially the danger involved in interpreting correlation as causation.

We also considered several regression models which are linear in the parameters (or can be so rendered) but are not necessarily linear in the variables and suggested the circumstances in which such models may be appropriate.

In concluding this chapter it is essential to comment briefly on the classical linear regression model, which is the foundation of most of regression analysis. It

Table 3.4 Anatomy of two-variable classical regression model

These things are assumed	These things are observed	These things are not observed	These things are imposed	These things are computed
True β_0 and β_1 exist		True β_0 and β_1	Some estimating criterion, e.g. least squares	$\hat{\beta}_0$ and $\hat{\beta}_1$
True u_i exist u_i have these properties: (i) $E(u_i) = 0$ (ii) $E(u_i^2) = \sigma^2$ (iii) $E(u_i u_j) = 0$ $\quad i \neq j$ Population of Y for given X in which		True u_i $E(u_i)$ $E(u_i^2)$		Residuals e_i $\bar{e}$ = mean of residuals = 0 $\hat{\sigma}^2$ = estimate of σ^2
$Y_i = \beta_0 + \beta_1 X_i + u_i$	Y and X in a given sample	Y not in the sample		$\hat{Y}_i$

Source: Adapted from S. Valavanis, *Econometrics*, McGraw-Hill Book Company, New York, 1959, p. 19.

should be noted that the classical model is a theoretical construct or abstraction because it is based on a set of assumptions which may be stringent or unrealistic. But such abstraction is often necessary in the initial stages of studying any field of knowledge. As our knowledge progresses, as we learn the tricks of the trade, we learn to live with or modify apparently unrealistic assumptions. Therefore, what is important initially is to know precisely what are the things that we assume, what are the things that we guess, and what are the things that we observe. Perhaps Table 3.4 will help the reader to keep this in mind.

EXERCISES

3.1 Establish the equivalency of the assumptions given in Table 3.1.

3.2 Consider the sample regression

$$Y_i = \hat{\beta}_0 + \hat{\beta}_1 X_i + e_i$$

Imposing the restrictions (a) $\sum e_i = 0$ and (b) $\sum e_i X_i = 0$, obtain the estimators $\hat{\beta}_0$ and $\hat{\beta}_1$ and show that they are identical with the least-squares estimators given in equations (3.1.11) and (3.1.12). This method of obtaining estimators is called the *analogy principle*. Give an intuitive justification for imposing restrictions (a) and (b).

3.3 Show that r^2 defined in (3.3.4) ranges between 0 and 1. You may use the Cauchy-Schwarz inequality which states that for any random variables X and Y the following relationship holds true:

$$[E(XY)]^2 \leq E(X^2)E(Y^2)$$

3.4 Let $\hat{\beta}_{yx}$ and $\hat{\beta}_{xy}$ represent the slopes in the regression of Y on X and X on Y, respectively. Show that

$$\hat{\beta}_{yx}\hat{\beta}_{xy} = r^2$$

where r is the coefficient of correlation between X and Y.

3.5 Spearman's rank correlation coefficient r_s is defined as follows:

$$r_s = 1 - \frac{6 \sum d^2}{N(N^2 - 1)}$$

where d = difference in the ranks assigned to the same individual or phenomenon and N = number of individuals or phenomena ranked. Derive r_s from r defined in (3.3.8).

Hint: Rank the X and Y values from 1 to N. Note that the sum of X and Y ranks is $N(N + 1)/2$ each and therefore their means are $(N + 1)/2$.

3.6 You are given the ranks of 10 students in midterm and final examinations in statistics. Compute Spearman's coefficient of rank correlation and interpret it:

	Student									
	A	B	C	D	E	F	G	H	I	J
Rank: Midterm	1	3	7	10	9	5	4	8	2	6
Rank: Final	3	2	8	7	9	6	5	10	1	4

3.7 The following table gives data on quit rate per 100 employees in manufacturing and the unemployment rate in manufacturing in the United States for the period of 1960–1972.

Note: The term *quit* refers to people leaving their jobs voluntarily.

Quit and unemployment rates in U.S. manufacturing, 1960–1972

Year	Quit rate per 100 employees, Y	Unemployment rate (%), X
1960	1.3	6.2
1961	1.2	7.8
1962	1.4	5.8
1963	1.4	5.7
1964	1.5	5.0
1965	1.9	4.0
1966	2.6	3.2
1967	2.3	3.6
1968	2.5	3.3
1969	2.7	3.3
1970	2.1	5.6
1971	1.8	6.8
1972	2.2	5.6

Source: Manpower Report of the President, 1973, tables C-10 and A-18.

(a) Plot the data in a scattergram.

(b) Assume that quit rate Y is linearly related to the unemployment rate X as $Y_i = \beta_0 + \beta_1 X_i + u_i$. Estimate β_0, β_1, and their standard errors.

(c) Compute r^2 and r.

(d) Interpret your results.

3.8 Based on a sample of 10 observations, the following results were obtained:

$$\sum Y_i = 1110 \quad \sum X_i = 1700 \quad \sum X_i Y_i = 205500 \quad \sum X^2 = 322000 \quad \sum Y^2 = 132100$$

with coefficient of correlation $r = 0.9758$. But on rechecking these calculations it was found that two pairs of observations were recorded:

Y	X		Y	X
90	120	instead of	80	110
140	220		150	210

What will be the effect of this error on r? Obtain the correct r.

3.9 The following table gives the rate of change (percent per year) of stock price indexes and consumer price indexes in selected countries for the post-World War II period.

Stock values and consumer prices, post-World War II period (through 1969)

| Country | Rate of change, % per year | |
	Stock prices, Y	Consumer prices, X
1. Australia	5.0	4.3
2. Austria	11.1	4.6
3. Belgium	3.2	2.4
4. Canada	7.9	2.4
5. Chile	25.5	26.4
6. Denmark	3.8	4.2
7. Finland	11.1	5.5
8. France	9.9	4.7
9. Germany	13.3	2.2
10. India	1.5	4.0
11. Ireland	6.4	4.0
12. Israel	8.9	8.4
13. Italy	8.1	3.3
14. Japan	13.5	4.7
15. Mexico	4.7	5.2
16. Netherlands	7.5	3.6
17. New Zealand	4.7	3.6
18. Sweden	8.0	4.0
19. United Kingdom	7.5	3.9
20. United States	9.0	2.1

Source: Phillip Cagen: *Common Stock Values and Inflation: The Historical Record of Many Countries*, National Bureau of Economic Research, Suppl., March, 1974, table 1, p. 4.

(*a*) Plot the data in a scattergram.

(*b*) Estimate the parameters in a linear regression of the rate of change of stock prices on the rate of change of consumer prices and obtain the r^2.

(*c*) Are common stocks a hedge against inflation? Are they a perfect hedge?

3.10 Let $X_i^* = (X_i - \bar{X})/S_x$ and $Y_i^* = (Y_i - \bar{Y})/S_y$, where S_x and S_y are standard deviations of X and Y in the sample. Show that in the model

$$X_i^* = \alpha + \beta Y_i^* + u_i$$

$\hat{\alpha} = 0$, and $\hat{\beta} = r$, the coefficient of correlation between X and Y.

Note: Variables X^* and Y^* are known as *standardized variables*. A variable is said to be standardized or in standard (deviation) units if it is expressed in terms of deviation from its mean value and divided by its sample standard deviation.

3.11 There are occasions when the two-variable PRF assumes the following form:

$$Y_i = \beta_i X_i + u_i$$

In this model the intercept term is absent or zero. The model is therefore known as *regression through the origin*. For this model show that

(*a*) $\hat{\beta}_1 = \dfrac{\sum X_i Y_i}{\sum X_i^2}$

(b) $\text{var}(\hat{\beta}_1) = \dfrac{\sigma^2}{\sum X_i^2}$

where σ^2 is estimated by $\hat{\sigma}^2 = \sum e_i^2/(N-1)$.

(c) $\sum e_i$ need not be zero.

3.12 Consider the following formulations of the two-variable PRF:

$$\text{Model I:} \quad Y_i = \beta_0 + \beta_1 X_i + u_i$$

$$\text{Model II:} \quad Y_i = \alpha_0 + \alpha_1(X_i - \bar{X}) + u_i$$

(a) Find the estimators of β_0 and α_0? Are they identical? Are their variances identical?

(b) Find the estimators of β_1 and α_1? Are they identical? Are their variances identical?

(c) What is the advantage, if any, of model II over model I?

3.13 Consider the following models:

$$\text{Model I:} \quad Y_i = \beta_0 + \beta_1 X_i + u_i$$

$$\text{Model II:} \quad Y_i^* = \alpha + \alpha_1 X_i^* + u_i$$

where Y^* and X^* are standardized variables as defined in Exercise 3.10. Show that $\hat{\alpha}_1 = \hat{\beta}_1(S_x/S_y)$ and hence *establish that although the regression coefficients are independent of the change of origin they are not independent of the change of scale.*

3.14 The following table gives data on Gross National Product for the United States.

Gross National Product in current dollars, 1971-2 to 1975-4

Year and quarter	GNP (billions of dollars)
1971-2	1056.2
-3	1072.4
-4	1091.2
1972-1	1127.0
-2	1156.7
-3	1181.4
-4	1219.4
1973-1	1265.0
-2	1287.8
-3	1319.7
-4	1352.7
1974-1	1370.9
-2	1391.0
-3	1424.4
-4	1441.3
1975-1	1433.6
-2	1460.6
-3	1528.5
-4	1572.5

Source: Federal Reserve Bank of St. Louis, *National Economics Trends*, February 1976, p. 12.

(a) Fit a model of the following type to the preceding data:

$$\ln Y_t = \beta_0 + \beta_1 X_t + u_t$$

where $Y_t =$ GNP at time t and $X =$ time, measured chronologically starting with 1 for 1971-2, 2 for 1971-3, and so on.

(b) How would you interpret β_1?

(c) What is the quarterly rate of growth of GNP and the corresponding annual rate of growth?

3.15 Fit a suitable linear regression model to the following data, which relate to the consumer price index and money supply in Japan for the period 1973-2 to 1975-3, and comment on your results.

Consumer prices and money supply in Japan, 1973-2 to 1975-3

Year and quarter	Consumer price index (1970 = 100)	Money supply (billions of yen)
1973-2	122.4	35,522
-3	126.1	36,631
-4	131.6	37,404
1974-1	144.5	38,675
-2	151.3	40,343
-3	157.0	40,978
-4	163.7	41,549
1975-1	166.3	42,853
-2	172.1	43,899
-3	173.6	45,402

Source: Federal Reserve Bank of St. Louis, *Rates of Change in Economic Data for Ten Industrial Countries*, February 17, 1976.

3.16 If in the models

$$\ln Y_i = \beta_0 + \beta_1 X_i + u_i$$

and

$$Y_i = \alpha_0 + \alpha_1 X_i + u_i$$

Y denotes consumption expenditure and X denotes income, show that the elasticity of consumption expenditure with respect to income is given by $E_1 = \beta_1 X_i$ and $E_2 = \alpha_1(X_i/Y_i)$, where E_1 and E_2 are elasticities. How would you interpret these elasticities?

Hint: The definition of elasticity between Y and X is $(dY/dX)(X/Y)$.

3.17 The Engel expenditure curve, named after the German statistician Ernst Engel (1821–1896), relates a consumer's expenditure on a commodity to his total income. Letting $Y =$ consumption expenditure on a commodity and $X =$ consumer income, consider the following models:

$$Y_i = \beta_0 + \beta_1(X_i) + u_i$$

$$Y_i = \beta_0 + \beta_1(1/X_i) + u_i$$

$$\ln Y_i = \ln \beta_0 + \beta_1 \ln X_i + u_i$$

$$\ln Y_i = \ln \beta_0 + \beta_1(1/X_i) + u_i$$

$$Y_i = \beta_0 + \beta_1 \ln X_i + u_i$$

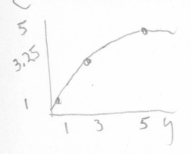

Which of the preceding model(s) would you choose for the Engel expenditure ,curve and why?

Hint: Interpret the various slope coefficients; find out the expressions for elasticity of expenditure with respect to income, etc.

3.18 Let r_1 = coefficient of correlation between N pairs of values (Y_i, X_i) and r_2 = coefficient of correlation between N pairs of values $(aX_i + b, cY_i + d)$, where a, b, c, and d are constants. Show that $r_1 = r_2$ and hence *establish the principle that the coefficient of correlation is invariant with respect to the change of scale and the change of origin.*

Hint: Apply the definition of r given in (3.3.8).

Note: The operations, aX_i, $X_i + b$, and $aX_i + b$ are known, respectively, as the *change of scale, change of origin,* and both *change of scale and origin.*

3.19 If r, the coefficient of correlation between N pairs of values (X_i, Y_i), is positive, then it follows that

(a) r between $(-X_i, -Y_i)$ is also positive.

(b) r between $(-X_i, Y_i)$ and that between $(X_i, -Y_i)$ can be either positive or negative.

(c) Both the slope coefficients β_{yx} and β_{xy} are positive, where β_{yx} = slope coefficient in the regression of Y on X and β_{xy} = slope coefficient in the regression of X on Y.

For each statement determine whether it is true or false.

3.20 If X_1, X_2, and X_3 are uncorrelated variables each having the same standard deviation, show that the coefficient of correlation between $X_1 + X_2$ and $X_2 + X_3$ is equal to $\frac{1}{2}$. Why is the correlation coefficient not zero?

3.21 Apply the model given in Exercise 3.10 to the consumption-income example given in Table 3.2 and show that the slope coefficient is, in fact, equal to the coefficient of correlation.

APPENDIX 3A

3A.1 DERIVATION OF LEAST-SQUARES ESTIMATORS

Differentiate (3.1.7) partially with respect to $\hat{\beta}_0$ and $\hat{\beta}_1$ to obtain

$$\frac{\partial(\sum e_i^2)}{\partial \hat{\beta}_0} = -2 \sum (Y_i - \hat{\beta}_0 - \hat{\beta}_1 X_i) \tag{1}$$

$$\frac{\partial(\sum e_i^2)}{\partial \hat{\beta}_1} = -2 \sum (Y_i - \hat{\beta}_0 - \hat{\beta}_1 X_i) X_i \tag{2}$$

Setting these two equations to zero, after algebraic simplification and manipulation, gives the estimators given in equations (3.1.11) and (3.1.12).

3A.2 VARIANCES AND STANDARD ERRORS OF LEAST-SQUARES ESTIMATORS

From (3.1.11) we have

$$\hat{\beta}_1 = \frac{\sum x_i y_i}{\sum x_i^2}$$

$$= \frac{\sum x_i(Y_i - \overline{Y})}{\sum x_i^2}$$

$$\hat{\beta}_1 = \frac{\sum x_i Y_i}{\sum x_i^2} - \frac{\bar{Y} \sum x_i}{\sum x_i^2}$$

$$= \frac{\sum x_i Y_i}{\sum x_i^2} \qquad \text{since } \sum x_i = 0$$

$$= \sum k_i Y_i \qquad \text{where } k_i = \frac{x_i}{\left(\sum x_i^2\right)} \tag{3}$$

which shows that $\hat{\beta}_1$ is a *linear estimator* because it is a linear function of Y.

$$\hat{\beta}_1 = \sum k_i Y_i = \sum k_i (\beta_0 + \beta_1 X_i + u_i) = \beta_1 + \sum k_i u_i \tag{4}$$

where use is made of the fact that $\sum k_i = 0$, $\sum k_i^2 = 1/\sum x_i^2$, and $\sum k_i x_i = \sum k_i X_i = 1$.

Given the assumptions about u_i, it follows that $E(\hat{\beta}_1) = \beta_1 + \sum k_i E(u_i) = \beta_1$, which shows that $\hat{\beta}_1$ is an unbiased estimator. (*Note:* The x's are nonstochastic and therefore can be treated like a constant for the purpose of taking mathematical expectation.)

Now by definition

$$\text{var}(\hat{\beta}_1) = E(\hat{\beta}_1 - \beta_1)^2$$

$$= E(\sum k_i u_i)^2 \qquad \text{using (4)}$$

$$= E(k_1^2 u_1^2 + k_2^2 u_2^2 + \cdots + k_N^2 u_N^2 + 2k_1 k_2 u_1 u_2$$

$$+ \cdots + 2k_{N-1} k_N u_{N-1} u_N) \tag{5}$$

Since by assumption, $E(u_i^2) = \sigma^2$ for each i, and $E(u_i u_j) = 0$ for $i \neq j$, it follows that

$$\text{var}(\hat{\beta}_1) = \sigma^2 \sum k_i^2$$

$$= \frac{\sigma^2}{\sum x_i^2} \qquad \text{using the definition of } k_i^2$$

$$= \text{equation (3.1.20)} \tag{6}$$

The variance of $\hat{\beta}_0$ can be obtained following the same line of reasoning given previously. Once the variance of $\hat{\beta}_0$ and $\hat{\beta}_1$ are obtained, their square roots give the corresponding standard errors.

3A.3 THE LEAST-SQUARES ESTIMATOR OF σ^2

Recall that

$$Y_i = \beta_0 + \beta_1 X_i + u_i \tag{7}$$

Therefore

$$\bar{Y} = \beta_0 + \beta_1 \bar{X} + \bar{u} \tag{8}$$

Subtracting (8) from (7) gives

$$y_i = \beta_1 x_i + (u_i - \bar{u}) \tag{9}$$

Also recall that

$$e_i = y_i - \hat{\beta}_1 x_i \tag{10}$$

Therefore, substituting (9) into (10) yields

$$e_i = \beta_1 x_i + (u_i - \bar{u}) - \hat{\beta}_1 x_i \tag{11}$$

Collecting terms, squaring, and summing on both sides, we obtain

$$\sum e_i^2 = (\hat{\beta}_1 - \beta_1)^2 \sum x_i^2 + \sum (u_i - \bar{u})^2 - 2(\hat{\beta}_1 - \beta_1) \sum x_i(u_i - \bar{u}) \tag{12}$$

Taking expectations on both sides gives

$$E(\sum e_i^2) = \sum x_i^2 E(\hat{\beta}_1 - \beta_1)^2 + E[\sum (u_i - \bar{u})^2] - 2E[(\hat{\beta}_1 - \beta_1) \sum x_i(u_i - \bar{u})]$$
$$= \quad\quad A \quad\quad + \quad\quad B \quad\quad + \quad C \tag{13}$$

Now by the assumptions of the classical linear regression model as well as some of the results of Sec. 3A.2, it can be verified that

$$A = \sigma^2$$
$$B = (N - 1)\sigma^2$$
$$C = -2\sigma^2$$

Therefore, substituting these values into (13) we obtain

$$E(\sum e_i^2) = (N - 2)\sigma^2 \tag{14}$$

Therefore, if we define

$$\hat{\sigma}^2 = \frac{\sum e_i^2}{N - 2} \tag{15}$$

its expected value is

$$E(\hat{\sigma}^2) = \frac{1}{N - 2} E(\sum e_i^2) = \sigma^2 \quad\quad \text{using (14)} \tag{16}$$

which shows that $\hat{\sigma}^2$ is an unbiased estimator of true σ^2.

3A.4 MINIMUM-VARIANCE PROPERTY OF LEAST-SQUARES ESTIMATORS (GAUSS-MARKOV THEOREM)

It was shown in Sec. 3A.2 that the least-squares estimator $\hat{\beta}_1$ is linear as well as unbiased (this holds true of $\hat{\beta}_0$ too). To show that these estimators are also minimum variance in the class of all linear unbiased estimators, consider the least-squares estimator $\hat{\beta}_1$:

$$\hat{\beta}_1 = \sum k_i Y_i$$

where
$$k_i = \frac{X_i - \bar{X}}{\sum (X_i - \bar{X})^2} = \frac{x_i}{\sum x_i^2} \qquad \text{(see Sec. 3A.2)} \tag{17}$$

which shows that $\hat{\beta}_1$ is a weighted average of the Y's with k_i serving as the weights.

Let us define an alternative linear estimator of β_1 as follows:

$$\beta_1^* = \sum w_i Y_i \tag{18}$$

where w_i are also weights, not necessarily equal to k_i. Now

$$\begin{aligned} E(\beta_1^*) &= \sum w_i E(Y_i) \\ &= \sum w_i(\beta_0 + \beta_1 X_i) \\ &= \beta_0 \sum w_i + \beta_1 \sum w_i X_i \end{aligned} \tag{19}$$

Therefore, for β_1^* to be unbiased, we must have

$$\sum w_i = 0 \tag{20}$$

and
$$\sum w_i X_i = 1 \tag{21}$$

Now

$$\begin{aligned} \text{var}(\beta_1^*) &= \text{var} \sum w_i Y_i \\ &= \sum w_i^2 \, \text{var}\, Y_i \\ &= \sigma^2 \sum w_i^2 \qquad [\text{Note: var } Y_i = \text{var } u_i = \sigma^2 \text{ (see Table 3.1).}] \\ &= \sigma^2 \sum \left(w_i - \frac{x_i}{\sum x_i^2} + \frac{x_i}{\sum x_i^2} \right)^2 \qquad \text{(Note the mathematical device)} \\ &= \sigma^2 \sum \left(w_i - \frac{x_i}{\sum x_i^2} \right)^2 + \sigma^2 \frac{\sum x_i^2}{(\sum x_i^2)^2} + 2\sigma^2 \sum \left(w_i - \frac{x_i}{\sum x_i^2} \right)\left(\frac{x_i}{\sum x_i^2} \right) \\ &= \sigma^2 \sum \left(w_i - \frac{x_i}{\sum x_i^2} \right)^2 + \sigma^2 \left(\frac{1}{\sum x_i^2} \right) \end{aligned} \tag{22}$$

because the last term in the next to the last step drops out. (Why?)

Since the last term in (22) is constant, the variance of (β_1^*) can be minimized only by manipulating the first term. If we let

$$w_i = \frac{x_i}{\sum x_i^2}$$

equation (22) reduces to

$$\begin{aligned} \text{var}(\beta_1^*) &= \frac{\sigma^2}{\sum x_i^2} \\ &= \text{var}(\hat{\beta}_1) \end{aligned} \tag{23}$$

In words, with weights $w_i = k_i$, which are the least-squares weights, the variance of the linear estimator β_1^* is equal to the variance of the least-squares estimator $\hat{\beta}_1$; otherwise var $(\beta_1^*) >$ var $(\hat{\beta}_1)$. To put it differently, if there is a minimum-variance linear unbiased estimator of β_1, it must be the least-squares estimator. Similarly it can be shown that $\hat{\beta}_0$ is a minimum-variance linear unbiased estimator of β_0.

3A.5 COMPUTER PRINTOUT OF THE CONSUMPTION-INCOME EXAMPLE

As pointed out in Sec. 1.7, throughout this book we shall make heavy use of the computer to obtain answers to the illustrative examples to familiarize the reader with some of the "packaged" programs. For the consumption-income data given in Table 3.2, we have used a time-sharing computer facility and obtained the results shown on the accompanying printout. Since this is the first time in the book that an actual computer printout is given, it may be helpful to comment on the output briefly. For expositional purposes, the printout is divided into 12 parts, each part being identified by a roman numeral. Throughout the printout the question mark symbol (?) means that the computer is asking a question and the user has to provide the answer, in most cases by simply typing yes or no on a typewriter at a terminal connected to the computer.

Part I: Gives the actual data used in the analysis. The first column gives the values of the Y variable, and the second column gives the values of the X variable. Each line starts with the question mark; the computer is asking, "What are the values?"

Part II: Print (?): Do you want the data fed in I to be printed for verification? If you want it, print YES; if not, print NO.

Part III: Changes (?): Are any data fed in I to be changed, say, because of errors? Answer YES or NO. If the answer is YES, the computer will tell you how to make the changes.

Part IV: Specify the dependent variable. In I the dependent variable is printed first. Therefore, the number 1 after the question mark tells the computer that it is the first variable which is to be treated as the dependent variable.

Part V: Specify the independent (i.e., explanatory) variable. In I the explanatory variable X was printed as the second variable. Therefore, the number 2 after the question mark tells the computer that it is the second variable that is to be treated as the independent variable.

Part VI: After completing the preceding steps, the computer begins to work and prints out the following information:
1. The regression coefficients and their standard errors. (*Note:* This particular program does not give the standard error of the intercept term.)
2. The t value (see Chap. 5 for an explanation).

3. The correlation coefficient r. (r^2 can be easily computed from this r.)

4. The standard error of estimate, which is nothing but the square root of $\hat{\sigma}^2$.

Part VII: This part gives the analysis of variance table, which is discussed fully in Chap. 5.

Part VIII: If the answer to the question "Do you wish to print the table of residuals ($= e_i$)" is YES, the computer will print out the actual and estimated Y values, the residuals, and the standardized residuals, that is, the residuals divided by the standard error of estimate. (We shall discuss this in a later chapter.) [Compare this part with Table 3.3, cols. (1), (9), and (10).]

Part IX: This part gives information about the smallest and largest residuals, information which is highly useful in finding out whether some of the data points are extreme. (This will be explained in Chap. 11.)

Part X: This part gives the scattergram of the actual and predicted or estimated Y values. Such a visual impression is often helpful in finding out the goodness of fit of the regression line.

Part XI: The user may want to use some of the output for further work. By printing YES, the output is saved.

Part XII: The role of the Durbin-Watson statistic will be explained in Chap. 11.

Comparing the calculations given in Table 3.3 and the computer printout, the utility of the computer can be readily appreciated. In just a page or so the printout gives all the essential summary of regression analysis. And, of course, this is done with a tremendous saving in time and energy.

COMPUTER PRINTOUT

```
I.    ?70,80
      ?65,100
      ?90,120
      ?95,140
      ?110,160
      ?115,180
      ?120,200
      ?140,220
      ?155,240
      ?150,260

II.   PRINT
      ?* NO

III.  CHANGE
      ?* NO

IV.   SPECIFY THE DEPENDENT VARIABLE
      ?* 1

V.    SPECIFY THE INDEPENDENT VARIABLE
      ?* 2
```

VI. INTERCEPT 24,45456
REGRESSION COEFFICIENT 0.50909
STANDARD ERROR OF REG. COEF. 0.357E-01 (= .0357)
COMPUTED T VALUE 14.243
CORRELATION COEFFICIENT 0.981
STANDARD ERROR OF ESTIMATE 6.493

VII. ANALYSIS OF VARIANCE FOR THE REGRESSION

SOURCE OF VARIATION	D.F.	SUM OF SQ.	MEAN SQ.	F VALUE
ATTRIBUTABLE TO REGRESSION	1	8552.730	8552.730	202.870
DEVIATION FROM REGRESSION	8	337.270	42.159	
TOTAL	9	8890.000		

VIII. DO YOU WISH TO PRINT THE TABLE OF RESIDUALS
?* YES

CASE NO.	Y OBSERVED	Y ESTIMATED	RESIDUAL	STD. RESID.
1	70.000	65.182	4.818	0.742
2	65.000	75.364	-10.364	-1.596
3	90.000	85.545	4.455	0.686
4	95.000	95.727	-0.727	-0.112
5	110.000	105.909	4.091	0.630
6	115.000	116.091	-1.091	-0.168
7	120.000	126.276	-6.273	-0.966
8	140.000	136.455	3.545	0.546
9	155.000	146.636	8.364	1.288
10	150.000	156.818	-6.818	-1.050

IX. TEST OF EXTREME RESIDUALS
RATIO OF RANGES FOR THE SMALLEST RESIDUAL 0.234
RATIO OF RANGES FOR THE LARGEST RESIDUAL 0.234
CRITICAL VALUE OF THE RATIO AT ALPHA = 0.10 0.409

X. DO YOU WISH TO PLOT Y OBSERVED AND Y ESTIMATED
?* YES

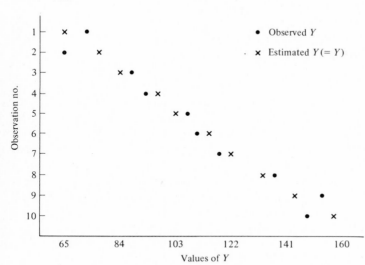

XI. DO YOU WISH TO KEEP ANY RESULTS
?* NO

XII. DO YOU WISH TO COMPUTE THE DURBIN-WATSON STATISTIC
?* YES
DURBIN-WATSON STATISTIC
2.680

FOUR

THE NORMALITY ASSUMPTION: CLASSICAL NORMAL LINEAR REGRESSION MODEL

In this chapter we continue to deal with the two-variable classical linear regression model but assume that the population disturbances u_i are normally distributed. Such a model is called a *two-variable classical normal linear regression model*. In what follows, we offer justification for the normality assumption for u_i and point out the consequences of this assumption.

4.1 THE PROBABILITY DISTRIBUTION OF DISTURBANCES u_i

Recall that for the application of the method of ordinary least squares (OLS) to the classical linear regression model we did not make any assumptions about the probability distribution of the disturbances u_i. The only assumptions made about u_i were that they had zero expectations, were uncorrelated, and had a constant variance. With these assumptions, we saw (in Chap. 3) that the OLS estimators $\hat{\beta}_0$, $\hat{\beta}_1$, and $\hat{\sigma}^2$ satisfy several desirable statistical properties, such as unbiasedness and minimum variance. If our objective is point estimation only, the OLS method will therefore suffice. But point estimation is only one aspect of statistical inference, the other being hypothesis testing.[1]

---

[1] What is known as the *classical theory of statistical inference* consists of two branches, namely, estimation (point as well as interval) and hypothesis testing. Point estimation was considered in Chap. 3. The topics of interval estimation and hypothesis testing, which are intimately connected, will be discussed fully in Chap. 5. Here it suffices to note that in hypothesis testing we are generally concerned with the relationship between the population quantities (parameters) and their sample counterparts (estimators).

Thus, our interest is not only in obtaining, say, $\hat{\beta}_1$, but in using it to make statements or inferences about true β_1. More generally, our goal is not merely to obtain the sample regression function (SRF), but to use it to draw inferences about the population regression function (PRF), as emphasized in Chap. 2.

Since our objective is estimation as well as hypothesis testing, we need to specify the probability distribution of the disturbances u_i. Why? The answer is not difficult. It was shown in App. 3A, Sec. 3A.2, that the OLS estimators $\hat{\beta}_0$ and $\hat{\beta}_1$ are both linear functions of u_i, which is random by assumption.[2] Therefore, the sampling or probability distributions of the OLS estimators will depend upon the assumptions made about the probability distribution of u_i. And since the probability distributions of these estimators are necessary to draw inferences about their population values, the nature of the probability distribution of u_i assumes an extremely important role in hypothesis testing.

Since the method of OLS does not make any assumption about the probabilistic nature of u_i, it is of little help for the purpose of drawing inferences about the PRF from SRF, the Gauss-Markov theorem notwithstanding. This void can be filled if we are willing to assume that the u's follow some probability distribution. For reasons to be explained shortly, in the regression context it is usually assumed that the u's follow the normal distribution.

4.2 THE NORMALITY ASSUMPTION

The classical *normal* linear regression assumes that each u_i is distributed *normally* with

$$\text{Mean:} \quad E(u_i) \quad = 0 \tag{4.2.1}$$

$$\text{Variance:} \quad E(u_i^2) \quad = \sigma^2 \tag{4.2.2}$$

$$\text{cov}\,(u_i, u_j): \quad E(u_i u_j) = 0 \qquad i \neq j \tag{4.2.3}$$

These assumptions may be more compactly stated as

$$u_i \sim N(0, \sigma^2) \tag{4.2.4}$$

where $\sim$ means "distributed as" and where N stands for the "normal distribution," the terms in the parenthesis representing the two parameters of the normal distribution, namely, the mean and the variance.

In passing it may be noted that for *two normally distributed variables zero covariance or correlation means independence of the two variables*. Therefore, with the normality assumption, (4.2.3) means that u_i and u_j are not only uncorrelated but also independently distributed.

---

[2] Note that these estimators are actually linear functions of the dependent variable Y. But Y is itself a linear function of u, as postulated in (2.4.2). Hence, the estimators are ultimately functions of u, which is random by assumption.

Why the normality assumption? There are several reasons.

1. As pointed out in Sec. 2.5, u_i represent the combined influence (on the dependent variable) of a large number of independent variables which are not explicitly introduced in the regression model. As noted, the influence of these omitted or neglected variables is hopefully small and at best random. Now by the celebrated *central limit theorem* of statistics it can be shown that if there is a large number of independent and identically distributed random variables, then, with a few exceptions, the distribution of their sum tends to a normal distribution as the number of such variables increases indefinitely.[3] It is this central limit theorem that provides a theoretical justification for the assumption of normality of u_i.

2. A variant of the central limit theorem states that even if the number of variables is not very large or if these variables are not strictly independent, their sum may still be normally distributed.[4]

3. With the normality assumption, the probability distributions of the OLS estimators can be easily derived because *it is a property of the normal distribution that any linear function of normally distributed variables is itself normally distributed.* It is shown later that under the normality assumption for u_i, the OLS estimators $\hat{\beta}_0$ and $\hat{\beta}_1$ are also normally distributed.

4. Finally, the normal distribution is a comparatively simple distribution involving only two parameters (mean and variance); it is very well-known, and its theoretical properties have been extensively studied in mathematical statistics.

4.3 PROPERTIES OF OLS ESTIMATORS UNDER THE NORMALITY ASSUMPTION

With the assumption of normality, the OLS estimators $\hat{\beta}_0$, $\hat{\beta}_1$, and $\hat{\sigma}^2$ have the following statistical properties:[5]

1. They are unbiased.
2. They have minimum variance. Combined with 1, this means they are *minimum-variance unbiased*, or efficient estimators.
3. Consistent; that is, as the sample size increases indefinitely, the estimators converge to their true population values.
4. $\hat{\beta}_0$ is *normally* distributed with

$$\text{Mean:} \quad E(\hat{\beta}_0) = \beta_0 \tag{4.3.1}$$

$$\text{var } (\hat{\beta}_0): \quad \sigma_{\hat{\beta}_0}^2 = \frac{\sum X_i^2}{N \sum x_i^2} \sigma^2 \tag{4.3.2}$$

---

[3] For a relatively simple discussion of the theorem, see Harald Cramer, *The Elements of Probability Theory and Some of Its Applications*, John Wiley & Sons, Inc., New York, 1955, pp. 114–116. One exception to the theorem is the Cauchy distribution; see M. G. Kendall and A. Stuart, *The Advanced Theory of Statistics*, vol. 1, Charles Griffin & Company, Ltd., London, 1960, pp. 248–249.

[4] For the various forms of the central limit theorem, see Harald Cramer, *Mathematical Methods of Statistics*, Princeton University Press, Princeton, N.J., 1946, chap. 17.

[5] The statistical properties of estimators are discussed fully in App. A.

or, more compactly,

$$\hat{\beta}_0 \sim N(\beta_0, \sigma_{\hat{\beta}_0}^2)$$

5. $\hat{\beta}_1$ is *normally* distributed with

$$\text{Mean:} \quad E(\hat{\beta}_1) = \beta_1$$

$$\text{var } (\hat{\beta}_1): \quad \sigma_{\hat{\beta}_1}^2 = \frac{\sigma^2}{\sum x_i^2} \tag{4.3.3}$$

or, more compactly,

$$\hat{\beta}_1 \sim N(\beta_1, \sigma_{\hat{\beta}_1}^2)$$

6. $(N - 2)\hat{\sigma}^2/\sigma^2$ is distributed as the χ^2 (chi-square) distribution with $N - 2$ df.
7. $(\hat{\beta}_0, \hat{\beta}_1)$ are distributed independently of $\hat{\sigma}^2$.
8. $\hat{\beta}_0$ and $\hat{\beta}_1$ *have minimum variance in the entire class of unbiased estimators, whether linear or not.* This result, which is due to Rao, is very powerful because unlike the Gauss-Markov theorem it is not restricted to the class of linear estimators only.[6]

The unbiasedness and minimum-variance properties of the OLS estimators have been proved in App. 3A. To show that $\hat{\beta}_0$ and $\hat{\beta}_1$ follow the normal distribution is easy. As noted in Chap. 3, $\hat{\beta}_0$ and $\hat{\beta}_1$ are linear functions of the stochastic disturbance term u_i (see fn. 2). Since the u_i are assumed to be normally distributed, then, following the rule that any linear function of normally distributed variables is itself normally distributed, it follows that $\hat{\beta}_0$ and $\hat{\beta}_1$ are themselves normally distributed with the means and variances given previously. The proof of the statement that $(N - 2)\hat{\sigma}^2/\sigma^2$ follows the χ^2 distribution with $N - 2$ df is slightly involved and may be found in the references.[7]

The important point to note is that the normality assumption enables us to derive the probability distributions of $\hat{\beta}_0$ (normal), $\hat{\beta}_1$ (normal), and $\hat{\sigma}^2$ (chi square). As we shall see in Chap. 5, this simplifies the task of establishing confidence intervals and testing (statistical) hypotheses.

In passing, note that if we assume that u_i is distributed normally with mean 0 and variance σ^2, then Y_i itself is normally distributed with mean and variance given by

$$\text{Mean:} \quad E(Y_i) = \beta_0 + \beta_1 X_i \tag{4.3.4}$$

$$\text{var } (Y_i) = \sigma^2 \tag{4.3.5}$$

More compactly, we can write

$$Y_i \sim N(\beta_0 + \beta_1 X_i, \sigma^2) \tag{4.3.6}$$

The proof of (4.3.6) follows from Table 3.1 and fn. 2 of this chapter.

---

[6] C. R. Rao, *Linear Statistical Inference and its Applications*, John Wiley & Sons, Inc., New York, 1965, p. 258.

[7] See, for example, Robert V. Hogg and Allen T. Craig, *Introduction to Mathematical Statistics*, 2d ed., The Macmillan Company, New York, 1965, p. 144.

4.4 THE METHOD OF MAXIMUM LIKELIHOOD (ML)

A general method of point estimation with some stronger theoretical properties as compared with the method of OLS is the method of *maximum likelihood* (ML). The general idea behind ML is as follows. Let $f(x, \theta)$ be the density function of the random variable X, and let θ be the parameter of the density function. If we observe a random sample of $X_1, X_2, \ldots, X_N$, then the ML estimator of θ is that value of θ that has the highest probability of generating the observed sample. In other words, the ML estimate of θ is that value which maximizes the density function $f(x, \theta)$. (An application is given in Exercise 4.1.)

We shall not pursue the ML method in this text for these reasons: First, it is rather involved. Secondly, assuming normality of u_i, the ML and OLS estimators of the regression coefficients, the β's, are identical, and this is true of the simple as well as multiple regressions. In small samples, the ML estimator of σ^2 is biased, whereas the OLS estimator of σ^2 is unbiased. However, as the sample size increases indefinitely, the ML and OLS estimators of σ^2 tend to be equal. Finally, the method of OLS with the added assumption of normality of u_i provides us with all the tools necessary for both estimation and hypothesis testing of the linear regression models. (For the verification of these statements, the interested reader should consult the references.[8])

4.5 SUMMARY AND CONCLUSIONS

In this chapter we considered the classical normal linear regression model. This model differs from the model considered in Chap. 3 in that it assumes that the population disturbances are normally distributed. With this assumption, we saw that the OLS estimators of β_0, β_1, and σ^2 follow well-known probability distributions. This considerably simplifies our task of statistical inference, that is, estimation of the parameters as well as testing hypotheses about them. That this is so, is shown in Chap. 5.

In passing, we mentioned very briefly an alternative method of point estimation, namely, the method of maximum likelihood. But with the normality assumption, the ML estimators are generally the same as the OLS estimators, especially if the sample size is large. Therefore, we shall not deal with the method of maximum likelihood in this text.

---

[8] See J. Johnston, *Econometric Methods*, 2d ed., McGraw-Hill Book Company, New York, 1972, p. 25, and Jan Kmenta, *Elements of Econometrics*, The Macmillan Company, New York, 1971, pp. 213–215.

EXERCISES

*4.1 *Maximum-likelihood estimation of two-variable regression model.* Assume that in the two-variable model $Y_i = \beta_0 + \beta_1 X_i + u_i$, the Y_i are normally and independently distributed with mean $= \beta_0 + \beta_1 X_i$ and variance $= \sigma^2$. As a result, the joint probability density function of $Y_1, Y_2, \ldots, Y_N$, given the preceding mean and variance, can be written as

$$f(Y_1, Y_2, \ldots, Y_N \mid \beta_0 + \beta_1 X_i, \sigma^2)$$

But in view of the independence of the Y's, this joint probability density function can be written as a product of N individual density functions as

$$f(Y_1, Y_2, \ldots, Y_N \mid \beta_0 + \beta_1 X_i, \sigma^2)$$
$$= f(Y_1 \mid \beta_0 + \beta_1 X_i, \sigma^2) f(Y_2 \mid \beta_0 + \beta_1 X_i, \sigma^2) \cdots f(Y_N \mid \beta_0 + \beta_1 X_i, \sigma^2) \quad (1)$$

where
$$f(Y_i) = \frac{1}{\sigma\sqrt{2\pi}} \exp\left\{ -\frac{1}{2} \frac{(Y_i - \beta_0 - \beta_1 X_i)^2}{\sigma^2} \right\} \quad (2)$$

which is the density function of a normally distributed variable with the given mean and variance.
Note: exp means e to the power the expression indicated by { }.

(a) Show that substituting (2) for each Y_i into (1) gives

$$f(Y_1, Y_2, \ldots, Y_N \mid \beta_0 + \beta_1 X_i, \sigma^2) = \frac{1}{\sigma^N (\sqrt{2\pi})^N} \exp\left\{ -\frac{1}{2} \sum \frac{(Y_i - \beta_0 - \beta_1 X_i)^2}{\sigma^2} \right\} \quad (3)$$

(b) If $Y_1, Y_2, \ldots, Y_N$ are known but β_0, β_1, and σ^2 are not known, the function in (3) is called a *likelihood function.* The method of maximum likelihood consists in estimating the unknowns in such a manner that the probability of observing the given Y is as high (or maximum) as possible. Therefore, we have to find the maximum of the function (3). This is now a straightforward exercise in differential calculus. For differentiation, it is easier to express equation (3) in the log form as follows: Using natural log, we obtain

$$\ln f(Y_1, Y_2, \ldots, Y_N \mid \beta_0 + \beta_1, \sigma^2) = -N \ln \sigma - \frac{N}{2} \ln(\pi) - \frac{1}{2} \sum \frac{(Y_i - \beta_0 - \beta_1 X_i)^2}{\sigma^2} \quad (4)$$

Differentiating equation (4) with respect to β_0 and β_1, respectively, show that the maximum-likelihood estimators of β_0 and β_1 are identical with the least-squares estimators. How would you account for this equality?

(c) Show that the ML estimator of σ^2 is $\sum e_i^2 / N$, which differs from the OLS estimator, which is $\sum e_i^2 / (N - 2)$. Is the ML estimator of σ^2 biased in small samples? And in large samples?
Hint: To obtain the ML estimator of σ^2, differentiate (4) with respect to σ^2.

*4.2 "If two random variables are statistically independent, the coefficient of correlation between the two is zero. But the converse is not necessarily true; that is, zero correlation does not imply statistical independence. However, if two variables are normally distributed, zero correlation necessarily implies statistical independence." Verify this statement for the following joint probability density function of two normally distributed variables Y_1 and Y_2. (This joint probability density function is known as the *bivariate normal probability density function*):

$$f(Y_1, Y_2) = \frac{1}{2\pi\sigma_1\sigma_2\sqrt{1-\rho^2}} \exp\left\{ -\frac{1}{2(1-\rho^2)} \left[\left(\frac{Y_1 - \mu_1}{\sigma_1}\right)^2 - 2\rho \frac{(Y_1 - \mu_1)(Y_2 - \mu_2)}{\sigma_1\sigma_2} + \left(\frac{Y_2 - \mu_2}{\sigma_2}\right)^2 \right] \right\}$$

where $\mu_1 =$ mean of Y_1, $\mu_2 =$ mean of Y_2, $\sigma_1 =$ standard deviation of Y_1, $\sigma_2 =$ standard deviation of Y_2, and $\rho =$ coefficient of correlation between Y_1 and Y_2.

* Optional.

TWO-VARIABLE REGRESSION: INTERVAL ESTIMATION AND HYPOTHESIS TESTING[1]

As pointed out in Chap. 4, estimation and hypothesis testing constitute the two major branches of classical statistics. The theory of estimation consists of two parts: point estimation and interval estimation. We have discussed point estimation thoroughly in the previous two chapters where we introduced the OLS and ML methods of point estimation. In this chapter we first consider interval estimation and then take up the topic of hypothesis testing, a topic intimately related to interval estimation.

5.1 INTERVAL ESTIMATION: SOME BASIC IDEAS

To fix the ideas, consider the hypothetical consumption-income example of Chap. 3. Equation (3.4.1) shows that the estimated marginal propensity to consume (MPC) $\hat{\beta}_1$ is 0.5091, which is a single (point) estimate of the unknown population MPC β_1. How reliable is this estimate? As noted in Chap. 3, because of sampling fluctuations, a single estimate is likely to differ from the true value, although in repeated sampling its mean value is expected to be equal to the true value. (*Note:* $E(\hat{\beta}_1) = \beta_1$.) Now in statistics the reliability of a point estimator is

---

[1] The discussion which follows presumes that the reader is familiar with basic notions of statistical inference such as confidence interval, hypothesis testing, level of significance or probability of type I error, type II error, etc. The reader wishing to refresh his or her knowledge of these concepts is advised to read App. A before proceeding further.

measured by its standard error or variance. Therefore, instead of relying on the point estimate alone, we may give the probability that the point estimator lies in a certain range or interval around the true parameter, say, within 2 or 3 standard errors. This is roughly the idea behind interval estimation.

To be more specific, assume that we want to find out how "close" is, say, $\hat{\beta}_1$ to β_1. For this purpose we may try to find out two positive numbers δ and α, the latter lying between 0 and 1, such that the probability that the interval $(\hat{\beta}_1 - \delta, \hat{\beta}_1 + \delta)$ contains the true β_1 is $1 - \alpha$. Symbolically,

$$\Pr(\hat{\beta}_1 - \delta \leq \beta_1 \leq \hat{\beta}_1 + \delta) = 1 - \alpha \tag{5.1.1}$$

Such an interval, if it exists, is known as the *confidence interval;* $1 - \alpha$ is known as the *confidence coefficient;* and $\alpha(0 < \alpha < 1)$ is known as the *level of significance.*[2] The endpoints of the confidence interval are known as the *confidence limits* (also known as *critical* values), $\hat{\beta}_1 - \delta$ being the *lower confidence limit* and $\hat{\beta}_1 + \delta$ the *upper confidence limit.* In passing, it may be noted that in practice α and $1 - \alpha$ are often expressed in percentage forms as 100α and $100(1 - \alpha)$ percent.

Equation (5.1.1) shows that an *interval estimator,* in contrast to a point estimator, is an interval constructed in such a manner that it has a specified probability $1 - \alpha$ of including within its limits the true value of the parameter. For example, if $\alpha = 0.05$, or 5 percent, (5.1.1) would read: The probability that the (random) interval shown there includes the true β_1 is 0.95, or 95 percent. The interval estimator thus gives a range of values within which the true β_1 may lie.

It is very important to know the following aspects of interval estimation:

1. Equation (5.1.1) does not say that the probability of β_1 lying between the given limits is $1 - \alpha$. Since β_1, although an unknown, is assumed to be some fixed number, either it lies in the interval or it does not. What (5.1.1) states is that using the method described in this chapter, the probability of constructing an interval which contains β_1 is $1 - \alpha$.

2. The interval (5.1.1) is a *random interval;* that is, it will vary from one sample to the next because it is based on $\hat{\beta}_1$, which is random. (Why?)

3. Since the confidence interval is random, the probability statements attached to it should be understood in the long-run sense, that is, repeated sampling. More specifically, (5.1.1) means: If in repeated sampling confidence intervals like it are constructed a great many times on the $1 - \alpha$ probability basis, then, in the long run, on the average, such intervals will enclose in $1 - \alpha$ of the cases the true value of the parameter.

4. As noted in 2, the interval (5.1.1) is random so long as $\hat{\beta}_1$ is not known. But once we have a specific sample and once we obtain a specific numerical value of $\hat{\beta}_1$, the interval (5.1.1) is no longer random; it is fixed. In this case, we cannot make the probabilistic statement (5.1.1); that is, we cannot say that the probability is

---

[2] Also known as the *probability of committing type I error.* Type I error consists in rejecting a true hypothesis, whereas type II error consists in accepting a false hypothesis. (This is discussed more fully in App. A.)

$1 - \alpha$ that a given *fixed* interval includes the true β_1: In this situation β_1 is either in the fixed interval or outside it. Thus the probability is either 1 or 0.

How are the confidence intervals constructed? From the discussion above one may expect that if the sampling or probability distributions of the estimators are known, one can make confidence interval statements such as (5.1.1). In Chap. 4 we saw that under the assumption of normality of the disturbances u_i the OLS estimators $\hat{\beta}_0$ and $\hat{\beta}_1$ are themselves normally distributed and that the OLS estimator $\hat{\sigma}^2$ is related to the χ^2 (chi-square) distribution. It would then seem that the task of constructing confidence intervals is a simple one. Although this may be the case, we need to digress a bit and consider some of the probability distributions related to the normal distribution which will be immensely helpful in the discussion that follows.

5.2 NORMAL, t, χ^2, AND F DISTRIBUTIONS: A DIGRESSION

The normal distribution was introduced in Chap. 4. Some of the distributions related to the normal distribution are given in the following theorems without proof.[3]

Theorem 5.1: If $Z_1, Z_2, \ldots, Z_N$ are normally and independently distributed random variables such that $Z_i \sim N(\mu_i, \sigma_i^2)$, then the sum $Z = \sum k_i Z_i$, where k_i are constants not all zero, is also distributed normally with mean $\sum k_i \mu_i$ and variance $\sum k_i^2 \sigma_i^2$; that is, $Z \sim N(\sum k_i \mu_i, \sum k_i^2 \sigma_i^2)$.

Theorem 5.2: If $Z_1, Z_2, \ldots, Z_N$ are normally and independently distributed normal variables such that each $Z_i \sim N(0, 1)$, that is, a standardized normal variable, then $\sum Z_i^2$ follows the chi-square distribution with N df. Symbolically, $\sum Z_i^2 \sim \chi_N^2$, where N denotes the df.

Theorem 5.3: If $Z_1, Z_2, \ldots, Z_N$ are independently distributed random variables each following a chi-square distribution with k_i df, then the sum $\sum Z_i$ also follows a chi-square distribution with $k = \sum k_i$ df.

Theorem 5.4: If Z_1 is a standardized normal variable $[Z_1 \sim N(0, 1)]$ and another variable Z_2 follows the chi-square distribution with k df and is independent of Z_1, the variable defined as

$$t = \frac{Z_1}{\sqrt{Z_2/\sqrt{k}}} = \frac{Z_1 \sqrt{k}}{\sqrt{Z_2}} \tag{5.2.1}$$

follows Student's t distribution with k df.

---

[3] See App. A for a brief discussion of various probability distributions and their properties. For proofs of the theorems, refer to Alexander M. Mood, Franklin A. Graybill, and Duane C. Boes, *Introduction to the Theory of Statistics*, McGraw-Hill Book Company, New York, 1974, pp. 239–249.

Theorem 5.5: If Z_1 and Z_2 are independently distributed chi-square variables with k_1 and k_2 df, respectively, then the variable

$$F = \frac{Z_1/k_1}{Z_2/k_2} \tag{5.2.2}$$

has the F distribution with k_1 and k_2 df.

In the remainder of this chapter we shall see how Theorems 5.1 to 5.5 aid us in establishing confidence intervals and test hypotheses.

5.3 CONFIDENCE INTERVALS FOR REGRESSION COEFFICIENTS β_0 AND β_1

It was shown in Chap. 4, Sec. 4.3, that with the normality assumption for u_i, the OLS estimators $\hat{\beta}_0$ and $\hat{\beta}_1$ are themselves normally distributed with means and variances given therein. Therefore, for example, the variable

$$
\begin{aligned}
Z &= \frac{\hat{\beta}_1 - \beta_1}{\text{se}(\hat{\beta}_1)} \\
&= \frac{(\hat{\beta}_1 - \beta_1)\sqrt{\sum x_i^2}}{\sigma}
\end{aligned} \tag{5.3.1}
$$

is a standardized normal variable. It therefore seems that we can use the normal distribution to make probabilistic statements about $\hat{\beta}_1$ provided the true population variance σ^2 is known. If σ^2 is known, an important property of a normally distributed variable with mean μ and variance σ^2 is that the area under the normal curve between $\mu \pm \sigma$ is about 68 percent, that between the limits $\mu \pm 2\sigma$ is about 95 percent, and that between $\mu \pm 3\sigma$ is about 99.7 percent.

But σ^2 is rarely known, and in practice it is determined by the unbiased estimator $\hat{\sigma}^2$. Replacing σ by $\hat{\sigma}$, (5.3.1) may be written as

$$
\begin{aligned}
t &= \frac{\hat{\beta}_1 - \beta_1}{\text{se}(\hat{\beta}_1)} \\
&= \frac{(\hat{\beta}_1 - \beta_1)\sqrt{\sum x_i^2}}{\hat{\sigma}}
\end{aligned} \tag{5.3.2}
$$

where the $\text{se}(\hat{\beta}_1)$ now refers to the estimated standard error. It can be shown (see App. 5A, Sec. 5A.1) that the t variable defined previously follows the t distribution with $N - 2$ df. [Note the difference between (5.3.1) and (5.3.2).] Therefore, instead of using the normal distribution, we can use the t distribution to establish a confidence interval for β_1 as follows:

$$\Pr\left(-t_{\alpha/2} \le t \le t_{\alpha/2}\right) = 1 - \alpha \tag{5.3.3}$$

where the t value in the middle of this double inequality is the t value given by

(5.3.2) and where $t_{\alpha/2}$ is the value of the t variable obtained from the t distribution for $\alpha/2$ level of significance and $N - 2$ df. Substitution of (5.3.2) into (5.3.3) yields

$$\Pr\left[-t_{\alpha/2} \leq \frac{\hat{\beta}_1 - \beta_1}{\text{se}(\hat{\beta}_1)} \leq t_{\alpha/2}\right] = 1 - \alpha \tag{5.3.4}$$

Rearranging (5.3.4), we obtain

$$\Pr\left[\hat{\beta}_1 - t_{\alpha/2}\text{se}(\hat{\beta}_1) \leq \beta_1 \leq \hat{\beta}_1 + t_{\alpha/2}\text{se}(\hat{\beta}_1)\right] = 1 - \alpha \tag{5.3.5}$$

Equation (5.3.5) provides the $100(1 - \alpha)$ percent confidence interval for β_1. Returning to our illustrative consumption-income example, in Chap. 3, Sec. 3.4, we found that $\hat{\beta}_1 = 0.5091$, $\text{se}(\hat{\beta}_1) = 0.0357$, and df $= 8$. If we assume $\alpha = 5$ percent, that is, 95 percent confidence coefficient, then, the t table shows that for 8 df the critical $t_{\alpha/2} = t_{0.025} = 2.306$. Substituting these values in (5.3.5), the reader should verify that the 95 percent confidence interval for β_1 is as follows:

$$0.4268 \leq \beta_1 \leq 0.5914 \tag{5.3.6}$$

The interpretation of the preceding confidence interval is: Given the confidence coefficient of 95 percent, in the long run, in 95 out of 100 cases intervals like (0.4268, 0.5914) will contain the true β_1. But note that we cannot say that the probability is 95 percent that the specific interval 0.4268 to 0.5914 contains the true β_1 because this interval is now fixed and no longer random and, therefore, β_1 either lies in it or does not: The probability that the specified fixed interval includes the true β_1 is therefore 1 or 0. Following this discussion, the reader should verify that the 95 percent confidence interval for β_0 of the consumption-income example is as follows:

$$9.6643 \leq \beta_0 \leq 39.2545 \tag{5.3.7}$$

5.4 CONFIDENCE INTERVAL FOR σ^2

As pointed out in Chap. 4, Sec. 4.3, under the normality assumption, the variable

$$\chi^2 = (N - 2)\frac{\hat{\sigma}^2}{\sigma^2} \tag{5.4.1}$$

follows the χ^2 distribution with $N - 2$ df.[4] Therefore, we can use the χ^2 distribution to establish confidence interval for σ^2:

$$\Pr\left(\chi^2_{1 - \alpha/2} \leq \chi^2 \leq \chi^2_{\alpha/2}\right) = 1 - \alpha \tag{5.4.2}$$

where the χ^2 value in the middle of this double inequality is as given by (5.4.1) and where $\chi^2_{1 - \alpha/2}$ and χ^2_{α} are two values of χ^2 obtained from the chi-square table for

---

[4] For proof, see Robert V. Hogg and Allen T. Craig, *Introduction to Mathematical Statistics*, 2d ed., The Macmillan Company, New York, 1965, p. 144.

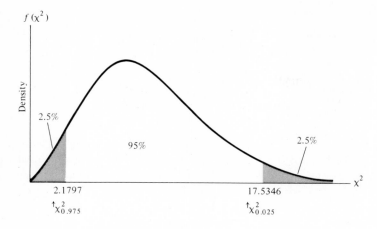

Figure 5.1 The 95 percent confidence interval for $\chi^2(8\ \text{df})$.

$N - 2$ df in such a manner that they cut off $100(\alpha/2)$ percent tail areas of the χ^2 distribution, as shown in Fig. 5.1.

Substituting χ^2 from (5.4.1) into (5.4.2) and rearranging the terms, we obtain

$$\Pr \left[(N - 2)\frac{\hat{\sigma}^2}{\chi^2_{\alpha/2}} \leq \sigma^2 \leq (N - 2)\frac{\hat{\sigma}^2}{\chi^2_{1 - \alpha/2}} \right] = 1 - \alpha \qquad (5.4.3)$$

which gives the $100(1 - \alpha)$ percent confidence interval for σ^2.

To illustrate, consider this example. From Chap. 3, Sec. 3.4, we obtain $\hat{\sigma}^2 = 42.1591$ and df $= 8$. If α is chosen at 5 percent, the chi-square table for 8 df gives the following critical values: $\chi^2_{0.025} = 17.5346$, and $\chi^2_{0.975} = 2.1797$. These values show that the probability of a chi-square value exceeding 17.5346 is 2.5 percent and that of 2.1797 is 97.5 percent. Therefore, the interval between these two values is the 95 percent confidence interval for χ^2, as shown diagrammatically in Fig. 5.1. (Note the skewed characteristic of the chi-square distribution.)

Substituting the data of our example into (5.4.3), the reader should verify that the 95 percent confidence interval for σ^2 is as follows:

$$19.2310 \leq \sigma^2 \leq 154.7038 \qquad (5.4.4)$$

The interpretation of this interval is: If we establish 95 percent confidence limits on σ^2 and if we maintain a priori that these limits will include true σ^2, we shall be right in the long run 95 percent of the time.

5.5 HYPOTHESIS TESTING: GENERAL COMMENTS

Having discussed the problem of point and interval estimation, we shall now consider the topic of hypothesis testing. In this section we discuss briefly some general aspects of this topic; App. A gives some additional details.

The problem of statistical hypothesis testing may be stated simply as follows: *Is a given observation or finding compatible with some stated hypothesis or not?* The word "compatible," as used here, means "sufficiently" close to the hypothesized value to lead us to accept the stated hypothesis. Thus, if some theory or prior experience leads us to believe that the true slope coefficient β_1 of the consumption-income example is unity, is the observed $\hat{\beta}_1 = 0.5091$ obtained from the sample of Table 3.2 consistent with the stated hypothesis? If it is, we may accept the hypothesis; otherwise, we may reject it.

In the language of statistics, the stated hypothesis is known as the *null hypothesis* and is denoted by the symbol H_0. The null hypothesis is usually tested against an *alternative hypothesis*, denoted by H_1, which may state, for example, that true β_1 is different from unity. The alternative hypothesis may be *simple* or *composite*.[5] For example, $H_1: \beta_1 = 1.5$ is a simple hypothesis, but $H_1: \beta_1 \neq 1.5$ is a composite hypothesis.

The theory of hypothesis testing is concerned with developing rules or procedures for deciding whether to accept or reject the null hypothesis. There are two mutually complementary approaches for devising such rules, namely, *confidence interval* and *test of significance*. Both these approaches predicate that the variable (statistic or estimator) under consideration has some probability distribution and that hypothesis testing involves making statements or assertions about the value(s) of the parameter(s) of such distribution. For example, we know that with the normality assumption $\hat{\beta}_1$ is normally distributed with mean equal to β_1 and variance given by (4.3.3). If we hypothesize that $\beta_1 = 1$, we are making an assertion about one of the parameters of the normal distribution, namely, the mean. Most of the statistical hypotheses encountered in this text will be of this type—making assertions about one or more values of the parameters of some assumed probability distribution such as the normal, F, t, or χ^2. How this is accomplished is discussed in the following two sections.

5.6 HYPOTHESIS TESTING: THE CONFIDENCE-INTERVAL APPROACH

To illustrate the confidence-interval approach, once again we revert to the consumption-income example. As we know, the estimated MPC $\hat{\beta}_1$ is 0.5091. Now suppose we assume

$$H_0: \beta_1 = 0.3$$

$$H_1: \beta_1 \neq 0.3$$

[5] A statistical hypothesis is called a *simple hypothesis* if it specifies the precise value(s) of the parameter(s) of a probability density function; otherwise, it is called a *composite hypothesis*. For example, in the normal pdf$(1/\sigma\sqrt{2\pi}) \exp \{-\frac{1}{2}[(X - \mu)/\sigma]^2\}$, if we assert that $H_1: \mu = 15$ and $\sigma = 2$, it is a simple hypothesis; but if $H_1: \mu = 15$ and $\sigma > 15$, it is a composite hypothesis, because the standard deviation does not have a specific value.

Note that the null hypothesis is a simple hypothesis whereas the alternative hypothesis is composite. Is the observed $\hat{\beta}_1$ compatible with H_0?

To answer this question, let us refer to the confidence interval (5.3.6). We know that in the long run intervals like (0.4268, 0.5914) will contain true β_1 with 95 percent probability. Consequently, in the long run (i.e., repeated sampling) such intervals provide a range or limits within which true β_1 may lie with a confidence coefficient of, say, 95 percent. Thus the confidence interval provides a set of plausible null hypotheses. Therefore, if β_1 under H_0 falls within the $100(1 - \alpha)$ percent confidence interval, we may accept the null hypothesis; if it lies outside the interval, we may reject it.

The confidence-interval approach to hypothesis testing thus consists in first finding out the appropriate confidence interval and then verifying whether the null hypothesized value lies inside that interval or outside it. For our hypothetical example, $H_0: \beta_1 = 0.3$ clearly lies outside the 95 percent confidence interval for β_1. Hence we may reject the hypothesis; the probability of observing such a value of $\hat{\beta}_1$ (given $\beta_1 = 0.3$) is less than 2.5 percent.

5.7 HYPOTHESIS TESTING: THE TEST-OF-SIGNIFICANCE APPROACH

An alternative but complementary approach to the confidence-interval method of testing statistical hypotheses is the test-of-significance approach developed along independent lines by R. A. Fisher and jointly by Neyman and Pearson.[6] Broadly speaking, a test of significance is a procedure by which sample results are used to verify the truth or falsity of a null hypothesis. The key idea behind tests of significance is that of a *test statistic* (estimator) and the sampling distribution of such a statistic under the null hypothesis. The decision to accept or reject H_0 is made on the basis of the value of the test statistic obtained from the data at hand.

As an illustration, recall that under the normality assumption the variable

$$t = \frac{\hat{\beta}_1 - \beta_1}{\text{se}(\hat{\beta}_1)}$$

$$= \frac{(\hat{\beta}_1 - \beta_1)\sqrt{\sum x_i^2}}{\hat{\sigma}} \tag{5.3.2}$$

follows the t distribution with $N - 2$ df. If the value of true β_1 is specified under the null hypothesis, the t value of (5.3.2) can readily be computed from the available sample, and therefore it can serve as a test statistic. And since this test statistic

---

[6] Details may be found in E. L. Lehman, *Testing Statistical Hypothesis*, John Wiley & Sons, Inc., New York, 1959.

follows the t distribution, confidence-interval statements such as the following can be made:

$$\Pr\left[-t_{\alpha/2} \le \frac{\hat{\beta}_1 - \beta_1^*}{\text{se}(\hat{\beta}_1)} \le t_{\alpha/2}\right] = 1 - \alpha \qquad (5.7.1)$$

where β_1^* is the value of β_1 under H_0 and where $-t_{\alpha/2}$ and $t_{\alpha/2}$ are the values of t obtained from the t table for $(\alpha/2)$ level of significance and $N - 2$ df [cf. (5.3.4)].

Rearranging (5.7.1), we obtain

$$\Pr\left[\beta_1^* - t_{\alpha/2}\,\text{se}(\hat{\beta}_1) \le \hat{\beta}_1 \le \beta_1^* + t_{\alpha/2}\,\text{se}(\hat{\beta}_1)\right] = 1 - \alpha \qquad (5.7.2)$$

which gives the interval in which $\hat{\beta}_1$ will fall with $1 - \alpha$ probability, given $\beta_1 = \beta_1^*$. In the language of hypothesis testing, the $100(1 - \alpha)$ percent confidence interval established in (5.7.2) is known as the *region of acceptance* (of the null hypothesis) and the *region(s)* outside the confidence interval is (are) called the *region(s) of rejection* (of H_0) or the *critical region(s)*. As noted previously, the confidence limits, the endpoints of the confidence interval, are also called *critical values*.

The intimate connection between the confidence-interval and test-of-significance approaches to hypothesis testing can now be seen by comparing (5.3.5) with (5.7.2). In the confidence-interval procedure we try to establish limits within which the true but unknown β_1 may lie, whereas in the test-of-significance approach we hypothesize some value for β_1 and try to see whether the computed $\hat{\beta}_1$ lies within reasonable (confidence) limits around the hypothesized value.

Once again let us revert to our consumption-income example. We know that $\hat{\beta}_1 = 0.5091$, $\text{se}(\hat{\beta}_1) = 0.0357$, and df $= 8$. If we assume $\alpha = 5$ percent, $t_{\alpha/2} = 2.306$. If we let $H_0: \beta_1 = \beta_1^* = 0.3$ and $H_1: \beta_1 \ne 0.3$, (5.7.2) becomes

$$\Pr(0.2177 \le \hat{\beta}_1 \le 0.3823) = 0.95 \qquad (5.7.3)$$

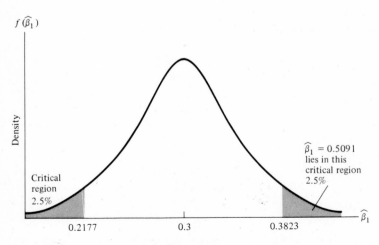

Figure 5.2 The 95 percent confidence interval for $\hat{\beta}_1$ under the hypothesis that $\beta_1 = 0.3$.

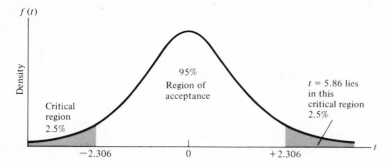

Figure 5.3 The 95 percent confidence interval for t (8 df).

as shown diagrammatically in Fig. 5.2. Since the observed $\hat{\beta}_1$ lies in the critical region, we may reject the null hypothesis that true $\beta_1 = 0.3$.

In practice, there is no need to estimate (5.7.2) explicitly. One can compute the t value in the middle of the double inequality given by (5.7.1) and see whether it lies between the critical t values or outside them. For our example,

$$t = \frac{0.5091 - 0.3}{0.0357} = 5.86 \tag{5.7.4}$$

which clearly lies in the critical region of Fig. 5.3. The conclusion remains the same; namely, we reject H_0.

Since we use the t distribution, the preceding testing procedure is called appropriately the t *test*. In the language of significance tests, a statistic is said to be *statistically significant* if the value of the test statistic lies in the critical region. In this case the null hypothesis is rejected. By the same token, a test is said to be *statistically insignificant* if the value of the test statistic lies in the acceptance region. In this situation, the null hypothesis may be accepted. In our example, the t test is significant and hence we may reject the hypothesis.

Before concluding our discussion of hypothesis testing, it may be noted that the testing procedure outlined previously is known as a *two-sided*, or *two-tail*, test-of-significance procedure in that we consider the two extreme tails of the relevant probability distribution, the rejection regions, and reject the null hypothesis if it lies in either tail. But this was because our H_1 was a two-sided composite hypothesis; $\beta_1 \neq 0.3$ means β_1 is either greater than or less than 0.3. But suppose prior experience suggests to us that the MPC is expected to be greater than 0.3. In this case we have: $H_0: \beta_1 = 0.3$ and $H_1: \beta_1 > 0.3$. Although H_1 is still a composite hypothesis, it is now one-sided. To test this hypothesis, we use the *one-tail test*, as shown in Fig. 5.4.

The test procedure is the same as before except that the upper confidence limit or critical value now corresponds to $t_\alpha = t_{.05}$, that is, the 5 percent level. As Fig. 5.4 shows, we need not consider the lower tail of the t distribution in this case. Whether one uses a two- or one-tail test of significance will depend upon how the

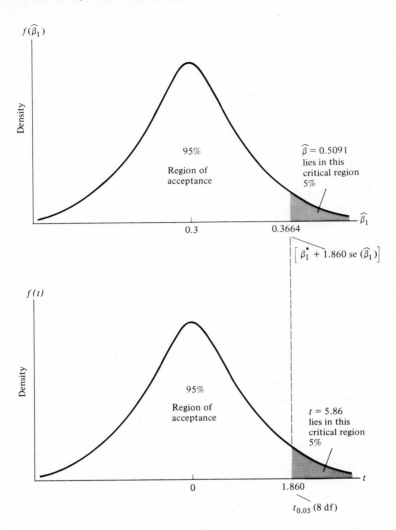

Figure 5.4 One-tail test of significance.

alternative hypothesis is formulated, which, in turn, may depend upon some a priori considerations or prior empirical experience.

As another illustration of the test-of-significance methodology, consider the following variable:

$$\chi^2 = (N - 2)\frac{\hat{\sigma}^2}{\sigma^2} \tag{5.4.1}$$

which, as noted previously, follows the χ^2 distribution with $N - 2$ df. For the hypothetical example, $\hat{\sigma}^2 = 42.1591$ and df $= 8$. If we postulate that $H_0: \sigma^2 = 85$ vs. $H_1: \sigma^2 \neq 85$, equation $(5.4.1)$ provides the test statistic for H_0. Substituting the appropriate values in (5.4.1), it can be found that under H_0, $\chi^2 = 3.97$. If we assume $\alpha = 5$ percent, the critical χ^2 values are 2.1797 and 17.5346. Since the computed χ^2 lies between these limits, the data support the null hypothesis and we may accept it. (See Fig. 5.1.) This test procedure is called very appropriately the *chi-square test of significance*.

5.8 REGRESSION ANALYSIS AND ANALYSIS OF VARIANCE

In this section we study regression analysis from the point of view of the analysis of variance and introduce the reader to an illuminating and complementary way of looking at the statistical inference problem.

In Chap. 3, Sec. 3.3, we developed the following identity:

$$\sum y_i^2 = \sum \hat{y}_i^2 + \sum e_i^2 = \hat{\beta}_1^2 \sum x_i^2 + \sum e_i^2 \tag{3.3.2}$$

that is, TSS = ESS + RSS, which decomposes the total sum of squares (TSS) into two components: explained sum of squares (ESS) and residual sum of squares (RSS). A study of these components of TSS is known as the *analysis of variance* (AOV) from the regression viewpoint.

Associated with any sum of squares is its df, the number of independent observations on which it is based. TSS has $N - 1$ df because we lose 1 df in computing the sample mean $\bar{Y}$. RSS has $N - 2$ df. (Why?) (*Note:* This is true only for the two-variable regression model with the intercept β_0 present.) ESS has 1 df (again true of the two-variable case only), which follows from the fact that ESS = $\hat{\beta}_1^2 \sum x_i^2$ is a function of $\hat{\beta}_1$ only since $\sum x_i^2$ is known.

Let us arrange the various sums of squares and their associated df in Table 5.1, which is the standard form of the AOV table, sometimes called *ANOVA table*. Given the entries of Table 5.1, we now consider the following variable:

$$F = \frac{\text{MSS of ESS}}{\text{MSS of RSS}}$$

$$= \frac{\hat{\beta}_1^2 \sum x_i^2}{\sum e_i^2/(N - 2)} \tag{5.8.1}$$

Table 5.1 AOV table for the two-variable regression model

Source of variation	SS	df	MSS†
Due to regression (ESS)	$\sum \hat{y}_i^2 = \hat{\beta}_1^2 \sum x_i^2$	1	$\hat{\beta}_1^2 \sum x_i^2$
Due to residuals (RSS)	$\sum e_i^2$	$N - 2$	$\dfrac{\sum e_i^2}{N - 2} = \hat{\sigma}^2$
TSS	$\sum y_i^2$	$N - 1$	

† Mean sum of squares which is obtained by dividing SS by their df.

Assuming that the disturbances u_i are normally distributed and $H_0: \beta_1 = 0$, it can be shown that the F of (5.8.1) satisfies the conditions of Theorem 5.5 (Sec. 5.2) and therefore follows the F distribution with 1 and $N - 2$ df. (See App. 5A, Sec. 5A.2.)

What use can be made of the above F ratio? It can be shown that[7]

$$E(\hat{\beta}_1^2 \sum x_i^2) = \sigma^2 + \beta_1^2 \sum x_i^2 \qquad (5.8.2)$$

and

$$E \frac{\sum e_i^2}{N - 2} = E(\hat{\sigma}^2) = \sigma^2 \qquad (5.8.3)$$

(Note that β_1 and σ^2 appearing on the right sides of these equations are the true parameters.) Therefore, if β_1 is, in fact, zero, equations (5.8.2) and (5.8.3) both provide us with identical estimates of true σ^2. In this situation, the explanatory variable X has no linear influence on Y whatsoever and the entire variation in Y is explained by the random disturbances u_i. If, on the other hand, β_1 is not zero, (5.8.2) and (5.8.3) will be different and part of the variation in Y will be ascribable to X. Therefore, the F ratio of (5.8.1) provides a test of the null hypothesis H_0: $\beta_1 = 0$. Since all the quantities entering into this equation can be obtained from the available sample, this F ratio provides a test statistic to test the null hypothesis that true β_1 is zero. All that needs to be done is to compute the F ratio and compare it with the critical F value obtained from the F tables at the chosen level of significance.

To illustrate, let us continue with our consumption-income example. The AOV table for this example is already given in the computer printout in App. 3A, Sec. 3A.5. The computed F value is seen to be 202.87. If α is chosen at 5 percent, the critical F value for 1 and 8 df is 5.32. Obviously, the computed F value is statistically significant, and we may reject the null hypothesis that income X has no influence on consumption expenditure.

There is an interesting relationship between the F test of significance discussed previously and the t test encountered earlier. It can be shown that *the square of the t value with $N - k$ df is an F value with 1 and $N - k$ df.* (*Note:* The numerator df of the F ratio must be 1 for this statement to be true.) If we assume $H_0: \beta_1 = 0$, then, for the consumption-income example the t value is found to be 14.26 by applying (5.3.2). This t value has 8 df. Under the same hypothesis, the F value was 202.87 with 1 and 8 df. Hence, $(14.26)^2 = F$ value, save for the rounding errors.

5.9 APPLICATION OF REGRESSION ANALYSIS: THE PROBLEM OF PREDICTION

On the basis of the sample data of Table 3.2 we obtained the following sample regression:

$$\hat{Y}_i = 24.4545 + 0.5091 X_i \qquad (3.4.2)$$

---

[7] For proof, see K. A. Brownlee, *Statistical Theory and Methodology in Science and Engineering,* John Wiley & Sons, Inc., New York, 1960, pp. 278-280.

where $\hat{Y}_i$ is the estimator of true $E(Y_i)$ corresponding to given X. What use can be made of this *historical regression?* One use is to "predict" or "forecast" the future consumption expenditure Y corresponding to some given level of income X. Now there are two kinds of predictions: (1) prediction of the conditional mean value of Y corresponding to a chosen X, say, X_0, that is the point on the population regression line itself (see Fig. 2.2), and (2) prediction of an individual Y value corresponding to X_0. We shall call these two predictions the *mean prediction* and *individual prediction.*

Mean Prediction[8]

To fix the ideas, assume that $X_0 = 100$ and we want to predict $E(Y_0 | X_0 = 100)$. Now it can be shown that the historical regression (3.4.2) provides the point estimate of this mean prediction as follows:

$$\hat{Y}_0 = \hat{\beta}_0 + \hat{\beta}_1 X_0$$

$$= 24.4545 + 0.5091(100)$$

$$= 75.3676 \tag{5.9.1}$$

where $\hat{Y}_0 = $ estimator of $E(Y_0 | X_0)$. It can be proved that this point predictor is a best linear unbiased estimator (BLUE).

Since $\hat{Y}_0$ is an estimator, it is likely to be different from its true value. The difference between the two values will give some idea about the prediction or forecast error. To assess this error, we need to find out the sampling distribution of $\hat{Y}_0$. It can be shown that $\hat{Y}_0$ above is normally distributed with mean $(\beta_0 + \beta_1 X_0)$ and the variance given by the following formula:

$$\text{var}(\hat{Y}_0) = \sigma^2 \left[\frac{1}{N} + \frac{(X_0 - \bar{X})^2}{\sum x_i^2} \right] \tag{5.9.2}$$

Replacing the unknown σ^2 by its unbiased estimator $\hat{\sigma}^2$, it follows that the variable

$$t = \frac{\hat{Y}_0 - (\beta_0 + \beta_1 X_0)}{\text{se}(\hat{Y}_0)} \tag{5.9.3}$$

follows the t distribution with $N - 2$ df. The t distribution can therefore be used to derive confidence intervals for the true $E(Y_0 | X_0)$ and test hypotheses about it in the usual manner, namely,

$$\Pr \left[\hat{\beta}_0 + \hat{\beta}_1 X_0 - t_{\alpha/2} \, \text{se}(\hat{Y}_0) \le \beta_0 + \beta_1 X_0 \le \hat{\beta}_0 + \hat{\beta}_1 X_0 + t_{\alpha/2} \, \text{se}(\hat{Y}_0) \right] = 1 - \alpha$$

$$\tag{5.9.4}$$

where $\text{se}(\hat{Y}_0)$ is obtained from (5.9.2).

---

[8] For the proofs of the various statements made consult J. Johnston, *Econometric Methods,* McGraw-Hill Book Company, 2d ed., New York, 1972, pp. 38–43.

For our data (see Table 3.3),

$$\text{var}\,(\hat{Y}_0) = 42.159 \left[\frac{1}{10} + \frac{(100-170)^2}{33,000} \right]$$

$$= 10.4873$$

and $\qquad \text{se}(\hat{Y}_0) = 3.2383$

Therefore, the 95 percent confidence interval for true $E(Y_0 \mid X_0) = \beta_0 + \beta_1 X_0$ is given by

$$[75.3676 - 2.306(3.2383) \le E(Y_0 \mid X = 100) \le 75.3676 + 2.306(3.2383)]$$

that is,

$$[67.8965 \le E(Y \mid X = 100) \le 82.8325] \qquad (5.9.5)$$

Thus, given $X_0 = 100$, in repeated sampling, 95 out of 100 intervals like (5.9.5) will include the true mean value; the single best estimate of the true mean value is of course the point estimate 75.3676.

If we obtain 95 percent confidence intervals like (5.9.5) for each of the X values given in Table 3.2, we obtain what is known as the *confidence interval*, or *confidence band*, for the population regression function, which is shown in Fig. 5.5.

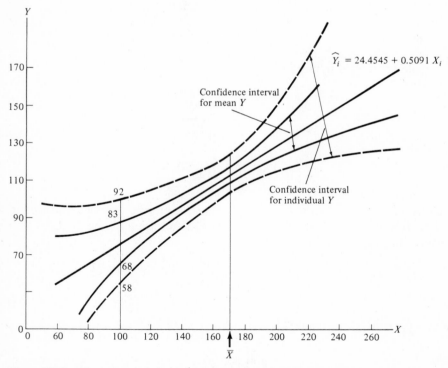

Figure 5.5 Confidence intervals (bands) for mean Y and individual Y values.

Individual Prediction

If our interest lies in predicting an individual Y value Y_0 corresponding to a given X value, say, X_0, it can be proved that a best linear unbiased estimator of Y_0 is also given by (5.9.1) but its variance is as follows:

$$\text{var}\,(Y_0) = \sigma^2 \left[1 + \frac{1}{N} + \frac{(X_0 - \bar{X})^2}{\sum x_i^2} \right] \tag{5.9.6}$$

It can be shown further that Y_0 also follows the normal distribution with mean and variance given by (5.9.1) and (5.9.6), respectively. Substituting $\hat{\sigma}^2$ for the unknown σ^2, it follows that the variable $t = (Y_0 - \hat{Y}_0)/\text{se}(Y_0)$ also follows the t distribution. Therefore, the t distribution can be used to draw inference about the true Y_0. Continuing with our consumption-income example, the point prediction of Y_0 is 75.3676, the same as that of $\hat{Y}_0$, and its variance is 52.6470 (the reader should verify this calculation). Therefore, the 95 percent confidence interval for Y_0 corresponding to $X_0 = 100$ is seen to be

$$(58.6353 \le Y_0 | X_0 = 100 \le 92.0955) \tag{5.9.7}$$

Comparing this interval with (5.9.5), it can be seen that the confidence interval for individual Y_0 is wider than that for the mean value of Y_0. (Why?) Computing confidence intervals like (5.9.7) conditional upon the X values given in Table 3.2, we obtain the 95 percent confidence band for the individual Y values corresponding to these X values. This confidence band along with the confidence band for $\hat{Y}_0$ associated with the same X's is shown in Fig. 5.5.

Notice an important feature of the confidence bands shown in Fig. 5.5. The width of these bands is smallest when $X_0 = \bar{X}$. (Why?) However, the width widens sharply as X_0 moves away from $\bar{X}$. (Why?) This would suggest that the predictive ability of the *historical* sample regression line falls markedly as X_0 departs progressively from $\bar{X}$. Therefore, one should exercise great caution in "extrapolating" the historical regression line to predict $\hat{Y}_0$ or Y_0 associated with a given X_0 which is far removed from the sample mean $\bar{X}$.

5.10 REPORTING THE RESULTS OF REGRESSION ANALYSIS

There are various ways of reporting the results of regression analysis, but in this text we shall use the following format, employing the consumption-income example of Chap. 3 as an illustration:

$$\hat{Y}_i = 24.4545 + 0.5091X_i \qquad r^2 = 0.9621$$

$$(6.4138) \quad (0.0357) \qquad \text{df} = 8$$

$$t = (3.8128)(14.2605) \tag{5.10.1}$$

In equation (5.10.1) the figures in the first set of parentheses are the estimated standard errors of the various regression coefficients and the figures in the second set of parentheses are the estimated t values computed from equation (5.3.2) under the null hypothesis that the true population value of each regression coefficient individually is zero (for example, $3.8128 = 24.4545 \div 6.4138$).

One advantage of reporting regression results in the preceding form is that we can see at once whether each of the estimated regression coefficients is individually statistically significant, that is, significantly different from zero. Of course, any other null hypothesis can be tested by making use of (5.3.2) and the estimated standard errors reported in (5.10.1). The "zero" null hypothesis is a kind of straw man, the objective being to find out whether Y is related at all to a given explanatory variable.

5.11 SUMMARY AND CONCLUSIONS

Estimation and hypothesis testing make up the two branches of classical statistics. Having discussed the estimation problem thoroughly in Chaps. 3 and 4, in this chapter we considered the problem of hypothesis testing. Simply stated, hypothesis testing is concerned with this question: Is a given finding compatible with some stated hypothesis or not? There are two mutually complementary approaches to answering this question, namely, confidence interval and test of significance.

Underlying the confidence-interval procedure is the concept of interval estimation. An interval estimator, in contradistinction with a point estimator, is an interval or range constructed in such a manner that it has a specified probability of including within its limits the true value of the unknown parameter. The interval thus constructed is known as a confidence interval. If the (null) hypothesized value of the parameter falls inside the confidence interval, the hypothesis may be accepted; if it falls outside the interval, the hypothesis may be rejected. In short, the confidence interval provides a set of plausible hypotheses about the values of the unknown parameters.

In the significance-test procedure, instead of constructing a confidence interval for the value of the unknown parameter, one develops a test statistic or criterion and examines its sampling distribution under the null hypothesis. The test statistic usually follows a well-defined probability distribution such as the normal, t, or chi square. The test statistic computed from the available sample is compared against its critical value(s) from the relevant probability distribution. If the computed test statistic exceeds the critical value(s), the null hypothesis may be rejected; otherwise it may be accepted.

In this chapter we also considered the analysis-of-variance approach to regression analysis and showed how it supplements the confidence-interval and test-of-significance approaches to hypothesis testing. Finally, we showed how the sample regression line obtained from the given data can be used for the purpose of forecasting and discussed the problems involved in extrapolating the sample regression line indiscriminately.

EXERCISES

5.1 Refer to Exercise 3.9.

(a) Compute the standard errors of the estimates of the parameters and estimate σ^2.

(b) Establish 95 percent confidence intervals for β_0, β_1, and σ^2.

(c) Test the following hypotheses at the 5 percent level of significance: (i) $\beta_1 = 0$, (ii) $\beta_0 = 0$.

(d) Can you test the hypothesis that $\beta_0 = \beta_1 = 0$ simultaneously by applying the t test? If not, why not?

(e) Predict the average rate of change in stock prices given that the rate of change in consumer prices is 6 percent and find the standard error of prediction.

(f) Predict the rate of change of an individual stock price given that the rate of change in consumer price is 6 percent and find the standard error of prediction.

(g) Test the hypothesis that $\beta_1 = 0$ using the AOV technique. Does the F test support the conclusion in (c)(i) above? Why?

5.2 The AOV table for Exercise 3.7 is as follows:

Source of variation	SS	df	MSS
Due to regression	2.153	1	2.153
Due to residual	1.144	11	0.104
Total	3.297	12	

Based on the preceding data, test the null hypothesis that the quit rate is not linearly related to the unemployment rate.

5.3 The following table gives indexes of compensation per hour and output per hour (i.e., labor productivity) for the United States total private economy for the period 1971-2 to 1975-4.

Year and quarter	Index of compensation per hour (1967 = 100)	Index of output per hour (1967 = 100)
1971-2	131.0	107.0
-3	133.3	108.4
-4	134.1	107.9
1972-1	137.3	109.0
-2	138.9	110.6
-3	140.4	114.4
-4	143.0	113.1
1973-1	147.6	114.4
-2	149.5	113.2
-3	152.1	113.3
-4	155.5	113.2
1974-1	158.4	111.7
-2	163.4	111.0
-3	168.2	110.5
-4	172.1	109.4
1975-1	176.6	109.8
-2	179.3	114.4
-3	182.3	114.0
-4	185.6	114.3

Source: Federal Reserve Bank of St. Louis, *National Economic Trends*, February 27, 1976.

(a) Use a suitable linear regression model to find out whether there is any relationship between average labor productivity and average compensation.

Hint: Plot the scattergram first.

′ (b) Use the t and the F tests to test the hypothesis that there is no association between productivity and compensation.

5.4 Set up the analysis-of-variance table for Exercise 3.15 and test the null hypothesis that changes in money supply have no relationship to the consumer prices.

5.5 Show that the coefficient of determination r^2 defined in (3.3.5) can be computed alternatively as

$$r_{Y\hat{Y}}^2 = \frac{[\sum (Y_i - \bar{Y})(\hat{Y}_i - \bar{Y})]^2}{\sum (Y_i - \bar{Y})^2 \sum (\hat{Y}_i - \bar{Y})^2}$$

$$= \frac{(\sum y_i \hat{y}_i)^2}{(\sum y_i^2)(\sum \hat{y}_i^2)}$$

where Y_i = actual Y, $\hat{Y}_i$ = estimated Y, and $\bar{Y} = \bar{\hat{Y}}$ = mean of Y. In words, the coefficient of determination r^2 is the squared correlation coefficient between actual and estimated Y.

Hint: Apply the definition of r given in (3.3.8) and recall that $\sum y_i \hat{y}_i = \sum (\hat{y}_i + e_i)\hat{y}_i = \sum \hat{y}_i^2$.

Note: The preceding relationship holds true even if there is more than one explanatory variable in the model; that is, it holds true of the multiple regression models discussed in Chap. 6.

5.6 R. A. Fisher has derived the sampling distribution of the correlation coefficient defined in (3.3.8). If it is assumed that the variables X and Y are jointly normally distributed, that is, if they come from a bivariate normal distribution (see Exercise 4.2), then under the assumption that the population correlation coefficient ρ is zero, it can be shown that $t = r\sqrt{N-2}/\sqrt{1-r^2}$ follows Student's t distribution with $N - 2$ df.[9] Show that this t value is identical with the t value given in (5.3.2) under the null hypothesis that $\beta_1 = 0$. Hence establish that under the same null hypothesis $F = t^2$ (see Sec. 5.8).

5.7 The capital market line (CML) of portfolio theory[10] postulates a linear relationship between expected return and risk (measured by the standard deviation) for efficient portfolios as follows:

$$E_i = \beta_0 + \beta_1 \sigma_i$$

where E_i = expected return on portfolio i and σ_i = standard deviation of return. You are given the following data on expected return and standard deviation of the portfolios of 10 mutual funds in the United States for the period 1954–1963. Check whether the data support the theory.

Name of mutual fund	Average annual return, %	Standard deviation of annual return, %
Boston Fund	12.4	12.1
Delaware Fund	14.4	21.4
Equity Fund	14.6	18.7
Fundamental Investors	16.0	21.7
Investors Mutual	11.3	12.4
Loomis-Sales Mutual Fund	10.0	10.4
Massachusetts Investors Trust	16.2	20.6
New England Fund	10.4	10.2
Putnam Fund of Boston	13.1	16.0
Wellington Fund	11.3	12.0

Source: Jack Clark Francis, *Investments: Analysis and Management,* McGraw-Hill Book Company, New York, 1972, table 14-5, p. 410.

[9] If ρ is, in fact, zero, Fisher has shown that r follows the same t distribution provided either X or Y is normally distributed. But if ρ is not equal to zero, both variables must be normally distributed.

[10] See William F. Sharpe, *Portfolio Theory and Capital Markets,* McGraw-Hill Book Company, New York, 1970, p. 83.

5.8 To measure the elasticity of substitution between capital and labor inputs, Arrow, Chenery, Minhas, and Solow, the authors of the now famous CES (constant elasticity of substitution) production function, used the following model:

$$\log \left(\frac{V}{L}\right) = \log \beta_0 + \beta_1 \log W + u$$

where (V/L) = value added per unit of labor, L = labor input, and W = real wage rate. The coefficient β_1 measures the elasticity of substitution between labor and capital. Fit the preceding model to the following data and test the hypothesis that the elasticity of substitution is not statistically significantly different from 1.

Industry	$\log (V/L)$	$\log W$
Wheat flour	3.6973	2.9617
Sugar	3.4795	2.8532
Paints and varnishes	4.0004	3.1158
Cement	3.6609	3.0371
Glass and glassware	3.2321	2.8727
Ceramics	3.3418	2.9745
Plywood	3.4308	2.8287
Cotton textiles	3.3158	3.0888
Woolen textiles	3.5062	3.0086
Jute textiles	3.2352	2.9680
Chemicals	3.8823	3.0909
Aluminum	3.7309	3.0881
Iron and steel	3.7716	3.2256
Bicycles	3.6601	3.1025
Sewing machines	3.7554	3.1354

Source: Damodar Gujarati, "A Test of ACMS Production Function: Indian Industries, 1958," *Indian Journal of Industrial Relations*, July 1966, vol. 2, no. 1, pp. 95–97.

5.9 The monetarists or quantity theorists maintain that national income is determined largely by the quantity of money. To test this hypothesis, consider the following models:

$$\text{GNP}_t = \beta_0 + \beta_1 M_t + u_t$$

$$\ln \text{GNP}_t = \ln \alpha_0 + \alpha_1 \ln M_t + u_t$$

where GNP = gross national product, M = money supply, and t = time. Apply the preceding models to the data in the table that follows.

(a) Which of the preceding models support the monetarists' theory?

(b) Which model gives a better fit? How would you compare the r^2 values of the two models?

(c) How would you interpret the slope coefficients of the two models?

(d) The *income velocity* is defined as the "ratio of national income to money supply" and its inverse is defined as the "Cambridge k." The stability of the income velocity, or Cambridge k, has been of great interest to monetary economists. How would you find out whether the income velocity, or Cambridge k, was stable over the period given in the table?

Hint: Develop a suitable regression model.

Gross National Product and money supply, U.S., 1972-1 to 1975-2

Year and quarter	GNP (billions of dollars)	Money supply (billions of dollars)
1972-1	1127.0	237.5
-2	1156.7	242.3
-3	1181.4	247.4
-4	1219.4	252.9
1973-1	1365.0	257.6
-2	1287.8	261.7
-3	1319.7	265.3
-4	1352.7	268.7
1974-1	1370.9	272.7
-2	1391.0	276.5
-3	1424.4	279.4
-4	1441.3	282.2
1975-1	1433.6	282.6
-2	1460.6	287.8

Source: Federal Reserve Bank of St. Louis, *Rates of Change in Economic Data for Ten Industrial Countries*, February 17, 1976.

5.10 Suppose the equation of an indifference curve between two goods is

$$X_i Y_i = \beta_0 + \beta_1 X_i$$

How would you estimate the parameters of this model? Apply the preceding model to the following data and comment on your results:

Consumption of good X: 1   2   3   4   5

Consumption of good Y: 4   3.5   2.8   1.9   0.8

APPENDIX 5A

5A.1 DERIVATION OF EQUATION (5.3.2)

Let

$$Z_1 = \frac{\hat{\beta}_1 - \beta_1}{se(\hat{\beta}_1)}$$

$$= \frac{(\hat{\beta}_1 - \beta_1)\sqrt{x_i^2}}{\sigma} \tag{1}$$

and

$$Z_2 = (N - 2)\frac{\hat{\sigma}^2}{\sigma^2} \tag{2}$$

Provided σ is known, Z_1 follows the standardized normal distribution; that is, $Z_1 \sim N(0, 1)$. (Why?) Z_2 follows the chi-square distribution with $N - 2$ df. (For proof, see fn. 4.) Therefore, by virtue of Theorem 5.4, the variable

$$t = \frac{Z_1 \sqrt{N - 2}}{\sqrt{Z_2}} \tag{3}$$

follows the t distribution with $N - 2$ df. Substitution of (1) and (2) into (3) gives equation (5.3.2).

5A.2 DERIVATION OF EQUATION (5.8.1)

Equation (1) of Sec. 5A.1 shows that $Z_1 \sim N(0, 1)$. Therefore, by Theorem 5.2, the quantity

$$Z_1^2 = \frac{(\hat{\beta}_1 - \beta_1)^2 \sum x_i^2}{\sigma^2}$$

follows the χ^2 distribution with 1 df. As noted in Sec. 5A.1,

$$Z_2 = (N - 2)\frac{\hat{\sigma}^2}{\sigma^2} = \frac{\sum e_i^2}{\sigma^2}$$

also follows the χ^2 distribution with $N - 2$ df. Moreover, as noted in Sec. 4.3, Z_2 is distributed independently of Z_1. Then applying Theorem 5.5, it follows that

$$F = \frac{Z_1^2/1}{Z_2/(N - 2)}$$
$$= \frac{(\hat{\beta}_1 - \beta_1)^2(\sum x_i^2)}{\sum e_i^2/(N - 2)}$$

follows the F distribution with 1 and $N - 2$ df, respectively. Under the null hypothesis $H_0 : \beta_1 = 0$, the preceding F ratio reduces to equation (5.8.1).

SIX

MULTIPLE REGRESSION ANALYSIS: THE PROBLEM OF ESTIMATION

The two-variable model studied extensively in the previous two chapters is often inadequate in practice. In our consumption-income example, for instance, it was assumed implicitly that only income X affects consumption Y. But economic theory is seldom so simple for, besides income, a number of other variables are also likely to affect consumption expenditure. An obvious example is wealth of the consumer. As another example, the demand for a commodity is likely to depend, not only on its own price, but also on the prices of other competing or complementary goods, income of the consumer, social status, etc. Therefore, we need to extend our simple two-variable regression model to cover models involving more than two variables. This leads us to the discussion of multiple regression models, i.e., models in which the dependent variable Y depends on two or more explanatory variables.

The simplest possible multiple regression model is three-variable regression, with one dependent variable and two explanatory variables. In this and the next chapter we shall study this model, and in Chap. 8 we shall generalize it to more than three variables. Throughout, we are concerned with multiple linear regression models, that is, models linear in the parameters; they may or may not be linear in the variables.

6.1 THE THREE-VARIABLE MODEL: NOTATION AND ASSUMPTIONS

Generalizing the two-variable population regression function (PRF) (2.4.2), we may write the three-variable PRF as

$$Y_i = \beta_1 + \beta_2 X_{2i} + \beta_3 X_{3i} + u_i \qquad (6.1.1)$$

where Y is the dependent variable, X_2 and X_3 the explanatory variables, u the stochastic disturbance term, and i the ith observation. For the purpose of this and the next chapter, however, we shall write equation (6.1.1) in a slightly different but more revealing notation due to Yule, as follows:[1]

$$Y_i = \beta_{1.23} + \beta_{12.3}X_{2i} + \beta_{13.2}X_{3i} + u_i \qquad (6.1.2)$$

where the subscripted numbers attached to the coefficients are interpreted as follows: Subscript 1 denotes the dependent variable Y, 2 denotes the explanatory variable X_2, and 3 denotes the explanatory variable X_3. (*Note:* An alternative notation for Y_i is X_{1i}. Thus the subscript 1 representing Y is quite appropriate.)

$\beta_{1.23}$ in equation (6.1.2) is the intercept term. As usual, it gives the mean or average effect on Y of all the variables excluded from the model, although its mechanical interpretation is the average value of Y when X_2 and X_3 are set equal to zero. The coefficients $\beta_{12.3}$ and $\beta_{13.2}$ are called the *partial regression coefficients*, and their meaning will be explained shortly.

The Yule notation looks rather complex but is actually quite self-explanatory. Its greatest advantage is that it clearly reveals the number of variables in the analysis and also indicates which is the dependent variable and which are the explanatory variables.

Each variable carries two subscripts: The first refers to the variable and the second to the observation number with the convention that the subscript 1 always refer to the dependent variable Y. Thus, X_{24} means the fourth observation on variable X_2. Each parameter carries three subscripts. Those to the left of the point are called *primary subscripts*, and those to the right of the point are called *secondary subscripts*. The first primary subscript always denotes the dependent variable Y, and the second primary subscript indicates the variable to which the β coefficient is attached. The secondary subscript(s) indicates which other variable(s) is present in the model.

Assumptions of the Model

We continue to operate within the framework of the classical linear regression model first introduced in Chap. 3. Specifically, we assume that

$$E(u_i) = 0 \qquad \text{for each } i \qquad (3.1.1)$$

$$\text{cov}\,(u_i, u_j) = 0 \qquad i \neq j \qquad (3.1.2)$$

$$\text{var}\,(u_i) = \sigma^2 \qquad \text{for each } i \qquad (3.1.3)$$

$$\text{cov}\,(u_i, X_{2i}) = \text{cov}\,(u_i, X_{3i}) = 0 \qquad (3.1.5)[2]$$

---

[1] G. U. Yule, "On the Theory of Correlation for any number of variables, treated by a new system of notation," *Proceedings of Royal Society, A,* vol. 79, 1907, pp. 182–193.

[2] This assumption is automatically fulfilled if X_2 and X_3 are nonstochastic and (3.1.1) holds.

To this list we now add another assumption, namely, the assumption of *no multicollinearity, which means that no exact linear relationship exists between the explanatory variables.* Formally, no multicollinearity means there exists no set of numbers λ_2 and λ_3, not both zero, such that

$$\lambda_2 X_{2i} + \lambda_3 X_{3i} = 0 \tag{6.1.3}$$

If such a linear relationship exists, then X_2 and X_3 are said to be *collinear*, or *linearly dependent.* On the other hand, if (6.1.3) holds true only when $\lambda_2 = \lambda_3 = 0$, then X_2 and X_3 are said to be *linearly independent.*

Although we shall consider the problem of multicollinearity in depth in Chap. 9, intuitively the logic behind the assumption of no multicollinearity is not too difficult to grasp. Suppose that in (6.1.2) Y, X_2, and X_3 represent consumption expenditure, income, and wealth of the consumer, respectively. In postulating that consumption expenditure is linearly related to income and wealth, economic theory presumes that wealth and income may have some independent influence on consumption. If not, there is no sense in including both income and wealth variables in the model. In the extreme, if there is an exact linear relationship between income and wealth, we have only one independent variable, not two, and there is no need to include both the variables.[3] In short, the assumption of no multicollinearity requires that in the theoretical population regression function we include only those variables which are not linear functions of some of the variables in the model. Whether this can always be accomplished in practice is another matter, and we shall explore it extensively in Chap. 9.

6.2 INTERPRETATION OF MULTIPLE REGRESSION EQUATION

Given the assumptions of the classical regression model, it follows that, on taking the conditional expectation of Y on both sides of (6.1.2), we obtain

$$E(Y_i \mid X_2, X_3) = \beta_{1.23} + \beta_{12.3} X_{2i} + \beta_{13.2} X_{3i} \tag{6.2.1}$$

In words, equation (6.2.1) gives the conditional mean or expected value of Y conditional upon the given or fixed values of the variables X_2 and X_3. Therefore, as in the two-variable case, multiple regression analysis is conditional regression analysis conditional upon the fixed values of the explanatory variables, and what we obtain is the average or mean value of Y for the fixed values of the X variables.

---

[3] We shall see in Chap. 9 what happens if there is such an exact linear relationship between variables.

6.3 THE MEANING OF PARTIAL REGRESSION COEFFICIENTS

The meaning of *partial* regression coefficient is as follows: $\beta_{12.3}$ measures the change in the mean value of Y, $E(Y_i \mid X_2, X_3)$, per unit change in X_2, holding X_3 constant. In other words, it gives the slope of $E(Y_i \mid X_2, X_3)$ with respect to X_2, holding X_3 constant.[4] Similarly, $\beta_{13.2}$ measures the change in the mean value of Y per unit change in X_3, holding X_2 constant. The utility of the Yule notation should now be clear.

What precisely is the meaning of the term *holding constant*?[5] To understand this, assume that Y represents output and X_2 and X_3 represent labor and capital inputs, respectively. Assume further that both X_2 and X_3 are required in the production of Y and the proportions in which they can be employed in the production of Y can be varied. Now suppose we increase the labor input by a unit which results in some increase in the output (the gross marginal product of labor).[6] Can we ascribe the resulting change in output exclusively to the labor input X_2? If we were to do so, we would be *inflating* the contribution of X_2 to Y; X_2 gets "credit" for that portion of the change in Y that is due to the concomitant increase in the capital input. Therefore, to assess the "true" contribution of X_2 (the net marginal product of labor) to the change in Y, we must somehow "control" the influence of X_3. Similarly, to assess the true contribution of X_3, we must also control the influence of X_2.

How do we go about this control procedure? For concreteness, assume that we want to control the linear influence of the capital input X_3 in measuring the impact of a unit change in the labor input X_2 on the output. To this end, we may proceed as follows.

Stage I Regress Y on X_3 only as follows:

$$Y_i = \hat{\beta}_{1.3} + \hat{\beta}_{13} X_{3i} + w_i \tag{6.3.1}$$

Equation (6.3.1) is nothing but a two-variable regression, save the new but self-explanatory notation, where w_i is the (sample) residual term.

Stage II Regress X_2 on X_3 only as follows:

$$X_{2i} = \hat{\beta}_{2.3} + \hat{\beta}_{23} X_{3i} + v_i \tag{6.3.2}$$

---

[4] The calculus-minded reader will notice at once that $\beta_{12.3}$ and $\beta_{13.2}$ are partial derivatives of $E(Y_i \mid X_2, X_3)$ with respect to X_2 and X_3.

[5] The terms *controling, holding constant, allowing or accounting for the influence of,* and *correcting the influence of* are all synonymous and will be used interchangeably in this text.

[6] Since labor and capital are both required in production, this increase may lead to some increase in capital; the amount of change in the latter will depend on the technology of production.

where v_i is also the residual term. Now

$$w_i = Y_i - \hat{\beta}_{1.3} - \hat{\beta}_{13} X_{3i}$$

$$= Y_i - \hat{Y}_i \tag{6.3.3}$$

and

$$v_i = X_{2i} - \hat{\beta}_{2.3} - \hat{\beta}_{23} X_{3i}$$

$$= X_{2i} - \hat{X}_{2i} \tag{6.3.4}$$

where $\hat{Y}_i$ and $\hat{X}_{2i}$ are the estimated values from the regression equations (6.3.1) and (6.3.2), respectively.

What do the residuals w_i and v_i imply? w_i represents the value of Y_i after removing the (linear) influence on it of X_3, and similarly v_i represents the value of X_{2i} after removing the (linear) influence on it of X_3. So to speak, w_i and v_i are "purified" Y_i and X_{2i}, i.e., purified of the influence (contamination?) of X_3. Therefore, we now proceed as follows.

Stage III Regress w_i on v_i as follows:

$$w_i = a_0 + a_1 v_i + z_i \tag{6.3.5}$$

where z_i is also the sample residual term. Then a_1 should give us an estimate of the "true" effect of a unit change in X_2 on Y,(that is, net marginal product of labor) or the true slope of Y with respect to X_2, that is, an estimate of $\beta_{12.3}$.

In practice, however, there is no need to go through the preceding cumbersome and time-consuming procedure for a_1 can be estimated directly from the formula given in Sec. 6.4 [see equation (6.4.7)]. The three-stage procedure is merely a pedagogic device to drive home the meaning of "partial" regression coefficient.

6.4 OLS AND ML ESTIMATION OF THE PARTIAL REGRESSION COEFFICIENTS

To estimate the parameters of the three-variable regression model (6.1.2), we use the method of ordinary least squares (OLS) introduced in Chap. 3.

OLS Estimators

To find the OLS estimators, let us first write the sample regression function (SRF) corresponding to the PRF of (6.1.2) as follows:

$$Y_i = \hat{\beta}_{1.23} + \hat{\beta}_{12.3} X_{2i} + \hat{\beta}_{13.2} X_{3i} + e_i \tag{6.4.1}$$

where e_i is the residual term, the sample counterpart of the stochastic disturbance term u_i.

As noted in Chap. 3, the OLS procedure consists in so choosing the values of the unknown parameters that the residual sum of squares (RSS) $\sum e_i^2$ is as small as possible. Symbolically,

$$\min \sum e_i^2 = \sum (Y_i - \hat{\beta}_{1.23} - \hat{\beta}_{12.3} X_{2i} - \hat{\beta}_{13.2} X_{3i})^2 \tag{6.4.2}$$

where the RSS is obtained by simple algebraic manipulations of (6.4.1). Now the most straightforward procedure to obtain the estimators which will minimize (6.4.2) is to differentiate it with respect to the unknowns, set the resulting expressions to zero, and solve them simultaneously. As shown in App. 6A, Sec. 6A.1, this procedure gives the following *normal equations* [cf. equations (3.1.9) and (3.1.10)]:

$$\bar{Y} = \hat{\beta}_{1.23} + \hat{\beta}_{12.3} \bar{X}_2 + \hat{\beta}_{13.2} \bar{X}_3 \tag{6.4.3}$$

$$\sum Y_i X_{2i} = \hat{\beta}_{1.23} \sum X_{2i} + \hat{\beta}_{12.3} \sum X_{2i}^2 + \hat{\beta}_{13.2} \sum X_{2i} X_{3i} \tag{6.4.4}$$

$$\sum Y_i X_{3i} = \hat{\beta}_{1.23} \sum X_{3i} + \hat{\beta}_{12.3} \sum X_{2i} X_{3i} + \hat{\beta}_{13.2} \sum X_{3i}^2 \tag{6.4.5}$$

From equation (6.4.3) we see at once that

$$\hat{\beta}_{1.23} = \bar{Y} - \hat{\beta}_{12.3} \bar{X}_2 - \hat{\beta}_{13.2} \bar{X}_3 \tag{6.4.6}$$

which is the OLS estimator of the population intercept $\beta_{1.23}$. Note the similarity between this estimator and its two-variable counterpart given in equation (3.1.12).

Following the convention of letting the lowercase letters denote deviations from sample mean values, one can derive the following formulas from the normal equations (6.4.3) to (6.4.5):

$$\hat{\beta}_{12.3} = \frac{(\sum y_i x_{2i})(\sum x_{3i}^2) - (\sum y_i x_{3i})(\sum x_{2i} x_{3i})}{(\sum x_{2i}^2)(\sum x_{3i}^2) - (\sum x_{2i} x_{3i})^2} \tag{6.4.7}[7]$$

$$\hat{\beta}_{13.2} = \frac{(\sum y_i x_{3i})(\sum x_{2i}^2) - (\sum y_i x_{2i})(\sum x_{2i} x_{3i})}{(\sum x_{2i}^2)(\sum x_{3i}^2) - (\sum x_{2i} x_{3i})^2} \tag{6.4.8}$$

which give the OLS estimators of the population partial regression coefficients $\beta_{12.3}$ and $\beta_{13.2}$, respectively.

In passing note: (1) equations (6.4.7) and (6.4.8) are symmetrical in nature because one can be obtained from the other by interchanging the roles of X_2 and X_3; (2) the denominators of these two equations are identical; and (3) the three-variable case is a natural extension of the two-variable case.

Variances and Standard Errors of OLS Estimators

Having obtained the OLS estimators of the partial regression coefficients, we can derive the variances and standard errors of these estimators in the manner indicated in App. 3A, Sec. 3A.2. As in the two-variable case, we need the standard

---

[7] This estimator is equal to a_1 of (6.3.5). For proof, see App. 6A, Sec. 6A.2.

errors for two main purposes: to establish confidence intervals and to test statistical hypotheses. The relevant formulas are as follows:[8]

$$\text{var}\,(\hat{\beta}_{12.3}) = \frac{\sum x_{3i}^2}{(\sum x_{2i}^2)(\sum x_{3i}^2) - (\sum x_{2i}x_{3i})^2}\,\sigma^2 \tag{6.4.9}$$

$$\text{se}(\hat{\beta}_{12.3}) = +\sqrt{\text{var}\,(\hat{\beta}_{12.3})} \tag{6.4.10}$$

$$\text{var}\,(\hat{\beta}_{13.2}) = \frac{\sum x_{2i}^2}{(\sum x_{2i}^2)(\sum x_{3i}^2) - (\sum x_{2i}x_{3i})^2}\,\sigma^2 \tag{6.4.11}$$

$$\text{se}(\hat{\beta}_{13.2}) = +\sqrt{\text{var}\,(\hat{\beta}_{13.2})} \tag{6.4.12}$$

where σ^2 is the (homoscedastic) variance of the population disturbances u_i.

Following the argument of App. 3A, Sec. 3A.3, the reader can verify that an unbiased estimate of σ^2 is given by

$$\hat{\sigma}^2 = \frac{\sum e_i^2}{N - 3} \tag{6.4.13}$$

Note the similarity between this estimator of σ^2 and its two-variable counterpart $[\hat{\sigma}^2 = (\sum e_i^2)/(N - 2)]$. Note that the degrees of freedom are now $N - 3$ because in estimating $\sum e_i^2$ we must first estimate $\beta_{1.23}$, $\beta_{12.3}$, and $\beta_{13.2}$, which consume 3 df. (The argument is quite general. Thus, in the four-variable case, the df will be $N - 4$.)

The estimator $\hat{\sigma}^2$ can be computed from (6.4.13) once the residuals e_i are available, but it can also be obtained more readily by using the following relation (for proof, see App. 6A, Sec. 6A.3):

$$\sum e_i^2 = \sum y_i^2 - \hat{\beta}_{12.3} \sum y_i x_{2i} - \hat{\beta}_{13.2} \sum y_i x_{3i} \tag{6.4.14}$$

which is the three-variable counterpart of the relation given in (3.1.25).

Properties of OLS Estimators

Since we are still operating within the framework of the classical linear regression model, the OLS estimators of the partial regression coefficients satisfy the Gauss-Markov theorem given in Sec. 3.3, which states that in the class of all linear unbiased estimators, the OLS estimators have the minimum variance.

In passing, note the following features of the sample regression function (6.4.1).

1. As in the two-variable case, the three-variable regression line (surface) passes through the means $\overline{Y}$, $\overline{X}_2$, and $\overline{X}_3$. This follows at once from equation (6.4.3).

---

[8] The derivations of these formulas are easier using the matrix notation. Hence the proofs are deferred until Chap. 8. Also, the variance and standard error of $\hat{\beta}_{1.23}$ will be given in Chap. 8 because its algebraic expression is rather involved.

2. The mean value of the estimated $Y_i (= \hat{Y}_i)$ is equal to the mean value of the actual Y_i, which is easy to see:

$$
\begin{aligned}
\hat{Y}_i &= \hat{\beta}_{1.23} + \hat{\beta}_{12.3} X_{2i} + \hat{\beta}_{13.2} X_{3i} \\
&= (\bar{Y} - \hat{\beta}_{12.3} \bar{X}_2 - \hat{\beta}_{13.2} \bar{X}_3) + \hat{\beta}_{12.3} X_{2i} + \hat{\beta}_{13.2} X_{3i} \\
&= \bar{Y} + \hat{\beta}_{12.3}(X_{2i} - \bar{X}_2) + \hat{\beta}_{13.2}(X_{3i} - \bar{X}_3) \\
&= \bar{Y} + \hat{\beta}_{12.3} x_{2i} + \hat{\beta}_{13.2} x_{3i}
\end{aligned}
\tag{6.4.15}
$$

Summing both sides of equation (6.4.15) over the sample values and dividing through by the sample size N gives $\hat{\bar{Y}} = \bar{Y}$. (*Note:* $\sum x_{2i} = \sum x_{3i} = 0$.) Notice that by virtue of (6.4.15), we can write

$$
\hat{y}_i = \hat{\beta}_{12.3} x_{2i} + \hat{\beta}_{13.2} x_{3i}
\tag{6.4.16}
$$

and hence the SRF (6.4.1) can be written in the *deviation form* as

$$
y_i = \hat{y}_i + e_i = \hat{\beta}_{12.3} x_{2i} + \hat{\beta}_{13.2} x_{3i} + e_i
\tag{6.4.17}
$$

where, as usual, lowercase letters indicate deviations from mean values.

3. $\sum e_i = \bar{e} = 0$. (Why?)

4. The residual e_i are uncorrelated with $\hat{Y}_i$, that is, $\sum e_i \hat{Y}_i = 0$. (Why?)

5. The residuals e_i are uncorrelated with X_{2i} and X_{3i}; that is, $\sum e_i X_{2i} = \sum e_i X_{3i} = 0$. (Why?)

6. As noted in Chap. 4, for the purpose of hypothesis testing we assume that the disturbances u_i are normally distributed with mean 0 and variance σ^2. With this assumption, the estimators $\hat{\beta}_{12.3}$, $\hat{\beta}_{13.2}$, and $\hat{\beta}_{1.23}$ are themselves normally distributed with means equal to $\beta_{12.3}$, $\beta_{13.2}$, and $\beta_{1.23}$, respectively, and with the variances given previously. The proof is simple. Consider, for example, equation (6.4.7), which gives the estimator of $\beta_{12.3}$. Knowing that the X's are nonstochastic, it is clear from this formula that $\hat{\beta}_{12.3}$ is a linear function of Y. But if u_i is assumed to be normally distributed, Y_i is also normally distributed. (Why?) Therefore, $\hat{\beta}_{12.3}$, being a linear function of Y, is itself normally distributed by virtue of the fact that any linear function of a normally distributed variable is itself normally distributed. The knowledge that with the normality assumption the OLS estimators of the multiple regression models are themselves normally distributed is extremely useful in hypothesis testing, as we shall see in Chap. 7.

7. Following the logic of the two-variable model given in Chap. 4, under the normality assumption it can be shown that $(N - 3)\hat{\sigma}^2/\sigma^2$ follows the χ^2 distribution with $N - 3$ df. This fact enables us to test hypothesis about the true σ^2, as we shall see in Chap. 7.

We noted briefly in Chap. 4 that under the normality assumption the OLS and maximum-likelihood (ML) estimators of the regression coefficients of the two-variable model are identical. This equality extends to models containing any number of variables. The proof of the statement can be found in the references given in Chap. 4. However, this is not true of the estimator of σ^2. It can be shown that the ML estimator of σ^2 is $\sum e_i^2/N$ regardless of the number of variables in the model, whereas the OLS estimator of σ^2 is $\sum e_i^2/(N-2)$ in the two-variable case, $\sum e_i^2/(N-3)$ in the three-variable case, and $\sum e_i^2/(N-k)$ in the case of a k-variable model. In other words, the OLS estimator of σ^2 takes into account the number of degrees of freedom, whereas the ML estimator does not. Of course, if N is very large, the ML and OLS estimators of σ^2 will tend to be close to each other.

6.5 THE MULTIPLE COEFFICIENT OF DETERMINATION R^2 AND THE MULTIPLE COEFFICIENT OF CORRELATION R

In the two-variable case we saw that r^2 as defined in (3.3.4) measures the goodness of fit of the regression equation; that is, it gives the proportion or percentage of the total variation in the dependent variable Y explained by the (single) explanatory variable X. This notion of r^2 can be easily extended to regression models containing more than two variables. Thus, in the three-variable model we would like to know the proportion of the variation in Y explained by the variables X_2 and X_3 jointly. The quantity that gives this information is known as the *multiple coefficient of determination* and is denoted by R^2; conceptually it is akin to r^2.

To derive R^2, we may follow the derivation of r^2 given in Sec. 3.3. Recall that

$$Y_i = \hat{\beta}_{1.23} + \hat{\beta}_{12.3}X_{2i} + \hat{\beta}_{13.2}X_{3i} + e_i$$
$$= \hat{Y}_i + e_i \qquad (6.5.1)$$

where $\hat{Y}_i$ is the estimated value of Y_i from the fitted regression line and is an estimator of true $E(Y_i|X_{2i}, X_{3i})$. Shifting to lowercase letters to indicate deviations from the mean values, equation (6.5.1) may be written as

$$y_i = \hat{\beta}_{12.3}x_{2i} + \hat{\beta}_{13.2}x_{3i} + e_i \qquad \text{(Why?)}$$
$$= \hat{y}_i + e_i \qquad (6.5.2)$$

Squaring (6.5.2) on both sides and summing over the sample values, we obtain

$$\sum y_i^2 = \sum \hat{y}_i^2 + \sum e_i^2 + 2\sum \hat{y}_i e_i$$
$$= \sum \hat{y}_i^2 + \sum e_i^2 \qquad \text{(Why?)} \qquad (6.5.3)$$

Verbally, equation (6.5.3) states that total sum of squares (TSS) equals explained sum of squares (ESS) + residual sum of squares (RSS). Now substituting for $\sum e_i^2$ from (6.4.14), we obtain

$$\sum y_i^2 = \sum \hat{y}_i^2 + \sum y_i^2 - \hat{\beta}_{12.3}\sum y_i x_{2i} - \hat{\beta}_{13.2}\sum y_i x_{3i}$$

which, on rearranging, gives

$$\text{ESS} = \sum \hat{y}_i^2 = \hat{\beta}_{12.3}\sum y_i x_{2i} + \hat{\beta}_{13.2}\sum y_i x_{3i} \qquad (6.5.4)$$

Now, by definition

$$R^2 = \frac{\text{ESS}}{\text{TSS}}$$

$$= \frac{\hat{\beta}_{12.3} \sum y_i x_{2i} + \hat{\beta}_{13.2} \sum y_i x_{3i}}{\sum y_i^2} \qquad (6.5.5)^9$$

[Cf. (6.5.5) with (3.3.5).]

Since the quantities entering (6.5.5) are generally computed routinely, R^2 can be computed easily. Note that R^2, like r^2, lies between 0 and 1. If it is 1, it means that the fitted regression line explains 100 percent of the variation in Y. On the other hand, if it is 0, the model does not explain any of the variation in Y. Typically, however, R^2 lies between these extreme values. The fit of the model is said to be "better" the closer is R^2 to 1.

Recall that in the two-variable case we defined the quantity r as the coefficient of correlation and indicated that it measures the degree of (linear) association between two variables. The three or more variable analog of r is the coefficient of *multiple correlation*, denoted by R, and it is a measure of the degree of association between Y and all the explanatory variables jointly. Although r can be positive or negative, R is always taken to be positive. In practice, however, R is of little importance. The more meaningful quantity is R^2.

6.6 AN ILLUSTRATIVE EXAMPLE: THE COBB-DOUGLAS PRODUCTION FUNCTION

By way of illustrating the ideas introduced thus far in this chapter, consider the celebrated *Cobb-Douglas production function*, which may be written in Yule's notation as

$$Y_i = \beta_{1.23} X_{2i}^{\beta_{12.3}} X_{3i}^{\beta_{13.2}}$$

This equation may be expressed more conveniently in logarithmic form as

$$\ln Y_i = \beta_0 + \beta_{12.3} \ln X_{2i} + \beta_{13.2} \ln X_{3i} \qquad (6.6.1)$$

where Y = output, X_2 = labor input, X_3 = capital input, and $\beta_0 = \ln \beta_{1.23}$.

The properties of the Cobb-Douglas production function are quite well known. For example, $\beta_{12.3}$ and $\beta_{13.2}$ measure the elasticities of output with respect to labor and capital (see Exercise 6.2). The sum $\beta_{12.3} + \beta_{13.2}$ gives information about returns to scale, that is, the response of output to a proportionate change in the inputs. If $\beta_{12.3} + \beta_{13.2} = 1$, then there are constant returns to scale; doubling the inputs will double the output. If the sum is less than 1, there are

---

[9] Note that R^2 can also be computed as follows: $R^2 = 1 - \sum e_i^2 / \sum y_i^2$. (Why?) Note also that the R^2 in (6.5.5) can be denoted by $R_{1.23}^2$ to indicate that there are two explanatory variables X_2 and X_3 in the model.

decreasing returns to scale; doubling the inputs will less than double the output. Finally, if the sum is greater that 1, there are increasing returns to scale; doubling the inputs will more than double the output.

As a test of the model, we obtained the data given in Table 6.1 and we fitted the Cobb-Douglas production function to these data by the method of OLS. The computer printout of the outcome is given in App. 6A, Sec. 6A.4. From the printout, we obtain the following regression:

$$\ln Y_i = -3.3384 + 1.4988 \ln X_2 + 0.4899 \ln X_3$$

$$(0.5398) \qquad\qquad (0.1020)$$

$$t = (2.7765) \qquad\qquad (4.8005)$$

$$R^2 = 0.8890 \qquad \mathrm{df} = 12 \tag{6.6.2}$$

In presenting the results shown in equation (6.6.2), we have followed the convention first introduced in Sec. 5.10. The figures in the first set of parentheses represent the estimated standard errors of the partial regression coefficients. (*Note:* The computer program used did not compute the standard error of the intercept term. Many computer programs do not generally present the standard error of the intercept term because in most applications the intercept term is of lesser importance.) The figures in the second set of parentheses are the estimated t values. The df refer to the degrees of freedom used in the computation of the RSS.

Table 6.1 Real gross product, man days, and real capital input in the agricultural sector of Taiwan, 1958–1972

Year	Real gross product (millions of NT $)†, Y	Man days (millions of days), X_2	Real capital input (millions of NT $), X_3
1958	16,607.7	275.5	17,803.7
1959	17,511.3	274.4	18,096.8
1960	20,171.2	269.7	18,271.8
1961	20,932.9	267.0	19,167.3
1962	20,406.0	267.8	19,647.6
1963	20,831.6	275.0	20,803.5
1964	24,806.3	283.0	22,076.6
1965	26,465.8	300.7	23,445.2
1966	27,403.0	307.5	24,939.0
1967	28,628.7	303.7	26,713.7
1968	29,904.5	304.7	29,957.8
1969	27,508.2	298.6	31,585.9
1970	29,035.5	295.5	33,474.5
1971	29,281.5	299.0	34,821.8
1972	31,535.8	288.1	41,794.3

† New Taiwan dollars.

Source: Thomas Pei-Fan Chen, "*Economic Growth and Structural Change in Taiwan—1952–1972, A Production Function Approach*," unpublished Ph.D. thesis, Dept. of Economics, Graduate Center, City University of New York, June 1976, table II.

From equation (6.6.2) it is seen that in the Taiwanese agricultural sector for the period 1958–1972 the output elasticities of labor and capital were 1.4988 and 0.4899, respectively. In other words, over the period of study, holding the capital input constant, a 1 percent increase in the labor input led on the average to about a 1.5 percent increase in the output. Similarly, holding the labor input constant, a 1 percent increase in the capital input led on the average to about 0.5 percent increase in the output. Adding the two output elasticities, we obtain 1.9887, which gives the value of the returns to scale parameter. As is evident, over the period of the study, the Taiwanese agricultural sector was characterized by increasing returns to scale.[10]

From a purely statistical viewpoint, the estimated regression line fits the data quite well. The R^2 value of 0.8990 means that about 89 percent of the variation in the (log of) output is explained by the (log of) labor and capital. In Chap. 7, we shall see how the estimated standard errors can be used to test hypotheses about the "true" values of the parameters of the Cobb-Douglas production function for the Taiwanese economy (see Exercise 7.1).

6.7 COMPARING TWO OR MORE R^2 VALUES: THE ADJUSTED R^2

An important property of R^2 is that it is a nondecreasing function of the number of explanatory variables present in the model; as the number of explanatory variables increases, R^2 almost invariably increases and never decreases. (For proof, see Sec. 6.9.) Stated differently, an additional X variable will not decrease R^2. To see this, recall the definition of the coefficient of determination:

$$R^2 = \frac{\text{ESS}}{\text{TSS}}$$

$$= 1 - \frac{\text{RSS}}{\text{TSS}}$$

$$= 1 - \frac{\sum e_i^2}{\sum y_i^2} \tag{6.7.1}$$

Now $\sum y_i^2$ is independent of the number of X variables in the model because it is simply $\sum (Y_i - \bar{Y})^2$. The RSS $\sum e_i^2$, however, depends on the number of explanatory variables (including the intercept term) present in the model. Intuitively, it is clear that as the number of X variables increases, $\sum e_i^2$ is bound to decrease (at least it will not increase); hence R^2 as defined in (6.7.1) will increase. In view of this, in comparing two regression models with the *same dependent variable* but

[10] We abstain from the question of the appropriateness of the model from the theoretical viewpoint as well as the question of whether one can measure returns to scale from time-series data.

differing number of X variables, one should be very wary of choosing the model with the highest R^2.

To compare two R^2's, one must take into account the number of X variables present in the model. This can be done readily if we consider an alternative coefficient of determination, which is as follows:

$$\bar{R}^2 = 1 - \frac{\sum e_i^2/(N-k)}{\sum y_i^2/(N-1)} \tag{6.7.2}$$

where k = the number of parameters in the model *including the intercept term*. (In the three-variable regression, $k = 3$. Why?) The R^2 thus defined is known as the *adjusted* R^2. The term *adjusted* means adjusted for the df associated with the sums of squares entering into (6.7.1): $\sum e_i^2$ has $N - k$ df in a model involving k parameters, which include the intercept term, and $\sum y_i^2$ has $N - 1$ df. (Why?) For the three-variable case, we know that $\sum e_i^2$ has $N - 3$ df.

Equation (6.7.2) can also be written as

$$\bar{R}^2 = 1 - \frac{\hat{\sigma}^2}{S_y^2} \tag{6.7.3}$$

where $\hat{\sigma}^2$ is the residual variance, an unbiased estimator of true σ^2, and S_y^2 is the sample variance of Y.

It is easy to see that $\bar{R}^2$ and R^2 are related because, substituting (6.7.1) into (6.7.2), we obtain

$$\bar{R}^2 = 1 - (1 - R^2)\frac{N-1}{N-k} \tag{6.7.4}$$

It is immediately apparent from equation (6.7.4) that (1) for $k > 1$, $\bar{R}^2 < R^2$, which implies that as the number of X variables increases, the adjusted R^2 is increasingly less than the unadjusted R^2; and (2) $\bar{R}^2$ can be negative, although R^2 is necessarily nonnegative. In case $\bar{R}^2$ turns out to be negative in an application, its value is taken as zero. (The reader should verify that for the Cobb-Douglas example given earlier the $\bar{R}^2$ is 0.8705, which is less than the R^2 value of 0.8890.)

It is crucial to note that in comparing two models on the basis of the coefficient of determination, whether adjusted or not, the *dependent variable must be the same;* the explanatory variables may take any form. Thus for the models

$$\ln Y_i = \beta_0 + \beta_{12.3}X_{2i} + \beta_{13.2}X_{3i} \tag{6.7.5}$$

$$Y_i = \alpha_0 + \alpha_{12.3}X_{2i} + \alpha_{13.2}X_{3i} \tag{6.7.6}$$

the computed R^2's cannot be compared. The reason is as follows: By definition, R^2 measures the proportion of the variation in the dependent variable accounted for by the explanatory variables. Therefore, in equation (6.7.5) R^2 measures the proportion of *variation in* $\ln Y$ explained by X_2 and X_3, whereas in equation

(6.7.6) it measures the proportion of the variation in Y, and the two are not the same thing.[11]

To compare the R^2 values of equations (6.7.5) and (6.7.6) we may proceed as follows: Estimate ln $\hat{Y}_i$ from model (6.7.5), obtain their antilog values, and then compute r^2 between antilog ln $\hat{Y}_i$ and Y_i, as suggested in Exercise 5.5. This r^2 is comparable with the R^2 value of model (6.7.6). Alternatively, obtain $\hat{Y}_i$ from model (6.7.6), convert them into ln $\hat{Y}_i$, and finally compute r^2 between ln $\hat{Y}_i$ and ln Y_i, as suggested previously. This r^2 value is comparable with the R^2 value of model (6.7.5). For a concrete application, see Exercise 6.1.

In concluding this section, a warning is in order: Sometimes researchers play the game of maximizing $\bar{R}^2$, that is, choosing the model that gives the highest $\bar{R}^2$. But this may be dangerous. For in regression analysis our objective is not to obtain a high $\bar{R}^2$ per se but rather to obtain dependable estimates of the true population regression coefficients and draw statistical inferences about them. In empirical analysis it is not unusual to obtain a very high $\bar{R}^2$ but find that some of the regression coefficients are either statistically insignificant or have signs which are contrary to a priori expectations. Therefore, the researcher should be more concerned about the logical or theoretical relevance of the explanatory variables to the dependent variable and their statistical significance. If in this process we obtain a high $\bar{R}^2$, well and good; on the other hand, if $\bar{R}^2$ is low, it does not mean the model is bad.

6.8 PARTIAL CORRELATION COEFFICIENT

In Chap. 3 we introduced the coefficient of correlation r as a measure of the degree of linear association between two variables. For the three-variable regression model we can compute three correlation coefficients: r_{12} (correlation between Y and X_2), r_{13} (correlation coefficient between Y and X_3), and r_{23} (correlation between X_2 and X_3). These correlation coefficients are called *simple correlation coefficients*, or *correlation coefficients of zero order*. These coefficients can be computed by the definition of correlation coefficient given in (3.3.8).

But now consider this question: Does, say, r_{12}, in fact, measure the "true" degree of association between Y and X_2 when a third variable X_3 may be associated with both of them? This question is analogous to the following question: Does the regression coefficient β_{12} measure the "true" slope of Y with respect to X_2 when X_3 is present in the model? The answer should be apparent by now. In general, r_{12} is not likely to reflect the "true" degree of association between Y and X_2 in the presence of X_3. As a matter of fact, it is likely to give a "false" impression of the nature of association between Y and X_2, as will be

---

[11] Note that a change in ln Y gives a relative or proportional change in Y, whereas a change in Y gives an absolute change. Therefore, var $\hat{Y}_i$/var $Y_i \neq$ var (ln $\hat{Y}_i$)/var (ln Y_i); that is, the two coefficients of determination are not the same.

shown shortly. Therefore, what we need is a correlation coefficient that is independent of the influence, if any, of X_3 on X_2 and Y. Such a correlation coefficient can be obtained and is known appropriately as the *partial correlation coefficient*. Conceptually, it is similar to the partial regression coefficient. We define

$r_{12.3}$ = partial correlation coefficient between Y and X_2, holding X_3 constant

$r_{13.2}$ = partial correlation coefficient between Y and X_3, holding X_2 constant

$r_{23.1}$ = partial correlation coefficient between X_2 and X_3, holding Y constant

One way of computing the preceding partial correlation coefficients is as follows: Recall the three-stage procedure discussed in Sec. 6.3. In the third stage we regressed w_i on v_i, which were purified Y_i and X_{2i}, that is, purified of the linear influence of X_3. Therefore, if we now compute the simple coefficient of correlation between w_i and v_i, we should obtain $r_{12.3}$ because the variable X_3 is now held constant. Symbolically,

$$r_{wv} = r_{12.3}$$

$$= \frac{\sum (w_i - \bar{w})(v_i - \bar{v})}{\sqrt{\sum (w_i - \bar{w})^2 \sum (v_i - \bar{v})^2}}$$

$$= \frac{\sum w_i v_i}{\sqrt{\sum w_i^2 \sum v_i^2}} \tag{6.8.1}$$

where use is made of the fact that $\bar{w} = \bar{v} = 0$. (Why?)

From the preceding discussion it is clear that the partial correlation between Y and X_2 holding X_3 constant is nothing but the simple (or zero-order) correlation coefficient between residuals from the regression of Y on X_3 and X_2 on X_3, respectively. $r_{13.2}$ and $r_{23.1}$ are to be interpreted similarly.

In reality, one need not go through the three-stage procedure to compute the partial correlations because they can be easily obtained from the simple, or zero-order, correlation coefficients as follows (for proofs, see the Exercises):[12]

$$r_{12.3} = \frac{r_{12} - r_{13}r_{23}}{\sqrt{(1 - r_{13}^2)(1 - r_{23}^2)}} \tag{6.8.2}$$

$$r_{13.2} = \frac{r_{13} - r_{12}r_{23}}{\sqrt{(1 - r_{12}^2)(1 - r_{23}^2)}} \tag{6.8.3}$$

$$r_{23.1} = \frac{r_{23} - r_{12}r_{13}}{\sqrt{(1 - r_{12}^2)(1 - r_{13}^2)}} \tag{6.8.4}$$

The partial correlations given in the equations (6.8.2) to (6.8.4) are called *first-order correlation coefficients*. By *order* we mean the number of secondary sub-

---

[12] Most computer programs for multiple regression analysis routinely compute the simple correlation coefficients; hence the partial correlation coefficients can be readily computed.

scripts. Thus $r_{12.34}$ would be the correlation coefficient of order two, $r_{12.345}$ would be the correlation coefficient of order three, and so on. As noted previously, r_{12}, r_{13}, and so on, are called *simple*, or *zero-order*, *correlations*. The interpretation of, say, $r_{12.34}$ is that it gives the coefficient of correlation between Y and X_2, holding X_3 and X_4 constant.

Interpretation of Simple and Partial Correlation Coefficients

In the two-variable case, the simple r had a straightforward meaning: It measured the degree of (linear) association (and not causation) between the dependent variable Y and the single explanatory variable X. But once we go beyond the two-variable case, we need to pay careful attention to the interpretation of the simple correlation coefficient. From (6.8.2), for example, we observe:

1. Even if $r_{12} = 0$, $r_{12.3}$ will not be zero unless r_{13} or r_{23} or both are zero.

2. If $r_{12} = 0$ and r_{13} and r_{23} are nonzero and of the same sign, $r_{12.3}$ will be negative, whereas if they are of the opposite signs, it will be positive. An example will make this point clear. Let $Y = $ crop yield, $X_2 = $ rainfall, and $X_3 = $ temperature. Assume $r_{12} = 0$, that is, no association between crop yield and rainfall. Assume further that r_{13} is positive and r_{23} is negative. Then, as (6.8.2) shows, $r_{12.3}$ will be positive; that is, holding temperature constant, there is a positive association between yield and rainfall. This seemingly paradoxical result, however, is not surprising. Since temperature X_3 affects both yield Y and rainfall X_2, in order to find out the net relationship between crop yield and rainfall, we need to remove the influence of the "nuisance" variable temperature. This example shows how one might be misled by the simple coefficient of correlation.

3. $r_{12.3}$ and r_{12} (and similar comparisons) need not have the same sign.

4. In the two-variable case we have seen that r^2 lies between 0 and 1. The same property holds true of the squared partial correlation coefficients. Using this fact, the reader should verify that one can obtain the following expression from (6.8.2):

$$0 \leq r_{12}^2 + r_{13}^2 + r_{23}^2 - 2r_{12}r_{13}r_{23} \leq 1 \tag{6.8.5}$$

which gives the interrelationships among the three zero-order correlation coefficients. Similar expressions can be derived from equations (6.8.3) and (6.8.4).

5. Suppose that $r_{13} = r_{23} = 0$. Does this mean that r_{12} is also zero? The answer is obvious from (6.8.5). The fact that Y and X_3 and X_2 and X_3 are uncorrelated does not mean that Y and X_2 are uncorrelated.

In passing it may be pointed out that the expression $r_{12.3}^2$ may be called the *coefficient of partial determination* and may be interpreted as the proportion of the variation in Y not explained by the variable X_3 that has been explained by the inclusion of X_2 into the model (see Exercise 6.10). Conceptually it is similar to R^2.

6.9 SOME INTERESTING RELATIONSHIPS

In this section we collect some interesting relationships between partial and simple regression coefficients, between partial regression coefficients and partial correlation coefficients, and between R^2 and simple and partial correlation coefficients. Most of these relationships can be derived from basic definitions, and the topics covered in this chapter and are therefore relegated to the exercises.

Relationship between Partial and Simple Regression Coefficients and Simple Correlations

$$\hat{\beta}_{12.3} = \frac{\hat{\beta}_{12} - \hat{\beta}_{13}\hat{\beta}_{32}}{1 - \hat{\beta}_{23}\hat{\beta}_{32}} = \frac{r_{12} - r_{13}r_{23}}{1 - r_{23}^2}\frac{s_1}{s_2} \tag{6.9.1}$$

$$\hat{\beta}_{13.2} = \frac{\hat{\beta}_{13} - \hat{\beta}_{12}\hat{\beta}_{23}}{1 - \hat{\beta}_{32}\hat{\beta}_{23}} = \frac{r_{13} - r_{12}r_{23}}{1 - r_{23}^2}\frac{s_1}{s_3} \tag{6.9.2}$$

where $\hat{\beta}_{13}$ is the slope coefficient in the regression of Y and X_3, $\hat{\beta}_{23}$ is the slope coefficient in the regression of X_2 on X_3, and so on, and where s_1, s_2, and s_3 are sample standard deviations of variables Y, X_2, and X_3. The coefficients β_{13}, and so on, are called *simple, gross,* or *two-variable regression coefficients.*

Relationship between Partial Regression Coefficients and Partial Correlation Coefficients

$$\hat{\beta}_{12.3} = r_{12.3}\left(\frac{\sum e_{1.3i}^2}{\sum e_{2.3i}^2}\right)^{1/2} \tag{6.9.3}$$

$$\hat{\beta}_{13.2} = r_{13.2}\left(\frac{\sum e_{1.2i}^2}{\sum e_{3.2i}^2}\right)^{1/2} \tag{6.9.4}$$

where $\sum e_{1.3i}^2$ is the RSS in the regression of Y on X_3, and so on. From (3.3.2) and (3.3.5), the RSS $\sum e_{1.3i}^2$ can be expressed as $\sum y_i^2(1 - r_{13}^2)$.

Relationship between R^2 and Simple and Partial Correlation Coefficients

$$R^2 = \frac{r_{12}^2 + r_{13}^2 - 2r_{12}r_{13}r_{23}}{1 - r_{23}^2} \tag{6.9.5}$$

$$R^2 = r_{12}^2 + (1 - r_{12}^2)r_{13.2}^2 \tag{6.9.6}$$

$$R^2 = r_{13}^2 + (1 - r_{13}^2)r_{12.3}^2 \tag{6.9.7}$$

In concluding this section, we note the following: It was stated previously that R^2 will not decrease if an additional explanatory variable is introduced into the model, which can be seen clearly from (6.9.6). This equation states that the proportion of the variation in Y explained by X_2 and X_3 jointly is the sum of two parts: the part explained by X_2 alone $(= r_{12}^2)$ and the part not explained by X_2 $(= 1 - r_{12}^2)$ times the proportion that is explained by X_3 after holding the influence of X_2 constant. Now $R^2 > r_{12}^2$ so long as $r_{13.2}^2 > 0$. At worst, $r_{13.2}^2$ will be zero, in which case $R^2 = r_{12}^2$.

6.10 SUMMARY AND CONCLUSIONS

In this chapter we introduced the simplest possible multiple regression model, namely, the three-variable linear regression. Although in many ways a straightforward extension of the two-variable case, the three-variable model introduced several new concepts, such as partial regression coefficients, partial correlation coefficients, multiple correlation coefficient, adjusted and unadjusted R^2, and coefficient of partial determination. We also considered some interrelationships among these coefficients and pointed out the pitfalls involved in interpreting simple correlation coefficients in the context of multiple regression analysis.

In Chap. 7 we shall take up the companion problem of confidence interval estimation and hypothesis testing and extend some of the ideas introduced in Chap. 5.

EXERCISES

6.1 The following table gives data on real gross product, labor input, and real capital input in the Taiwanese manufacturing sector.

Year	Real gross product (millions of NT \$)†, Y	Labor input (per thousand persons), X_2	Real capital input (millions of NT \$), X_3
1958	8911.4	281.5	120,753
1959	10,873.2	284.4	122,242
1960	11,132.5	289.0	125,263
1961	12,086.5	375.8	128,539
1962	12,767.5	375.2	131,427
1963	16,347.1	402.5	134,267
1964	19,542.7	478.0	139,038
1965	21,075.9	553.4	146,450
1966	23,052.0	616.7	153,714
1967	26,128.2	695.7	164,783
1968	29,563.7	790.3	176,864
1969	33,376.6	816.0	188,146
1970	38,354.3	848.4	205,841
1971	46,868.3	873.1	221,748
1972	54,308.0	999.2	239,715

† New Taiwan dollars.

Source: Thomas Pei-Fan Chen, "Economic Growth and Structural Change in Taiwan—1952–1972, A Production Function Approach," unpublished Ph.D. thesis, Dept. of Economics, Graduate Center, City University of New York, June 1976, table II.

(a) Fit the following models to the preceding data:

$$Y_i = \beta_0 + \beta_{12.3} X_{2i} + \beta_{13.2} X_{3i} + u_i$$

$$\ln Y_i = \alpha_0 + \alpha_{12.3} \ln X_{2i} + \alpha_{13.2} \ln X_{3i} + u_i$$

(b) Which model gives a better fit and why?

(c) How would you compare the R^2 values of the two models? (Show your calculations.)

(d) How would you compute the output elasticities with respect to labor and capital for the first model?

(e) How do the results for the manufacturing sector differ from that for the agricultural sector given in Table 6.1?

*6.2 Show that $\beta_{12.3}$ and $\beta_{13.2}$ in (6.6.1) do, in fact, give output elasticities of labor and capital.

6.3 (a) Examine whether the following version of the Phillips curve provides a good fit to the United States data given in the table and interpret your results:

$$Y = \beta_{1.23} + \beta_{12.3} X_i + \beta_{13.2} X_i^2 + u_i$$

where Y = rate of change of money wages and X = unemployment rate.

Note: Y may be computed by subtracting the previous year's earnings from the current year's earnings and dividing by the previous year's earnings.

(b) What is the rationale for introducing the square of the unemployment rate in the model? A priori, would you expect $\beta_{13.2}$ to be positive or negative?

Average hourly earnings and unemployment rate, U.S. total manufacturing sector, 1959–1971

Year	Average hourly earnings, $	Unemployment rate, %
1959	2.19	6.1
1960	2.26	6.2
1961	2.32	7.8
1962	2.39	5.8
1963	2.46	5.7
1964	2.53	5.0
1965	2.61	4.0
1966	2.72	3.2
1967	2.83	3.6
1968	3.01	3.3
1969	3.19	3.3
1970	3.36	5.6
1971	3.56	6.8

Source: Manpower Report of the President, March 1973, unemployment rates from table A-18, p. 151, and hourly earnings from table C-3, p. 191.

6.4 Show that (6.8.1) and (6.8.2) are equivalent.

6.5 How would you prove that a_0 in equation (6.3.5) is zero?

6.6 Establish equations (6.9.1) and (6.9.2).

6.7 Derive equations (6.9.3) and (6.9.4).

6.8 Establish equations (6.9.5) to (6.9.7).

6.9 How would you derive equations (6.8.3) and (6.8.4)?

6.10 Show that $r_{12.3}^2 = (R^2 - r_{13}^2)/(1 - r_{13}^2)$ and interpret the equation.

6.11 Show that $\hat{\beta}_{12.3}\hat{\beta}_{23.1}\hat{\beta}_{31.2} = r_{12.3}r_{23.1}r_{31.2}$,

Note: In general, $\beta_{31.2} \neq \beta_{13.2}$ but $r_{31.2} = r_{13.2}$. (Why?)

6.12 If the relation $\alpha_1 X_1 + \alpha_2 X_2 + \alpha_3 X_3 = 0$ holds true for all values of X_1, X_2, and X_3, find out the values of the three partial correlation coefficients.

6.13 Is it possible to obtain the following from a set of data?
  (a) $r_{23} = 0.9$, $r_{13} = -0.2$, $r_{12} = 0.8$.
  (b) $r_{12} = 0.6$, $r_{23} = -0.9$, $r_{31} = -0.5$.
  (c) $r_{21} = 0.01$, $r_{13} = 0.66$, $r_{23} = -0.7$.

6.14 If $Z = aX + bY$ and $W = cX - dY$, and if the correlation coefficient between X and Y is r but Z and W are uncorrelated, show that $\sigma_z \sigma_w = (a^2 + b^2)\sigma_x \sigma_y (1 - r^2)^{1/2}$, where σ_z, σ_w, σ_x, and σ_y are the standard deviations of the four variables and where a, b, c, and d are constants.

6.15 Consider the following simple demand function for money:

$$M_t = \beta_0 Y_t^{\beta_1} r_t^{\beta_2} e^{u_t}$$

where M_t = aggregate real cash balances at time t, Y_t = aggregate real national income at time t, and r_t = long-term interest rate.

  (a) Given the following data, estimate the elasticities of aggregate real cash balances with respect to aggregate real income and the long-term interest rate.

Data on money, national income, and implicit price deflator for India, 1948–1965

Year	Nominal money (crores of rupees)	Nominal net income (per 100 crores of rupees)	Implicit price deflator	Long-term interest rate (%)
1948–1949	1898.69	86.5	100.00	3.03
1949–1950	1880.29	90.1	102.15	3.07
1950–1951	1979.49	95.3	107.68	3.15
1951–1952	1803.79	99.7	109.56	3.41
1952–1953	1764.71	98.2	103.81	3.66
1953–1954	1793.97	104.8	104.49	3.64
1954–1955	1920.63	96.1	93.48	3.70
1955–1956	2216.95	99.8	95.23	3.74
1956–1957	2341.89	113.1	102.82	3.99
1957–1958	2413.16	113.9	104.59	4.18
1958–1959	2526.02	126.9	108.15	4.13
1959–1960	2720.22	129.5	109.19	4.05
1960–1961	2868.61	141.4	111.19	4.06
1961–1962	3045.82	148.0	113.32	4.16
1962–1963	3309.98	154.0	115.70	4.49
1963–1964	3752.12	172.1	123.19	4.66
1964–1965	4880.06	200.1	132.96	4.80

Note: One crore rupees is equal to ten million rupees. A rupee is approximately equal to about 12 cents at 1975 prices.

Source: Damodar Gujarati, "The Demand for Money in India," *The Journal of Development Studies*, vol. V, no. 1, 1968, pp. 59–64.

(b) If instead of fitting the preceding demand function you were to fit the model $(M/Y)_t = \alpha r_t^\beta$, how would you interpret the results? Show the necessary computations.

Note: To convert the nominal quantities into real quantities, divide the former by the implicit price deflator.

6.16 If $X_3 = a_1 X_1 + a_2 X_2$, where a_1 and a_2 are constants, show that the three partial correlations are numerically equal to 1, $r_{13.2}$ having the sign of a_1, $r_{23.1}$ the sign of a_2, and $r_{12.3}$ the opposite sign of a_1/a_2.

6.17 Under what conditions will $\hat{\beta}_{12.3}$ and $\hat{\beta}_{13.2}$ be equal to the simple regression coefficients $\hat{\beta}_{12}$ and $\hat{\beta}_{13}$?

6.18 From the following data estimate the partial regression coefficients, their standard errors, and the adjusted and unadjusted R^2 values:

$$\bar{Y} = 367{,}693 \qquad \bar{X}_2 = 402.760 \qquad \bar{X}_3 = 8.0$$

$$\sum (Y_i - \bar{Y})^2 = 66042.269 \qquad \sum (X_{2i} - \bar{X}_2)^2 = 84855.096 \qquad \sum (X_{3i} - \bar{X})^2 = 280.000$$

$$\sum (Y_i - \bar{Y})(X_{2i} - \bar{X}_2) = 74778.346 \qquad \sum (Y_i - \bar{Y})(X_{3i} - \bar{X}_3) = 4250.900$$

$$\sum (X_{2i} - \bar{X})(X_{3i} - \bar{X}_3) = 4796.000 \qquad \text{and} \qquad N = 15$$

6.19 In general $R^2 \neq r_{12}^2 + r_{13}^2$, but it is so only if $r_{23} = 0$. Comment.

6.20 In the three-variable case there are three zero-order correlation coefficients r_{12}, r_{13}, r_{23} and three first-order correlation coefficients $r_{12.3}, r_{13.2}, r_{23.1}$. How many zero-order and first-order correlations can you obtain in the four-variable case? In the n-variable case?

6.21 Prove that $r_{12.3}^2 = \hat{\beta}_{12.3}\hat{\beta}_{21.3}$, $r_{13.2}^2 = \hat{\beta}_{13.2}\hat{\beta}_{31.2}$, and $r_{23.1}^2 = \hat{\beta}_{23.1}\hat{\beta}_{32.1}$ and interpret. Can you establish a similar expression for the two-variable case?

6.22 Show that the variances of $\hat{\beta}_{12.3}$ and $\hat{\beta}_{13.2}$ given in (6.4.9) and (6.4.11) can also be expressed as

$$\text{var}(\hat{\beta}_{12.3}) = \frac{\sigma^2}{\sum x_2^2 (1 - r_{23}^2)}$$

$$\text{var}(\hat{\beta}_{13.2}) = \frac{\sigma^2}{\sum x_3^2 (1 - r_{23}^2)}$$

where $r_{23} =$ coefficient of correlation between X_2 and X_3.

  Hint: $r_{23}^2 = (\sum x_2 x_3)^2 / (\sum x_2^2 \sum x_3^2)$.

APPENDIX 6A

6A.1 DERIVATION OF OLS ESTIMATORS GIVEN IN EQUATIONS (6.4.3) TO (6.4.5)

Differentiating

$$\sum e_i^2 = \sum (Y_i - \hat{\beta}_{1.23} - \hat{\beta}_{12.3}X_{2i} - \hat{\beta}_{13.2}X_{3i})^2 \qquad (6.4.2)$$

partially with respect to the three unknowns and setting the resulting expressions to zero, we obtain

$$\frac{\partial \sum e_i^2}{\partial \hat{\beta}_{1.23}} = 2 \sum (Y_i - \hat{\beta}_{1.23} - \hat{\beta}_{12.3}X_{2i} - \hat{\beta}_{13.2}X_{3i})(-1) = 0$$

$$\frac{\partial \sum e_i^2}{\partial \hat{\beta}_{12.3}} = 2 \sum (Y_i - \hat{\beta}_{1.23} - \hat{\beta}_{12.3} X_{2i} - \hat{\beta}_{13.2} X_{3i})(-X_{2i}) = 0$$

$$\frac{\partial \sum e_i^2}{\partial \hat{\beta}_{13.2}} = 2 \sum (Y_i - \hat{\beta}_{1.23} - \hat{\beta}_{12.3} X_{2i} - \hat{\beta}_{13.2} X_{3i})(-X_{3i}) = 0$$

Simplifying the preceding equations, we obtain equations (6.4.3) to (6.4.5).
In passing, note that the three preceding equations can also be written as

$$\sum e_i = 0$$

$$\sum e_i X_{2i} = 0$$

$$\sum e_i X_{3i} = 0$$

which show the properties of the least-squares fit, namely, that the residuals sum to zero and that they are uncorrelated with the explanatory variables X_2 and X_3.

6A.2 EQUIVALENCE BETWEEN a_1 OF (6.3.5) AND $\hat{\beta}_{12.3}$ OF (6.4.7)

To show that a_1 of (6.3.5) and $\hat{\beta}_{12.3}$ of (6.4.7) are identical. The OLS estimator of a_1 is

$$a_1 = \frac{\sum (w_i - \bar{w})(v_i - \bar{v})}{\sum (v_i - \bar{v})^2}$$

$$= \frac{\sum w_i v_i}{\sum v_i^2} \qquad \text{since } \bar{w} = \bar{v} = 0 \qquad \text{(Why?)}$$

Since $\bar{w} = \bar{v} = 0$, equations (6.3.1) and (6.3.2) can be written as

$$y_i = \hat{\beta}_{13} x_{3i} + w_i \qquad \text{and} \qquad x_{2i} = \hat{\beta}_{23} x_{3i} + v_i$$

where the small letters, as usual, denote deviations from mean values.
Substituting for w_i and v_i from the preceding equations into the equation for a_1, we obtain

$$a_1 = \frac{\sum (y_i - \hat{\beta}_{13} x_{3i})(x_{2i} - \hat{\beta}_{23} x_{3i})}{\sum (x_{2i} - \hat{\beta}_{23} x_{3i})^2}$$

$$= \frac{\sum yx_{2i} - \hat{\beta}_{23} \sum y_i x_{3i} - \hat{\beta}_{13} \sum x_{2i} x_{3i} + \hat{\beta}_{13} \hat{\beta}_{23} \sum x_3^2}{\sum x_2^2 + \hat{\beta}_{23}^2 \sum x_{3i}^2 - 2\hat{\beta}_{23} \sum x_{2i} x_{3i}}$$

Noting that $\hat{\beta}_{23} = \sum x_{2i} x_{3i} / \sum x_{3i}^2$, and so on, the reader should verify that a_1 above does, in fact, reduce to $\hat{\beta}_{12.3}$ given in (6.4.7).

6A.3 DERIVATION OF EQUATION (6.4.14)

Recall that

$$e_i = Y_i - \hat{\beta}_{1.23} - \hat{\beta}_{12.3} X_{2i} - \hat{\beta}_{13.2} X_{3i}$$

which can also be written as

$$e_i = y_i - \hat{\beta}_{12.3} x_{2i} - \hat{\beta}_{13.2} x_{3i}$$

where small letters, as usual, indicate deviations from mean values.
    Now

$$\sum e_i^2 = \sum (e_i e_i)$$
$$= \sum e_i(y_i - \hat{\beta}_{12.3} x_{2i} - \hat{\beta}_{13.2} x_{3i})$$
$$= \sum e_i y_i$$

where use is made of the fact that $\sum e_i x_{2i} = \sum e_i x_{3i} = 0$. (Why?)
Now

$$\sum e_i y_i = \sum y_i e_i = \sum y_i(y_i - \hat{\beta}_{12.3} x_{2i} - \hat{\beta}_{13.2} x_{3i})$$

that is,

$$\sum e_i^2 = \sum y_i^2 - \hat{\beta}_{12.3} \sum y_i x_{2i} - \hat{\beta}_{13.2} \sum y_i x_{3i}$$

which is the required result.

6A.4 COMPUTER PRINTOUT OF THE COBB-DOUGLAS PRODUCTION FUNCTION FITTED TO THE TAIWANESE AGRICULTURAL SECTOR

The following printout follows the format of the printout first introduced in Sec. 3A.5.

Y (Real Gross Product)	X_2 (Man-days)	X_3 (Real Capital Input)	ln Y	ln X_2	ln X_3
16607.699	275.500	17803.699	9.718	5.619	9.787
17511.301	274.400	18096.801	9.771	5.615	9.803
20171.199	269.700	18271.801	9.912	5.597	9.813
20932.898	267.000	19167.301	9.949	5.587	9.861
20406.000	267.800	19647.602	9.924	5.590	9.886
20831.602	275.000	20803.500	9.944	5.617	9.943
24806.301	283.000	22076.602	10.119	5.645	10.002
26465.801	300.700	23445.199	10.184	5.706	10.062
27403.000	307.500	24939.000	10.218	5.728	10.124
28628.699	303.700	26713.699	10.262	5.716	10.193
29904.500	304.700	29957.801	10.306	5.719	10.308
27508.199	298.600	31585.898	10.222	5.699	10.360
29035.500	295.500	33474.500	10.276	5.689	10.419
29281.500	299.000	34821.801	10.285	5.700	10.458
31535.801	288.100	41794.301	10.359	5.663	10.641

```
ANALYSIS
?* MULTIPLE REGRESSION

SPECIFY THE DEPENDENT VARIABLE
?* 4(= ln Y)

HOW MANY INDEPENDENT VARIABLES
?* 2

SPECIFY THESE VARIABLES
?* 5,6(ln X₂, ln X₃)
```

VARIABLE	REG. COEFF.	STD. ERROR COEFF.	COMPUTED T
5	1.49877	0.53980	2.77651
6	0.48986	0.10204	4.80047
INTERCEPT	-3.33844		

MULTIPLE CORRELATION 0.94288 (ADJUSTED R = 0.93303)
STANDARD ERROR OF ESTIMATE 0.07481

ANALYSIS OF VARIANCE FOR THE REGRESSION

SOURCE OF VARIATION	D.F.	SUM OF SQ.	MEAN SQ.	F VALUE
ATTRIBUTABLE TO REGRESSION	2	0.538	0.269	48.069
DEVIATION FROM REGRESSION	12	0.067	0.560 E-02	
TOTAL	14	0.605		

```
DO YOU WISH TO PRINT THE TABLE OF RESIDUALS
?* YES
```

CASE NO	Y OBSERVED	Y ESTIMATED	RESIDUAL	STD. RESIDUAL
1	9.718	9.877	−0.159	−2.128
2	9.771	9.879	−0.108	−1.447
3	9.912	9.858	0.544E-01	0.727
4	9.949	9.866	0.083	1.110
5	9.924	9.883	0.410E-01	0.548
6	9.944	9.950	−0.616E-02	−0.082
7	10.119	10.022	0.096	1.289
8	10.184	10.143	0.408E-01	0.545
9	10.218	10.207	0.118E-01	0.158
10	10.262	10.222	0.405E-01	0.541
11	10.306	10.283	0.230E-01	0.308
12	10.222	10.278	−0.561E-01	−0.750
13	10.276	10.291	−0.149E-01	−0.199
14	10.285	10.328	−0.434E-01	−0.580
15	10.359	10.362	−0.300E-02	−0.401E-01

Note: 0.544E-01 means 0.0544, etc.

TEST OF EXTREME RESIDUALS
RATIO OF RANGES FOR THE SMALLEST RESIDUAL	0.483
RATIO OF RANGES FOR THE LARGEST RESIDUAL	0.276
CRITICAL VALUE OF THE RATIO AT ALPHA = 0.10	0.472

DO YOU WISH TO PLOT Y OBSERVED AND Y ESTIMATED
?* YES

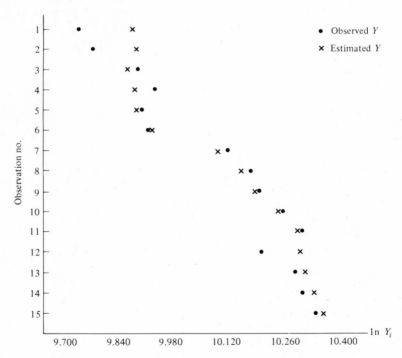

DO YOU WISH TO COMPUTE THE DURBIN-WATSON STATISTIC
?* YES

DURBIN WATSON STATISTIC
0.8901

SEVEN

MULTIPLE REGRESSION ANALYSIS: THE PROBLEM OF INFERENCE

This chapter is a continuation of Chap. 5 and extends the ideas of interval estimation and hypothesis testing developed there to models involving three or more variables. Although in many ways the concepts developed in Chap. 5 can be applied straightforwardly to the multiple regression model, there are a few additional features that are special to such models, and it is these features which will receive more attention in this chapter.

7.1 THE NORMALITY ASSUMPTION ONCE AGAIN

We know by now that if our sole objective is point estimation of the parameters of the regression models, the method of ordinary least squares (OLS), which does not make any assumption about the probability distribution of the disturbances u_i, will suffice. But if our objective is estimation as well as inference, then, as argued in Chaps. 4 and 5, we need to assume that the u_i follow some probability distribution.

For reasons already clearly spelled out, we assumed that the u_i follow the normal distribution with zero mean and constant variance σ^2. We continue to make the same assumption for multiple regression models. With the normality assumption and following the discussion of Chap. 4, the OLS estimators of the partial regression coefficients, which are identical with the maximum-likelihood

123

(ML) estimators, are best linear unbiased estimators (BLUE).[1] Moreover, the estimators $\hat{\beta}_{12.3}$, $\hat{\beta}_{13.2}$, and $\hat{\beta}_{1.23}$ are themselves normally distributed with means equal to true $\beta_{12.3}$, $\beta_{13.2}$, and $\beta_{1.23}$ and the variances given in Chap. 6. Furthermore, $(N - 3)\hat{\sigma}^2/\sigma^2$ follows the χ^2 distribution with $N - 3$ df, and the three OLS estimators are distributed independently of $\hat{\sigma}^2$. The proofs follow the two-variable case discussed in App. 3A. As a result and following Chap. 5, it can be shown that replacing σ^2 by its unbiased estimator $\hat{\sigma}^2$ in the computation of the standard errors, the variables

$$t = \frac{\hat{\beta}_{1.23} - \beta_{1.23}}{\text{se}(\hat{\beta}_{1.23})} \tag{7.1.1}$$

$$t = \frac{\hat{\beta}_{12.3} - \beta_{12.3}}{\text{se}(\hat{\beta}_{12.3})} \tag{7.1.2}$$

$$t = \frac{\hat{\beta}_{13.2} - \beta_{13.2}}{\text{se}(\hat{\beta}_{13.2})} \tag{7.1.3}$$

each follows the t distribution with $N - 3$ df.

Note that the df are now $N - 3$ because in computing $\sum e_i^2$ and hence $\hat{\sigma}^2$ we first need to estimate the three partial regression coefficients, which therefore put three restrictions on the residual sum of squares (RSS) (following this logic in the four-variable case there will be $N - 4$ df, and so on). Therefore, the t distribution can be used to establish confidence intervals as well as test statistical hypotheses about the true population partial regression coefficients. Similarly, the χ^2 distribution can be used to test hypotheses about the true σ^2. To demonstrate the actual mechanics, we use the following illustrative example.

7.2 AN ILLUSTRATIVE EXAMPLE

Suppose that we want to study the behavior of personal consumption expenditure in the United States over the past several years. To this end, we use the following simple model:

$$E(Y \mid X_2, X_3) = \beta_{1.23} + \beta_{12.3}X_{2i} + \beta_{13.2}X_{3i} \tag{7.2.1}$$

where Y = personal consumption expenditure (PCE), X_2 = personal disposable (after-tax) income (PDI), and X_3 = time measured in years. Equation (7.2.1) postulates that PCE is linearly related to PDI and time or the *trend variable*. In most multiple regression analysis involving time-series data it is a common practice to introduce the time or trend variable in addition to several other explanatory variables. This is done for the following reasons.

---

[1] With the normality assumption, the OLS estimators $\hat{\beta}_{12.3}$, $\hat{\beta}_{13.2}$, and $\hat{\beta}_{1.23}$ are minimum-variance estimators in the entire class of unbiased estimators, whether linear or not. See C. R. Rao, *Linear Statistical Inference and Its Applications*, John Wiley & Sons, Inc., New York, 1965, p. 258.

1. Our interest may be simply to find out how the dependent variable behaves over time. For example, charts are often drawn showing, say, the behavior of GNP, employment, unemployment, stock prices, etc., over several time periods. A look at such charts often reveals whether the general movement of the time series under consideration is upward (upward trend), downward (downward trend), or trendless (i.e., no discernible pattern). In such an analysis we may not be interested in the causes behind the upward or downward trend; our objective may be simply to describe the data over time.

2. Many a time the trend variable is a surrogate for a basic variable affecting Y. But this basic variable may not be directly observable or, if observable, data on it may not be available or may be difficult to obtain. For instance, in production theory technology is one such variable. We may feel the impact of technology, but we may not know how to measure it. Therefore, it may be "convenient" to assume that technology is some function of the time measured chronologically. In some situations it may be believed that a measurable variable affecting Y is so closely related to time that it is easier (costwise, at least) to introduce the time variable itself rather than the basic variable. For example, in (7.2.1), time X_3 may very well represent population. The aggregate PCE increases as population increases, and population may very well have some (linear) relationship with time.

As a test of the model (7.2.1), we obtained the data in Table 7.1. The estimated

Table 7.1 Personal consumption expenditure and personal disposal income in the U.S., 1956–1970, billions of 1958 dollars

PCE, Y	PDI, X_2	Time, X_3
281.3	309.3	1956 = 1
288.1	316.1	1957 = 2
290.0	318.8	1958 = 3
307.3	333.0	1959 = 4
316.1	340.3	1960 = 5
322.5	350.5	1961 = 6
338.4	367.2	1962 = 7
353.3	381.2	1963 = 8
373.7	408.1	1964 = 9
397.7	434.8	1965 = 10
418.1	458.9	1966 = 11
430.1	477.5	1967 = 12
452.7	499.0	1968 = 13
469.1	513.5	1969 = 14
476.9	533.2	1970 = 15

Source: Survey of Current Business, U.S. Department of Commerce, various issues.

regression line is as follows (see the computer printout in App. 7A, Sec. 7A.1, for details):

$$\hat{Y}_i = 53.1603 + 0.7266X_{2i} + 2.7363X_{3i}$$

$$(13.0261) \quad (0.0487) \quad\quad (0.8486)$$

$$t = (4.0811) \quad (14.9060) \quad\quad (3.2246) \quad\quad\quad (7.2.2)$$

$$df = 12 \quad\quad \begin{matrix} R^2 = 0.9988 \\ \bar{R}^2 = 0.9986 \end{matrix}$$

where, following the format of equation (5.10.1), the figures in the first set of parentheses are the estimated standard errors and those in the second set are the t values under the null hypothesis that the relevant population coefficient has a value of zero.

The interpretation of equation (7.2.2) is as follows: If X_2 and X_3 are both fixed at zero, the average or mean value of the personal consumption expenditure (reflecting the influence of all the omitted variables) is estimated at approximately 53.16 billions of 1958 dollars. As cautioned before, in most cases the intercept term has no economic meaning. The partial regression coefficient 0.7266 means that, holding all other variables constant (X_3 in the present case), as personal income increases, say, by $1, the mean consumption expenditure increases by about 73 cents. By the same token, if X_2 is held constant, the mean personal consumption expenditure is estimated to increase at the rate of 2.7 billions of dollars per year. The R^2 value of 0.9988 shows that the two explanatory variables explain about 99.9 percent of the variation in personal consumption expenditure in the United States over the period 1956–1970. The adjusted R^2 shows that after taking into account the df, X_2 and X_3 still explain about 99.8 percent of the variation in Y.

7.3 HYPOTHESIS TESTING ABOUT INDIVIDUAL PARTIAL REGRESSION COEFFICIENTS

If we invoke the assumption that $u_i \sim N(0, \sigma^2)$, then, as noted in Sec. 7.1, we can use the t test to test a hypothesis about any *individual* partial regression coefficient. To illustrate the mechanics, consider our numerical example. Let us postulate that

$$H_0: \beta_{12.3} = 0 \quad \text{and} \quad H_1: \beta_{12.3} \neq 0$$

The null hypothesis states that, holding X_3 constant, personal disposable income has no (linear) influence on personal consumption expenditure.[2] To test the null

---

[2] In most empirical investigations, the null hypothesis is stated in this form, that is, taking the extreme position (a kind of straw man) that there is no relationship between the dependent variable and the explanatory variable under consideration. The idea here is to find out whether the relationship between the two is a trivial one to begin with.

hypothesis, we use the t test given in (7.1.2). Following Chap. 5, if the computed t value exceeds the critical t value at the chosen level of significance, we may reject the hypothesis; otherwise, we may accept it. For our example, using (7.1.2) and noting that $\beta_{12.3} = 0$ under the null hypothesis, we obtain

$$t = \frac{0.7266}{0.0487} = 14.9060 \qquad (7.3.1)$$

If we assume $\alpha = 0.05$, $t_{\alpha/2} = 2.179$ for 12 df. [*Note:* We are using the two-tail t test. (Why?)] Since the computed t value of 14.9060 far exceeds the critical t value of 2.170, we may reject the null hypothesis and say that $\hat{\beta}_{12.3}$ is statistically significant, that is, significantly different from zero. Graphically, the situation is shown in Fig. 7.1.

In Chap. 5 we saw the intimate connection between hypothesis testing and confidence-interval estimation. For our example, the 95 percent confidence interval for $\beta_{12.3}$ is

$$\hat{\beta}_{12.3} - t_{\alpha/2} \, \text{se}(\hat{\beta}_{12.3}) \leq \beta_{12.3} \leq \hat{\beta}_{12.3} + t_{\alpha/2} \, \text{se}(\hat{\beta}_{12.3})$$

which in our case becomes

$$0.7266 - 2.179(0.0487) \leq \beta_{12.3} \leq 0.7266 + 2.179(0.0487)$$

that is,

$$0.6205 \leq \beta_{12.3} \leq 0.8327 \qquad (7.3.2)$$

that is, $\beta_{12.3}$ lies between 0.6205 and 0.8327 with a 95 percent confidence coefficient. This means that if 100 samples of size 15 are selected and 100 confidence intervals like $\hat{\beta}_{12.3} \pm t_{\alpha/2} \, \text{se}(\hat{\beta}_{12.3})$ are constructed, we expect 95 of them to contain the true population parameter $\beta_{12.3}$. Since the null hypothesized value of zero does not lie in the interval (7.3.2), we can reject the null hypothesis that $\beta_{12.3} = 0$ with 95 percent confidence coefficient. Thus, whether we use the t

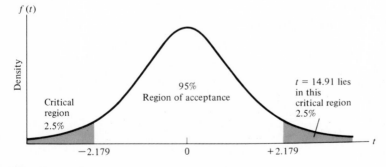

Figure 7.1 95 percent confidence interval for t (12 df).

test of significance as in (7.3.1) or the confidence-interval estimation as in (7.3.2), we reach the same conclusion. But this should not be surprising in view of the close connection between confidence-interval estimation and hypothesis testing.

Following the procedure just described, we can test hypotheses about other parameters of the model (7.2.1) from the information presented in equation (7.2.2). If, for example, we assume that $\alpha = 0.05$ and hypothesize that each of the true partial regression coefficients is *individually* equal to zero, then, it is apparent from (7.2.2) that each estimated partial regression coefficient is statistically significant, that is, significantly different from zero, because the computed t value in each case exceeds the critical t value; *individually* we may reject the (individual) null hypothesis.

7.4 TESTING THE OVERALL SIGNIFICANCE OF THE SAMPLE REGRESSION

Throughout the previous section we were concerned with testing the significance of the estimated partial regression coefficients individually, that is, under the separate hypothesis that each true population partial regression coefficient was zero. But now consider the following hypothesis:

$$H_0: \beta_{12.3} = \beta_{13.2} = 0 \tag{7.4.1}$$

This null hypothesis is a joint hypothesis that $\beta_{12.3}$ and $\beta_{13.2}$ are jointly or simultaneously equal to zero. A test of such a hypothesis is called a test of the *overall significance* of the observed or estimated regression line, that is, whether Y is linearly related to both X_2 and X_3.

Can the joint hypothesis in (7.4.1) be tested by testing the significance of $\hat{\beta}_{12.3}$ and $\hat{\beta}_{13.2}$ individually as in Sec. 7.3? The answer is no, and the reasoning is as follows.

In testing the individual significance of an observed partial regression coefficient in Sec. 7.3, we assumed implicitly that each test of significance was based on a different (i.e., independent) sample. Thus, in testing the significance of $\hat{\beta}_{12.3}$ under the hypothesis that $\beta_{12.3} = 0$, it was assumed tacitly that the testing was based on a different sample than the one used in testing the significance of $\hat{\beta}_{13.2}$ under the null hypothesis that $\beta_{13.2} = 0$. But to test the joint hypothesis of (7.4.1), if we use the same sample data (Table 7.1), we shall be violating the assumption underlying the test procedure.[3] The matter can be put differently: In (7.3.2) we established the 95 percent confidence interval for $\beta_{12.3}$. But if we use the same sample data to establish confidence interval for $\beta_{13.2}$, say, with a confidence coefficient of 95 percent, we cannot assert that both $\beta_{12.3}$ and $\beta_{13.2}$ lie in their respective confidence intervals with a probability of $(1 - \alpha)(1 - \alpha) = (0.95)(0.95)$.

---

[3] In any given sample the cov $(\hat{\beta}_{12.3}, \hat{\beta}_{13.2})$ may not be zero; that is, $\hat{\beta}_{12.3}$ and $\hat{\beta}_{13.2}$ may be correlated. (More on this in Chap. 8.)

In other words, although the statements

$$\Pr[\hat{\beta}_{12.3} - t_{\alpha/2}\,\mathrm{se}(\hat{\beta}_{12.3}) \leq \beta_{12.3} \leq \hat{\beta}_{12.3} + t_{\alpha/2}\,\mathrm{se}(\hat{\beta}_{12.3})] = 1 - \alpha$$

$$\Pr[\hat{\beta}_{13.2} - t_{\alpha/2}\,\mathrm{se}(\hat{\beta}_{13.2}) \leq \beta_{13.2} \leq \hat{\beta}_{13.2} + t_{\alpha/2}\,\mathrm{se}(\hat{\beta}_{13.2})] = 1 - \alpha$$

are individually true, it is not true that

$$\Pr[\hat{\beta}_{12.3} \pm t_{\alpha/2}\,\mathrm{se}(\hat{\beta}_{12.3}), \, \hat{\beta}_{13.2} \pm t_{\alpha/2}\,\mathrm{se}(\hat{\beta}_{13.2})] = (1 - \alpha)^2$$

because the intervals are not independent when the same data are used to derive them.

The upshot of the preceding argument is that for a given example (sample) only one confidence interval or only one test of significance can be obtained. How, then, does one test the simultaneous null hypothesis that $\beta_{12.3} = \beta_{13.2} = 0$? The answer is provided in the next section.

7.5 THE ANALYSIS-OF-VARIANCE APPROACH TO TESTING THE OVERALL SIGNIFICANCE OF AN OBSERVED MULTIPLE REGRESSION

For reasons given in Sec. 7.4, we cannot use the usual t test to test the joint hypothesis that the true partial slope coefficients are zero simultaneously. However, this joint hypothesis can be tested by the *analysis-of-variance* (AOV) technique first introduced in Sec. 5.8, which can be demonstrated as follows.

Recall the identity

$$\sum y_i^2 = \hat{\beta}_{12.3} \sum y_i x_{2i} + \hat{\beta}_{13.2} \sum y_i x_{3i} + \sum e_i^2 \qquad (7.5.1)$$

$$\text{TSS} = \qquad\qquad \text{ESS} \qquad\qquad\quad + \text{RSS}$$

TSS has, as usual, $N - 1$ df and RSS has $N - 3$ df for reasons already discussed. ESS has 2 df since it is a function of $\hat{\beta}_{12.3}$ and $\hat{\beta}_{13.2}$. Therefore, following the AOV procedure discussed in Sec. 5.8, we can set up Table 7.2.

Table 7.2 AOV table for the three-variable regression

Source of variation	SS	df	MSS
Due to regression (ESS)	$\hat{\beta}_{12.3} \sum y_i x_{2i} + \hat{\beta}_{13.2} \sum y_i x_{3i}$	2	$\dfrac{\hat{\beta}_{12.3} \sum y_i x_{2i} + \hat{\beta}_{13.2} \sum y_i x_{3i}}{2}$
Due to residual (RSS)	$\sum e_i^2$	$N - 3$	$\hat{\sigma}^2 = \dfrac{\sum e_i^2}{N - 3}$
Total	$\sum y_i^2$	$N - 1$	

Now it can be shown[4] that under the assumption of normal distribution for u_i and the null hypothesis $\beta_{12.3} = \beta_{13.2} = 0$, the variable

$$F = \frac{(\hat{\beta}_{12.3} \sum y_i x_{2i} + \hat{\beta}_{13.2} \sum y_i x_{3i})/2}{\sum e_i^2/(N-3)} \tag{7.5.2}$$

is distributed as the F distribution with 2 and $N-3$ df.

What use can be made of the preceding F ratio? It can be proved[5] that under the assumption that the $u_i \sim N(0, \sigma^2)$,

$$E \frac{\sum e_i^2}{N-3} = E(\hat{\sigma}^2) = \sigma^2 \tag{7.5.3}$$

With the additional assumption that $\beta_{12.3} = \beta_{13.2} = 0$, it can be shown that

$$\frac{E(\hat{\beta}_{12.3} \sum y_i x_{2i} + \hat{\beta}_{13.2} \sum y_i x_{3i})}{2} = \sigma^2 \tag{7.5.4}$$

Therefore, if the null hypothesis is true, both (7.5.3) and (7.5.4) give identical estimates of true σ^2. This should not be surprising because if there is a trivial relationship between Y and X_2 and X_3, the sole source of variation in Y is due to the random forces represented by u_i. If, however, the null hypothesis is false, that is, X_2 and X_3 definitely influence Y, the equality between (7.5.3) and (7.5.4) will not hold. In this case, the ESS will be relatively larger than the RSS, taking due account of their respective df. Therefore, the F value of (7.5.2) provides a test of the null hypothesis that the true slope coefficients are simultaneously zero. If the F value computed from (7.5.2) exceeds the critical F value from the F table at the α percent level of significance, we reject H_0; otherwise we accept it.

Turning to our example, we obtain Table 7.3 (see the computer printout in App. 7A, Sec. 7A.1). Using (7.5.2), we obtain

$$F = \frac{32982.5502}{6.4308} = 5128.8781 \tag{7.5.5}$$

If we use the 5 percent level of significance, the critical F value for 2 and 12 df, $F_{0.05}(2, 12)$, is 3.89. Obviously the computed F value is significant, and hence we may reject the null hypothesis. (If the null hypothesis were true, the probability of obtaining an F value of as much as 5129 is less than 5 in 100.) If the level of significance is assumed to be 1 percent, $F_{0.01}(2, 12) = 6.93$. The computed F still exceeds this critical value by a large margin. We still reject the null hypothesis; if the null hypothesis were true, the chance of obtaining an F value of 5129 is less than 1 in 100.[6]

---

[4] See K. A. Brownlee, *Statistical Theory and Methodology in Science and Engineering*, John Wiley & Sons, Inc., New York, 1960.

[5] *Ibid.*

[6] By convention, in this case we say that the computed F value is highly significant because the probability of commiting the type I error (i.e., the level of significance) is very low—1 in 100.

Table 7.3 AOV table for the illustrative example

Source of variation	SS	df	MSS
Due to regression	65,965.1003	2	32,982.5502
Due to residuals	77.1690	12	6.4308
Total	66,042.2693	14	

7.6 AN IMPORTANT RELATIONSHIP BETWEEN R^2 AND F

There is an intimate relationship between the coefficient of determination R^2 and the F test used in the analysis of variance. Assuming the normal distribution for the disturbances u_i and the null hypothesis that $\beta_{12.3} = \beta_{13.2} = 0$, we have seen that

$$F = \frac{\text{ESS}/2}{\text{RSS}/(N-3)} \tag{7.6.1}$$

is distributed as the F distribution with 2 and $N-3$ df.

More generally, in the k-variable case (including intercept), if we assume that the disturbances are normally distributed and that the null hypothesis is

$$H_0: \beta_{12.34\ldots k} = \beta_{13.24\ldots k} = \cdots = \beta_{1k.234\ldots k-1} = 0 \tag{7.6.2}$$

then it follows that

$$F = \frac{\text{ESS}/(k-1)}{\text{RSS}/(N-k)} \tag{7.6.3}$$

follows the F distribution with $k-1$ and $N-k$ df. (*Note:* The total number of parameters to be estimated is k, of which one is the intercept term.)

Let us manipulate (7.6.3) as follows:

$$F = \frac{N-k}{k-1} \frac{\text{ESS}}{\text{RSS}}$$

$$= \frac{N-k}{k-1} \frac{\text{ESS}}{\text{TSS} - \text{ESS}}$$

$$= \frac{N-k}{k-1} \frac{\text{ESS}/\text{TSS}}{1 - (\text{ESS}/\text{TSS})}$$

$$= \frac{N-k}{k-1} \frac{R^2}{1 - R^2}$$

$$= \frac{R^2/(k-1)}{(1-R^2)/(N-k)} \tag{7.6.4}$$

Table 7.4 AOV table in terms of R^2

Source of variation	SS	df	MSS†
Due to regression	$R^2(\sum y_i^2)$	2	$R^2(\sum y_i^2)/2$
Due to residuals	$(1 - R^2)(\sum y_i^2)$	$N - 3$	$(1 - R^2)(\sum y_i^2)/(N - 3)$
Total	$\sum y_i^2$	$N - 1$	

† Note that in computing the F value there is no need to multiply R^2 and $1 - R^2$ by $\sum y_i^2$ because it drops out, as shown in (7.6.5).

where use is made of the definition $R^2 = \text{ESS}/\text{TSS}$. Equation (7.6.4) shows how F and R^2 are related. These two statistics vary directly. When $R^2 = 0$, F is zero ipso facto. The larger the R^2, the greater the F value. In the limit, when $R^2 = 1$, F is infinite. Thus the F test, which is a measure of the overall significance of the estimated regression, is also a test of significance of R^2. In other words, testing the null hypothesis (7.6.2) is equivalent to testing the null hypothesis that (the population) R^2 is zero.

For the three-variable case (7.6.4) becomes

$$F = \frac{R^2/2}{(1 - R^2)/(N - 3)} \tag{7.6.5}$$

By virtue of the close connection between F and R^2, the AOV Table 7.2 can be recast as Table 7.4.

For our illustrative example, the reader should verify that the F of (7.6.5) is 4994, which is approximately equal to the F value of (7.5.5), the difference being due to the rounding errors. As before, the F value is highly significant, and we can reject the null hypothesis that Y is not linearly related to X_2 and X_3.

7.7 THE "INCREMENTAL," OR "MARGINAL," CONTRIBUTION OF AN EXPLANATORY VARIABLE

Let us return to our illustrative example. We know from (7.2.2) that the coefficient of X_2 (income) and X_3 (trend) are statistically significantly different from zero on the basis of *separate* t tests. We have also seen that the regression line obtained is itself significant on the basis of the F test given in (7.5.2) or (7.6.5). Now suppose that we introduce X_2 and X_3 *sequentially;* that is, we first regress Y on X_2 and assess its significance and then add X_3 to the model to find out whether it contributes anything (of course, the order in which X_2 and X_3 enter can be reversed). By contribution we mean whether the addition of the variable to the model increases the ESS (and thus R^2) "significantly" in relation to the RSS. This contribution may appropriately be called the *incremental*, or *marginal*, contribution of an explanatory variable.

The topic of incremental contribution is an important one in practice. In most

Table 7.5 AOV table for regression (7.7.1)

Source of variation	SS	df	MSS
ESS (due to X_2)	65898.2353	1	65898.2353
RSS	144.0340	13	11.0800
Total	66042.2693	14	

empirical investigations the researcher may not be completely sure whether it is worth adding an X variable to the model knowing that several other X variables are already present in the model. One does not wish to include variable(s) which contribute very little toward ESS. By the same token, one does not want to exclude variable(s) which substantially increase ESS. But how does one decide whether an X variable significantly reduces RSS? The analysis-of-variance technique can be easily extended to answer this question.

Suppose we first regress Y (personal consumption expenditure) on X_2 (personal disposable income) and obtain the following regression:

$$\hat{Y}_i = \hat{\beta}_{1.2} + \hat{\beta}_{12}X_{2i}$$

$$= 12.742 + 0.8812X_{2i} \qquad (7.7.1)$$
$$(4.663) \quad (0.0114)$$

$$t = (2.663)(77.2982) \quad r^2 = 0.9989$$

Under the null hypothesis $\beta_{12} = 0$, it can be seen that the estimated t value of 77.2982 ($= 0.8812/0.0114$) is obviously statistically significant either at the 5 or 1 percent level of significance. Thus, X_2 significantly affects Y. The AOV table for regression (7.7.1) is given as Table 7.5.

Assuming the disturbances u_i to be normally distributed and the null hypothesis $\beta_{12} = 0$, we know that

$$F = \frac{65898.235}{11.080} = 5947.494 \qquad (7.7.2)$$

follows the F distribution with 1 and 13 df. This F value is obviously significant at the usual levels of significance. Thus, as before, we can reject the hypothesis that $\beta_{12} = 0$. Incidentally, note that $t^2 = (77.2982)^2 = 5975.012$, which is equal to the F value of (7.7.2) save the rounding error. But this should not be surprising because, as noted in Chap. 5, under the same null hypothesis and the same level of significance, the square of t value with $N - 2$ df is equal to the F value with 1 and $N - 2$ df.

Having run the regression (7.7.1), let us suppose we decide to add X_3 to the model and obtain the multiple regression (7.2.2). The questions we want to answer are: (1) What is the marginal, or incremental, contribution of X_3 knowing that X_2 is already in the model and that it is significantly related to Y? (2) Is the incremen-

Table 7.6 AOV table to assess incremental contribution of a variable(s)

Source of variation	SS	df	MSS
ESS due to X_2 alone	$Q_1 = \hat{\beta}_{12}^2 \sum x_2^2$	1	$\dfrac{Q_1}{1}$
ESS due to the addition of X_3	$Q_2 = Q_3 - Q_1$	1	$\dfrac{Q_2}{1}$
ESS due to both X_2, X_3	$Q_3 = \hat{\beta}_{12.3} \sum y_i x_{2i} + \hat{\beta}_{13.2} \sum y_i x_{3i}$	2	$\dfrac{Q_3}{2}$
RSS	$Q_4 = Q_5 - Q_3$	$N-3$	$\dfrac{Q_4}{N-3}$
Total	$Q_5 = \sum y_i^2$	$N-1$	

tal contribution statistically significant? (3) What is the criterion for adding variables into the model? These questions can be answered by the AOV technique. To see this, let us construct Table 7.6. For our numerical example, Table 7.6 becomes Table 7.7.

To assess the incremental contribution of X_3 after allowing for the contribution of X_2, we form

$$F = \frac{Q_2/\text{df}}{Q_4/\text{df}}$$

$$= \frac{Q_2/1}{Q_4/12} \tag{7.7.3}$$

$$F = \frac{66.865}{6.430}$$

$$= 10.3973 \tag{7.7.4}$$

Now under the usual assumption of the normality of the u_i and the null hypothesis that $\beta_{13.2} = 0$, it can be shown that the F of (7.7.3) follows the F distribution

Table 7.7 AOV table for the illustrative example: incremental analysis

Source of variation	SS	df	MSS
ESS due to X_2 alone	$Q_1 = 65898.2353$	1	65898.2353
ESS due to the addition of X_3	$Q_2 = 66.8647$	1	66.8647
ESS due to X_2 and X_3	$Q_3 = 65965.1000$	2	32982.5500
RSS	$Q_4 = 77.1693$	12	6.4302
Total	$Q_5 = 66042.2693$	14	

with 1 and 12 df. From $(7.7.4)$ it is obvious that the observed F value is significant at the 1 percent level of significance. Thus we may reject the null hypothesis; addition of X_3 to the model significantly reduces the RSS or, what comes to the same thing, significantly increases ESS and hence the R^2 value. Therefore, X_3 should be added to the model.

Recall that in $(7.2.2)$ we obtained the t value of 3.2246 for the coefficient of X_3 under $H_0: \beta_{13.2} = 0$. Now $t^2 = (3.2246)^2 = 10.3980 = F$ value given in $(7.7.4)$ save for the rounding errors. But this is expected in view of the close relationship between F and t^2, as noted previously.

The F-test procedure just outlined provides a formal method of deciding whether a variable should be added to a regression model. In practice, however, a variable is often retained in the model even though it does not reduce the RSS significantly in the sense of the F test. (Why?) Oftentimes researchers are faced with the task of choosing from several competing models involving the same dependent variable but with different explanatory variables. As a matter of ad hoc choice, these researchers frequently choose the model which gives the highest adjusted $\bar{R}^2$. Therefore if the inclusion of a variable increases $\bar{R}^2$, it is retained in the model although it does not reduce RSS significantly in the statistical sense. The question then becomes: When does the adjusted $\bar{R}^2$ increase? It can be shown that $\bar{R}^2$ *will increase if the t value of the coefficient of the newly added variable is larger than 1 in absolute value*, where the t value is computed under the hypothesis that the population value of the said coefficient is zero.[7] Thus, under this hypothesis, we see that the t value of the coefficient of the trend variable in our illustrative example is 3.2246, which is greater than 1; hence the inclusion of the trend variable will increase $\bar{R}^2$. (In our example, X_3 also happens to be statistically significant.)

7.8 TESTING THE SIGNIFICANCE OF CORRELATION COEFFICIENTS

In this and the previous chapters we have come across several correlation coefficients, namely, simple correlation r, r_{12}, and so on, partial correlation $r_{12.3}$, and so on, multiple correlation R, coefficient of determination R^2, and partial coefficient of determination $r_{12.3}^2$, and so on. But so far we have said very little about their statistical significance (see Exercise 5.6) except for R^2, which is related to the F distribution. This is not because the subject is unimportant, but simply because the test procedure often requires the use of what may be called *correlation models* rather than the regression models.

Our emphasis in this text is primarily on regression models. In such models we study the behavior of the dependent variable Y conditional upon the fixed (in

---

[7] For proof, see Dennis J. Aigner, *Basic Econometrics*, Prentice-Hall, Inc., Englewood Cliffs, N.J., 1971, pp. 91–92.

repeated sampling) values of the explanatory variables, the X's. In other words, the X variables are assumed to be either nonstochastic or, if stochastic, independent of the disturbances u_i. In correlation models, on the other hand, it is assumed that Y as well as the X's are stochastic and that they have some (well-defined) joint probability distribution. Generally it is assumed that these variables follow (a multivariate) normal distribution. Furthermore, correlation models treat all variables symmetrically; that is, there is no distinction between dependent and explanatory variables. In regression models, on the contrary, we specify one variable as the dependent variable and the other(s) as the explanatory or determining variables.

This fundamental difference between correlation and regression models has an important bearing on the test procedure of correlation coefficients. If the X variables are assumed to be nonstochastic, or fixed, as in regression models, the probability distribution of various sample correlation coefficients depends on the values chosen for the nonstochastic X variables and in many cases the test procedure becomes extremely complicated to be of any practical use. In this situation tests of significance of observed correlation coefficients may not be carried out. Of course, we may still use the correlation coefficients but only as a descriptive device. If, on the other hand, the interest is in correlation models, the testing procedure has been studied extensively by several authors and various tests of significance are readily available. The interested reader may look them up in the references.[8] We shall not pursue these tests of significance in this text.

7.9 SUMMARY AND CONCLUSIONS

With this chapter we conclude regression analysis in its " purest " form, that is, under the idealistic assumptions of the classical linear model. Given these assumptions, we have seen how to tackle the twin problems of estimation and inference. In particular, we have seen how to estimate the simple and partial regression coefficients and their standard errors, simple and partial coefficients of correlations, and simple and multiple coefficients of determination. Similarly, we have seen how the estimators are related to their population values by using the techniques of confidence intervals, hypothesis testing, and analysis of variance. In developing these topics we have come across several probability distributions such as the normal, t, F, and χ^2 and have shown how these distributions help us to attack the problem of statistical inference.

Chapters 1 to 7, therefore, have introduced the reader to the " core " of regression analysis under the most "idealistic" conditions. But from now on we must inject some "reality" into our analysis and find out what happens if some or all the assumptions of the standard model are relaxed.

---

[8] A comparatively simple discussion can be found in G. Udny Yule and M. G. Kendall, *An Introduction to the Thoery of Statistics*, Charles Griffin & Company, Ltd., London, 1953, chaps. 17–19.

Before we turn to this task, however, in Chap. 8 we shall introduce the classical linear regression model in matrix notation. This chapter provides a convenient summary, in matrix form, of Chaps. 1 to 7. But more importantly, it shows why matrix algebra is such a useful tool when we go beyond two- or three-variable regression models.

EXERCISES

7.1 Refer to Exercise 6.1.
  (a) Are $\hat{\beta}_{12.3}$ and $\hat{\beta}_{13.2}$ individually statistically significant?
  (b) Are they statistically different from unity?
  (c) Are $\hat{\alpha}_{12.3}$ and $\hat{\alpha}_{13.2}$ statistically significant individually?
  (d) Do the data support the hypothesis that $\beta_{12.3} = \beta_{13.2} = 0$.
  (e) Test the hypothesis that $\alpha_{12.3} = \alpha_{13.2} = 0$.
  (f) How would you compute the output elasticities of labor and capital for the first model? For the second model?
  (g) Which of the models do you prefer? Why?
  (h) Compare the R^2's of the two models.
You may use the 5 percent level of significance.

7.2 Refer to Exercise 6.3.
  (a) Test the overall significance of the estimated regression.
  (b) What is the incremental contribution of X_i^2?
  (c) Would you keep X_i^2 in the model on the basis of the F test? On the basis of R^2?

7.3 Refer to Exercise 6.15.
  (a) What are the real income and interest rate elasticities of real cash balances?
  (b) Are the preceding elasticities statistically significant individually?
  (c) Test the overall significance of the estimated regression.
  (d) Is the income elasticity of demand for real cash balances significantly different from unity?
  (e) Should the interest rate variable be retained in the model? Why?

7.4 Continue with Exercise 6.15. Suppose that we run the following regression:

$$M_t^n = \alpha_0 \, Y_t^{\alpha_1} r_t^{\alpha_2} P_t^{\alpha_3}$$

where M_t^n = aggregate *nominal* money cash balances at time t, Y_t = aggregate real income at time t, r_t = long-term interest rate at time t, and P_t = implicit price deflator at time t (as a measure of general price level).
  (a) Run the preceding regression and interpret the results.
  (b) Compare the results of this regression with those obtained from the regression of Exercise 6.15.
  (c) A priori, what would be the value of α_3? Why?
  (d) What can you say about "money illusion" in the Indian economy for the period 1948–1965?

7.5 Continuing with Exercise 7.4, consider the following demand for money function:

$$M_t^n = \lambda_0 (Y_t^n)^{\lambda_1} r_t^{\lambda_2} p_t^{\lambda_3}$$

where, in addition to the definitions given in Exercise 7.4, Y_t^n stands for aggregate nominal net national income.
  (a) Run the preceding regression and comment on your results.
  (b) Compare the results of this regression with those obtained from Exercises 6.15 and 7.4.
  (c) What is the relationship, if any, between α_1 and λ_1?

7.6 Assuming both that Y and $X_2, X_3, \ldots, X_k$ are jointly normally distributed and the null hypothesis that the population partial correlations are individually equal to zero, R. A. Fisher has shown that

$$t = \frac{r_{12.34\ldots k}\sqrt{N-k-2}}{\sqrt{1-r^2_{12.34\ldots k}}}$$

follows the t distribution with $N-k-2$ df, where k is the kth-order partial correlation coefficient and where N is the total number of observations. (*Note:* $r_{12.3}$ is a first-order partial correlation coefficient, $r_{12.34}$ is a second-order partial correlation coefficient, and so on.) Refer to Exercise 6.18. Assuming Y and X_2 and X_3 to be jointly normally distributed, compute the three partial correlations $r_{12.3}, r_{13.2}$, and $r_{23.1}$ and test their significance under the hypothesis that the corresponding population correlations are individually equal to zero.

7.7 Recall the illustrative example of the chapter:

$$Y_i = \beta_{1.23} + \beta_{12.3}X_{2i} + \beta_{13.2}X_{3i} + u_i$$

where Y = personal consumption expenditure (PCE), X_2 = personal disposable income (PDI), and X_3 = time. One reason for introducing the time variable X_3 is to avoid the problem of "spurious" correlation. In data involving economic time series (such as PCE and PDI) it often happens that they tend to move in the same direction, reflecting an upward or downward trend. Therefore, if one were to regress, say, PCE on PDI only and obtain a high R^2 value, this high value may not reflect the true association between PCE and PDI; it may reflect simply the common trend present in them. To avoid such a spurious association between economic time series, one may proceed in two ways: Assuming that the time series exhibit a linear trend, one may introduce the time variable expressly into the model, as we have done in our illustrative example. As a result, $\beta_{12.3}$ now reflects the true association between PCE and PDI, that is, association net of the (linear) time effect. Alternatively, one can *detrend* variables Y and X_2 and run the regression on the detrended Y and X_2. Assuming, again, a linear time trend, the detrending can be effected by the three-stage procedure discussed in Chap. 6. First regress Y on X_3 (time) and obtain the residuals from this regression, say, w_i. Second, regress X_2 on X_3 and obtain the residuals from this regression, say, v_i. Finally, regress w_i on v_i, which are both free of the (linear) influence of time. The slope coefficient from this regression will reflect the true association between Y and X_2 and should, therefore, be equal to $\beta_{12.3}$.

Apply the preceding detrending procedure to the illustrative example discussed in the chapter and verify that the slope coefficient in the regression of detrended Y on detrended X_2 is equal to $\beta_{12.3}$.

7.8 Suppose you want to study the behavior of sales of a product, say, automobiles over a number of years and suppose someone suggests you try the following models:

$$Y_t = \beta_0 + \beta_1 t$$
$$Y_t = \alpha_0 + \alpha_1 t + \alpha_2 t^2$$

where Y_t = sales at time t and t = time measured in years. The first model postulates that sales is a linear function of time, whereas the second model states that it is a quadratic function of time.

(*a*) Discuss the properties of these models.

(*b*) How would you decide between the two models?

(*c*) In what situations will the quadratic model be useful?

(*d*) Try to obtain data on automobile sales in the United States over the past 20 years and see which of the models fits the data well.

7.9 In studying the demand for farm tractors in the United States for the periods 1921–1941 and 1948–1957, Griliches[9] obtained the following results:

$$\log Y_t = \text{constant} - 0.519 \, \log X_{2i} - 4.933 \, \log X_{3i} \qquad R^2 = 0.793$$
$$\qquad\qquad\qquad (0.231) \qquad\qquad (0.477)$$

[9] Z. Griliches, "The Demand for a Durable Input: Farm Tractors in the United States, 1921–1957," in *The Demand for Durable Goods*, Arnold C. Harberger (ed.), The University of Chicago Press, Chicago, 1960, table 1, p. 192.

where Y_t = value of stock of tractors on farms as of January 1, in 1935–1939 dollars, X_2 = index of prices paid for tractors divided by an index of prices received for all crops at time $t - 1$, X_3 = interest rate prevailing in year $t - 1$, and where the estimated standard errors are given in the parentheses.

(a) Interpret the preceding regression.

(b) Are the estimated slope coefficients individually statistically significant? Are they significantly different from unity?

(c) Use the analysis-of-variance technique to test the significance of the overall regression. *Hint:* Use the R^2 variant of the AOV technique.

(d) How would you compute the interest-rate elasticity of demand for farm tractors?

(e) How would you test the significance of estimated R^2?

7.10 Consider the following wage-determination equation for the British economy[10] for the period 1950–1969:

$$W_t = 8.582 + 0.364(PF)_t + 0.004(PF)_{t-1} - 2.560U_t$$
$$\quad (1.129) \ (0.080) \qquad (0.072) \qquad \quad (0.658)$$

$$R^2 = 0.873 \qquad df = 15$$

where W = wages and salaries per employee, PF = prices of final output at factor cost, U = unemployment in Great Britain as a percentage of the total number of employees in Great Britain, and t = time. (The figures in the parentheses are the estimated standard errors.)

(a) Interpret the preceding equation.

(b) Are the estimated coefficients individually significant?

(c) What is the rationale for the introduction of $(PF)_{t-1}$?

(d) Should the variable $(PF)_{t-1}$ be dropped from the model? Why?

(e) How would you compute the elasticity of wages and salaries per employee with respect to the unemployment rate U?

7.11 A variation of the wage-determination equation given in Exercise 7.10 is as follows:[11]

$$W_t = 1.073 + 5.288V_t - 0.116X_t + 0.054M_t + 0.046M_{t-1}$$
$$\quad (0.797) \ (0.812) \quad (0.111) \quad (0.022) \quad (0.019)$$

$$R^2 = 0.934 \qquad df = 14$$

where W is as before, V = unfilled job vacancies in Great Britain as a percentage of the total number of employees in Great Britain, X = gross domestic product per person employed, M = import prices, and M_{t-1} = import prices in the previous (or lagged) year. (The estimated standard errors are given in the parentheses.)

(a) Interpret the preceding equation.

(b) Which of the estimated coefficients are individually statistically significant?

(c) What is the rationale for the introduction of the X variable? A priori, is the sign of X expected to be negative?

(d) What is the purpose of introducing both M_t and M_{t-1} in the model?

(e) Which of the variables may be dropped from the model? Why?

(f) Test the overall significance of the observed regression.

[10] Taken from *Prices and Earnings in 1951–1969: An Econometric Assessment*, Dept. of Employment, HMSO, 1971, eq. (19), p. 35.

[11] *Ibid.*, eq. (67), p. 37.

APPENDIX 7A

7A.1 COMPUTER PRINTOUT OF THE PERSONAL CONSUMPTION EXPENDITURE AND PERSONAL DISPOSABLE INCOME REGRESSION

Data

Y (PCE)	X_2 (PDI)	X_3 (Time)
281.4	309.3	1
288.1	316.1	2
290.0	318.8	3
307.3	333.0	4
316.1	340.3	5
322.5	350.5	6
338.4	367.2	7
353.3	381.2	8
373.7	408.1	9
397.7	434.8	10
418.1	458.9	11
430.1	477.5	12
452.7	499.0	13
469.1	513.5	14
476.9	533.2	15

ANALYSIS
?* MULTIPLE REGRESSION

SPECIFY THE DEPENDENT VARIABLE
?* 1 (= Y)

HOW MANY INDEPENDENT VARIABLES
?* 2

SPECIFY THESE VARIABLES
?* 2, 3(X_2,X_3)

VARIABLE	REG. COEF.	STD. ERROR COEF.	COMPUTED T
2	0.7266	0.0487	14.9060
3	2.7363	0.8486	3.2246

INTERCEPT 53.1603
MULTIPLE CORRELATION 0.9994   (ADJUSTED R = 0.9993)
STANDARD ERROR OF ESTIMATE 2.5359

ANALYSIS OF VARIANCE FOR THE REGRESSION

SOURCE OF VARIATION	D.F.	SUM OF SQ.	MEAN SQ.	F VALUE
ATTRIBUTABLE TO REGRESSION	2	65965.1003	32982.5502	5128.8781
DEVIATION FROM REGRESSION	12	77.1690	6.4308	
TOTAL	14	66042.2693		

DO YOU WISH TO PRINT THE TABLE OF RESIDUALS
?* YES

CASE NO	Y OBSERVED	Y ESTIMATED	RESIDUAL
1	281.4	280.631	0.768
2	288.1	288.309	−0.209
3	290.0	293.007	−3.007
4	307.3	306.061	1.238
5	316.1	314.101	1.998
6	322.5	324.249	−1.749
7	338.4	339.119	−0.719
8	353.3	352.027	1.272
9	373.7	374.309	−0.609
10	397.7	396.445	1.254
11	418.1	416.693	1.406
12	430.1	432.944	−2.844
13	452.7	451.302	1.397
14	469.1	464.573	4.526
15	476.9	481.624	−4.724

TEST OF EXTREME RESIDUALS

RATIO OF RANGES FOR THE SMALLEST RESIDUAL	0.307
RATIO OF RANGES FOR THE LARGEST RESIDUAL	0.423
CRITICAL VALUE OF THE RATIO AT ALPHA = 0.10	0.472

DO YOU WISH TO PLOT Y OBSERVED AND Y ESTIMATED
?* YES

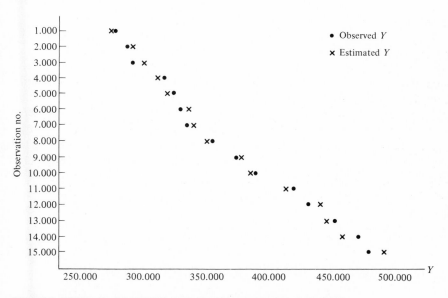

DO YOU WISH TO COMPUTE THE DURBIN-WATSON STATISTIC
?* YES

DURBIN-WATSON STATISTIC
2.3062

EIGHT

THE MATRIX APPROACH TO LINEAR REGRESSION MODEL*

This chapter presents the classical linear regression model involving k variables (Y and $X_2, X_3, \ldots, X_k$) in matrix algebra notation. Conceptually, the k-variable model is a logical extension of the two- and three-variable models considered thus far in this text. Therefore, this chapter presents very few new concepts save for the matrix notation.[1]

A great advantage of matrix algebra over scalar algebra (elementary algebra dealing with scalars or real numbers) is that it provides a compact method of handling regression models involving any number of variables; once the k-variable model is formulated and solved in matrix notation, the solution applies to one, two, three, or any number of variables.

8.1 THE k-VARIABLE LINEAR REGRESSION MODEL

Generalizing the two-and three-variable linear regression models, the k-variable population regression model (PRF) involving the dependent variable Y and $k - 1$ explanatory variables $X_2, X_3, \ldots, X_k$ may be written as

$$\text{PRF}: Y_i = \beta_1 + \beta_2 X_{2i} + \beta_3 X_{3i} + \cdots + \beta_k X_{ki} + u_i \qquad i = 1, 2, 3, \ldots, N \tag{8.1.1}$$

---

* This is an optional chapter and can be skipped without loss of continuity.

[1] Readers not familiar with matrix algebra should review App. B before proceeding any further. Appendix B provides the essentials of matrix algebra needed to follow this chapter.

where β_1 = the intercept, β_2 to β_k = partial slope coefficients, u = stochastic disturbance term, and i = ith observation, N being the size of the population.[2] The PRF (8.1.1) is to be interpreted in the usual manner: It gives the mean or expected value of Y conditional upon the fixed (in repeated sampling) values of $X_2, X_3, \ldots, X_k$, that is, $E(Y \mid X_{2i}, X_{3i}, \ldots, X_{ki})$.

Equation (8.1.1) is a short-hand expression for the following set of N simultaneous equations:

$$Y_1 = \beta_1 + \beta_2 X_{21} + \beta_3 X_{31} + \cdots + \beta_k X_{k1} + u_1$$
$$Y_2 = \beta_1 + \beta_2 X_{22} + \beta_3 X_{32} + \cdots + \beta_k X_{k2} + u_2$$

$$\cdots\cdots\cdots\cdots\cdots\cdots\cdots\cdots\cdots\cdots\cdots\cdots\cdots\cdots\cdots\cdots\cdots$$ (8.1.2)

$$Y_N = \beta_1 + \beta_2 X_{2N} + \beta_3 X_{3N} + \cdots + \beta_k X_{kN} + u_N$$

Let us write the system of equations (8.1.2) in an alternative but more illuminating way as follows:

$$
\begin{bmatrix} Y_1 \\ Y_2 \\ \vdots \\ Y_N \end{bmatrix}
=
\begin{bmatrix} 1 & X_{21} & X_{31} & \cdots & X_{k1} \\ 1 & X_{22} & X_{32} & \cdots & X_{k2} \\ \vdots & \vdots & \vdots & & \vdots \\ 1 & X_{2N} & X_{3N} & & X_{kN} \end{bmatrix}
\begin{bmatrix} \beta_1 \\ \beta_2 \\ \vdots \\ \beta_k \end{bmatrix}
+
\begin{bmatrix} u_1 \\ u_2 \\ \vdots \\ u_N \end{bmatrix}
$$ (8.1.3)

$$
\begin{array}{ccccccc}
\mathbf{y} & = & \mathbf{X} & & \boldsymbol{\beta} & + & \mathbf{u} \\
N \times 1 & & N \times k & & k \times 1 & & N \times 1
\end{array}
$$

where[3] $\mathbf{y}$ = $N \times 1$ column vector of observations on the dependent variable Y

$\mathbf{X}$ = $N \times k$ matrix giving N observations on $k - 1$ variables X_2 to X_k, the first column of 1s representing the intercept term. (This matrix is also known as the *data matrix*)

$\boldsymbol{\beta}$ = $k \times 1$ column vector of the unknown parameters $\beta_1, \beta_2, \ldots, \beta_k$

$\mathbf{u}$ = $N \times 1$ column vector of N disturbances u_i

Using the rules of matrix multiplication and addition, the reader should verify that the systems (8.1.2) and (8.1.3) are equivalent.

---

[2] For notational simplicity, from now on we shall drop the Yule notation introduced in Chaps. 6 and 7. It is understood that $\beta_2, \beta_3, \ldots, \beta_k$ are partial regression coefficients. Thus, β_2 means $\beta_{12.34\cdots k}$, $\beta_3 = \beta_{13.24\cdots k}$, and so on.

[3] Following the notation introduced in App. B, vectors will be represented by lowercase boldfaced letters and matrices will be represented by uppercase boldfaced letters.

System (8.1.3) is known as the *matrix representation of the general (k-variable) linear regression model*. It can be written more compactly as

$$\underset{N \times 1}{\mathbf{y}} = \underset{N \times k}{\mathbf{X}} \quad \underset{k \times 1}{\boldsymbol{\beta}} + \underset{N \times 1}{\mathbf{u}} \tag{8.1.4}$$

Where there is no confusion about the dimensions or orders of the matrix $\mathbf{X}$ and the vectors $\mathbf{y}$, $\boldsymbol{\beta}$, and $\mathbf{u}$, equation (8.1.4) may be written simply as

$$\mathbf{y} = \mathbf{X}\boldsymbol{\beta} + \mathbf{u} \tag{8.1.5}$$

As an illustration of the matrix representation, consider the two-variable consumption-income model considered in Chap. 3, namely, $Y_i = \beta_0 + \beta_1 X_i + u_i$, where Y is consumption expenditure and X is income. Using the data given in Table 3.2, the matrix formulation is

$$
\begin{bmatrix} 70 \\ 65 \\ 90 \\ 95 \\ 110 \\ 115 \\ 120 \\ 140 \\ 155 \\ 150 \end{bmatrix}
=
\begin{bmatrix} 1 & 80 \\ 1 & 100 \\ 1 & 120 \\ 1 & 140 \\ 1 & 160 \\ 1 & 180 \\ 1 & 200 \\ 1 & 220 \\ 1 & 240 \\ 1 & 260 \end{bmatrix}
\begin{bmatrix} \beta_0 \\ \beta_1 \end{bmatrix}
+
\begin{bmatrix} u_1 \\ u_2 \\ u_3 \\ u_4 \\ u_5 \\ u_6 \\ u_7 \\ u_8 \\ u_9 \\ u_{10} \end{bmatrix}
\tag{8.1.6}
$$

$$\underset{10 \times 1}{\mathbf{y}} = \underset{10 \times 2}{\mathbf{X}} \quad \underset{2 \times 1}{\boldsymbol{\beta}} + \underset{10 \times 1}{\mathbf{u}}$$

As in the two- and three-variable cases, our objective is to estimate the parameters of the multiple regression (8.1.1) and to draw inferences about them from the data at hand. In matrix notation this amounts to estimating $\boldsymbol{\beta}$ and drawing inferences about this $\boldsymbol{\beta}$. For the purpose of estimation, we may use the method of ordinary least squares (OLS) or the method of maximum likelihood (ML). But as noted before, these two methods yield identical estimates of the regression coefficients.[4] Therefore, we shall confine our attention to the method of OLS.

8.2 ASSUMPTIONS OF THE CLASSICAL LINEAR REGRESSION MODEL IN MATRIX NOTATION

In Table 8.1 we give the assumptions underlying the classical linear regression model in scalar notation and their equivalents in matrix notation. Assumption 1

---

[4] The proof that this is so in the k-variable case can be found in the footnote references given in Chap. 4.

Table 8.1 Assumptions of the classical linear regression model

Scalar notation	Matrix notation
1. $E(u_i) = 0$, for each i (3.1.1)	1. $E(\mathbf{u}) = \mathbf{0}$ (8.2.1) where $\mathbf{u}$ and $\mathbf{0}$ are $N \times 1$ column vectors, $\mathbf{0}$ being a null vector
2. $E(u_i u_j) = 0$ $i \neq j$, (3.1.2) $ = \sigma^2$ $i = j$ (3.1.3)	2. $E(\mathbf{uu'}) = \sigma^2 \mathbf{I}$ (8.2.2) where $\mathbf{I}$ is an $N \times N$ identity matrix
3. $X_2, X_3, \ldots, X_k$ are nonstochastic or fixed	3. The $N \times k$ matrix $\mathbf{X}$ is nonstochastic; that is, it consists of a set of fixed numbers
4. There is no exact linear relationship among the X variables, that is, no multicollinearity	4. The rank of $\dot{\mathbf{X}}$ is k ($=$ number of columns in $\mathbf{X}$) and k is less than N, the number of observations

given in (8.2.1) means that the expected value of the disturbance vector $\mathbf{u}$, that is, of each of its elements, is zero. More explicitly, $E(\mathbf{u}) = \mathbf{0}$ means

$$E \begin{bmatrix} u_1 \\ u_2 \\ \vdots \\ u_N \end{bmatrix} = \begin{bmatrix} E(u_1) \\ E(u_2) \\ \vdots \\ E(u_N) \end{bmatrix} = \begin{bmatrix} 0 \\ 0 \\ \vdots \\ 0 \end{bmatrix} \tag{8.2.3}$$

Assumption 2 [equation (8.2.2)] is a compact way of expressing the two assumptions given in (3.1.2) and (3.1.3) by the scalar notation. To see this, we can write

$$E(\mathbf{uu'}) = E \begin{bmatrix} u_1 \\ u_2 \\ \vdots \\ u_N \end{bmatrix} \begin{bmatrix} u_1 & u_2 & \cdots & u_N \end{bmatrix}$$

where $\mathbf{u'}$ is the transpose of the column vector $\mathbf{u}$, or a row vector. Performing the multiplication, we obtain

$$E(\mathbf{uu'}) = E \begin{bmatrix} u_1^2 & u_1 u_2 & \cdots & u_1 u_N \\ u_2 u_1 & u_2^2 & \cdots & u_2 u_N \\ \cdots & \cdots & \cdots & \cdots \\ u_N u_1 & u_N u_2 & \cdots & u_N^2 \end{bmatrix}$$

Applying the expectations operator E to each element of the preceding matrix, we obtain

$$E(\mathbf{uu'}) = \begin{bmatrix} E(u_1^2) & E(u_1 u_2) & \cdots & E(u_1 u_N) \\ E(u_2 u_1) & E(u_2^2) & \cdots & E(u_2 u_N) \\ \cdots & \cdots & \cdots & \cdots \\ E(u_N u_1) & E(u_N u_2) & \cdots & E(u_N^2) \end{bmatrix} \tag{8.2.4}$$

Because of the assumptions of homoscedasticity and no serial correlation, matrix (8.2.4) reduces to

$$E(\mathbf{uu}') = \begin{bmatrix} \sigma^2 & 0 & 0 & \cdots & 0 \\ 0 & \sigma^2 & 0 & \cdots & 0 \\ \multicolumn{5}{c}{\dotfill} \\ 0 & 0 & 0 & \cdots & \sigma^2 \end{bmatrix}$$

$$= \sigma^2 \begin{bmatrix} 1 & 0 & 0 & \cdots & 0 \\ 0 & 1 & 0 & \cdots & 0 \\ \multicolumn{5}{c}{\dotfill} \\ 0 & 0 & 0 & \cdots & 1 \end{bmatrix}$$

$$= \sigma^2 \mathbf{I} \tag{8.2.5}$$

where $\mathbf{I}$ is an $N \times N$ identity matrix.

Matrix (8.2.4) [and its representation given in (8.2.5)] is called the *variance-covariance matrix* of the disturbances u_i; the elements on the main diagonal of this matrix (running from the upper-left corner to the lower-right corner) give the variances, and the elements off the main diagonal give the covariances.[5] Note that the variance-covariance matrix is symmetric: The elements above and below the main diagonal are reflections of one another.

Assumption 3 states that the $N \times k$ matrix $\mathbf{X}$ is nonstochastic; that is, it consists of fixed numbers. As noted previously, our regression analysis is conditional regression analysis, conditional upon the fixed values of the X variables.

Assumption 4 states that the $\mathbf{X}$ matrix has full column rank equal to k, the number of columns in the matrix. This means that the columns of the X matrix are linearly independent; that is, there is no exact linear relationship among the X variables. In other words there is no multicollinearity. In scalar notation this is equivalent to saying that there exists no set of numbers $\lambda_1, \lambda_2, \ldots, \lambda_k$ not all zero such that [cf. (6.1.3)]

$$\lambda_1 X_{1i} + \lambda_2 X_{2i} + \cdots + \lambda_k X_{ki} = 0 \tag{8.2.6}$$

where $X_{1i} = 1$ for all i (to allow for the column of 1s in the X matrix.) In matrix notation, (8.2.6) can be represented as

$$\lambda'\mathbf{x} = 0 \tag{8.2.7}$$

where λ' is a $1 \times k$ row vector and x is $k \times 1$ column vector.

If an exact linear relationship such as (8.2.6) exists, the variables are said to be collinear. If, on the other hand, (8.2.6) holds true only if $\lambda_1 = \lambda_2 = \lambda_3 = \cdots = 0$, then the X variables are said to be linearly independent. An intuitive reason for the *no multicollinearity* assumption was given in Chap. 6, and we shall explore this assumption further in Chap. 9.

---

[5] By definition, the variance of $u_i = E[u_i - E(u_i)]^2$ and the covariance between u_i and $u_j = E[u_i - E(u_i)][u_j - E(u_j)]$. But because of the assumption $E(u_i) = 0$ for each i, we have the variance-covariance matrix (8.2.4).

8.3 OLS ESTIMATION

To obtain the OLS estimate of $\boldsymbol{\beta}$, let us first write down the k-variable sample regression (SRF):

$$Y_i = \hat{\beta}_1 + \hat{\beta}_2 X_{2i} + \hat{\beta}_3 X_{3i} + \cdots + \hat{\beta}_k X_{ki} + e_i \tag{8.3.1}$$

which can be written more compactly in matrix notation as

$$\mathbf{y} = \mathbf{X}\hat{\boldsymbol{\beta}} + \mathbf{e} \tag{8.3.2}$$

and in matrix form as

$$\begin{bmatrix} Y_1 \\ Y_2 \\ \vdots \\ Y_N \end{bmatrix} = \begin{bmatrix} 1 & X_{21} & X_{31} & \cdots & X_{k1} \\ 1 & X_{22} & X_{32} & \cdots & X_{k2} \\ \vdots & & & & \\ 1 & X_{2N} & X_{3N} & \cdots & X_{kN} \end{bmatrix} \begin{bmatrix} \hat{\beta}_1 \\ \hat{\beta}_2 \\ \vdots \\ \hat{\beta}_k \end{bmatrix} + \begin{bmatrix} e_1 \\ e_2 \\ \vdots \\ e_N \end{bmatrix} \tag{8.3.3}$$

$$\begin{array}{cccc} \mathbf{y} & = & \mathbf{X} & \hat{\boldsymbol{\beta}} & + & \mathbf{e} \\ N \times 1 & & N \times k & k \times 1 & & N \times 1 \end{array}$$

where $\hat{\boldsymbol{\beta}}$ is a k-element column vector of the OLS estimators of the regression coefficients and where $\mathbf{e}$ is an $N \times 1$ column vector of N residuals.

As in the two- and three-variable models, in the k-variable case the OLS estimators are obtained by minimizing

$$\sum e_i^2 = \sum (Y_i - \hat{\beta}_1 - \hat{\beta}_2 X_{2i} - \cdots - \hat{\beta}_k X_{ki})^2 \tag{8.3.4}$$

where $\sum e_i^2$ is the residual sum of squares (RSS). In matrix notation, this amounts to minimizing $\mathbf{e}'\mathbf{e}$ since

$$\mathbf{e}'\mathbf{e} = \begin{bmatrix} e_1 & e_2 & \cdots & e_N \end{bmatrix} \begin{bmatrix} e_1 \\ e_2 \\ \vdots \\ e_N \end{bmatrix} = e_1^2 + e_2^2 + \cdots + e_N^2 = \sum e_i^2 \tag{8.3.5}$$

Now from (8.3.2) we obtain

$$\mathbf{e} = \mathbf{y} - \mathbf{X}\hat{\boldsymbol{\beta}} \tag{8.3.6}$$

Therefore,

$$\mathbf{e}'\mathbf{e} = (\mathbf{y} - \mathbf{X}\hat{\boldsymbol{\beta}})'(\mathbf{y} - \mathbf{X}\hat{\boldsymbol{\beta}})$$
$$= \mathbf{y}'\mathbf{y} - 2\hat{\boldsymbol{\beta}}'\mathbf{X}'\mathbf{y} + \hat{\boldsymbol{\beta}}'\mathbf{X}'\mathbf{X}\hat{\boldsymbol{\beta}} \tag{8.3.7}$$

where use is made of the properties of the transpose of a matrix, namely, $(\mathbf{X}\hat{\boldsymbol{\beta}})' = \hat{\boldsymbol{\beta}}'\mathbf{X}'$; and since $\hat{\boldsymbol{\beta}}'\mathbf{X}'\mathbf{y}$ is a scalar (a real number), it is equal to its transpose $\mathbf{y}'\mathbf{X}\hat{\boldsymbol{\beta}}$.

Equation (8.3.7) is the matrix representation of (8.3.4). In the scalar notation, the method of OLS consists in so estimating $\beta_1, \beta_2, \ldots, \beta_k$ that $\sum e_i^2$ is as small as possible. This is accomplished by differentiating (8.3.4) partially with respect to $\hat{\beta}_1$ $\hat{\beta}_2, \ldots, \hat{\beta}_k$ and setting the resulting expressions to zero. This process yields k

simultaneous equations in k unknowns, the normal equations of the least-squares theory. As shown in App. 8A, Sec. 8A.1, these equations are as follows:

$$N\hat{\beta}_1 + \hat{\beta}_2 \sum X_{2i} + \hat{\beta}_3 \sum X_{3i} + \cdots + \hat{\beta}_k \sum X_{ki} = \sum Y_i$$

$$\hat{\beta}_1 \sum X_{2i} + \hat{\beta}_2 \sum X_{2i}^2 + \hat{\beta}_3 \sum X_{2i}X_{3i} + \cdots + \hat{\beta}_k \sum X_{2i}X_{ki} = \sum X_{2i}Y_i$$

$$\hat{\beta}_1 \sum X_{3i} + \hat{\beta}_2 \sum X_{3i}X_{2i} + \hat{\beta}_3 \sum X_{3i}^2 + \cdots + \hat{\beta}_k \sum X_{3i}X_{ki} = \sum X_{3i}Y_i \qquad (8.3.8)^6$$

$$\cdots\cdots\cdots\cdots\cdots\cdots\cdots\cdots\cdots\cdots\cdots\cdots\cdots\cdots\cdots$$

$$\hat{\beta}_1 \sum X_{ki} + \hat{\beta}_2 \sum X_{ki}X_{2i} + \hat{\beta}_3 \sum X_{ki}X_{3i} + \cdots + \hat{\beta}_k \sum X_{ki}^2 = \sum X_{ki}Y_i$$

In matrix form, the equations (8.3.8) can be represented as

$$\underbrace{\begin{bmatrix} N & \sum X_{2i} & \sum X_{3i} & \cdots & \sum X_{ki} \\ \sum X_{2i} & \sum X_{2i}^2 & \sum X_{2i}X_{3i} & \cdots & \sum X_{2i}X_{ki} \\ \sum X_{3i} & \sum X_{3i}X_{2i} & \sum X_{3i}^2 & \cdots & \sum X_{3i}X_{ki} \\ \cdots & \cdots & \cdots & & \cdots \\ \sum X_{ki} & \sum X_{ki}X_{2i} & \sum X_{ki}X_{3i} & \cdots & \sum X_{ki}^2 \end{bmatrix}}_{(\mathbf{X'X})} \underbrace{\begin{bmatrix} \hat{\beta}_1 \\ \hat{\beta}_2 \\ \hat{\beta}_3 \\ \vdots \\ \hat{\beta}_k \end{bmatrix}}_{\hat{\boldsymbol{\beta}}} = \underbrace{\begin{bmatrix} 1 & 1 & \cdots & 1 \\ X_{21} & X_{22} & \cdots & X_{2N} \\ X_{31} & X_{32} & \cdots & X_{3N} \\ \cdots & \cdots & & \cdots \\ X_{k1} & X_{k2} & \cdots & X_{kN} \end{bmatrix}}_{\mathbf{X'}} \underbrace{\begin{bmatrix} Y_1 \\ Y_2 \\ Y_2 \\ \vdots \\ Y_N \end{bmatrix}}_{\mathbf{y}}$$

$$(8.3.9)$$

or, more compactly, as

$$(\mathbf{X'X})\hat{\boldsymbol{\beta}} = \mathbf{X'y} \qquad (8.3.10)$$

Note these features of the $(\mathbf{X'X})$ matrix: (1) It gives the raw sums of squares and cross products of the X variables, one of which is the intercept term taking the value of 1 for each observation. The elements on the main diagonal give the raw sums of squares, and those off the main diagonal give the raw sums of cross products (by *raw* we mean in original units of measurement). (2) It is symmetrical since the cross product between X_{2i} and X_{3i} is the same as that between X_{3i} and X_{2i}. (3) It is of order $(k \times k)$, that is, k rows and k columns.

In (8.3.10) the known quantities are $(\mathbf{X'X})$ and $(\mathbf{X'y})$ (the cross product between the X variables and Y) and the unknown is $\hat{\boldsymbol{\beta}}$. Now using matrix algebra, if the inverse of $(\mathbf{X'X})$ exists, say, $(\mathbf{X'X})^{-1}$, then premultiplying both sides of (8.3.10) by this inverse, we obtain

$$(\mathbf{X'X})^{-1}(\mathbf{X'X})\hat{\boldsymbol{\beta}} = (\mathbf{X'X})^{-1}\mathbf{X'y}$$

But since $(\mathbf{X'X})^{-1}(\mathbf{X'X}) = \mathbf{I}$, an identity matrix of order $k \times k$, we get

$$\mathbf{I}\hat{\boldsymbol{\beta}} = (\mathbf{X'X})^{-1}\mathbf{X'y}$$

or

$$\hat{\boldsymbol{\beta}} = (\mathbf{X'X})^{-1}\mathbf{X'y} \qquad (8.3.11)$$

$$k \times 1 \quad k \times k \quad (k \times N)(N \times 1)$$

---

[6] These equations can be remembered easily. Start with the equation $Y_i = \hat{\beta}_1 + \hat{\beta}_2 X_{2i} + \hat{\beta}_3 X_{3i} + \cdots + \hat{\beta}_k X_{ki}$. Summing this equation over the N values gives the first equation in (8.3.8); multiplying it by X_2 on both sides and summing over N gives the second equation; multiplying it by X_3 on both sides and summing over N gives the third equation; and so on. In passing, note that the first equation in (8.3.8) gives at once $\hat{\beta}_1 = \bar{Y} - \hat{\beta}_2 \bar{X}_2 \cdots \hat{\beta}_k \bar{X}_k$ [cf. (6.4.6)].

Equation (8.3.11) is a fundamental result of the OLS theory in matrix notation. It shows how the $\hat{\beta}$ vector can be estimated from the given data. Although
(8.3.11) was obtained from (8.3.9), it can be obtained directly from (8.3.7) by
differentiating $e'e$ with respect to $\hat{\beta}$. The proof is given in App. 8A, Sec. 8A.2.

An Illustration

As an illustration of the matrix methods developed so far, let us rework the
consumption-income example of Chap. 3, whose data are reproduced in (8.1.6).
For the two-variable case we have

$$\hat{\beta} = \begin{bmatrix} \hat{\beta}_0 \\ \hat{\beta}_1 \end{bmatrix}$$

$$(\mathbf{X'X}) = \begin{bmatrix} 1 & 1 & 1 & \cdots & 1 \\ X_1 & X_2 & X_3 & \cdots & X_N \end{bmatrix} \begin{bmatrix} 1 & X_1 \\ 1 & X_2 \\ 1 & X_3 \\ & \cdots \\ 1 & X_N \end{bmatrix} = \begin{bmatrix} N & \sum X_i \\ \sum X_i & \sum X_i^2 \end{bmatrix}$$

and

$$\mathbf{X'y} = \begin{bmatrix} 1 & 1 & 1 & \cdots & 1 \\ X_1 & X_2 & X_3 & \cdots & X_N \end{bmatrix} \begin{bmatrix} Y_1 \\ Y_2 \\ Y_3 \\ \vdots \\ Y_N \end{bmatrix} = \begin{bmatrix} \sum Y_i \\ \sum X_i Y_i \end{bmatrix}$$

Using the data given in (8.1.6), we obtain

$$\mathbf{X'X} = \begin{bmatrix} 10 & 1700 \\ 1700 & 322000 \end{bmatrix}$$

and

$$\mathbf{X'y} = \begin{bmatrix} 1110 \\ 205500 \end{bmatrix}$$

Using the rules of matrix inversion given in App. B, it can be seen that the inverse
of the preceding $(\mathbf{X'X})$ matrix is

$$(\mathbf{X'X})^{-1} = \begin{bmatrix} 0.97576 & -0.005152 \\ -0.005152 & 0.0000303 \end{bmatrix}$$

Therefore,

$$\hat{\beta} = \begin{bmatrix} \hat{\beta}_0 \\ \hat{\beta}_1 \end{bmatrix} = \begin{bmatrix} 0.97576 & -0.005152 \\ -0.005152 & 0.0000303 \end{bmatrix} \begin{bmatrix} 1110 \\ 205500 \end{bmatrix}$$

$$= \begin{bmatrix} 24.3571 \\ 0.5079 \end{bmatrix}$$

Previously we obtained, $\hat{\beta}_0 = 24.4545$ and $\hat{\beta}_1 = 0.5091$, using the computer. The difference between the two estimates is due to the rounding errors. In passing, note that in working on a desk calculator it is essential to obtain results to several significant digits to minimize the rounding errors.

Variance-Covariance Matrix of $\hat{\boldsymbol{\beta}}$

The matrix methods enable us to develop formulas, not only for the variance of $\hat{\beta}_i$, any given element of $\hat{\boldsymbol{\beta}}$, but also for the covariance between any two elements of $\hat{\boldsymbol{\beta}}$, say, $\hat{\beta}_i$ and $\hat{\beta}_j$. We need these variances and covariances for the purpose of statistical inference.

By definition, the variance-covariance matrix of $\hat{\boldsymbol{\beta}}$ is [cf. (8.2.4)]:

$$\text{var-cov}\,(\hat{\beta}) = E\{[\hat{\boldsymbol{\beta}} - E(\hat{\boldsymbol{\beta}})][\hat{\boldsymbol{\beta}} - E(\hat{\boldsymbol{\beta}})]'\}$$

which can be written explicitly as

$$\text{var-cov}\,(\hat{\boldsymbol{\beta}}) = \begin{bmatrix} \text{var}\,(\hat{\beta}_1) & \text{cov}\,(\hat{\beta}_1, \hat{\beta}_2) & \cdots & \text{cov}\,(\hat{\beta}_1, \hat{\beta}_k) \\ \text{cov}\,(\hat{\beta}_2, \hat{\beta}_1) & \text{var}\,(\hat{\beta}_2) & \cdots & \text{cov}\,(\hat{\beta}_2, \hat{\beta}_k) \\ \hdashline \text{cov}\,(\hat{\beta}_k, \hat{\beta}_1) & \text{cov}\,(\hat{\beta}_k, \hat{\beta}_2) & \cdots & \text{var}\,(\hat{\beta}_k) \end{bmatrix} \quad (8.3.12)$$

It is shown in App. 8A, Sec. 8A.3, that the preceding variance-covariance matrix can be obtained from the following formula:

$$\text{var-cov}\,(\hat{\boldsymbol{\beta}}) = \sigma^2 (\mathbf{X}'\mathbf{X})^{-1} \quad (8.3.13)$$

where σ^2 is the homoscedastic variance of u_i and where $(\mathbf{X}'\mathbf{X})^{-1}$ is the inverse matrix appearing in the equation (8.3.11), which gives the OLS estimator $\hat{\boldsymbol{\beta}}$.

In the two- and three-variable linear regression models an unbiased estimator of σ^2 was given by $\hat{\sigma}^2 = \sum e_i^2/(N - 2)$ and $\hat{\sigma}^2 = \sum e_i^2/(N - 3)$, respectively. In the k-variable case, the corresponding formula is

$$\hat{\sigma}^2 = \frac{\sum e_i^2}{N - k}$$

$$= \frac{\mathbf{e}'\mathbf{e}}{N - k} \quad (8.3.14)$$

where there are now $N - k$ df. (Why?)

Although in principle $\mathbf{e}'\mathbf{e}$ can be computed from the estimated residuals, in practice it can be obtained directly as follows. Recalling that $\sum e_i^2 (= \text{RSS}) = \text{TSS} - \text{ESS}$, in the two-variable case

$$\sum e_i^2 = \sum y_i^2 - \hat{\beta}_1^2 \sum x_i^2 \quad (3.1.25)$$

and in the three-variable case

$$\sum e_i^2 = \sum y_i^2 - \hat{\beta}_2 \sum y_i x_{2i} - \hat{\beta}_3 \sum y_i x_{3i} \quad (6.4.14)$$

Extending this principle, it can be seen that for the k-variable model

$$\sum e_i^2 = \sum y_i^2 - \hat{\beta}_2 \sum y_i x_{2i} - \cdots - \hat{\beta}_k \sum y_i x_{ki} \qquad (8.3.15)$$

In matrix notation,

$$\text{TSS: } \sum y_i^2 = \mathbf{y'y} - N\bar{Y}^2 \qquad (8.3.16)$$

$$\text{ESS: } \hat{\beta}_2 \sum y_i x_{2i} + \cdots + \hat{\beta}_k \sum y_i x_{ki} = \hat{\boldsymbol{\beta}}'\mathbf{X'y} - N\bar{Y}^2 \qquad (8.3.17)$$

where the term $N\bar{Y}^2$ is known as the correction for mean.[7] Therefore,

$$\mathbf{e'e} = \mathbf{y'y} - \hat{\boldsymbol{\beta}}'\mathbf{X'y} \qquad (8.3.18)$$

Once $\mathbf{e'e}$ is estimated, $\hat{\sigma}^2$ can be easily computed from (8.3.14), which, in turn, will enable us to estimate the variance-covariance matrix (8.3.13).

For our illustrative example,

$$\mathbf{e'e} = 132100 - [24.4545 \quad 0.5091]\begin{bmatrix} 1110 \\ 205500 \end{bmatrix}$$

$$= 335.5$$

Hence, $\hat{\sigma}^2 = (335.5/8) = 41.9375$, which is approximately the value obtained previously in Chap. 3.

Properties of OLS Vector $\hat{\boldsymbol{\beta}}$

In the two- and three-variable cases we know that the OLS estimators are linear, unbiased, and in the class of all linear unbiased estimators they have minimum variance (the Gauss-Markov property). In short, the OLS estimators are best linear unbiased estimators (BLUE). This property extends to the entire $\hat{\boldsymbol{\beta}}$ vector; that is, $\hat{\boldsymbol{\beta}}$ is linear (each of its elements is a linear function of Y, the dependent variable). $E(\hat{\boldsymbol{\beta}}) = \boldsymbol{\beta}$, that is, the expected value of each element of $\hat{\boldsymbol{\beta}}$ is equal to the corresponding element of the true $\boldsymbol{\beta}$, and in the class of all linear unbiased estimators of $\boldsymbol{\beta}$, the OLS estimator $\hat{\boldsymbol{\beta}}$ has minimum variance.[8] As stated in the introduction, the k-variable case is in most cases a straightforward extension of the two- and three-variable cases.

8.4 THE COEFFICIENT OF DETERMINATION R^2 IN MATRIX NOTATION

The coefficient of determination R^2 has been defined as

$$R^2 = \frac{\text{ESS}}{\text{TSS}}$$

---

[7] *Note:* $\sum y_i^2 = \sum (Y_i - \bar{Y})^2 = \sum Y_i^2 - N\bar{Y}^2 = \mathbf{y'y} - N\bar{Y}^2$. Therefore, without the correction term, $\mathbf{y'y}$ will give simply the raw sum of squares, not the sum of squared deviations.

[8] For proofs, see Lester D. Taylor, *Probability and Mathematical Statistics*, Harper & Row, Publishers, Incorporated, New York, 1974, pp. 271–278.

In the two-variable case,

$$R^2 = \frac{\hat{\beta}_1^2 \sum x_i^2}{\sum y_i^2} \tag{3.3.5}$$

and in the three-variable case

$$R^2 = \frac{\hat{\beta}_2 \sum y_i x_{2i} + \hat{\beta}_3 \sum y_i x_{3i}}{\sum y_i^2} \tag{6.5.5}$$

Generalizing, we obtain for the k-variable case

$$R^2 = \frac{\hat{\beta}_2 \sum y_i x_{2i} + \hat{\beta}_3 \sum y_i x_{3i} + \cdots + \hat{\beta}_k \sum y_i x_{ki}}{\sum y_i^2} \tag{8.4.1}$$

Using (8.3.16) and (8.3.17), equation (8.4.1) can be written as

$$R^2 = \frac{\hat{\boldsymbol{\beta}}'\mathbf{X}'\mathbf{y} - N\bar{Y}^2}{\mathbf{y}'\mathbf{y} - N\bar{Y}^2} \tag{8.4.2}$$

which gives the matrix representation of R^2.

For our illustrative example,

$$\hat{\boldsymbol{\beta}}'\mathbf{X}'\mathbf{y} = [24.3571 \quad 0.5079] \begin{bmatrix} 1110 \\ 205500 \end{bmatrix}$$

$$= 131409.831$$

$$\mathbf{y}'\mathbf{y} = 132100$$

and $\qquad N\bar{Y}^2 = 123210$

Plugging these values in (8.4.2), it can be seen that $R^2 = 0.9224$, which is about the same as obtained before, save for the rounding errors.

8.5 HYPOTHESIS TESTING IN MATRIX NOTATION

For reasons spelled out in the previous chapters, if our objective is inference as well as estimation, we shall have to assume that the disturbances u_i follow some probability distribution. Also for reasons given previously, in regression analysis we usually assume that each u_i follows the normal distribution with zero mean and constant variance σ^2. In matrix notation, we have

$$\mathbf{u} \sim N(\mathbf{0}, \sigma^2 \mathbf{I}) \tag{8.5.1}$$

where $\mathbf{u}$ and $\mathbf{0}$ are $N \times 1$ column vectors and $\mathbf{I}$ is an $N \times N$ identity matrix, $\mathbf{0}$ being the null vector.

Given the normality assumption, we know that in two- and three-variable linear regression models: (1) the OLS estimators $\hat{\beta}_i$ and the ML estimators $\tilde{\beta}_i$ are identical, but the ML estimator $\tilde{\sigma}^2$ is biased although this bias can be removed by using the unbiased OLS estimator $\hat{\sigma}^2$; and (2) the OLS estimators $\hat{\beta}_i$, are also normally distributed. Generalizing, in the k-variable case it can be shown that

$$\hat{\boldsymbol{\beta}} \sim N[\boldsymbol{\beta}, \sigma^2(\mathbf{X}'\mathbf{X})^{-1}] \qquad (8.5.2)$$

that is, each element of $\hat{\boldsymbol{\beta}}$ is normally distributed with mean equal to the corresponding element of true $\boldsymbol{\beta}$ and the variance given by σ^2 times the appropriate diagonal element of the inverse matrix $(\mathbf{X}'\mathbf{X})^{-1}$.

Since in practice σ^2 is unknown, it is estimated by $\hat{\sigma}^2$. Then by the usual shift to the t distribution, it follows that each element of $\hat{\boldsymbol{\beta}}$ follows the t distribution with $N - k$ df. Symbolically,

$$t = \frac{\hat{\beta}_i - \beta_i}{\text{se}\,(\hat{\beta}_i)} \qquad (8.5.3)$$

with $N - k$ df, where $\hat{\beta}_i$ is any element of $\hat{\boldsymbol{\beta}}$.

The t distribution can therefore be used to test hypotheses about the true β_i as well as to establish confidence intervals about it. The actual mechanics have already been illustrated in Chaps. 5 and 7.

8.6 ANALYSIS OF VARIANCE IN MATRIX NOTATION

In Chap. 7 we developed the AOV technique (1) to test the overall significance of the estimated regression, that is, to test the null hypothesis that the true (partial) slope coefficients are simultaneously equal to zero, and (2) to assess the incremental contribution of an explanatory variable. The AOV technique can be easily extended to the k-variable case. Recall that the AOV technique consists in decomposing the TSS into two components: the ESS and the RSS. The matrix expressions for these three sums of squares are already given in (8.3.16), (8.3.17), and (8.3.18), respectively. The degrees of freedom associated with these sums of squares are $N - 1$, $k - 1$, and $N - k$, respectively. (Why?) Then, following Chap. 7, Table 7.2, we can set up Table 8.2.

Table 8.2 Matrix formulation of the AOV table for k-variable linear regression model

Source of variation	SS	df	MSS
Due to regression (that is, due to $X_2, X_3, \ldots, X_k$)	$\hat{\boldsymbol{\beta}}'\mathbf{X}'\mathbf{y} - N\bar{Y}^2$	$k - 1$	$\dfrac{\hat{\boldsymbol{\beta}}'\mathbf{X}'\mathbf{y} - N\bar{Y}^2}{k - 1}$
Due to residuals	$\mathbf{y}'\mathbf{y} - \hat{\boldsymbol{\beta}}'\mathbf{X}'\mathbf{y}$	$N - k$	$\dfrac{\mathbf{y}'\mathbf{y} - \hat{\boldsymbol{\beta}}'\mathbf{X}'\mathbf{y}}{N - k}$
Total	$\mathbf{y}'\mathbf{y} - N\bar{Y}^2$	$N - 1$	

Table 8.3 k-variable AOV table in matrix form in terms of R^2

Source of variation	SS	df	MSS
Due to regression (that is, due to $X_2, X_3, \ldots, X_k$)	$R^2(\mathbf{y'y} - N\bar{Y}^2)$	$k - 1$	$\dfrac{R^2(\mathbf{y'y} - N\bar{Y}^2)}{k - 1}$
Due to residuals	$(1 - R^2)(\mathbf{y'y} - N\bar{Y}^2)$	$N - k$	$\dfrac{(1 - R^2)(\mathbf{y'y} - N\bar{Y}^2)}{N - k}$
Total	$\mathbf{y'y} - N\bar{Y}^2$	$N - 1$	

Assuming that the disturbances u_i are normally distributed and the null hypothesis $\beta_2 = \beta_3 = \cdots = \beta_k = 0$, and following Chap. 7, it can be shown that

$$F = \frac{(\hat{\boldsymbol{\beta}}'\mathbf{X}'\mathbf{y} - N\bar{Y}^2)/(k - 1)}{(\mathbf{y'y} - \hat{\boldsymbol{\beta}}'\mathbf{X}'\mathbf{y})/(N - k)} \tag{8.6.1}$$

follows the F distribution with $k - 1$ and $N - k$ df.

In Chap. 7 we saw that under the assumptions stated previously, there is a close relationship between F and R^2, namely,

$$F = \frac{R^2/(k - 1)}{(1 - R^2)/(N - k)} \tag{7.6.4}$$

Therefore, the AOV Table 8.2 can be recast as Table 8.3. One advantage of Table 8.3 over Table 8.2 is that the entire analysis can be done in terms of R^2; one need not consider the term $(\mathbf{y'y} - N\bar{Y}^2)$ for it drops out in the F ratio.

8.7 MATRIX FORMULATION IN DEVIATION FORM

If the Y and X variables are measured in the deviation form, that is, as deviations from their sample means, there are a few changes in the formulas presented thus far. These changes are listed in Table 8.4.[9] As Table 8.4 shows, in the deviation form the correction for mean $N\bar{Y}^2$ drops out from the TSS and ESS. (Why?) This results in a change for the formula for R^2. Otherwise, most of the formulas developed in the original units of measurement hold true for the deviation form.

8.8 THE CORRELATION MATRIX

In the previous chapters we came across the zero-order, or simple, correlation coefficients r_{12}, r_{13}, r_{23} and the partial, or first-order, correlations $r_{12.3}, r_{13.2}$,

---

[9] In these days of high-speed computers there may not be need for the deviation form. But it simplifies formulas and therefore calculations if one is working with a desk calculator and dealing with large numbers.

Table 8.4 k-variable regression model in original units and in the deviation form†

Original units		Deviation form	
$y = X\hat{\beta} + e$	(8.3.2)	$y = X\hat{\beta} + e$	
		The column of 1s in the **X** matrix drops out. (Why?)	
$\hat{\beta} = (X'X)^{-1}X'y$	(8.3.11)	Same	
var-cov $(\hat{\beta}) = \sigma^2(X'X)^{-1}$	(8.3.13)	Same	
$e'e = y'y - \hat{\beta}'X'y$	(8.3.18)	Same	
$\sum y_i^2 = y'y - N\bar{Y}^2$	(8.3.16)	$\sum y_i^2 = y'y$	(8.7.1)
$ESS = \hat{\beta}'X'y - N\bar{Y}^2$	(8.3.17)	$ESS = \hat{\beta}'X'y$	(8.7.2)
$R^2 = \dfrac{\hat{\beta}'X'y - N\bar{Y}^2}{y'y - N\bar{Y}^2}$	(8.4.2)	$R^2 = \dfrac{\hat{\beta}'X'y}{y'y}$	(8.7.3)

† Note that although in both cases the symbols for the matrices and vectors are the same, in the deviation form the elements of the matrices and vectors are assumed to be deviations rather than the raw data. Note also that in the deviation form $\hat{\beta}$ is of order $k - 1$ and the var-cov $(\hat{\beta})$ is of order $(k - 1)(k - 1)$.

$r_{23.1}$ and their interrelationships. In the k-variable case, we shall have in all $k(k - 1)/2$ zero-order correlation coefficients (see Exercise 6.20). These $k(k - 1)/2$ correlations can be put into a matrix, called the *correlation matrix* **R**, as follows:

$$\mathbf{R} = \begin{bmatrix} r_{11} & r_{12} & r_{13} & \cdots & r_{1k} \\ r_{21} & r_{22} & r_{23} & \cdots & r_{2k} \\ \cdots\cdots\cdots\cdots\cdots\cdots\cdots \\ r_{k1} & r_{k2} & r_{k3} & \cdots & r_{kk} \end{bmatrix}$$

$$= \begin{bmatrix} 1 & r_{12} & r_{13} & \cdots & r_{1k} \\ r_{21} & 1 & r_{23} & \cdots & r_{2k} \\ \cdots\cdots\cdots\cdots\cdots\cdots\cdots \\ r_{k1} & r_{k2} & r_{k3} & \cdots & 1 \end{bmatrix} \qquad (8.8.1)$$

where the subscript 1, as before, denotes the dependent variable Y (r_{12} means correlation coefficient between Y and X_2, and so on) and where use is made of the fact the coefficient of correlation of a variable with respect to itself is always 1 ($r_{11} = r_{22} = \cdots = r_{kk} = 1$).

From the correlation matrix **R**, one can obtain correlation coefficients of first order (see Chap. 6) and of higher order such as $r_{12.34\ldots k}$. (See Exercise 8.4.) Many computer programs routinely compute the **R** matrix. We shall discuss the correlation matrix in our future work (see Chap. 9).

8.9 SUMMARY OF THE MATRIX APPROACH: AN ILLUSTRATIVE EXAMPLE

By way of summarizing the matrix approach to regression analysis, we shall present a numerical example involving three variables. Recall the illustrative example of Chap. 7, which involved the regression of aggregate personal consumption expenditure on aggregate personal disposable income and time for the period 1956–1970. It was stated there that the trend variable t may represent, among other things, aggregate or total population: Aggregate consumption expenditure is expected to increase as population increases. One way of isolating the influence of population is to convert the aggregate consumption expenditure and aggregate income figures to per capita or per head basis by dividing them by total population. A regression of per capita consumption expenditure on per capita income will then give the relationship between consumption expenditure and income net of population changes (or the scale effect). The trend variable may still be retained in the model as a "catch-all" for all other influences affecting consumption expenditure (e.g., technology). For empirical purposes, therefore, the regression model is

$$Y_i = \hat{\beta}_1 + \hat{\beta}_2 X_{2i} + \hat{\beta}_3 X_{3i} + e_i \tag{8.9.1}$$

where Y = per capita consumption expenditure, X_2 = per capita disposable income, and X_3 = time. The data required to run the regression (8.9.1) are given in Table 8.5.

Table 8.5 Per capita personal consumption expenditure (PPCE) and per capita personal disposable income (PPDI) in the U.S., 1956–1970, in 1958 dollars

PPCE, Y	PPDI, X_2	Time, X_3
1673	1839	1 (= 1956)
1688	1844	2
1666	1831	3
1735	1881	4
1749	1883	5
1756	1910	6
1815	1969	7
1867	2016	8
1948	2126	9
2048	2239	10
2128	2336	11
2165	2404	12
2257	2487	13
2316	2535	14
2324	2595	15 (= 1970)

Source: Economic Report of the President, January 1972, table B-16.

In matrix notation, our problem may be shown as follows:[10]

$$
\begin{bmatrix} 1673 \\ 1688 \\ 1666 \\ 1735 \\ 1749 \\ 1756 \\ 1815 \\ 1867 \\ 1948 \\ 2048 \\ 2128 \\ 2165 \\ 2257 \\ 2316 \\ 2324 \end{bmatrix}
=
\begin{bmatrix} 1 & 1839 & 1 \\ 1 & 1844 & 2 \\ 1 & 1831 & 3 \\ 1 & 1881 & 4 \\ 1 & 1883 & 5 \\ 1 & 1910 & 6 \\ 1 & 1969 & 7 \\ 1 & 2016 & 8 \\ 1 & 2126 & 9 \\ 1 & 2239 & 10 \\ 1 & 2336 & 11 \\ 1 & 2404 & 12 \\ 1 & 2487 & 13 \\ 1 & 2535 & 14 \\ 1 & 2595 & 15 \end{bmatrix}
\begin{bmatrix} \hat{\beta}_1 \\ \hat{\beta}_2 \\ \hat{\beta}_3 \end{bmatrix}
+
\begin{bmatrix} e_1 \\ e_2 \\ e_3 \\ e_4 \\ e_5 \\ e_6 \\ e_7 \\ e_8 \\ e_9 \\ e_{10} \\ e_{11} \\ e_{12} \\ e_{13} \\ e_{14} \\ e_{15} \end{bmatrix}
\qquad (8.9.2)
$$

$$
\begin{array}{cccc}
\mathbf{y} & = & \mathbf{X} & \hat{\boldsymbol{\beta}} + \mathbf{e} \\
15 \times 1 & & 15 \times 3 & 3 \times 1 \quad 15 \times 1
\end{array}
$$

From the preceding data we obtain the following quantities:

$$\bar{Y} = 1942.333 \qquad \bar{X}_2 = 2126.333 \qquad \bar{X}_3 = 8.0$$

$$\sum (Y_i - \bar{Y})^2 = 830121.333 \qquad \sum (X_{2i} - \bar{X}_2)^2 = 1103111.333$$

$$\sum (X_{3i} - \bar{X}_3)^2 = 280.0$$

$$
\mathbf{X'X} =
\begin{bmatrix} 1 & 1 & 1 & \cdots & 1 \\ X_{21} & X_{22} & X_{23} & \cdots & X_{2N} \\ X_{31} & X_{32} & X_{33} & \cdots & X_{3N} \end{bmatrix}
\begin{bmatrix} 1 & X_{21} & X_{31} \\ 1 & X_{22} & X_{32} \\ 1 & X_{23} & X_{33} \\ \vdots & \vdots & \vdots \\ 1 & X_{2N} & X_{3N} \end{bmatrix}
$$

$$
=
\begin{bmatrix} N & \sum X_{2i} & \sum X_{3i} \\ \sum X_{2i} & \sum X_{2i}^2 & \sum X_{2i} X_{3i} \\ \sum X_{3i} & \sum X_{2i} X_{3i} & \sum X_{3i}^2 \end{bmatrix}
$$

$$
=
\begin{bmatrix} 15 & 31895 & 120 \\ 31895 & 68922513 & 272144 \\ 120 & 272144 & 1240 \end{bmatrix}
\qquad (8.9.3)
$$

and

$$
\mathbf{X'y} =
\begin{bmatrix} 29135 \\ 62905821 \\ 247934 \end{bmatrix}
\qquad (8.9.4)
$$

---

[10] The calculations presented can be simplified considerably if we use the deviation form. (See Exercise 8.1.)

Using the rules of matrix inversion given in App. A, it can be seen that

$$(\mathbf{X'X})^{-1} = \begin{bmatrix} 37.232491 & -0.0225079 & 1.3366965 \\ -0.0225079 & 0.0000137 & -0.0008319 \\ 1.3366965 & -0.0008319 & 0.054034 \end{bmatrix} \tag{8.9.5}$$

Therefore

$$\hat{\boldsymbol{\beta}} = (\mathbf{X'X})^{-1}\mathbf{X'y} = \begin{bmatrix} 300.28625 \\ 0.74198 \\ 8.04356 \end{bmatrix} \tag{8.9.6}$$

The residual sum of squares can now be computed as

$$\sum e_i^2 = \mathbf{e'e}$$

$$= \mathbf{y'y} - \hat{\boldsymbol{\beta}}'\mathbf{X'y}$$

$$= 57420003 - [300.28625 \quad 0.74198 \quad 8.04356] \begin{bmatrix} 29135 \\ 62905821 \\ 247934 \end{bmatrix}$$

$$= 1976.85574 \tag{8.9.7}$$

whence we obtain

$$\hat{\sigma}^2 = \frac{\mathbf{e'e}}{12} = 164.73797 \tag{8.9.6}$$

The variance-covariance matrix for $\hat{\boldsymbol{\beta}}$ can therefore be shown as

$$\text{var-cov } (\hat{\boldsymbol{\beta}}) = \hat{\sigma}^2(\mathbf{X'X})^{-1} = \begin{bmatrix} 6133.65151 & -3.70794 & 220.20634 \\ -3.70794 & 0.00225 & -0.13705 \\ 220.20634 & -0.13705 & 8.90155 \end{bmatrix} \tag{8.9.9}$$

The diagonal elements of this matrix give the variances of $\hat{\beta}_1$, $\hat{\beta}_2$, and $\hat{\beta}_3$, respectively, and their positive square roots give the corresponding standard errors.

From the previous data, it can be readily verified that

$$\text{ESS: } \hat{\boldsymbol{\beta}}'\mathbf{X'y} - N\bar{Y}^2 = 828144.47786 \tag{8.9.10}$$

and

$$\text{TSS: } \mathbf{y'y} - N\bar{Y}^2 = 830121.333 \tag{8.9.11}$$

Therefore,

$$R^2 = \frac{\hat{\boldsymbol{\beta}}'\mathbf{X'y} - N\bar{Y}^2}{\mathbf{y'y} - N\bar{Y}^2}$$

$$= \frac{828144.47786}{830121.333}$$

$$= 0.99761 \tag{8.9.12}$$

Applying (6.7.3), the adjusted coefficient of determination can be seen to be

$$\bar{R}^2 = 0.99722 \tag{8.9.13}$$

Collecting our results thus far, we have

$$\hat{Y}_i = 300.28625 \; + 0.74198X_{2i} + 8.04356X_{3i}$$

$$(78.31763) \quad (0.04753) \quad \quad (2.98354) \quad \quad \quad (8.9.14)$$

$$t = \quad (3.83421) \; (15.61077) \quad \quad (2.69598)$$

$$R^2 = 0.99761 \quad \quad \bar{R}^2 = 0.99722 \quad \quad df = 12$$

The interpretation of (8.9.14) is this: If both X_2 and X_3 are fixed at zero value, the average value of per capita personal consumption expenditure is estimated at about \$300. As usual, this mechanical interpretation of the intercept should be taken with a grain of salt. The partial regression coefficient of 0.74198 means that, holding all other variables constant, an increase in income of, say, a dollar is accompanied by an increase in the mean per capita personal consumption expenditure of about 74 cents. In short, the marginal propensity to consume is estimated to be about 0.74 or 74 percent. Similarly, holding all other variables constant, the mean per capita personal consumption expenditure increased at the rate of about \$8 per year during the period of the study, 1956–1970. The R^2 value of 0.9976 shows that the two explanatory variables accounted for over 99 percent of the variation in per capita consumption expenditure in the United States over the period 1956–1970. Although $\bar{R}^2$ dips slightly, it is still very high.

Turning to the statistical significance of the estimated coefficients, we see from (8.9.14) that each of the estimated coefficients is *individually* statistically significant at, say, the 5 percent level of significance: The ratios of the estimated coefficients to their standard errors (that is, t ratios) are 3.83421, 15.61077, and 2.69598, respectively. Using a two-tail t test at the 5 percent level of significance, we see that the critical t value for 12 df is 2.179. Each of the computed t value exceeds this critical value. Hence, individually we may reject the null hypothesis that the true population value of the relevant coefficient is zero.

As noted previously, we cannot apply the usual t test to test the hypothesis that $\beta_2 = \beta_3 = 0$ simultaneously because the t-test procedure assumes that an independent sample is drawn every time the t test is applied. If the same sample is used to test hypothesis about β_2 and β_3 simultaneously, it is likely that the estimators $\hat{\beta}_2$ and $\hat{\beta}_3$ are correlated, thus violating the assumption underlying the t-test procedure.[11] As a matter of fact, a look at the variance-covariance matrix of $\hat{\beta}$ given in (8.9.9) shows that the estimators $\hat{\beta}_2$ and $\hat{\beta}_3$ are negatively correlated (the covariance between the two is -0.13705). Hence we cannot use the t test to test the null hypothesis that $\beta_2 = \beta_3 = 0$.

But recall that a null hypothesis like $\beta_2 = \beta_3 = 0$, simultaneously, can be tested by the analysis-of-variance technique and the attendant F test, which were

---

[11] See Sec. 7.4 for details.

Table 8.6 The AOV table for the data of Table 8.5

Source of variation	SS	df	MSS
Due to X_2, X_3	828144.47786	2	41407.23893
Due to residuals	1976.85574	12	164.73797
Total	830121.33360	14	

introduced in Chap. 7. For our problem, the analysis-of-variance table is Table 8.6. Under the usual assumptions, we obtain

$$F = \frac{41407.23893}{164.73797} = 251.352 \tag{8.9.15}$$

which is distributed as the F distribution with 2 and 12 df. The computed F value is obviously highly significant; we can reject the null hypothesis that $\beta_2 = \beta_3 = 0$, that is, that per capita personal consumption expenditure is not linearly related to per capita disposable income and trend.

In Sec. 8.8 we introduced the correlation matrix **R**. For our data, the correlation matrix is as follows:

$$\mathbf{R} = \begin{array}{c} Y \\ X_2 \\ X_3 \end{array} \begin{array}{ccc} Y & X_2 & X_3 \\ \begin{bmatrix} 1 & 0.9980 & 0.9743 \\ 0.9980 & 1 & 0.9664 \\ 0.9743 & 0.9664 & 1 \end{bmatrix} \end{array} \tag{8.9.16}$$

Note that in (8.9.16) we have bordered the correlation matrix by the variables of the model so that we can readily identify which variables are involved in the computation of the correlation coefficient. Thus the coefficient 0.9980 in the first row of matrix (8.9.16) tells us that it is the correlation coefficient between Y and X_2 (that is, r_{12}). From the zero-order correlations given in the correlation matrix (8.9.16) one can easily derive the first-order correlation coefficients. (See Exercise 8.7.)

8.10 SUMMARY AND CONCLUSIONS

The primary purpose of this chapter was to introduce the matrix approach to classical linear regression model. Although very few new concepts of regression analysis were introduced, the matrix notation provides a compact method of dealing with linear regression models involving any number of variables.

EXERCISES

8.1 For the illustrative example discussed in Sec. 8.9 the $X'X$ and $X'y$ using the data in the deviation form are as follows:

$$X'X = \begin{bmatrix} 1103111.333 & 16984 \\ 16984 & 280 \end{bmatrix}$$

and

$$X'y = \begin{bmatrix} 955099.333 \\ 14854.000 \end{bmatrix}$$

(a) Estimate β_2 and β_3.
(b) How would you estimate β_1?
(c) Estimate the variance of $\hat{\beta}_2$ and $\hat{\beta}_3$ and their covariances.
(d) Obtain R^2 and $\bar{R}^2$.
(e) Comparing your results with those given in Sec. 8.9, what are the advantages of the deviation form?

8.2 For the illustrative example of Chap. 7, you have been given the following data, where all the variables are measured in the deviation form, that is, as deviations from their sample means:

$$X'X = \begin{bmatrix} 84855.096 & 4250.900 \\ 4250.900 & 280.000 \end{bmatrix}$$

and

$$X'y = \begin{bmatrix} 74778.346 \\ 4250.900 \end{bmatrix}$$

Furthermore, $\bar{Y} = 367.693$, $\bar{X}_2 = 402.760$, and $\bar{X}_3 = 9.0$.
(a) Obtain $\hat{\beta}_2$ and $\hat{\beta}_3$ and their variances and covariances.
(b) Estimate the intercept term β_1.
(c) Calculate R^2.
(d) Using the calculated R^2, test the hypothesis that $\beta_2 = \beta_3 = 0$.

8.3 *Testing the equality of two regression coefficients.* Suppose that you are given the following regression model:

$$Y_i = \beta_1 + \beta_2 X_{2i} + \beta_3 X_{3i} + u_i$$

and you want to test the hypothesis that $\beta_2 = \beta_3$. Assuming that the u_i are normally distributed, it can be shown that

$$t = \frac{\hat{\beta}_2 - \hat{\beta}_3}{\sqrt{\text{var}(\hat{\beta}_2) + \text{var}(\hat{\beta}_3) - 2\,\text{cov}(\hat{\beta}_2, \hat{\beta}_3)}}$$

follows the t distribution with $N - 3$ df. (In general, for the k-variable case the df are $N - k$.) Therefore, the preceding t test can be used to test the null hypothesis $\beta_2 = \beta_3$.

Apply the preceding t test to test the hypothesis that the true values of β_2 and β_3 in the regression (8.9.14) are identical.

Hint: Use the var-cov matrix of β given in (8.9.9).

8.4 *Expressing higher-order correlations in terms of lower-order correlations.* Correlation coefficients of order p can be expressed in terms of correlation coefficients of order $p - 1$ by the following reduction formula:

$$r_{12.345\ldots(p-1)} = \frac{r_{12.345\ldots(p-1)} - \left[r_{1p.345\ldots(p-1)}\, r_{2p.345\ldots(p-1)}\right]}{\sqrt{\left[1 - r_{1p.345\ldots(p-1)}^2\right]}\sqrt{\left[1 - r_{2p.345\ldots(p-1)}^2\right]}}$$

Thus,

$$r_{12.3} = \frac{r_{12} - r_{13}r_{23}}{\sqrt{1 - r_{13}^2}\sqrt{1 - r_{23}^2}}$$

as found in Chap. 6.

You are given the following correlation matrix:

$$\mathbf{R} = \begin{array}{c} \\ Y \\ X_2 \\ X_3 \\ X_4 \\ X_5 \end{array} \begin{array}{c} \begin{array}{ccccc} Y & X_2 & X_3 & X_4 & X_5 \end{array} \\ \begin{bmatrix} 1 & 0.44 & -0.34 & -0.31 & -0.14 \\ & 1 & 0.25 & -0.19 & -0.35 \\ & & 1 & 0.44 & 0.33 \\ & & & 1 & 0.85 \\ & & & & 1 \end{bmatrix} \end{array}$$

Find

(a) $r_{12.345}$ (b) $r_{12.34}$ (c) $r_{12.3}$
(d) $r_{13.245}$ (e) $r_{13.24}$ (f) $r_{13.2}$

8.5 *Expressing higher-order regression coefficients in terms of lower-order regression coefficients.* A regression coefficient of order p can be expressed in terms of a regression coefficient of order $p-1$ by the following reduction formula:

$$\hat{\beta}_{12.345\ldots p} = \frac{\hat{\beta}_{12.345\ldots(p-1)} - [\hat{\beta}_{1p.345\ldots(p-1)}\hat{\beta}_{p2.345\ldots(p-1)}]}{1 - \hat{\beta}_{2p.345\ldots(p-1)}\hat{\beta}_{p2.345\ldots(p-1)}}$$

Thus,

$$\hat{\beta}_{12.3} = \frac{\hat{\beta}_{12} - \hat{\beta}_{13}\hat{\beta}_{32}}{1 - \hat{\beta}_{23}\hat{\beta}_{32}}$$

as shown in (6.9.1).

Using the preceding formula, find expressions for the following regression coefficients in terms of lower-order regression coefficients: $\hat{\beta}_{12.3456}$, $\hat{\beta}_{12.345}$, and $\hat{\beta}_{12.34}$.

8.6 Establish the following identity:

$$\hat{\beta}_{12.3}\hat{\beta}_{23.1}\hat{\beta}_{31.2} = r_{12.3}r_{23.1}r_{31.2}$$

8.7 For the correlation matrix $\mathbf{R}$ given in (8.9.16) find all the first-order partial correlation coefficients.

8.8 In studying the variation in crime rates in certain large cities in the United States, Ogburn obtained the following data:[12]

			Y	X_2	X_3	X_4	X_5
$\bar{Y} = 19.9$	$S_1 = 7.9$	Y	1	0.44	−0.34	−0.31	−0.14
$\bar{X}_2 = 49.2$	$S_2 = 1.3$	X_2		1	0.25	−0.19	−0.35
$\bar{X}_3 = 10.2$	$S_3 = 4.6$	$\mathbf{R} = X_3$			1	0.44	0.33
$\bar{X}_4 = 481.4$	$S_4 = 74.4$	X_4				1	0.85
$\bar{X}_5 = 41.6$	$S_5 = 10.8$	X_5					1

where Y = crime rate, number of known offences per thousand of population
  X_2 = percentage of male inhabitants
  X_3 = percentage of total inhabitants who are foreign-born males
  X_4 = number of children under 5 years of age per thousand married women between ages 15 and 44 years
  X_5 = church membership, number of church members 13 years of age and over per 100 of total population 13 years of age and over; S_1 to S_5 are the sample standard deviations of variables Y through X_5 and $\mathbf{R}$ is the correlation matrix

[12] W. F. Ogburn, "Factors in the Variation of Crime among Cities," *Journal of American Statistical Association*, vol. 30, 1935.

(a) Treating Y as the dependent variable, obtain the regression of Y on the four X variables and interpret the estimated regression.

(b) Obtain $r_{12.3}$, $r_{14.35}$ and $r_{15.34}$.

(e) Obtain R^2 and test the hypothesis that all partial slope coefficients are simultaneously equal to zero.

8.9 The following table gives data on output and total cost of production of a commodity in the short run.

Output	Total cost, $
1	193
2	226
3	240
4	244
5	257
6	260
7	274
8	297
9	350
10	420

To test whether the preceding data suggest the U-shaped average and marginal cost curves typically encountered in the short run, one can use the following model:

$$Y_i = \beta_1 + \beta_2 X_i + \beta_3 X_i^2 + \beta_4 X_i^3 + u_i$$

where Y = total cost and X = output. The additional explanatory variables X_i^2 and X_i^3 are derived from X.

(a) Express the data in the deviation form and obtain $(X'X)$, $(X'y)$, and $(X'X)^{-1}$.

(b) Estimate β_2, β_3, and β_4.

(c) Estimate the var-cov matrix of $\hat{\beta}$.

(d) Estimate β_1. Interpret $\hat{\beta}_1$ in the context of the problem.

(e) Obtain R^2 and $\bar{R}^2$.

(f) A priori, what are the signs of β_2, β_3, and β_4? Why?

(g) From the total cost function given previously obtain expressions for the marginal and average cost functions.

(h) Fit the average and marginal cost functions to the data and comment on the fit.

(i) If $\beta_3 = \beta_4 = 0$, what is the nature of the marginal cost function? How would you test the hypothesis that $\beta_3 = \beta_4 = 0$?

(j) How would you derive the total variable cost and average variable cost functions from the given data?

8.10 To study the labor force participation of urban poor families (families earning less than \$3943 in 1969), the data on page 164 were obtained from the 1970 Census of Population.

(a) Using the regression model $Y_i = \beta_1 + \beta_2 X_{2i} + \beta_3 X_{3i} + \beta_4 X_{4i} + u_i$, obtain the estimates of the regression coefficients and interpret your results.

(b) A priori what are the expected signs of the regression coefficients in the preceding model and why?

(c) How would you test the hypothesis that the overall unemployment rate has no effect on the labor force participation of the urban poor in the census tracts given in the preceding table?

(d) Should any variables be dropped from the preceding model? Why? *Unemployment-t*

(e) What other variables would you consider for inclusion in the model?

Labor force participation experience of the urban poor: census tracts, New York City, 1970

Tract no.	% in labor force, Y†	Mean family income, X_2	Mean family size, X_3	Unemployment rate, X_4‡
137	64.3	1998	2.95	4.4
139	45.4	1114	3.40	3.4
141	26.6	1942	3.72	1.1
142	87.5	1998	4.43	3.1
143	71.3	2026	3.82	7.7
145	82.4	1853	3.90	5.0
147	26.3	1666	3.32	6.2
149	61.6	1434	3.80	5.4
151	52.9	1513	3.49	12.2
153	64.7	2008	3.85	4.8
155	64.9	1704	4.69	2.9
157	70.5	1525	3.89	4.8
159	87.2	1842	3.53	3.9
161	81.2	1735	4.96	7.2
163	67.9	1639	3.68	3.6

† Y = family heads under 65 years old
‡ X_4 = percent of civilian labor force unemployed
   Source: Census Tracts: New York, Bureau of the Census, U.S. Department of Commerce, 1970.

8.11 In an application of the Cobb-Douglas production function the following results were obtained:

$$\ln Y_i = 2.3542 + 0.9576 \ln X_{2i} + 0.8242 \ln X_{3i}$$
$$(0.3022) \qquad (0.3571)$$

$$R^2 = 0.8432 \qquad df = 12$$

where Y = output, X_2 = labor input, and X_3 = capital input, and where the figures in parentheses are the estimated standard errors.

(a) As noted in Chap. 6, the coefficients of the labor and capital inputs in the preceding equation give the elasticities of output with respect to labor and capital. Test the hypothesis that these elasticities are *individually* equal to unity.

(b) Test the hypothesis that the labor and capital elasticities are equal, assuming (i) the covariance between the estimated labor and capital coefficient is zero, and (ii) it is -0.0972.

(c) How would you test the overall significance of the estimated regression equation given previously?

*8.12 Express the likelihood function for the k-variable regression model in matrix notation and show that $\tilde{\beta}$, the vector of maximum-likelihood estimators, is identical to $\hat{\beta}$, the vector of OLS estimators of the k-variable regression model.

8.13 *Regression using standardized variables.* Consider the following sample regression functions (SRFs):

$$Y_i = \hat{\beta}_1 + \hat{\beta}_2 X_{2i} + \hat{\beta}_3 X_{3i} + e_i \tag{1}$$

$$Y_i^* = b_1 + b_2 X_{2i}^* + b_3 X_{3i}^* + e_i^* \tag{2}$$

* Optional.

where $Y_i^* = \dfrac{Y_i - \bar{Y}}{s_y}$

$X_{2i}^* = \dfrac{X_{2i} - \bar{X}_2}{s_2}$

$X_{3i}^* = \dfrac{X_{3i} - \bar{X}_3}{s_3}$

where the s's denote the sample standard deviations. As noted in Chap. 3, Exercise 3.10, the starred variables above are known as the *standardized variables*. These variables have zero means and unit ($= 1$) standard deviations. Expressing all the variables in the deviation form, show that for model (2):

(a) $\mathbf{X'X} = \begin{bmatrix} 1 & r_{23} \\ r_{23} & 1 \end{bmatrix} N$

(b) $\mathbf{X'y} = \begin{bmatrix} r_{12} \\ r_{13} \end{bmatrix} N$

(c) $(\mathbf{X'X})^{-1} = \dfrac{1}{N(1 - r_{23}^2)} \begin{bmatrix} 1 & -r_{23} \\ -r_{23} & 1 \end{bmatrix}$

(d) $\hat{\boldsymbol{\beta}} = \begin{bmatrix} b_2 \\ b_3 \end{bmatrix} = \dfrac{1}{1 - r_{23}^2} \begin{bmatrix} r_{12} - r_{23} r_{13} \\ r_{13} - r_{23} r_{12} \end{bmatrix}$

(e) $b_1 = 0$

and establish the relationships between the b's and the $\hat{\beta}$'s.

(Note that in the preceding relations N denotes the sample size. r_{12}, r_{13}, and r_{23} denote the correlations between Y and X_2, between Y and X_3, and between X_2 and X_3, respectively.)

APPENDIX 8

8A.1 DERIVATIONS OF k NORMAL OR SIMULTANEOUS EQUATIONS

Differentiating

$$\sum e_i^2 = \sum (Y_i - \hat{\beta}_1 - \hat{\beta}_2 X_{2i} - \cdots - \hat{\beta}_k X_{ki})^2$$

partially with respect to $\hat{\beta}_1, \hat{\beta}_2, \ldots, \hat{\beta}_k$ we obtain

$$\frac{\partial \sum e_i^2}{\partial \hat{\beta}_1} = 2 \sum (Y_i - \hat{\beta}_1 - \hat{\beta}_2 X_{2i} - \cdots - \hat{\beta}_k X_{ki})(-1)$$

$$\frac{\partial \sum e_i^2}{\partial \hat{\beta}_2} = 2 \sum (Y_i - \hat{\beta}_1 - \hat{\beta}_2 X_{2i} - \cdots - \hat{\beta}_k X_{ki})(-X_{2i})$$

$$\cdots\cdots\cdots\cdots\cdots\cdots\cdots\cdots\cdots\cdots\cdots\cdots\cdots\cdots$$

$$\frac{\partial \sum e_i^2}{\partial \hat{\beta}_k} = 2 \sum (Y_i - \hat{\beta}_1 - \hat{\beta}_2 X_{ki} - \cdots - \hat{\beta}_k X_{ki})(-X_{ki})$$

Setting the preceding partial derivatives equal to zero and rearranging the terms, we obtain the k normal equations given in (8.3.8).

8A.2 MATRIX DERIVATION OF NORMAL EQUATIONS

From (8.3.7) we obtain

$$e'e = y'y - 2\hat{\beta}'X'y + \hat{\beta}'X'X\hat{\beta}$$

Using rules of matrix differentiation given in App. B, we obtain

$$\frac{\partial(e'e)}{\partial\hat{\beta}} = -2X'y + 2X'X\hat{\beta}$$

Setting the preceding equation to zero gives

$$(X'X)\hat{\beta} = X'y$$

whence $\hat{\beta} = (X'X)^{-1}X'y$, provided the inverse exists.

8A.3 VARIANCE-COVARIANCE MATRIX of $\hat{\beta}$

From (8.3.11) we obtain

$$\hat{\beta} = (X'X)^{-1}X'y$$

Substituting $y = X\beta + u$ into the preceding expression gives

$$\hat{\beta} = (X'X)^{-1}X'(X\beta + u)$$

$$= (X'X)^{-1}X'X\beta + (X'X)^{-1}X'u$$

$$= \beta + (X'X)^{-1}X'u \tag{1}$$

Therefore,
$$\hat{\beta} - \beta = (X'X)^{-1}X'u \tag{2}$$

By definition,
$$\text{var-cov}(\hat{\beta}) = E[(\hat{\beta} - \beta)(\hat{\beta} - \beta)']$$

$$= E\{[(X'X)^{-1}X'u][(X'X)^{-1}X'u]'\}$$

$$= E[(X'X)^{-1}X'uu'X(X'X)^{-1}] \tag{3}$$

where in the last step use is made of the fact that $(AB)' = B'A'$.

Noting that the X's are nonstochastic, on taking expectation of (3), we obtain

$$\text{var-cov}(\hat{\beta}) = (X'X)^{-1}X'E(uu')X(X'X)^{-1}$$

$$= (X'X)^{-1}X'\sigma^2 IX(X'X)^{-1}$$

$$= \sigma^2(X'X)^{-1}$$

which is the result given in (8.3.13). Note that in deriving the preceding result use is made of the assumption that $E(uu') = \sigma^2 I$.

TWO

VIOLATIONS OF
THE ASSUMPTIONS
OF THE CLASSICAL MODEL

In Part I we considered at length the classical normal linear regression model and showed how it can be used to handle the twin problems of statistical inference, namely, estimation and hypothesis testing, as well as the problem of prediction. But recall that this model is based on several simplifying assumptions, which are as follows.

Assumption 1 The conditional mean value of the population disturbance term u_i, conditional upon the given values of the explanatory variables (the X's), is zero.

Assumption 2 The conditional variance of u_i is constant or homoscedastic.

Assumption 3 There is no autocorrelation in the disturbances.

Assumption 4 The explanatory variables are either nonstochastic (i.e., fixed in repeated sampling) or, if stochastic, distributed independently of the disturbances u_i.

Assumption 5 There is no multicollinearity among the explanatory variables, the X's.

Assumption 6 The u's are normally distributed with mean and variance given by Assumptions 1 and 2.

With the preceding assumptions, we saw that the ordinary-least-squares (OLS) estimators of the regression coefficients are best linear unbiased estimators (BLUE) and, with the normality assumption, are distributed normally. As a result, it was possible to obtain interval estimators as well as to test hypotheses about true population regression coefficients.

In Part II, we take a closer look at the preceding assumptions and find out what happens to the properties of the OLS estimators if one or more of the assumptions are not fulfilled and what can be done in those cases.

We shall not discuss Assumptions 1, 4, and 6 at great length. The violation of Assumption 1 may not be very critical from a practical viewpoint because it may affect only the intercept of the regression. This can be seen as follows: Suppose we have the two-variable model

$$Y_i = \beta_0 + \beta_1 X_i + u_i$$

and suppose that $E(u_i)$, conditional upon X_i, is not zero but is equal to some constant k. Therefore, taking the conditional expectation of the preceding model, we obtain

$$E(Y_i \mid X_i) = \beta_0 + \beta_1 X_i + E(u_i \mid X_i)$$
$$= \beta_0 + \beta_1 X_i + k$$
$$= \alpha + \beta_1 X_i$$

where $\alpha = \beta_0 + k$. Therefore, if Assumption 1 is not fulfilled, we see that we cannot estimate the original β_0. But since in practice the intercept term is generally of little importance, we may not pay much attention to it; for most purposes the meaningful quantity is the slope coefficient β_1, which remains unaffected even if Assumption 1 is not satisfied.[1]

In Chap. 3 we discussed the rationale behind Assumption 4. We also stated there that our approach to (single-equation) regression models is conditional, conditional on the given values of the X variables. There is a good reason for this approach. Unlike scientists in other fields of knowledge, economists generally have no control over their data. More often than not, economists depend on secondary data, that is, data collected by someone else, such as the government and other organizations. Therefore, the practical strategy to follow is to assume that for the problem at hand the values of the explanatory variables are given even though the variables themselves may be intrinsically stochastic. Hence, the results of the regression analysis are conditional upon these given values. As long as this is understood, the theory developed in Part I can be legitimately applied in practice.

---

[1] It is very important to note that this statement is true only if $E(u_i) = k$ for each i. However, if $E(u_i) = k_i$, that is, a different constant for each i, $\hat{\beta}_1$ may be biased as well as inconsistent. In this case violation of Assumption 1 will be critical. For proofs and further details, see Peter Schmidt, *Econometrics*, Marcel Dekker, Inc., New York, 1976, pp. 36–39.

But as we shall see in Part IV, Assumption 4 is likely to be violated in the simultaneous-equation models, models involving more than one regression equation. In such models, the disturbance term in an equation is very likely to be correlated with one or more explanatory variables in that equation. In this circumstance, it can be proved (see Chap. 16) that the OLS estimators are not only biased but also inconsistent; that is, they remain biased even if the sample size increases indefinitely. But one can obtain a glimpse of the nature of the problem from the simple two-variable model of Chap. 3. In App. 3A, Sec. 3A.2, we showed that for the model $Y_i = \beta_0 + \beta_1 X_i + u_i$,

$$\hat{\beta}_1 = \beta_1 + \frac{\sum x_i u_i}{\sum x_i^2}$$

Now if u and x are correlated, the last term in the preceding equation will be nonzero. Therefore, $E(\hat{\beta}_1)$ will not be equal to β_1; that is, $\hat{\beta}_1$ will be biased. It is shown in Chap. 16 that this bias may not disappear even if the size of the sample increases indefinitely.

If the explanatory variable(s) and the disturbance term u_i are correlated or there is reason to believe them to be correlated, then, the method of ordinary least squares may not be applied. In Chap. 18 we shall discuss some alternative estimating techniques.

Assumption 6, the normality assumption, is not absolutely essential if our objective is estimation only. As noted in Chap. 3, the OLS estimators are BLUE regardless of whether the u_i are normally distributed or not. Moreover, if u_i are not normally distributed, it can be shown that the OLS estimators tend to be normally distributed as the sample size increases indefinitely. In short, the OLS estimators of the regression coefficients tend to be asymptotically normally distributed. But this is not true in small samples; without the normality assumption, the OLS estimators are not normally distributed in such samples. And since economists often do not have the luxury of large sample data, the normality assumption becomes extremely important for the purposes of hypothesis testing and prediction. Thus, with the twin problem of estimation and hypothesis testing in mind, and given the fact that small samples are the rule rather than the exception in most economic analyses, we shall continue to use the normality assumption.

This leaves us with Assumptions 2, 3, and 5, which we discuss in the following three chapters. Chapter 9 discusses the topic of multicollinearity, Chap. 10 considers the topic of heteroscedasticity, and Chap. 11 is devoted to the discussion of autocorrelation. In each of these three chapters we follow a common format, namely, we find out the nature of the problem, examine its consequences, suggest methods of detecting it, and offer remedial measures so that they may lead to estimators which possess the desirable statistical properties discussed in Part I.

NINE

MULTICOLLINEARITY

One of the assumptions of the classical linear regression model is that there is no multicollinearity among the explanatory variables included in the model. In this chapter we take a closer look at this assumption. Specifically, we seek answers to the following questions:

1. What is the nature of multicollinearity?
2. What are its consequences?
3. How does one detect it?
4. What remedial measures can be taken to alleviate the problem of multicollinearity?

9.1 THE NATURE OF MULTICOLLINEARITY

The term *multicollinearity* is due to Ragnar Frisch.[1] Originally it meant the existence of a "perfect," or exact, linear relationship among some or all explanatory variables of a regression model.[2] For the k-variable regression involving explanatory variable $X_1, X_2, \ldots, X_k$ (where $X_1 = 1$ for all observations to allow

---

[1] Ragnar Frisch, *Statistical Confluence Analysis by Means of Complete Regression Systems*, Institute of Economics, Oslo University, publ. no. 5, 1934.

[2] Strictly speaking, the term *multicollinearity* refers to the existence of more than one exact linear relationship, and the term *collinearity* refers to the existence of a single linear relationship. But this distinction is rarely maintained in practice, and multicollinearity refers to both the cases.

for the intercept term), an exact linear relationship is said to exist if the following condition is satisfied:

$$\lambda_1 X_1 + \lambda_2 X_2 + \cdots + \lambda_k X_k = 0 \tag{9.1.1}$$

where λ_1, λ_2, ..., λ_k are constants such that not all of them are zero simultaneously.

Today, however, the term multicollinearity is used in a broader sense to include the case of perfect multicollinearity, as shown by (9.1.1) as well as the case where the X variables are intercorrelated but not perfectly so as follows:[3]

$$\lambda_1 X_1 + \lambda_2 X_2 + \cdots + \lambda_2 X_k + v_i = 0 \tag{9.1.2}$$

where v_i is a stochastic error term.

To see the difference between *perfect* and *less than perfect* multicollinearity, assume, for example, that $\lambda_2 \neq 0$. Then, (9.1.1) can be written as

$$X_{2i} = -\frac{\lambda_1}{\lambda_2} X_{1i} - \frac{\lambda_3}{\lambda_2} X_{3i} - \cdots - \frac{\lambda_k}{\lambda_2} X_{ki} \tag{9.1.3}$$

which shows how X_2 is exactly linearly related to other variables or how it can be derived from a linear combination of other X variables. In this situation, the coefficient of correlation between the variable X_2 and the linear combination on the right-hand side of (9.1.3) is bound to be unity.

Similarly, if $\lambda_2 \neq 0$, equation (9.1.2) can be written as

$$X_{2i} = -\frac{\lambda_1}{\lambda_2} X_{1i} - \frac{\lambda_3}{\lambda_2} X_{3i} - \cdots - \frac{\lambda_k}{\lambda_2} X_{ki} - \frac{1}{\lambda_2} v_i \tag{9.1.4}$$

which shows that X_2 is not an exact linear combination of other X's because it is also determined by the stochastic error term v_i.

As a numerical example, consider the following hypothetical data:

X_2	X_3	X_3^*
10	50	52
15	75	75
18	90	97
24	120	129
30	150	152

It is apparent that $X_{3i} = 5X_{2i}$. Therefore, there is perfect collinearity between X_2 and X_3 since the coefficient of correlation r_{23} is unity. The variable X_3^* was

---

[3] If there are only two explanatory variables, *intercorrelation* can be measured by the zero-order or simple correlation coefficient. But if there are more than two X variables, intercorrelation can be measured by the partial correlation coefficients or by the multiple correlation coefficient R of one X variable with all other X variables taken together.

created from X_3 by simply adding to it the following numbers, which were taken from a table of random numbers: 2, 0, 7, 9, 2. Now there is no longer perfect collinearity between X_2 and X_3^*. However, the two variables are highly correlated because calculations will show that the coefficient of correlation between them is 0.9959.

In passing, note that multicollinearity, as we have just defined it, excludes only linear relationships among the X variables. It does not rule out nonlinear relationships among them. For example, consider the following regression model:

$$Y_i = \beta_0 + \beta_1 X_i + \beta_2 X_i^2 + \beta_3 X_i^3 + u_i \qquad (9.1.5)$$

where, say, Y = total cost of production and X = output. The variables X_i^2 (output squared) and X_i^3 (output cubed) are obviously functionally related to X_i, but the relationship is nonlinear. Therefore, models such as (9.1.5) do not violate the assumption of no multicollinearity. As a matter of fact, to depict the U-shaped average and marginal cost curves of economic theory, model (9.1.5) is very appropriate.

Why does the classical linear regression model assume that there is no multicollinearity among the X's? The reasoning is: If multicollinearity is perfect in the sense of (9.1.1), the regression coefficients of the X variables are indeterminate and their standard errors are infinite. If multicollinearity is less than perfect, as in (9.1.2), the regression coefficients, although determinate, possess large standard errors (in relation to the coefficients themselves), which means the coefficients cannot be estimated with great precision or accuracy. The proofs of these statements will be given in Secs. 9.2 and 9.3.

But before we turn to the proofs, it should be emphasized strongly that since the X's are assumed to be fixed or nonstochastic, *multicollinearity is essentially a sample (regression) phenomenon.*[4] When we postulate the theoretical or population regression function (PRF), we believe that all X variables included in the model have separate or independent influence on the dependent variable Y. But it may happen that in any given sample that is used to test the PRF some or all X variables are so highly collinear that we cannot isolate their individual influence on Y. So to speak, our sample lets us down although the theory says that all X's are important. In short, our sample may not be "rich" enough to accommodate all X variables in the analysis.

As an illustration, reconsider the consumption-income example of Chap. 3. Economists theorize that, besides income, the wealth of the consumer is also an important determinant of consumption expenditure. Thus we may write

$$\text{Consumption}_i = \beta_1 + \beta_2 \text{ income}_i + \beta_3 \text{ wealth}_i + u_i$$

---

[4] If there is reason to believe that the X variables are stochastic and are linearly related in the population, we should develop our PRF to take this into account. What we are saying is that even if the X's are not linearly related in the population, they may be so related in the sample. In this sense, multicollinearity is a sample phenomenon.

Now it may happen that when we obtain data on income and wealth, the two variables may be highly, if not perfectly, correlated: Wealthier people generally tend to have higher incomes. Thus, although in theory income and wealth are logical candidates to explain the behavior of consumption expenditure, in practice (i.e., in the sample) it may be difficult to disentangle the separate influences of income and wealth on consumption expenditure.

9.2 ESTIMATION IN THE PRESENCE OF PERFECT MULTICOLLINEARITY

It was stated previously that in the case of perfect multicollinearity the regression coefficients remain indeterminate and their standard errors are infinite. This can be demonstrated readily in terms of the three-variable regression model. Using the deviation form, where all the variables are expressed as deviations from their sample means, the three-variable regression model can be written as

$$y_i = \hat{\beta}_{12.3} x_{2i} + \hat{\beta}_{13.2} x_{3i} + e_i \tag{9.2.1}$$

Now from Chap. 6 we obtain

$$\hat{\beta}_{12.3} = \frac{(\sum y_i x_{2i})(\sum x_{3i}^2) - (\sum y_i x_{3i})(\sum x_{2i} x_{3i})}{(\sum x_{2i}^2)(\sum x_{3i}^2) - (\sum x_{2i} x_{3i})^2} \tag{6.4.7}$$

$$\hat{\beta}_{13.2} = \frac{(\sum y_i x_{3i})(\sum x_{2i}^2) - (\sum y_i x_{2i})(\sum x_{2i} x_{3i})}{(\sum x_{2i}^2)(\sum x_{3i}^2) - (\sum x_{2i} x_{3i})^2} \tag{6.4.8}$$

Assume that $X_{3i} = \lambda X_{2i}$, where $\lambda \neq 0$. Substituting this into, say, (6.4.7), we obtain

$$\hat{\beta}_{12.3} = \frac{(\sum y_i x_{2i})(\lambda^2 \sum x_{2i}^2) - (\lambda \sum y_i x_{2i})(\lambda \sum x_{2i}^2)}{(\sum x_{2i}^2)(\lambda^2 \sum x_{2i}^2) - \lambda^2 (\sum x_{2i}^2)^2}$$

$$= \frac{0}{0} \tag{9.2.2}$$

which is an indeterminate expression. The reader can verify that $\hat{\beta}_{13.2}$ is also indeterminate.

Why do we obtain the result shown in (9.2.2)? Recall the meaning of $\hat{\beta}_{12.3}$: It gives the average rate of change in Y as X_2 changes by a unit, holding X_3 constant. But if X_3 and X_2 are perfectly collinear, there is no way X_3 can be kept constant: As X_2 changes, so does X_3 by the factor λ. What it means, then, is that there is no way of disentangling the separate influences of X_2 and X_3 from the given sample: For practical purposes X_2 and X_3 are indistinguishable.[5]

Turning to the variances of $\hat{\beta}_{12.3}$ and $\hat{\beta}_{13.2}$, we obtain from Chap. 6:

$$\text{var}\,(\hat{\beta}_{12.3}) = \frac{\sum x_{3i}^2}{(\sum x_{2i}^2)(\sum x_{3i}^2) - (\sum x_{2i}x_{3i})^2}\,\sigma^2 \qquad (6.4.9)$$

$$\text{var}\,(\hat{\beta}_{13.2}) = \frac{\sum x_{2i}^2}{(\sum x_{2i}^2)(\sum x_{3i}^2) - (\sum x_{2i}x_{3i})^2}\,\sigma^2 \qquad (6.4.11)$$

Substituting $X_{3i} = \lambda X_{2i}$ into the preceding expressions, we see, for instance,

$$\text{var}\,(\hat{\beta}_{12.3}) = \frac{\lambda^2 \sum x_{2i}^2}{\lambda^2(\sum x_{2i}^2)^2 - \lambda^2(\sum x_{2i}^2)^2}\,\sigma^2$$

$$= \frac{\sigma^2}{0}$$

$$= \infty \qquad (9.2.3)$$

and similarly var $(\hat{\beta}_{13.2}) = \infty$. Thus the variances of both $\hat{\beta}_{12.3}$ and $\hat{\beta}_{13.2}$ are undefined and in effect "infinite." Hence the standard errors are also undefined and infinite.

9.3 ESTIMATION IN THE PRESENCE OF "HIGH" BUT "IMPERFECT" MULTICOLLINEARITY

The perfect multicollinearity situation is a pathological extreme. Generally, there is no exact linear relationship among the X variables, especially in data involving economic time series. Thus, turning to the three-variable model in the deviation form given in (9.2.1), instead of exact multicollinearity, we may have

$$x_{3i} = \lambda x_{2i} + v_i \qquad (9.3.1)$$

where $\lambda \neq 0$ and where v_i is a stochastic error term such that $\sum x_{2i}v_i = 0$. (Why?) In this case, estimation of the regression coefficients $\beta_{12.3}$ and $\beta_{13.2}$ may be possible. For example, substituting (9.3.1) into (6.4.7), we obtain

$$\hat{\beta}_{12.3} = \frac{(\sum y_i x_{2i})(\sum x_{2i}^2 + \sum v_i^2) - (\sum y_i x_{2i} + \sum y_i v_i)\sum x_{2i}^2}{\sum x_{2i}^2(\sum x_{2i}^2 + \sum v_i^2) - (\sum x_{2i}^2)^2} \qquad (9.3.2)$$

where use is made of $\sum x_{2i}v_i = 0$. A similar expression can be derived for $\hat{\beta}_{13.2}$.

---

[5] Another way of looking at the problem is as follows: In the three-variable case the three unknowns $\beta_{1.23}$, $\beta_{12.3}$, and $\beta_{13.2}$ can be estimated from the three normal equations given by (6.4.3), (6.4.4), and (6.4.5), provided these equations are independent. But if X_2 and X_3 are exactly linearly related, equations (6.4.4) and (6.4.5) cannot be independent. For example, if $X_3 = 2X_2$, equation (6.4.5) is twice equation (6.4.4). As a result, we have two, not three, independent equations to estimate the three unknowns. From elementary algebra we know that in this situation unique estimation of all the unknowns is not possible.

Table 9.1 The behavior of var $(\hat{\beta}_{12.3})$ **as correlation coefficient** r_{23} **increases**

Value of r_{23}	var $(\hat{\beta}_{12.3})$
0	$\dfrac{\sigma^2}{\sum x_{2i}^2}$
0.50	$(1.33)\dfrac{\sigma^2}{\sum x_{2i}^2}$
0.70	$(1.96)\dfrac{\sigma^2}{\sum x_{2i}^2}$
0.80	$(2.78)\dfrac{\sigma^2}{\sum x_{2i}^2}$
0.90	$(5.26)\dfrac{\sigma^2}{\sum x_{2i}^2}$
0.95	$(10.26)\dfrac{\sigma^2}{\sum x_{2i}^2}$
1.00	∞

Now, unlike (9.2.2), there is no reason to believe a priori that (9.3.2) cannot be estimated. Of course, if v_i is sufficiently small, say, very close to zero, (9.3.1) will indicate almost perfect collinearity and we shall be back to the indeterminate case (9.2.2).

Now let us see what happens to the variances of $\hat{\beta}_{12.3}$ and $\hat{\beta}_{13.2}$, which are given in Sec. 9.2. Using Exercise 6.22, these variances can be written alternatively as

$$\text{var} (\hat{\beta}_{12.3}) = \frac{\sigma^2}{\sum x_{2i}^2(1 - r_{23}^2)} \tag{9.3.3}$$

and

$$\text{var} (\hat{\beta}_{13.2}) = \frac{\sigma^2}{\sum x_{3i}^2(1 - r_{23}^2)} \tag{9.3.4}$$

where r_{23} is the coefficient of correlation between X_2 and X_3. It is apparent from the formulas (9.3.3) and (9.3.4) that as r_{23} tends toward 1, that is, as collinearity increases, the variances of the two estimators increase and in the limit when $r_{23} = 1$, they are infinite.

To give some idea about how fast the variances increase as r_{23} increases, consider Table 9.1, which shows that, starting with no collinearity, the variance of $\hat{\beta}_{12.3}$ increases rapidly. By the time $r = 0.80$, the variance is about 2.8 times the variance in the absence of collinearity, and by the time $r = 0.95$, it is tenfold higher.[6]

9.4 CONSEQUENCES OF MULTICOLLINEARITY

Properties of OLS Estimators

Recall that if the assumptions of the classical linear regression models are satisfied, the ordinary-least-squares (OLS) estimators of the regression coefficients are linear, unbiased, and have minimum variance; in short, they are best linear unbiased estimators (BLUE). Now it can be shown that even if multicollinearity is very high, the OLS estimators still retain the property of BLUE, but note the following.

Unbiasedness is a multisample or repeated sampling property. What it says is that, keeping the values of the X variable fixed, if one obtains repeated samples and computes the OLS estimators for each of these samples, then the average of the sample values will converge to the true population values of the estimators as the number of samples increases. But this says nothing about the properties of the estimators in any given sample.

It is true that collinearity does not destroy the property of minimum variance: In the class of all linear unbiased estimators, the OLS estimators have minimum variance; that is, they are efficient. But this does not mean that the variance of an OLS estimator will necessarily be small (in relation to the value of the estimator) in any given sample.

As noted in Sec. 9.1 multicollinearity is essentially a sample phenomenon. Therefore, the fact that the OLS estimators are BLUE despite multicollinearity is of little consolation in practice. We must see what happens or is likely to happen in any given sample.

Practical Consequences of Multicollinearity

As shown in Sec. 9.2, in case of perfect multicollinearity the OLS estimators are indeterminate and their variances and standard errors are undefined. If collinearity is severe but not perfect, then the following consequences ensue.

1. Although the OLS estimators may be obtainable, their standard errors tend to be large as the degree of collinearity between the variables increases. This was shown in Sec. 9.3 for the three-variable case and can be readily generalized to the k-variable case (see Exercise 9.3).

---

[6] In passing it may be noted that as r_{23} approaches 1, the covariance between $\hat{\beta}_{12.3}$ and $\hat{\beta}_{13.2}$ tends to infinity, and hence it becomes difficult to separate the effects of X_2 and X_3 from each other. This can be confirmed readily from the following formula:

$$\text{cov}\,(\hat{\beta}_{12.3}, \hat{\beta}_{13.2}) = \frac{-\sigma^2(r_{23})}{(1 - r_{23}^2)\sqrt{\sum x_{2i}^2 \sum x_{3i}^2}}$$

2. Because of the large standard errors, the confidence intervals for the relevant population parameters tend to be larger. Thus, in the three-variable case, if there is no collinearity $(r_{23} = 0)$, and assuming σ^2 is known, the 95 percent confidence interval for $\beta_{12.3}$ can be seen to be[7]

$$\Pr\left(\hat{\beta}_{12.3} - 1.96\sqrt{\frac{\sigma^2}{\sum x_{2i}^2}} \le \beta_{12.3} \le \hat{\beta}_{12.3} + 1.96\sqrt{\frac{\sigma^2}{\sum x_{2i}^2}}\right) = 0.95 \quad (9.4.1)$$

But if collinearity is severe, say, $r_{23} = 0.9$, then we see from Table 9.1 that the 95 percent confidence interval now is

$$\Pr\left[\hat{\beta}_{12.3} - (1.96)\sqrt{(5.26)}\sqrt{\frac{\sigma^2}{\sum x_{2i}^2}} \le \beta_{12.3} \le \hat{\beta}_{12.3} + (1.96)\sqrt{(5.26)}\sqrt{\frac{\sigma^2}{\sum x_{2i}^2}}\right]$$

$$= 0.95 \quad (9.4.2)$$

Therefore, the latter confidence interval is larger than the former by a factor of about $\sqrt{5.26} = 2.29$, or more than twice as large.

3. By virtue of 2, in cases of high multicollinearity, the sample data may be compatible with a diverse set of hypotheses. Hence the probability of accepting a false hypothesis (i.e., type II error) increases.

4. As noted, as long as multicollinearity is not perfect, estimation of the regression coefficients is possible but the estimates and their standard errors become very sensitive to even the slightest change in the data. To see this, consider Table 9.2.

Calculations will show that

$$\hat{Y}_i = 1.1939 + 0.4463 X_{2i} + 0.0030 X_{3i}$$

$$(0.7737) \quad (0.1848) \quad (0.0851)$$

$$t = (1.5431) \quad (2.4151) \quad (0.0358) \quad (9.4.3)$$

$$R^2 = 0.8101 \quad r_{23} = 0.5523$$

$$\text{cov}(\hat{\beta}_2, \hat{\beta}_3) = -0.000868 \quad df = 2$$

---

[7] Note that we are using the normal distribution because σ^2 is assumed to be known for convenience.

Table 9.2 Hypothetical data on Y, X_2, and X_3

Y	X_2	X_3
1	2	4
2	0	2
3	4	12
4	6	0
5	8	16

Table 9.3 Hypothetical data on Y,
X_2, **and** X_3

Y	X_2	X_3
1	2	4
2	0	2
3	4	0
4	6	12
5	8	16

Regression (9.4.3) shows that none of the regression coefficients are individually significant at the conventional 1 or 5 percent levels of significance, although $\hat{\beta}_2$ is significant at the 10 percent level on the basis of a one-tail t test.

Now consider Table 9.3. The only difference between Tables 9.2 and 9.3 is that the third and fourth values of X_3 are interchanged. Using the data of Table 9.3, we now obtain

$$\hat{Y}_i = \ 1.2108 \ + 0.4014X_{2i} + 0.0270X_{3i}$$

$$(0.7480) \quad (0.2721) \qquad (0.1252)$$

$$t = (1.6187) \quad (1.4752) \qquad (0.2158) \qquad (9.4.4)$$

$$R^2 = 0.8143 \qquad r_{23} = 0.8285$$

$$\text{cov} \ (\hat{\beta}_2, \hat{\beta}_3) = \ -0.0282 \qquad \text{df} = 2$$

As a result of a slight change in the data, we see that $\hat{\beta}_2$, which was statistically significant before at the 10 percent level of significance, is no longer significant even at that level. Also note that in (9.4.3) cov $(\hat{\beta}_2, \hat{\beta}_3) = \ -0.000868$ whereas in (9.4.4) it is -0.0282, a more than thirtyfold increase. All these changes may be attributable to increased multicollinearity: In (9.4.3) $r_{23} = 0.5523$, whereas in (9.4.4) it is 0.8285. Similarly, the standard errors of $\hat{\beta}_2$ and $\hat{\beta}_3$ increase between the two regressions, a usual symptom of collinearity.

5. If multicollinearity is high, one may obtain a high R^2, but none or very few estimated coefficients are statistically significant. Thus in regression (9.4.4) $R^2 = 0.8143$, meaning that about 81 percent of the variation in Y is explained by X_2 and X_3, and yet neither of the coefficients is individually statistically significant even at the 10 percent level of significance. Thus high multicollinearity may make it impossible to isolate the individual effects of the explanatory variables.

9.5 AN ILLUSTRATIVE EXAMPLE

To illustrate the various points made previously, let us reconsider the consumption-income example of Chap. 3. In Table 9.4 we reproduce the data of Table 3.2 and add to it data on wealth of the consumer. If we assume that

Table 9.4 Hypothetical data on consumption expenditure Y, income X_2, and wealth X_3

Y, $	X_2, $	X_3, $
70	80	810
65	100	1009
90	120	1273
95	140	1425
110	160	1633
115	180	1876
120	200	2052
140	220	2201
155	240	2435
150	260	2686

consumption expenditure is linearly related to income and wealth, then, based on Table 9.4, we obtain the following regression:

$$\hat{Y}_i = 24.7747 + 0.9415X_{2i} - 0.0424X_{3i}$$
$$(6.7525) \quad (0.8229) \quad\quad (0.0807)$$
$$t = (3.6690) \quad (1.1442) \quad (-0.5261)$$
$$R^2 = 0.9635 \quad\quad \bar{R}^2 = 0.9531 \quad\quad \text{df} = 7$$

(9.5.1)

Regression (9.5.1) shows that income and wealth together explain about 96 percent of the variation in consumption expenditure, and yet neither of the slope coefficients is individually statistically significant. Moreover, not only is the wealth variable statistically insignificant, but also it has a wrong sign. A priori, one would expect a positive relationship between consumption and wealth. Although $\hat{\beta}_2$ and $\hat{\beta}_3$ are individually statistically insignificant, if we test the hypothesis that $\beta_2 = \beta_3 = 0$ simultaneously, this hypothesis can be rejected, as Table 9.5 shows. Under the usual assumption we obtain

$$F = \frac{4282.7770}{46.3494}$$
$$= 92.4019$$

(9.5.2)

This F value is obviously highly significant.

Table 9.5 AOV table for the consumption-income-wealth example

Source of variation	SS	df	MSS
Due to regression	8565.5541	2	4282.7770
Due to residual	324.4459	7	46.3494

Our example shows dramatically what multicollinearity does. The fact that the F test is significant but the t values of X_2 and X_3 are individually insignificant means that the two variables are so highly correlated that it is impossible to isolate the individual impact of either income or wealth on consumption. As a matter of fact, if we regress X_3 on X_2, we obtain

$$\hat{X}_{3i} = 7.5454 + 10.1909X_{2i}$$

$$(29.4758) \quad (0.1643) \tag{9.5.3}$$

$$t = (0.2560) \quad (62.0405) \qquad R^2 = 0.9979$$

which shows that there is almost perfect collinearity between X_3 and X_2.

Now let us see what happens if we regress Y on X_2 only:

$$\hat{Y}_i = 24.4545 + 0.5091X_{2i}$$

$$(6.4138) \quad (0.0357) \tag{9.5.4}$$

$$t = (3.8128) \quad (14.2432) \qquad R^2 = 0.9621$$

In (9.5.1) the income variable was statistically insignificant, whereas now it is highly significant. If instead of regressing Y on X_2, we regress it on X_3, we obtain

$$\hat{Y}_i = 24.3480 + 0.0498X_{3i}$$

$$(6.3837) \quad (0.0037) \tag{9.5.5}$$

$$t = (3.8141) \quad (13.3576) \qquad R^2 = 0.9567$$

We see that wealth has now significant impact on consumption expenditure, whereas in (9.5.1) it had no effect on consumption expenditure.

Regressions (9.5.4) and (9.5.5) show very clearly that in situations of extreme multicollinearity dropping the highly collinear variable will often make the other X variable statistically significant. This would suggest that a way out of extreme collinearity is to drop the collinear variable, but we shall have more to say about it in Sec. 9.8.

9.6 DETECTION OF MULTICOLLINEARITY

Having studied the nature and consequences of multicollinearity, the natural question is: How does one know that collinearity is present in any given situation, especially in models involving more than two explanatory variables. There are several methods of detection, some of which are as follows.

1. Collinearity is often suspected when R^2 is high (say, between 0.7 and 1.0) and when zero-order correlations are also high but none or very few of the partial regression coefficients are individually statistically significant on the basis of the conventional t test. If R^2 is high, it will mean that the F test of the analysis-of-variance procedure in most cases will reject the null hypothesis that the true values of all the partial slope coefficients are simultaneously zero, the t test notwithstanding. Our consumption-income-wealth example shows vividly that

the F value is highly significant, although neither income nor wealth has an independent impact on consumption.

2. Although high zero-order correlations may suggest collinearity, it is not necessary that they be high to have collinearity in any specific case. To put the matter somewhat technically, *high zero-order correlations are a sufficient but not a necessary condition for the existence of multicollinearity because it can exist even through the zero-order or simple correlations are comparatively low* (say, less than 0.50). To see this, suppose we have a four-variable model

$$Y_i = \beta_1 + \beta_2 X_{2i} + \beta_3 X_{3i} + \beta_4 X_{4i} + u_i$$

and suppose that

$$X_{4i} = \lambda_2 X_{2i} + \lambda_3 X_{3i}$$

where λ_2 and λ_3 are constants, not both zero. Obviously, X_4 is an exact linear combination of X_2 and X_3, giving $R_{4.23}^2 = 1$.

Now recalling the formula (6.9.5) from Chap. 6, we can write

$$R_{4.23}^2 = \frac{r_{42}^2 + r_{43}^2 - 2r_{42}r_{43}r_{23}}{1 - r_{23}^2} \tag{9.6.1}$$

But since $R_{4.23}^2 = 1$ because of perfect collinearity, we obtain

$$1 = \frac{r_{42}^2 + r_{43}^2 - 2r_{42}r_{43}r_{23}}{1 - r_{23}^2} \tag{9.6.2}$$

Now it is not difficult to see that (9.6.2) is satisfied by $r_{42} = 0.5$, $r_{43} = 0.5$, and $r_{23} = -0.5$, which are not very high values.

Therefore, in models involving more than two explanatory variables, the simple or zero-order correlation will not provide an infallible guide to the presence of multicollinearity. Of course, if there are only two explanatory variables, the zero-order correlations will suffice.

3. As a result, it is suggested that one should look, not only at the zero-order correlations, but also at the partial correlation coefficients.[8] Thus, in the regression of Y on X_2, X_3, and X_4, if one finds that $R_{1.234}^2$ is very high but $r_{12.34}^2$, $r_{13.24}^2$, and $r_{14.23}^2$ are comparatively low, it may suggest that the variables X_2, X_3, and X_4 are highly intercorrelated and that at least one of these variables is superfluous.

Although a study of the partial correlations may be useful, there is no guarantee that they will provide an unfailing guide to multicollinearity, for it may happen that both R^2 and all the partial correlations are sufficiently high.

4. Since multicollinearity arises because one or more of the explanatory variables are exact or approximate linear combinations of the other explanatory variables, one way of finding out which X variable is related to other X variables is to regress each X_i on the remaining X variables and compute the corresponding

---

[8] See D. E. Farrar and R. R. Glauber, "Multicollinearity in Regression Analysis: The Problem Re-visited," *Review of Economics and Statistics*, vol. 49, pp. 92–107, 1967.

R^2, which we designate as R_i^2. Then, following the relationship between F and R^2 established in (7.6.4), the variable

$$F_i = \frac{R_{x_i \cdot x_2 x_3 \cdots x_k}^2/(k-2)}{(1 - R_{x_i \cdot x_2 x_2 \cdots x_k}^2)/(N - k + 1)} \tag{9.6.3}$$

follows the F distribution with $k - 2$ and $N - k + 1$ df. In equation (9.6.3) N stands for the sample size, k stands for the number of explanatory variables including the intercept term, and $R_{x_i \cdot x_2 x_3 \cdots x_k}^2$ is the coefficient of determination in the regression of variable X_i on the remaining variables.[9]

If the computed F exceeds the critical F_i at the chosen level of significance, it is taken to mean that the particular X_i is collinear with other X's; if it does not exceed the critical F_i, we say that it is not collinear with other X's, in which case we may retain that variable in the model. If F_i is statistically significant, we will still have to decide whether the particular X_i should be dropped from the model. This question will be taken up in Sec. 9.8.

The methods discussed previously provide us with some means of assessing the presence of multicollinearity in any application of the regression model. But it should be noted that the criteria suggested are to some extent "fishing expeditions." Which of the preceding methods will enable one to detect multicollinearity will depend on the nature of the problem.

9.7 MULTICOLLINEARITY AND PREDICTION

It is said that if the sole purpose of regression analysis is prediction, then multicollinearity is not a serious problem because the higher the R^2, the better the prediction.[10] But this may be so only if the collinearity existing among the X variables in a given sample will also continue to exist in the future.

If, however, the approximate linear relationship among the X's in a sample does not continue into the future (samples), prediction will be increasingly uncertain.[11] Moreover, if the objective of the analysis is not only prediction but also reliable estimation of the parameters, serious multicollinearity will be a problem because we have seen that it leads to large standard errors of the estimators.

9.8 REMEDIAL MEASURES

What can be done if multicollinearity is serious? As in the case of detection, there are no infallible guides because multicollinearity is essentially a sample problem.

---

[9] For example, $R_{x_2}^2$ can be obtained by regressing X_{2i} as follows: $X_{2i} = \alpha_1 + \alpha_3 X_{3i} + \alpha_4 X_{4j} + \cdots + \alpha_k X_{ki} + v_i$, where v_i is a disturbance term.

[10] See R. C. Geary, "Some Results about Relations between Stochastic Variables: A Discussion Document," *Review of International Statistical Institute*, vol. 31, pp. 163–181, 1963.

[11] For an excellent discussion, see E. Malinvaud, *Statistical Methods of Econometrics*, 2d ed., North-Holland Publishing Company, Amsterdam, 1970, pp. 220–221.

However, the following rules of thumb can be tried, the success depending on the severity of the collinearity problem.

1. *A priori information.* Suppose we consider the model

$$Y_i = \beta_1 + \beta_2 X_{2i} + \beta_3 X_{3i} + u_i$$

where Y = consumption, X_2 = income, and X_3 = wealth. As noted before, income and wealth variables tend to be highly collinear. But suppose a priori we believe that $\beta_3 = 0.10\beta_2$; that is, the rate of change of consumption with respect to wealth is one-tenth the corresponding rate with respect to income. We can then run the following regression:

$$Y_i = \beta_1 + \beta_2 X_{2i} + 0.10\beta_2 X_{3i} + u_i$$
$$= \beta_1 + \beta_2 X_i + u_i$$

where $X_i = X_{2i} + 0.1X_{3i}$. Once we obtain $\hat{\beta}_2$, we can estimate $\hat{\beta}_3$ from the postulated relationship between β_2 and β_3.

How does one obtain a priori information? It could come either from economic theory or from previous empirical work in which the collinearity problem happens to be less serious.

2. *Combing cross-sectional and time-series data.* A variant of the extraneous or a priori information technique suggested previously is the combination of cross-sectional and time-series data, known as *pooling the data.* Suppose we want to study the demand for automobiles in the United States and assume we have time-series data on the number of cars sold, average price of the car, and consumer income. Suppose also that

$$\ln Y_t = \beta_1 + \beta_2 \ln P_t + \beta_3 \ln I_t + u_t$$

where Y = number of cars sold, P = average price, I = income, and t = time. Our objective is to estimate the price elasticity β_2 and income elasticity β_3.

Now in time-series data the price and income variables generally tend to be highly collinear. Therefore, if we run the preceding regression, we shall be faced with the usual multicollinearity problem. A way out of this has been suggested by Tobin.[12] He suggests that if we have cross-sectional data (such as generated by consumer panels or budget studies conducted by various private and governmental agencies), we can obtain a fairly reliable estimate of the income elasticity β_3 because in such data, which are at a point in time, the prices do not vary much. Let the cross-sectionally estimated income elasticity be $\hat{\beta}_3$. Using this estimate, the preceding time-series regression may be written as

$$Y_t^* = \beta_1 + \beta_2 \ln P_t + u_t$$

where $Y^* = \ln Y - \hat{\beta}_3 \ln I$, and represents that value of Y after removing from it

[12] J. Tobin, "A Statistical Demand Function for Food in the U.S.A.," *Journal of the Royal Statistical Society,* ser. A, pp. 113–141, 1950.

the effect of income. We can now obtain an estimate of the price elasticity β_2 from the preceding regression.

Although it is an appealing technique, pooling the time-series and cross-section data in the manner just suggested may create problems of interpretation, because we are assuming implicitly that the cross-sectionally estimated income elasticity is the same thing as that which would be obtained from a pure time-series analysis.[13] Nonetheless, the technique has been used in many applications and is worthy of consideration in situations where the cross-sectional estimates do not vary substantially from one cross section to another. An example of this technique is provided in Exercise 9.18.

3. *Dropping a variable(s) and specification bias.* When faced with severe multicollinearity, one of the "simplest" things to do is to drop one of the collinear variables. Thus, in our consumption-income-wealth illustration, when we drop the wealth variable, we obtain regression (9.5.4), which shows that whereas in the original model the income variable was statistically insignificant, it is now "highly" significant.

But in dropping a variable from the model we may be committing a *specification bias*, or *specification error*. Specification bias arises from incorrect specification of the model used in the analysis. Thus, if economic theory says that income and wealth should both be included in the model explaining the consumption expenditure, dropping the wealth variable would constitute specification bias.[14]

To see the consequences of specification bias, let the "true" or "correctly" specified model be

$$Y_i = \beta_1 + \beta_2 X_{2i} + \beta_3 X_{3i} + u_i \tag{9.8.1}$$

But suppose we use the following "incorrect" or "misspecified" model:

$$Y_i = \alpha_1 + \alpha_2 X_{2i} + v_i \tag{9.8.2}$$

We know that

$$\hat{\alpha}_2 = \frac{\sum y_i x_{2i}}{\sum x_{2i}^2} \tag{9.8.3}$$

and

$$\hat{\beta}_2 = \frac{(\sum y_i x_{2i})(\sum x_{3i}^2) - (\sum y_i x_{3i})(\sum x_{2i} x_{3i})}{(\sum x_{2i}^2)(\sum x_{3i}^2) - (\sum x_{2i} x_{3i})^2} \tag{9.8.4}$$

It can now be shown from (9.8.3) and (9.8.4) that

$$E(\hat{\alpha}_2) = \beta_2 + b_{32}\beta_3 \tag{9.8.5}$$

---

[13] For a thorough discussion and application of the pooling technique, see Edwin Kuh, *Capital Stock Growth: A Micro-Econometric Approach*, North-Holland Publishing Company, Amsterdam, 1963, chaps. 5 and 6.

[14] For a simple discussion of different types of specification errors, see Chap. 15 and Jan Kmenta, *Elements of Econometrics*, The Macmillan Company, New York, 1971, sec. 10-4, pp. 391–405.

where b_{32} = slope coefficient in the regression of X_3 on X_2 (see Exercise 9.10). Therefore, it is obvious from (9.8.5) that $\hat{\alpha}_2$ will be a biased estimate of β_2 as long as b_{32} is different from zero (it is assumed that β_3 is different from zero; otherwise there is no sense in including X_3 in the original model).[15] Of course, if b_{32} is zero, we have no multicollinearity problem to begin with. It is also clear from (9.8.5) that if both b_{32} and β_3 are positive, $E(\hat{\alpha}_2)$ will be greater than β_2; hence on the average $\hat{\alpha}_2$ will overestimate β_2, leading to a positive bias. Similarly, if the product $b_{32}\beta_3$ is negative, on the average $\hat{\alpha}_2$ will underestimate β_2, leading to a negative bias.

From the preceding discussion it is clear that dropping a variable from the model to alleviate the problem of multicollinearity may lead to the specification bias. Hence the remedy may be worse than the disease in some situations because while multicollinearity may prevent effective estimation of the parameters of the model, omitting a variable may seriously mislead us as to the true values of the parameters.

4. *Transformation of variables.* Suppose we have time-series data on consumption expenditure, income, and wealth. One reason for high multicollinearity between income and wealth in such data is that over time both the variables tend to move in the same direction. One way of minimizing this dependence is to proceed as follows.

If the relation

$$Y_t = \beta_1 + \beta_2 X_{2t} + \beta_3 X_{3t} + u_t \qquad (9.8.6)$$

holds at time t, it must also hold at time $t - 1$ because the origin of time is arbitrary anyway. Therefore, we have

$$Y_{t-1} = \beta_1 + \beta_2 X_{2,t-1} + \beta_3 X_{3,t-1} + u_{t-1} \qquad (9.8.7)$$

If we subtract (9.8.7) from (9.8.6), we obtain

$$Y_t - Y_{t-1} = \beta_2(X_{2t} - X_{2,t-1}) + \beta_3(X_{3t} - X_{3,t-1}) + v_t \qquad (9.8.8)$$

where $v_t = u_t - u_{t-1}$. Equation (9.8.8) is known as the *first difference* form because we run the regression, not on the original variables, but on the differences of successive values of the variables.

The first difference regression model often reduces the severity of multicollinearity because although the levels of X_2 and X_3 may be highly correlated, there is no a priori reason to believe that their differences will also be highly correlated.

The first difference transformation, however, creates some additional problems. The error term v_t appearing in (9.8.8) may not satisfy one of the assumptions of the classical linear regression model, namely, that the disturbances are not serially correlated. As we shall see in Chap. 11, if the original u_t is serially independent or uncorrelated, the error term v_t obtained previously will in most cases be

---

[15] Note further that if b_{32} does not approach zero as the sample size is increased indefinitely, then $\hat{\alpha}_2$ will be not only biased but also inconsistent.

serially correlated. Again the remedy may be worse than the disease! Moreover, there is a loss of one observation due to the differencing procedure, and therefore the degrees of freedom are reduced by one. In a small sample this could be a factor one would wish at least to take into consideration. Furthermore, the first differencing procedure may not be appropriate in cross-sectional data where there is no logical ordering of the observations.

5. *Additional or new data.* Since multicollinearity is a sample feature, it is possible that in another sample involving the same variables collinearity may not be as serious as in the first sample. Sometimes simply increasing the size of the sample (if possible) may attenuate the collinearity problem. For example, in the three-variable model we saw that

$$\text{var} \left(\hat{\beta}_{12.3} \right) = \frac{\sigma^2}{\sum x_{2i}^2 (1 - r_{23}^2)}$$

Now as the sample size increases, $\sum x_{2i}^2$ will generally increase. (Why?) Therefore, for any given r_{23}, the variance of $\hat{\beta}_{12.3}$ will decrease, thus decreasing the standard error, which will enable us to estimate $\beta_{12.3}$ more precisely.

There are several other statistical techniques which can be used to minimize the collinearity problem, but they are rather advanced and beyond the scope of this book. The interested reader may consult the references.[16]

One caution needs to be borne in mind: In regression analysis when one obtains insignificant t values for the regression coefficients, there is often the temptation to blame this lack of significance on multicollinearity. But the real culprit may not be collinearity but something else, say, the specification bias. Perhaps the model used in the analysis is wrongly specified or the theoretical support for the model is too weak. Therefore, before the researcher blames insignificant t values on multicollinearity, it would be wise to consider whether the model is sound in theory. Perhaps a search of the literature may suggest an alternative specification of the model.

9.9 SUMMARY AND CONCLUSIONS

One of the assumptions of the classical linear regression model is that there is no multicollinearity among the explanatory variables, the X's. Broadly interpreted, multicollinearity refers to the situation where there is either an exact or approximately exact linear relationship among the X variables.

The consequences of multicollinearity are as follows: If there is perfect collinearity among the X's, their regression coefficients are indeterminate and their standard errors are infinite. If collinearity is high but not perfect, estimation of

---

[16] The techniques of factor analysis and principal components may be used to resolve the multicollinearity problem. A readable discussion of these techniques may be found in Donald F. Morrison, *Multivariate Statistical Methods*, McGraw-Hill Book Company, New York, 1967, chaps. 7 and 8. But note that matrix algebra is required to follow these chapters.

regression coefficients is possible but their standard errors tend to be large. As a result, the population values of the coefficients cannot be estimated precisely.

Although there are no sure methods of detecting collinearity, there are several indicators of it, which are as follows:

1. The clearest sign of multicollinearity is when R^2 is very high but none of the regression coefficients is statistically significant on the basis of the conventional t test. This is, of course, an extreme case.

2. In models involving just two explanatory variables, a fairly good idea of collinearity can be obtained by examining the zero-order, or simple, correlation coefficient between the two variables. If this correlation is high, multicollinearity is generally the culprit.

3. However, the zero-order correlation coefficients can be misleading in models involving more than two X variables since it is possible to have low zero-order correlations and yet find high multicollinearity. In situations like these, one needs to examine the partial correlation coefficients.

4. If R^2 is high but the partial correlations are low, multicollinearity is a possibility. Here one or more variables may be superfluous. But if R^2 is high and the partial correlations are also high, multicollinearity may not be readily detectable.

5. Therefore, one may regress each of the X_i variables on the remaining X variables in the model and find out the corresponding coefficients of determination R_i^2. A high R_i^2 would suggest that X_i is highly correlated with the rest of the X's. Therefore, one may drop that X_i from the model, provided it does not lead to serious specification bias.

Detection of multicollinearity is half the battle. The other half is concerned with how to get rid of the problem. Again there are no sure methods, only a few rules of thumb. Some of these rules are: (1) using extraneous or prior information, (2) combining cross-sectional and time-series data, (3) omitting a highly collinear variable, (4) transforming data, and (5) obtaining additional or new data. Of course, which of these rules will work in practice will depend on the nature of the data and severity of the collinearity problem.

EXERCISES

9.1 In the k-variable linear regression model there are k normal equations to estimate the k unknowns. These normal equations are given in (8.3.8). Assume that X_k is a perfect linear combination of the remaining X variables. How would you show that in this case it is impossible to estimate the k regression coefficients?

*9.2 In matrix notation we saw in Chap. 8 that

$$\hat{\beta} = (X'X)^{-1}X'y$$

(a) What happens to $\hat{\beta}$ when there is perfect collinearity among the X's?

(b) How would you know if perfect collinearity exists?

* Optional.

*9.3 Using matrix notation, we obtained in (8.3.13)

$$\text{var-cov } (\hat{\boldsymbol{\beta}}) = \sigma^2 (\mathbf{X'X})^{-1}$$

What happens to the above var-cov matrix when (a) there is perfect multicollinearity and (b) when collinearity is high but not perfect.

*9.4 Consider the following correlation matrix:

$$\mathbf{R} = \begin{array}{c} \\ X_2 \\ X_3 \\ \\ X_k \end{array} \begin{array}{c} \begin{array}{cccc} X_2 & X_3 & \cdots & X_k \end{array} \\ \left[\begin{array}{cccc} 1 & r_{23} & \cdots & r_{2k} \\ r_{32} & 1 & \cdots & r_{3k} \\ \cdots\cdots\cdots\cdots\cdots \\ r_{k2} & r_{k3} & \cdots & 1 \end{array} \right] \end{array}$$

How would you find out from the correlation matrix whether (a) there is perfect collinearity, (b) there is less than perfect collinearity, and (c) the X's are uncorrelated.

Hint: You may use $|\mathbf{R}|$ to answer these questions, where $|\mathbf{R}|$ denotes the determinant of $\mathbf{R}$.

9.5 Consider the following set of hypothetical data:

Y	X_2	X_3
−10	1	1
−8	2	3
−6	3	5
−4	4	7
−2	5	9
0	6	11
2	7	13
4	8	15
6	9	17
8	10	19
10	11	21

If you want to fit the model $Y_i = \beta_1 + \beta_2 X_{2i} + \beta_3 X_{3i} + u_i$, can you estimate the three unknowns? Why or why not?

9.6 In case the regression in Exercise 9.5 cannot be estimated, how can the model be modified so that some or all the coefficients can be estimated?

9.7 Recall Chap. 7, Sec. 7, where we considered the marginal or incremental contribution of an explanatory variable. The example discussed there involved the regression of personal consumption expenditure Y on personal disposable income X_2 and the trend X_3. When we introduced variable X_2 into the model first and then variable X_3, we obtained Table 7.7. But suppose we introduce X_3 first and then X_2. The AOV table corresponding to this change is as follows:

AOV table when X_3 enters first

Source of variation	SS	df	MSS
ESS due to X_3 alone	$Q_1 = 64536.2529$	1	64536.2529
ESS due to addition of X_2	$Q_2 = 1428.8471$	1	1428.8471
ESS due to X_2 and X_3	$Q_3 = 65965.1000$	2	32982.5500
Due to residual	$Q_4 = 77.1693$	12	6.4310
Total	$Q_5 = 66042.2693$		

Although the ESS due to X_2 and X_3 together is the same in both the tables, its allocation between the two X's is different. In Table 7.7, where X_2 enters first, its contribution to ESS is 65898.2353, but when it enters marginally as in the preceding table, its contribution is only 1428.8471. The same thing is true of X_3. How would you explain this phenomenon?

9.8 If the relation $\lambda_1 X_{1i} + \lambda_2 X_{2i} + \lambda_3 X_{3i} = 0$ holds true for all values of λ_1, λ_2, and λ_3, estimate $r_{12.3}, r_{13.2}$, and $r_{23.1}$. Also find out $R^2_{1.23}$, $R^2_{2.13}$, and $R^2_{3.12}$. What is the degree of multicollinearity in this situation?

9.9 Consider the following model:

$$Y_t = \beta_1 + \beta_2 X_t + \beta_3 X_{t-1} + \beta_4 X_{t-2} + \beta_5 X_{t-3} + \beta_6 X_{t-4} + u_t$$

where Y = consumption, X = income, and t = time. The preceding model postulates that consumption expenditure at time t is a function of income not only at time t but also income through previous periods. Thus consumption expenditure in the first quarter of 1976 is a function of income in that quarter and the four quarters of 1975. Such models are called *distributed lag models*, and we shall discuss them in a later chapter.

(a) Would you expect multicollinearity in such models and why?

(b) If collinearity is expected, how would you resolve the problem?

9.10 Establish equation (9.8.5).

Hint: Divide the numerator and denominator of (9.8.4) by $(\sum x^2_{2i})(\sum x^2_{3i})$ and simplify.

9.11 Consider the illustrative example of Sec. 9.5. How would you reconcile the difference in the marginal propensity to consume obtained from (9.5.1) and (9.5.4)?

9.12 In data involving economic time series such as GNP, money supply, prices, income, unemployment, etc., multicollinearity is usually suspected. Why?

9.13 Suppose in the model

$$Y_i = \beta_1 + \beta_2 X_{2i} + \beta_3 X_{3i} + u_i$$

r_{23}, the coefficient of correlation between X_2 and X_3, is zero. Therefore, someone suggests that you run the following regressions:

$$Y_i = \alpha_1 + \alpha_2 X_{2i} + u_{1i}$$

$$Y_i = \gamma_1 + \gamma_3 X_{3i} + u_{2i}$$

(a) Will $\hat{\alpha}_2 = \hat{\beta}_2$ and $\hat{\gamma}_3 = \hat{\beta}_3$? Why?

(b) Will $\hat{\beta}_1$ equal $\hat{\alpha}_1$ or $\hat{\gamma}_1$ or some combination thereof?

(c) Will var $(\hat{\beta}_2)$ = var $(\hat{\alpha}_2)$ and var $(\hat{\beta}_3)$ = var $(\hat{\gamma}_3)$?

9.14 Refer to the illustrative example of Chap. 6 where we fitted the Cobb-Douglas production function to the Taiwanese agricultural sector. The results of the regression given in (6.6.2) show that both the labor and capital coefficients are individually statistically significant.

(a) Find out whether the variables labor and capital are highly correlated.

(b) If your answer to (a) is affirmative, would you drop, say, the labor variable from the model and regress the output variable on capital input only?

(c) If you do so, what kind of specification bias is committed? Find out the nature of this bias.

9.15 Refer to Exercise 8.9. For this problem the correlation matrix is as follows:

	X_i	X_i^2	X_i^3
X_i	1	0.9742	0.9284
X_i^2		1.0	0.9872
X_i^3			1.0

(a) "Since the zero-order correlations are very high, there must be serious multicollinearity." Comment.

(b) Would you drop variables X_i^2 and X_i^3 from the model?

(c) If you drop them, what will happen to the value of the coefficient of X_i?

9.16 *Stepwise regression.* In deciding on the "best" set of explanatory variables for a regression model, researchers often follow the method of stepwise regression. In this method one proceeds either by introducing the X variables one at a time (stepwise forward regression) or by including all the possible X variables in one multiple regression and rejecting them one at a time (stepwise backward regression). The decision to add or drop a variable is usually made on the basis of the contribution of that variable to the ESS, as judged by the F test. Knowing what you do now about multicollinearity, would you recommend either procedure? Why or why not?[17]

*9.17 *Orthogonal explanatory variables.* Suppose in the model

$$Y_i = \beta_1 + \beta_2 X_{2i} + \beta_3 X_{3i} + \cdots + \beta_k X_{ki} + u_i$$

X_2 to X_k are all uncorrelated. Such variables are called *orthogonal variables*. If this is the case:

(a) What will be the structure of the $(\mathbf{X'X})$ matrix?

(b) How would you obtain $\hat{\boldsymbol{\beta}} = (\mathbf{X'X})^{-1}\mathbf{X'y}$?

(c) What will be the nature of the var-cov matrix of $\hat{\boldsymbol{\beta}}$?

(d) Suppose you have run the regression and afterward you want to introduce another orthogonal variable, say, X_{k+1} into the model? Do you have to recompute all the previous coefficients $\hat{\beta}_1$ to $\hat{\beta}_k$? Why or why not?

9.18 Klein and Goldberger attempted to fit the following regression model to the United States economy:

$$Y_i = \beta_1 + \beta_2 X_{2i} + \beta_3 X_{3i} + \beta_4 X_{4i} + u_i$$

where Y = consumption, X_2 = wage income, X_3 = nonwage, nonfarm income, and X_4 farm income. But since X_2, X_3, and X_4 are expected to be highly collinear, they obtained estimates of β_3 and β_4 from cross-sectional analysis as follows: $\beta_3 = 0.75\beta_2$ and $\beta_4 = 0.625\beta_2$. Using these estimates, they reformulated their consumption function as follows:

$$Y_i = \beta_1 + \beta_2(X_{2i} + 0.75X_{3i} + 0.625X_{4i}) + u_i = \beta_1 + \beta_2 Z_i + u_i$$

where $Z_i = X_{2i} + 0.75X_{3i} + 0.625X_{4i}$.

(a) Fit the modified model to the following data and obtain estimates of β_1 to β_4.

(b) How would you interpret the variable Z?

Year	Y	X_2	X_3	X_4	Year	Y	X_2	X_3	X_4
1936	62.8	43.41	17.10	3.96	1946	95.7	76.73	28.26	9.76
1937	65.0	46.44	18.65	5.48	1947	98.3	75.91	27.91	9.31
1938	63.9	44.35	17.09	4.37	1948	100.3	77.62	32.30	9.85
1939	67.5	47.82	19.28	4.51	1949	103.2	78.01	31.39	7.21
1940	71.3	51.02	23.24	4.88	1950	108.9	83.57	35.61	7.39
1941	76.6	58.71	28.11	6.37	1951	108.5	90.59	37.58	7.98
1945†	86.3	87.69	30.29	8.96	1952	111.4	95.47	35.17	7.42

Source: L. R. Klein and A. S. Goldberger, *An Economic Model of the United States, 1929–1952,* North Holland Publishing Company, Amsterdam, 1964, p. 131.

† The data for the war years 1942–1944 are missing. The data for other years are billions of 1939 dollars.

[17] See if your reasoning agrees with that of Arthur S. Goldberg and D. B. Jochems, "Note on Stepwise Least-Squares," *Journal of the American Statistical Association,* pp. 105–110, March 1961.

* Optional.

9.19 (a) Show that if $r_{1i} = 0$ for $i = 2, 3, \ldots, k$, then

$$R_{1.23 \cdots k} = 0$$

(b) What is the importance of this finding for the regression of variable $X_1 (= Y)$ on $X_2, X_3, \ldots,$ X_k?

9.20 Suppose all the zero-order correlation coefficients of $X_1 (= Y)$, $X_2, \ldots, X_k$ are equal to r.
   (a) What is the value of $R^2_{1.23 \cdots k}$?
   (b) What are the values of the first-order correlation coefficients?

TEN

HETEROSCEDASTICITY

An important assumption of the classical linear regression model is that the disturbances u_i appearing in the population regression function are homoscedastic; that is, they all have the same variance. In this chapter we examine the validity of this asumption and find out what happens if this assumption is not fulfilled. As in Chap. 9, we seek answers to the following questions:

1. What is the nature of heteroscedasticity?
2. What are its consequences?
3. How does one detect it?
4. What are the remedial measures?

10.1 THE NATURE OF HETEROSCEDASTICITY

As noted in Chap. 3, one of the important assumptions of the classical linear regression model is that the variance of each disturbance term u_i, conditional on the chosen values of the explanatory variables, is some constant number equal to σ^2. This is the assumption of *homoscedasticity*, or *equal* (homo) *spread* (scedasticity), that is, *equal variance*. Symbolically,

$$E(u_i^2) = \sigma^2 \qquad i = 1, 2, \ldots, N \qquad (10.1.1)$$

Diagrammatically, in the two-variable regression model homoscedascity can be shown as in Fig. 3.3, which, for convenience, is reproduced as Fig. 10.1. As Fig. 10.1 shows, the conditional variance of Y_i (which is equal to that of u_i),

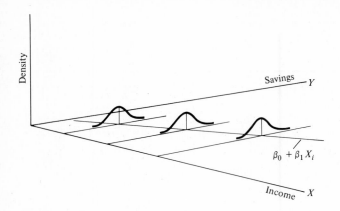

Figure 10.1 Homoscedastic disturbances.

conditional upon the given X_i, remains the same regardless of the values taken by the variable X.

In contrast, consider Fig. 10.2, which shows that the conditional variance of Y_i increases as X increases. Here, the variances of Y_i are not the same. Hence there is heteroscedasticity. Symbolically,

$$E(u_i^2) = \sigma_i^2 \tag{10.1.2}$$

Notice the subscript on σ^2, which reminds us that the conditional variances of u_i ($=$ conditional variance of Y_i) are no longer constant.

To make the difference between homoscedasticity and heteroscedasticity clear, assume that in the two-variable model $Y_i = \beta_0 + \beta_1 X_i + u_i$, Y represents savings and X represents income. Figures 10.1 and 10.2 show that as income increases, savings on the average also increase. But in Fig. 10.1 the variance of

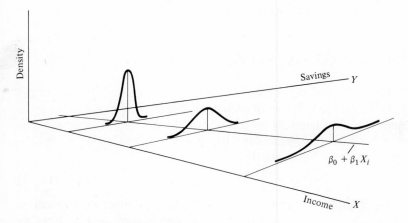

Figure 10.2 Heteroscedastic disturbances.

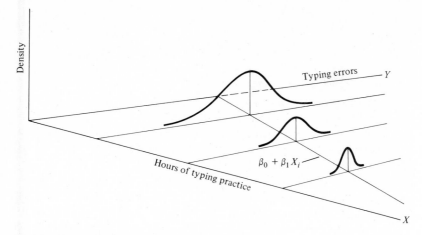

Figure 10.3 Illustration of heteroscedasticity.

savings remain the same at all levels of income, whereas in Fig. 10.2 it increases with income. It seems that in Fig. 10.2 the higher-income families on the average save more than the lower-income families, but there is also more variability in their savings.

There are several reasons why the variances of u_i may be variable, some of which are as follows.[1]

1. Following the *error-learning models*, as people learn, their errors of behavior become smaller over time. In this case, σ_i^2 is expected to decrease. As an example, consider Fig. 10.3, which relates the number of typing errors made in a given time period on a test to the hours put in typing practice. As Fig. 10.3 shows, as the number of hours of typing practice increases, the average number of typing errors as well as their variances decreases.

2. As incomes grow, people have more *discretionary income*[2] and hence more scope for choice about the disposition of their income. Hence σ_i^2 is likely to increase with income. Thus in the regression of savings on income one is likely to find σ_i^2 increasing with income (as in Fig. 10.2) because people have more choices about their savings behavior. Similarly, companies with larger profits are generally expected to show greater variability in their dividend policies than companies with lower profits. Also, *growth-oriented* companies are likely to show more variability in their dividend payout ratio than established companies.

3. As data collecting techniques improve, σ_i^2 is likely to decrease. Thus, banks which have sophisticated data processing equipment are likely to commit fewer errors in the monthly or quarterly statements of their customers than banks without such facilities.

---

[1] See Stefan Valavanis, *Econometrics*, McGraw-Hill Book Company, New York, 1959, p. 48.

[2] As Valavanis puts it, "Income grows, and people now barely discern dollars whereas previously they discerned dimes," *ibid.*, p. 48.

It should be noted that the problem of heteroscedasticity is likely to be more common in cross-sectional than time-series data. In cross-sectional data, one usually deals with members of a population at a given point in time, such as individual consumers or their families, firms, industries, or geographical subdivision, such as state, county, or city, etc. Moreover, these members may be of different sizes, such as small, medium, or large firms or low, medium, or high income. In time-series data, on the other hand, the variables tend to be of similar orders of magnitude because one generally collects the data for the same entity over a period of time. Examples are GNP, consumption expenditure, savings, or employment in the United States, say, for the period 1950 to 1975.

As an illustration of heteroscedasticity likely to be encountered in cross-sectional analysis, consider Table 10.1. This table gives data on compensation per employee in 10 nondurable goods manufacturing industries classified by the employment size of the firm or the establishment for the year 1958. Also given in the table are average productivity figures for the nine employment classes.

Although the industries differ in their output composition, Table 10.1 shows clearly that on the average large firms pay more than the small firms. As an example, firms employing one to four employees paid on the average about $3396,

Table 10.1 Compensation per employee ($) in nondurable manufacturing industries according to employment size of establishment

Industry	Employment size (average no. of employees)								
	1–4	5–9	10–19	20–49	50–99	100–249	250–499	500–999	1000–2499
Food and kindred products	2994	3295	3565	3907	4189	4486	4676	4968	5342
Tobacco products	1721	2057	3336	3320	2980	2848	3072	2969	3822
Textile mill products	3600	3657	3674	3437	3340	3334	3225	3163	3168
Apparel and related products	3494	3787	3533	3215	3030	2834	2750	2967	3453
Paper and allied products	3498	3847	3913	4135	4445	4885	5132	5342	5326
Printing and publishing	3611	4206	4695	5083	5301	5269	5182	5395	5552
Chemicals and allied products	3875	4660	4930	5005	5114	5248	5630	5870	5876
Petroleum and coal products	4616	5181	5317	5337	5421	5710	6316	6455	6347
Rubber and plastic products	3538	3984	4014	4287	4221	4539	4721	4905	5481
Leather and leather products	3016	3196	3149	3317	3414	3254	3177	3346	4067
Average compensation	3396	3787	4013	4104	4146	4241	4387	4538	4843
Standard deviation	743.7	851.4	727.8	746.3	929.9	1080.6	1243.2	1307.7	1112.5
Average productivity	9355	8584	7962	8275	8389	9418	9795	10281	11750

Source: *The Census of Manufactures,* U.S. Department of Commerce, 1958 (computed).

whereas those employing 1000 to 2499 on the average paid about \$4843. But note that the standard deviation of compensation also generally increases with the employment size of the establishment, suggesting that the higher the average pay, the higher its variability.

Suppose we want to run the regression

$$\text{Average compensation}_i = \beta_0 + \beta_1 \text{ average productivity}_i + u_i$$

where i refers to the ith employment-size class. If we were to run the preceding regression using the data given in Table 10.1, we would most likely encounter heteroscedasticity. Of course, we would have to find out whether the standard deviations of compensation presented in Table 10.1 are statistically significantly different. We shall take up this question in Sec. 10.4, where we shall also examine some of the estimating techniques which take into account heteroscedasticity.

10.2 CONSEQUENCES OF HETEROSCEDASTICITY

Recall that if all the assumptions of the classical linear regression model are fulfilled, the OLS estimators are BLUE; that is, in the class of all linear unbiased estimators they have the minimum variance. In short, they are efficient. Now if we keep all but the homoscedasticity assumption, it can be shown that *the OLS estimators are still unbiased and consistent but they are no longer efficient in small as well as large samples* (*i.e., asymptotically*). In other words, in repeated sampling the OLS estimators on the average are equal to their true population values (the unbiasedness property), and as the sample size increases indefinitely they converge to their true values (the consistency property) but their variances are no longer minimum even if the sample size increases indefinitely (the asymptotic efficiency property).

To fix the ideas, let us revert to the two-variable model:

$$Y_i = \beta_0 + \beta_1 X_i + u_i$$

Now letting $E(u_i^2) = \sigma_i^2$ but retaining all other OLS assumptions, it can be shown that the method of *weighted least squares* (see Sec. 10.4) gives the BLUE of β_1, say, β_1^*, which is as follows:

$$\beta_1^* = \frac{(\sum w_i)(\sum w_i X_i Y_i) - (\sum w_i X_i)(\sum w_i Y_i)}{(\sum w_i)(\sum w_i X_i^2) - (\sum w_i X_i)^2} \tag{10.2.1}$$

and its variance is given by

$$\text{var}(\beta_1^*) = \frac{\sum w_i}{(\sum w_i)(\sum w_i X_i^2) - (\sum w_i X_i)^2} \tag{10.2.2}$$

where

$$w_i = \frac{1}{\sigma_i^2} \tag{10.2.3}$$

The estimator β_1^* is known as the *weighted least-squares estimator* for reasons stated in Sec. 10.4.

On the other hand, the usual OLS estimator of β_1 is

$$\hat{\beta}_1 = \frac{\sum x_i y_i}{\sum x_i^2} \tag{10.2.4}$$

and under heteroscedasticity its variance can be shown to be (see Exercise 10.1)

$$\text{var}\,(\hat{\beta}_1) = \frac{\sum x_i^2 \sigma_i^2}{(\sum x_i^2)^2} \tag{10.2.5}$$

Now from App. 3A, Sec. 3A.2, it is easy to verify that $\hat{\beta}_1$ is still unbiased; as a matter of fact, the unbiasedness property does not require that the disturbances u_i be homoscedastic. But the variance of $\hat{\beta}_1$ given in (10.2.5) is different from (actually greater than) the variance of β_1^* given in (10.2.2), and we stated previously that β_1^* is BLUE. The gist of our analysis, then, is that $\hat{\beta}_1$, although unbiased, is inefficient; its variance is larger than necessary (i.e., larger than the variance of β_1^*).

In practice it may happen that we do not know whether heteroscedasticity exists in a given situation. Therefore, we may mistakenly use the usual OLS formulas derived under the assumption of homoscedasticity even though the true situation may be one of heteroscedasticity. What are the consequences of this action? To answer this question, let us continue with our two-variable model. As before, the OLS estimator of $\hat{\beta}_1$ is given by (10.2.4), and because of the homoscedasticity assumption its variance is given by the usual formula, namely,

$$\text{var}\,(\hat{\beta}_1) = \frac{\sigma^2}{\sum x_i^2} \tag{10.2.6}$$

Now if heteroscedasticity is present, we should use (10.2.5) even if the variance thus obtained is inefficient.[3] To see the consequences of using (10.2.6) instead of (10.2.5), let us posit that

$$\sigma_i^2 = \sigma^2 k_i \tag{10.2.7}$$

where k_i are some constant (nonstochastic) weights, not necessarily all equal.[4] Equation (10.2.7) states that the heteroscedastic variances are proportional to k_i, σ^2 being the factor of proportionality. (*Note:* Unlike σ_i^2, σ^2 is a constant.)

---

[3] The reason for this is that under heteroscedasticity the usual OLS estimator of σ^2, namely, $\hat{\sigma}^2$, is no longer unbiased. As a result the usual estimating formula var $(\hat{\beta}_1) = \hat{\sigma}^2/\sum x_i^2$ is biased. As a matter of fact, it can be shown that

$$E\,\frac{\hat{\sigma}^2}{\sum x_i^2} = \frac{-N(\sum x_i^2 \sigma_i^2) + (N-1)(\sum x_i^2)(\sum \sigma_i^2)}{N(N-2)(\sum x_i^2)^2}$$

which is obviously different from (10.2.5). For proof, see J. Kmenta, *Elements of Econometrics*, The Macmillan Company, New York, 1971, pp. 250–254.

[4] As we shall see in Sec. 10.4, these weights might be some known functions of the explanatory variable(s), the X's.

Substituting (10.2.7) into (10.2.5), we obtain

$$\text{var } (\hat{\beta}_1) = \frac{\sigma^2 \sum x_i^2 k_i}{(\sum x_i^2)^2}$$

$$= \frac{\sigma^2 \sum x_i^2 k_i}{(\sum x_i^2)(\sum x_i^2)}$$

$$= \text{var } (\hat{\beta}_1^{\text{OLS}}) \frac{(\sum x_i^2 k_i)}{(\sum x_i^2)} \tag{10.2.8}$$

where var $(\hat{\beta}_1^{\text{OLS}})$ is the variance of $\hat{\beta}_1$ under the assumption of homoscedasticity, as given by (10.2.6).

It is clear from (10.2.8) that if x_i^2 and k_i are, say, positively correlated, which may very well be true of most economic data, and if $(\sum x_i^2 k_i)/(\sum x_i^2)$ is greater than 1, the variance of $\hat{\beta}_1$ under heteroscedasticity will be larger than its variance under homoscedasticity. Thus, in this situation the usual OLS formula (10.2.6) will underestimate the true variance of $\hat{\beta}_1$ given by (10.2.5), which is inefficient to begin with. As a result, we shall be underestimating the true standard error of $\hat{\beta}_1$. Therefore, we shall overestimate the t value associated with the estimated $\hat{\beta}_1$ [recall that under the null hypothesis $\beta_1 = 0$, $t = \hat{\beta}_1/\text{se}(\hat{\beta}_1)$], which might lead to the conclusion that in the specific case at hand $\hat{\beta}_1$ is statistically significant. Of course, if the true variance given by (10.2.5) were known, the "correct" t value may show that $\hat{\beta}_1$ is, in fact, statistically insignificant. Hence, heteroscedasticity is potentially a very troublesome problem.

The upshot of the preceding discussion is as follows:

1. When heteroscedasticity is present or suspected, *in theory* the BLUE of β_1 is the weighted least-squares estimator β_1^*, not the conventional estimator $\hat{\beta}_1$, although the latter is unbiased.

2. The variance of $\hat{\beta}_1$ derived under the assumption of heteroscedasticity and given by (10.2.5) is no longer minimum; it is the variance of β_1^* given in (10.2.2) which is minimum.

3. In view 2, if we use the variance formula given in (10.2.5) instead of (10.2.2), the confidence interval for β_1 is unnecessarily wide and the tests of significance are less powerful.

4. The situation becomes worse if in heteroscedastic situations instead of using (10.2.5), which is inefficient as is, we use the usual OLS formula (10.2.6) to estimate the variance of $\hat{\beta}_1$. As noted previously, (10.2.6) is a biased estimator of (10.2.5), the bias stemming from the fact that the conventional estimator of σ^2, $\hat{\sigma}^2$, is no longer unbiased. The nature of the bias depends on the relationship between σ_i^2 and the values taken by the explanatory variable(s).

5. As a consequence of 4, in heteroscedastic situations if we mistakenly continue to apply the traditional OLS formulas (derived under the assumption of homoscedasticity), we are likely to draw totally misleading conclusions because the usual t and F tests are very much likely to exaggerate the statistical significance of the conventionally estimated parameters. Therefore, in cases of heteroscedasticity

the conventional OLS estimator (10.2.6) is inappropriate. We should at least use (10.2.5) even though the variance thus obtained is not minimum. Ideally, of course, we should use (10.2.2), replacing $\hat{\beta}_1$ by β_1^*.

Although in specific cases and under specific hypotheses about the form of σ_i^2 one can find out the nature of the bias involved in erroneously applying the usual homoscedastic variance and standard error formulas of the OLS estimators, in general, it is not possible to detect the bias so readily. This is because the nature of the bias in the estimated variances depends on the nature of heteroscedasticity itself (i.e., the form of σ_i^2) as well as the nature of the particular X values appearing in the sample at hand (this can be readily seen from the equation given in fn. 3).[5] In practice one rarely knows what the true σ_i^2 is. Hence, despite its theoretical superiority, the weighted least-squares estimator β_1^* cannot be easily obtained. In practice, one usually makes some ad hoc assumptions about σ_i^2 to deal with the problem of heteroscedasticity. Equation (10.2.7) represents one such assumption, and we shall come across some others in Sec. 10.4.

10.3 DETECTION OF HETEROSCEDASTICITY

As with multicollinearity, the important practical question is: How does one know that heteroscedasticity is present in a specific situation? Again, as in the case of multicollinearity, there are no hard and fast rules for detecting heteroscedasticity, only a few rules of thumb. But this is inevitable because σ_i^2 can be known only if we have the entire Y population corresponding to the chosen X's, such as the population shown in Table 2.1 or Table 10.1. But such data are an exception rather than the rule in most economic investigations. In this respect the econometrician differs from scientists in fields such as agriculture and biology where they have a good deal of control over their subjects. More often than not, in economic studies there is only one sample Y value corresponding to a particular value of X. And there is no way one can know σ_i^2 from just one Y observation. Therefore, in most cases involving econometric investigations, heteroscedasticity may be a matter of "speculation" or, as one author puts it, "ad-hockery." (The term is due to Professor Zvi Griliches.)

With the preceding caveat in mind, let us examine some of the informal and "formal" methods of detecting heteroscedasticity.

1. *Nature of the problem.* Very often the nature of the problem under consideration suggests whether heteroscedasticity is likely to be encountered. For example, following the pioneering work of Prais and Houthakker on family budget studies, where they found that the residual variance around the regression of consumption on income increased with income, it is now generally assumed

---

[5] For an excellent but rather advanced discussion, see Stephen M. Goldfeld and Richard E. Quandt, *Nonlinear Methods in Econometrics*, North-Holland Publishing Company, Amsterdam, 1972, chap. 3.

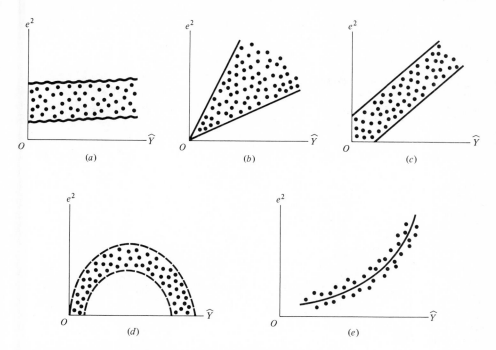

Figure 10.4 Hypothetical patterns of estimated squared residuals.

that in similar surveys one can expect unequal variances among the disturbances.[6] As a matter of fact, in cross-sectional data involving heterogeneous units, hetero-scedasticity may be the rule rather than the exception. Thus, in a cross-sectional analysis involving the investment expenditure in relation to sales, rate of interest, etc., heteroscedasticity is generally expected if small-, medium-, and large-size firms are sampled together.

2. *Graphical method.* If there is no a priori or empirical information about the nature of heteroscedasticity, in practice one can do the regression analysis on the assumption that there is no heteroscedasticity and then do a post mortem examin-ation of the estimated residual squared e_i^2 to see if they exhibit any systematic pattern. Although e_i^2 are not the same thing as u_i^2, they can be used as proxies especially if the sample size is sufficiently large.[7] An examination of the RSS may reveal patterns such as those shown in Fig. 10.4.

In Fig. 10.4, e_i^2 are plotted against $\hat{Y}_i$, the estimated Y_i from the regression line, the idea being to find out whether the estimated mean value of Y is systema-tically related to the squared residual. In Fig. 10.4a we see that there is no

[6] S. J. Prais and H. S. Houthakker, *The Analysis of Family Budgets*, The Cambridge University Press, New York, 1955.

[7] For the relationship between e_i and u_i, see E. Malinvaud, *Statistical Methods of Econometrics*, North-Holland Publishing Company, Amsterdam, 1970, pp. 88–89.

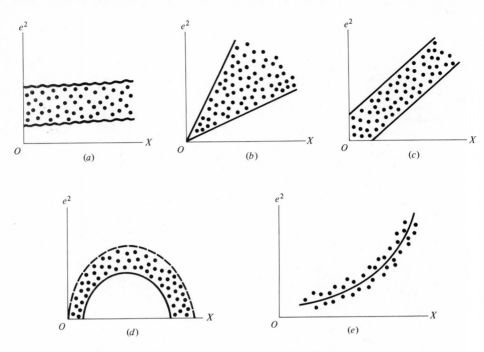

Figure 10.5 Scattergram of estimated squared residuals against X.

systematic pattern between the two variables, suggesting that perhaps no hetero-scedasticity is present in the data. Figure 10.4b to e, however, exhibits definite patterns. For instance, Fig. 10.4c suggests a linear relationship whereas Fig. 10.4d and e indicate a quadratic relationship between e_i^2 and $\hat{Y}_i$. Using such knowledge, albeit informal, one may transform the data in such a manner that the transformed data do not exhibit heteroscedasticity. In Sec. 10.4 we shall examine several such transformations.

Instead of plotting e_i^2 against $\hat{Y}_i$, one may plot them against one of the explanatory variables especially if plotting e_i^2 against $\hat{Y}_i$ results in the pattern shown in Fig. 10.4a. Such a plot, which is shown in Fig. 10.5, may reveal patterns similar to those given in Fig. 10.4. (In the case of the two-variable model, plotting e_i^2 against $\hat{Y}_i$ is equivalent to plotting it against X_i, and therefore Fig. 10.5 is similar to Fig. 10.4. But this is not the situation when we consider a model involving two or more X variables; in this instance, e_i^2 may be plotted against any X variable included in the model.)

A pattern such as that shown in Fig. 10.5c, for instance, suggests that the variance of the disturbance term is linearly related to the X variable. Thus, if in the regression of savings on income, one finds a pattern such as that shown in Fig. 10.5c, it suggests that the heteroscedastic variance may be *proportional* to the value of the income variable. This knowledge may help us in transforming our data in such a manner that in the regression on the transformed data the variance of the disturbance is homoscedastic. We shall return to this topic in the next section.

3. *Park test.*[8] Park formalizes the graphical method by suggesting that σ_i^2 is some function of the explanatory variable X_i. The functional form he suggested was

$$\sigma_i^2 = \sigma^2 X_i^\beta e^{v_i}$$

or
$$\ln \sigma_i^2 = \ln \sigma^2 + \beta \ln X_i + v_i \qquad (10.3.1)$$

where v_i is the stochastic disturbance term.

Since σ_i^2 is generally not known, Park suggests using e_i^2 as a proxy and running the following regression:

$$\ln e_i^2 = \ln \sigma^2 + \beta \ln X_i + v_i$$

$$= \alpha + \beta \ln X_i + v_i \qquad (10.3.2)$$

If β turns out to be statistically significant, it would suggest that heteroscedasticity is present in the data. If it turns out to be insignificant, we may accept the assumption of homoscedasticity. The Park test is thus a two-stage procedure. In the first stage we run the OLS regression disregarding the heteroscedasticity question. We obtain e_i from this regression, and then in the second stage we run the regression (10.3.2).

Although empirically appealing, the Park test has some problems. Goldfeld and Quandt have argued that the error term v_i entering into (10.3.2) may not satisfy the OLS assumptions and may itself be heteroscedastic.[9] Nonetheless, as a strictly suggestive method, one may use the Park test.

To illustrate the Park approach, we use the data given in Table 10.1 to run the following regression:

$$Y_i = \beta_0 + \beta_1 X_i + u_i$$

where Y = average compensation in thousands of dollars, X = average productivity in thousands of dollars and i = ith employment size of the establishment. The results of the regression were as follows:

$$\hat{Y}_i = 1999.0466 + 0.2323 X_i$$

$$(0.1000) \qquad\qquad\qquad (10.3.3)$$

$$t = (2.323) \qquad R^2 = 0.4356$$

The results reveal that the estimated slope coefficient is significant at the 5 percent level on the basis of a one-tail t test. The equation shows that as labor

[8] R. E. Park, "Estimation with Heteroscedastic Error Terms," *Econometrica*, vol. 34, no. 4, p. 888, October 1966.

[9] Goldfeld and Quandt, *op. cit.*, pp. 93–94.

productivity increases by, say, a dollar, labor compensation on the average increases by about 23 cents.

The residuals obtained from regression (10.3.3) were regressed on X_i as suggested in equation (10.3.2), giving the following results:

$$\ln e_i^2 = 35.9010 - 2.8099 \ln X_i$$

$$(4.216) \tag{10.3.4}$$

$$t = (-0.667) \qquad R^2 = 0.0595$$

Obviously, there is no statistically significant relationship between the two variables. Following the Park test, one may conclude that there is no heteroscedasticity in the error variance.[10]

4. *Glejser test.*[11] The Glejser test is similar in spirit to the Park test. After obtaining the residuals e_i from the OLS regression, Glejser suggests regressing the absolute values of e_i, $|e_i|$, on the X variable that is thought to be closely associated with σ_i^2. In his experiments, Glejser used the following functional forms:

$$|e_i| = \beta_1 X_i + v_i$$

$$|e_i| = \beta_1 \sqrt{X_i} + v_i$$

$$|e_i| = \beta_1 \frac{1}{X_i} + v_i$$

$$|e_i| = \beta_1 \frac{1}{\sqrt{X_i}} + v_i$$

$$|e_i| = \beta_0 + \beta_1 X_i + v_i$$

$$|e_i| = \sqrt{\beta_0 + \beta_1 X_i} + v_i$$

$$|e_i| = \sqrt{\beta_0 + \beta_1 X_i^2} + v_i$$

where v_i is the error term.

Again as an empirical or practical matter, one may use the Glejser approach. But Goldfeld and Quandt point out that the error term v_i has some problems in that its expected value is nonzero, it is serially correlated (see Chap. 11), and ironically it is heteroscedastic.[12] An additional difficulty with the Glejser method is that models such as

$$|e_i| = \sqrt{\beta_0 + \beta_1 X_i} + v_i \qquad \text{and} \qquad |e_i| = \sqrt{\beta_0 + \beta_1 X_i^2}$$

are nonlinear in the parameters and therefore cannot be estimated with the usual OLS procedure.

---

[10] The particular functional form chosen by Park is only suggestive. A different functional form may reveal significant relationship. For example, one may use e_i^2 instead of $\ln e_i^2$ as the dependent variable.

[11] H. Glejser, "A New Test for Heteroscedasticity," *Journal of the American Statistical Association,* vol. 64, pp. 316–323, 1969.

[12] For details, see Goldfeld and Quandt, *op. cit.,* chap. 3.

Glejser has found that for large samples the first four of the preceding models give generally satisfactory results in detecting heteroscedasticity. As a practical matter, therefore, the Glejser technique may be used for large samples and may be used in the small samples strictly as a qualitative device to learn something about heteroscedasticity.

5. *Spearman's rank correlation test.* In Exercise 3.5 we defined the Spearman's rank correlation coefficient as

$$r_s = 1 - 6 \left[\frac{\sum d_i^2}{N(N^2 - 1)} \right] \tag{10.3.5}$$

where d_i = difference in the ranks assigned to two different characteristics of the *i*th individual or phenomenon and N = number of individuals or phenomena ranked. The preceding rank correlation coefficient can be used to detect heteroscedasticity as follows: Assume $Y_i = \beta_0 + \beta_1 X_i + u_i$.

Step I Fit the regression to the data on Y and X and obtain the residuals e_i.

Step II Ignoring the sign of e_i, that is, taking their absolute value $|e_i|$, rank both $|e_i|$ and X_i according to an ascending or descending order and compute the Spearman's rank correlation coefficient given previously.

Step III Assuming that the population rank correlation coefficient ρ_s to be zero and $N > 8$, the significance of the sample r_s can be tested by the t test as follows:[13]

$$t = \frac{r_s \sqrt{N - 2}}{\sqrt{1 - r_s^2}} \tag{10.3.6}$$

with df $= N - 2$.

If the computed t value exceeds the critical t value, we may accept the hypothesis of heteroscedasticity; otherwise we may reject it. If the regression model involves more than one X variable, r_s can be computed between $|e_i|$ and each of the X variables separately and can be tested for statistical significance by the t test given above.

As an illustration, refer to Exercise 5.7, which requires the estimation of the capital market line of the portfolio theory. Since the data related to 10 mutual funds of differing sizes and investment goals, a priori one might expect heteroscedasticity. To test this hypothesis, we apply the rank correlation technique. Table 10.2 gives the necessary data required in the analysis.

Applying formula (10.3.5), we obtain

$$r_s = 1 - 6 \frac{126.5}{10(100 - 1)}$$

$$= 0.2333 \tag{10.3.7}$$

---

[13] See G. Udny Yule and M. G. Kendall, *An Introduction to the Theory of Statistics*, Charles Griffin & Company, Ltd., London, 1953, p. 455.

Table 10.2 Illustration of rank correlation method

X, Standard deviation of annual returns	$\|e_i\|$, Absolute value of residual	Rank of X	Rank of $\|e_i\|$	d	d^2
12.4	1.017	5	9	−4	16
14.4	1.260	7	10	−3	9
14.6	0.181	8	4	4	16
16.0	0.202	9	5	4	16
11.3	0.221	3.5	6	−2.5	6.25
10.0	0.602	1	7	−6	36
16.2	0.908	10	8	2	4
10.4	0.110	2	3	−1	1
13.1	0.077	6	2	4	16
11.3	0.038	3.5	1	2.5	6.25
				0	126.5

Notes: (a) The values of X and $\|e\|$ are ranked in ascending order. (b) Since two of X values are identical, their rank is tied.

Source: Exercise 5.7.

Applying the t test given in (10.3.6), we obtain

$$t = \frac{(0.2333)(\sqrt{8})}{\sqrt{1 - 0.0544}}$$

$$= 0.6786 \tag{10.3.8}$$

For 8 df this t value is not significant even at the 10 percent level of significance. Thus, there is no evidence of systematic relationship between the explanatory variable and the absolute values of the residuals, which might suggest that there is no heteroscedasticity.

In addition to the tests discussed previously, one may use Bartlett's homogeneity-of-variance test. But this test requires that we have data of the type given in Table 10.1, which provides us with several estimates of the variance of the phenomenon under consideration. The actual mechanics of the test are slightly involved and are presented in Exercise 10.2.

10.4 REMEDIAL MEASURES

As we have seen, heteroscedasticity does not destroy the unbiasedness and consistency properties of the OLS estimators, but they are no longer efficient, not even asymptotically (i.e., large sample size). This lack of efficiency makes the usual hypothesis-testing procedure of dubious value. Therefore, remedial measures are clearly called for. There are two approaches to remediation: when σ_i^2 is known and when σ_i^2 is not known.

When σ_i^2 Is Known: The Method of Weighted Least Squares

When σ_i^2 is known or can be estimated, the most straightforward method of dealing with heteroscedasticity is by means of the *weighted least squares*. To illustrate this method, consider the two variable model

$$\text{PRF}: Y_i = \beta_0 + \beta_1 X_i + u_i$$

$$\text{SRF}: Y_i = \hat{\beta}_0 + \hat{\beta}_1 X_i + e_i$$

The usual or unweighted least-squares method consists in minimizing RSS: $\sum e_i^2 = \sum (Y_i - \hat{\beta}_0 - \hat{\beta}_1 X_i)^2$ with respect to the unknowns. In minimizing this RSS, the unweighted least-squares method gives implicitly the same weight to each e_i^2. Thus, in the hypothetical scattergram of Fig. 10.6, points A, B, and C all have the same weight in computing $\sum e_i^2$. Obviously, in this case the e_i^2 associated with point C will dominate the RSS.

The method of weighted least squares does take into account the extreme points, such as C in Fig. 10.6, by minimizing, not the usual or unweighted RSS, but the following RSS:

$$\min: \sum e_i^2 = \sum w_i (Y_i - \beta_0^* - \beta_1^* X_i)^2 \tag{10.4.1}$$

where w_i, the weights, are some constant (nonstochastic) numbers and where β_0^* and β_1^* are weighted least-squares estimators. The w_i are chosen in such a manner

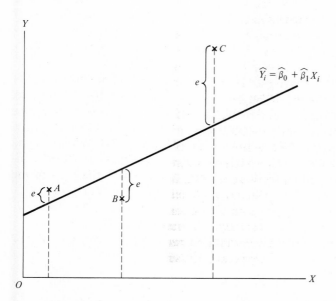

Figure 10.6 Hypothetical scattergram.

that the extreme observations (for example, C in Fig. 10.6) receive smaller weights. If σ_i^2 is known, one can let

$$w_i = \frac{1}{\sigma_i^2} \tag{10.4.2}$$

that is, weight each observation inversely proportional to σ_i^2. This scheme of weighting will "discount" heavily observations which come from populations with larger variances, such as point C in Fig. 10.6.

The mechanics of minimizing (10.4.1) follows the usual calculus techniques and is given in App. 10A, Sec. 10A.1. The results of the minimization procedure are as follows:

$$\beta_0^* = \frac{\sum w_i Y_i}{\sum w_i} - \beta_1^* \frac{\sum w_i X_i}{\sum w_i}$$

$$= \bar{Y}^* - \beta_1^* \bar{X}^* \tag{10.4.3}$$

where $\bar{Y}^*$ and $\bar{X}^*$ are weighted sample means with w_i serving as the weights and

$$\beta_1^* = \frac{\sum w_i y_i^* x_i^*}{\sum w_i x_i^{*2}} \tag{10.4.4}$$

where $y_i^* = Y_i - \bar{Y}^*$ and $x_i^* = X_i - \bar{X}^*$ represent deviations from the weighted sample means. In Exercise 10.12 the reader is asked to show that β_1^* given in (10.4.4) is precisely the weighted least-squares estimator given in (10.2.1). It is left as an exercise for the reader to show that the variance of β_1^* is as shown in (10.2.2). Notice at once that if $w_1 = w_2 = w_3 = \cdots = w_N$, that is, each observation has the same weight, the weighted least-squares estimators given previously coincide with the usual or unweighted least-squares estimators.

When σ_i^2 Is Not Known

In econometric studies prior knowledge of σ_i^2 is a rarity. As a result, the method of weighted least squares discussed previously cannot be used readily. In practice, therefore, one may resort to some ad hoc, albeit reasonably plausible, assumptions about σ_i^2 and transform the original regression model in such a way that the transformed model will satisfy the assumption of homoscedasticity. Without some such transformation, the problem of heteroscedasticity becomes practically insoluble. We now illustrate some of these transformations with the help of the two-variable model

$$Y_i = \beta_0 + \beta_1 X_i + u_i$$

Several possible assumptions about the pattern of heteroscedasticity are now considered.

Assumption 1

$$E(u_i^2) = \sigma^2 X_i^2 \tag{10.4.5}$$

If as a matter of "speculation," graphical methods, or Park and Glejser approaches it is believed that the variance of u_i is proportional to the square of the explanatory variable X, one may transform the original model as follows. Divide the original model through by X_i:

$$\frac{Y_i}{X_i} = \frac{\beta_0}{X_i} + \beta_1 + \frac{u_i}{X_i}$$

$$= \beta_0 \frac{1}{X_i} + \beta_1 + v_i \tag{10.4.6}$$

where v_i is the transformed disturbance term and is equal to u_i/X_i. Now it is easy to verify that

$$E(v_i^2) = E\left(\frac{u_i}{X_i}\right)^2 = \frac{1}{X_i^2} E(u_i^2)$$

$$= \sigma^2 \quad \text{using (10.4.5)}$$

Hence the variance of v_i is now homoscedastic, and one may proceed to apply OLS to the transformed equation (10.4.6), regressing Y_i/X_i on $1/X_i$.

Notice that in the transformed regression, the intercept term β_1 is the slope coefficient in the original equation and the slope coefficient β_0 is the intercept term in the original model. Therefore, to get back to the original model we shall have to multiply the estimated (10.4.6) by X_i. An application of this transformation is given in Exercise 10.10.

Assumption 2

$$E(u_i^2) = \sigma^2 X_i \tag{10.4.7}$$

If it is believed that the variance of u_i instead of being proportional to the squared X_i is proportional to X_i itself, then the original model can be transformed as follows:

$$\frac{Y_i}{\sqrt{X_i}} = \frac{\beta_0}{\sqrt{X_i}} + \beta_1 \sqrt{X_i} + \frac{u_i}{\sqrt{X_i}}$$

$$= \beta_0 \frac{1}{\sqrt{X_i}} + \beta_1 \sqrt{X_i} + v_i \tag{10.4.8}$$

where $v_i = u_i/\sqrt{X_i}$ and where $X_i > 0$.

Given Assumption 2, it can be readily verified that $E(v_i^2) = \sigma^2$, a homoscedastic situation. Therefore, one may proceed to apply OLS to (10.4.8), regressing $Y_i/\sqrt{X_i}$ on $1/\sqrt{X_i}$ and $\sqrt{X_i}$.

Note an important feature of the transformed model: It has no intercept term. Therefore, one will have to use the "regression through the origin" model to estimate β_0 and β_1 (see Exercise 3.11 for a description of this model). Having run (10.4.8), one can get back to the original model simply by multiplying (10.4.8) by $\sqrt{X_i}$.

Assumption 3

$$E(u_i^2) = \sigma^2 [E(Y_i)]^2 \tag{10.4.9}$$

Equation (10.4.9) postulates that the variance of u_i is proportional to the square of the expected value of Y (see Fig. 10.4e). Now

$$E(Y_i) = \beta_0 + \beta_1 X_i$$

Therefore, if we transform the original equation as follows:

$$\frac{Y_i}{E(Y_i)} = \frac{\beta_0}{E(Y_i)} + \beta_1 \frac{X_i}{E(Y_i)} + \frac{u_i}{E(Y_i)}$$

$$= \beta_0 \left(\frac{1}{E(Y_i)}\right) + \beta_1 \frac{X_i}{E(Y_i)} + v_i \tag{10.4.10}$$

where $v_i = u_i/E(Y_i)$, it can be seen that $E(v_i^2) = \sigma^2$; that is, the disturbances v_i are homoscedastic. Hence, it is regression (10.4.10) that will satisfy the homoscedasticity assumption of the classical linear regression model.

The transformation (10.4.10) is, however, inoperational because $E(Y_i)$ depends on β_0 and β_1, which are unknown. Of course, we know $\hat{Y}_i = \hat{\beta}_0 + \hat{\beta}_1 X_i$, which is an estimate of $E(Y_i)$. Therefore, we may proceed in two steps: First we run the usual OLS regression disregarding the heteroscedasticity problem and obtain $\hat{Y}_i$. Then, using the estimated $\hat{Y}_i$, we transform our model as follows:

$$\frac{Y_i}{\hat{Y}_i} = \beta_0 \left(\frac{1}{\hat{Y}_i}\right) + \beta_1 \left(\frac{X_i}{\hat{Y}_i}\right) + v_i \tag{10.4.11}$$

where $v_i = (u_i/\hat{Y}_i)$. In step 2, we run the regression (10.4.11). Although $\hat{Y}_i$ are not exactly $E(Y_i)$, they are consistent estimators; that is, as the sample size increases indefinitely, they converge to true $E(Y_i)$. Hence, the transformation (10.4.11) will do in practice if the sample size is reasonably large.

Assumption 4 Log transformation If, instead of running the regression $Y_i = \beta_0 + \beta_1 X_i + u_i$, we run

$$\ln Y_i = \beta_0 + \beta_1 \ln X_i + u_i \tag{10.4.12}$$

very often it reduces heteroscedasticity. This is because log transformation compresses the scales in which the variables are measured, thereby reducing a tenfold difference between two values to a twofold difference. Thus, the number 80 is 10 times the number 8, but $\ln 80 \, (= 4.3820)$ is only twice as large as $\ln 8 \, (= 2.0794)$.

An additional advantage of the log transformation is that the slope coefficient β_1 measures the elasticity of Y with respect to X, that is, the percentage change in Y for a percentage change in X. For example, if Y is consumption and X is income, β_1 in (10.4.12) will measure income elasticity, whereas in the original model β_1 measures only the rate of change of mean consumption for a unit change in income. It is one reason why the log models are quite popular in empirical econometrics. (For some of the problems associated with log transformation, see Exercise 10.4.)

To conclude our discussion of the remedial measures, it should be reemphasized that all the transformations discussed previously are ad hoc; we are essentially speculating about the nature of σ_i^2. Which of the transformations discussed previously will work will depend on the nature of the problem and the severity of heteroscedasticity. There are some additional problems with the transformations we have considered. For example, when we go beyond the two-variable model we may not know a priori which of the X variables should be chosen for transforming the data[14] Then there is the problem of *spurious correlation*. This term, due to Karl Pearson, refers to the situation where correlation is found to be present between the ratios of variables even though the original variables are uncorrelated or random.[15] Thus, in the model $Y_i = \beta_0 + \beta_1 X_i + u_i$, Y and X may not be correlated; but in the transformed model $Y_i/X_i = \beta_0(1/X_i) + \beta_1 + v_i$, Y_i/X_i and $1/X_i$ are often found to be correlated. Therefore, the reader should be aware of some of the problems associated with the commonly used transformations in econometric studies.

10.5 SUMMARY AND CONCLUSIONS

A critical assumption of the classical linear regression model is that the disturbances u_i all have the same variance. If this assumption is not satisfied, we have heteroscedasticity. Heteroscedasticity does not destroy the unbiasedness and consistency properties of the usual OLS estimators. But these estimators are no longer minimum variance or efficient. In other words, they are no longer BLUE. The BLUE estimators are provided by the method of weighted least squares.

If we continue to use the usual OLS estimators in cases of heteroscedasticity, the variances of these estimators are no longer provided by the usual OLS estimators. For example, in the two-variable case, the traditional estimator of the variance of $\hat{\beta}_1$ is $\sigma^2/\sum x_i^2$, whereas under heteroscedasticity it is $\sum x_i^2 \sigma_i^2/(\sum x_i^2)^2$. Therefore, in heteroscedastic situations we should at least use the latter estimator. But note that this latter variance is no longer minimum variance; hence the confidence intervals based on it will be unnecessarily wide and the tests of significance less powerful.

---

[14] However, as a practical matter, one may plot e_i^2 against each variable and decide which X variable may be used for transforming the data (see Fig. 10.5).

[15] For example, if X_1, X_2, and X_3 are mutually uncorrelated $r_{12} = r_{13} = r_{23} = 0$ and we find that the (values of the) ratios X_1/X_3 and X_2/X_3 are correlated, then there is spurious correlation. "More generally, correlation may be described as spurious if it is induced by the method of handling the data and is not present in the original material." M. G. Kendall and W. R. Buckland, *A Dictionary of Statistical Terms*, Hafner Publishing Company, Inc., New York, 1972, p. 143.

The situation can be potentially serious if we (erroneously) disregard heteroscedasticity and use the conventional OLS estimators of the variances. Thus, in the two-variable case if we use $\sigma^2/\sum x_i^2$ instead of $\sum x_i^2 \sigma_i^2/(\sum x_i^2)^2$ (which is inefficient to begin with), the t and F tests of significance based on it will be highly misleading because in situations of heteroscedasticity the usual estimator of σ^2, $\hat{\sigma}^2$, is no longer unbiased. As a result, the variance $\sigma^2/\sum x_i^2$ is also no longer unbiased. As noted, in some situations the conventional formula $\sigma^2/\sum x_i^2$ will underestimate $\sum x_i^2 \sigma_i^2/(\sum x_i^2)^2$. Therefore, estimates may be declared statistically significant when, in fact, they are not and confidence intervals for the parameters will be narrower (giving the air of great precision) when, in fact, they are much wider. In short, if heteroscedasticity is suspected, the formula $\sigma^2/\sum x_i^2$ should not be applied.

Although it is easier to document the consequences of heteroscedasticity, it is not so easy to detect it because in econometric investigations, more often than not there is only one Y value corresponding to the given X value, making it impossible to find out σ_i^2 from that single observation. As a consequence, some roundabout and informal methods of detecting heteroscedasticity have been devised. These methods generally examine the residuals obtained from the usual least-squares procedure to see if they exhibit systematic patterns. If they do, they might suggest ways of transforming the original model under consideration in such a manner that in the transformed equation the disturbances have constant variance.

If the heteroscedastic variances σ_i^2 are known, the most straightforward method of resolving the problem is by means of the weighted least squares which minimizes the importance of extreme observations by weighting them in proportion inverse to their variances. Knowledge of σ_i^2 is generally a rarity. As a result, one usually makes some plausible assumption about the nature of σ_i^2 and transforms the data to make the disturbances in the transformed data homoscedastic. In this chapter we examined several commonly used transformations and pointed out their special features. We also noted some of the problems associated with such transformations.

EXERCISES

10.1 Establish equation (10.2.5).
   Hint: From App. 3A, Sec. 3A.2, we have

$$\text{var}(\hat{\beta}_1) = E(\sum k_i u_i)^2$$

where $k_i = x_i/\sum x_i^2$ and $E(u_i^2) = \sigma_i^2$.

10.2 *Bartlett's homogeneity-of-variance test.*[16] Suppose there are k independent sample variances s_1^2, $s_2^2, \ldots, s_k^2$ with $f_1, f_2, \ldots, f_k$ df, each from populations which are normally distributed with mean μ and variance σ_i^2. Suppose further that we want to test the null hypothesis $H_0: \sigma_1^2 = \sigma_2^2 = \cdots = \sigma_k^2 = \sigma^2$; that is, each sample variance is an estimate of the same population variance σ^2.

---

[16] The test was first given in Bartlett's "Properties of Sufficiency and Statistical Tests," *Proceedings of the Royal Society of London, A,* 160, p. 268, 1937.

If the null hypothesis is true, then

$$s^2 = \frac{\sum_{i=1}^{k} f_i s_i^2}{\sum f_i} = \frac{\sum f_i s_i^2}{f}$$

where $f = \sum_{i=1}^{k} f_i$ provides an estimate of the common (pooled) estimate of the population variance σ^2.

Bartlett has shown that the null hypothesis can be tested by the ratio A/B, which is approximately distributed as the χ^2 distribution with $k - 1$ df, where

$$A = f \ln s^2 - \sum (f_i \ln s_i^2)$$

and

$$B = 1 + \frac{1}{3(k-1)} \left[\sum \left(\frac{1}{f_i}\right) - \frac{1}{f} \right]$$

Apply the Bartlett test to the data of Table 10.1 to test the hypothesis that population variances of employee compensation are the same in each employment size of the establishment.

Hint: The df for each sample variance is 9.

10.3 (*a*) Can you estimate the parameters of the models

$$|e_i| = \sqrt{\beta_0 + \beta_1 X_i} + v_i$$
$$|e_i| = \sqrt{\beta_0 + \beta_1 X_i^2} + v_i$$

by the method of ordinary least squares? Why or why not?

(*b*) If not, can you suggest a method, informal or formal, of estimating the parameters of such models?

10.4 Although log models as shown in equation (10.4.12) often reduce heteroscedasticity, one has to pay careful attention to the properties of the disturbance term of such models. For example, the model

$$Y_i = \beta_0 X_i^{\beta_1} u_i \tag{1}$$

can be written as

$$\ln Y_i = \ln \beta_0 + \beta_1 \ln X_i + \ln u_i \tag{2}$$

(*a*) If $\ln u_i$ is to have zero expectation, what must be the distribution of u_i?
(*b*) If $E(u_i) = 1$, will $E(\ln u_i) = 0$? Why or why not?
(*c*) If $E(\ln u_i)$ is not zero, what can be done to make it zero?

10.5 The following data represent average labor productivity and standard deviation of labor productivity for the nine employment-size classes shown in Table 10.1.

Employment size (no. of employees)	Average productivity, $	Standard deviation of productivity, $
1–4	9355	2487
5–9	8584	2642
10–19	7962	3055
20–49	8275	2706
50–99	8389	3119
100–249	9418	4493
250–499	9795	4910
500–999	10,281	5893
1000–2499	11,750	5550

Source: *The Census of Manufactures*, U.S. Department of Commerce, 1958 (computed).

(a) Plot average productivity against standard deviation of productivity.

(b) Does the scattergram suggest that a model of the following type fits the data reasonably well?

$$Y_i = \beta_0 + \beta_1 X_i + u_i$$

where Y = standard deviation, X = average productivity, and i = ith employment class.

(c) What can you say about the nature of heteroscedasticity, if any, present in the data?

10.6 The following table gives data on sales/cash ratio in U.S. manufacturing industries classified by the asset size of the establishment for the period 1971-I to 1973-IV. (The data are on a quarterly basis.) The sales/cash ratio may be regarded as a measure of income velocity in the corporate sector, that is, the number of times a dollar turns over.

Asset size (millions of dollars)

Year and quarter	1–10	10–25	25–50	50–100	100–250	250–1000	1000+
1971-I	6.696	6.929	6.858	6.966	7.819	7.557	7.860
-II	6.826	7.311	7.299	7.081	7.907	7.685	7.351
-III	6.338	7.035	7.082	7.145	7.691	7.309	7.088
-IV	6.272	6.265	6.874	6.485	6.778	7.120	6.765
1972-I	6.692	6.236	7.101	7.060	7.104	7.584	6.717
-II	6.818	7.010	7.719	7.009	8.064	7.457	7.280
-III	6.783	6.934	7.182	6.923	7.784	7.142	6.619
-IV	6.779	6.988	6.531	7.146	7.279	6.928	6.919
1973-I	7.291	7.428	7.272	7.571	7.583	7.053	6.630
-II	7.766	9.071	7.818	8.692	8.608	7.571	6.805
-III	7.733	8.357	8.090	8.357	7.680	7.654	6.772
-IV	8.316	7.621	7.766	7.867	7.666	7.380	7.072

Source: *Quarterly Financial Report for Manufacturing Corporations*, Federal Trade Commission and the Securities and Exchange Commission, U.S. government, various issues (computed).

(a) For each asset size compute the mean and standard deviation of the sales/cash ratio.

(b) Plot the mean value against the standard deviation as computed in (a), using asset size as the unit of observation.

(c) By means of a suitable regression model decide whether standard deviation of the ratio increases with the mean value. If not, how would you rationalize the result?

(d) If there is a statistically significant relationship between the two, how would you transform the data so that there is no heteroscedasticity?

10.7 The data in the following table refer to median salaries of women and men economists by field of specialization for the year 1964.

(a) Find the average salary and the standard deviation of salary of the two groups of economists.

(b) Is there significant difference between the two standard deviations? (You may use the Bartlett test.)

(c) Suppose you want to predict men economists' median salary from women economists' median salary. Develop a suitable linear regression model for this purpose. If you expect heteroscedasticity in such a model, how will you deal with it?

	Median salaries (thousands of dollars)	
Field of specialization	Women	Men
Business finance, etc.	9.3	13.0
Labor economics	10.3	12.0
Monetary-fiscal	8.0	11.6
General economic theory	8.7	10.8
Population, welfare programs, etc.	12.0	11.5
Economic systems and development	9.0	12.2

Source: *The Structure of Economists' Employment and Salaries,* Committee on the National Science Foundation Report on the Economics Profession, *American Economic Review,* vol. 55, no. 4, p. 62, December 1965.

10.8 The following data give economists' median salaries classified by degree attained and age:

	Median salaries (thousands of dollars)	
Age, years	M.A.	Ph.D.
25–29	8.0	8.8
30–34	9.2	9.6
35–39	11.0	11.0
40–44	12.8	12.5
45–49	14.2	13.6
50–54	14.7	14.3
55–59	14.5	15.0
60–64	13.5	15.0
65–69	12.0	15.0

Source: The Structure of Economists' Employment and Salaries, Committee on National Science Foundation Report on the Economics Profession, *American Economic Review,* vol. 55, no. 4, p. 37, December 1965.

(*a*) Are the variances of median salaries of economists with M.A. and Ph.D. degrees equal?

(*b*) If they are, how would you test the hypothesis that the average median salaries for the two groups are the same?

(*c*) Economists with an M.A. degree earned more than their Ph.D. counterparts between the ages 35 and 54. How would you explain this finding if you believe that a Ph.D. economist should earn more than an M.A. economist?

10.9 For the data given in Table 10.1, regress average compensation Y on average productivity X, treating employment size as the unit of observation and interpret your results, and verify your results from those given in (10.3.3).

(*a*) From the preceding regression obtain the residuals e_i.

(*b*) Regress e_i on Y_i. If there is significant relationship between the two, what can you conclude?

(*c*) Following the Park test, regress $\ln e_i^2$ on $\ln X_i$ and verify the regression (10.3.4).

(*d*) Following the Glejser approach, regress $|e_i|$ on X_i and then regress $|e_i|$ on $\sqrt{X_i}$ and comment on your results.

(*e*) Find the rank correlation between $|e_i|$ and X_i and comment on the nature of heteroscedasticity, if any, present in the data.

10.10 In a survey of some 9966 economists in 1964 the following data were obtained:

Age, years	Median salary, $
20–24	7800
25–29	8400
30–34	9700
35–39	11,500
40–44	13,000
45–49	14,800
50–54	15,000
55–59	15,000
60–64	15,000
65–69	14,500
70+	12,000

Source: The Structure of Economists' Employment and Salaries, Committee on the National Science Foundation Report on the Economics Profession, *American Economic Review*, vol. 55, no. 4, p. 36, December 1965.

(*a*) Develop a suitable regression model explaining median salary in relation to age.

Note: For the purpose of regression assume that the median salaries refer to the midpoint of the age interval. Thus, $7800 refers to age 22.5 years, and so on. For the last age interval, assume that the maximum age is 75 years.

(*b*) Assuming that the variance of the disturbance term is proportional to the square of age, transform the data so as to make the resulting disturbance term homoscedastic.

(*c*) Repeat (*b*) assuming that the variance is proportional to age. Which of the transformations seems to be plausible?

(*d*) If none of the preceding transformations seem plausible, assume that the variance term is proportional to the conditional expectation of median salary, conditional upon the given age. How would you transform the data so that the resulting variance is homoscedastic?

10.11 The following table gives data on special drawing rights (SDRs), also known as *paper gold*, and balance of payments for 10 countries for the year 1974.

Since the SDRs are used as an international currency, its size is expected to be related to the balance of payments position of a country.

(*a*) From the data given, is there a discernible relationship between the SDRs and the balance of payments? Answer by regressing the former on the latter.

(*b*) Using your results in (*a*), test separately the following hypothesis; the disturbance variance is proportional to the

    (i) square of the balance of payment value

    (ii) conditional expected value of the SDRs conditional upon the value of the balance of payments

(*c*) Can you use the log transformation discussed in the text to transform the data? Why or why not?

(*d*) Apply the rank correlation test to e_i obtained from the regression in (*a*) and the balance of payments figures. Can you say anything about heteroscedasticity based on this test?

Country	SDRs (millions of dollars)	Balance of payments (millions of dollars)
Belgium	715	346
Canada	574	26
France	248	−83†
Germany	1763	−466
Italy	221	−4633
Japan	529	1241
Netherlands	595	985
Sweden	131	−802
United Kingdom	843	−4355
United States	2370	−8374

† Negative sign denotes balance of payment deficit.

Source: International Financial Statistics, International Monetary Fund, December 1975.

10.12 Show that equation (10.4.4) can alternatively be written as

$$\beta_1^* = \frac{\sum w_i X_i Y_i - (\sum w_i X_i \sum w_i Y_i / \sum w_i)}{\sum w_i X_i^2 - [(\sum w_i X_i)^2 / \sum w_i]}$$

Further show that when $w_i = w$ (a constant), β_1^* is equal to the first equation in (3.1.11).

APPENDIX 10A

10A.1 THE METHOD OF WEIGHTED LEAST SQUARES

To illustrate the method, we use the two-variable model $Y_i = \beta_0 + \beta_1 X_i + u_i$. The unweighted least-squares method minimizes

$$\sum e_i^2 = \sum (Y_i - \hat{\beta}_0 - \hat{\beta}_1 X_i)^2 \tag{1}$$

to obtain the estimates, whereas the weighted least-squares method minimizes the weighted residual sum of squares:

$$\sum w_i e_i^2 = \sum w_i (Y_i - \beta_0^* - \beta_1^* X_i)^2 \tag{2}$$

where β_0^* and β_1^* are the weighted least-squares estimators and where the weights w_i are such that

$$w_i = \frac{1}{\sigma_i^2} \tag{3}$$

that is, the weights are inversely proportional to the variance of u_i or Y_i conditional upon the given X_i, it being understood that var $(u_i | X_i) = $ var $(Y_i | X_i) = \sigma_i^2$.

Differentiating (2) with respect to β_0^* and β_1^*, we obtain

$$\frac{\partial \sum w_i e_i^2}{\partial \beta_0^*} = 2 \sum w_i (Y_i - \beta_0^* - \beta_1^* X_i)(-1)$$

$$\frac{\partial \sum w_i e_i^2}{\partial \beta_1^*} = 2 \sum w_i (Y_i - \beta_0^* - \beta_1^* X_i)(-X_i)$$

Setting the preceding expressions equal to zero, we obtain the following two normal equations:

$$\sum w_i Y_i = \beta_0^* \sum w_i + \beta_1^* \sum w_i X_i \tag{4}$$

$$\sum w_i X_i Y_i = \beta_0^* \sum w_i X_i + \beta_1^* \sum w_i X_i^2 \tag{5}$$

Notice the similarity between these normal equations and the normal equations of the unweighted least squares.

Now letting

$$\bar{X}^* = \frac{\sum w_i X_i}{\sum w_i}$$

$$\bar{Y}^* = \frac{\sum w_i Y_i}{\sum w_i}$$

and

$$x_i^* = X_i - \bar{X}^* \qquad y_i^* = Y_i - \bar{Y}^*$$

we solve (4) and (5) simultaneously to obtain

$$\beta_0^* = \bar{Y}^* - \beta_1^* \bar{X}^* \tag{6}$$

$$\beta_1^* = \frac{\sum w_i x_i^* y_i^*}{\sum w_i x_i^{*2}} \tag{7}$$

Note that if $w_1 = w_2 = \cdots = w_N = w$, the weighted least-squares estimators coincide with the unweighted least-squares estimators.

ELEVEN

AUTOCORRELATION

An important assumption of the classical linear model presented in Part I is that there is no autocorrelation or serial correlation among the disturbances u_i entering into the population regression function. In this chapter, we take a critical look at this assumption with a view to seeking answers to the following questions:

1. What is the nature of autocorrelation?
2. What are the theoretical and practical consequences of autocorrelation?
3. Since the assumption of nonautocorrelation relates to the unobservable disturbances u_i, how does one know that there is autocorrelation in any given situation?
4. How does one remedy the problem of autocorrelation?

11.1 THE NATURE OF THE PROBLEM

The term *autocorrelation* may de defined as "correlation between members of series of observations ordered in time [as in time-series data] or space [as in cross-sectional data]."[1] In the regression context, the classical linear regression model assumes that such autocorrelation does not exist in the disturbances u_i. Symbolically,

$$E(u_i u_j) = 0 \qquad i \neq j \qquad (3.1.2)$$

---

[1] Maurice G. Kendall and William R. Buckland, *A Dictionary of Statistical Terms*, Hafner Publishing Company, Inc., New York, 1971, p. 8.

Put simply, the classical model assumes that the disturbance term relating to any observation is not influenced by the disturbance term relating to any other observation. For example, if we are dealing with quarterly time-series data involving the regression of output on labor and capital inputs and if, say, there is a labor strike affecting output in one quarter, there is no reason to believe that this disruption will be carried over to the next quarter. That is, if output is lower this quarter, there is no reason to expect it to be lower next quarter. Similarly, if we are dealing with cross-sectional data involving the regression of family consumption expenditure on family income, the effect of an increase of one family's income on its consumption expenditure is not expected to affect the consumption expenditure of another family.

However, if there is such a dependence, we have autocorrelation. Symbolically,

$$E(u_i u_j) \neq 0 \qquad i \neq j \tag{11.1.1}$$

In this situation, the disruption caused by a strike this quarter may very well affect output next quarter or the increases in the consumption expenditure of one family may very well prompt another family to increase its consumption expenditure if it wants to keep up with the Joneses.

Before we find out why autocorrelation exists, it is essential to clear up some terminological questions. Although it is now a common practice to treat the terms *autocorrelation* and *serial correlation* synonymously, some authors prefer to distinguish the two terms. For example, Tintner defines autocorrelation as "lag correlation of a given series with itself, lagged by a number of time units," whereas he reserves the term serial correlation to "lag correlation between two different series."[2] Thus, correlation between two time series such as $u_1, u_2, \ldots, u_{10}$ and $u_2, u_3, \ldots, u_{11}$, where the former is the latter series lagged by one time period, is *autocorrelation*, whereas correlation between times series such as $u_1, u_2, \ldots, u_{10}$ and $v_2, v_3, \ldots, v_{11}$, where u and v are two different time series, is called *serial correlation*. Although the distinction between the two terms may be useful, in this book we shall treat them synonymously.

It may be interesting to visualize some of the plausible patterns of auto- and nonautocorrelation, which are given in Fig. 11.1. Figure 11.1a to d shows that there is a discernible pattern among the u's. Figure 11.1a shows a cyclical pattern; Fig. 11.1b and c suggest an upward or downward linear trend in the disturbances; whereas Fig. 11.1d indicates that both linear and quadratic trend terms are present in the disturbances. It is only Fig. 11.1e which indicates no systematic pattern, supporting the nonautocorrelation assumption of the classical linear regression model.

The natural question is: Why does serial correlation occur? There are several reasons, some of which are as follows:

1. *Inertia.* A salient feature of most economic time series is inertia, or slug-

---

[2] Gerhard Tintner, *Econometrics*, John Wiley & Sons, Inc., New York, 1965, science ed., p. 187.

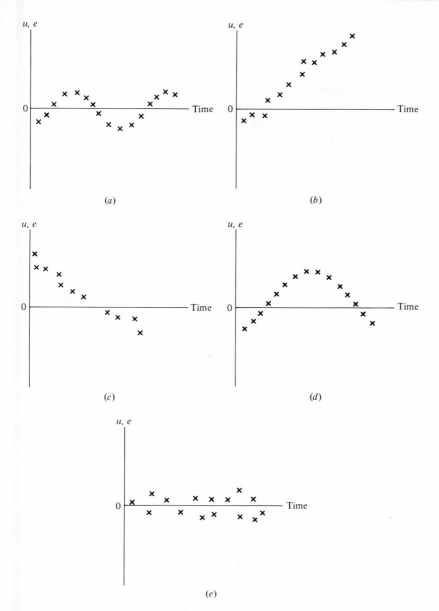

Figure 11.1 Patterns of autocorrelation.

gishness. As is well known, time series such as GNP, price indexes, production, employment, and unemployment exhibit (business) cycles. Starting at the bottom of the recession, when economic recovery starts, most of these series start moving upward. In this upswing, the value of a series at one point in time is greater than its previous value. Thus there is a "momentum" built into them, and it continues until something happens (e.g., increase in interest rate or taxes or both) to slow them down. Therefore, in regressions involving time-series data, successive observations are likely to be interdependent.

2. *Specification bias: excluded variables case.* In empirical analysis it is often the case that the researcher starts with a plausible regression model which may not be the most "perfect" one. After the regression analysis, the researcher does the postmortem examination to find out whether the results accord with a priori expectations. If not, surgery is begun. For example, the researcher may plot the residuals e_i obtained from the fitted regression and may observe patterns such as those shown in Fig. 11.1a to d. These residuals (which are proxies for u_i) may suggest that some variables which were originally candidates but were not included in the model for a variety of reasons should be included. This is the case of *excluded variable* specification bias. It very often happens that inclusion of such variables removes the correlation pattern observed among the residuals. For example, suppose we have the following demand model:

$$Y_t = \beta_1 + \beta_2 X_{2t} + \beta_3 X_{3t} + \beta_4 X_{4t} + u_t \tag{11.1.2}$$

where Y = quantity of beef demanded, X_2 = price of beef, X_3 = consumer income, X_4 = price of pork, and t = time.[3] However, for some reasons we run the following regression:

$$Y_t = \beta_1 + \beta_2 X_{2t} + \beta_3 X_{3t} + v_t \tag{11.1.3}$$

Now if (11.1.2) is the "correct" model or the "truth" or true relation, running (11.1.3) is tantamount to letting $v_t = \beta_4 X_{4t} + u_t$. And to the extent the price of pork affects the consumption of beef, the error or disturbance term v will reflect a systematic pattern, thus creating (false) autocorrelation. A simple test of this would be to run both (11.1.2) and (11.1.3) and see whether autocorrelation, if any, observed in model (11.1.3) disappears when (11.1.2) is run.[4] The actual mechanics of detecting autocorrelation will be discussed in Sec. 11.3 where we will show that a plot of the residuals from regressions (11.1.2) and (11.1.3) will often shed considerable light on serial correlation.

3. *Specification bias: incorrect functional form.* Suppose the "true" or correct model in a cost-output study is as follows:

$$\text{Marginal cost}_i = \beta_1 + \beta_2 \text{ output}_i + \beta_3 \text{ output}_i^2 + u_i \tag{11.1.4}$$

but we fit the following model:

$$\text{Marginal cost}_i = \alpha_1 + \alpha_2 \text{ output}_i + v_i \tag{11.1.5}$$

The marginal cost curve corresponding to the "true" model is shown in Fig. 11.2 along with the "incorrect" linear cost curve.

---

[3] As a matter of convention, we shall use the subscript t to denote time-series data and the usual subscript i for cross-sectional data.

[4] If it is found that the real problem is one of specification bias, not autocorrelation, then as shown in Sec. 9.8, the OLS estimators of the parameters in (11.1.3) may be biased as well as inconsistent.

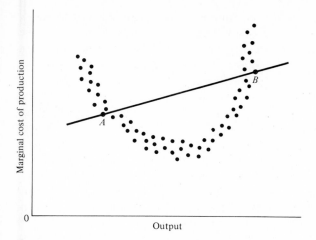

Figure 11.2 Specification bias: incorrect functional form.

As Fig. 11.2 shows, between points A and B the linear marginal cost curve will consistently overestimate the true marginal cost, whereas beyond these points it will consistently underestimate the true marginal cost. This is to be expected, because the disturbance term v_i is, in fact, equal to output$^2 + u_i$, and hence catch the systematic effect of the output^2 term on marginal cost. In this case, v_i will reflect autocorrelation because of the use of an incorrect functional form.

4. *Cobweb phenomenon.* The supply of many agricultural commodities reflect the so-called "Cobweb phenomenon" where supply reacts to price with a lag of one time period because supply decisions take time to implement (the gestation period). Thus, at the beginning of this year's planting of crop farmers are influenced by the price prevailing last year so that their supply function is

$$\text{Supply}_t = \beta_0 + \beta_1 P_{t-1} + u_t \tag{11.1.6}$$

Suppose at the end of period t, price P_t turns out to be lower than P_{t-1}. Therefore, in period $t + 1$ farmers may very well decide to produce less than they did in period t. Obviously, in this situation the disturbances u_i are not expected to be random because if the farmers overproduce in year t, they are likely to reduce their production in $t + 1$, and so on, leading to a Cobweb pattern.

5. *Lags.* In a time-series regression of consumption expenditure on income, it is not uncommon to find that the consumption expenditure in the current period depends, among other things, on the consumption expenditure of the previous period. That is,

$$\text{Consumption}_t = \beta_1 + \beta_2 \text{ income}_t + \beta_3 \text{ consumption}_{t-1} + u_t \tag{11.1.7}$$

Regression such as (11.1.7) is known as *autoregression* because one of the explanatory variables is the lagged value of the dependent variable. (We shall study such models in Chap. 12). The rationale for a model such as (11.1.7) is simple. Consumers do not change their consumption habits frequently because of psychological, technological, or institutional reasons. Now if we neglect the lagged term in (11.1.7), the resulting error term will reflect a systematic pattern due to the influence of lagged consumption on current consumption.

6. "*Manipulation*" *of data.* In empirical analysis, the raw data are often "manipulated." For example, in time-series regressions involving quarterly data, such data are usually derived from the monthly data by simply adding three monthly observations and dividing the sum by 3. This averaging introduces smoothness into the data by dampening the fluctuations in the monthly data. Therefore, the graph plotting the quarterly data looks much smoother than the monthly data, and this smoothness may itself lend to a systematic pattern in the disturbances, thereby introducing autocorrelation. Another source of manipulation is *interpolation* or *extrapolation* of data. For example, the Census of Population is conducted every 10 years in this country, the last being in 1970 and the one before that in 1960. Now if there is a need to obtain data for some year within the intercensus period 1960–1970, the common practice is to interpolate on the basis of some ad hoc assumptions. All such data "massaging"

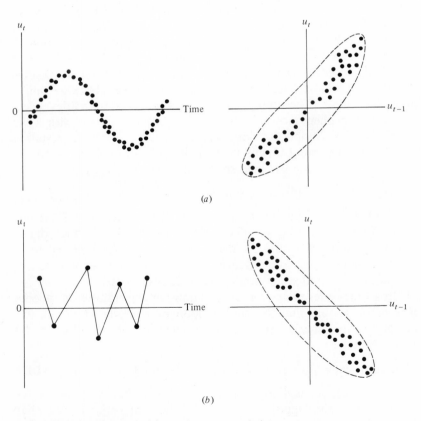

(a)

(b)

Figure 11.3 (a) Positive and (b) negative autocorrelation

techniques might impose upon the data a systematic pattern which might not exist in the original data.

Before concluding this section, it may be noted that the problem of autocorrelation is usually more common in time-series data, although it can and does occur in cross-sectional data. In time-series data, the observations are ordered in chronological order. Therefore, there is likely to be intercorrelations among successive observations especially if the time interval between successive observations is short, such as a day, a week, or a month rather than a year. There is generally no such chronological order in the cross-sectional data, although in some cases a similar order may exist. Hence in a cross-sectional regression of consumption expenditure on income where the units of observations are 50 states of the United States, it is possible that the data are so arranged that they fall into groups such as the South, Southwest, North, etc. Since the consumption pattern is likely to differ from one geographical region to another, although substantially similar within any given region, the estimated residuals from the regression may exhibit a systematic pattern associated with the regional differences. The point to note is that although autocorrelation is usually predominant in time-series data, it can occur in cross-sectional data. Some authors call autocorrelation in cross-sectional data *spatial autocorrelation*, that is, correlation in space rather than over time.

It should be noted also that autocorrelation can be positive as well as negative, although most economic time series generally exhibit positive autocorrelation because most of them either move upward or downward over extended time periods and do not exhibit a constant up-and-down movement such as that shown in Fig. 11.3*b*.

11.2 CONSEQUENCES OF AUTOCORRELATION

Recall that if all the assumptions of the classical linear regression model are satisfied, the Gauss-Markov theorem (Chap. 3) states that in the class of all linear unbiased estimators, the OLS estimators are best; that is, they have minimum variance. In short, they are efficient. Now, if we retain all but the nonautocorrelation assumption of the classical model, the OLS estimators have the following properties:

1. They are unbiased; that is, in repeated sampling (conditional upon the fixed X's) their average values are equal to their true population values.
2. They are consistent; that is, as the sample size increases indefinitely, they collapse on to their true values.
3. However, as in the case of heteroscedasticity, they are no longer efficient (minimum variance) in small as well as large samples (i.e., asymptotically).

As a result, if we persist in applying OLS in situations of autocorrelation, the following consequences ensue.

1. Even if we allow for serial correlation in the conventionally computed OLS estimators and their variances, the estimators are still inefficient (as compared with the BLUEs). Therefore, the confidence intervals are unnecessarily wide and the tests of significance less powerful.

2. If we disregard the autocorrelation problem completely and continue to apply the classical OLS formulas (derived under the assumption of no autocorrelation), the consequences are likely to be far more serious because:

(a) The residual variance $\hat{\sigma}^2$ is likely to underestimate the true σ^2.

(b) Even if σ^2 is not underestimated, the variances and standard errors of the OLS estimators are likely to underestimate the true variances and standard errors and as a result of (a) and (b)

(c) The usual t and F tests of significance are no longer valid, and if applied, are likely to give seriously misleading conclusions about the statistical significance of the estimated regression coefficients.

3. Although the OLS estimators are unbiased, which is a repeated sampling property, in any particular sample they are likely to give a distorted picture of their true population values, as we shall show shortly. In other words, the OLS estimators become sensitive to sampling fluctuations.

To establish some of the propositions stated previously, let us revert to the two-variable model

$$Y_t = \beta_0 + \beta_1 X_t + u_t \qquad (11.2.1)$$

where t denotes the observation at time t. Now to make any headway, we must assume the mechanism that generates the u_t. This is inevitable since u_t are unobservable. As a starting point or first approximation, one can assume that the disturbances are generated as follows:

$$u_t = \rho u_{t-1} + \varepsilon_t \qquad -1 < \rho < +1 \qquad (11.2.2)$$

where ρ is known as the *coefficient of autocovariance* and where ε_t is the stochastic disturbance such that it satisfies all the OLS assumptions, namely,

$$E(\varepsilon_t) = 0$$
$$\text{var } (\varepsilon_t) = \sigma^2 \qquad (11.2.3)$$
$$\text{cov } (\varepsilon_t, \varepsilon_{t+s}) = 0 \qquad s \neq 0$$

The scheme (11.2.2) is known as *Markov first-order autoregressive scheme*, or simply a *first-order autoregressive scheme*. The name *autoregressive* is appropriate because (11.2.2) can be interpreted as the regression of u_t on itself lagged one period. It is first-order because only u_t and its immediate past value are involved. If the model were $u_t = \rho u_{t-2} + \varepsilon_t$, it would be a second-order autoregressive scheme, and so on. In passing it may be noted that ρ, the coefficient of autocovariance, can also be interpreted as the *first-order coefficient of autocorrelation*, or, more accurately, the *coefficient of autocorrelation* of lag 1.[5]

What (11.2.2) postulates is that the movement or shift in u_t consists of two parts; a part ρu_{t-1}, which accounts for a systematic shift, and the other ε_t, which is purely random.

With the first-order autoregressive scheme, it can be shown that

$$\text{var}\,(\beta_1^*) = \frac{\sigma^2}{\sum\limits_{t=1}^{N} x_t^2}\left(1 + \rho\,\frac{\sum\limits_{t=1}^{N-1} x_t x_{t+1}}{\sum\limits_{t=1}^{N} x_t^2} + 2\rho^2\,\frac{\sum\limits_{t=1}^{N-2} x_t x_{t+2}}{\sum\limits_{t=1}^{N} x_t^2} + \cdots + 2\rho^{N-1}\,\frac{x_1 x_N}{\sum\limits_{t=1}^{N} x_t^2}\right)$$

$$(11.2.4)$$

where var (β_1^*) is the variance of the *usual* OLS estimator under (first-order) serial correlation.[6] In contrast, the usual (homoscedastic) formula for the variance of OLS estimator is

$$\text{var}\,(\hat{\beta}_1) = \frac{\sigma^2}{\sum\limits_{t=1}^{N} x_t^2} \qquad (11.2.5)$$

---

[5] This name can be easily justified. By definition, the (population) coefficient of correlation between u_t and u_{t-1} is

$$\rho = \frac{E\{[u_t - E(u_t)][u_{t-1} - E(u_{t-1})]\}}{\sqrt{\text{var}\,(u_t)}\sqrt{\text{var}\,(u_{t-1})}}$$

$$= \frac{E(u_t u_{t-1})}{\text{var}\,(u_{t-1})}$$

since $E(u_t) = 0$ for each t and var $(u_t) = $ var (u_{t-1}) because we are retaining the assumption of homoscedasticity. The reader can see that ρ is also the slope coefficient in the regression of u_t on u_{t-1}.

[6] For proof, see J. Johnston, *Econometric Methods*, 2d ed., McGraw-Hill Book Company, New York, 1972, p. 247. But it is crucial to note that var (β_1^*) is still not minimum because $\hat{\beta}_1 = \sum x_i y_i / \sum x_i^2$ is no longer BLUE. Assuming first-order autoregressive scheme, the BLUE of β_1, call it b_1, is given by

$$b_1 = \frac{\sum (x_t - \rho x_{t-1})(y_t - \rho y_{t-1})}{\sum (x_t - \rho x_{t-1})^2} + C$$

and its variance is given by

$$\text{var}\,(b_1) = \frac{\sigma^2}{\sum (x_t - \rho x_{t-1})^2} + D$$

where C and D are correction factors which may be disregarded in practice. (For proofs, see Jan Kmenta, *Elements of Econometrics*, The Macmillan Company, New York, 1971, pp. 274–275.) It is var (b_1) and not var (β_1^*) which is minimum, although the latter does take into account (first-order) serial correlation. In passing, note that if $\rho = 0$, b_1 coincides with β_1 and var (β_1^*) and var (b_1) both coincide with var $(\hat{\beta}_1)$ given in (11.2.5). Note further that although no longer BLUE, $\hat{\beta}_1$ is still unbiased, which can be readily verified from App. 3A, Sec. 3A.2.

Comparing (11.2.5) with (11.2.4), we see at once that the former excludes all but the first term in the parentheses of (11.2.4). Now if ρ is positive (which is true of most economic time series) and the X's are positively correlated (also true of most economic time series), then it is clear that

$$\text{var}(\hat{\beta}_1) < \text{var}(\beta_1^*) \tag{11.2.6}$$

that is, the usual OLS variance of $\hat{\beta}_1$ underestimates its true variance (under first-order serial correlation). Therefore, under the assumed conditions, we should use var (β_1^*), not var $(\hat{\beta}_1)$. [Ideally, of course we should use the BLUE estimator b_1 and its variance given in fn. 6. But if this is not done, we should at least use var (β_1^*).]

If we use var $(\hat{\beta}_1)$, we shall be inflating the precision or accuracy (i.e., underestimate the standard error) of the estimator $\hat{\beta}_1$. As a result, in computing the t ratio as $t = \hat{\beta}_1/\text{se}(\hat{\beta}_1)$ (under the hypothesis that $\beta_1 = 0$), we shall be overestimating the t value and hence the statistical significance of the estimated β_1. But as in the case of heteroscedasticity, this is not the end of the matter because σ^2 itself is likely to be underestimated. Recall that for the classical two-variable linear regression model

$$\hat{\sigma}^2 = \frac{\sum e_t^2}{N-2} \tag{11.2.7}$$

provides an unbiased estimator of σ^2; that is, $E(\hat{\sigma}^2) = \sigma^2$. But if there is autocorrelation, given by the first-order autoregressive scheme, it can be shown that

$$E(\hat{\sigma}^2) = \frac{\sigma^2\{N - [2/(1-\rho)] - 2\rho r\}}{N-2} \tag{11.2.8}$$

where $r = \sum_{t=1}^{N-1} x_t x_{t-1}/\sum_{t=1}^{N} x_t^2$, which can be interpreted as the (sample) correlation coefficient between successive values of the X's.[7] If ρ and r are both positive (not an unlikely assumption for most economic time series), it is apparent from (11.2.8) that $E(\hat{\sigma}^2) < \sigma^2$; that is, the usual residual variance formula, on the average, will underestimate the true σ^2. In other words, $\hat{\sigma}^2$ will be biased downward. Needless to say, this bias in $\hat{\sigma}^2$ will be transmitted to var $(\hat{\beta}_1)$ because in practice we estimate the latter by the formula $\hat{\sigma}^2/\sum x_t^2$.

To see how OLS is likely to underestimate σ^2 and the variance of $\hat{\beta}_1$, let us conduct the following experiment.[8] Suppose in the model (11.2.1) we "know" that the true $\beta_0 = 1$ and $\beta_1 = 0.8$. Therefore, the stochastic PRF is

$$Y_t = 1.0 + 0.8X_t + u_t \tag{11.2.9}$$

Hence, $\qquad\qquad E(Y_t|X_t) = 1.0 + 0.8X_t \tag{11.2.10}$

---

[7] See S. M. Goldfeld and R. E. Quandt, *Nonlinear Methods in Econometrics*, North-Holland Publishing Company, Amsterdam, 1972, p. 183.

[8] The experiment presented is an example of the so-called "Monte Carlo method."

Table 11.1 A hypothetical example of positively autocorrelated error terms

ε_t†	$u_t = 0.7u_{t-1} + \varepsilon_t$
0	0	$u_0 = 5$ (assumed)
1	0.464	$u_1 = 0.7(5) + 0.464 = 3.9640$
2	2.0262	$u_2 = 0.7(3.964) + 2.0262 = 4.8010$
3	2.455	$u_3 = 0.7(4.8010) + 2.455 = 5.8157$
4	−0.323	$u_4 = 0.7(5.8157) - 0.323 = 3.7480$
5	−0.068	$u_5 = 0.7(3.7480) - 0.068 = 2.5556$
6	0.296	$u_6 = 0.7(2.5556) + 0.296 = 2.0849$
7	−0.288	$u_7 = 0.7(2.0849) - 0.288 = 1.1714$
8	1.298	$u_8 = 0.7(1.1714) + 1.298 = 2.1180$
9	0.241	$u_9 = 0.7(2.1180) + 0.241 = 1.7236$
10	−0.957	$u_{10} = 0.7(1.7236) - 0.957 = 0.2495$

† Obtained from *A Million Random Digits and One Hundred Thousand Deviates*, Rand Corporation, Santa Monica, Calif., 1950.

which gives the true population regression line. Let us assume that u_t are generated by the first-order autoregressive scheme as follows:

$$u_t = 0.7u_{t-1} + \varepsilon_t \tag{11.2.11}$$

where ε_t satisfy all the OLS assumptions. We assume further for convenience that the ε_t are normally distributed with zero mean and unit ($= 1$) variance. Equation (11.2.11) postulates that the successive disturbances are positively correlated, with a coefficient of autocorrelation of $+0.7$, a rather high degree of dependence.

Now, using a table of random normal numbers with zero mean and unit variance, we generated 10 random numbers shown in Table 11.1 by the scheme (11.2.11). To start off the scheme, we need to specify the initial value of u, say, $u_0 = 5$.

Plotting the u_t generated in Table 11.1, we obtain Fig. 11.4, which shows that initially each successive u_t is higher than its previous value and subsequently it is generally smaller than its previous value, showing, in general, a positive autocorrelation.

Now suppose the values of X are fixed at $1, 2, 3, \ldots, 10$. Then, given these X's, we can generate a sample of 10 Y values from (11.2.9) and the values of u_t given in Table 11.1. The details are given in Table 11.2. Using the data of Table 11.2, if we regress Y on X, we obtain the following (sample) regression:

$$\hat{Y}_t = \quad 6.5452 + 0.3051X_t$$
$$(0.6153) \quad (0.0992)$$
$$t = (10.6366) \quad (3.0763) \tag{11.2.12}$$
$$r^2 = 0.5419 \qquad \hat{\sigma}^2 = 0.8114$$

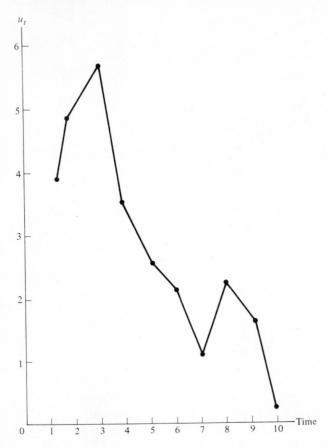

Figure 11.4 Correlation generated by the scheme $u_t = 0.7u_{t-1} + \varepsilon_t$ (Table 11.1).

Table 11.2 Generation of Y sample values

X_t	u_t†	$Y_t = 1.0 + 0.8X_t + u_t$
1	3.9640	$Y_1 = 1.0 + 0.8(1)\ \ + 3.9640 = 5.7640$
2	4.8010	$Y_2 = 1.0 + 0.8(2)\ \ + 4.8010 = 7.4010$
3	5.8157	$Y_3 = 1.0 + 0.8(3)\ \ + 5.8157 = 9.2157$
4	3.7480	$Y_4 = 1.0 + 0.8(4)\ \ + 3.7480 = 7.9480$
5	2.5556	$Y_5 = 1.0 + 0.8(5)\ \ + 2.5556 = 7.5556$
6	2.0849	$Y_6 = 1.0 + 0.8(6)\ \ + 2.0849 = 7.8849$
7	1.1714	$Y_7 = 1.0 + 0.8(7)\ \ + 1.1714 = 7.7714$
8	2.1180	$Y_8 = 1.0 + 0.8(8)\ \ + 2.1180 = 9.5180$
9	1.7236	$Y_9 = 1.0 + 0.8(9)\ \ + 1.7236 = 9.9236$
10	0.2495	$Y_{10} = 1.0 + 0.8(10) + 0.2495 = 9.2495$

† Obtained from Table 11.1.

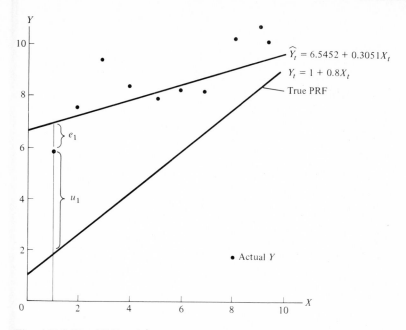

Figure 11.5 True PRF and the estimated regression line for the data of Table 11.2.

whereas the true regression line is as given by (11.2.10). Both the regression lines are given in Figure 11.5, which shows clearly how much the fitted regression line distorts the true regression line; it seriously underestimates the true slope coefficient but overestimates the true intercept. (But note that the OLS estimators are still unbiased.)

Figure 11.5 also shows why the true variance of u_i is likely to be underestimated by the estimator $\hat{\sigma}^2$, which is computed from the e_i: The e_i are generally close to the fitted line (which is due to the OLS procedure) but deviate substantially from the true PRF. Hence, they do not give a correct picture of u_i. To gain some insight into the extent of underestimation of true σ^2, suppose we conduct another sampling experiment. Keeping the X_t and ε_t given in Tables 11.1 and 11.2, let us assume $\rho = 0$, that is, no autocorrelation. The new sample of Y values thus generated is given in Table 11.3.

The regression based on Table 11.3 is as follows:

$$\hat{Y}_t = 2.5339 + 0.6146 X_t$$

$$(0.6684) \quad (0.1087)$$

$$t = (3.7910) \quad (5.6541)$$

$$r^2 = 0.7998 \qquad \hat{\sigma}^2 = 0.9752$$

(11.2.13)

This regression is much closer to the "truth" because the Y's are now essentially random. Notice that $\hat{\sigma}^2$ has increased from 0.8114 ($\rho = 0.7$) to 0.9752 ($\rho = 0$). Also

Table 11.3 Sample of Y values with zero serial correlation

X_t	$\varepsilon_t = u_t$ †	$Y_t = 1.0 + 0.8X_t + \varepsilon_t$
1	0.464	2.264
2	2.026	4.626
3	2.455	5.855
4	−0.323	3.877
5	−0.068	4.932
6	0.296	6.096
7	−0.288	6.312
8	1.298	8.698
9	0.241	8.441
10	−0.957	8.043

† Since there is no autocorrelation, the u_t and ε_t are identical. The ε_t are from Table 11.1.

notice that the standard errors of $\hat{\beta}_0$ and $\hat{\beta}_1$ have increased. This is in accord with the theoretical results considered previously.

11.3 DETECTING AUTOCORRELATION

As demonstrated in Sec. 11.2, autocorrelation is potentially a serious problem. Remedial measures are therefore surely called for. Of course, before one does anything, it is essential to find out whether autocorrelation exists in a given situation. In this section we shall consider a few commonly used tests of serial correlation and relegate others to the exercises.

Graphical Method

Recall that the assumption of nonautocorrelation of the classical model relates to the population disturbances u_i, which cannot be observed directly. What we have instead are their proxies, the residuals e_i, which can be obtained from the usual OLS procedure. Although the e_i are not the same thing as u_i, the two are related, which can be demonstrated as follows.

For the two-variable model

$$Y_i = \beta_0 + \beta_1 X_i + u_i$$

or in the deviation form

$$y_i = \beta_1 x_i + (u_i - \bar{u}) \tag{11.3.1}$$

Table 11.4 Actual and estimated Y and residuals in the regression $Y_t = \beta_0 + \beta_1 X_t + u_t$, where $Y_t =$ quit rate and $X_t =$ unemployment rate

Year	Actual Y, %	Estimated $Y(= \hat{Y})$, %	Residuals, e_t
1960	1.3	1.592	−0.292
1961	1.2	1.134	0.066
1962	1.4	1.706	−0.306
1963	1.4	1.735	−0.335
1964	1.5	1.935	−0.435
1965	1.9	2.221	−0.321
1966	2.6	2.450	0.150
1967	2.3	2.336	−0.036
1968	2.5	2.422	0.078
1969	2.7	2.422	0.278
1970	2.1	1.763	0.337
1971	1.8	1.420	0.380
1972	2.2	1.763	0.437

Source: Exercise 3.7.

where $y_i = (Y_i - \bar{Y})$ and $x_i = (X_i - \bar{X})$. (*Note:* $\bar{u}$ and $E(u_i)$ are not the same.) We know that

$$e_i = y_i - \hat{\beta}_1 x_i$$
$$= [\beta_1 x_i + (u_i - \bar{u})] - \hat{\beta}_1 x_i$$
$$= (\beta_1 - \hat{\beta}_1)x_i + (u_i - \bar{u}) \tag{11.3.2}$$

Now

$$\hat{\beta}_1 = \beta_1 + \frac{\sum x_i u_i}{\sum x_i^2} \qquad \text{using App. 3A, Sec. 3A.2} \tag{11.3.3}$$

therefore, substituting (11.3.3) into (11.3.2), we obtain

$$e_i = (u_i - \bar{u}) - x_i \left[\frac{\sum x_i u_i}{\sum x_i^2} \right] \tag{11.3.4}$$

As a result, if there is any autocorrelation among the u's, it will be reflected in the e's by virtue of (11.3.4). Therefore, e_i can be examined for possible clues about the nature of serial correlation in u_i. In a time series this can be done by plotting e_t against time, as shown in Fig. 11.1. If patterns such as Fig. 11.1a to d are seen, one can suspect autocorrelation, whereas if the pattern is as shown in Fig. 11.1e, perhaps there is no autocorrelation.

An examination of residuals as just indicated may itself suggest ways of attacking the serial correlation problem. For example, if the residuals exhibit the pattern of Fig. 11.1b, they might suggest that a linear trend or time variable could be included in the model. If the pattern of residuals is as shown in Fig. 11.1d, it

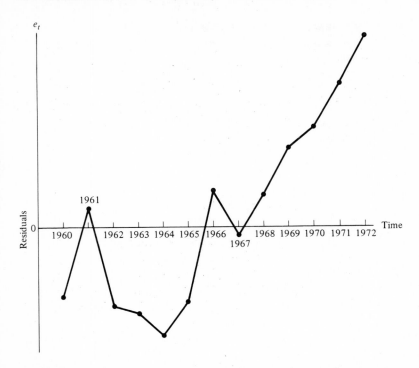

Figure 11.6 Residuals from the regression of quit rate on the unemployment rate.

might indicate that a second-degree as well as a first-degree time variable should be included in the model.

As an illustration of the graphical method, Table 11.4 gives the residuals estimated from the regression of Exercise 3.7, which involves regressing the quit rate on the unemployment rate. Plotting the residuals against time, we obtain Fig. 11.6. It is amply clear from Fig. 11.6 that the residuals are nonrandom. Up to 1964 (except 1961) the residuals are increasingly negative, whereas beginning in 1966 (except for 1967) they are increasingly positive. Thus there is positive autocorrelation among the residuals. (The reader can verify this by plotting e_t against e_{t-1}.)

Figure 11.6 shows almost a cyclical pattern in the e_t. It suggests that another variable which moves cyclically with the quit rate should be introduced into the model. For example, accession rate (number of new hires per 100 employees), which is an indicator of the demand for labor, may be included in the model because, other things remaining the same, the higher the accession rate, the higher the quit rate.

The greatest virtue of the graphical method is its simplicity. No matter whether the regression model includes 1 explanatory variable or 10, the residuals can be easily plotted against time. A few regression (packaged) programs now routinely compute and print out such residuals. Such a printout is a great visual aid in determining whether autocorrelation is present in a given case.

The graphical method can be supplemented by analytical methods which provide a test statistic to indicate whether the nonrandom pattern observed in the estimated e_i is statistically significant. The most celebrated of these methods is the Durbin-Watson d statistic.

Durbin-Watson d Test[9]

The Durbin-Watson d statistic is defined as

$$d = \frac{\sum\limits_{t=2}^{t=N} (e_t - e_{t-1})^2}{\sum\limits_{t=1}^{t=N} e_t^2} \tag{11.3.5}$$

which is simply the ratio of the sum of squared differences in successive residuals to the RSS. Note that in the numerator of the d statistic the number of observations is $N - 1$ because one observation is lost in taking successive differences.

A great advantage of the d statistic is that it is based on the estimated residuals, which are routinely computed in regression analysis. Because of this advantage, it is now a common practice to report the Durbin-Watson d along with summary statistics such as R^2, adjusted R^2, t ratios, etc. Although it is now used routinely, it is important to note the assumptions underlying the d statistic:

1. The regression model includes an intercept term. If such term is not present, as in the case of the regression through the origin, it is essential to rerun the regression including the intercept term to obtain the RSS.
2. The explanatory variables, the X's, are nonstochastic, or fixed in repeated sampling.
3. The disturbances u_t are generated by the first-order autoregressive scheme: $u_t = \rho u_{t-1} + \varepsilon_t$.
4. The regression model does not include lagged value(s) of the dependent variable as one of the explanatory variables. Thus, the test is inapplicable to models of the following type:

$$Y_t = \beta_1 + \beta_2 X_{2t} + \beta_3 X_{3t} + \cdots + \beta_k X_{kt} + \gamma Y_{t-1} + u_t \tag{11.3.6}$$

where Y_{t-1} is the one-period lagged value of Y. Such models are known as *autoregressive models*. We shall examine them fully in Chap. 12.

The exact sampling or probability distribution of the d statistic given in (11.3.5) is difficult to derive because, as Durbin and Watson have shown, it depends in a complicated way on the X values present in a given sample. This should be understandable because d is computed from e_i, which are, of course,

---

[9] J. Durbin and G. S. Watson, "Testing for Serial Correlation in Least-Squares Regression," *Biometrika*, vol. 38, pp. 159–177, 1951.

dependent on the given X's. Therefore, unlike the t, F, or χ^2 tests, there is no unique critical value which will lead to the rejection or the acceptance of the null hypothesis that there is no first-order serial correlation in the disturbances u_i. However, Durbin and Watson were successful in deriving a lower bound d_L and an upper bound d_U such that if the computed d from (11.3.5) lies outside these critical values, a decision can be made regarding the presence of positive or negative serial correlation. Moreover, these limits depend only on the number of observations N and the number of explanatory variables and do not depend on the values taken by these explanatory variables. These limits, for N going from 15 to 100 and up to 5 explanatory variables, have been tabulated by Durbin and Watson and are reproduced in App. D, Table 5.

The actual test procedure can be explained better with the aid of Fig. 11.7, which shows that the limits of d are 0 and 4. This can be established as follows: Expand (11.3.5) to obtain

$$d = \frac{\sum e_t^2 + \sum e_{t-1}^2 - 2 \sum e_t e_{t-1}}{\sum e_t^2} \tag{11.3.7}$$

Since $\sum e_t^2$ and $\sum e_{t-1}^2$ differ in only one observation, they are approximately equal. Therefore, setting $\sum e_{t-1}^2 = \sum e_t^2$, (11.3.7) may be written as

$$d \doteq 2\left(1 - \frac{\sum e_t e_{t-1}}{\sum e_t^2}\right) \tag{11.3.8}$$

where $\doteq$ means approximately.

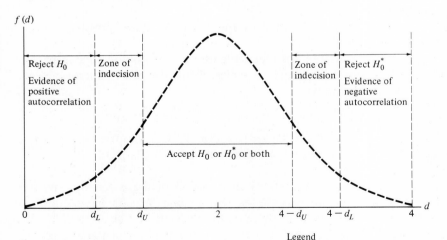

Legend

H_0 : No positive autocorrelation

H_0^* : No negative autocorrelation

Figure 11.7 Durbin-Watson d statistic.

Now let us define

$$\hat{\rho} = \frac{\sum e_t e_{t-1}}{\sum e_t^2}$$

(11.3.9)

as the sample first-order coefficient of autocorrelation, an estimator of ρ. (See fn. 5.) Using (11.3.9), (11.3.8) can be expressed as

$$d \doteq 2(1 - \hat{\rho})$$

(11.3.10)

It is apparent from equation (11.3.10) that if $\hat{\rho} = 0, d = 2$; that is, if there is no serial correlation (of the first-order), d is expected to be about 2. Therefore, as a rule of thumb, if d is found to be 2 in an application, one may assume that there is no first-order autocorrelation, either positive or negative. If $\hat{\rho} = +1$, indicating perfect positive correlation in the residuals, $d \doteq 0$. Therefore, the closer is d to 0, the greater the evidence of positive serial correlation. This should be evident from (11.3.5) because if there is positive autocorrelation, the e_t's will be bunched together and their differences will therefore tend to be small. As a result, the numerator sum of squares will be smaller in comparison with the denominator sum of squares, which remains a unique value for any given regression.

If $\hat{\rho} = -1$, that is, there is perfect negative correlation among successive residuals, $d \doteq 4$. Hence, the closer is d to 4, the greater the evidence of negative serial correlation. Again, looking at (11.3.5), this is understandable. For if there is negative autocorrelation, a positive e_t will tend to be followed by a negative e_t and vice versa so that $|e_t - e_{t-1}|$ will usually be greater than $|e_t|$. Therefore, the numerator of d will be comparatively larger than the denominator.

The mechanics of the Durbin-Watson test is as follows, assuming that the assumptions underlying the test are fulfilled:

1. Run the OLS regression and obtain the residuals e_i.
2. Compute d from (11.3.5). (Most computer programs now do this routinely.)
3. For the given sample size and given number of explanatory variables, find out the critical d_L and d_U values.
4. If the null hypothesis H_0 is that there is no positive serial correlation, then if

$$d < d_L: \text{reject } H_0$$

$$d > d_U: \text{do not reject } H_0$$

$$d_L \leq d \leq d_U: \text{the test is inconclusive}[10]$$

---

[10] However, Theil and Nagar have shown that the upper limit d_U "is approximately equal to the true significance limit in all those cases in which the behavior of the explanatory variables is smooth in the sense that their first and second differences are small compared with the range of the corresponding variable itself." See Henri Theil, *Principles of Econometrics*, John Wiley & Sons, Inc., New York, 1971, p. 201.

5. If the null hypothesis H_0 is that there is no negative serial correlation, then if

$$d > 4 - d_L: \text{reject } H_0$$

$$d < 4 - d_U: \text{do not reject } H_0$$

$$4 - d_U \le d \le 4 - d_L: \text{the test is inconclusive}$$

6. If H_0 is two-sided, namely, that there is no positive or negative serial autocorrelation, then if

$$d < d_L: \text{reject } H_0$$

$$d > 4 - d_L: \text{reject } H_0$$

$$d_U < d < 4 - d_U: \text{do not reject } H_0$$

or $$\left. \begin{array}{c} d_L \le d \le d_U \\ 4 - d_U \le d \le 4 - d_L \end{array} \right\} \text{the test is inconclusive}$$

As the preceding steps indicate, a great drawback of the d test is that if it falls in the *indecisive zone*, or *region of ignorance*, one cannot conclude whether autocorrelation does or does not exist. In this case one may resort to other tests (some of which are given by way of exercises) or obtain additional data or a different sample. It is also to be noted that the minimum number of observations required to refer to the Durbin-Watson tables is 15. The reason is that in a sample of fewer than 15 observations it becomes very difficult to draw any definitive conclusions about autocorrelation by examining the estimated residuals.

As a demonstration of the d test, consider the illustrative example of Chap. 6, which involves the regression of the log of output on the logs of labor and capital inputs. The results of this regression including the estimated residuals are given in the computer printout of App. 6A, Sec. 6A.4. From the information given there, it can be readily verified that $d = 0.8901$. Now for $N = 15$ and two explanatory variables, the critical d values at the 5 percent level of significance are $d_L = 0.95$ and $d_U = 1.54$. If the null hypothesis is that there is no positive serial correlation, we see that the estimated d value is less than the critical d_L, suggesting that the null hypothesis can be rejected.

In using the Durbin-Watson test, it is essential to note that it cannot be applied in violation of its assumptions. In particular, it should not be used to test for serial correlation in autoregressive models, that is, models containing lagged value(s) of the dependent variable as explanatory variable(s). If applied mistakenly, the d value in such cases will often be around 2, which is the value of d expected in the absence of first-order autocorrelation [see (11.3.10)]. Hence there is built-in bias against discovering serial correlation in such models.[11] This does not mean that autoregressive models do not suffer from the autocorrelation problem. As we

[11] For details, see Marc Nerlove and Kenneth F. Wallis, "Use of the Durbin-Watson Statistic in Inappropriate Situations," *Econometrica*, vol. 34, no. 1, pp. 235–238, January 1966.

shall see in a later chapter, Durbin has developed the so-called h statistic to test serial correlation in such models.

11.4 REMEDIAL MEASURES

Since in the presence of serial correlation the OLS estimators are inefficient, it is essential to seek remedial measures. The remedy, however, depends on what knowledge one has about the nature of interdependence among the disturbances. We distinguish two situations: when the structure of autocorrelation is known and when it is not known.

When the Structure of Autocorrelation Is Known

Since the disturbances u_t are unobservable, the nature of serial correlation is often a matter of speculation or practical exigencies. In practice, it is usually assumed that the u_t follow the first-order autoregressive scheme, namely,

$$u_t = \rho u_{t-1} + \varepsilon_t \tag{11.4.1}$$

where $|\rho| < 1$ and where the ε_t follow the OLS assumptions of zero expected value, constant variance, and nonautocorrelation, as shown in (11.2.3).

Assuming the validity of (11.4.1), the serial correlation problem can be satisfactorily resolved if ρ, the coefficient of autocorrelation, is known. To see this, let us revert to the two-variable model:[12]

$$Y_t = \beta_0 + \beta_1 X_t + u_t \tag{11.4.2}$$

If (11.4.2) holds true at time t, it also holds true at time $t - 1$. Hence,

$$Y_{t-1} = \beta_0 + \beta_1 X_{t-1} + u_{t-1} \tag{11.4.3}$$

Multiplying (11.4.3) by ρ on both sides, we obtain

$$\rho Y_{t-1} = \rho\beta_0 + \rho\beta_1 X_{t-1} + \rho u_{t-1} \tag{11.4.4}$$

Subtracting (11.4.4) from (11.4.2) gives

$$(Y_t - \rho Y_{t-1}) = \beta_0(1 - \rho) + \beta_1 X_t - \rho\beta_1 X_{t-1} + (u_t - \rho u_{t-1})$$
$$= \beta_0(1 - \rho) + \beta_1(X_t - \rho X_{t-1}) + \varepsilon_t \tag{11.4.5}$$

where in the last step use is made of (11.4.1).

Since ε_t satisfy all the OLS assumptions, one can proceed to apply OLS to (11.4.5) and obtain estimators with all the optimum properties (unbiasedness, minimum variance, etc.). Regression (11.4.5) is known as the *generalized difference*

---

[12] It does not matter whether the model has more than one explanatory variable because autocorrelation is a property of the u_t's.

equation. It involves regressing Y on X, not in the original form, but in the difference form, which is obtained by subtracting a proportion $(= \rho)$ of the value of a variable in the previous time period from its value in the current time period. In this differencing procedure, we lose one observation because the first observation has no predecessor. To avoid this loss of one observation, the first observation on Y and X is transformed as follows:[13]

$$Y_1 \sqrt{1 - \rho^2} \quad \text{and} \quad X_1 \sqrt{1 - \rho^2}$$

When ρ Is Not Known

Although straightforward to apply, the generalized difference regression is generally difficult to run because ρ is rarely known in practice. Therefore, alternative methods need to be devised. Some of these methods are as follows.

1. *The first difference method.* Since ρ lies between 0 and ± 1, one could start from two extreme positions. At one extreme we could assume that $\rho = 0$, that is, no serial correlation, and at the other extreme we could let $\rho = \pm 1$, that is, perfect positive or negative autocorrelation. As a matter of fact, when a regression is run, one generally assumes that there is no autocorrelation and then lets the Durbin-Watson or other tests show whether this assumption is justified. If, however, $\rho = +1$, the generalized difference equation (11.4.5) reduces to the first difference equation as

$$Y_t - Y_{t-1} = \beta_1(X_t - X_{t-1}) + (u_t - u_{t-1})$$
$$= \beta_1(X_t - X_{t-1}) + \varepsilon_t$$

or
$$\Delta Y_t = \beta_1 \, \Delta X_t + \varepsilon_t \tag{11.4.6}$$

where Δ, called *delta*, is the first difference operator and is a symbol or operator (like the expected-value operator E) for successive differences of two values. (*Note:* Generally an operator is a symbol for expressing a mathematical operation.) In running (11.4.6) all one has to do is to form the first differences of both the dependent and explanatory variables and use them as inputs in the regression analysis.

Note an important feature of the first-difference model: There is no intercept term in it. Hence, to run (11.4.6), the regression through the origin model (see Exercise 3.11) will have to be used. But suppose that the original model were

$$Y_t = \beta_0 + \beta_1 X_t + \beta_2 t + u_t \tag{11.4.7}$$

---

[13] It is important that the first Y and X observations be so transformed; otherwise the generalized difference regression may do no better than the usual OLS procedure. On this, see J. Johnston, *op. cit.,* chap. 8.

where t is the trend variable and where u_t follows the first-order autoregressive scheme. The reader can verify that the first-difference transformation of (11.4.7) is as follows:

$$\Delta Y_t = \beta_1 \Delta X_t + \beta_2 + \varepsilon_t \qquad (11.4.8)$$

where $\Delta Y_t = Y_t - Y_{t-1}$ and $\Delta X_t = X_t - X_{t-1}$. Equation (11.4.8) shows that there is an intercept term in the first-difference form, which is in contrast to (11.4.6). But of course, β_2 is the coefficient of the trend variable in the original model. Hence, *if there is an intercept term in the first-difference form, it signifies that there was a linear trend term in the original model and the intercept term is, in fact, the coefficient of the trend variable.* If β_2, for instance, is positive in (11.4.8), it means that there is an upward trend in Y after allowing for the influence of all other variables.

Instead of assuming $\rho = +1$, if we assume that $\rho = -1$, that is, perfect negative serial correlation (which is not typical of economic time series), the generalized difference equation (11.4.5) now becomes

$$Y_t + Y_{t-1} = 2\beta_0 + \beta_1(X_t + X_{t-1}) + \varepsilon_t$$

or

$$\frac{Y_t + Y_{t-1}}{2} = \beta_0 + \beta_1 \frac{X_t + X_{t-1}}{2} + \frac{\varepsilon_t}{2} \qquad (11.4.9)$$

The preceding model is known as the (two-period) *moving average* regression model because we are regressing the value of one moving average on another.[14]

The first-difference transformation presented previously is quite popular in applied econometrics since it is easy to perform. But note that this transformation rests on the assumption that $\rho = +1$; that is, the disturbances are perfectly positively correlated. If this is not the case, the remedy may be worse than the disease. But how does one find out whether the assumption of $\rho = +1$ is justifiable in a given situation? The answer is now given.

2. *ρ Based on Durbin-Watson d statistic.* Recall that earlier we established the following relation:

$$d \doteq 2(1 - \hat{\rho}) \qquad (11.3.10)$$

or

$$\hat{\rho} \doteq 1 - \frac{d}{2} \qquad (11.4.10)$$

which suggests a simple way of obtaining an estimate of ρ from the estimated d statistic. It is clear from (11.4.10) that the first-difference assumption that $\rho = +1$ is valid only if $d = 0$ or approximately so. It is also clear that when $d = 2$, $\hat{\rho} = 0$ and when $d = 4$, $\hat{\rho} = -1$. Therefore, the d statistic provides us with a ready-made method of obtaining an estimate of ρ. But note that the relation (11.4.10) is only

---

[14] Since $(Y_t + Y_{t-1})/2$ and $(X_t + X_{t-1})/2$ are averages of two adjacent values they are called *two-period averages*. They are moving because in computing these averages in successive periods we drop one observation and add another. Hence, $(Y_{t+1} + Y_t)/2$ would be the next two-period average, etc.

an approximate one and may not hold true for small samples. For small samples, Theil and Nagar have suggested the following relation:[15]

$$\hat{\rho} = \frac{N^2(1 - d/2) + k^2}{N^2 - k^2} \qquad (11.4.11)$$

where N = total number of observations, d = Durbin-Watson d, and k = number of coefficients (including the intercept) to be estimated.

It is easy to verify that for large N the Theil-Nagar formulation coincides with the relation (11.4.10). Once ρ is estimated from (11.4.10) or (11.4.11), one can transform the data using the generalized difference equation (11.4.5) and proceed to the usual OLS estimation. Note that the first Y and X observations will have to be multiplied by $\sqrt{1 - \hat{\rho}^2}$ to avoid the loss of the first observation. An example of the transformation discussed previously is given in Sec. 11.5.

In addition to the methods already suggested, there are several other methods of estimating ρ, such as the Cochrane and Orcutt iterative method, Hildreth and Lu scanning procedure, and Durbin two-step procedure. Since these methods can be computationally time-consuming and since there are some statistical problems with each one of them, it is best to leave them to the exercises. (See Exercises 11.5 to 11.7.)

11.5 AN ILLUSTRATIVE EXAMPLE

As an illustration of the methods discussed in Sec. 11.4, we consider the following example (Table 11.5).

The regression model chosen for empirical investigation was

$$\ln \text{HWI}_t = \beta_0 + \beta_1 \ln U_t + u_t$$

Assuming that all the OLS assumptions are fulfilled, the estimated regression is

$$\ln \text{HWI}_t = \quad 3.1698 - 1.5316 \ln U_t$$

$$(0.0487) \quad (0.0719)$$

$$t = (65.0883)(21.3018) \qquad (11.5.1)$$

$$R^2 = 0.9516 \qquad d = 0.9021$$

Assume, further, that the null hypothesis is that $\rho = 0$ and the alternative hypothesis is that $\rho > 0$. At the 5 percent level of significance the critical d values for 24 observations and 1 explanatory variable are $d_L = 1.27$ and $d_U = 1.45$. Since the computed d of 0.9021 is less than d_L, we reject the null hypothesis. There is definite evidence of positive autocorrelation.

---

[15] H. Theil and A. L. Nagar, "Testing the Independence of Regression Disturbances," *Journal of the American Statistical Association*, vol. 56, pp. 793–806, 1961. They assume that the explanatory variables move smoothly; especially the first and second differences of these variables are small in absolute value in relation to the range of the values of the variables themselves.

Table 11.5 Relationship between help-wanted index HWI and the unemployment rate U

Year and quarter	HWI, 1957–1959 = 100	U, %
1962-1	104.66	5.63
2	103.53	5.46
3	97.30	5.63
4	95.96	5.60
1963-1	98.83	5.83
2	97.23	5.76
3	99.06	5.56
4	113.66	5.63
1964-1	117.00	5.46
2	119.66	5.26
3	124.33	5.06
4	133.00	5.06
1965-1	143.33	4.83
2	144.66	4.73
3	152.33	4.46
4	178.33	4.20
1966-1	192.00	3.83
2	186.00	3.90
3	188.00	3.86
4	193.33	3.70
1967-1	187.66	3.66
2	175.33	3.83
3	178.00	3.93
4	187.66	3.96

Source: Damodar Gujarati, "The Relation Between Help-Wanted Index and the Unemployment Rate: A Statistical Analysis, 1962–1967," *The Quarterly Review of Economics and Business*, vol. 8, pp. 67–73, 1968.

Since our regression suffers from the autocorrelation problem, remedial measures are called for. One remedial measure would be to obtain an estimate of ρ (assuming first-order autoregressive mechanism) and use it to transform our data in the manner of the generalized difference equation (11.4.5). And since the Durbin-Watson d is available, we can use the Theil-Nagar technique to obtain an estimate of ρ as follows:

$$\hat{\rho} = \frac{(24)^2(1 - 0.9021/2) + (2)^2}{(24)^2 - (2)^2}$$

$$= 0.5598 \tag{11.5.2}$$

Using this estimate we transform our data as follows:

$$(\ln \text{HWI}_t - 0.5598 \ln \text{HWI}_{t-1}) \quad \text{and} \quad (\ln U_t - 0.5598 \ln U_{t-1})$$

that is, subtract 0.5598 times the previous value of the variable from its current value. The first value of HWI and U will be transformed as follows:

$$\sqrt{(1 - 0.5598^2)} \ln \text{HWI}_1 \quad \text{and} \quad \sqrt{(1 - 0.5598^2)} \ln U_1$$

Let us denote these transformed variables by $\ln (\text{HWI}_t^*)$ and $\ln (U_t^*)$. The regression on these transformed variables is as follows:

$$\ln \text{HWI}_t^* = \quad 1.4091 - 1.4604 \ln U_t^*$$

$$(0.0397) \quad (0.1320)$$

$$t = (35.4937)(11.0636) \tag{11.5.3}$$

$$R^2 = 0.8466 \quad d = 1.7438$$

The reader can easily verify that the regression (11.5.3) does not suffer from the serial correlation problem.

In passing, note that the intercept term in (11.5.3) is, in fact, an estimate of $\beta_0(1 - \rho)$, as can be seen from (11.4.5). Therefore, an estimate of β_0 can be obtained as $\hat{\beta}_0(1 - 0.5598) = 1.4091$; that is, $\hat{\beta}_0 = 3.2010$.

11.6 SUMMARY AND CONCLUSIONS

One of the important assumptions of the classical linear regression model is that the errors or disturbances u_i entering into the population regression function are random or uncorrelated. If this assumption is violated, we have the problem of serial or autocorrelation.

Autocorrelation can arise for several reasons. Examples are inertia, or sluggishness, of most economic time series, specification bias resulting from excluding some relevant variables from the model or using an incorrect functional form, the Cobweb phenomenon, exclusion of lagged variables, and data manipulation.

Although the OLS estimators remain unbiased as well as consistent in the presence of autocorrelation, they are no longer efficient. As a result, the usual t and F tests of significance cannot be legitimately applied. Hence remedial measures are needed. The remedy depends on the nature of interdependence among the disturbances u_i. But since the disturbances are unobservable, the common practice is to assume that they are generated by some plausible mechanism. The mechanism that is commonly used is the Markov first-order autoregressive scheme, which assumes that the disturbance in the current time period is linearly related to the disturbance term in the previous time period, the coefficient of autocorrelation providing the extent of interdependence. If the first-order scheme is valid and the coefficient of autocorrelation is known, the serial correlation problem can be easily attacked by transforming the data following the generalized difference equation procedure. Since the coefficient of autocorrelation is not known a priori, we considered several methods of estimating it. Some of these methods are ad hoc, and some are based on the data themselves. In practice these methods have been proved to be quite useful.

Of course, before remediation comes detection. Although there are several methods of finding out whether serial correlation is present in a given instance, the most celebrated among these is the Durbin-Watson d statistic. The d statistic is now routinely computed along with the summary statistics such as the R^2, t ratios, etc. In this chapter, we pointed out the assumptions underlying the d test as well as some of its restrictions.

EXERCISES

11.1 Given a sample of 50 observations and four explanatory variables, what can you say about autocorrelation if (a) $d = 1.05$? (b) $d = 1.40$? (c) $d = 2.50$? (d) $d = 3.97$?

11.2 In studying the movement in the production workers' share in the value added (i.e., labor's share), the following models were considered by Gujarati.[16]

$$\text{Model } A: Y_t = \beta_0 + \beta_1 t + u_t$$

$$\text{Model } B: Y_t = \alpha_0 + \alpha_1 t + \alpha_2 t^2 + u_t$$

where Y = labor's share and t = time. Based on the annual data for 1949–1964, the following results were obtained for the primary metal industry:

$$\text{Model } A: \hat{Y}_t = 0.4529 - 0.0041t \qquad R^2 = 0.5284 \qquad d = 0.8252$$

$$(-3.9608)$$

$$\text{Model } B: \hat{Y}_t = 0.4786 - 0.0127t + 0.0005t^2$$

$$(-3.2724) \quad (2.7777)$$

$$R^2 = 0.6629 \qquad d = 1.82$$

where the figures in the parentheses are t ratios.

(a) Is there serial correlation in model A? In model B?
(b) What accounts for the serial correlation?
(c) How would you distinguish between "pure" autocorrelation and specification bias?

11.3 *Detecting autocorrelation: von Neumann ratio test.*[17] Assuming that the residuals e_t are random drawings from normal distribution, von Neumann has shown that for *large N*, the ratio

$$\frac{\delta^2}{s^2} = \frac{\sum (e_t - e_{t-1})^2/(N-1)}{\sum (e_t - \bar{e})^2/N} \qquad Note: \bar{e} = 0 \text{ in OLS}$$

called the *von Neumann ratio*, is approximately normally distributed with

$$\text{Mean: } E\frac{\delta^2}{s^2} = \frac{2N}{N-1}$$

and variance

$$\text{var}\frac{\delta^2}{s^2} = 4N^2\frac{N-2}{(N+1)(N-1)^3}$$

[16] Damodar Gujarati, "Labor's Share in Manufacturing Industries," *Industrial and Labor Relations Review*, vol. 23, no. 1, pp. 65–75, October 1969.

[17] J. von Neumann, "Distribution of the Ratio of the Mean Square Successive Difference to the Variance," *Annals of Mathematical Statistics*, vol. 12, pp. 367–395, 1941.

(a) If N is sufficiently large, how would you use the von Neumann ratio to test for autocorrelation?

(b) What is the relationship between the Durbin-Watson d and the ratio?

(c) The d statistic lies between 0 and 4. What are the corresponding limits for the von Neumann ratio?

(d) Since the ratio depends on the assumption that the e's are random drawings from normal distribution, how valid is this assumption for the OLS residuals?

(e) Suppose in an application the ratio was found to be 2.88 with 100 observations. Test the hypothesis that there is no serial correlation in the data.

Note: B. I. Hart has tabulated the critical values of the von Neumann ratio for sample size of up to 60 observations.[18]

11.4 *Detecting serial correlation: the run test.* Refer to the residuals e, given in Table 11.4. Suppose we simply note down the signs of these residuals, which are as follows:

$$- + - - - - + - + + + + +$$

We define a run as an uninterrupted sequence of one symbol or attribute, such as $+$ or $-$. We further define the length of a run as the number of elements in the run. In the preceding sequence there are six runs: a run of one minus, a run of one plus, a run of four minuses (i.e., length of 4), a run of one plus, a run of one minus, and a final run of five pluses.

By examining how runs behave in a strictly random sequence of observations one can derive a test of randomness of runs. For example, are the 6 runs observed in the preceding sequence of 13 observations too many or too few as compared with the number of runs expected in a strictly random sequence of 13 observations? If there are too many runs, it would mean that in our example the e's change sign frequently, thus indicating negative serial correlation (cf. Fig. 11.3b). Similarly, if there are too few runs, they may suggest positive autocorrelation, as in Fig. 11.3a.

Now letting N = total number of observations, N_1 = number of $+$ symbols, N_2 = number of $-$ symbols $(N = N_1 + N_2)$, and n = number of runs, it can be shown that for $N_1 > 10$ and $N_2 > 10$, the number of runs n is distributed normally with

$$\text{Mean} = E(n) = \frac{2N_1 N_2}{N_1 + N_2} + 1$$

$$\text{var }(n) = \frac{2N_1 N_2 (2N_1 N_2 - N_1 - N_2)}{(N_1 + N_2)^2 (N_1 + N_2 - 1)}$$

Hence, the normal distribution can be used to find out whether the number of runs observed in an application is statistically significant.

If N_1 or N_2 is smaller than 10, Swed and Eisenhart have developed special tables which give critical values of the runs expected in a random sequence of N observations. These tables are given in App. D, Table 6.

(a) What is the advantage of the run test over other tests considered in this text?

(b) If in a sample of 80 observations it was found that there were 30 pluses, 50 minuses, and 25 runs. Is the sequence random?

(c) Use the Swed and Eisenhart tables to test for randomness in the e's observed in Table 11.4.

(d) If you have the following sequence of observations

$$+ + + + + + + + + + - - - - - - - - - -$$

what can you say about serial correlation? What does serial correlation mean in this situation?

---

[18] The table may be found in Johnston, *op. cit.*, pp. 432–433.

11.5 *Estimating ρ: the Cochrane-Orcutt procedure.*[19] Assuming the first-order autoregressive scheme

$$u_t = \rho u_{t-1} + \varepsilon_t \tag{1}$$

where $-1 < \rho < 1$ and where ε_t satisfies the usual OLS assumptions, Cochrane and Orcutt suggest estimating ρ from the OLS residuals as

$$e_t = \hat{\rho} e_{t-1} + v_t \tag{2}$$

that is,

$$\hat{\rho} = \frac{\sum e_t e_{t-1}}{\sum e_{t-1}^2} \tag{3}$$

Using $\hat{\rho}$ obtained previously, the generalized difference equation (11.4.5) can be approximated by

$$Y_t - \hat{\rho} Y_{t-1} = \beta_0(1 - \hat{\rho}) + \beta_1(X_t - \hat{\rho} X_{t-1}) + e_t \tag{4}$$

Not knowing a priori that the "first-stage" $\hat{\rho}$ obtained is the "best" estimate of ρ, Cochrane and Orcutt suggest obtaining a "second-stage" estimate of ρ as follows:

$$e_t^* = \hat{\rho} e_{t-1}^* + w_t$$

that is,

$$\hat{\rho} = \frac{\sum e_t^* e_{t-1}^*}{\sum e_{t-1}^{*2}} \tag{5}$$

where e^*'s are the residuals obtained from equation (4) and $\hat{\rho}$ is the *second-stage* estimate of ρ. Using this second-stage estimate, the data can be transformed again using the generalized difference equation. This iterative process can go on until the successive estimates of ρ do not differ substantially from one another.

(*a*) What are the advantages of the Cochrane and Orcutt procedure?

(*b*) How does one know that the ρ obtained in the "final" stage is the "best" one?

11.6 *Estimating ρ: the Hildreth-Lu scanning or search procedure.*[20] Since in the first-order autoregressive scheme

$$u_t = \rho u_{t-1} + \varepsilon_t$$

ρ is expected to lie between -1 and $+1$, Hildreth and Lu suggest a systematic "scanning" or search procedure to locate it. They recommend selecting ρ between -1 and $+1$ using, say, 0.1 unit intervals and transforming the data by the generalized difference equation (11.4.5). Thus, one may choose ρ from $-0.9, -0.8, \ldots, 0.8, 0.9$. For each chosen ρ we run the generalized difference equation and obtain the associated RSS: $\sum e_t^2$. Hildreth and Lu suggest choosing that ρ which minimizes the RSS (hence maximizing the R^2). If further refinement is needed, they suggest using smaller unit intervals, say, 0.01 unit such as $-0.99, -0.98, \ldots, 0.90, 0.91$, and so on.

(*a*) What are the advantages of the Hildreth-Lu procedure?

(*b*) How does one know that the ρ value ultimately chosen to transform the data will, in fact, guarantee minimum $\sum e_t^2$?

[19] D. Cochrane and G. H. Orcutt, "Application of Least Squares Regressions to Relationships Containing Autocorrelated Error Terms," *Journal of the American Statistical Association*, vol. 44, pp. 32–61, 1949.

[20] G. Hildreth and J. Y. Lu, "Demand Relations with Autocorrelated Disturbances," Michigan State University, *Agricultural Experiment Station*, Tech. Bull. 276, November 1960.

11.7 *Estimating ρ: the Durbin two-stage procedure.*[21] Assuming the first-order autoregressive scheme, Durbin suggests a two-step procedure for resolving the serial correlation problem. In step I, an estimate of ρ is obtained from the generalized difference equation (11.4.5) by writing it as follows:

$$Y_t = \beta_0(1 - \rho) + \beta_1 X_t - \rho\beta_1 X_{t-1} + \rho Y_{t-1} + \varepsilon_t$$

If the preceding regression is run, the coefficient of Y_{t-1} will provide an estimate of ρ. Using the estimate of ρ thus obtained, in step II the data are transformed via the generalized difference equation (11.4.5).

(a) What are the merits of the Durbin two-step procedure?

(b) Is ρ thus obtained likely to be unbiased? Consistent?

(c) Is there more than one way of obtaining ρ from the preceding equation? If so, which estimate will you choose and why?

(d) Since Y_{t-1}, the lagged value of the dependent variable, appears as an explanatory variable in the preceding equation, does the preceding regression violate any of the assumptions of the classical linear regression model? If so, can the equation be estimated by the method of OLS?

11.8 You are given the following data:

Y, Personal consumption expenditure (billions of 1958 dollars)	X, time	$\hat{Y}$, estimated Y†	e_t, residuals
281.4	1 (= 1956)	261.4208	19.9791
288.1	2	276.6026	11.4973
290.0	3	291.7844	− 1.7844
307.3	4	306.9661	0.3338
316.1	5	322.1479	− 6.0479
322.5	6	337.3297	− 14.8297
338.4	7	352.5115	− 14.1115
353.3	8	367.6933	− 14.3933
373.7	9	382.8751	− 9.1751
397.7	10	398.0569	− 0.3569
418.1	11	413.2386	4.8613
430.1	12	428.4206	1.6795
452.7	13	443.6022	9.0977
469.1	14	458.7840	10.3159
476.9	15 (= 1970)	473.9658	2.9341

† Obtained from the regression $Y_t = \beta_0 + \beta_1 X_t + u_t$.

(a) Verify that Durbin-Watson $d = 0.4147$.

(b) Is there positive serial correlation in the disturbances?

(c) If so, estimate ρ by the
  (i) Theil-Nagar method
  (ii) Durbin two-stage procedure
  (iii) Cochrane-Orcutt method

(d) Use the Theil-Nagar method to transform the data and run the regression on the transformed data.

(e) Does the regression estimated in (d) exhibit autocorrelation? If so, how would you get rid of it?

[21] J. Durbin, "Estimation of Parameters in Time-Series Regression Models," *Journal of the Royal Statistical Society*, ser. B, vol. 22, pp. 139–153, 1960.

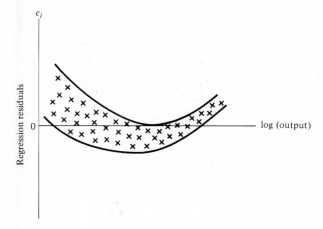

Figure 11.8 Regression residuals from the Nerlove study. (*Adapted from Marc Nerlove, "Return to Scale in Electric Supply," in Measurement in Economics, Carl F. Christ et al., eds., Stanford University Press, Stanford, Calif., 1963.*)

11.9 In measuring returns to scale in electricity supply, Nerlove used cross-sectional data of 145 privately owned utilities in the United States for the period 1955 and regressed the log of total cost on the logs of output, wage rate, price of capital, and price of fuel. He found that the residuals estimated from this regression exhibited "serial" correlation, as judged by the Durbin-Watson d. To seek a remedy, he plotted the estimated residuals on the log of output and obtained Fig. 11.8.

(*a*) What does Fig. 11.8 show?

(*b*) How can you get rid of "serial" correlation in the preceding situation?

11.10 The residuals from a regression when plotted against time gave the scattergram in Fig. 11.9. The encircled "extreme" residual is called an *outlier*. An outlier is an observation whose value exceeds the values of other observations in the sample by a large amount, perhaps three or four standard deviations away from the mean value of all the observations.

(*a*) What are the reasons for the existence of the outlier(s)?

(*b*) If there is an outlier(s), should that observation(s) be discarded and the regression run on the remaining observations?

(*c*) Is the Durbin-Watson d applicable in the presence of the outlier(s)?

11.11 Verify equation (11.4.8).

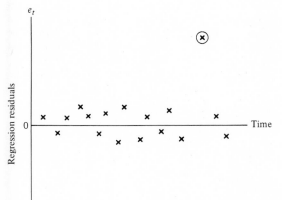

Figure 11.9 Hypothetical regression residuals plotted against time.

*11.12 Assume the first-order autoregressive scheme $u_t = \rho u_{t-1} + \varepsilon_t$, where ε_t satisfies the assumptions of the classical linear regression model.

    (a) Show that var $(u_t) = \sigma^2/(1 - \rho^2)$, where $\sigma^2 = $ var (ε_t).

    (b) What is the covariance between u_t and u_{t-1}? Between u_t and u_{t-2}? Generalize your results.

    (c) Write down the variance-covariance matrix of the u's.

    (d) If $\rho = 1$, what happens to the variance of u_t? What implications does it have for the first-difference transformation?

11.13 Apply the Durbin two-step procedure to the illustrative example given in Sec. 11.5 and compare your results.

11.14 Refer to Exercise 3.9. Obtain the residuals and find out if there is autocorrelation in the data? How would you transform the data in case serial correlation is detected?

11.15 Refer to equation (11.2.4). Assume that $\rho \neq 0$ but the X's are mutually uncorrelated. What happens to the var (β_1^*)? What can you say about autocorrelation in this situation?

11.16 Refer to equation (11.2.8). Assume $r = 0$ but $\rho \neq 0$. What is the effect on $E(\hat\sigma^2)$ if (a) $0 < \rho < 1$ and (b) $-1 < \rho < 0$? When will the bias in $\hat\sigma^2$ be reasonably small?

11.17 Refer to Tables 11.1 and 11.2. Using ε_t and X_t given there, generate a sample of ten Y values from the model

$$Y_t = 3.0 + 0.5X_t + u_t$$

where $u_t = 0.9u_{t-1} + \varepsilon_t$. Assume $u_0 = 10$. Comment on your results.

11.18 Show that for large N, the Theil-Nagar estimate of ρ is equal to the estimate given by equation (11.4.10).

11.19 Refer to Exercise 8.9. Omitting the variables X^2 and X^3, run the regression and examine the residuals for "serial" correlation. If serial correlation is found, how would you rationalize it? What remedial measures would you suggest?

11.20 Based on the Durbin-Watson d statistic, how would you distinguish "pure" autocorrelation from specification bias?

11.21 Suppose in the model

$$Y_t = \beta_0 + \beta_1 X_t + u_t$$

the u's are in fact serially independent. What would happen in this situation if assuming that $u_t = \rho u_{t-1} + \varepsilon_t$ we use the generalized difference regression

$$Y_t - \rho Y_{t-1} = \beta_0(1 - \rho) + \beta_1 X_t - \rho\beta_1 X_{t-1} + \varepsilon_t$$

Discuss in particular the properties of the disturbance term ε_t.

11.22 Refer to Exercise 6.15. A priori autocorrelation is expected in such data. Therefore, it is suggested that you regress the log of real money supply on the logs of real national income and long-term interest rate in the first-difference form. Run this regression, and then rerun the regression in the original form. Is the assumption underlying the first-difference transformation satisfied? If not, what kinds of biases are likely to result from such a transformation? Illustrate with the data at hand.

11.23 In a study of the determination of prices of final output at factor cost in the United Kingdom, the following results were obtained on the basis of annual data for the period 1951–1969:

$$PF_t = 2.033 + 0.273W_t - 0.521X_t + 0.256M_t + 0.028M_{t-1} + 0.121PF_{t-1}$$

$$(0.992)\ (0.127)\qquad (0.099)\qquad (0.024)\qquad (0.039)\qquad\qquad (0.119)$$

$$R^2 = 0.984 \qquad d = 2.54$$

* Optional.

where PF = prices of final output at factor cost, W = wages and salaries per employee, X = gross domestic product per person employed, M = import prices, M_{t-1} = import prices lagged 1 year, and PF_{t-1} = prices of final output at factor cost in the previous year.[22]

"Since for 18 observations and five explanatory variables, the 5 percent lower and upper d values are 0.71 and 2.06, the estimated d value of 2.54 indicates that there is no positive autocorrelation." Comment.

11.24 Give circumstances under which each of the following methods of estimating the first-order coefficient of autocorrelation ρ may be appropriate:

(*a*) First-difference regression
(*b*) Moving average regression
(*c*) Theil-Nagar transform
(*d*) Cochrane and Orcutt iterative procedure
(*e*) Hildreth-Lu scanning procedure
(*f*) Durbin two-step procedure

11.25 Will $\hat{\beta}_0$ = 3.2010 obtained from the regression (11.5.3) provide an unbiased estimate of the true β_0? Why or why not?

[22] *Source: Prices and Earnings in 1951–1969: An Econometric Assessment*, Department of Employment, Her Majesty's Stationery Office, 1971, table no. C, p. 37, equation no. 63.

THREE

TOPICS IN ECONOMETRICS

In Part I we introduced the classical linear regression model with all its assumptions. In Part II we examined in detail the consequences that ensue when one or more of the assumptions are not satisfied and what can be done about them. In Part III we turn to a study of some selected but commonly encountered econometric techniques.

In Chap. 12, we consider regression models that include current as well as past, or lagged, values of the explanatory variables in addition to models that include lagged value(s) of the dependent variable as one of the explanatory variables. These models are called, respectively, the *distributed-lag and autoregressive* models. Although such models are extremely useful in empirical econometrics, they pose some special estimating problems because they violate one or more assumptions of the classical regression model. We consider these special problems and examine the appropriate remedial measures.

In Chap. 13, we consider the role of *qualitative* explanatory variables in regression analysis. The qualitative variables, called *dummy variables*, are a device of incorporating into the regression model variables which cannot be readily quantified, such as sex, religion, and color, and yet influence the behavior of the dependent variable.

In Chap. 14, we allow the dependent variable in a regression model itself to be qualitative in nature. Such models are used in situations where the dependent variable is of the "yes" or "no" type, such as ownership of house, car, and

253

household appliances or possession of an attribute, such as membership in a trade union or professional society. Models which include yes–no-type dependent variables are called *dichotomous*, or *dummy, dependent-variable regression models*. We consider their special features because they violate some of the assumptions of the classical linear regression model; we also consider some remedies.

Chapter 15 is devoted to a brief discussion of several assorted topics in econometrics, including (1) the errors of measurement in the dependent and explanatory variables, (2) a priori restrictions on the regression coefficients, (3) nonlinear-in-the-parameter regression models, and (4) specification bias or error. In each case we examine the nature of the topic and point out its relevance for empirical analysis.

With Chap. 15 we conclude our discussion of the single-equation regression models that we began in Chap. 1. These fifteen chapters cover most of the major areas in single-equation econometric models.

TWELVE

AUTOREGRESSIVE AND DISTRIBUTED-LAG MODELS

In regression analysis involving time-series data, if the regression model includes not only the current but the lagged (past) values of the explanatory variables (the X's), it is called a *distributed-lag model*. Whereas, if the model includes one or more lagged values of the dependent variable among its explanatory variables, it is called an *autoregressive model*. Thus,

$$Y_t = \alpha + \beta_0 X_t + \beta_1 X_{t-1} + \beta_2 X_{t-2} + u_t$$

represents a distributed-lag model, whereas

$$Y_t = \alpha + \beta X_t + \gamma Y_{t-1} + u_t$$

is an example of an autoregressive model.

Autoregressive and distributed-lag models are used extensively in econometric analysis, and in this chapter we take a close look at such models with a view to finding out:

1. What is the role of lags in economics?
2. What are the reasons for the lags?
3. Is there any theoretical justification for the commonly used lagged models in empirical econometrics?
4. What is the relationship, if any, between autoregressive and distributed-lag models? Can one be derived from the other?
5. What are some of the statistical problems involved in estimating such models?

12.1 THE ROLE OF "TIME," OR "LAG," IN ECONOMICS

In economics the dependence of a variable Y (the dependent variable) on another variable(s) X (the explanatory variable) is rarely instantaneous. Very often, Y responds to X with a lapse of time. Such a lapse of time is called a *lag*. To illustrate the nature of the lag, we consider several examples.

Example 12.1 The consumption function Suppose a person receives a salary increase of $2000 in annual pay, and suppose that this is a "permanent" increase in the sense that the increase in salary is maintained. What will be the effect of this increase in income on the person's annual consumption expenditure?

Now it is a common experience that following such a gain in income, by and large, people do not rush to spend all the increase immediately. Thus, our recipient may decide to increase consumption expenditure by $800 in the first year following the salary increase in income, by another $600 in the next year, and by another $400 in the following year, saving the remainder. By the end of the third year, the person's annual consumption expenditure will be increased by $1800. We can thus write the consumption function as

$$Y_t = \text{constant} + 0.4X_t + 0.3X_{t-1} + 0.2X_{t-2} + u_t \qquad (12.1.1)$$

where Y is consumption expenditure and X is income.

Equation (12.1.1) shows that the effect of an increase in income of $2000 is spread, or distributed, over a period of 3 years. Models such as (12.1.1) are therefore called *distributed-lag models* because the effect of a given cause (income) is spread over a number of time periods. Geometrically, the distributed-lag model (12.1.1) is shown in Fig. 12.1. More generally we may write

$$Y_t = \alpha + \beta_0 X_t + \beta_1 X_{t-1} + \beta_2 X_{t-2} + \cdots + \beta_k X_{t-k} + u_t \qquad (12.1.2)$$

which is a distributed-lag model with a finite lag of k time periods. The coefficient β_0 is known as the *short-run*, or *impact*, *multiplier* because it gives the change in the mean value of Y following a unit change in X in the same time period. $\beta_1, \beta_2, \ldots, \beta_k$ are called *delay*, or *interim*, *multipliers* because they measure the impact on mean Y of a unit change in X in various previous time periods. And

$$\sum_{i=0}^{k} \beta_i = \beta_0 + \beta_1 + \beta_2 + \cdots + \beta_k = \beta \qquad (12.1.3)$$

is called the *long-run*, or *total*, *distributed-lag multiplier* provided the sum β exists (to be discussed elsewhere).

Returning to (12.1.1), we see that the short-run multiplier, which is nothing but the short-run marginal propensity to consume (MPC), is 0.4, whereas the long-run multiplier, which is the long-run marginal propensity to

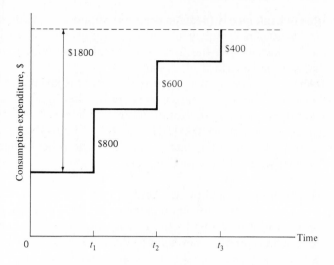

Figure 12.1 Example of distributed lags.

consume, is $0.4 + 0.3 + 0.2 = 0.9$. The meaning is that following $1 increase in income, the consumer will increase his or her level of consumption by about 40 cents in the year of increase, by another 30 cents in the next year, and by yet another 20 cents in the following year. The long-run impact of an increase of $1 in income is thus 90 cents.

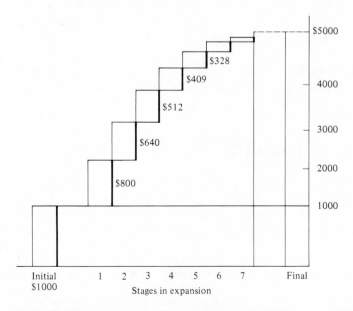

Figure 12.2 Cumulative expansion in bank deposits (initial reserve $1000 and 20 percent reserve requirement).

Example 12.2 Creation of bank money (demand deposits) Suppose the Federal Reserve System pours $1000 of new money into the banking system by buying government securities. What will be the total amount of bank money, or demand deposits, that will be generated ultimately?

Following the fractional reserve system, if we assume that the law requires banks to keep a 20 percent reserve backing for the deposits they create, then by the well-known multiplier process the total amount of demand deposits that will be generated will be equal to $1000 [1/(1 − 0.8)] = $5000. Of course, $5000 in demand deposits will not be created overnight. The process takes time, which can be shown schematically in Fig. 12.2.

Example 12.3 Link between money and prices According to the monetarists, inflation is essentially a monetary phenomenon in the sense that a continuous increase in the general price level is due to the rate of expansion in money supply far in excess of the amount of money actually demanded by the economic units. Of course, this link between inflation and changes in money supply is not instantaneous. Studies have shown that the lag between the two is anywhere from 3 to about 12 quarters.

Example 12.4 Lag between R&D expenditure and productivity The decision to invest in research and development (R&D) expenditure and its ultimate payoff in terms of increased productivity involves considerable lag, actually several lags, such as, "... the lag between the investment of funds and the time inventions actually begin to appear, the lag between the invention of an idea or device and its development up to a commercially applicable stage, and the lag which is introduced by the process of diffusion: it takes time before all the old machines are replaced by the better new ones."[1]

The preceding examples are only a sample of the use of lag in economics. Undoubtedly, the reader can produce several examples from his or her own experience.

12.2 THE REASONS FOR LAGS[2]

Although the examples cited in Sec. 12.1 point out the nature of lagged phenomena, they do not fully explain why lags occur. There are three main reasons.

1. *Psychological reasons.* Due to the force of habit (inertia), people do not change their consumption habits immediately following a price decrease or an

[1] Zvi Griliches, "Distributed Lags: A Survey," *Econometrica*, vol. 36, no. 1, pp. 16–49, January 1967.

[2] This section leans heavily on *Distributed Lags and Demand Analysis for Agricultural and Other Commodities*, Agricultural Handbook No. 141, U.S. Department of Agriculture, June 1958. (The author of this monograph is Marc Nerlove.)

income increase perhaps because the process of change may involve some immediate disutility. Thus, those who become instant millionaires by winning lotteries may not change the life styles to which they were accustomed for a long time because they may not know how to react to such a windfall gain immediately. Of course, given reasonable time, they may learn to live with their newly acquired fortune. Also, people may not know whether a change is "permanent" or "transitory." Thus, my reaction to an increase in my income will depend on whether the increase is permanent or just transitory. If it is only a once-for-all increase and in succeeding periods my income returns to its previous level, I may save the entire increase, whereas someone else in my position might decide to "live it up."

2. *Technological reasons.* Suppose the price of capital relative to labor declines, making substitution of capital for labor economically feasible. Of course, addition of capital takes time (the gestation period). Moreover, if the drop in price is expected to be temporary, firms may not rush to substitute capital for labor, especially if they expect that after the temporary drop the price of capital may increase beyond its previous level. Sometimes, imperfect knowledge also accounts for lags. At present the market for electronic pocket calculators is glutted with all kinds of calculators with varying computational features and prices. Moreover, since their introduction in the late 1960s, the prices of most calculators have dropped dramatically. As a result, prospective consumers for the calculator may hestitate to buy until they have had time to look into the features and prices of all the competing brands. Moreover, they may hesitate to buy in the expectation of further decline in price or useful innovations.

3. *Institutional reasons.* These reasons also contribute to lags. For example, contractual obligations may prevent firms from switching from one source of labor or raw material to another. As another example, those who have placed funds in long-term savings accounts for fixed durations such as 1 year, 3 years, or 7 years, are essentially "locked in" even though money market conditions may be such that higher yields are available elsewhere. Similarly, employers often give their employees a choice among several health insurance plans, but once a choice is made, an employee may not switch to another plan for at least 1 year. Although this may be done for administrative convenience, the employee is locked in for 1 year.

For the reasons just discussed, lag occupies a central role in economics. This is clearly reflected in the short-run–long-run methodology of economics. It is for this reason we say that short-run price or income elasticities are generally smaller (in absolute value) than the corresponding long-run elasticities or that short-run marginal propensity to consume is generally smaller than long-run marginal propensity to consume.

12.3 ESTIMATION OF DISTRIBUTED-LAG MODELS

Granted that distributed-lag models play a highly useful role in economics, how does one estimate such models? Specifically, suppose we have the following distributed-lag model in one explanatory variable:[3]

$$Y_t = \alpha + \beta_0 X_t + \beta_1 X_{t-1} + \beta_2 X_{t-2} + \cdots + u_t \qquad (12.3.1)$$

where we have not defined the length of the lag, that is, how far back into the past we want to go. Such a model is called an *infinite* (lag) *model* whereas a model of the type (12.1.2) is called a *finite* (lag) *distributed-lag model* because the length of the lag k is specified. We shall continue to use (12.3.1) because it is easy to handle mathematically, as we shall see.[4]

How do we estimate the α and β's of (12.3.1)? We may adopt two approaches: ad hoc estimation and a priori restrictions on the β's by assuming that the β's follow some systematic pattern. We shall consider ad hoc estimation in this section and the other approach in the next section.

Ad Hoc Estimation of Distributed-Lag Models

Since the explanatory variable X_t is assumed to be nonstochastic (or at least uncorrelated with the disturbance term u_t), X_{t-1}, X_{t-2}, and so on, are nonstochastic, too. Therefore, in principle, the ordinary least squares (OLS) can be applied to (12.3.1). This is the approach taken by Alt[5] and Tinbergen.[6] They suggest that to estimate (12.3.1) one may proceed *sequentially*; that is, first regress Y_t on X_t, then regress Y_t on X_t and X_{t-1}, then regress Y_t on X_t, X_{t-1}, and X_{t-2}, and so on. This sequential procedure stops when the regression coefficients of the lagged variables start becoming statistically insignificant and/or the coefficient of at least one of the variables changes signs from positive to negative or vice versa. Following this precept, Alt regressed fuel-oil consumption Y on new orders X. Based on the quarterly data for the period 1930–1939, the results were as follows:

$$\hat{Y}_t = 8.37 + 0.171 X_t$$

$$\hat{Y}_t = 8.27 + 0.111 X_t + 0.064 X_{t-1}$$

$$\hat{Y}_t = 8.27 + 0.109 X_t + 0.071 X_{t-1} - 0.055 X_{t-2}$$

$$\hat{Y}_t = 8.32 + 0.108 X_t + 0.063 X_{t-1} + 0.022 X_{t-2} - 0.020 X_{t-3}$$

Alt chose the second regression as the "best" one because in the last two equations the sign of X_{t-2} was not stable and in the last equation the sign of X_{t-3} was negative, which may be difficult to interpret economically.

---

[3] If there is more than one explanatory variable in the model, each variable may have a lagged effect on Y. For simplicity only, we assume one explanatory variable.

[4] In practice, however, the coefficients of the distant X values are expected to have negligible effect on Y.

[5] F. F. Alt, "Distributed Lags," *Econometrica*, vol. 10, pp. 113–128, 1942.

[6] J. Tinbergen, "Long-Term Foreign Trade Elasticities," *Metroeconomica*, vol. 1, pp. 174–185, 1949.

Although seemingly straightforward, ad hoc estimation suffers from many drawbacks, such as the following.

1. There is no a priori guide as to what is the maximum length of the lag.

2. As one estimates successive lags, there are fewer degrees of freedom left, making statistical inference somewhat shaky. Economists are not usually that lucky to have a long series of data so that they can go on estimating numerous lags.

3. More importantly, in economic time-series data, successive values (lags) tend to be highly correlated; hence multicollinearity rears its ugly head. As noted in Chap. 9, multicollinearity leads to inefficient estimation; that is, the standard errors tend to be large in relation to the estimated coefficients. As a result, based on the routinely computed t ratios, we may tend to declare (erroneously) that a lagged coefficient(s) is statistically insignificant. But this lack of statistical significance may be due to multicollinearity and not to the fact that a coefficient is really insignificant.

In view of the preceding problems, the ad hoc estimation procedure has very little to recommend it. Clearly, some prior or theoretical considerations must be brought to bear upon the various β's if we are to make headway with the estimation problem.

12.4 THE KOYCK APPROACH TO DISTRIBUTED-LAG MODELS[7]

Koyck has proposed an ingenious method of estimating distributed-lag models. Suppose we start with the infinite-lag distributed-lag model (12.3.1). Assuming that the β's are all of the same sign, Koyck assumes that they decline geometrically as follows:

$$\beta_k = \beta_0 \lambda^k \qquad k = 0, 1, \ldots \qquad (12.4.1)$$

where λ, such that $0 < \lambda < 1$, is known as the *rate of decline, or decay*, of the distributed lag and where $1 - \lambda$ is known as the *speed of adjustment*.

What (12.4.1) postulates is that each successive β coefficient is numerically less than each preceding β (this follows since $\lambda < 1$), implying that as one goes back into the distant past, the effect of that lag on Y_t becomes progressively smaller, a quite plausible assumption. After all, current and recent past incomes are expected to affect current consumption expenditure more heavily than income in the distant past. Geometrically, the Koyck scheme is depicted in Fig. 12.3.

By assuming nonnegative values for λ, Koyck rules out the β's from changing sign, and by assuming $\lambda < 1$, he gives lesser weight to the distant β's than the

[7] L. M. Koyck, *Distributed Lags and Investment Analysis*, North-Holland Publishing Company, Amsterdam, 1954.

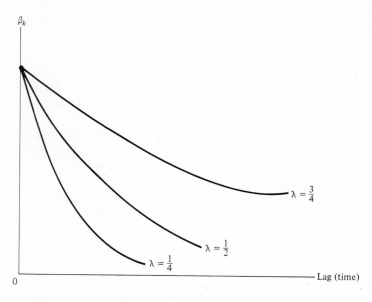

Figure 12.3 Koyck scheme (declining geometric distribution).

current ones. Moreover, the Koyck scheme ensures that the sum of the β's, which gives the long-run multiplier, is a finite amount, namely,

$$\sum_{k=0}^{\infty} \beta_k = \beta_0\left(\frac{1}{1-\lambda}\right)$$
(12.4.2)[8]

As a result of (12.4.1), the infinite-lag model (12.3.1) may be written as

$$Y_t = \alpha + \beta_0 X_t + \beta_0 \lambda X_{t-1} + \beta_0 \lambda^2 X_{t-2} + \cdots + u_t$$
(12.4.3)

As it stands, the model is still not amenable to easy estimation since there remain a large (literally infinite) number of parameters to be estimated and the parameter λ enters in a highly nonlinear form: Strictly speaking, the method of linear (in the parameters) regression analysis cannot be applied to such a model. But now Koyck suggests an ingenious way out. He lags (12.4.3) by one period to obtain

$$Y_{t-1} = \alpha + \beta_0 X_{t-1} + \beta_0 \lambda X_{t-2} + \beta_0 \lambda^2 X_{t-3} + \cdots + u_{t-1}$$
(12.4.4)

He then multiplies (12.4.4) by λ to obtain

$$\lambda Y_{t-1} = \lambda\alpha + \lambda\beta_0 X_{t-1} + \beta_0 \lambda^2 X_{t-2} + \beta_0 \lambda^3 X_{t-3} + \cdots + \lambda u_{t-1}$$
(12.4.5)

[8] This is because

$$\sum \beta_k = \beta_0(1 + \lambda + \lambda^2 + \lambda^3 + \cdots) = \beta_0\left(\frac{1}{1-\lambda}\right)$$

since the expression in the parenthesis on the right side is an infinite geometric series whose sum is $1/(1-\lambda)$ provided $0 < \lambda < 1$.

Subtracting (12.4.5) from (12.4.3), he gets

$$Y_t - \lambda Y_{t-1} = \alpha(1 - \lambda) + \beta_0 X_t + (u_t - \lambda u_{t-1}) \tag{12.4.6}$$

or, rearranging,

$$Y_t = \alpha(1 - \lambda) + \beta_0 X_t + \lambda Y_{t-1} + v_t \tag{12.4.7}$$

where $v_t = (u_t - \lambda u_{t-1})$.

The procedure just described is known as the *Koyck transformation*. Comparing (12.4.7) with (12.3.1), we see the tremendous simplification accomplished by Koyck. Whereas before we had to estimate α and an infinite number of β's, we now have to estimate only three unknowns: α, β_0, and λ. Now there is no reason to expect multicollinearity. In a sense multicollinearity is resolved by replacing X_{t-1}, $X_{t-2}, \ldots$, by a single variable, namely, Y_{t-1}. But note the following features of the Koyck transformation.

1. We started with a distributed-lag model but ended up with an autoregressive model because Y_{t-1} appears as one of the explanatory variables. This shows how one can "convert" a distributed-lag model into an autoregressive model.

2. The appearance of Y_{t-1} is likely to create some statistical problems. Y_{t-1}, like Y_t, is stochastic, which means that we have a stochastic explanatory variable in the model. Recall that the classical least-squares theory is predicated on the assumption that the explanatory variables are either nonstochastic or, if stochastic, are distributed independently of the stochastic disturbance term. Hence we must find out if Y_{t-1} satisfies this assumption. (We shall return to this point in Sec. 12.7.)

3. In the original model (12.3.1) the disturbance term was u_t, whereas in the transformed model it is $v_t = (u_t - \lambda u_{t-1})$. Now the statistical properties of v_t depend on what is assumed about the statistical properties of u_t. For, as shown later, if the original u_t's are serially uncorrelated, the v_t's are serially correlated. Therefore, we may have to face up to the serial correlation problem in addition to the stochastic explanatory variable Y_{t-1}. We shall do that in Sec. 12.7.

12.5 RATIONALIZATION OF THE KOYCK MODEL: THE ADAPTIVE EXPECTATION MODEL

Although very neat, the Koyck model (12.4.7) is ad hoc since it was obtained by a purely algebraic process; it is devoid of any theoretical underpinning. But this gap can be filled if we start from a different perspective. Suppose we postulate the following model:

$$Y_t = \beta_0 + \beta_1 X_t^* + u_t \tag{12.5.1}$$

where Y = demand for money (real cash balances)
X^* = equilibrium, optimum, expected, or normal rate of interest
u = error term

Equation (12.5.1) postulates that the demand for money is a function of *expected* (in the sense of anticipation) rate of interest.

Since the expectational variable X^* is not directly observable, let us propose the following hypothesis about how expectations are formed:

$$X_t^* - X_{t-1}^* = \gamma(X_t - X_{t-1}^*) \tag{12.5.2[9]}$$

where γ, such that $0 < \gamma \leq 1$, is known as the *coefficient of expectation*. Hypothesis (12.5.2) is known as the *adaptive expectation, progressive expectation*, or *error learning* hypothesis, popularized by Cagan[10] and Friedman.[11]

What (12.5.2) states is that expectations are revised each period by a fraction γ of the gap between the current value of the variable and its previous expected value. Thus, for our model this would mean that expectations about interest rate are revised each period by a fraction γ of the discrepancy between the rate of interest observed in the current period and its anticipated value in the previous period. Another way of stating this would be to write (12.5.2) as

$$X_t^* = \gamma X_t + (1 - \gamma)X_{t-1}^* \tag{12.5.3}$$

which shows that the expected value of the rate of interest at time t is a weighted average of the actual value of the interest rate at time t and its value expected in the previous period, with weights of γ and $1 - \gamma$, respectively. If $\gamma = 1$, $X_t^* = X_t$, meaning that expectations are realized immediately and fully, that is, in the same time period. If, on the other hand, $\gamma = 0$, $X_t^* = X_{t-1}^*$, meaning that expectations are static.

Substituting (12.5.3) into (12.5.1), we obtain

$$\begin{aligned} Y_t &= \beta_0 + \beta_1[\gamma X_t + (1 - \gamma)X_{t-1}^*] + u_t \\ &= \beta_0 + \beta_1 \gamma X_t + \beta_1(1 - \gamma)X_{t-1}^* + u_t \end{aligned} \tag{12.5.4}$$

Now lag (12.5.1) one period, multiply it by $1 - \gamma$, and subtract the product from (12.5.4). After simple algebraic manipulations, we obtain

$$\begin{aligned} Y_t &= \gamma\beta_0 + \gamma\beta_1 X_t + (1 - \gamma)Y_{t-1} + u_t - (1 - \gamma)u_{t-1} \\ &= \gamma\beta_0 + \gamma\beta_1 X_t + (1 - \gamma)Y_{t-1} + v_t \end{aligned} \tag{12.5.5}$$

where $v_t = u_t - (1 - \gamma)u_{t-1}$.

The similarity between the adaptive expectation model (12.5.5) and the Koyck model (12.4.7) should be readily apparent although the interpretations of the coefficients in the two models are different. Note that like the Koyck model, the

---

[9] Sometimes the model is also expressed as

$$X_t^* - X_{t-1}^* = \gamma(X_{t-1} - X_{t-1}^*)$$

[10] P. Cagan, "The Monetary Dynamics of Hyper Inflations," in M. Friedman (ed.), *Studies in the Quantity Theory of Money*, University of Chicago Press, Chicago, 1956.

[11] Milton Friedman, *A Theory of the Consumption Function*, National Bureau of Economic Research, Princeton University Press, Princeton, N.J., 1957.

adaptive expectation model is autoregressive and its error term is similar to the Koyck error term. But the adaptive expectation model has a much stronger theoretical base than the Koyck model. (We shall return to the estimation of the adaptive expectation model in Sec. 12.7.)

12.6 ANOTHER RATIONALIZATION OF THE KOYCK MODEL: THE STOCK ADJUSTMENT, OR PARTIAL ADJUSTMENT, MODEL

The adaptive expectation model is one way of rationalizing the Koyck model. Another rationalization is provided by Marc Nerlove in the so-called *stock adjustment*, or *partial adjustment*, model.[12] To illustrate this model, consider the flexible accelerator model of economic theory which assumes that there is an *equilibrium, optimal, desired,* or *long-run* amount of capital stock needed to produce a given output under the given state of technology, rate of interest, etc. For simplicity assume that this desired level of capital Y_t^* is a linear function of output X as follows:

$$Y_t^* = \beta_0 + \beta_1 X_t + u_t \qquad (12.6.1)$$

Since the desired level of capital is not directly observable, Nerlove postulates the following hypothesis, known as the *partial adjustment*, or *stock adjustment, hypothesis*:

$$Y_t - Y_{t-1} = \delta(Y_t^* - Y_{t-1}) \qquad (12.6.2)[13]$$

where δ, such that $0 < \delta \leq 1$, is known as the *coefficient of adjustment* and where $Y_t - Y_{t-1}$ = actual change and $(Y_t^* - Y_{t-1})$ = desired change.

Note: Sometimes the model is also written as

$$Y_t - Y_{t-1} = \delta(Y_{t-1}^* - Y_{t-1})$$

Equation (12.6.2) postulates that the actual change in capital stock (investment) in any given time period t is some fraction δ of the desired change for that period. If $\delta = 1$, it means that the actual stock of capital is equal to the desired stock; that is, actual stock adjusts to the desired stock instantaneously (in the same time period). However, if $\delta = 0$, it means that nothing changes since actual stock at time t is the same as that observed in the previous time period. Typically, δ is expected to lie between these extremes since adjustment to the desired stock of capital is likely to be incomplete because of rigidity, inertia, contractual obliga-

---

[12] See *Distributed Lags and Demand Analysis for Agricultural and Other Commodities, op. cit.*

[13] Some authors do not add the stochastic disturbance term u_t to the relation (12.6.1) but add it to this relation, believing that if the former is truly equilibrium relation, there is no scope for the error term, whereas the adjustment mechanism can be imperfect and may require the disturbance term.

tions, etc. Hence the name *partial adjustment model.* Note that the adjustment mechanism (12.6.2) alternatively can be written as

$$Y_t = \delta Y_t^* + (1 - \delta)Y_{t-1} \qquad (12.6.3)$$

showing that the observed capital stock at time t is a weighted average of the desired capital stock at that time and the capital stock existing in the previous time period, δ and $(1 - \delta)$ being the weights. Now substitution of (12.6.1) into (12.6.3) gives

$$Y_t = \delta(\beta_0 + \beta_1 X_t + u_t) + (1 - \delta)Y_{t-1}$$
$$= \delta\beta_0 + \delta\beta_1 X_t + (1 - \delta)Y_{t-1} + \delta u_t \qquad (12.6.4)$$

This model is called the *partial adjustment model.*

The partial adjustment model resembles both the Koyck and adaptive expectation models in that it is autoregressive. But it has a much simpler disturbance term: the original disturbance term u_t multiplied by a constant δ. But bear in mind that although similar in appearance, the adaptive expectation and partial adjustment models are conceptually very much different. The former is based on uncertainty (about the future course of prices, interest rates, etc.), whereas the latter is due to technical or institutional rigidities, inertia, cost of change, etc. However, both these models are theoretically much sounder than the Koyck model.

12.7 ESTIMATION OF AUTOREGRESSIVE MODELS

From our discussion thus far we have the following three models:

Koyck

$$Y_t = \alpha(1 - \lambda) + \beta_0 X_t + \lambda Y_{t-1} + (u_t - \lambda u_{t-1}) \qquad (12.4.7)$$

Adaptive expectation

$$Y_t = \gamma\beta_0 + \gamma\beta_1 X_t + (1 - \gamma)Y_{t-1} + [u_t - (1 - \gamma)u_{t-1}] \qquad (12.5.5)$$

Partial adjustment

$$Y_t = \delta\beta_0 + \delta\beta_1 X_t + (1 - \delta)Y_{t-1} + \delta u_t \qquad (12.6.4)$$

All these models have the following common form:

$$Y_t = \alpha_0 + \alpha_1 X_t + \alpha_2 Y_{t-1} + v_t \qquad (12.7.1)$$

that is, they are all autoregressive in nature. Therefore, we must now look at the estimation problem of such models, because the classical least squares may not be directly applicable to them. The reason is twofold: the presence of stochastic explanatory variables and the possibility of serial correlation.

Now, as noted previously, for the application of the classical least-squares theory, it must be shown that the stochastic explanatory variable Y_{t-1} is distributed independently of the disturbance term v_t. To determine whether this is so, it is essential to know the properties of v_t. If we assume that the original distur-bance term u_t satisfies all the classical assumptions, such as $E(u_t) = 0$, var $(u_t) = \sigma^2$ (the assumption of homoscedasticity), and cov $(u_t, u_{t+s}) = 0$ for $s \neq 0$ (the assumption of no autocorrelation), v_t may not inherit all these properties. Consider, for example, the error term in the Koyck model, which is $v_t = (u_t - \lambda u_{t-1})$. Given the assumptions about u_t, it is easy to show that v_t is serially correlated because

$$E(v_t v_{t-1}) = -\lambda\sigma^2 \qquad (12.7.2)[14]$$

which is nonzero (unless λ happens to be zero). And since Y_{t-1} appears in the Koyck model as an explanatory variable, it is bound to be correlated with v_t (via the presence of u_{t-1} in it). As a matter of fact, it can be shown that

$$\text{cov } [Y_{t-1}, (u_t - \lambda u_{t-1})] = -\lambda\sigma^2 \qquad (12.7.3)$$

which is the same as (12.7.2). The reader can verify that the same holds true of the adaptive expectation model.

What is the implication of the finding that in the Koyck model as well as the adaptive expectation model the stochastic explanatory variable Y_{t-1} is correlated with the error term v_t? As noted in the introduction to Part II, if an explanatory variable in a regression model is correlated with the stochastic disturbance term, the OLS estimators are not only biased but also not even consistent; that is, even if the sample size is increased indefinitely, the estimators do not approximate their true population values.[15] Therefore, estimation of the Koyck and adaptive expec-tation models by the usual OLS procedure may yield seriously misleading results.

The partial adjustment model is different, however. In this model $v_t = \delta u_t$, where $0 < \delta \leq 1$. Therefore, if u_t satisfies the assumptions of the classical linear regression model given previously, so will δu_t. Therefore, OLS estimation of the partial adjustment model will yield consistent estimates although the estimates tend to be biased (in finite or small samples).[16] Intuitively, the reason for consist-ency is this: Although Y_{t-1} depends on u_{t-1} and all the previous disturbance terms, it is not related to the current error term u_t. Therefore, as long as u_t is serially independent, Y_{t-1} will also be independent or at least uncorrelated with u_t, thereby satisfying an important assumption of OLS, namely, noncorrelation between the explanatory variable(s) and the stochastic disturbance term.

Although OLS estimation of the stock, or partial, adjustment model provides consistent estimation because of the simple structure of the error term in such a

---

[14] $E(v_t v_{t-1}) = E(u_t - \lambda u_{t-1})(u_{t-1} - \lambda u_{t-2})$

$\qquad = -\lambda E(u_{t-1})^2 \qquad$ since covariances between u's are zero by assumption

$\qquad = -\lambda\sigma^2$

[15] The proof is beyond the scope of this book and may be found in Griliches, *op. cit.*, pp. 36–38. However, see Chap. 16 for an outline of the proof in another context.

[16] For proof, see J. Johnston, *Econometric Methods*, 2d ed., McGraw-Hill Book Company, New York, 1972, pp. 274ff.

model, one should not assume that it applies rather than the Koyck or adaptive expectation model. The reader is strongly advised against doing so. A model should be chosen on the basis of strong theoretical considerations, not simply because it leads to easy statistical estimation. Every model should be considered on its own merit, paying due attention to the stochastic disturbances appearing therein. If in models such as the Koyck or adaptive expectation model OLS cannot be straightforwardly applied, methods need to be devised to resolve the estimation problem. Several alternative estimation methods are available although some of them may be computationally tedious. In the following section we consider one such relatively simple method.

12.8 THE METHOD OF INSTRUMENTAL VARIABLES

The reason why OLS cannot be applied to the Koyck or adaptive expectation model is that the explanatory variable Y_{t-1} tends to be correlated with the error term v_t. If somehow this correlation can be removed, one can apply OLS to obtain consistent estimates, as noted previously. (*Note:* There will be some small sample bias.) How can this be accomplished? Liviatan has proposed the following solution.[17]

Let us suppose that we find a " proxy " for Y_{t-1} which is highly correlated with Y_{t-1} but is uncorrelated with v_t, where v_t is the error term appearing in the Koyck or adaptive expectation model. Such a proxy is called an *instrumental variable*.[18] Liviatan suggests X_{t-1} as the instrumental variable for Y_{t-1} and further suggests that the parameters of the regression (12.7.1) can be obtained by solving the following normal equations:

$$\sum Y_t = N\hat{\alpha}_0 + \hat{\alpha}_1 \sum X_t + \hat{\alpha}_2 \sum Y_{t-1}$$
$$\sum Y_t X_t = \hat{\alpha}_0 \sum X_t + \hat{\alpha}_1 \sum X_t^2 + \hat{\alpha}_2 \sum Y_{t-1} X_t \qquad (12.8.1)$$
$$\sum Y_t X_{t-1} = \hat{\alpha}_0 \sum X_{t-1} + \hat{\alpha}_1 \sum X_t X_{t-1} + \hat{\alpha}_2 \sum Y_{t-1} X_{t-1}$$

Notice that if we were to apply OLS directly to (12.7.1), the usual OLS normal equations would be (see Sec. 6.4)

$$\sum Y_t = N\hat{\alpha}_0 + \hat{\alpha}_1 \sum X_t + \hat{\alpha}_2 \sum Y_{t-1}$$
$$\sum Y_t X_t = \hat{\alpha}_0 \sum X_t + \hat{\alpha}_1 \sum X_t^2 + \hat{\alpha}_2 \sum Y_{t-1} X_t \qquad (12.8.2)$$
$$\sum Y_t Y_{t-1} = \hat{\alpha}_0 \sum Y_{t-1} + \hat{\alpha}_1 \sum X_t Y_{t-1} + \hat{\alpha}_2 \sum Y_{t-1}^2$$

The difference between the two sets of normal equations should be readily apparent. Liviatan has shown that the α's estimated from (12.8.1) are consistent whereas

---

[17] N. Liviatan, "Consistent Estimation of Distributed Lags," *International Economic Review*, vol. 4, pp. 44–52, January 1963.
[18] Such instrumental variables are used frequently in simultaneous-equations models (see Chap. 18).

those estimated from (12.8.2) may not be consistent. This is because Y_{t-1} and $v_t[=u_t - \lambda u_{t-1} \text{ or } u_t - (1 - \gamma)u_{t-1}]$ may be correlated whereas X_t and X_{t-1} are uncorrelated with v_t. (Why?)

Although easy to apply in practice, the Liviatan technique is likely to suffer from the multicollinearity problem because X_t and X_{t-1}, which enter in the normal equations of (12.8.1), are likely to be highly correlated (as noted in Chap. 11, most economic time-series typically exhibit a high degree of correlation between successive values). The implication, then, is that although the Liviatan procedure yields consistent estimates, the estimators are likely to be inefficient.[19]

12.9 DETECTING AUTOCORRELATION IN AUTOREGRESSIVE MODELS: DURBIN h TEST

As we have seen, it is the likely serial correlation in the errors v_t that make the estimation problem in the autoregressive model rather complex: In the stock adjustment model the error term v_t did not have (first-order) serial correlation if the error term u_t in the original model was serially uncorrelated, whereas in the Koyck and adaptive expectation models v_t was serially correlated even if u_t was serially independent. The question, then, is: How does one know if there is serial correlation in the error term appearing in the autoregressive models?

As noted in Chap. 11, the Durbin-Watson d statistic may not be used to detect (first-order) serial correlation in autoregressive models, because the computed d value in such models generally tends toward 2, which is the value of d expected in a truly random sequence. In other words, if we routinely compute the d statistic for such models, there is a built-in bias against discovering (first-order) serial correlation. Despite this, many researchers compute the d value for want of anything better. Recently, however, Durbin himself has proposed a *large-sample* test of first-order serial correlation in autoregressive models.[20] This test, called the h *statistic*, is as follows:

$$h = \hat{\rho}\sqrt{\frac{N}{1 - N[\text{var}(\hat{\alpha}_2)]}} \tag{12.9.1}$$

where N = sample size, var $(\hat{\alpha}_2)$ = variance of the coefficient of the lagged Y_{t-1}, and $\hat{\rho}$ = estimate of the first-order serial correlation ρ, which is given by the equation (11.3.9).

For large sample size, Durbin has shown that if $\rho = 0$, the h statistic follows the standardized normal distribution, that is, the normal distribution with zero mean and unit variance. Hence the statistical significance of an observed h can

[19] To see how the efficiency of the estimators can be improved, consult Lawrence R. Klien, *A Textbook of Econometrics*, 2d ed., Prentice-Hall, Inc., Englewood Cliffs, N.J., 1974, p. 99.

[20] J. Durbin, "Testing for Serial Correlation in Least-Squares Regression when Some of the Regressors Are Lagged Dependent Variables," *Econometrica*, vol. 38, pp. 410–421, 1970.

easily be determined from the standardized normal distribution table (see App. D, Table D.1).

In practice there is no need to compute $\hat{\rho}$ because we have seen in Chap. 11 that it can be approximated from the estimated d as follows:

$$\hat{\rho} \doteq 1 - \tfrac{1}{2}d \qquad (11.4.10)$$

where d is the usual Durbin-Watson statistic.[21] Therefore, (12.9.1) can be written as

$$h \doteq \left(1 - \frac{1}{2}d\right)\sqrt{\frac{N}{1 - N[\operatorname{var}(\hat{\alpha}_2)]}} \qquad (12.9.2)$$

As an illustration, suppose in an application involving 100 observations it was found that $d = 1.9$ and var $(\hat{\alpha}_2) = 0.005$. Therefore

$$h = \left[1 - \frac{1}{2}(1.9)\right]\sqrt{\frac{100}{1 - 100(.005)}}$$

$$= 0.7071$$

At, say, the 5 percent level of significance the critical h value from the normal distribution table is 1.645. Since the computed h is less than the critical h, we may accept the hypothesis that there is no (first-order) serial correlation in the data.

Note these features of the h statistic:

1. It does not matter how many X variables or how many lagged values of Y are included in the regression model. To compute h, we need consider only the variance of the coefficient of lagged Y_{t-1}.
2. The test is not applicable if $[N \operatorname{var}(\hat{\alpha}_2)]$ exceeds 1 (why?). In practice, though, this does not usually happen.
3. Since the test is meant for large samples, its application in small samples is not strictly justified. The small-sample properties of the test are not yet fully established.[22]

12.10 AN ILLUSTRATIVE EXAMPLE

Refer to Exercise 6.15, which gives annual data on stock of money, national income, prices, and long-run interest rate in India for the period 1948–1949 to 1964–1965. Suppose we postulate the following demand for money relation:[23]

---

[21] Note that this d value itself may not be used to test for serial correlation in the autoregressive models. It merely provides an *input* for the computation of the h statistic.

[22] See G. S. Maddala and A. S. Rao, "Tests for Serial Correlation in Regression Models with Lagged Dependent Variable and Serially Correlated Errors," *Econometrica*, vol. 41, no. 4, pp. 761–774, 1973.

[23] For a similar model, see Gregory C. Chow, "On the Long-Run and Short-Run Demand for Money," *Journal of Political Economy*, vol. 74, no. 2, pp. 111–131, 1966. Note that one advantage of the multiplicative function is that the exponents of the variables give direct estimates of elasticities (see Chap. 3).

$$M_t^* = \beta_0 R_t^{\beta_1} Y_t^{\beta_2} e^{u_t} \tag{12.10.1}$$

where M_t^* = desired, or long-run, demand for money (real cash balances)

R_t = long-term interest rate, %

Y_t = aggregate real national income

For statistical estimation, (12.10.1) may be expressed conveniently in log form as

$$\ln M_t^* = \ln \beta_0 + \beta_1 \ln R_t + \beta_2 \ln Y_t + u_t \tag{12.10.2}$$

Since the desired demand variable is not directly observable, let us assume the stock adjustment hypothesis, namely,

$$\frac{M_t}{M_{t-1}} = \left(\frac{M_t^*}{M_{t-1}}\right)^{\delta} \qquad 0 < \delta \le 1 \tag{12.10.3}$$

Equation (12.10.3) states that a constant percentage (why?) of the discrepancy between the actual and desired real cash balances is eliminated within a single period (year). In log form, equation (12.10.3) may be expressed as

$$\ln M_t - \ln M_{t-1} = \delta(\ln M_t^* - \ln M_{t-1}) \tag{12.10.4}$$

Substituting $\ln M_t^*$ from (12.10.2) into equation (12.10.4) and rearranging, we obtain

$$\ln M_t = \delta \ln \beta_0 + \beta_1 \delta \ln R_t + \beta_2 \delta \ln Y_t + (1 - \delta) \ln M_{t-1} + \delta u_t \quad (12.10.5)[24]$$

which may be called the *short-run demand function* for money (why?). Assuming that u_t and hence δu_t satisfies the usual OLS assumptions, the regression results based on the given data were as follows:

$$\ln M_t = 1.6207 - 0.1024 \ln R_t + 0.6869 \ln Y_t + 0.5284 \ln M_{t-1}$$

$$(1.2404)(0.3678) \qquad (0.3427) \qquad (0.2007)$$

$$t = (1.3066)(-0.2784) \qquad (2.0108) \qquad (2.6328)$$

$$R^2 = 0.9227 \qquad d = 1.8624 \tag{12.10.6}[25]$$

The estimated short-run demand function shows that the short-run interest elasticity is statistically insignificant but the short-run income elasticity is statistically significant at the 5 percent level of significance (one-tail test). The coefficient of adjustment is $\delta = 1 - 0.5284 = 0.4716$, implying that about 47 percent of the discrepancy between the desired and actual real cash balances is eliminated in a

---

[24] In passing note that this model is essentially nonlinear in the parameters. Therefore, although OLS may give an unbiased estimate of, say, $\beta_1 \delta$ taken together, it may not give unbiased estimates of β_1 and δ individually, especially if the sample is small.

[25] Note this feature of the estimated standard errors. The standard error of, say, the coefficient of $\ln R_t$ refers to the standard error of $\hat{\beta}_1 \hat{\delta}$, an estimator of $\beta_1 \delta$. There is no simple way to obtain the standard errors of $\hat{\beta}_1$ and $\hat{\delta}$ individually from the standard error of $\hat{\beta}_1 \hat{\delta}$, especially if the small is relatively small. For large samples, however, individual standard errors of $\hat{\beta}_1$ and $\hat{\delta}$ can be obtained approximately, but the computations are involved. See Jan Kmenta, *Elements of Econometrics*, The Macmillan Company, New York, 1971, p. 444.

year. To get back to the long-run demand function (12.10.2), all that needs to be done is to divide the short-run demand function through by δ (why?) and drop the ln M_{t-1} term. The results are

$$\ln M_t^* = 2.2520 - 0.2169 \ln R_t + 1.4565 \ln Y_t \qquad (12.10.7)[26]$$

As can be seen, the long-run income elasticity of demand for money 1.4565 is substantially greater than the corresponding short-run elasticity 0.6869.

Note that the estimated Durbin-Watson d is 1.8624, which is close to 2. This substantiates our previous remark that in the autoregressive models the computed d is generally close to 2. Therefore, we cannot trust the computed d to find out whether there was serial correlation in our data. Although our sample size is rather small, rendering the h test strictly speaking inappropriate, we present it nonetheless to illustrate the mechanics behind its computation. Using the estimated d value and formula (12.9.2), we obtain

$$h = \left[1 - \frac{1}{2}(1.8624) \right] \sqrt{\frac{17}{1 - 17(0.0403)}}$$

$$= 0.50$$

where the variance of the lagged dependent variable is obtained from the estimated standard error of that variable, namely, $(0.2007)^2$.

Although the estimated h is rather small, leading to the acceptance of the hypothesis that there is no serial correlation (of the first order), this conclusion should be taken with a grain of salt in view of the smallness of the sample.

12.11 THE ALMON APPROACH TO DISTRIBUTED-LAG MODELS: THE ALMON POLYNOMIAL LAG[27]

Although used extensively in practice, the Koyck distributed-lag model is based on the assumption that the β coefficients decline geometrically as the lag lengthens (see Fig. 12.3). This assumption may be too restrictive in some situations. Consider, for example, Fig. 12.4.

In Fig. 12.4a it is assumed that the β's increase at first and then decrease, whereas in Fig. 12.4c it is assumed that they follow a cyclical pattern. Obviously, the Koyck scheme of distributed-lag models will not work in these cases. However, looking at Fig. 12.4a and c, it seems that one can express β_i as a function of i, the length of the lag (time), and fit suitable curves to reflect the functional

---

[26] Note that we have not presented the standard errors of the estimated coefficients for reasons discussed in fn. 25.

[27] Shirley Almon, "The Distributed Lag Between Capital Appropriations and Expenditures," *Econometrica*, vol. 33, pp. 178–196, January 1965.

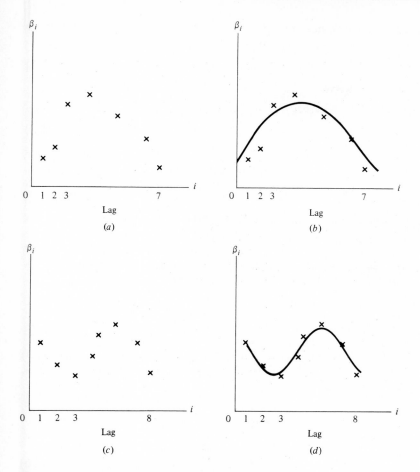

Figure 12.4 Almon polynomial-lag scheme.

relationship between the two, as indicated in Fig. 12.4*b* and *d*. This is precisely the approach suggested by Shirley Almon. To illustrate her technique, let us revert to the finite distributed-lag model considered previously, namely,

$$Y_t = \alpha + \beta_0 X_t + \beta_1 X_{t-1} + \beta_2 X_{t-2} + \cdots + \beta_k X_{t-k} + u_t \quad (12.1.2)$$

which may be written more compactly as

$$Y_t = \alpha + \sum_{i=0}^{k} \beta_i X_{t-i} + u_t \quad (12.11.1)$$

Following a theorem in mathematics, known as *Weierstrass's theorem*, Almon assumes that β_i can be approximated by a suitable-degree polynomial in i, the length of the lag.[28] For instance, if the lag scheme shown in Fig. 12.4a applies, we can write

$$\beta_i = a_0 + a_1 i + a_2 i^2 \tag{12.11.2}$$

which is a quadratic, or second-degree, polynomial in i (see Fig. 12.4b). However, if the β's follow the pattern of Fig. 12.4c, we can write

$$\beta_i = a_0 + a_1 i + a_2 i^2 + a_3 i^3 \tag{12.11.3}$$

which is a third-degree polynomial in i (see Fig. 12.4d). More generally, we may write

$$\beta_i = a_0 + a_1 i + a_2 i^2 + \cdots + a_m i^m \tag{12.11.4}$$

which is an mth-degree polynomial in i. It is assumed that m (the degree of the polynomial) is less than k (the maximum length of the lag).

To explain how the Almon scheme works, let us assume that the β's follow the pattern shown in Fig. 12.4a and, therefore, the second-degree polynomial approximation is appropriate. Substituting (12.11.2) into (12.11.1), we obtain

$$Y_t = \alpha + \sum_{i=0}^{k} (a_0 + a_1 i + a_2 i^2) X_{t-i} + u_t$$

$$= \alpha + a_0 \sum_{i=0}^{k} X_{t-i} + a_1 \sum_{i=0}^{k} i X_{t-i} + a_2 \sum_{i=0}^{k} i^2 X_{t-i} + u_t \tag{12.11.5}$$

Defining

$$Z_{0t} = \sum_{i=0}^{k} X_{t-i}$$

$$Z_{1t} = \sum_{i=0}^{k} i X_{t-i} \tag{12.11.6}$$

$$Z_{2t} = \sum_{i=0}^{k} i^2 X_{t-i}$$

we may write (12.11.5) as

$$Y_t = \alpha + a_0 Z_{0t} + a_1 Z_{1t} + a_2 Z_{2t} + u_t \tag{12.11.7}$$

In the Almon scheme Y is regressed on the constructed variables Z, not the original X variables. Note that (12.11.7) can be estimated by the usual OLS procedure. The estimates of α and a_i thus obtained will have all the desirable statistical properties provided the stochastic disturbance term u satisfies the assumptions of the classical linear regression model. In this respect, the Almon technique has a distinct advantage over the Koyck method because, as we have

---

[28] Broadly speaking, the theorem states that on a finite closed interval any continuous function may be approximated uniformly by a polynomial of a suitable degree.

seen, the latter has some serious estimation problems which result from the presence of the stochastic explanatory variable Y_{t-1} and its likely correlation with the disturbance term.

Once the a's are estimated from (12.11.7), the original β's can be estimated from (12.11.2) [or more generally from (12.11.4)] as follows:

$$\hat{\beta}_0 = \hat{a}_0$$
$$\hat{\beta}_1 = \hat{a}_0 + \hat{a}_1 + \hat{a}_2$$
$$\hat{\beta}_2 = \hat{a}_0 + 2\hat{a}_1 + 4\hat{a}_2 \qquad (12.11.8)$$
$$\hat{\beta}_3 = \hat{a}_0 + 3\hat{a}_1 + 9\hat{a}_2$$
$$\dots\dots\dots\dots\dots\dots\dots\dots$$
$$\hat{\beta}_k = \hat{a}_0 + k\hat{a}_1 + k^2\hat{a}_2$$

Before we apply the Almon technique, we must resolve the following practical problems.

1. The maximum length of the lag k must be specified in advance. This is a major weakness of the Almon technique; the researcher must decide the appropriate length of the lag. In practice, one hopes that k is reasonably small. Thus, in a regression involving quarterly data for 10 years, we may want to use a maximum lag of 8 or 10 quarters. If, however, we have only annual data for 10 years, we may not want to use more than 2 or 3 year's lag. In any event, the researcher must decide the maximum value of k.

2. Having specified k, the degree of the polynomial m must also be specified. Generally, the degree of the polynomial should be at least one more than the number of turning points in the curve relating β_i to i. Thus, in Fig. 12.4a there is only one turning point; hence a second-degree polynomial will be a good approximation. In Fig. 12.4c there are two turning points; hence a third-degree polynomial will provide a good approximation. A priori, however, one may not know the number of turning points, and therefore, the choice of m is largely subjective. However, theory may suggest a particular shape in some cases. In practice, one hopes that a fairly low-degree polynomial (say, $m = 2$ or 3) will give good results. Having chosen a particular value of m, if we want to find out whether a higher-degree polynomial will give a better fit, we can proceed as follows.

Suppose we must decide between the second- and third-degree polynomials. For the second-degree polynomial the estimating equation is as given by (12.11.7). For the third-degree polynomial the corresponding equation is

$$Y_t = \alpha + a_0 Z_{0t} + a_1 Z_{1t} + a_2 Z_{2t} + a_3 Z_{3t} + u_t \qquad (12.11.9)$$

where $Z_{3t} = \sum_{i=0}^{k} i^3 X_{t-i}$. After running regression (12.11.9), if we find that a_2 is statistically significant but a_3 is not, we may assume that the second-degree polynomial provides a reasonably good approximation.

However, we must beware of the problem of multicollinearity, which is likely to arise because of the way the Z's are constructed from the X's, as shown in (12.11.6) [see also (12.11.10)]. As shown in Chap. 9, in cases of serious multicollinearity, $\hat{a}_3$ may turn out to be statistically insignificant, not because the true a_3 is zero, but simply because the sample at hand does not allow us to assess the separate impact of Z_3 on Y. Therefore, in our illustration, before we accept the conclusion that the third-degree polynomial is not the correct choice, we must make sure that the multicollinearity problem is not serious enough, which can be done by applying the techniques discussed in Chap. 9.

Thus, as a strictly empirical matter, the choice of the degree of the polynomial can be based on the statistical significance of successive a_i coefficients in models like (12.11.9) provided the multicollinearity problem is taken into account.

3. Once m and k are specified, the Z's can be readily constructed. For instance, if $m = 2$ and $k = 5$, the Z's are

$$Z_{0t} = \sum_{i=0}^{5} X_{t-i} = (X_t + X_{t-1} + X_{t-2} + X_{t-3} + X_{t-4} + X_{t-5})$$

$$Z_{1t} = \sum_{i=0}^{5} i . X_{t-i} = (X_{t-1} + 2X_{t-2} + 3X_{t-3} + 4X_{t-4} + 5X_{t-5}) \qquad (12.11.10)$$

$$Z_{2t} = \sum_{i=0}^{5} i^2 . X_{t-i} = (X_{t-1} + 4X_{t-2} + 9X_{t-3} + 16X_{t-4} + 25X_{t-5})$$

Notice that the Z's are linear combinations of the original X's. Also notice why the Z's are likely to exhibit multicollinearity.

Before proceeding to a numerical example, it may be interesting to note the advantages of the Almon method. First, it provides a flexible method of incorporating a variety of lag structures (see Exercise 12.16). The Koyck technique, on the other hand, is quite rigid in that it assumes that the β's decline geometrically. Second, unlike the Koyck technique, in the Almon method we do not have to worry about the presence of the lagged dependent variable as an explanatory variable in the model and the problems it creates for estimation. Finally, if a sufficiently low-degree polynomial can be fitted, the number of coefficients to be estimated (the a's) is considerably smaller than the original number of coefficients (the β's).

But let us reemphasize the problems with the Almon technique. First, the degree of the polynomial as well as the maximum value of the lag is largely a subjective decision. Second, for reasons noted previously, the Z variables are likely to exhibit multicollinearity. Therefore, in models like (12.11.9) the estimated a's are likely to show large standard errors (relative to the values of these coefficients), thereby rendering one or more such coefficients statistically insignificant on the basis of the conventional t test. But this does not necessarily mean that one or more of the original β coefficients will also be statistically insignificant. (The proof of this statement is slightly involved but is suggested in Exercise 12.17.) As a result, the multicollinearity problem may not be as serious as one might think.

A Numerical Example

To illustrate the Almon technique, Table 12.1 gives data on inventories Y and sales X in the United States manufacturing sector for the period 1955–1974. For illustrative purposes, assume that inventories depend on sales in the current year and in the three preceding years as follows:

$$Y_t = \alpha + \beta_0 X_t + \beta_1 X_{t-1} + \beta_2 X_{t-2} + \beta_3 X_{t-3} + u_t \qquad (12.11.11)$$

Furthermore, assume that β_i can be approximated by a second-degree polynomial as shown in (12.11.2). Then, following (12.11.5), we may write

$$Y_t = \alpha + a_0 Z_{0t} + a_1 Z_{1t} + a_2 Z_{2t} + u_t \qquad (12.11.12)$$

where

$$Z_{0t} = \sum_{i=0}^{3} X_{t-i} = (X_t + X_{t-1} + X_{t-2} + X_{t-3})$$

$$Z_{1t} = \sum_{i=0}^{3} i X_{t-i} = (X_{t-1} + 2X_{t-2} + 3X_{t-3}) \qquad (12.11.13)$$

$$Z_{2t} = \sum_{i=0}^{3} i^2 X_{t-i} = (X_{t-1} + 4X_{t-2} + 9X_{t-3})$$

Table 12.1 Inventories Y and sales X in United States manufacturing industries, 1955–1974 (millions of dollars)

Year	Y	X	Z_0	Z_1	Z_2
1955	45,069	26,480	...	...	...
1956	50,642	27,740	...	...	...
1957	51,871	28,736	...	...	...
1958	50,070	27,280	110,236	163,656	378,016
1959	52,707	30,219	113,975	167,972	391,884
1960	53,814	30,796	117,031	170,987	397,963
1961	54,939	30,896	119,191	173,074	397,192
1962	58,213	33,113	125,024	183,145	426,051
1963	60,043	35,032	129,837	187,293	433,861
1964	63,383	37,335	136,376	193,946	445,548
1965	68,221	41,003	146,483	206,738	475,480
1966	77,965	44,869	158,239	220,769	505,631
1967	84,655	46,449	169,656	238,880	544,896
1968	90,875	50,282	182,603	259,196	594,952
1969	97,074	53,555	195,155	277,787	639,899
1970	101,645	52,859	203,145	293,466	672,724
1971	102,445	55,917	212,613	310,815	719,617
1972	107,719	62,017	224,348	322,300	749,348
1973	120,870	71,398	242,191	332,428	761,416
1974	147,135	82,078	271,410	363,183	822,719

Source: Data on inventories and sales from *Economic Report of the President*, table C-41, p. 297, February 1975.

The Z variables thus constructed are shown in Table 12.1. Using the data on Y and the Z's, we obtain the following regression:

$$Y_t = -8140.7564 + 0.6612Z_{0t} + 0.9020Z_{1t} - 0.4322Z_{2t}$$

$$(1992.9809) \quad (0.1655) \quad (0.4831) \quad (0.1665) \qquad (12.11.14)$$

$$t = \quad (-4.0847) \quad (3.9960) \quad (1.8671) \quad (-2.5961)$$

$$\bar{R}^2 = 0.9961 \qquad \mathrm{df} = 13$$

(*Note:* Since we are assuming a 3-year lag, the total number of observations is reduced from 20 to 17.)

From the estimated a coefficients given in equation (12.11.14), we estimate the β coefficients from the relation (12.11.8) as follows:

$$\hat{\beta}_0 = \hat{a}_0 = 0.6612$$

$$\hat{\beta}_1 = (\hat{a}_0 + \hat{a}_1 + \hat{a}_2) = (0.6612 + 0.9020 - 0.4322) = 1.1310$$

$$\hat{\beta}_2 = (\hat{a}_0 + 2\hat{a}_2 + 4\hat{a}_2) = [0.6612 + 2(0.9020) - 4(0.4322)] = 0.7364$$

$$\hat{\beta}_3 = (\hat{a}_0 + 3\hat{a}_1 + 9\hat{a}_2) = [0.6612 + 3(0.9020) - 9(0.4322)] = -0.5226$$

Thus, the estimated distributed-lag model corresponding to (12.11.12) is

$$Y_t = -8140.7564 + 0.6612X_t + 1.1310X_{t-1} + 0.7364X_{t-2} - 0.5426X_{t-3}$$

$$(1992.9803) \quad (0.1655) \quad (0.1798)^{29} \quad (0.1625)^{29} \quad (0.2307)^{29}$$

$$t = \quad (-4.0847) \quad (3.9960) \quad (6.2903) \quad (4.5317) \quad (-2.3520)$$

$$(12.11.15)$$

Geometrically, the estimated β_i are shown in Fig. 12.5.

[29] These standard errors are computed from the formula given in Exercise 12.17.

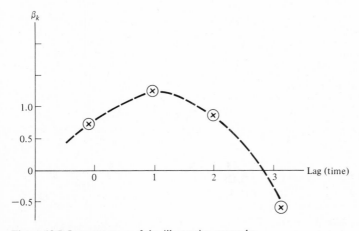

Figure 12.5 Lag structure of the illustrative example.

Our numerical example may be used to point out a few additional features of the Almon procedure:

1. The standard errors of the a coefficients are directly obtainable from the OLS regression (12.11.14), but the standard errors of some of the $\hat{\beta}$ coefficients, the objective of primary interest, cannot be so obtained. But these standard errors can be easily computed from the standard errors of the estimated a coefficients by using a well-known formula from statistics, which is given in Exercise 12.17.[30]

2. The $\hat{\beta}$'s obtained in (12.11.15) are called *unrestricted estimates* in the sense that no a priori restrictions are placed on them. In some situations, however, one may want to impose the so-called *endpoint* restrictions on the β's by assuming that β_0 and β_k (the current and kth lagged coefficient) are zero. Because of psychological, institutional, or technological reasons, the value of the explanatory variable in the current period may not have any impact on the current value of the dependent variable, thereby justifying the zero value for β_0. By the same token, beyond a certain time period k the explanatory variable may not have any impact on the dependent variable, thus supporting the assumption that β_k is zero.[31] Sometimes the β's are estimated with the restriction that the sum of all the β coefficients is unity. (To see how such restrictions are taken into account, the reader is referred to the Almon article, fn. 27.)

12.12 SUMMARY AND CONCLUSIONS

Because of psychological, technological, and institutional reasons, it takes time to make and execute economic decisions. As a result, an economic dependent variable Y may respond to an economic determining variable X with a lapse of time. Such a lapse of time is called a *lag*, and regression models which take into account such lags are called *regression models involving lagged variables*, or *lagged regression models*.

There are two types of lagged variables: lagged explanatory variables, which are either nonstochastic or, if stochastic, distributed independently of the stochastic disturbance term, and lagged dependent variables. Regression models which include the current as well as lagged values of the nonstochastic X variables are called *distributed-lag models* because the effect of an explanatory variable(s) on the dependent variable is spread or distributed over several time periods. However, regression models which include the lagged values of the dependent variables among the explanatory variables are called *autoregressive models;* such models involve regression of the dependent variables on itself lagged certain time periods.

---

[30] Some computer programs on regression analysis with the Almon lag option now routinely compute these standard errors.

[31] In the current example one may note the negative value for $\hat{\beta}_3$. If such a negative value makes no sense in light of theory, one may wish to restrict $\beta_3 = 0$ and reestimate the lag structure.

If a distributed-lag model contains several lags, its estimation by OLS, although possible in principle, is difficult in practice because it consumes too many degrees of freedom and because it is likely to lead to a serious multi-collinearity problem. As is well known, if there is multicollinearity, the OLS estimators, although unbiased, are inefficient. Therefore, unconstrained estimation of a large number of lags is practically out of the question; some a priori restrictions need to be imposed on the various lagged coefficients. One such procedure is the extensively used Koyck distributed-lag model, which assumes that the coefficients of the lagged terms decline geometrically as one goes into the distant past. With this assumption, a model involving an undefined number of lags can be reduced to a model that contains only the current values of the nonstoch-astic X variable(s) and a single lagged value of the dependent variable as its explanatory variables.

Although a superb achievement, the simplification is not without a price: The Koyck model creates some serious statistical problems in that it includes a stoch-astic explanatory variable (lagged Y_{t-1}) which may very well be correlated with the stochastic disturbance term. In this situation econometric theory shows that the OLS estimators are not only biased but inconsistent as well; that is, even if the sample size is increased indefinitely, the estimators do not converge to their true population values. In short, they remain biased asymptotically. Therefore, alterna-tive estimating techniques are called for. In this chapter we considered one such alternative, namely, the *method of instrumental variables*. The key idea behind this method is to replace the lagged stochastic explanatory variable Y_{t-1} by another variable which is highly correlated with Y_{t-1} but uncorrelated with the distur-bance term. The estimates obtained by these methods are consistent.

The Koyck model, although popular in empirical econometrics, does not have a solid theoretical underpinning. This void is bridged by the adaptive expectation model used by Cagan and others and the stock adjustment, or partial adjustment, model developed by Nerlove. These models take into account how economic agents form expectations about uncertain economic events and how they make adjustments when their expectations do not match the reality. A unique feature of both these models is that in their final form they resemble the Koyck model in that they are also autoregressive and employ the same variables. The adaptive expecta-tion model faces the same estimation problem as does the Koyck model. The partial adjustment model, however, can be estimated by the usual OLS method.

It was noted in Chap. 11 that the Durbin-Watson d statistic is not meaningful for testing autocorrelation (of first-order) in autoregressive models because in such models the d value hovers around 2, which is the value expected in a truly random sequence. Recently, Durbin himself has suggested the so-called h statistic to test for serial correlation in autoregressive models. However, this test is designed for large samples only.

An alternative to the Koyck approach to the distributed-lag models is Shirley Almon's polynomial distributed-lag model. Based on Weierstrass's theorem in mathematics, Almon assumes that the lagged coefficients β_i can be approximated by a suitable-degree polynomial in i, the length of the lag. Although the Almon technique avoids some of the estimation problems associated with the Koyck model, its practical weakness is that both the degree of the polynomial and the maximum length of the lag must be specified in advance by the user of the technique.

Despite the estimation problems, the distributed-lag and autoregressive models have proved extremely useful in empirical economics because they make the otherwise static economic theory a dynamic one by taking into account explicitly the role of time. Such models help us to distinguish between the short- and long-run response of the dependent variable to a unit change in the value of the explanatory variable(s). Thus, for estimating short- and long-run price, income, substitution, and other similar elasticities these models have proved to be highly useful.[32]

EXERCISES

12.1 Consider the following model:

$$Y_t^* = \alpha + \beta_0 X_t + u_t$$

where Y^* = desired, or long-run, business expenditure for new plant and equipment, X_t = sales, and t = time. Using the stock adjustment model, estimate the parameters of the long- and short-run demand function for expenditure on new plant and equipment from the following data.

Business expenditure for new plant and equipment Y and sales X in United States manufacturing industries, 1960–1973 (billions of dollars)

Year	Y	X	Year	Y	X
1960	15.09	30.796	1967	28.51	46.449
1961	14.33	30.896	1968	28.37	50.282
1962	15.06	33.113	1969	31.68	53.555
1963	16.22	35.032	1970	31.95	52.859
1964	19.34	37.335	1971	29.99	55.917
1965	23.44	41.003	1972	31.35	62.017
1966	28.20	44.869	1973	38.01	71.398

Source: Economic Report of the President, tables C-40 and C-41, pp. 296–297, 1975.

12.2 Use the data of Exercise 12.1 but consider the following model:

$$Y_t^* = \beta_0 X_t^{\beta_1} e^{u_t}$$

Based on the stock adjustment model, estimate the short- and long-run elasticities of expenditure on new plant and equipment with respect to sales. Compare your results with Exercise 12.1.

[32] For applications of these models, see Arnold C. Harberger, ed., *The Demand for Durable Goods,* The University of Chicago Press, Chicago, 1960.

12.3 Use the data of Exercise 12.1 but assume that

$$Y_t = \alpha + \beta X_t^* + u_t$$

where X_t^* are the desired sales. Estimate the parameters of this model and compare the results with those obtained in Exercise 12.1. How would you decide which is the appropriate model?

12.4 Establish equation (12.7.3).

12.5 Consider the model

$$Y_t = \alpha + \beta_1 X_{1t} + \beta_2 X_{2t} + \beta_3 Y_{t-1} + v_t$$

Suppose Y_{t-1} and v_t are correlated. To remove the correlation, suppose we use the following instrumental variable approach: First regress Y_t on X_{1t} and X_{2t} and obtain the estimated $\hat{Y}_t$ from this regression. Then regress

$$Y_t = \alpha + \beta_1 X_{1t} + \beta_2 X_{2t} + \beta_3 \hat{Y}_{t-1} + v_t$$

where $\hat{Y}_{t-1}$ are estimated from the first-stage regression.
   (a) How does this procedure remove the correlation between Y_{t-1} and v_t in the original model?
   (b) What are the advantages of the recommended procedure over the Liviatan approach?

*12.6 *Mean, or average, lag.* By *mean*, or *average, lag* is meant the average length of time it takes for a (unit) change in the explanatory variable X to be transferred to the dependent variable Y.
   (a) Show that for the Koyck model the mean lag is $\lambda/(1 - \lambda)$.
   (b) If λ is relatively large, what are its implications?

12.7 *Median lag.* The median lag is the time required for the first half of the total change in Y following a unit sustained change in X. For the Koyck model, the median lag is as follows:

$$\text{Koyck model: Median lag} = -\left(\frac{\log 2}{\log \lambda}\right)$$

where λ is the Koyck rate of decline of the lagged coefficients.
   (a) Evaluate the median lag for $\lambda = 0.2, 0.4, 0.6, 0.8$.
   (b) Is there any systematic relationship between the value of λ and the value of the median lag?

12.8 Suppose

$$M_t = \alpha + \beta_1 Y_t^* + \beta_2 R_t^* + u_t$$

where M = demand for real cash balances, Y^* = expected real income, and R^* = expected interest rate. Assume that expectations are formulated as follows:

$$Y_t^* = \gamma_1 Y_t + (1 - \gamma_1)Y_{t-1}^*$$

$$R_t^* = \gamma_2 R_t + (1 - \gamma_2)R_{t-1}^*$$

where γ_1 and γ_2 are coefficients of expectation, both lying between 0 and 1.
   (a) How would you express M_t in terms of the observable quantities?
   (b) What estimation problems do you foresee?

12.9 Consider the model

$$Y_t^* = \alpha + \beta X_t^* + u_t$$

where Y^* = desired stock of capital and X^* = expected level of output.
   (a) Assuming the stock adjustment model for Y^* and the adaptive expectations model for X^*, reduce the model to observable quantities.

* Optional.

(b) Pay due attention to the stochastic properties of the model and discuss some of the estimating problems.

(c) Compare your analysis with that given by Roger N. Waud.[33]

12.10 *Serial correlation model.* Consider the following model:

$$Y_t = \alpha + \beta X_t + u_t$$

Assume that u_t follows Markov first-order autoregressive scheme given in Chap. 11, namely,

$$u_t = \rho u_{t-1} + \varepsilon_t$$

where ρ is the coefficient of (first-order) autocorrelation and where ε_t satisfies all the assumptions of the classical OLS. Then, as shown in Chap. 11, the model

$$Y_t = \alpha(1 - \rho) + \beta(X_t - \rho X_{t-1}) + \rho Y_{t-1} + \varepsilon_t$$

will have a serially independent error term, making OLS estimation possible. But this model, called the *serial correlation model,* very much resembles the Koyck, adaptive expectation, and partial adjustment models? How would you know in any given situation which of the preceding models is appropriate?[34]

12.11 Consider the Koyck (or for that matter the adaptive expectation) model given in (12.4.7), namely,

$$Y_t = \alpha(1 - \lambda) + \beta_0 X_t + \lambda Y_{t-1} + (u_t - \lambda u_{t-1})$$

Suppose in the original model u_t follows the first-order autoregressive scheme $u_t - \rho u_{t-1} = \varepsilon_t$, where ρ is the coefficient of autocorrelation and where ε_t satisfies all the classical OLS assumptions.

(a) If $\rho = \lambda$, can the Koyck model be estimated by OLS?

(b) Will the estimates thus obtained be unbiased? Consistent? Why or why not?

(c) How reasonable is it to assume that $\rho = \lambda$?

12.12 *Triangular, or arithmetic, distributed-lag model.*[35] This model assumes that the stimulus (explanatory variable) exerts its greatest impact in the current time period and then declines by equal decrements to zero as one goes into the distant past. Geometrically, it is shown in Fig. 12.6. Following this distribution suppose we run the following succession of regressions:

$$Y_t = \alpha + \beta\left(\frac{2X_t + X_{t-1}}{3}\right)$$

$$Y_t = \alpha + \beta\left(\frac{3X_t + 2X_{t-1} + X_{t-2}}{6}\right)$$

$$Y_t = \alpha + \beta\left(\frac{4X_t + 3X_{t-1} + 2X_{t-2} + X_{t-1}}{10}\right)$$

etc., and choose the regression that gives the highest R^2 as the "best" regression. Comment on this strategy.

[33] " Misspecification in the 'Partial Adjustment' and 'Adaptive Expectations' Models," *International Economic Review,* vol. 9, no. 2, pp. 204–217, June 1968.

[34] For a discussion of the serial correlation model, see Zvi Griliches, " Distributed Lags: A Survey," *Econometrica,* vol. 35, no. 1, p. 34, January 1967.

[35] This model was proposed by Irving Fisher in "Note on a Short-cut Method for Calculating Distributed Lags," *International Statistical Bulletin,* pp. 323–328, 1937.

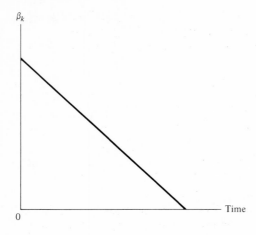

Time

Figure 12.6 Triangular or arithmetic lag scheme (Fisher's).

12.13 Based on the quarterly data for the period 1950–1960, F. R. Brechling obtained the following demand function for labor for the British economy (the figures in parentheses are standard errors):[36]

$$\dot{E}_t = 14.22 \ + 0.172Q_t - 0.028t - 0.0007t^2 - 0.297E_{t-1}$$

$$(2.61) \quad (0.014) \quad (0.015) \quad (0.0002) \quad (0.033)$$

$$\bar{R}^2 = 0.76 \qquad d = 1.37$$

where $\dot{E}_t = (E_t - E_{t-1})$
Q = output
t = time

The preceding equation was based on the assumption that the desired level of employment E_t^* is a function of output, time, and time squared and the hypothesis that $E_t - E_{t-1} = \delta(E_t^* - E_{t-1})$, where δ, the coefficient of adjustment, lies between 0 and 1.

(a) Interpret the preceding regression.
(b) What is the value of δ?
(c) Derive the long-run demand function for labor from the estimated short-run demand function.
(d) How would you test for serial correlation in the preceding model?

12.14 In studying the farm demand for tractors, Griliches used the following model:[37]

$$T_t^* = \alpha X_{1,t-1}^{\beta_1} X_{2,t-1}^{\beta_2}$$

where T^* = desired stock of tractors
X_1 = relative price of tractors
X_2 = interest rate

Using the stock adjustment model, he obtained the following results for the period 1921–1957:

$$\log T_t = \text{constant} - 0.218 \log X_{1,t-1} - 0.855 \log X_{2,t-1} + 0.864 \log T_{t-1}$$

$$(0.051) \qquad (0.170) \qquad (0.035)$$

$$R^2 = 0.987$$

[36] F. P. R. Brechling, "The Relationship between Output and Employment in British Manufacturing Industries," *Review of Economic Studies*, vol. 32, July 1965.

[37] Zvi Griliches, "The Demand for a Durable Input: Farm Tractors in the United States, 1921–1957," in Arnold C. Harberger, ed., *The Demand for Durable Goods*, The University of Chicago Press, Chicago, 1960.

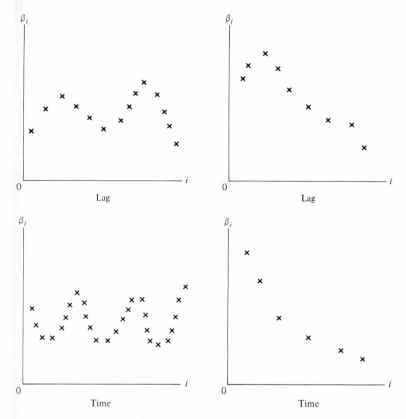

Figure 12.7 Hypothetical lag structures.

where the figures in the parentheses are the estimated standard errors.

(a) What is the estimated coefficient of adjustment?

(b) What are the short- and long-run price elasticities?

(c) What are the corresponding interest elasticities?

(d) What are the reasons for high or low rate of adjustment in the present model?

12.15 Whenever the lagged dependent variable appears as an explanatory variable, the R^2 is usually much higher than when it is not included. What are the reasons for it?

12.16 Consider the lag patterns in Fig. 12.7. What degree polynomials would you fit to the lag structures and why?

12.17 Consider the equation (12.11.4)

$$\beta_i = a_0 + a_1 i + a_2 i^2 + \cdots + a_m i^m$$

To obtain the variance of $\hat{\beta}_i$ from the variances of $\hat{a}_i$, we use the following formula:

$$\text{var} (\hat{\beta}_i) = \text{var} (\hat{a}_0 + \hat{a}_1 i + \hat{a}_2 i^2 + \cdots + \hat{a}_m i^m)$$

$$= \sum_{j=0}^{m} i^{2j} \text{ var} (\hat{a}_j) + 2 \sum_{j<p} i^{(j+p)} \text{ cov} (\hat{a}_j \hat{a}_p)$$

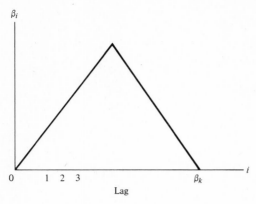

Figure 12.8 Inverted-V distributed-lag model.

(a) Using the preceding formula, find the variance of $\hat{\beta}_i$ expressed as

$$\hat{\beta}_i = \hat{a}_0 + \hat{a}_1 i + \hat{a}_2 i^2$$

$$\hat{\beta}_i = \hat{a}_0 + \hat{a}_1 i + \hat{a}_2 i^2 + \hat{a}_3 i^3$$

(b) If the variances of $\hat{a}_i$ are large relative to themselves, will the variance of $\hat{\beta}_i$ be large also? Why or why not?

12.18 Fit the Almon polynomial distributed-lag model to the data of Exercise 12.1 by assuming that $i = 4$ and $m = 2$. How do you know whether the suggested lag model fits the data reasonably well?

*****12.19** Consider the following distributed-lag model:

$$Y_t = \alpha + \beta_0 + \beta_1 X_{t-1} + \beta_2 X_{t-2} + \beta_3 X_{t-3} + \beta_4 X_{t-4} + u_t$$

Assume that β_i can be adequately expressed by the second-degree polynomial as follows:

$$\beta_i = a_0 + a_1 i + a_2 i^2$$

How would you estimate the β's if we want to impose the restriction that $\beta_0 = \beta_4 = 0$?

*****12.20** *The inverted-V distributed-lag model.* Consider the k-period finite distributed-lag model

$$Y_t = \alpha + \beta_0 X_t + \beta_1 X_{t-1} + \beta_2 X_{t-2} + \cdots + \beta_k X_{t-k} + u_t$$

DeLeeuw has proposed the structure for the β's as in Fig. 12.8,[38] where the β's follow the inverted-V shape. Assuming for simplicity that k (the maximum length of the lag) is an even number, and further assuming that β_0 and β_k are zero, DeLeeuw suggests the following scheme for the β's:

$$\beta_i = i\beta \qquad 0 \le i \le \frac{k}{2}$$

$$= (k - i)\beta \qquad \frac{k}{2} \le i < k$$

How would you use the DeLeeuw scheme to estimate the parameters of the preceding k-period distributed-lag model?

* Optional.

[38] See his article, "The Demand for Capital Goods by Manufacturers: A Study of Quarterly Time Series," *Econometrica*, vol. 30, no. 3, pp. 407–423, July 1962.

THIRTEEN

REGRESSION ON DUMMY VARIABLES

The purpose of this chapter is to consider the role of qualitative explanatory variables in regression analysis. It will be shown that the introduction of qualitative variables, often called *dummy variables*, makes the linear regression model an extremely flexible tool that is capable of handling many interesting problems encountered in empirical studies.

13.1 THE NATURE OF DUMMY VARIABLES

In regression analysis it frequently happens that the dependent variable is influenced, not only by variables which can be readily quantified on some well-defined scale (e.g., income, output, prices, costs, height, and temperature), but also by variables which are essentially qualitative in nature (e.g., sex, race, color, religion, nationality, wars, earthquakes, strikes, political upheavals, and changes in government economic policy). For example, holding all other factors constant, female college teachers are found to earn less than their male counterparts, and nonwhites are found to earn less than whites. This may result from sex or racial discrimination, but whatever the reason, qualitative variables such as sex and race do influence the dependent variable and clearly should be included among the explanatory variables.

Since such qualitative variables usually indicate the presence or absence of a "quality" or an attribute, such as male or female, black or white, or Catholic or non-Catholic, one method of "quantifying" such attributes is by constructing artificial variables which take on values of 1 or 0, 0 indicating the absence of an attribute and 1 indicating the presence (or possession) of that attribute. For example, 1 may indicate that a person is a male, and 0 may designate a female; or 1 may indicate that a person is a college graduate, and 0 that he is not, and so on. Variables which assume such 0 and 1 values are called *dummy variables*.[1] Alternative names are *indicator variables, binary variables, categorical variables, qualitative variables*, and *dichotomous variables*.

Dummy variables can be used in regression models just as easily as quantitative variables. As a matter of fact, a regression model may contain explanatory variables that are exclusively dummy, or qualitative, in nature. Such models are called *analysis-of-variance (AOV) models*. As an example, consider the following model:

$$Y_i = \alpha + \beta D_i + u_i \qquad (13.1.1)$$

where Y = annual salary of a college teacher
$\quad D_i = 1 \qquad$ if male college teacher
$\quad\quad = 0 \qquad$ otherwise (i.e., female teacher)

Note that (13.1.1) is like the two-variable regression models encountered previously except that instead of a quantitative X variable we have a dummy variable D (hereafter, we shall designate all the dummy variables by the letter D).

Model (13.1.1) may enable us to find out whether sex makes any difference in a college teacher's salary, assuming, of course, that all other variables such as age, degree attained, and years of experience are held constant. Assuming that the disturbances satisfy the usual assumptions of the classical linear regression model, we obtain from (13.1.1)

Mean salary of female college teacher $\quad E(Y_i|D_i = 0) = \alpha$

Mean salary of male college teacher $\quad\quad E(Y_i|D_i = 1) = \alpha + \beta$

that is, the intercept term α gives mean salary of female college teachers and the *slope* coefficient β tells by how much the mean salary of a male college teacher differs from the mean salary of his female counterpart, $\alpha + \beta$ reflecting the mean salary of the male college teacher.

A test of the null hypothesis that there is no sex discrimination ($H_0: \beta = 0$) can be easily made by running regression (13.1.1) in the usual manner and finding out whether on the basis of the t test the estimated $\hat{\beta}$ is statistically significant.

AOV models of type (13.1.1), although common in fields such as sociology, psychology, education, and market research, are not that common in economics. Typically, in most economic research a regression model contains some explanatory variables that are quantitative and some that are qualitative. Regression models containing an admixture of quantitative and qualitative variables are

---

[1] It is not absolutely essential that dummy variables take the values of 0 and 1. The pair (0, 1) can be transformed into any other pair by a linear function such that $Z = a + bD(b \neq 0)$, where a and b are constants and where $D = 1$ or 0. When $D = 1$, we have $Z = a + b$; and when $D = 0$, we have $Z = a$. Thus, the pair (0, 1) becomes $(a, a + b)$.

called *analysis-of-covariance* (*ACOV*) *models*, and in this chapter we shall be largely dealing with such models.

13.2 REGRESSION ON ONE QUANTITATIVE VARIABLE AND ONE QUALITATIVE VARIABLE WITH TWO CLASSES, OR CATEGORIES

As an example of the ACOV model, let us modify model (13.1.1) as follows:

$$Y_i = \alpha_0 + \alpha_1 D_i + \beta X_i + u_i \tag{13.2.1}$$

where Y_i = annual salary of a college teacher
X_i = years of teaching experience
$D_i = 1$ if male
$\quad\ = 0$ otherwise

Model (13.2.1) contains one quantitative variable (years of teaching experience) and one qualitative variable (sex) which has two classes (or levels, classifications, or categories), namely, male and female.

What is the meaning of (13.2.1)? Assuming, as usual, that $E(u_i) = 0$, we see that

Mean salary of a female college teacher

$$E(Y_i \mid X_i, D_i = 0) = \alpha_0 + \beta X_i \tag{13.2.2}$$

Mean salary of a male college teacher

$$E(Y_i \mid X_i, D_i = 1) = (\alpha_0 + \alpha_1) + \beta X_i \tag{13.2.3}$$

Geometrically, we have the situation shown in Fig. 13.1 (for illustration, it is assumed that $\alpha_1 > 0$). In words, model (13.2.1) postulates that the male and female college teachers' salary functions in relation to the years of teaching experience have the same slope (β) but different intercepts. In other words, it is assumed that the level of the male teacher's mean salary is different from that of the female teacher's mean salary (by α_1) but the rate of change in the mean annual salary by years of experience is the same for both sexes.

If the assumption of common slope is valid,[2] a test of the hypothesis that the two regressions (13.2.2) and (13.2.3) have the same intercept (i.e., there is no sex discrimination) can be made easily by running the regression (13.2.1) and noting the statistical significance of the estimated $\hat{\alpha}_1$ on the basis of the traditional t test. If the t test shows that $\hat{\alpha}_1$ is statistically significant, we reject the null hypothesis that the male and female college teachers' levels of mean annual salary are the same.

Before proceeding further, note the following features of the dummy-variable regression model considered previously:

---

[2] The validity of this assumption can be tested by the procedure outlined in Sec. 13.6.

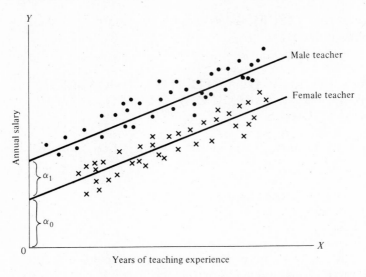

Figure 13.1 Hypothetical scattergram between annual salary and years of teaching experience of college teachers.

1. To distinguish the two categories, male and female, we have introduced only one dummy variable D_i. For if $D_i = 1$ always denotes a male, when $D_i = 0$ we know that it is a female since there are only two possible outcomes. Hence, one dummy variable suffices to distinguish two categories. Assuming that the regression model contains an intercept term, if we were to write model (13.2.1) as

$$Y_i = \alpha_0 + \alpha_1 D_{1i} + \alpha_2 D_{2i} + \beta X_i + u_i \qquad (13.2.4)$$

where Y_i and X_i are as defined before

$$
\begin{aligned}
D_{1i} &= 1 &&\text{if male teacher} \\
&= 0 &&\text{otherwise} \\
D_{2i} &= 1 &&\text{if female teacher} \\
&= 0 &&\text{otherwise}
\end{aligned}
$$

then model (13.2.4), as it stands, cannot be estimated because of perfect collinearity between D_1 and D_2. To see this, suppose we have a sample of three male teachers and two female teachers. The data matrix will look something like that following:

		D_1	D_2	X
Male	Y_1	1	1	0	X_1
Male	Y_2	1	1	0	X_2
Female	$Y_3 = 1$	0	1	X_3
Male	Y_4	1	1	0	X_4
Female	Y_5	1	0	1	X_5

The first column on the right-hand side of the preceding data matrix represents the common intercept term α_0. Now it can be seen readily that $D_1 = 1 - D_2$

or $D_2 = 1 - D_1$; that is, D_1 and D_2 are perfectly collinear. And as shown in Chap. 9, in cases of perfect multicollinearity the usual OLS estimation is not possible. There are various ways of resolving this problem, but the simplest one is to assign the dummies the way we did for model (13.2.1), namely, use only one dummy variable if there are two levels or classes of the qualitative variable. In this case, the preceding data matrix will not have the column labeled D_2, thus avoiding the perfect multicollinearity problem. The general rule is this: *If a qualitative variable has m categories, introduce only m − 1 dummy variables.* In our example, sex has two categories, and hence we introduced only a single dummy variable. If this rule is not followed, we shall fall into what might be called the *dummy-variable trap*, that is, the situation of perfect multicollinearity.

2. The assignment of 1 and 0 values to two categories, such as male and female, is arbitrary in the sense that in our example we could have assigned $D = 1$ for female and $D = 0$ for male. In this situation, the two regressions obtained from (13.2.1) will be

$$\text{Female teacher} \quad E(Y_i \mid X_i, D_i = 1) = (\alpha_0 + \alpha_1) + \beta X_i \qquad (13.2.5)$$

$$\text{Male teacher} \quad E(Y_i \mid X_i, D_i = 0) = \alpha_0 + \beta X_i \qquad (13.2.6)$$

Now as contrasted with (13.2.2) and (13.2.3), in the preceding models α_1 tells by how much the mean salary of a female college teacher differs from the mean salary of a male college teacher. In this case, if there is sex discrimination, α_1 is expected to be negative whereas before it was expected to be positive. Therefore, in interpreting the results of the models which use the dummy variables it is critical to know how the 1 and 0 values are assigned.

3. The group, category, or classification that is assigned the value of 0 is often referred to as the *base, control, comparison,* or *omitted* category. It is the base in the sense that comparisons are made with that category. Thus in model (13.2.1) the female teacher is the base category. Note that the (common) intercept term α_0 is the intercept term for the base category in the sense that if we run the regression with $D = 0$, that is, on females only, the intercept will be α_0. Also note that which category serves as the base category is a matter of choice sometimes dictated by a priori considerations.

4. The coefficient α_1 attached to the dummy variable D can be called the *differential intercept coefficient* because it tells by how much the value of the intercept term of the category that receives the value of 1 differs from the intercept coefficient of the base category.

13.3 REGRESSION ON ONE QUANTITATIVE VARIABLE AND ONE QUALITATIVE VARIABLE WITH MORE THAN TWO CLASSES

Suppose that based on the cross-sectional data we want to regress the annual expenditure on health care by an individual on the income and education of the individual. Since the variable *education* is qualitative in nature, suppose we consider three mutually exclusive levels of education: less than high school, high school, and college. Now, unlike the previous case, we have more than two categories of the qualitative variable education. Therefore, following the rule that the number of dummies be one less than the number of categories of the variable, we should introduce two dummies to take care of the three levels of education. Assuming that the three educational groups have a common slope but different intercepts in the regression of annual expenditure on health care on annual income, we can use the following model:

$$Y_i = \alpha_0 + \alpha_1 D_{1i} + \alpha_2 D_{2i} + \beta X_i + u_i \tag{13.3.1}$$

where Y_i = annual expenditure on health care
   X_i = annual income
   $D_1 = 1$ if high school education
    $= 0$ otherwise
   $D_2 = 1$ if college education
    $= 0$ otherwise

Note that in the preceding assignment of the dummy variables we are arbitrarily treating the "less than high school education" category as the base category. Therefore, the intercept α_0 will reflect the intercept for this category. The differential intercepts α_1 and α_2 tell by how much the intercepts of the other two

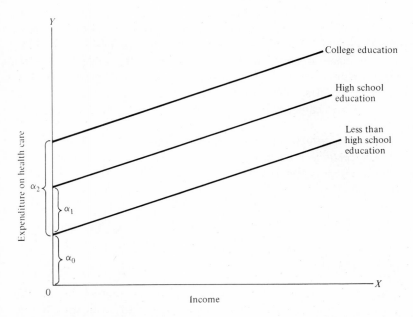

Figure 13.2 Expenditure on health care in relation to income for three levels of education.

categories differ from the intercept of the base category, which can be readily checked as follows: Assuming $E(u_i) = 0$, we obtain from (13.3.1)

$$E(Y_i|D_1 = 0, D_2 = 0, X_i) = \alpha_0 + \beta X_i \qquad (13.3.2)$$

$$E(Y_i|D_1 = 1, D_2 = 0, X_i) = (\alpha_0 + \alpha_1) + \beta X_i \qquad (13.3.3)$$

$$E(Y_i|D_1 = 0, D_2 = 1, X_i) = (\alpha_0 + \alpha_2) + \beta X_i \qquad (13.3.4)$$

which are, respectively, the mean health care expenditure functions for the three levels of education, namely, less than high school, high school, and college. Geometrically, the situation is shown in Fig. 13.2 (for illustrative purposes it is assumed that $\alpha_2 > \alpha_1$).

After running regression (13.3.1), one can easily find out whether the differential intercepts α_1 and α_2 are individually statistically significant, that is, different from the base group. A test of the hypothesis that $\alpha_1 = \alpha_2 = 0$ simultaneously can also be made by the AOV technique and the attendant F test, as shown in Chap. 7.

In passing, note that the interpretation of regression (13.3.1) will change if we were to adopt a different scheme of assigning the dummy variables. Thus, if we assign $D_1 = 1$ to "less than high school education" category and $D_2 = 1$ to "high school education category," the base category will then be "college education" and all comparisons will be in relation to this category.

13.4 REGRESSION ON ONE QUANTITATIVE VARIABLE AND TWO QUALITATIVE VARIABLES

The technique of dummy variable can be easily extended to handle more than one qualitative variable. Let us revert to the college teacher's salary regression (13.2.1), but now assume that in addition to income and sex the color of the teacher is also an important determinant of salary. For simplicity, assume that color has two categories: black and white. We can now write (13.2.1) as

$$Y_i = \alpha_0 + \alpha_1 D_{1i} + \alpha_2 D_{2i} + \beta X_i + u_i \qquad (13.4.1)$$

where Y_i and X_i = annual salary and years of teaching experience
$\qquad D_1 = 1 \qquad$ if male
$\qquad \quad = 0 \qquad$ otherwise
$\qquad D_2 = 1 \qquad$ if white
$\qquad \quad = 0 \qquad$ otherwise

Notice that each of the two qualitative variables, sex and color, has two categories and hence needs one dummy variable for each. Note also that the omitted, or base, category now is "black female teacher."

Assuming $E(u_i) = 0$, we can obtain the following regressions from (13.4.1):

Mean salary for black female teacher

$$E(Y_i|D_1 = 0, D_2 = 0, X_i) = \alpha_0 + \alpha_1 X_i \qquad (13.4.2)$$

Mean salary for black male teacher

$$E(Y_i | D_1 = 1, D_2 = 0, X_i) = (\alpha_0 + \alpha_1) + \beta X_i \qquad (13.4.3)$$

Mean salary for white female teacher

$$E(Y_i | D_1 = 0, D_2 = 1, X_i) = (\alpha_0 + \alpha_2) + \beta X_i \qquad (13.4.4)$$

Mean salary for white male teacher

$$E(Y_i | D_1 = 1, D_2 = 1, X_i) = (\alpha_0 + \alpha_1 + \alpha_2) + \beta X_i \qquad (13.4.5)$$

Once again, it is assumed that the preceding regressions differ only in the intercept coefficient but not in the slope coefficient β.

An OLS estimation of (13.4.1) will enable us to test a variety of hypotheses. Thus, if α_2 is statistically significant, it will mean that color does affect a teacher's salary. Similarly, if α_1 is statistically significant, it will mean that sex also affects a teacher's salary. If both these differential intercepts are statistically significant, it would mean sex as well as color is an important determinant of teachers' salaries.

A Generalization

Following the preceding discussion, we can extend our model to include more than one quantitative variable and more than two qualitative variables. The only precaution to be taken is that the number of dummies for each qualitative variable should be one less than the number of categories of that variable. An example is given in the following section.

13.5 THE ECONOMICS OF "MOONLIGHTING": AN APPLICATION

A person holding two or more jobs, one primary and one or more secondary, is known as a *moonlighter*. Shisko and Rostker were interested in finding out what factors determined the wages of moonlighters.[3] Based on a sample of 318 moonlighters, they obtained the following regression, which is given in the notation used by the authors:

$$w_m = 37.07 + 0.403w_0 - 90.06 \text{ race} + 75.51 \text{ urban}$$

$$(0.062) \qquad (24.47) \qquad (21.60)$$

$$+ 47.33 \text{ Hisch} + 113.64 \text{ reg} + 2.26 \text{ age} \qquad (13.5.1)$$

$$(23.42) \qquad (27.62) \qquad (0.94)$$

$$R^2 = 0.34 \qquad \text{df} = 311$$

---

[3] Robert Shisko and Bernard Rostker, "The Economics of Multiple Job Holding," *The American Economic Review*, vol. 66, no. 3, pp. 298–308, June 1976.

where w_m = moonlighting wage (cents/hour)

$\quad w_0$ = primary wage (cents/hours)

$\quad$ Race = 0 $\quad$ if white

$\qquad$ = 1 $\quad$ nonwhite

$\quad$ Urban = 0 $\quad$ nonurban

$\qquad$ = 1 $\quad$ urban

$\quad$ Reg = 0 $\quad$ nonwest

$\qquad$ = 1 $\quad$ west

$\quad$ Hisch = 0 $\quad$ nongraduate

$\qquad$ = 1 $\quad$ high school graduate

$\quad$ Age = age, years

In model (13.5.1) there are two quantitative explanatory variables, w_0 and age, and four qualitative variables. Note that the coefficients of all these variables are statistically significant at the 5 percent level. What is interesting to note is that all the qualitative variables affect moonlighting wages significantly. For instance, holding all other factors constant, the level of hourly wages is expected to be higher by about 47 cents for the high school graduate than those with less than high school education.

From regression (13.5.1) one can derive several individual regressions, two of which are as follows: The mean hourly wage rate of white, nonurban, nonwest, nongraduate moonlighters (i.e., when all the dummies take a value of zero) is

$$w_m = 37.07 + 0.403w_0 + 2.26 \text{ age} \qquad (13.5.2)$$

The mean hourly wage rate of a nonwhite, urban, west, high school graduate (i.e., when all the dummies are equal to 1) is

$$w_m = 183.49 + 0.403w_0 + 2.26 \text{ age} \qquad (13.5.3)$$

13.6 COMPARING TWO REGRESSIONS[4]

Until now, in the models considered in this chapter we assumed that the qualitative variables affect the intercept but not the slope coefficient of various subgroup regressions. But the assumption of the constancy of the slope coefficient between groups can be tested by the dummy variables. To see how this is done, let us revert to the college teachers' salary regression considered in Sec. 13.2. Suppose that instead of running regression (13.2.1), which assumes that the salary regressions differ in the intercept but not in the slope coefficient, we run the following separate regressions:

---

[4] The material in this section draws heavily on the author's articles, "Use of Dummy Variables in Testing for Equality Between Sets of Coefficients in Two Linear Regressions: A Note," and "Use of Dummy Variables . . .: A Generalization," both published in the *American Statistician*, vol. 24, nos. 1 and 5, pp. 50–52 and 18–21, 1970.

Female college teacher's salary regression

$$Y_i = \lambda_0 + \lambda_1 X_i + u_i \qquad i = 1, 2, \ldots, N_1 \qquad (13.6.1)$$

Male college teacher's salary regression

$$Y_i = \gamma_0 + \gamma_1 X_i + u_i \qquad i = 1, 2, \ldots, N_2 \qquad (13.6.2)$$

Note that the number of observations N_1 and N_2 in the two groups need not be the same.

Now regressions (13.6.1) and (13.6.2) present the following four possibilities:

1. $\lambda_0 = \gamma_0$ and $\lambda_1 = \gamma_1$; that is, the two regressions are identical.
2. $\lambda_0 \neq \gamma_0$ but $\lambda_1 = \gamma_1$; that is, the two regressions differ only in their locations (i.e., intercepts).
3. $\lambda_0 = \gamma_0$ but $\lambda_1 \neq \gamma_1$; that is, the two regressions have the same intercepts but different slopes.
4. $\lambda_0 \neq \gamma_0$ and $\lambda_1 \neq \gamma_1$; that is, the two regressions are completely different.

All these possibilities are depicted in Fig. 13.3.

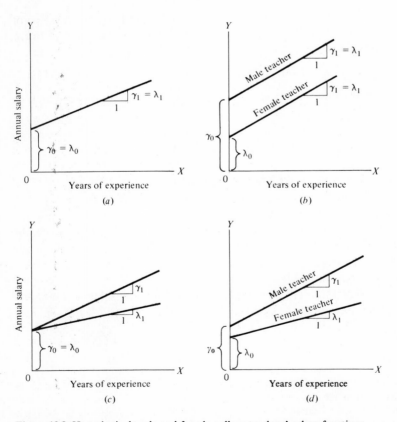

Figure 13.3 Hypothetical male and female college teachers' salary functions.

From the data at hand, one can run the two individual regressions (13.6.1) and (13.6.2) and then use suitable statistical techniques to test all the preceding possibilities. One such technique, known as the *Chow test*,[5] uses the AOV technique and the attendant F test and is given in Exercise 13.10. However, all the preceding possibilities can be tested if we "pool" all the N_1 and N_2 observations together and estimate the following regression:[6]

$$Y_i = \alpha_0 + \alpha_1 D_i + \beta_1 X_i + \beta_2 (D_i X_i) + u_i \qquad (13.6.3)$$

where Y_i = annual salary of a college teacher
$\quad X_i$ = years of teaching experience
$\quad D_i = 1 \qquad$ if male
$\quad\quad = 0 \qquad$ if female

Model (13.6.3) differs from (13.2.1) in that it has an additional variable $D_i X_i$.

To see the implication of model (13.6.3) and assuming that $E(u_i) = 0$, we obtain

$$E(Y_i | D_i = 0, X_i) = \alpha_0 + \beta_1 X_i \qquad (13.6.4)$$

$$E(Y_i | D_i = 1, X_i) = (\alpha_0 + \alpha_1) + (\beta_1 + \beta_2) X_i \qquad (13.6.5)$$

which are, respectively, the mean salary functions for female and male college teachers, and are the same as (13.6.1) and (13.6.2) with $\lambda_0 = \alpha_0$, $\lambda_1 = \beta_1$, $\gamma_0 = (\alpha_0 + \alpha_1)$, and $\gamma_1 = (\beta_1 + \beta_2)$. Therefore, estimating (13.6.3) is equivalent to estimating the two individual salary functions (13.6.1) and (13.6.2).

In model (13.6.3), α_1 is the differential intercept, as previously, and β_2 is the *differential slope coefficient*, indicating by how much the slope coefficient of a male teacher's salary function differs from the slope coefficient of a female teacher's salary function. Note how the introduction of the dummy variable D in the *multiplicative* form (D multiplied by X) enables us to differentiate between slope coefficients of the two groups, just as the introduction of the dummy variable in the *additive form* enabled us to distinguish between the intercepts of the two groups.

The advantages of estimating (13.6.3) over estimating the two regressions (13.6.1) and (13.6.2) individually can now be readily seen:

1. We need to run only a single regression because the individual regressions can easily be deduced from it in the manner indicated by equations (13.6.4) and (13.6.5).
2. The single regression can be used to test a variety of hypotheses. Thus, if the differential intercept coefficient α_1 is statistically insignificant, we may accept

---

[5] Gregory C. Chow, "Tests of Equality Between Sets of Coefficients in Two Linear Regressions," *Econometrica*, vol. 28, no. 3, 1960.
[6] The pooling technique implicitly assumes that u_i in (13.6.1) and (13.6.2) have the same properties, especially common variance.

the hypothesis that the two regressions have a common intercept. Similarly, if the differential slope coefficient β_2 is statistically insignificant, we may accept the hypothesis that the two regressions have a common slope. The test of the hypothesis that $\alpha_1 = \beta_2 = 0$ simultaneously can also be made by the AOV technique discussed in Chap. 7.
3. Finally, pooling increases the df and hence improves the relative precision of the estimated parameters.

13.7 TESTING THE EQUIVALENCY OF TWO REGRESSIONS: AN ILLUSTRATION

Since there are situations which may require comparing two regressions, we illustrate the technique introduced in Sec. 13.6 with the aid of the following example: In studying the relationship between the unemployment rate and the unfilled job-vacancy rate in Great Britain for the period 1958-IV to 1971-II, the author obtained the scattergram shown in Fig. 13.4.[7] As the figure shows, beginning with

---

[7] Damodar Gujarati, "The Behaviour of Unemployment and Unfilled Vacancies: Great Britain, 1958–1971," *The Economic Journal*, vol. 82, pp. 195–202, March 1972.

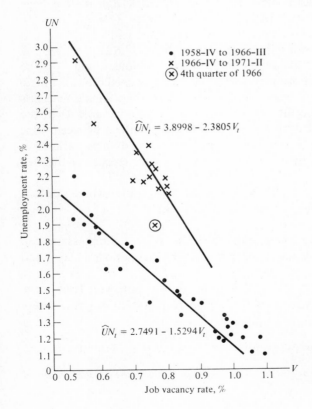

Figure 13.4 Scattergram of unemployment rate and job-vacancy rate, Great Britain, 1958–IV to 1971–II.

the fourth quarter of 1966, the unemployment-vacancy relationship seems to have changed; the curve relating the two seems to have shifted upward starting with that quarter. This upward shift implies that for a given job-vacancy rate there is more unemployment as of the fourth quarter of 1966 than before. In his study the author found that a plausible cause for the upward shift was that in October 1966 (that is, the fourth quarter) the then Labor government liberalized the National Insurance Act by replacing the flat-rate system of short-term unemployment benefits by a mixed system of flat-rate and (previous) earnings related benefits, which obviously increased the level of unemployment benefits. If unemployment benefits are increased, the unemployed are likely to take a longer time to look for a job, thus reflecting a higher amount of unemployment for any given job-vacancy rate.

To find out whether the observed drift in the unemployment–job-vacancy relationship beginning in the fourth quarter of 1966 was statistically significant, the author used the following model:

$$UN_t = \alpha_0 + \alpha_1 D_t + \beta_1 V_t + \beta_2 (D_t V_t) + u_t \qquad (13.7.1)$$

where UN = unemployment rate, %
V = job vacancy rate, %
$D = 1$ for period beginning in 1966-IV
    $= 0$ for period before 1966-IV
t = time, measured in quarters

Based on 51 quarterly observations for the period 1958-IV to 1971-II the following results were obtained (the actual data used are given in App. 13A, Sec. 13A.1; the reader may want to examine these data, as they show how one introduces dummy variables):

$$UN_t = 2.7491 + 1.1507D_t - 1.5294V_t - 0.8511(D_t V_t)$$

$$(0.3171) \quad (0.1218) \quad (0.4294) \qquad\qquad (13.7.2)$$

$$t = (3.6288)(-12.5552) \ (-1.9819) \quad R^2 = 0.9072$$

Judged by the usual criteria, the estimated regression gives an excellent fit. Note that both the differential intercept and slope coefficients are statistically significant at the 5 percent level. Thus one may accept the hypothesis that there definitely was a shift in the UN-V relationship beginning in the fourth quarter of 1966.

From the preceding regression we can derive the following regressions:

1958-IV to 1966-III $UN_t = 2.7491 - 1.5294V_t$ (13.7.3)

1966-IV to 1971-II $UN_t = (2.7491 + 1.15) - (1.5294 + 0.8511)V_t$

$$= 3.8998 - 2.3805V_t \qquad\qquad (13.7.4)$$

which are shown in Fig. 13.4. These regressions show that in the period beginning in 1966-IV the UN-V curve has a much steeper slope and higher intercept than in the period beginning in 1958-IV.

13.8 THE USE OF DUMMY VARIABLES IN SEASONAL ANALYSIS

Many economic time series based on monthly or quarterly data exhibit seasonal patterns (regular oscillatory movement). Examples are sales of department stores at Christmas time, demand for money (cash balances) by households at holiday times, demand for ice cream and soft drinks during the summer, and prices of crops right after the harvesting season. Often it is desirable to remove the seasonal factor, or *component*, from a time series so that one may concentrate on the other components, such as the trend.[8] The process of removing the seasonal component from a time series is known as *deseasonalization*, or *seasonal adjustment*, and the time series thus obtained is called the *deseasonalized*, or *seasonally adjusted*, time series. Important economic time series, such as the consumer price index, the wholesale price index, the index of industrial production, are usually published in the seasonally adjusted form.

There are several methods of deseasonalizing a time series, but we shall consider only one of these methods, namely, the *method of dummy variables*.[9] To illustrate how the dummy variables can be used to deseasonalize economic time series, suppose that we want to regress profits of United States manufacturing corporations on their sales for the quarterly periods of 1965–1970. The relevant data without seasonal adjustment are given in App. 13A, Sec. 13A.2, which also shows how one prepares the *data matrix* to incorporate dummy variables. A look at these data reveals an interesting pattern. Both profits and sales are higher in the second quarter than in either the first quarter or the third quarter of each year. Perhaps the second quarter exhibits some seasonal effect. To investigate this, we proceed as follows:

$$\text{Profits}_t = \alpha_0 + \alpha_1 D_{1t} + \alpha_2 D_{2t} + \alpha_3 D_{3t} + \beta(\text{sales})_t + u_t \qquad (13.8.1)$$

where $D_1 = 1$ for second quarter
      $= 0$ otherwise
      $D_2 = 1$ for third quarter
      $= 0$ otherwise
      $D_3 = 1$ for fourth quarter
      $= 0$ otherwise

Note that we are assuming that the variable "season" has four classes, the four quarters of a year, thereby requiring the use of three dummy variables. Thus, if there is a seasonal pattern present in various quarters, the estimated differential intercepts α_1, α_2, and α_3, if statistically significant, will reflect it. It is possible that

---

[8] A time series may contain four components: a seasonal, a cyclical, a trend, and one that is strictly random.

[9] Some other methods are the ratio-to-moving-average method, link-relative method, and percentage-of-annual-average method. For a nontechnical discussion of these methods, see Morris Hamburg, *Statistical Analysis for Decision Making*, Harcourt, Brace & World, Inc., New York, 1970, pp. 563–575.

only some of these differential intercepts are statistically significant so that only some quarters may reflect it. But model (13.8.1) is general enough to accommodate all these cases. (Note we treat the first quarter of the year as the base quarter.)

Using the data given in App. 13A, Sec. 13A.2, we obtain the following results (profit and sales figures are in millions of dollars):

$$Profits_t =$$

$$6688.3789 + 1322.8938D_{1t} - 217.8037D_{2t} + 183.8597D_{3t} + 0.0383(sales)_t$$

$$(638.4753) \qquad (632.2561) \qquad (654.2937) \qquad (0.0115)$$

$$t = (2.0720) \qquad (-0.3445) \qquad (0.2810) \qquad (3.3313)$$

$$R^2 = 0.4256 \qquad (13.8.2)$$

The results show that only the sales coefficient and differential intercept associated with the second quarter are statistically significant at the 5 percent level.[10] Thus one may conclude that there is some seasonal factor operating in the second quarter of each year. The sales coefficient of 0.0383 tells that after taking into account the seasonal effect, if sales increase, say, by \$1, the average profits are expected to increase by about 4 cents.

In the formulation of model (13.8.1), it was assumed that only the intercept term differs between quarters, the slope coefficient of the sales variable being the same in each quarter. But this assumption can be tested by the procedure discussed in Sec. 13.6 and is relegated to Exercise 13.17.

---

[10] If desired, one may rerun the regression using just one dummy to distinguish the second quarter from the remaining quarters of the year.

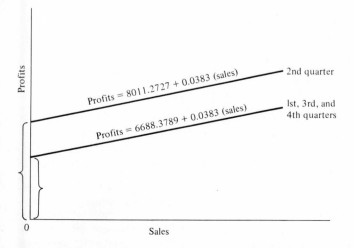

Figure 13.5 Relationship between profits and sales in U.S. manufacturing corporations, 1965–I to 1970–II.

From the estimated regression (13.8.2) we can derive the following individual regressions (by omitting D_{2t} and D_{3t}):

First, third, and fourth quarters

$$\text{Profits}_t = 6688.3789 + 0.0383(\text{sales})_t$$

Second quarter

$$\text{Profits}_t = 8011.2727 + 0.0383(\text{sales})_t \qquad (13.8.3)$$

Geometrically, these regressions can be seen in Fig. 13.5.

13.9 PIECEWISE LINEAR REGRESSION

To illustrate yet another use of dummy variables, consider Fig. 13.6, which shows how a hypothetical business company remunerates its sales representatives. It pays commissions based on sales in such a manner that up to a certain level, the *target*, or *threshold*, level X^*, there is one (stochastic) commission structure and beyond that level another. (*Note:* Besides sales, there are other factors which affect sales commission. Assume that these other factors are represented by the stochastic disturbance term.) More specifically, it is assumed that sales commission increases linearly with sales until the threshold level X^* after which also it increases linearly with sales but at a much faster rate. Thus, we have a *piecewise linear regression* consisting of two pieces or segments, which are labeled I and II in Fig. 13.6, and the commission function changes its slope at the threshold value.

Given the data on commission, sales, and the value of the threshold level X^*, the technique of dummy variables can be used to estimate the (differing) slopes of

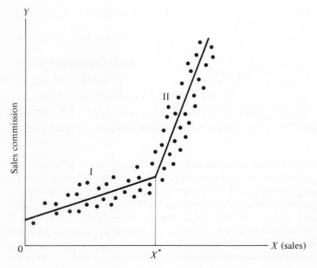

Figure 13.6 Hypothetical relationship between sales commission and sales volume. (*Note:* The intercept on the Y axis denotes minimum guaranteed commission.)

the two segments of the piecewise linear regression shown in Fig. 13.6. We proceed as follows:

$$Y_i = \alpha_0 + \beta_1 X_i + \beta_2 (X_i - X^*) D_i + u_i \tag{13.9.1}$$

where Y_i = sales commission

X_i = volume of sales generated by the sales person
X^* = threshold value of sales (known in advance)
$D = 1$ if $X_i > X^*$
   $= 0$ if $X_i < X^*$

Assuming $E(u_i) = 0$, we see at once that

$$E(Y_i | D_i = 0, X_i, X^*) = \alpha_0 + \beta_1 X_i \tag{13.9.2}$$

which gives the mean sales commission up to the target level X^* and

$$E(Y_i | D_i = 1, X_i, X^*) = \alpha_0 - \beta_2 X^* + (\beta_1 + \beta_2) X_i \tag{13.9.3}$$

which gives the mean sales commission beyond the target level X^*.

Thus, β_1 gives the slope of the regression line in segment I, and $\beta_1 + \beta_2$ gives the slope of the regression line in segment II of the piecewise linear regression shown in Fig. 13-6. A test of the hypothesis that there is no "break" in the regression at the threshold value X^* can be conducted easily by noting the statistical significance of the estimated differential slope coefficient $\hat{\beta}_2$.

13.10 SUMMARY AND CONCLUSIONS

The purpose of this chapter was to show how qualitative, or dummy, variables taking values of 1 and 0 can be introduced into regression models alongside quantitative variables. As the illustrations in the chapter show, the dummy variables are essentially a data classifying device in that they divide a sample into various subgroups based on qualities, or attributes (sex, marital status, race, religion, etc.), and *implicitly* run individual regressions for each such subgroup. Now if there are differences in the response of the dependent variable to the variation in the quantitative variables in the various subgroups, they will be reflected in the differences in the intercepts or slope coefficients, or both, of the various subgroup regressions.

Although a versatile tool, the dummy-variable technique needs to be handled carefully. First, if the regression model contains a constant term, the number of dummy variables must be one less than the number of classifications of each qualitative variable. Second, the coefficients attached to the dummy variables must always be interpreted in relation to the base group, that is, the group that gets the value of zero. Finally, if a model has several qualitative variables with several classes, introduction of the dummy variables can consume a large number of degrees of freedom. Therefore, one should always weigh the number of dummy variables to be introduced into the model against the total number of observations available for study.

EXERCISES

13.1 If you have monthly data over a number of years, how many dummy variables will you introduce to test the following hypotheses:

(a) All the 12 months of the year exhibit seasonal patterns.

(b) Only February, April, June, August, October, and December exhibit seasonal patterns.

13.2 Refer to regression (13.5.1), which explains the determination of moonlighter's hourly wages. From this equation derive the hourly wage equations for the following types of moonlighters:

(a) White, nonurban, western resident, and high school graduate

(b) Nonwhite, urban, nonwestern resident, and non-high school graduate

(c) White, nonurban, nonwest resident, and high school graduate

13.3 *Interaction effects.* Suppose that we modify the college teachers' salary regression (13.4.1) as follows:

$$Y_i = \alpha_0 + \alpha_1 D_{1i} + \alpha_2 D_{2i} + \alpha_3(D_{1i}D_{2i}) + \beta X_i + u_i$$

where Y_i = annual salary of a college teacher

X_i = years of teaching experience

$D_1 = 1$ if male and zero otherwise

$D_2 = 1$ if white and zero otherwise

(a) The term $(D_{1i}D_{2i})$ represents the *interaction effect*. What is meant by this expression?

(b) What is the meaning of the coefficient α_3?

(c) Find $E(Y_i | D_1 = 1, D_2 = 1, X_i)$ and interpret it.

13.4 In studying the effect of a number of qualitative attributes on the prices charged for movie admissions in a large metropolitan area for the period 1961–1964, R. D. Lampson obtained the following regression for the year 1961:[11]

$$Y = 4.13 + 5.77D_1 + 8.21D_2 - 7.68D_3 - 1.13D_4$$
$$\quad\quad\;\;(2.04)\quad\;(2.67)\quad\;(2.51)\quad\;(1.78)$$

$$+ \; 27.09D_5 + 31.46 \log X_1 + 0.81X_2 + 3 \text{ other dummy variables}$$
$$\;\;(3.58)\quad\quad(13.78)\quad\quad\;\;(0.17)$$
$$R^2 = 0.961$$

where D_1 = theatre location: 1 if suburban, 0 if city center

D_2 = theatre age: 1 if less than 10 years since construction or major innovation, 0 otherwise

D_3 = type of theatre: 1 if outdoor, 0 if indoor

D_4 = parking: 1 if provided, 0 otherwise

D_5 = screening policy: 1 if first run, 0 otherwise

X_1 = average percentage unused seating capacity per showing

X_2 = average film rental, cents per ticket charged by the distributor

Y = adult evening admission price, cents

and where the figures in parentheses are standard errors.

(a) Comment on the results.

(b) How would you rationalize the introduction of the variable X_1?

(c) How would you explain the negative value of the coefficient of D_4?

13.5 Refer to regression (13.8.1). How would you test the hypothesis

(a) $\alpha_1 = \alpha_2$

(b) $\alpha_1 = \alpha_3$

(c) If $\alpha_1 \neq \alpha_0$ and $\alpha_2 \neq \alpha_0$ statistically, does it mean that $\alpha_1 \neq \alpha_2$? not necessarily

Hint: var $(A + B) = $ var $(A) + $ var $(B) + 2$ cov (A, B) and var $(A - B) = $ var $(A) + $ var $(B) - 2$ cov (A, B).

[11] R. D. Lampson, "Measured Productivity and Price Change: Some Empirical Evidence on Service Industry Bias, Motion Picture Theaters," *Journal of Political Economy*, vol. 78, March/April 1970.

13.6 (a) How would you obtain the standard errors of the regression coefficients in models (13.7.3) and (13.7.4), which were estimated from the "pooled" regression (13.7.2)?

(b) To obtain numerical answers, what additional information, if any, is required?

13.7 As stated in the text, the estimates of the regression coefficients obtained from (13.6.3) will be identical with those obtained from the individual estimation of two regressions (13.6.1) and (13.6.2). Will this also be true of $\hat{\sigma}^2$, the estimator of the true variance of σ^2; that is, will $\hat{\sigma}^2$ obtained from (13.6.3) be the same as that obtained from (13.6.1) or (13.6.2)? Why or why not?

13.8 *Deseasonalizing data.* The illustrative example of Sec. 13.8 showed how the dummy variables can be used to take into account the seasonal effects. After estimating regression (13.8.2), we found that only the dummy associated with the second quarter of a year was statistically significant, indicating that only the second quarter exhibited some seasonal effect. Therefore, one method of deseasonalizing the data would be to subtract from the profits and sales figures of the second quarter of each year the value of 1322.8938 (millions of dollars), the value of the dummy coefficient for the second quarter, and run the regression of profits on sales using the data thus transformed.

(a) Transform the preceding data and run the regression. Do not introduce any dummy variables in this regression. (Why?)

(b) Compare the coefficient of the sales variable in the estimated regression using the transformed data with that given in (13.8.2). Are these two coefficients expected to be identical statistically? Why?

13.9 *Pooling cross-sectional and time-series data.* Suppose you have data on output, labor, and capital inputs for N firms in an industry for T time periods and suppose you want to fit a production function of the following type:

$$Y_{it} = \alpha + \beta_1 X_{1it} + \beta_2 X_{2it} + u_{it} \qquad \begin{aligned} i &= 1, 2, 3, \ldots, N \\ t &= 1, 2, 3, \ldots, T \end{aligned}$$

where Y = output

X_1 = capital input

X_2 = labor input

Assuming you have the relevant data, you are asked to develop models such that

(a) Firms differ in *managerial efficiency*, the differences affecting only the intercept α; this may be called the *firm effect*.

(b) All firms are of equal managerial efficiency, but the intercept α shifts from year to year; this may be called the *year effect*.

(c) The intercept of the preceding production function is affected by the firm as well as the year effect.

(d) What assumption do you make about the disturbance term u_{it}?

13.10 *Testing the equality of two regressions: the Chow test.* Consider the following data:

Personal savings and income data, U.K. 1946–1963 (millions of pounds)

Period I: 1946–1954	Savings	Income	Period II: 1955–1963	Savings	Income
1946	0.36	8.8	1955	0.59	15.5
1947	0.21	9.4	1956	0.90	16.7
1948	0.08	10.0	1957	0.95	17.7
1949	0.20	10.6	1958	0.82	18.6
1950	0.10	11.0	1959	1.04	19.7
1951	0.12	11.9	1960	1.53	21.1
1952	0.41	12.7	1961	1.94	22.8
1953	0.50	13.5	1962	1.75	23.9
1954	0.43	14.3	1963	1.99	25.2

Source: Central Statistical Office, U.K.

There seems to be a change in the response of savings to income between the two periods. Therefore, we consider the following regressions:

$$\text{Period } I: \quad Y_{1t} = \alpha_1 + \beta_1 X_t + u_{1t} \quad t = 1, 2, \ldots, 9 \tag{1}$$

$$\text{Period } II: \quad Y_{2t} = \alpha_2 + \beta_2 X_t + u_{2t} \quad t = 1, 2, \ldots, 9 \tag{2}$$

where Y and X are savings and income, respectively, and where the subscripts 1 and 2 on the variables refer to the two periods.

Now to find out whether the two regressions differ, either in the intercepts or slopes, or both, Chow outlines the following steps:

Step I Combine all the N_1 and N_2 observations of the two periods and run the following single "pooled" regression: (*Note:* In the present example, $N_1 = N_2 = 9$, but they need not be always the same):

$$Y_t = \alpha + \beta X_t + u_t$$

From this regression obtain the residual sum of squares (RSS), say, S_1, with df $= N_1 + N_2 - k$, where k is the number of parameters estimated. In this example, $k = 2$.

Step II Run the two individual regressions (1) and (2) and obtain their RSS, say, S_2 and S_3, with df $= N_1 - k$ and $N_2 - k$, respectively. k in this case is 2. Add these two SS, say $S_4 = S_2 + S_3$ with df $= N_1 + N_2 - 2k$.

Step III Obtain $S_5 = S_1 - S_4$.

Step IV Apply the F test as follows:

$$F = \frac{S_5/k}{S_4/(N_1 + N_2 - 2k)}$$

with df $= k, N_1 + N_2 - 2k$. If the computed F exceeds the critical F, reject the hypothesis that the two regressions are the same.

Apply the Chow test to the previous data.

13.11 To test whether the savings-income regressions are the same for the two time periods given in Exercise 13.10, suppose we use the dummy-variable techniques as follows:

$$Y_t = \alpha_0 + \alpha_1 D_t + \beta_1 X_t + \beta_2(D_t X_t) + u_t \quad t = 1, 2, \ldots, N_1 + N_2$$

where Y and X are savings and income, respectively, and $D_t = 1$ for observations in the first period and 0 for the observations in the second period.

(a) Estimate the preceding regression.

(b) Compare your results with those obtained in Exercise 13.10 by applying the Chow test.

(c) What are the advantages, if any, of the dummy-variable method over the Chow test?

13.12 In the dummy-variable regression model of Exercise 13.11 instead of using 1 and 0 values for the dummy D, use the values $Z_t = a + bD_t$, where $D = 1$ and 0 and where $a = 2$ and $b = 3$. Compare the two results.

13.13 In examining the behavior of the help-wanted index in relation to the unemployment rate in the United States for the quarterly periods of 1951-I to 1968-II, Gujarati divided his sample period into 10 subperiods to reflect business fluctuations observed during the period of study and fitted the following model:

$$HWI = \alpha_1 + \alpha_2 D_2 + \alpha_3 D_3 + \alpha_4 D_4 + \alpha_5 D_5 + \alpha_6 D_6 + \alpha_7 D_7 + \alpha_8 D_8$$

$$+ \alpha_9 D_9 + \alpha_{10} D_{10} + \beta_1 \frac{1}{U_1} + \beta_2 \frac{1}{U_2} + \beta_3 \frac{1}{U_3}$$

$$+ \beta_4 \frac{1}{U_4} + \beta_5 \frac{1}{U_5} + \beta_6 \frac{1}{U_6} + \beta_7 \frac{1}{U_7} + \beta_8 \frac{1}{U_8}$$

$$+ \beta_9 \frac{1}{U_9} + \beta_{10} \frac{1}{U_{10}}$$

where the D's are the dummy variables taking values of 1 or 0 for periods 2 through 10, HWI is the help-wanted index, U is the unemployment rate, and subscripts on U refer to the various time periods.

The regressions were as follows:

Period	α's	β's
1951-I to 1952-IV	$\alpha_1 = 56.4169$ (24.8530)	$\beta_1 = 208.3110$ (77.9402)
1953-I to 1954-III	$\alpha_2 = -22.1640$ (25.3457)	$\beta_2 = 241.1890$ (16.5722)
1954-IV to 1955-III	$\alpha_3 = -99.7531$ (34.1371)	$\beta_3 = 655.8030$ (107.0860)
1955-IV to 1957-I	$\alpha_4 = 87.7070$ (76.3868)	$\beta_4 = -51.5983$ (296.4690)
1957-II to 1958-II	$\alpha_5 = -44.2291$ (26.5035)	$\beta_5 = 410.8780$ (45.7821)
1958-III to 1959-IV	$\alpha_6 = -71.4072$ (29.3326)	$\beta_6 = 679.0280$ (90.1965)
1960-I to 1961-II	$\alpha_7 = -36.1858$ (29.0280)	$\beta_7 = 468.9000$ (88.0691)
1961-III to 1962-IV	$\alpha_8 = -7.8388$ (35.1229)	$\beta_8 = 346.2400$ (144.4920)
1963-I to 1966-IV	$\alpha_9 = -114.3650$ (25.8529)	$\beta_9 = 940.5190$ (32.7320)
1967-I to 1968-II	$\alpha_{10} = 35.1292$ (51.8413)	$\beta_{10} = 351.2390$ (170.9560)
	$R^2 = 0.9814 \qquad d = 1.74$	

Note: The figures in the parentheses are the estimated standard errors.

Source: Damodar Gujarati, "Cyclical Behavior of Help-Wanted Index and the Unemployment Rate," *The Review of Economics and Statistics,* vol. 51, no. 4, p. 483, November 1969.

(*a*) Find out which of the differential intercepts are statistically significant.

(*b*) Note that the β's give direct estimates of the slope coefficients in the various subperiods. How would you test the hypothesis that, say, $\beta_2 = \beta_3$?

(*c*) Suppose you were to fit the model

$$HWI = (\alpha_1 + \alpha_2 D_2 + \cdots + \alpha_{10} D_{10}) + \beta_1 U + \beta_2 U_2 + \cdots + \beta_{10} U_{10}$$

How would your results differ from those shown previously?

(*d*) How would you write the model to incorporate differential intercepts as well as differential slope coefficients?

13.14 Fit a piecewise linear regression to the following data, regressing total cost of production on output, where it is known that the total cost function changes its slope at the output level of 5500 units.

Total cost, dollars	Output
256	1000
414	2000
634	3000
778	4000
1003	5000
1839	6000
2081	7000
2423	8000
2734	9000
2914	10,000

13.15 The following table gives quarterly data (not seasonally adjusted) on the sale of mutual fund shares by the mutual fund industry for the period 1968–1973.

Sale of mutual fund shares (millions of dollars)

Year	Quarter			
	I	II	III	IV
1968	1564	1654	1607	1994
1969	2129	1658	1428	1503
1970	1381	1039	975	1230
1971	1304	1288	1108	1446
1972	1398	1176	1099	1219
1973	1382	888	933	1156

Source: *1974 Mutual Fund Fact Book,* Investment Company Institute, Washington, D.C. (The figures are rounded to the nearest million dollars.)

Consider the following model:

$$\text{Sales}_t = \alpha_0 + \alpha_1 D_1 + \alpha_2 D_2 + \alpha_3 D_3 + u_t$$

where $D_1 = 1$ for the second quarter, 0 otherwise
$D_2 = 1$ for the third quarter, 0 otherwise
$D_3 = 1$ for the fourth quarter, 0 otherwise

(a) Estimate the preceding regression.
(b) How would you interpret the α's?
(c) How would you use the estimated α's to deseasonalize the sales data.

13.16 Use the data of Exercise 13.15 but use the following model:

$$\text{Sales}_t = \alpha_1 D_1 + \alpha_2 D_2 + \alpha_3 D_3 + \alpha_4 D_4 + u_t$$

where the D's are the dummy variables taking values of 1 or 0 in quarters 1 to 4.

(a) How would you estimate the preceding equation?

(b) Does the preceding equation violate the rule that the number of dummies should be one less than the number of classifications (quarters)?

(c) Compare your results with those obtained in Exercise 13.15.

13.17 Refer to the data given in App. 13A, Sec. 13A.2, and regression (13.8.2). Develop a regression model to test the hypothesis that the slope as well as the intercept term of the regression of profits on sales is different for the second quarter of the year as compared with the remaining quarters. Show the necessary calculations.

13.18 (a) Repeat Exercise 13.11 but assign $D = 1$ to the observations in the second period and $D = 0$ to the observations in the first period and compare your results.

(b) What general conclusion can you draw regarding the assignment of the dummy variable in applications involving only two classifications or two time periods?

13A.1 DATA MATRIX FOR REGRESSION (13.7.2)

Year and quarter	Unemployment rate UN, %	Job-vacancy rate V, %	D	DV	Year and quarter	Unemployment rate UN, %	Job-vacancy rate V, %	D	DV
1958-IV	1.915	0.510	0	0	1965-I	1.201	0.997	0	0
1959-I	1.876	0.541	0	0	-II	1.192	1.035	0	0
-II	1.842	0.541	0	0	-III	1.259	1.040	0	0
-III	1.750	0.690	0	0	-IV	1.192	1.086	0	0
-IV	1.648	0.771	0	0	1966-I	1.089	1.101	0	0
1960-I	1.450	0.836	0	0	-II	1.101	1.058	0	0
-II	1.393	0.908	0	0	-III	1.243	0.987	0	0
-III	1.322	0.968	0	0	-IV	1.623	0.819	1	0.819
-IV	1.260	0.998	0	0	1967-I	1.821	0.740	1	0.740
1961-I	1.171	0.968	0	0	-II	1.990	0.661	1	0.661
-II	1.182	0.964	0	0	-III	2.114	0.660	1	0.660
III	1.221	0.952	0	0	-IV	2.115	0.698	1	0.698
-IV	1.340	0.849	0	0	1968-I	2.150	0.695	1	0.695
1962-I	1.411	0.748	0	0	-II	2.141	0.732	1	0.732
-II	1.600	0.658	0	0	-III	2.167	0.749	1	0.749
-III	1.780	0.562	0	0	-IV	2.107	0.800	1	0.800
-IV	1.941	0.510	0	0	1969-I	2.104	0.783	1	0.783
1963-I	2.178	0.510	0	0	-II	2.056	0.800	1	0.800
-II	2.067	0.544	0	0	-III	2.170	0.794	1	0.794
-III	1.942	0.568	0	0	-IV	2.161	0.790	1	0.790
-IV	1.764	0.677	0	0	1970-I	2.225	0.757	1	0.757
1964-I	1.532	0.794	0	0	-II	2.241	0.746	1	0.746
-II	1.455	0.838	0	0	-III	2.366	0.739	1	0.739
-III	1.409	0.885	0	0	-IV	2.324	0.707	1	0.707
-IV	1.296	0.978	0	0	1971-I	2.516†	0.583†	1	0.583†
					-II	2.909	0.524†	1	0.524†

† Preliminary estimates.

Source: Damodar Gujarati, "The Behaviour of Unemployment and Unfilled Vacancies: Great Britain, 1958–1971," *The Economic Journal*, vol. 82, p. 204, March 1972.

13A.2 DATA MATRIX FOR REGRESSION (13.8.2)

Year and quarter	Profits (millions of dollars)	Sales (millions of dollars)	D_1	D_2	D_3
1965-I	10,503	114,862	0	0	0
-II	12,092	123,968	1	0	0
-III	10,834	121,454	0	1	0
-IV	12,201	131,917	0	0	1
1966-I	12,245	129,911	0	0	0
-II	14,001	140,976	1	0	0
-III	12,213	137,828	0	1	0
-IV	12,820	145,465	0	0	1
1967-I	11,349	136,989	0	0	0
-II	12,615	145,126	1	0	0
-III	11,014	141,536	0	1	0
-IV	12,730	151,776	0	0	1
1968-I	12,539	148,862	0	0	0
-II	14,849	158,913	1	0	0
-III	13,203	155,727	0	1	0
-IV	14,947	168,409	0	0	1
1969-I	14,151	162,781	0	0	0
-II	15,949	176,057	1	0	0
-III	14,024	172,419	0	1	1
-IV	14,315	183,327	0	0	1
1970-I	12,381	170,415	0	0	0
-II	13,991	181,313	1	0	0
-III	12,174	176,712	0	1	0
-IV	10,985	180,370	0	0	1

Notes: $D_1 = 1$ for the second quarter, 0 otherwise
$D_2 = 1$ for the third quarter, 0 otherwise
$D_3 = 1$ for the fourth quarter, 0 otherwise

Source: Data on profits and sales pertain to the entire manufacturing sector and are from *Quarterly Financial Report for Manufacturing Corporations*, U.S. Federal Trade Commission and the U.S. Securities and Exchange Commission.

CHAPTER
FOURTEEN

REGRESSION ON DUMMY DEPENDENT VARIABLE

In the dummy-variable regression models considered in Chap. 13, it was assumed implicitly that the dependent variable Y was quantitative whereas the explanatory variables were either quantitative or qualitative or a mixture thereof. In this chapter we consider very briefly regression models in which the dependent variable itself can be dichotomous in nature, taking a 1 or 0 value, and point out some of the interesting estimation problems associated with such models.

14.1 DUMMY DEPENDENT VARIABLE

Suppose we want to study the labor-force participation of adult males as a function of the unemployment rate, average wage rate, family income, education, etc. Now a person is either in the labor force or is not. Hence, the dependent variable, labor-force participation, can take only two values: 1 if the person is in the labor force and 0 if he or she is not.

Consider another example. Suppose we want to study the union membership status of college professors as a function of several quantitative and qualitative variables. Now a college professor either belongs to a union or does not. Therefore, the dependent variable, union membership status, is a dummy variable taking on values of 0 or 1, 0 implying no union membership and 1 implying union membership.

There are several such examples where the dependent variable is dichotomous. Thus, a family either owns a house or it does not, it has disability insurance or it does not, both husband and wife are in the labor force or only one person is, and so on. Similarly, a certain drug is effective in curing an illness or it is not. A unique feature of all these examples is that the dependent variable is of the type that it elicits a yes or no response; that is, it is dichotomous in nature.

To see how models involving dummy dependent variables can be handled, consider the following simple model:

$$Y_i = \alpha + \beta X_i + u_i \tag{14.1.1}$$

where X = family income
$\quad\ Y = 1 \quad$ if the family owns a house
$\quad\quad\ = 0 \quad$ if it does not own a house

Models, such as (14.1.1), which express the dichotomous Y_i as a linear function of the explanatory variable(s) X_i, are called *linear probability models* (**LPM**) since $E(Y_i|X_i)$, the conditional expectation of Y_i given X_i, can be interpreted as the *conditional probability* that the event will occur given X_i; that is, Pr $(Y_i = 1|X_i)$. Thus, in the preceding case, $E(Y_i|X_i)$ gives the probability of a family owning a car whose income is the given amount X_i. The justification of the name LPM for models like (14.1.1) can be seen as follows.

Assuming $E(u_i) = 0$, as usual, we obtain

$$E(Y_i|X_i) = \alpha + \beta X_i \tag{14.1.2}$$

Now letting P_i = probability that $Y_i = 1$ (that is, that the event occurs) and $1 - P_i$ = probability that $Y_i = 0$ (that is, that the event does not occur), the variable Y_i has the following distribution:

Y_i	Probability
0	$1 - P_i$
1	$\dfrac{P_i}{1}$

Therefore, by the definition of mathematical expectation, we obtain

$$E(Y_i) = 0(1 - P_i) + 1(P_i)$$
$$= P_i \tag{14.1.3}$$

Comparing (14.1.2) with (14.1.3), we can equate

$$E(Y_i|X_i) = \alpha + \beta X_i = P_i \tag{14.1.4}$$

that is, the conditional expectation of the model (14.1.1) can, in fact, be interpreted as the conditional probability of Y_i.

Since the probability P_i must lie between 0 and 1, we have the restriction

$$0 \le E(Y_i|X_i) \le 1 \tag{14.1.5}$$

that is, the conditional expectation, or conditional probability, must lie between 0 and 1.

14.2 ESTIMATION OF LINEAR PROBABILITY MODELS

It seems that (14.1.1) is like any other regression model, hence its parameters can be estimated by the usual ordinary least-squares (OLS) procedure. But now we must face some special problems, which are as follows:

1. *Nonnormality of the disturbances u_i.* Although OLS does not require the disturbances (u's) to be normally distributed, we assumed them to be so distributed for the purpose of statistical inference, that is, hypothesis testing, etc. But the assumption of normality for u_i is no longer tenable for the LP models because, like Y_i, u_i takes on only two values. To see this, we write (14.1.1) as

$$u_i = Y_i - \alpha - \beta X_i \tag{14.2.1}$$

Now when

$$Y_i = 1 \qquad u_i = 1 - \alpha - \beta X_i$$

and when

$$\tag{14.2.2}$$

$$Y_i = 0 \qquad u_i = -\alpha - \beta X_i$$

Obviously, u_i cannot be assumed to be normally distributed.

But the nonfulfillment of the normality assumption may not be as critical as it appears because we know that the OLS point estimates still remain unbiased (recall that if the objective is point estimation, the normality assumption is inconsequential). Furthermore, as sample size increases indefinitely, it can be shown that the OLS estimators tend to be normally distributed generally.[1] Therefore, in large samples the statistical inference of the LPM will follow the usual OLS procedure under the normality assumption.

2. *Heteroscedastic variances of the disturbances.* Even if $E(u_i) = 0$ and $E(u_i u_j) = 0$, for $i \neq j$ (that is, no serial correlation), it can no longer be maintained that the disturbances u_i are homoscedastic. To see this, the u's given in (14.2.2) have the following probability distribution:

u_i	Probability
$-\alpha - \beta X_i$	$1 - P_i$
$1 - \alpha - \beta X_i$	P_i
	1

The preceding probability distribution follows from the probability distribution for Y_i given previously.

Now, by definition,

$$\text{var}(u_i) = E[u_i - E(u_i)]^2$$

$$= E(u_i^2) \qquad \text{for } E(u_i) = 0 \text{ by assumption}$$

---

[1] The proof is based on the central limit theorem and may be found in E. Malinvaud, *Statistical Methods of Econometrics*, Rand McNally & Company, Chicago, 1966, pp. 195–197.

Therefore, using the preceding probability distribution of u_i, we obtain

$$\text{var}(u_i) = E(u_i^2) = (-\alpha - \beta X_i)^2(1 - P_i) + (1 - \alpha - \beta X_i)^2(P_i)$$

$$= (-\alpha - \beta X_i)^2(1 - \alpha - \beta X_i) + (1 - \alpha - \beta X_i)^2(\alpha + \beta X_i)$$

$$= (\alpha + \beta X_i)(1 - \alpha - \beta X_i) \tag{14.2.3}$$

Or $\quad \text{var}(u_i) = E(Y_i|X_i)[1 - E(Y_i|X_i)]$

$$= P_i(1 - P_i) \tag{14.2.4}$$

where use is made of the fact that $E(Y_i|X_i) = \alpha + \beta X_i = P_i$. Equation (14.2.4) shows that the variance of u_i is heteroscedastic because it depends on the conditional expectation of Y, which, of course, depends on the value taken by X. Thus, ultimately the variance of u_i depends on X and is thus not homoscedastic.

Now we know that in the presence of heteroscedasticity the OLS estimators, although unbiased, are not efficient; that is, they do not have minimum variance. But again the problem of heteroscedasticity is not insurmountable. In Chap. 10 we discussed several methods of handling the heteroscedasticity problem. Since the variance of u_i depends on the expected value of Y conditional upon the X value, as shown in (14.2.3), one way of resolving the heteroscedasticity problem is to transform the data by dividing both sides of the model (14.1.1) by

$$\sqrt{E(Y_i|X_i)[1 - E(Y_i|X_i)]} = \sqrt{P_i(1 - P_i)} = \text{say}, \sqrt{w_i}$$

$$\frac{Y_i}{\sqrt{w_i}} = \frac{\alpha}{\sqrt{w_i}} + \beta \frac{X_i}{\sqrt{w_i}} + \frac{u_i}{\sqrt{w_i}} \tag{14.2.5}$$

The disturbance term in (14.2.5) will now be homoscedastic. (Why?) Therefore, one may proceed to the OLS estimation of (14.2.5).

Of course, the true $E(Y_i|X_i)$ is not known; hence w_i are unknown. To estimate w_i, we may use the following two-step procedure:

Step I Run the OLS regression on (14.1.1) despite the heteroscedasticity problem and obtain $\hat{Y}_i =$ estimate of true $E(Y_i|X_i)$. Then, obtain $\hat{w}_i = \hat{Y}_i(1 - \hat{Y}_i)$, the estimate of w_i.

Step II Use the estimated $\hat{w}_i$ to transform the data as in (14.2.5), and run the OLS regression on the data thus transformed.[2]

3. *Nonfulfillment of* $0 \le E(Y_i|X) \le 1$. Since $E(Y_i|X)$ in the linear probability models measures the conditional probability of the event Y occurring given X, it must necessarily lie between 0 and 1. Although this is true a priori, there is no guarantee that $\hat{Y}_i$, the estimators of $E(Y_i|X_i)$, will necessarily fulfill this restriction, and this is the real problem with the OLS estimation of the LPM. There are

---

[2] For the justification of this procedure, see Arthur S. Goldberger, *Econometric Theory*, John Wiley & Sons, Inc., New York, 1964, pp. 249–250.

two ways of finding out whether the estimated $\hat{Y}_i$ lie between 0 and 1. One is to estimate the LPM by the usual OLS method and find out whether the estimated $\hat{Y}_i$ lie between 0 and 1. If some are less than 0 (that is, negative), $\hat{Y}_i$ is assumed to be zero for those cases; if they are greater than 1, they are assumed to be 1. The second procedure is to devise an estimating technique that will guarantee that the estimated conditional probabilities $\hat{Y}_i$ will lie between 0 and 1. Several such methods are available, but we shall not pursue them here[3] (but see Exercise 14.4).

We conclude this chapter with an illustrative example.

14.3 COHEN-REA-LERMAN STUDY[4]

In a study prepared for the U.S. Department of Labor, Cohen, Rea, and Lerman were interested in examining the labor-force participation of various categories of labor as a function of several socioeconomic-demographic variables. In all their regressions, the dependent variable was a dummy, taking a value of 1 if a person is in the labor force, 0 if he or she is not. In Table 14.1 we reproduce one of their several dummy-dependent variable regressions.

[3] An excellent reference is S. M. Goldfeld and R. E. Quandt, *Nonlinear Methods in Econometrics*, North-Holland Publishing Company, Amsterdam, 1972, chap. 4. Another reference from an applied viewpoint is Robert S. Pindyck and Daniel Rubinfeld, *Econometric Models and Economic Forecasts*, McGraw-Hill Book Company, New York, 1976, chap. 8.

[4] Malcolm S. Cohen, Samuel A. Rea, Jr., and Robert I. Lerman, *A Micro Model of Labor Supply*, BLS Staff Paper 4, U.S. Department of Labor, 1970.

Table 14.1 Labor-force participation

Regression of women, age 22 and over, living in largest 96 standard metropolitan statistical areas (SMSA) (dependent variable: in or out of the labor force during 1966)

Explanatory variable	Coefficient	t ratio
Constant	0.4368	15.4
Marital status		
Married, spouse present	...	...
Married, other	0.1523	13.8
Never married	0.2915	22.0
Age		
22–54	...	...
55–64	−0.0594	−5.7
65 and over	−0.2753	−9.0
Years of schooling		
0–4	...	...
5–8	0.1255	5.8
9–11	0.1704	7.9
12–15	0.2231	10.6
16 and over	0.3061	13.3

Table 14.1 Labor-force participation (*continued*)

Explanatory variable	Coefficient	t ratio
Unemployment rate (1966), %		
Under 2.5	...	...
2.5–3.4	−0.0213	−1.6
3.5–4.0	−0.0269	−2.0
4.1–5.0	−0.0291	−2.2
5.1 and over	−0.0311	−2.4
Employment change (1965–1966), %		
Under 3.5	...	...
3.5–6.49	0.0301	3.2
6.5 and over	0.0529	5.1
Relative employment opportunities, %		
Under 62	...	...
62–73.9	0.0381	3.2
74 and over	0.0571	3.2
FILOW, $		
Less than 1500 or negative	...	...
1500–7499	−0.1451	−15.4
7500 and over	−0.2455	−24.4
Interaction (marital status and age)		
Marital status Age		
Other 55–64	−0.0406	−2.1
Other 65 and over	−0.1391	−7.4
Never married 55–64	−0.1104	−3.3
Never married 65 and over	−0.2045	−6.4
Interaction (age and years of schooling completed)		
Age Years of schooling		
65 and over 5–8	−0.0885	−2.8
65 and over 9–11	−0.0848	−2.4
65 and over 12–15	−0.1288	−4.0
65 and over 16 and over	−0.1628	−3.6

$$R^2 = 0.175$$
No. of observations = 25,143

Notes: ··· indicates the base or omitted category.

FILOW: family income less own wage and salary income.

Source: Malcolm S. Cohen, Samuel A. Rea, Jr., and Robert I. Lerman, *A Micro Model of Labor Supply*, BLS Staff Paper 4, U.S. Department of Labor, 1970, table F-6, pp. 212–213.

Before interpreting the results, note these features: The preceding regression was estimated using the OLS. To correct for heteroscedasticity, the authors used the two-stage procedure outlined previously in some of their regressions but found that the standard errors of the estimates thus obtained did not differ materially from those obtained without correction for heteroscedasticity. Perhaps this is due to the sheer size of the sample, namely, about 25,000. Because of this large sample size, the estimated t values may be tested for statistical significance by the usual OLS procedure even though the error term takes dichotomous values. The estimated R^2 of 0.175 may seem rather low, but in view of the large sample size, this R^2 is still significant on the basis of the F test given in Sec. 7.6. Finally, notice how the authors have blended quantitative and qualitative variables and how they have taken into account the interaction effects.

Turning to the interpretations of the findings, each slope coefficient gives the rate of change in the conditional probability of the event occurring for a given unit change in the value of the explanatory variable. For instance, the coefficient of -0.2753 attached to the variable "age 65 and over" means, holding all other factors constant, the probability of participation in the labor force by women in this age group is smaller by about 27 percent (as compared with the base category of women aged 22 to 54). By the same token, the coefficient of 0.3061 attached to the variable "16 or more years of schooling" means, holding all other factors constant, the probability of women with this much education participating in the labor force is higher by about 31 percent (as compared with women with less than 5 years of schooling, the base category).

Now consider the interaction term marital status and age. The table shows that the labor-force participation probability is higher by some 29 percent for those women who were never married (as compared with the base category) and smaller by about 28 percent for those women who are 65 and over (again in relation to the base category). But the probability of participation of women who were never married and are 65 or over is smaller by about 20 percent as compared with the base category. This implies that women aged 65 and over but never married are likely to participate in the labor force more than those who are aged 65 and over and are married or fall into the "other" category.

Following this procedure, the reader can easily interpret the rest of the coefficients given in Table 14.1. From the given information, it is easy to obtain the estimates of the conditional probabilities of labor-force participation of the various categories. Thus, if we want to find the probability for married women (other), aged 22 to 54, with 12 to 15 years of schooling, with an unemployment rate of 2.5 to 3.4 percent, employment change of 3.5 to 6.49 percent, relative employment opportunities of 74 percent and over and with FILOW of $7500 and over, we obtain

$$0.4368 + 0.1523 + 0.2231 - 0.0213 + 0.0301 + 0.0571 - 0.2455 = 0.6326$$

In other words, the probability of labor-force participation by women with the preceding characteristics is estimated to be about 63 percent.

14.4 SUMMARY AND CONCLUSIONS

In this chapter we considered models in which the dependent variable is dichotomous, taking on values of 1 or 0. Such models are used in situations where the dependent variable elicits a yes or no response, such as purchase or nonpurchase of an appliance, a house, or any other product and participation or nonparticipation in an activity like work or union membership. Models with dummy dependent variables, when expressed as linear functions of the explanatory variables (which may be quantitative or qualitative or both), are called *linear probability models* (LPM) because the expected values of the dependent variable conditional upon the given values of the explanatory variables can be interpreted as the conditional probabilities of the event occurring.

The linear probability models pose some special estimating problems in that (1) the disturbances are nonnormal, (2) they have heteroscedastic variances, and (3) the estimated conditional probabilities may not lie between the logical limits of 1 and 0. The problems of nonnormality is not as serious as it sounds because the estimates obtained by the usual OLS procedure are still unbiased. Moreover, in large samples, one can use the OLS methodology to test hypothesis, etc. The problem of heteroscedasticity can also be handled by transforming the data. The really serious problem is that the estimated conditional probabilities may not lie between the 0 and 1 limits. But here, too, one can resort to special estimating techniques that guarantee that the estimated conditional probabilities do, in fact, lie between 0 and 1.

EXERCISES

14.1 The following table gives hypothetical data on house ownership Y ($1 =$ owns a house, $0 =$ does not own a house) and family income X for 40 families (in thousands of dollars).

Family	Y	X	Family	Y	X
1	0	8	21	1	22
2	1	16	22	1	16
3	1	18	23	0	12
4	0	11	24	0	11
5	0	12	25	1	16
6	1	19	26	0	11
7	1	20	27	1	20
8	0	13	28	1	18
9	0	9	29	0	11
10	0	10	30	0	10
11	1	17	31	1	17
12	1	18	32	0	13
13	0	14	33	1	21
14	1	20	34	1	20
15	0	6	35	0	11
16	1	19	36	0	8
17	1	16	37	1	17
18	0	10	38	1	16
19	0	8	39	0	7
20	1	18	40	1	17

(a) Fit a linear probability model to the preceding data and interpret the resulting equation.

(b) For each family, obtain the estimated Y. How would you treat the estimated Y which are either negative or in excess of 1?

14.2 Refer to Exercise 14.1. Since in the linear probability model the stochastic error term is expected to be heteroscedastic, use the two-step procedure given in the text and reestimate the model.

(*Note:* If some estimated Y_i are negative, assume them to be zero. Similarly, if some of the estimated Y_i are equal to or greater than 1, treat them as equal to 1.)

14.3 In studying the purchase of durable goods Y ($Y = 1$ if purchased, $Y = 0$ if no purchase), as a function of several variables for a total of 762 households, Janet A. Fisher[5] obtained the following results:

Explanatory variable	Coefficient	Standard error
Constant	0.1411	$\cdots$
1957 Disposable income, X_1	0.0251	0.0118
X_1^2, X_2	-0.0004	0.0004
Checking accounts, X_3	-0.0051	0.0108
Savings accounts, X_4	0.0013	0.0047
U.S. Savings Bonds, X_5	-0.0079	0.0067
Housing status: rent, X_6	-0.0469	0.0937
Housing status: own, X_7	0.0136	0.0712
Monthly rent, X_8	-0.7540	1.0983
Monthly mortgage payments, X_9	-0.9809	0.5162
Personal noninstallment debt, X_{10}	-0.0367	0.0326
Age, X_{11}	0.0046	0.0084
Age squared, X_{12}	-0.0001	0.0001
Marital status, X_{13} (1 = married)	0.1760	0.0501
Number of children, X_{14}	0.0398	0.0358
X_{14}^2, X_{15}	-0.0036	0.0072
Purchase plans, X_{16}	0.1760	0.0384
(1 if planned; 0 otherwise)		
$R^2 = 0.1336$		

Notes: All financial variables are in thousands of dollars.
Housing status: Rent (1 if rents; 0 otherwise)
Housing status: Own (1 if owns; 0 otherwise)
Source: Janet A. Fisher, "An Analysis of Consumer Good Expenditure," *The Review of Economics and Statistics*, vol. 64, no. 1, table 1, p. 67.

(*a*) Comment generally on the fit of the equation.

(*b*) How would you interpret the coefficient of -0.0051 attached to checking account variable? How would you rationalize the negative sign for this variable?

(*c*) What is the rationale behind introducing the age-squared and number of children-squared variables? Why is the sign negative in both cases?

(*d*) Assuming values of zero for all but the income variable, find out the conditional probability of a household whose income is $20,000 purchasing a durable good.

(*e*) Estimate the conditional probability of owning durable good(s), given: $X_1 = \$15,000$, $X_3 = \$3000$, $X_4 = \$5000$, $X_6 = 0$, $X_7 = 1$, $X_8 = \$500$, $X_9 = \$300$, $X_{10} = 0$, $X_{11} = 35$, $X_{13} = 1$, $X_{14} = 2$, $X_{16} = 0$.

[5] See her article, "An Analysis of Consumer Good Expenditure," *The Review of Economics and Statistics*, vol. 64, no. 1, pp. 64–71, 1962.

*14-4 *The logit model.* A serious problem with the linear probability model considered in the text is that the estimated Y values, which are conditional probabilities, may not lie between the 0 and 1 limits. A model that guarantees that this will be the case is the *logit model.* This model can be developed as follows. Let

$$P_i = \text{probability that the } i\text{th family owns a house}$$

$$1 - P_i = \text{probability that it does not own a house}$$

Assuming that income is the only significant determinant of house purchase, consider the model

$$\ln \left(\frac{P_i}{1 - P_i} \right) = \alpha + \beta \ln X_i \qquad (1)$$

where X is income.

(a) The term in parenthesis on the left-hand side represents nothing but the log of the odds in favor of owning the house by a family. And equation (1) postulates that the log of this odds ratio is a linear function of the log of income. β therefore gives the income elasticity of the odds in favor of owning a house. Why?

The left-hand side of (1) is known as the *logit of house ownership*, the name *logit* coming from the logistic function, which can be written as

$$P_i = \frac{1}{1 + e^{-\alpha - \beta \ln X_i}} \qquad (2)$$

Verify that (2) can be transformed into (1).

(b) An advantage of the logit function (1) is that it guarantees that the estimated probabilities will lie between 0 and 1. Prove this.

(c) How would you fit the logit function (1), assuming you have the data on income?[6]

14.5 Verify that the R^2 value given in Table 14.1 is statistically significant.

* Optional.

[6] For answer and other details, see Henry Theil, *Principles of Econometrics*, John Wiley & Sons, Inc., New York, 1971, sec. 12.5.

FIFTEEN

SINGLE-EQUATION MODELS: SOME FURTHER TOPICS

To round off our discussion of single-equation models, we mention a few additional topics without any extended discussion. For details, the reader may consult the references.

15.1 ERRORS OF MEASUREMENT

All along we have assumed implicitly that the dependent variable Y and the explanatory variables, the X's, are measured without any errors. Thus, in the regression of consumption expenditure on income and wealth of households, we assume that the data on these variables are "accurate"; they are not *guess estimates*, extrapolated, interpolated, or rounded off in any systematic manner, such as to the nearest hundredth dollar, and so on. Unfortunately, this ideal is not met in practice for a variety of reasons, such as nonresponse errors, reporting errors, and computing errors. Whatever the reasons, errors of measurement is a potentially troublesome problem, as the following discussion shows.

Errors of Measurement in the Dependent Variable Y

Consider the following model:

$$Y_i^* = \alpha + \beta X_i + u_i \tag{15.1.1}$$

where $Y_i^* =$ "permanent" consumption expenditure[1]
$\quad X_i =$ current income
$\quad u_i =$ stochastic disturbance term

---

[1] This phrase is due to Milton Friedman.

Since Y_i^* is not directly measurable, we may use an observable expenditure variable Y_i such that

$$Y_i = Y_i^* + \varepsilon_i \tag{15.1.2}$$

where ε_i denote errors of measurement in Y_i^*. Therefore, instead of estimating (15.1.1), we estimate

$$\begin{aligned} Y_i &= (\alpha + \beta X_i + u_i) + \varepsilon_i \\ &= \alpha + \beta X_i + (u_i + \varepsilon_i) \\ &= \alpha + \beta X_i + v_i \end{aligned} \tag{15.1.3}$$

where $v_i = u_i + \varepsilon_i$ is a composite error term, containing the population disturbance term (which may be called the *error term* in the equation) and the measurement error term.

For simplicity assume that $E(u_i) = E(\varepsilon_i) = 0$, cov $(X_i, u_i) = 0$ (which is the assumption of the classical linear regression), and cov $(X_i, \varepsilon_i) = 0$; that is, the errors of measurement in Y_i^* are uncorrelated with X_i, and cov $(u_i, \varepsilon_i) = 0$; that is, the equation error and the measurement error are uncorrelated. With these assumptions, it can be seen that β estimated from either (15.1.1) or (15.1.3) will be an unbiased estimator of the true β (see Exercise 15.1); that is, the errors of measurement in the dependent variable Y do not destroy the unbiasedness property of the OLS estimators. However, the variances and standard errors of β estimated from (15.1.1) and (15.1.3) will be different because, employing the usual formulas (see Chap. 3), we obtain

Model (15.1.1) $\qquad$ var $(\hat{\beta}) = \dfrac{\sigma_u^2}{\sum x_i^2}$ $\qquad\qquad$ (15.1.4)

Model (15.1.3) $\qquad$ var $(\hat{\beta}) = \dfrac{\sigma_v^2}{\sum x_i^2}$

$$= \frac{\sigma_u^2 + \sigma_\varepsilon^2}{\sum x_i^2} \tag{15.1.5}$$

Obviously, the latter variance is larger than the former.[2] Therefore, although the errors of measurement in the dependent variable still give unbiased estimates of the parameters and their variances, the estimated variances are now larger than in the case where there are no such errors of measurement.

Errors of Measurement in the Explanatory Variable X

Now assume that instead of (15.1.1), we have the following model:

$$Y_i = \alpha + \beta X_i^* + u_i \tag{15.1.6}$$

---

[2] But note that this variance is still unbiased because under the stated conditions the composite error term $v_i = u_i + \varepsilon_i$ still satisfies the assumptions underlying the method of least squares.

where Y_i = current consumption expenditure
X_i^* = "permanent" income
u_i = disturbance term (equation error)

Suppose instead of observing X_i^*, we observe

$$X_i = X_i^* + w_i \tag{15.1.7}$$

where w_i represents errors of measurement in X_i^*. Therefore, instead of estimating (15.1.6), we estimate

$$
\begin{aligned}
Y_i &= \alpha + \beta(X_i - w_i) + u_i \\
&= \alpha + \beta X_i + (u_i - \beta w_i) \\
&= \alpha + \beta X_i + z_i
\end{aligned} \tag{15.1.8}
$$

where $z_i = u_i - \beta w_i$, a compound of equation and measurement errors.

Now even if we assume that w_i has zero mean, is serially independent, and is uncorrelated with u_i, we can no longer assume that the composite error term z_i is independent of the explanatory variable X_i. For, we have [assuming $E(z_i) = 0$]

$$
\begin{aligned}
\operatorname{cov}(z_i, X_i) &= E[z_i - E(z_i)][X_i - E(X_i)] \\
&= E(u_i - \beta w_i)(w_i) \qquad \text{using (15.1.7)} \\
&= E(-\beta w_i^2) \\
&= -\beta \sigma_w^2
\end{aligned} \tag{15.1.9}
$$

Thus, the explanatory variable and the error term in (15.1.8) are correlated, which violates the crucial assumption of the classical linear regression model that the explanatory variable is uncorrelated with the stochastic disturbance term. If this assumption is violated, then, as we saw in Chap. 12, Sec. 12.7, the OLS estimators are not only biased but also inconsistent; they remain biased asymptotically (that is, even if the sample size increases indefinitely).

Therefore, the errors of measurement pose a serious problem when they are present in the explanatory variable(s) because they make consistent estimation of the parameters impossible. Of course, as we saw, if they are present only in the dependent variable, the parameters remain unbiased and hence they are consistent, too.

If errors of measurement are suspected in the explanatory variable(s), one should try to find out other variables, the *instrumental variables* (see Chap. 12), which while highly correlated with the original X variables are themselves uncorrelated with the error term. But this is easier said than done. In practice it is not easy to find out such variables; we are often in the situation of complaining about the bad weather without being able to do much about it. Unfortunately, econometric theory has not much solace to offer either. In reality, what is usually done is to "assume away" the errors of measurement problem by supposing that they are not present; if they are present, we suppose that they are of sufficiently small magnitude so that we can proceed with the usual estimation procedure.

15.2 LINEAR EQUALITY RESTRICTIONS: RESTRICTED LEAST SQUARES

There are occasions where economic theory may suggest that the coefficients in a regression model satisfy some linear equality restrictions. For instance, consider the Cobb-Douglas production function

$$Y_i = \alpha X_{1i}^{\beta_1} X_{2i}^{\beta_2} e^{u_i} \tag{15.2.1}$$

where $Y = $ output, X_1 and $X_2 = $ inputs. Written in log form, the equation becomes

$$\ln Y_i = \ln \alpha + \beta_1 \ln X_{1_i} + \beta_2 \ln X_{2_i} + u_i \tag{15.2.2}$$

Now if there are constant returns to scale (equiproportional change in the output for an equiproportional change in the inputs), economic theory would suggest that

$$\beta_1 + \beta_2 = 1 \tag{15.2.3}$$

which is an example of a linear equality restriction.[3]

How does one find out if there are constant returns to scale, that is, if the restriction (15.2.3) is fulfilled? There are two approaches. The simplest procedure is to estimate (15.2.2) in the usual manner without taking into account the restriction (15.2.3) explicitly. This is called the *unrestricted* or *unconstrained* regression. Having estimated β_1 and β_2, a test of the hypothesis or restriction (15.2.3) can be conducted by the t test as follows:

$$t = \frac{(\hat{\beta}_1 + \hat{\beta}_2) - 1}{\sqrt{\text{var}\,(\hat{\beta}_1) + \text{var}\,(\hat{\beta}_2) + 2\,\text{cov}\,(\hat{\beta}_1, \hat{\beta}_2)}} \tag{15.2.4[4]}$$

If the t value thus computed exceeds the critical t value at the chosen level of significance, we reject the hypothesis of constant returns to scale; otherwise we may accept it.

The procedure just described is a kind of postmortem examination because we try to find out whether the linear restriction is satisfied after estimating the "unrestricted" regression. A direct approach would be to incorporate the restriction (15.2.3) into the estimating procedure at the outset. In the present example, this can be done easily. From (15.2.3) we see that

$$\beta_1 = 1 - \beta_2 \tag{15.2.5}$$

or

$$\beta_2 = 1 - \beta_1 \tag{15.2.6}$$

Therefore, using either of these equalities we can eliminate one of the β

---

[3] If we had $\beta_1 + \beta_2 < 1$, this would be an example of linear inequality restriction. To handle such restrictions, one needs to use mathematical programming techniques.

[4] Note that the denominator of this equation gives the standard error of $\hat{\beta}_1 + \hat{\beta}_2$. (Why?)

coefficients in (15.2.2) and estimate the resulting equation. Thus, if we use (15.2.5), we can write (15.2.2) as

$$\ln Y_i = \ln \alpha + (1 - \beta_2) \ln X_{1_i} + \beta_2 \ln X_{2_i} + u_i$$

$$= \ln \alpha + \ln X_{1_i} + \beta_2(\ln X_{2_i} - \ln X_{1_i}) + u_i$$

or $\qquad \ln Y_i - \ln X_{1_i} = \ln \alpha + \beta_2(\ln X_{2_i} - \ln X_{1_i}) + u_i \qquad (15.2.7)$

Notice how the original equation (15.2.2) is transformed. Once we estimate β_2 from (15.2.7), β_1 can be easily estimated from the relation (15.2.5). Needless to say, this procedure will guarantee that the sum of the estimated coefficients of the two inputs will equal 1.

The procedure outlined in (15.2.7) is known as *restricted least squares*. This procedure can be generalized to models containing more than two explanatory variables and more than one linear equality restriction. The generalization can be found in Theil.[5]

How do we compare the unrestricted and restricted least-squares regressions? In other words, how do we know that, say, the restriction (15.2.3) is valid? This can be tested by applying the F test as follows: Let

$\sum e_1^2$ = RSS of the unrestricted regression (15.2.2)

$\sum e_2^2$ = RSS of the restricted regression (15.2.7)

m = number of linear restrictions (1 in the present example)

k = number of parameters in the unrestricted regression

N = number of observations

Then,

$$F = \frac{(\sum e_2^2 - \sum e_1^2)/m}{\sum e_1^2/(N - k)} \qquad (15.2.8)$$

follows the F distribution with m, $N - k$ df.

If the computed F value is statistically insignificant, one may accept the hypothesis that the linear restriction(s) is valid. If, on the other hand, the estimated F value is statistically significant, it means that the restricted and unrestricted regressions are different; hence one may reject the hypothesis that the parameters obey the linear restriction(s).

15.3 NONLINEAR (IN-THE-PARAMETERS) REGRESSIONS

This text is concerned mainly with regression models that are linear in the parameters, but there are some situations where the linear-in-the-parameters regres-

---

[5] Henri Theil, *Principles of Econometrics*, John Wiley & Sons, Inc., New York, 1971, pp. 43–45.

sion methodology is not applicable.[6] For example, consider the following formulation of the Cobb-Douglas production function:

$$Y_i = \alpha X_{1i}^{\beta_1} X_{2i}^{\beta_2} + u_i \tag{15.3.1}$$

The difference between (15.2.1) and (15.3.1) lies in the specification of the error term u_i. With the specification of the error term as in (15.2.1), it was possible to transform the Cobb-Douglas production function so that in the resulting transformation given in (15.2.2) the model was at least linear in the (economically meaningful) parameters β_1 and β_2 although nonlinear in the parameter α. But there is no way the model (15.3.1) could be linearized even in the parameters β_1 and β_2. Models such as (15.3.1) are called *intrinsically nonlinear models*, whereas models such as (15.2.1) can be called *intrinsically linear models* because they can be linearized by suitable transformations. [*Recall:* As noted in Chap. 3, in model (15.2.2) unbiased estimation of β_1 and β_2 is possible, but this is not true of α. However, in practice the intercept term is generally of little economic significance.]

Intrinsically nonlinear models cannot be estimated directly by the OLS procedure. As a matter of fact, following the least-squares principle, if one were to minimize for model (15.3.1)

$$\sum u_i^2 = \sum (Y_i - \alpha X_{1i}^{\beta_1} X_{2i}^{\beta_2})^2 \tag{15.3.2}$$

the resulting expressions become highly nonlinear and are not easily solvable. (See Exercise 15.3.)

To solve intrinsically nonlinear regression models, several estimation techniques are available, but they are beyond the scope of this book. (However, see Exercise 15.14.) An excellent source is Goldfeld and Quandt,[7] and another source written from an applied viewpoint is Draper and Smith.[8]

15.4 SPECIFICATION BIAS

In regression analysis it is assumed implicitly that the model used in an empirical investigation is the "true," or the "correct," model. If for some reason, the model chosen is "incorrect," or "inappropriate," then we have what is known as the *specification bias*, or *specification error*. In Chaps. 9 and 11 we looked at this problem briefly and showed that if a regression model omits a variable(s) from the model incorrectly, then the coefficients of the variables included in the model are likely to be biased if the omitted variable(s) is correlated with the variables

---

[6] See, for example, the Glejser model considered in Chap. 10, namely, $|e_i| = \sqrt{\beta_0 + \beta_1 X_i}$, where e_i are the OLS residuals. (See Exercise 10.3.)

[7] S. M. Goldfeld and R. E. Quandt, *Nonlinear Methods in Econometrics*, North-Holland Publishing Company, Amsterdam, 1972.

[8] Norman Draper and Harry Smith, *Applied Regression Analysis*, John Wiley & Sons, Inc., New York, 1966, chap. 10.

included in the model. An example was given in Secs. 9.8 and 11.1. Omission of a relevant variable is only one type of specification error. There are others:

1. Inclusion of irrelevant variables
2. Use of a linear model where a nonlinear (in the parameters) model is called for
3. Incorrect specification of the error term, e.g., specifying the error term in the Cobb-Douglas model as in (15.2.1) instead of as in (15.3.1)
4. Use of the wrong functional form

If it is known that a specification error of the preceding types is committed, appropriate remedial measures can be taken,[9] but very often one does not know whether a specification error has been committed. The usual procedure is to develop a model, taking whatever help the theory has to offer, and try to modify the model on the basis of the outcome. Thus, if in the fitted model one finds that some of the estimated coefficients are statistically insignificant or have wrong signs, then one begins modifying the model. Thus, more often than not, model building is a trial-and-error process because very often our theory is not strong enough to tell us precisely the number of explanatory variables or the form in which they should be introduced. Thus, in the regression of consumption expenditure on income and wealth, economic theory may not be able to tell whether one should use a model that is linear in the variables or linear in the logarithms of these variables. Therefore, the stricture that the model used in empirical analysis is "correctly" specified should be taken with a grain of salt.

EXERCISES

15.1 Show that β estimated from either (15.1.1) or (15.1.3) provides an unbiased estimate of true β.

*15.2 Following Frieman's permanent income hypothesis, we may write

$$Y_i^* = \alpha + \beta X_i^* \tag{1}$$

where $Y_i^* =$ "permanent" consumption expenditure
$X_i^* =$ "permanant" income

Instead of observing the "permanent" variables, we observe

$$Y_i = Y_i^* + u_i$$

$$X_i = X_i^* + v_i$$

where Y_i and X_i are the quantities that can be observed or measured and where u_i and v_i are measurement errors in Y^* and X^*, respectively.

Using the observable quantities, we can write the consumption function as

$$Y_i = \alpha + \beta(X_i - v_i) + u_i$$

$$= \alpha + \beta X_i + (u_i - \beta v_i) \tag{2}$$

---

[9] For a thorough discussion, see Jan Kmenta, *Elements of Econometrics*, The Macmillan Company, New York, 1971, pp. 391–405.

* Optional.

Assuming that (1) $E(u_i) = E(v_i) = 0$, (2) var $(u_i) = \sigma_u^2$ and var $(v_i) = \sigma_v^2$, (3) cov $(Y_i^*, u_i) = 0$, cov $(X_i^*, v_i) = 0$, and (4) cov $(u_i, X_i^*) = $ cov $(v_i, Y_i^*) = $ cov $(u_i, v_i) = 0$, show that in large samples β estimated from (2) can be expressed as

$$\text{plim } (\hat{\beta}) = \frac{\beta}{1 + (\sigma_v^2/\sigma_{x*}^2)}$$

(a) What can you say about the nature of the bias in $\hat{\beta}$?

(b) If the sample size increased indefinitely, will the estimated β tend to equality with the true β?

15.3 Differentiate (15.3.2) with respect to α, β_1, and β_2 and set the resulting expressions to zero.

(a) What is the nature of the equations thus obtained?

(b) Why is it not possible to estimate the three unknowns by the usual OLS method?

(c) Can you suggest a procedure of estimating the unknown parameters?

15.4 Refer to Exercise 6.1. Estimate the parameters of the log-linear model given there imposing the restriction $\alpha_{12.3} + \alpha_{13.2} = 1$ and compare your results with the regression estimated without imposing this restriction. How would you decide which is the better model, the restricted or the unrestricted?

15.5 Suppose that the "true" model is

$$Y_i = \beta_1 + \beta_2 X_{2i} + u_i \tag{3}$$

but we add an "irrelevant" variable X_3 to the model (irrelevant in the sense that the true β_3 coefficient attached to the variable X_3 is zero), and estimate

$$Y_i = \beta_1 + \beta_2 X_{2i} + \beta_3 X_{3i} + v_i \tag{4}$$

(a) Would the R^2 and the adjusted R^2 for model (4) be larger than that for model (3)?

(b) Are the estimates of β_1 and β_2 obtained from (4) unbiased?

(c) Does the inclusion of the "irrelevant" variable X_3 affect the variances of $\hat{\beta}_1$ and $\hat{\beta}_2$?

*15.6 Suppose the "true" model is

$$Y_i = \beta X_i u_i \tag{5}$$

where the error term u_i is such that ln (u_i) satisfies the assumptions of the classical normal linear model; namely, it has zero mean and constant variance. But suppose, we fit the following model:

$$Y_i = \beta X_i + v_i \tag{6}$$

(a) Would the β estimated from (6) be an unbiased estimator of true β?

(b) If β estimated previously is biased, is it consistent, that is, does the bias disappear as the sample size increases?

15.7 Consider the following two models:

$$Model\ I \quad \text{Consumption}_i = \alpha_0 + \alpha_1 \text{ income}_i + u_i$$

$$Model\ II \quad \text{Consumption}_i = \beta_0 + \beta_1 \text{ wealth}_i + v_i$$

Suppose we contend that model I is the "truth." How would you go about verifying the "truth"?

15.8 *Capital asset pricing model.* The capital asset pricing model (CAPM) of modern investment theory postulates the following relationship between the average rate of return of a security (common stock), measured over a certain period, and the volatility of the security, called the *Beta coefficient* (volatility is measure of risk):

$$\bar{R}_i = \alpha_0 + \alpha_1(\beta_i) + u_i \tag{7}$$

where $\bar{R}_i$ = average rate of return on security i

β_i = true beta coefficient of security i

u_i = stochastic disturbance term

The true β_i is not directly observable but is measured as follows:

$$r_{it} = \alpha_0 + \beta^* r_{m_t} + e_t \tag{8}$$

where r_{it} = rate of return of security i for time t

r_{m_t} = market rate of return for time t (this rate is the rate of return on some broad market index, such as the S & P index of industrial securities)

e_t = residual term

and where β^* is an estimate of the "true" beta coefficient. In practice, therefore, instead of estimating (7), one estimates

$$\bar{R}_i = \alpha_0 + \alpha_1(\beta_i^*) + u_i \tag{9}$$

where β_i^* are obtained from the regression (8). But since β_i^* are estimated, the relationship between true β and β^* can be written as

$$\beta_i^* = \beta_i + v_i \tag{10}$$

where v_i can be called the *errors of measurement*.

(a) What will be the effect of this error of measurement on the estimate of α_1?

(b) Will the α_1 estimated from (9) provide an unbiased estimate of true α_1? If not, is it a consistent estimate of α_1? If not, what remedial measures do you suggest?

15.9 Consider the following "true" (Cobb-Douglas) production function

$$\ln Y_i = \alpha_0 + \alpha_1 \ln L_{1i} + \alpha_2 \ln L_{2i} + \alpha_3 \ln K_i + u_i \tag{11}$$

where Y = output

L_1 = production labor

L_2 = nonproduction labor

K = capital

But suppose the regression actually used in empirical investigation is

$$\ln Y_i = \beta_0 + \beta_1 \ln L_{1i} + \beta_2 \ln K_i + u_i \tag{12}$$

Assuming you have cross-sectional data on the relevant variables,

(a) Will $E(\hat{\beta}_1) = \alpha_1$ and $E(\hat{\beta}_2) = \alpha_3$?

(b) Will the answer in (a) hold if it is known that L_2 is an *irrelevant* input in the production function? Show the necessary derivations.

15.10 The residual sum of squares from the restricted least-squares regression is never less than the corresponding sum of squares from the unrestricted least-squares regression." Comment.

15.11 Offer an intuitive justification for the F test given in (15.2.8).

15.12 Under what conditions will the t and the F tests of significance, designed to test the validity of linear restrictions, give identical results?

15.13 Can the regression (15.2.7) be expressed as

$$\ln \left(\frac{Y_i}{X_{1i}} \right) = \ln \alpha + \beta_2 \ln \left(\frac{X_{2i}}{X_{1i}} \right) + u_i$$

How would you interpret the preceding regression if X_1 = labor input and X_2 = capital input?

15.14 Consider the following production function, which is known as the *constant elasticity of substitution* (CES) *production function*:

$$Y_i = \gamma[\delta K_i^{-\rho} + (1 - \delta)L^{-\rho}]^{-v/\rho} e^{u_i}$$

where Y_i = output

K_i = capital input

L_i = labor input

and where the parameters γ, δ, ν, and ρ are called, respectively, the *efficiency, distribution, returns to scale*, and *substitution parameters*. Since the CES production function is nonlinear in the parameters, it cannot be estimated readily by OLS. However, the function can be "linearized" by using the mathematical technique of Taylor's series as follows:

$$\ln Y_i = \beta_0 + \beta_1 \ln K_i + \beta_2 \ln L_i + \beta_3 \left[\ln \left(\frac{K_i}{L_i} \right) \right]^2 + u_i$$

where $\beta_0 = \ln \gamma$
$\quad \beta_1 = \nu\delta$
$\quad \beta_2 = \nu(1 - \delta)$
$\quad \beta_3 = -\frac{1}{2}\rho\nu\delta(1 - \delta)$

(a) How would you estimate the parameters of the CES production function from the estimated β coefficients?

(b) Can you obtain the standard errors of the parameters of the production function from the standard errors of the estimated β's?

(c) Illustrate your answers to (a) and (b) by fitting the "linearized" CES production function to the data of Exercise 6.1.

FOUR

SIMULTANEOUS-EQUATIONS MODELS

A casual look at the published empirical work in business and economics will reveal that many economic relationships are of the single-equation type. That is why we devoted the first three parts of this book to the discussion of the single-equation regression models. In such models, one variable (the dependent variable Y) is expressed as a linear function of one or more other variables (the explanatory variables, the X's). In such models an implicit assumption is that the cause-and-effect relationship, if any, between Y and the X's is unidirectional: The explanatory variables are the *cause* and the dependent variable is the *effect*.

However, there are situations where there is a two-way flow of influence among economic variables; that is, one economic variable affects another economic variable(s) and is, in turn, affected by it (them). Thus, in the regression of money M on the rate of interest R, the single-equation methodology assumes implicitly that the rate of interest is fixed (say, by the Federal Reserve System) and tries to find out the response of money demanded to the changes in the level of the interest rate. But what happens if the rate of interest depends on the demand for money? In this case, the conditional regression analysis made in this book thus far may not be appropriate because now M depends on R and R depends on M. Thus, we need to consider two equations, one relating M to R and another relating R to M. And this leads us to consider simultaneous-equations models, models in which there is more than one regression equation, one for each interdependent variable.

In the remaining three chapters of this book, we present a very elementary and often heuristic introduction to the complex subject of *simultaneous-equations models*, the details being left for the references.

In Chap. 16, we provide several examples of simultaneous-equations models and show why the method of ordinary least squares considered previously is generally inapplicable to estimate the parameters of each of the equations in the model.

In Chap. 17, we consider the so-called identification problem. If in a system, of simultaneous equations containing two or more equations it is not possible to obtain numerical values of each parameter in each equation because the equations are *observationally indistinguishable*, or look too much like one another, then we have the identification problem. Thus, in the regression of quantity Q on price P, is the resulting equation a demand function or a supply function? For Q and P enter into both functions. Therefore, if we have data on Q and P only and no other information, it will be difficult if not impossible to identify the regression as the demand or supply function. It is essential to resolve the identification problem before one proceeds to estimation because if we do not know what we are estimating, estimation per se is meaningless. In Chap. 17 we offer various methods of solving the identification problem.

In Chap. 18, we consider several estimation methods that are designed specifically for estimating the simultaneous-equations models and consider their merits and limitations.

SIXTEEN

SIMULTANEOUS-EQUATIONS MODELS

In this and the following two chapters we discuss the simultaneous-equations models. In particular, we discuss their special features, their estimation, and some of the statistical problems associated with them.

16.1 THE NATURE OF SIMULTANEOUS-EQUATIONS MODELS

In Parts I to III of this text we were concerned exclusively with single-equation models, i.e., models in which there was a single dependent variable Y and one or more explanatory variables, the X's. In such models the emphasis was on estimating and/or predicting the average value of Y conditional upon the fixed values of the X variables. The cause-and-effect relationship in such models therefore ran from the X's to the Y.

But there are many situations where such a one-way or unidirectional cause-and-effect relationship is not meaningful. This occurs if Y is not only determined by the X's, but some of the X's are, in turn, determined by Y. In short, there is a two-way, or simultaneous, relationship between Y and (some of) the X's, which makes the distinction between *dependent* and *explanatory* variables of dubious value. It is better to lump together a set of variables which can be determined simultaneously by the remaining set of variables. This is precisely what is done in simultaneous-equations models. In such models there is more than one equation—one for each of the *mutually*, or *jointly*, dependent or *endogenous* variables.[1] And unlike the single-equation models, in the simultaneous-equations models one may not estimate the parameters of a single equation without taking into account information provided by other equations in the system.

What happens if the parameters of each equation are estimated by applying, say, the method of OLS, disregarding other equations in the system? Recall that one of the crucial assumptions of the method of OLS is that the explanatory X variables are either nonstochastic or if stochastic (random) are distributed independently of the stochastic disturbance term. If neither of these conditions is met, then, as shown later, the least-squares estimators are not only biased but also inconsistent; that is, as the sample size increases indefinitely, the estimators do not converge to their true (population) values. Thus, in the following hypothetical system of equations[2]

$$Y_{1i} = \beta_{10} + \beta_{12} Y_{2i} + \gamma_{11} X_{1i} + u_{1i} \tag{16.1.1}$$

$$Y_{2i} = \beta_{20} + \beta_{21} Y_{1i} + \gamma_{21} X_{1i} + u_{2i} \tag{16.1.2}$$

where Y_1 and Y_2 are mutually dependent, or endogenous, variables and X_1 an exogenous variable and where u_1 and u_2 are the stochastic disturbance terms, the variables Y_1 and Y_2 are both stochastic. Therefore, unless it can be shown that the stochastic explanatory variable Y_2 in (16.1.1) is distributed independently of u_1 and the stochastic explanatory variable Y_1 in (16.1.2) is distributed independently of u_2, application of the classical OLS to these equations individually will lead to inconsistent estimates.

In the remainder of this chapter we give a few examples of simultaneous-equations models and show the bias involved in the direct application of the least-squares method to such models. After discussing the so-called identification problem in Chap. 17, in Chap. 18 we discuss some of the special methods developed to handle the simultaneous-equations models.

16.2 EXAMPLES OF SIMULTANEOUS-EQUATIONS MODELS

Example 16.1 Demand-and-supply model As is well known, the price P of a commodity and the quantity Q sold are determined by the intersection of the demand-and-supply curves for that commodity. Thus, assuming for simplicity that the demand-and-supply curves are linear and adding the stochastic disturbance terms u_1 and u_2, the empirical demand-and-supply function may be written as

---

[1] In the context of the simultaneous-equations models, the jointly dependent variables are called *endogenous variables* and the variables that are truly nonstochastic or can be so regarded are called the *exogenous*, or *predetermined*, *variables*. (More on this in Chap. 17.)

[2] These economical but self-explanatory notations will be generalized to more than two equations in Chap. 17.

Demand function $\qquad Q_t^d = \alpha_0 + \alpha_1 P_t + u_{1t} \quad \alpha_1 < 0 \qquad (16.2.1)$

Supply function $\qquad Q_t^s = \beta_0 + \beta_1 P_t + u_{2t} \quad \beta_1 > 0 \qquad (16.2.2)$

Equilibrium condition $\quad Q_t^d = Q_t^s$

where Q^d = quantity demanded
$\qquad Q^s$ = quantity supplied
$\qquad t$ = time

and the α's and β's are the parameters. A priori, α_1 is expected to be negative (downward-sloping demand curve), and β_1 is expected to be positive (upward-sloping supply curve).

Now it is not too difficult to see that P and Q are jointly dependent variables. If, for example, u_{1t} in (16.2.1) changes because of changes in other variables affecting Q_t^d (such as income, wealth, and tastes), the demand curve will shift upward if u_{1t} is positive and downward if u_{1t} is negative. These shifts are shown in Fig. 16.1.

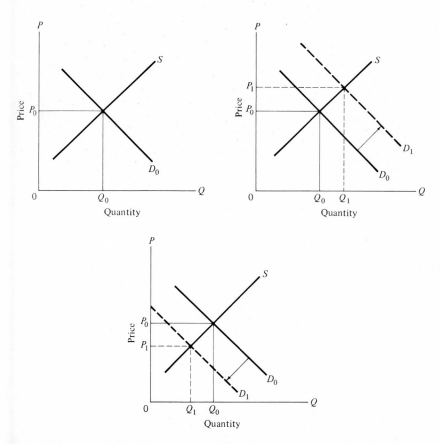

Figure 16.1 Interdependence of price and quantity.

As the figure shows, a shift in the demand curve changes both P and Q. Similarly, a change in u_{2t} (because of strikes, weather, import or export restrictions, etc.) will shift the supply curve, again affecting both P and Q. Because of this simultaneous dependence between Q and P, u_{1t} and P_t in (16.2.1) and u_{2t} and P_t in (16.2.2) cannot be independent. Therefore, a regression of Q on P as in (16.2.1) would violate an important assumption of the classical linear regression model, namely, the assumption of no correlation between the explanatory variable(s) and the disturbance term.

Example 16.2 Keynesian model of income determination Consider the simple keynesian model of income determination:

$$\text{Consumption function} \quad C_t = \beta_0 + \beta_1 Y_t + u_t \quad 0 < \beta_1 < 1 \quad (16.2.3)$$

$$\text{Income identity} \qquad Y_t = C_t + I_t(= S_t) \qquad\qquad (16.2.4)$$

where C = consumption expenditure
  Y = income
  I = investment (assumed exogenous)
  S = savings
  t = time
  u = stochastic disturbance term
β_0 and β_1 = parameters

The parameter β_1 is known as the *marginal propensity to consume* (**MPC**) (the amount of extra consumption expenditure resulting from an extra dollar of income). From economic theory, β_1 is expected to lie between 0 and 1. Equation (16.2.3) is the (stochastic) consumption function, and (16.2.4) is the na-

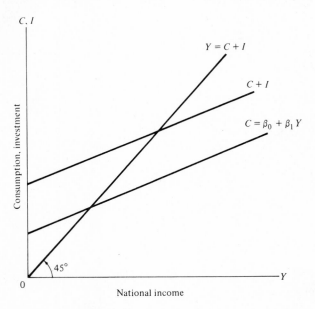

Figure 16.2 Keynesian model of income determination.

tional income identity signifying that total income is equal to total consumption expenditure plus total investment expenditure, it being understood that total investment expenditure is equal to total savings. Diagrammatically, we have Fig. 16.2.

From the postulated consumption function and Fig. 16.2 it is clear that C and Y are interdependent and that Y_t in (16.2.3) is not expected to be independent of the disturbance term because when u_t shifts (because of a variety of factors subsumed in the error term), then the consumption function also shifts, which, in turn, affects Y_t. Therefore, once again the classical least-squares method is inapplicable to (16.2.3). If applied, it is shown later that the estimators thus obtained will be inconsistent.

Example 16.3 Wage-price models Consider the following Phillips-type model of money-wage and price determination:

$$\dot{W}_t = \alpha_0 + \alpha_1 UN_t + \alpha_2 \dot{P}_t + u_{1t} \tag{16.2.5}$$

$$\dot{P}_t = \beta_0 + \beta_1 \dot{W}_t + \beta_2 \dot{R}_t + \beta_3 \dot{M}_t + u_{2t} \tag{16.2.6}$$

where $\dot{W}$ = rate of change of money wages
UN = unemployment rate, %
$\dot{P}$ = rate of change of prices
$\dot{R}$ = rate of change of cost of capital
$\dot{M}$ = rate of change of price of imported raw material
t = time
u_1, u_2 = stochastic disturbances.

Since the price variable $\dot{P}$ enters into the wage equation and the wage variable $\dot{W}$ enters into the price equation, the two variables are jointly dependent. Therefore, these stochastic explanatory variables are expected to be correlated with the relevant stochastic disturbances, once again rendering the classical OLS method inapplicable to estimate the parameters of the two equations individually.

Example 16.4 Walrasian model of general equilibrium[3] The walrasian model of general equilibrium theory provides a classic example of interdependence among various sectors of the economy. Omitting the stochastic disturbances for the moment and letting

$X_1, X_2, \ldots, X_n$: quantities of goods produced in the economy

$P_1, P_2, \ldots, P_n$: their prices

$Y_1, Y_2, \ldots, Y_m$: quantities of productive services or inputs

$W_1, W_2, \ldots, W_m$: their prices

---

[3] Leon Walras, *Elements of Pure Economics*, George Allen & Unwin, Ltd., London, 1954 (English ed.).

the walrasian system of general equilibrium can be expressed as

$$\textit{Demand functions} \quad X_1 = f(P_1, P_2, \ldots, P_n, W_1, W_2, \ldots, W_m)$$
$$X_2 = f(P_1, P_2, \ldots, P_n, W_1, W_2, \ldots, W_m)$$
$$\cdots\cdots\cdots\cdots\cdots\cdots\cdots\cdots\cdots\cdots\cdots\cdots\cdots \quad (16.2.7)$$
$$X_n = f(P_1, P_2, \ldots, P_n, W_1, W_2, \ldots, W_m)$$

These n equations define the market demand for n goods in terms of the prices of these goods and the prices of m inputs.

$$\textit{Supply functions} \quad P_1 = a_{11} W_1 + a_{12} W_2 + \cdots + a_{1m} W_m$$
$$P_2 = a_{21} W_1 + a_{22} W_2 + \cdots + a_{2m} W_m$$
$$\cdots\cdots\cdots\cdots\cdots\cdots\cdots\cdots\cdots\cdots\cdots\cdots\cdots \quad (16.2.8)$$
$$P_n = a_{n1} W_1 + a_{n2} W_2 + \cdots + a_{nm} W_m$$

where a_{ij} is the number of units of the jth productive service used to produce a unit of the ith commodity; these a_{ij} are known as the *coefficients of production*. Each supply function states that the price of a unit of X_i is equal to its cost of production, which is equal to the amount of the inputs used in its production times the prices of the inputs. In addition, in the set of equations

$$a_{11} X_1 + a_{21} X_2 + \cdots + a_{n1} X_n = Y_1$$
$$a_{12} X_1 + a_{22} X_2 + \cdots + a_{n2} X_n = Y_2$$
$$\cdots\cdots\cdots\cdots\cdots\cdots\cdots\cdots\cdots\cdots\cdots\cdots\cdots \quad (16.2.9)$$
$$a_{1m} X_1 + a_{2m} X_2 + \cdots + a_{nm} X_n = Y_m$$

we have the equilibrium conditions for the input market, which state that the total amount of inputs required (to produce the n goods) must be equal to the total amount available. Thus there are in all $n + n + m$ or $2n + m$ equations to determine the $2n + m$ unknowns in the system: n prices of n goods, m prices of m inputs, and n quantities of n goods.

We are not concerned here as to how Walras obtained the solution to the system. What is important to note is the nature of interdependence of goods produced and consumed in the economy and their prices: Thus, consumption of beef does not depend on the price of beef alone but also on the prices of pork and other competing products.

Example 16.5 Econometric models An extensive use of simultaneous-equations models has been made in the econometric models built by several econometricians. An early pioneer in this field was Professor Lawrence Klein of the Wharton School of the University of Pennsylvania. His initial model, known as *Klein's model I*, is as follows.

Consumption function
$$C_t = \beta_0 + \beta_1 P_t + \beta_2 (W + W')_t$$
$$+ \beta_3 P_{t-1} + u_{1t}$$

Investment function
$$I_t = \beta_4 + \beta_5 P_t + \beta_6 P_{t-1} + \beta_7 K_{t-1} + u_{2t}$$

Demand for labor
$$W_t = \beta_8 + \beta_9 (Y + T - W')_t$$
$$+ \beta_{10} (Y + T - W')_{t-1}$$
$$+ \beta_{11} t + u_{3t}$$

Identity
$$Y_t + T_t = C_t + I_t + G_t \qquad (16.2.10)$$

Identity
$$Y_t = W'_t + W_t + P_t$$

Identity
$$K_t = K_{t-1} + I_t$$

where
C = consumption expenditure
I = investment expenditure
G = government expenditure
P = profits
W = private wage bill
W' = government wage bill
K = capital stock
T = taxes
Y = income after tax
t = time
u_1, u_2, and u_3 = stochastic disturbances[4]

In the preceding model the variables C, I, W, Y, P, and K are treated as jointly dependent, or endogenous, variables and the variables P_{t-1}, K_{t-1}, and Y_{t-1} are treated as predetermined.[5] In all, there are six equations (including the three identities) to study the interdependence of six endogenous variables.

In Chap. 18 we shall see how such econometric models are estimated. For the time being, note that because of the interdependence among the endogenous variables, in general they are not independent of the stochastic disturbance terms, which therefore makes it inappropriate to apply the method of OLS to an individual equation in the system. For, as shown in Sec. 16.3, the estimators thus obtained are inconsistent; they do not converge to their true population values even when the sample size is very large.

---

[4] L. R. Klein, *Economic Fluctuations in the United States*, 1921–1941, John Wiley & Sons, Inc., New York, 1950.

[5] The model builder will have to specify which of the variables in a model are endogenous and which are predetermined. K_{t-1} and Y_{t-1} are predetermined because at time t their values are known. (More on this in Chap. 17.)

16.3 THE SIMULTANEOUS-EQUATIONS BIAS: INCONSISTENCY OF OLS ESTIMATORS

As stated previously, the method of least squares may not be applied to estimate a single equation embedded in a system of simultaneous equations if one or more of the explanatory variables are correlated with the disturbance term in that equation because the estimators thus obtained are inconsistent. To show this, let us revert to the simple keynesian model of income determination given in Example 16.2. Suppose that we want to estimate the parameters of the consumption function (16.2.3). Assuming that $E(u_t) = 0$, $E(u_t^2) = \sigma^2$, $E(u_t u_{t+j}) = 0$ (for $j \neq 0$), and cov $(I_t, u_t) = 0$, which are the assumptions of the classical linear regression model, we first show that Y_t and u_t in (16.2.3) are correlated and then prove that $\hat{\beta}_1$ is an inconsistent estimator of β_1.

To prove that Y_t and u_t are correlated, we proceed as follows: Substitute (16.2.3) into (16.2.4) to obtain

$$Y_t = \beta_0 + \beta_1 Y_t + u_t + I_t$$

that is,

$$Y_t = \frac{\beta_0}{1 - \beta_1} + \frac{1}{1 - \beta_1} I_t + \frac{1}{1 - \beta_1} u_t \tag{16.3.1}$$

Now

$$E(Y_t) = \frac{\beta_0}{1 - \beta_1} + \frac{1}{1 - \beta_1} I_t \tag{16.3.2}$$

where use is made of the fact that $E(u_t) = 0$ and that I_t being exogenous, or predetermined (because it is fixed in advance), its expected value is I_t.

Therefore, subtracting (16.3.2) from (16.3.1) results in

$$Y_t - E(Y_t) = \frac{u_t}{1 - \beta_1} \tag{16.3.3}$$

Moreover,

$$u_t - E(u_t) = u_t \quad \text{(Why?)} \tag{16.3.4}$$

whence

$$\text{cov } (Y_t, u_t) = E[Y_t - E(Y_t)][u_t - E(u_t)]$$

$$= \frac{E(u_t^2)}{1 - \beta_1} \quad \text{using (16.3.3) and (16.3.4)}$$

$$= \frac{\sigma^2}{1 - \beta_1} \tag{16.3.5}$$

Since σ^2 is positive by assumption (why?), the covariance between Y and u given in (16.3.5) is bound to be different from zero.[6] As a result, Y_t and u_t in (16.2.3) are

---

[6] It will be greater than zero as long as β_1, the MPC, lies between 0 and 1, and it will be negative if β_1 is greater than unity. Of course, a value of MPC greater than unity would not make much economic sense. In reality, therefore, the covariance between Y_t and u_t is expected to be positive.

expected to be correlated, which violates the assumption of the classical linear regression model that the disturbances are independent or at least uncorrelated with the explanatory variables. As noted previously, the OLS estimators in this situation are inconsistent.

To show that the OLS estimator $\hat{\beta}_1$ is an inconsistent estimator of β_1 because of correlation between Y_t and u_t, we proceed as follows:

$$\hat{\beta}_1 = \frac{\sum (C_t - \bar{C})(Y_t - \bar{Y})}{\sum (Y_t - \bar{Y})^2}$$

$$= \frac{\sum c_t y_t}{\sum y_t^2}$$

$$= \frac{\sum C_t y_t}{\sum y_t^2} \tag{16.3.6}$$

where the lowercase letters, as usual, indicate deviations from the (sample) mean values. Substituting for C_t from (16.2.3), we obtain

$$\hat{\beta}_1 = \frac{\sum (\beta_0 + \beta_1 Y_t + u_t)y_t}{\sum y_t^2}$$

$$= \beta_1 + \frac{\sum y_t u_t}{\sum y_t^2} \tag{16.3.7}$$

where in the last step use is made of the fact that $\sum y_t = 0$ and $(\sum Y_t y_t / \sum y_t^2) = 1$. (Why?)

Now an estimator is said to be consistent if its *probability limit*,[7] or *plim* for short, is equal to its true (population) value. Therefore, to show that $\hat{\beta}_1$ of (16.3.7) is inconsistent, we must show that its plim is not equal to the true β_1. Applying the rules of probability limit to (16.3.7), we obtain[8]

$$\text{plim } (\hat{\beta}_1) = \text{plim } (\beta_1) + \text{plim } \left(\frac{\sum y_t u_t}{\sum y_t^2}\right)$$

$$= \text{plim } (\beta_1) + \text{plim } \left(\frac{\sum y_t u_t / N}{\sum y_t^2 / N}\right)$$

$$= \beta_1 + \frac{\text{plim } (\sum y_t u_t / N)}{\text{plim } (\sum y_t^2 / N)} \tag{16.3.8}$$

where in the second step we have divided $\sum y_t u_t$ and $\sum y_t^2$ by the total number of observations in the sample N so that the quantities in the brackets are now the sample covariance between Y and u and the sample variance of Y, respectively.

---

[7] See App. A for the definition of probability limit.

[8] As stated in App. A, the plim of a constant (for example, β_1) is the same constant and the plim of $(A/B) = \text{plim } (A)/\text{plim } (B)$. Note, however, that $E(A/B) \neq E(A)/E(B)$.

In words, (16.3.8) states that the probability limit of $\hat{\beta}_1$ is equal to true β_1 plus the ratio of the plim of the sample covariance between Y and u to the plim of the sample variance of Y. Now as the sample size N increases indefinitely, one would expect the sample covariance between Y and u to approximate the true population covariance $E[Y_t - E(Y_t)][u_t - E(u_t)]$, which from (16.3.5) is equal to $[\sigma^2/(1 - \beta_1)]$. Similarly, as N tends to infinity, the sample variance of Y will approximate its population variance, say, σ_Y^2. Therefore, equation (16.3.8) may be written as

$$\text{plim } (\hat{\beta}_1) = \beta_1 + \frac{\sigma^2/(1 - \beta_1)}{\sigma_Y^2}$$

$$= \beta_1 + \frac{1}{1 - \beta_1}\left(\frac{\sigma^2}{\sigma_Y^2}\right) \tag{16.3.9}$$

Given that $0 < \beta_1 < 1$ and that σ^2 and σ_Y^2 are both positive, it is obvious from equation (16.3.9) that plim $(\hat{\beta}_1)$ will always be greater than β_1; that is, $\hat{\beta}_1$ will overestimate the true β_1.[9] In other words, $\hat{\beta}_1$ is a biased estimator, and the bias will not disappear no matter how large the sample size.

16.4 SUMMARY AND CONCLUSIONS

The purpose of this chapter was to introduce the simultaneous-equations models—models in which there is more than one dependent variable and more than one equation. This is in contrast to the single-equation models considered heretofore in which there was only one equation relating a single dependent variable to a set of explanatory variables which were either nonstochastic or, if stochastic, were (assumed to be) distributed independently of the stochastic disturbance term. A unique feature of the simultaneous-equations models is that the dependent variable in one equation may appear as an explanatory variable in another equation of the system. Therefore, such a *dependent explanatory* variable becomes stochastic and is usually correlated with the disturbance term of the equation in which it appears as an explanatory variable. In this situation the classical least-squares method may not be applied because the estimators thus obtained are inconsistent; that is, they do not converge to their true values no matter how large the sample.

Since simultaneous-equations models are used frequently, especially in the econometric models of the economy, alternative estimating techniques have been developed by various authors. Some of these techniques will be discussed in Chap. 18. But before we turn to them, it is essential to deal with the so-called problem of identification, a problem that comes logically before estimation. This is done in Chap. 17.

---

[9] In general, however, the direction of the bias will depend on the structure of the particular model and the true values of the regression coefficients.

EXERCISES

16.1 You are given the following data on Y (Gross National Product), C (consumer expenditure), and I (gross private domestic investment), all measured in billions of 1958 dollars:

Year	Y	C	I	Year	Y	C	I
1957	452.5	288.2	68.8	1966	658.1	418.1	109.3
1958	447.3	290.1	60.9	1967	675.2	430.1	101.2
1959	475.9	307.3	73.6	1968	706.6	452.7	105.2
1960	487.7	316.1	72.4	1969	725.6	469.1	110.5
1961	497.2	322.5	69.0	1970	722.5	477.5	103.4
1962	529.8	338.4	79.4	1971	746.3	496.4	111.1
1963	551.0	353.3	82.5	1972	792.5	527.3	125.0
1964	581.1	373.7	87.8	1973	839.2	552.1	138.1
1965	617.8	397.7	99.2	1974†	821.1	539.9	126.3

† Data for 1974 are preliminary estimates.
Source: Economic Report of the President, p. 250, February 1975.

Assume that C is linearly related to Y as in the simple keynesian model of income determination of Example 16.2. Obtain OLS estimates of the parameters of the consumption function. (Save the results for another look at the same data using the methods developed in Chap. 18.)

*16.2 (*a*) For the demand-and-supply model of Example 16.1, obtain the expression for the probability limit of $\hat{\alpha}_1$.

(*b*) Under what conditions will this probability limit be equal to the true α_1?

16.3 Gallaway and Smith developed a simple model for the United States economy, which is as follows:[10]

$$Y_t = C_t + I_t + G_t$$

$$C_t = \beta_1 + \beta_2 YD_{t-1} + \beta_3 M_t + u_{1t}$$

$$I_t = \beta_4 + \beta_5(Y_{t-1} - Y_{t-2}) + \beta_6 Z_{t-1} + u_{2t}$$

$$G_t = \beta_7 + \beta_8 G_{t-1} + u_{3t}$$

where
Y = Gross National Product
C = personal consumption expenditure
I = gross private domestic investment
G = government expenditure plus net foreign investment
YD = disposable, or after-tax, income
M = money supply at the beginning of the quarter
Z = property income before taxes
t = time
u_1, u_2, and u_3 = stochastic disturbances

All variables are measured in the first difference form.

* Optional.
[10] See their article, "A Quarterly Econometric Model of the United States," *Journal of American Statistical Association*, vol. 56, 1961.

Based on the quarterly from 1948–1957, the authors applied the least-squares method to each equation individually and obtained the following results:

$$C_t = 0.09 + 0.43\,YD_{t-1} + 0.23M_t \qquad R^2 = 0.23$$

$$I_t = 0.08 + 0.43(Y_{t-1} - Y_{t-2}) + 0.48Z_t \qquad R^2 = 0.40$$

$$G_t = 0.13 + 0.67G_{t-1} \qquad R^2 = 0.42$$

(a) How would you justify the use of the single-equation least-squares method in this case?

(b) Why are the R^2 values rather low?

16.4 G. Menges developed the following econometric model for the West German economy:

$$Y_t = \beta_0 + \beta_1 Y_{t-1} + \beta_2 I_t + u_{1t}$$

$$I_t = \beta_3 + \beta_4 Y_t + \beta_5 Q_t + u_{2t}$$

$$C_t = \beta_6 + \beta_7 Y_t + \beta_8 C_{t-1} + \beta_9 P_t + u_{3t}$$

$$Q_t = \beta_{10} + \beta_{11} Q_{t-1} + \beta_{12} R_t + u_{4t}$$

where Y = national income
  I = net capital formation
  C = personal consumption
  Q = profits
  P = cost of living index
  R = industrial productivity
  t = time
  u's = stochastic disturbances

(a) Which of the variables would you regard as endogenous and which as exogenous?

(b) Is there any equation in the system which can be estimated by the single-equation least-squares method?

(c) What is the reason behind including the variable P in the consumption function?

16.5 Develop a simultaneous-equations model for the supply of and demand for dentists in the United States. Specify the endogenous and exogenous variables in the model.

16.6 Develop a simple model of the demand for and supply of money in the United States and compare your model with those developed by Brunner and Meltzer[11] and Teigen.[12]

16.7 In their article, "A Model of the Distribution of Branded Personal Products in Jamaica,"[13] John U. Farley and Harold J. Levitt developed the following model (the personal products considered were shaving cream, skin cream, sanitary napkins, and toothpaste):

$$Y_{1i} = \alpha_1 + \beta_1 Y_{2i} + \beta_2 Y_{3i} + \beta_3 Y_{4i} + u_{1i}$$

$$Y_{2i} = \alpha_2 + \beta_4 Y_{1i} + \beta_5 Y_{5i} + \gamma_1 X_{1i} + \gamma_2 X_{2i} + u_{2i}$$

$$Y_{3i} = \alpha_3 + \beta_6 Y_{2i} + \gamma_3 X_{3i} + u_{3i}$$

$$Y_{4i} = \alpha_4 + \beta_7 Y_{2i} + \gamma_4 X_{4i} + u_{4i}$$

$$Y_{5i} = \alpha_5 + \beta_8 Y_{2i} + \beta_9 Y_{3i} + \beta_{10} Y_{4i} + u_{5i}$$

[11] "Some Further Evidence on Supply and Demand Functions for Money," *Journal of Finance*, vol. 19, May 1964.

[12] "Demand and Supply Functions for Money in the United States," *Econometrica*, vol. 32, no. 4, October 1964.

[13] *Journal of Marketing Research*, pp. 362–368, November 1968.

where Y_1 = percent of stores stocking the product

Y_2 = sales in units per month

Y_3 = index of direct contact with importer and manufacturer for the product

Y_4 = index of wholesale activity in the area

Y_5 = index of depth of brand stocking for the product (i.e., average number of brands of the product stocked by stores carrying the product)

X_1 = target population for the product

X_2 = income per capita in the parish where the area is

X_3 = distance from the population center of gravity to Kingston

X_4 = distance from population center to nearest wholesale town

(*a*) Can you identify the endogenous and exogenous variables in the preceding model?

(*b*) Can one or more equations in the model be estimated by the method of least squares? Why or why not?

16.8 To study the relationship between advertising expenditure and sales of cigarettes, Frank Bass used the following model:[14]

$$Y_{1t} = \alpha_1 + \beta_1 Y_{3t} + \beta_2 Y_{4t} + \gamma_1 X_{1t} + \gamma_2 X_{2t} + u_{1t}$$

$$Y_{2t} = \alpha_2 + \beta_3 Y_{3t} + \beta_4 Y_{4t} + \gamma_3 X_{1t} + \gamma_4 X_{2t} + u_{2t}$$

$$Y_{3t} = \alpha_3 + \beta_5 Y_{1t} + \beta_6 Y_{2t} + u_{3t}$$

$$Y_{4t} = \alpha_4 + \beta_7 Y_{1t} + \beta_8 Y_{2t} + u_{4t}$$

where Y_1 = logarithm of sales of filter cigarettes (number of cigarettes) divided by population over age 20

Y_2 = logarithm of sales of nonfilter cigarettes (number of cigarettes) divided by population over age 20

Y_3 = logarithm of advertising dollars for filter cigarettes divided by population over age 20 divided by advertising price index

Y_4 = logarithm of advertising dollars for nonfilter cigarettes divided by population over age 20 divided by advertising price index

X_1 = logarithm of disposable personal income divided by population over age 20 divided by consumer price index

X_2 = logarithm of price per package of nonfilter cigarettes divided by consumer price index

(*a*) In the preceding model the Y's are endogenous and the X's are exogenous. Why does the author assume X_2 to be exogenous?

(*b*) If X_2 is treated as an endogenous variable, how would you modify the preceding model?

(*c*) Should the price of filter cigarettes be included as an additional variable into the model? If so, would you regard it endogenous or exogenous? If endogenous, how would you modify the original model?

(*d*) Can one or more of the equations in the Bass model be estimated by the method of least squares? Justify your answer.

---

[14] See his article, "A Simultaneous Equation Regression Study of Advertising and Sales of Cigarettes," *Journal of Marketing Research*, vol. 6, pp. 291–300, August 1969.

SEVENTEEN

THE IDENTIFICATION PROBLEM

In this chapter we consider the nature and significance of the identification problem. The crux of the identification problem is as follows: Recall the demand-and-supply model introduced in Chap. 16, Sec. 16.2. Suppose that we have time-series data on Q and P only and no additional information (such as income of the consumer, price prevailing in the previous period, and weather condition). The identification problem then consists in seeking an answer to this question: Given only the data on P and Q, how do we know whether we are estimating the demand function or the supply function? Alternatively, if we *think* we are fitting a demand function, how do we guarantee that it is, in fact, the demand function that we are estimating and not something else?

A moment's reflection will reveal that an answer to the preceding question is necessary before one proceeds to estimate the parameters of our demand function. In this chapter we shall show how the identification problem is resolved. We first introduce a few notations and definitions and then illustrate the identification problem with several examples. This is followed by the rules that may be used to find out whether an equation in a simultaneous-equations model is identified, that is, whether it is the relationship that we are actually estimating, be it the demand or supply function or something else.

17.1 NOTATIONS AND DEFINITIONS

To facilitate our discussion, we introduce the following notations and definitions:

The general M equations model in M endogenous, or jointly dependent, variables may be written as Eq. (17.1.1):

$$Y_{1t} = \qquad \beta_{12}\,Y_{2t} + \beta_{13}\,Y_{3t} + \cdots + \beta_{1M}\,Y_{Mt}$$
$$+\,\gamma_{11}\,X_{1t} + \gamma_{12}\,X_{2t} + \cdots + \gamma_{1K}\,X_{Kt} + u_{1t}$$

$$Y_{2t} = \beta_{21}\,Y_{1t} + \qquad + \beta_{23}\,Y_{3t} + \cdots + \beta_{2M}\,Y_{Mt}$$
$$+\,\gamma_{21}\,X_{1t} + \gamma_{22}\,X_{2t} + \cdots + \gamma_{2K}\,X_{Kt} + u_{2t}$$

$$Y_{3t} = \beta_{31}\,Y_{1t} + \beta_{32}\,Y_{2t} + \qquad \cdots + \beta_{3M}\,Y_{Mt}$$
$$+\,\gamma_{31}\,X_{1t} + \gamma_{32}\,X_{2t} + \cdots + \gamma_{3K}\,X_{Kt} + u_{3t}$$

$$\cdots\cdots\cdots\cdots\cdots\cdots\cdots\cdots\cdots\cdots\cdots\cdots\cdots\cdots\cdots\cdots\cdots\cdots$$

$$Y_{MT} = \beta_{M1}\,Y_{1t} + \beta_{M2}\,Y_{2t} + \cdots + \beta_{M,\,M-1}\,Y_{M-1,\,t}$$
$$+\,\gamma_{M1}\,X_{1t} + \gamma_{M2}\,X_{2t} + \cdots + \gamma_{MK}\,X_{Kt} + u_{Mt}$$

$$(17.1.1)$$

where $Y_1, Y_2, \ldots, Y_M = M$ endogenous, or jointly dependent, variables

$X_1, X_2, \ldots, X_K = K$ predetermined variables (one of these X variables may take a value of unity to allow for the intercept term in each equation)

$u_1, u_2, \ldots, u_M = M$ stochastic disturbances

$t = 1, 2, \ldots, N$ = total number of observations

β's = coefficients of the endogenous variables

γ's = coefficients of the predetermined variables

In passing, note that not each and every variable need appear in each equation. As a matter of fact, it is shown in Sec. 17.2 that this must not be the case if an equation is to be identified.

As equation (17.1.1) shows, the variables entering a simultaneous-equations model are of two types: *endogenous*, that is, those (whose values are) determined within the model; and *predetermined*, that is, those (whose values are) determined outside the model. The endogenous variables are regarded as stochastic, whereas the predetermined variables are treated as nonstochastic.

The predetermined variables are divided into two categories: exogenous, current as well as lagged, and lagged endogenous. Thus, X_{1t} is a current (present-time) exogenous variable, whereas $X_{1(t-1)}$ is a lagged exogenous variable, with a lag of one time period. $Y_{1(t-1)}$ is a lagged endogenous variable with a lag of one time period, but since the value of $Y_{1(t-1)}$ is known at the current time t, it is regarded as nonstochastic; hence a predetermined variable.[1] In short, current exogenous, lagged exogenous, and lagged endogenous variables are deemed predetermined; their values are not determined by the model in the current time period.

---

[1] It is assumed implicitly here that the stochastic disturbances, the u's, are serially uncorrelated. If this is not the case, Y_{t-1} will be correlated with the current period disturbance term u_t. Hence we cannot treat it as predetermined.

It is up to the model builder to specify which variables are endogenous and which are predetermined. Although (noneconomic) variables, such as temperature and rainfall, are clearly exogenous or predetermined, the model builder must exercise great care in classifying economic variables as endogenous or pre-determined: He or she must defend the classification on a priori or theoretical grounds.

The equations appearing in (17.1.1) are known as the *structural*, or *behavioral*, equations because they may portray the structure (of an economic model) of an economy or the behavior of an economic agent (e.g., consumer or producer). The parameters β's and γ's are known as the *structural parameters or coefficients*.

From the structural equations one can solve for the M endogenous variables and derive the *reduced-form equations* and the associated *reduced-form coefficients*. A reduced-form equation is one which expresses an endogenous variable solely in terms of the predetermined variables and the stochastic disturbances. To illustrate, consider the keynesian model of income determination encountered in Chap. 16:

Consumption function $\quad C_t = \beta_0 + \beta_1 Y_t + u_t \qquad 0 < \beta_1 < 1 \qquad$ (16.2.3)

Income identity $\qquad Y_t = C_t + I_t \qquad$ (16.2.4)

In this model C (consumption) and Y (income) are the endogenous variables and I (investment expenditure) is treated as an exogenous variable. Both these equations are structural equations, (16.2.4) being an identity. As usual, the MPC β_1 is assumed to lie between 0 and 1.

If (16.2.3) is substituted into (16.2.4), we obtain, after simple algebraic manipulation,

$$Y_t = \Pi_0 + \Pi_1 I_t + w_t \qquad (17.1.2)$$

where

$$\Pi_0 = \frac{\beta_0}{1 - \beta_1}$$

$$\Pi_1 = \frac{1}{1 - \beta_1} \qquad (17.1.3)$$

$$w_t = \frac{u_t}{1 - \beta_1}$$

Equation (17.1.2) is a reduced-form equation; it expresses the endogenous variable Y solely as a function of the exogenous variable I and the stochastic disturbance term u. Π_0 and Π_1 are the associated reduced-form coefficients. Notice that these reduced-form coefficients are nonlinear combinations of the structural coefficient(s).

Substituting the value of Y from (17.1.2) into C of (16.2.3), we obtain another reduced-form equation:

$$C_t = \Pi_2 + \Pi_3 I_t + w_t \qquad (17.1.4)$$

where
$$\Pi_2 = \frac{\beta_0}{1 - \beta_1} \qquad \Pi_3 = \frac{\beta_1}{1 - \beta_1} \tag{17.1.5}$$

$$w_t = \frac{u_t}{1 - \beta_1}$$

The reduced-form coefficients, such as Π_1 and Π_3, are also known as *impact multipliers*, because they measure the impact on the endogenous variable of a unit change in the value of the exogenous variable. If in the preceding keynesian model the investment expenditure is increased by, say, \$1 and if the MPC is assumed to be 0.8, then from (17.1.3) we obtain $\Pi_1 = 5$. This means that increasing the investment by \$1 will *eventually* lead to an increase in income of \$5, that is, a fivefold increase. Similarly, under the assumed conditions, (17.1.5) shows that $\Pi_3 = 4$, meaning that \$1 increase in investment expenditure will lead eventually to \$4 increase in consumption expenditure.

In the context of econometric models, equations such as (16.2.4) or $Q_t^d = Q_t^s$ (quantity demanded equal to quantity supplied) are known as the *equilibrium conditions*. Identity (16.2.4) states that aggregate income Y must be equal to aggregate consumption (i.e., consumption expenditure plus investment expenditure). When equilibrium is achieved, the endogenous variables assume their equilibrium values. How are these equilibrium values obtained? Given the values of exogenous variables, and taking mathematical expectation, it is clear that the reduced-form equations give the equilibrium values of the relevant endogenous variables. Thus, (17.1.2) gives the equilibrium value of income, and (17.1.4) gives the equilibrium value of consumption. The impact multipliers then give the rate of change of these equilibrium values when the equilibrium is "disturbed" by changes in the exogenous variable(s).[2]

Notice an interesting feature of the reduced-form equations. Since only the predetermined variables and stochastic disturbances appear on the right-hand sides of these equations, and since the predetermined variables are assumed to be nonstochastic and hence independent of the disturbance terms, the OLS method can be applied to estimate the coefficients of the reduced-form equations (the Π's). From the estimated reduced-form coefficients one may estimate the structural coefficients (the β's), as shown later. This procedure is known as *indirect least squares* (ILS), and the estimated structural coefficients are called ILS estimates.

We shall study the ILS method in greater detail in Chap. 18. In the meantime, note that since the reduced-form coefficients can be estimated by the OLS method, and since these coefficients are combinations of the structural coefficients, the possibility exists that the structural coefficients can be "retrieved" from the reduced-form coefficients, and it is in the estimation of the structural parameters that we may be ultimately interested. How does one retrieve the structural

---

[2] In econometric models the exogenous variables play a crucial role. Very often, such variables are under the direct control of the government. Examples are the rate of personal and corporate taxes, subsidies, unemployment compensation, etc.

coefficients from the reduced-form coefficients? The answer is given in Sec. 17.2, an answer that brings out the crux of the identification problem.

17.2 THE IDENTIFICATION PROBLEM

By the *identification problem* we mean whether numerical estimates of the parameters of a structural equation can be obtained from the estimated reduced-form coefficients. If this can be done, we say that the particular equation is *identified*. If this cannot be done, then we say that the equation under consideration is *unidentified*, or *underidentified*.

An identified equation may be either *exactly* (or *fully* or *just*) *identified* or *overidentified*. It is said to be exactly identified if unique numerical values of the structural parameters can be obtained. It is said to be overidentified if more than one numerical value can be obtained for some of the parameters of the structural equations. The circumstances under which each of these cases occurs will be shown in the following discussion.

The identification problem arises because different sets of structural coefficients may be compatible with the same set of data. To put the matter differently, a given reduced-form equation may be compatible with different structural equations or different hypotheses (models), and it may be difficult to tell which particular hypothesis (model) we are investigating. In the remainder of this section we consider several examples to show the nature of the identification problem.

Underidentification

Consider once again the demand-and-supply model (16.2.1) and (16.2.2), together with the market-clearing, or equilibrium, condition that demand is equal to supply. By the equilibrium condition, we obtain

$$\alpha_0 + \alpha_1 P_t + u_{1t} = \beta_0 + \beta_1 P_t + u_{2t} \tag{17.2.1}$$

Solving (17.2.1), we obtain the equilibrium price

$$P_t = \Pi_0 + v_t \tag{17.2.2}$$

where

$$\Pi_0 = \frac{\beta_0 - \alpha_0}{\alpha_1 - \beta_1} \tag{17.2.3}$$

$$v_t = \frac{u_{2t} - u_{1t}}{\alpha_1 - \beta_1} \tag{17.2.4}$$

Substituting P_t from (17.2.2) into (16.2.1) or (16.2.2), we obtain the following equilibrium quantity:

$$Q_t = \Pi_1 + w_t \tag{17.2.5}$$

where
$$\Pi_1 = \frac{\alpha_1 \beta_0 - \alpha_0 \beta_1}{\alpha_1 - \beta_1} \qquad (17.2.6)$$

$$w_t = \frac{\alpha_1 u_{2t} - \beta_1 u_{1t}}{\alpha_1 - \beta_1} \qquad (17.2.7)$$

Incidentally, note that the error terms v_t and w_t are linear combinations of the original error terms u_1 and u_2.

Equations (17.2.2) and (17.2.5) are reduced-form equations. Now our demand-and-supply model contains four structural coefficients $\alpha_0, \alpha_1, \beta_0$, and β_1, but there is no unique way of estimating them. Why? The answer lies in the two reduced-form coefficients given in (17.2.3) and (17.2.6). These reduced-form coefficients contain all four structural parameters, but there is no way in which the four structural unknowns can be estimated from only two reduced-form coefficients. Recall from high school algebra that to estimate four unknowns we must have four (independent) equations, and, in general, to estimate k unknowns we must have k (independent) equations.

What all this means is that given time-series data on P (price) and Q (quantity) and no other information, there is no way the researcher can guarantee

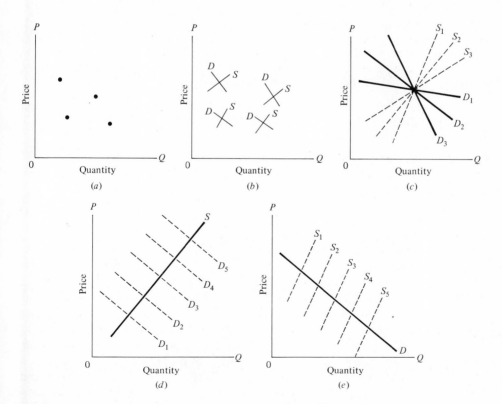

Figure 17.1 Hypothetical supply-and-demand functions and the identification problem.

whether he or she is estimating the demand function or the supply function. For, a given P_t and Q_t represent simply the point of intersection of the appropriate demand-and-supply curves because of the equilibrium condition that demand is equal to supply. To see this clearly, consider the scattergram shown in Fig. 17.1.

Figure 17.1a gives a few scatter points relating Q to P. Each scatter point represents the intersection of a demand and a supply curve, as shown in Fig. 17.1b. Now consider a single scatter point, such as that shown in Fig. 17.1c. There is no way we can be sure which demand-and-supply curve of a whole family of curves shown in that panel generated that point. Clearly, some additional information about the nature of the demand-and-supply curves is needed. For example, if the demand curve shifts over time because of changes in income, tastes, etc., but the supply curve remains relatively stable, as in Fig. 17.1d, the scatter points trace out a supply curve. In this situation, we say that the supply curve is identified. By the same token, if the supply curve shifts over time because of changes in weather conditions (in the case of agricultural commodities) or other extraneous factors but the demand curve remains relatively stable, as in Fig. 17.1e, the scatter points trace out a demand curve. In this case, we say that the demand curve is identified.

There is an alternative and perhaps more illuminating way of looking at the identification problem. Suppose we multiply (16.2.1) by λ $(0 \leq \lambda \leq 1)$ and (16.2.2) by $1 - \lambda$ to obtain the following equations (*note:* we drop the superscripts on Q):

$$\lambda Q_t = \lambda \alpha_0 + \lambda \alpha_1 P_t + \lambda u_{1t} \tag{17.2.8}$$

$$(1 - \lambda)Q_t = (1 - \lambda)\beta_0 + (1 - \lambda)\beta_1 P_t + (1 - \lambda)u_{2t} \tag{17.2.9}$$

Adding these two equations gives the following *linear combination* of the original demand-and-supply equations:

$$Q_t = \gamma_0 + \gamma_1 P_t + w_t \tag{17.2.10}$$

where
$$\gamma_0 = \lambda \alpha_0 + (1 - \lambda)\beta_0$$

$$\gamma_1 = \lambda \alpha_1 + (1 - \lambda)\beta_1 \tag{17.2.11}$$

$$w_t = \lambda u_{1t} + (1 - \lambda)u_{2t}$$

The "bogus," or "mongrel," equation (17.2.10) is *observationally indistinguishable* from either (16.2.1) or (16.2.2) because they all involve the regression of Q on P. Therefore, if we have time-series data on P and Q only, any of (16.2.1), (16.2.2), and (17.2.10) may be compatible with the same data. In other words, the same data may be compatible with the "hypothesis" (16.2.1), (16.2.2), or (17.2.10), and there is no way we can tell which one of these hypotheses we are testing.

For an equation to be identified, that is, for its parameters to be estimated, it must be shown that the given set of data will not produce a structural equation that looks similar in appearance to the one in which we are interested. If we set out to estimate the demand function, we must show that the given data is not consistent with the supply function or some mongrel equation.

Just, or Exact, Identification

The reason we could not identify the preceding demand function or the supply function was that the same variables P and Q are present in both functions and there is no additional information, such as that indicated in Fig. 17.1*d* or *e*. But suppose we consider the following demand-and-supply model:

Demand function $Q_t = \alpha_0 + \alpha_1 P_t + \alpha_2 I_t + u_{1t}$ $\alpha_1 < 0, \alpha_2 > 0$ (17.2.12)

Supply function $Q_t = \beta_0 + \beta_1 P_t + u_{2t}$ $\beta_1 > 0$ (17.2.13)

where I = income of the consumer, an exogenous variable, and all other variables are as defined previously.

Notice that the only difference between the preceding model and our original demand-and-supply model is that there is an additional variable in the demand function, namely, income. From economic theory of demand we know that income is usually an important determinant of demand for most goods and services. Therefore, its inclusion in the demand function will give us some additional information about consumer behavior. For most commodities income is expected to have a positive effect on consumption ($\alpha_2 > 0$).

Using the market-clearing mechanism, quantity demanded = quantity supplied, we have

$$\alpha_0 + \alpha_1 P_t + \alpha_2 I_t + u_{1t} = \beta_0 + \beta_1 P_t + u_{2t} \qquad (17.2.14)$$

Solving equation (17.2.14) provides the following equilibrium value of P_t:

$$P_t = \Pi_0 + \Pi_1 I_t + v_t \qquad (17.2.15)$$

where the reduced-form coefficients are

$$\Pi_0 = \frac{\beta_0 - \alpha_0}{\alpha_1 - \beta_1}$$

$$\Pi_1 = -\frac{\alpha_2}{\alpha_1 - \beta_1} \qquad (17.2.16)$$

and

$$v_t = \frac{u_{2t} - u_{1t}}{\alpha_1 - \beta_1}$$

Substituting the equilibrium value of P_t into the preceding demand or supply function, we obtain the following equilibrium quantity:

$$Q_t = \Pi_2 + \Pi_3 I_t + w_t \qquad (17.2.17)$$

where

$$\Pi_2 = \frac{\alpha_1 \beta_0 - \alpha_0 \beta_1}{\alpha_1 - \beta_1}$$

$$\Pi_3 = -\frac{\alpha_2 \beta_1}{\alpha_1 - \beta_1} \qquad (17.2.18)$$

and

$$w_t = \frac{\alpha_1 u_{2t} - \beta_1 u_{1t}}{\alpha_1 - \beta_1}$$

Since (17.2.15) and (17.2.17) are both reduced-form equations, the OLS method can be applied to estimate their parameters. Now the demand-and-supply model (17.2.12) and (17.2.13) contains five structural coefficients α_0, α_1, α_2, β_0, and β_1. But there are only four equations to estimate them, namely, the four reduced-form coefficients Π_0, Π_1, Π_2, and Π_3 given in (17.2.16) and (17.2.18). Hence unique solution of all the structural coefficients is not possible. But it can be readily shown that the parameters of the supply function can be identified (estimated) because

$$\beta_0 = \Pi_2 - \beta_1 \Pi_0$$
$$\beta_1 = \frac{\Pi_3}{\Pi_1}$$

(17.2.19)

But there is no unique way of estimating the parameters of the demand function; therefore, it remains underidentified. Incidentally, note that the structural coefficient β_1 is a nonlinear function of the reduced-form coefficients, which poses some problems when it comes to estimating the standard error of the estimated β_1, as we shall see in Chap. 18.

To verify that the demand function (17.2.12) cannot be identified (estimated), let us multiply it by λ ($0 < \lambda \leq 1$) and (17.2.13) by $1 - \lambda$ and add them up to obtain the following "mongrel" equation:

$$Q_t = \gamma_0 + \gamma_1 P_t + \gamma_2 I_t + w_t$$

(17.2.20)

where

$$\gamma_0 = \lambda\alpha_0 + (1 - \lambda)\beta_0$$
$$\gamma_1 = \lambda\alpha_1 + (1 - \lambda)\beta_1$$

(17.2.21)

$$\gamma_2 = \lambda\alpha_2$$

and

$$w_t = \lambda u_{1t} + (1 - \lambda)u_{2t}$$

Equation (17.2.20) is observationally indistinguishable from the demand function (17.2.12) although it is distinguishable from the supply function (17.2.13), which does not contain the variable I as an explanatory variable. Hence the demand function remains unidentified.

Notice an interesting fact: It is the presence of an additional variable in the demand function that enables us to identify the supply function! Why? The inclusion of the income variable in the demand equation provides us some additional information about the variability of the function, as indicated in Fig. 17.1d. The figure shows how the intersection of the stable supply curve with the shifting demand curve (on account of changes in income) enables us to trace (identify) the supply curve. As will be shown shortly, very often the identifiability of an equation depends on whether it excludes one or more variables which are included in other equations in the model.

But suppose we consider the following demand-and-supply model:

Demand function $\quad Q_t = \alpha_0 + \alpha_1 P_t + \alpha_2 I_t + u_{1t} \qquad \alpha_1 < 0,\, \alpha_2 > 0 \qquad$ (17.2.12)

Supply function $\quad Q_t = \beta_0 + \beta_1 P_t + \beta_2 P_{t-1} + u_{2t} \qquad \beta_1 > 0,\, \beta_2 > 0 \qquad$ (17.2.22) where the demand function remains as before but the supply function includes an additional explanatory variable, price lagged one period. The supply function postulates that the quantity of a commodity supplied depends on its current and previous period's price, a model often used to explain the supply of many agricultural commodities. Note that P_{t-1} is a predetermined variable because its value is known at time t.

By the market-clearing mechanism we have

$$\alpha_0 + \alpha_1 P_t + \alpha_2 I_t + u_{1t} = \beta_0 + \beta_1 P_t + \beta_2 P_{t-1} + u_{2t} \qquad (17.2.23)$$

Solving this equation, we obtain the following equilibrium price:

$$P_t = \Pi_0 + \Pi_1 I_t + \Pi_2 P_{t-1} + v_t \qquad (17.2.24)$$

where

$$\Pi_0 = \frac{\beta_0 - \alpha_0}{\alpha_1 - \beta_1}$$

$$\Pi_1 = -\frac{\alpha_2}{\alpha_1 - \beta_1} \qquad (17.2.25)$$

$$\Pi_2 = \frac{\beta_2}{\alpha_1 - \beta_1}$$

$$v_t = \frac{u_{2t} - u_{1t}}{\alpha_1 - \beta_1}$$

Substituting the equilibrium price into the demand or supply equation, we obtain the corresponding equilibrium quantity:

$$Q_t = \Pi_3 + \Pi_4 I_t + \Pi_5 P_{t-1} + w_t \qquad (17.2.26)$$

where the reduced-form coefficients are

$$\Pi_3 = \frac{\alpha_1 \beta_0 - \alpha_0 \beta_1}{\alpha_1 - \beta_1}$$

$$\Pi_4 = -\frac{\alpha_2 \beta_1}{\alpha_1 - \beta_1} \qquad (17.2.27)$$

$$\Pi_5 = \frac{\alpha_1 \beta_2}{\alpha_1 - \beta_1}$$

and

$$w_t = \frac{\alpha_1 u_{2t} - \beta_1 u_{1t}}{\alpha_1 - \beta_1}$$

The demand-and-supply model given in equations (17.2.12) and (17.2.22) contain six structural coefficients α_0, α_1, α_2, β_0, β_1, and β_2, and there are six reduced-form coefficients Π_0, Π_1, Π_2, Π_3, Π_4, and Π_5 to estimate them. Thus, we have six equations in six unknowns, and normally we should be able to obtain unique estimates. Therefore, the parameters of both the demand-and-supply equations can be identified, and the system as a whole can be identified. (In Exercise 17.2 the reader is asked to express the six structural coefficients in terms of the six reduced-form coefficients given previously to show that unique estimation of the model is possible.)

To check that the preceding demand-and-supply functions are identified, we can also resort to the device of multiplying the demand equation (17.2.12) by λ $(0 \leq \lambda \leq 1)$ and the supply equation (17.2.22) by $1 - \lambda$ and add them to obtain a mongrel equation. This mongrel equation will contain both the predetermined variables I_t and P_{t-1}; hence it will be observationally different from the demand as well as the supply equation because the former does not contain P_{t-1} and the latter does not contain I_t.

Overidentification

For certain goods and services, income as well as wealth of the consumer is an important determinant of demand. Therefore, let us modify the demand function (17.2.12) as follows, keeping the supply function as before:

$$\text{Demand function} \quad Q_t = \alpha_0 + \alpha_1 P_t + \alpha_2 I_t + \alpha_3 R_t + u_{1t} \quad (17.2.28)$$

$$\text{Supply function} \quad Q_t = \beta_0 + \beta_1 P_t + \beta_2 P_{t-1} + u_{2t} \quad (17.2.22)$$

where in addition to the variables already defined, R represents wealth; for most goods and services, wealth, like income, is expected to have a positive effect on consumption.

Equating demand to supply, we obtain the following equilibrium price and quantity:

$$P_t = \Pi_0 + \Pi_1 I_t + \Pi_2 R_t + \Pi_3 P_{t-1} + v_t \quad (17.2.29)$$

$$Q_t = \Pi_4 + \Pi_5 I_t + \Pi_6 R_t + \Pi_7 P_{t-1} + w_t \quad (17.2.30)$$

where

$$\Pi_0 = \frac{\beta_0 - \alpha_0}{\alpha_1 - \beta_1} \qquad \Pi_1 = -\frac{\alpha_2}{\alpha_1 - \beta_1}$$

$$\Pi_2 = -\frac{\alpha_3}{\alpha_1 - \beta_1} \qquad \Pi_3 = \frac{\beta_2}{\alpha_1 - \beta_1}$$

$$\Pi_4 = \frac{\alpha_1 \beta_0 - \alpha_0 \beta_1}{\alpha_1 - \beta_1} \qquad \Pi_5 = -\frac{\alpha_2 \beta_1}{\alpha_1 - \beta_1} \qquad (17.2.31)$$

$$\Pi_6 = -\frac{\alpha_3 \beta_1}{\alpha_1 - \beta_1} \qquad \Pi_7 = \frac{\alpha_1 \beta_2}{\alpha_1 - \beta_1}$$

$$w_t = \frac{\alpha_1 u_{2t} - \beta_1 u_{1t}}{\alpha_1 - \beta_1} \qquad v_t = \frac{u_{2t} - u_{1t}}{\alpha_1 - \beta_1}$$

The preceding demand-and-supply model contains seven structural coefficients, but there are eight equations to estimate them—the eight reduced-form coefficients given in (17.2.31); that is, the number of equations is greater than the number of unknowns. As a result, unique estimation of all the parameters of our model is not possible, which can be shown easily. From the preceding reduced-form coefficients, we can obtain

$$\beta_1 = \frac{\Pi_6}{\Pi_2} \tag{17.2.32}$$

or
$$\beta_1 = \frac{\Pi_5}{\Pi_1} \tag{17.2.33}$$

that is, there are two estimates of the price coefficient in the supply function, and there is no guarantee that these two values or solutions will be identical.[3] Moreover, since β_1 appears in the denominators of all the reduced-form coefficients, the ambiguity in the estimation of β_1 will be transmitted to other estimates, too.

Why was the supply function identified in the model (17.2.12) and (17.2.22) but not in the system (17.2.28) and (17.2.22), although in both cases the supply function remains the same? The answer is that we have "too much," or an oversufficiency, of information to identify the supply curve. This is the opposite of the case of underidentification, where there is too little information. The oversufficiency of the information results from the fact that in the model (17.2.12) and (17.2.22) the exclusion of the income variable from the supply function was enough to identify it, but in the model (17.2.28) and (17.2.22) the supply function excludes not only the income variable but also the wealth variable. In other words, in the latter model we put "too many" restrictions on the supply function by requiring it to exclude more variables than necessary to identify it. However, this does not imply that overidentification is necessarily bad because we shall see in Chap. 18 how we can handle the problem of too much information, or too many restrictions.

We have now exhausted all the cases. As the preceding discussion shows, an equation in a simultaneous-equations model may be underidentified or identified (either over or just). The model as a whole is identified if each equation in it is identified. To secure identification, we resort to the reduced-form equations. But in Sec. 17.3, we consider an alternative and perhaps less time-consuming method of determining whether or not an equation in a simultaneous-equations model is identified.

17.3 RULES FOR IDENTIFICATION

As the examples in Sec. 17.2 show, in principle it is possible to resort to the reduced-form equations to determine the identification of an equation in a system

---

[3] Notice the difference between under- and overidentification. In the former case, it is impossible to obtain estimates of the structural parameters, whereas in the latter case, there may be several estimates of one or more structural coefficients.

of simultaneous equations. But these examples also show how time-consuming and laborious the process can be. Fortunately, it is not essential to use this procedure. The so-called *order and rank conditions* of identification lighten the task by providing a systematic routine.

To understand the order and rank conditions, we introduce the following notations:

M = number of endogenous variables in the model

m = number of endogenous variables in a given equation

K = number of predetermined variables in the model

k = number of predetermined variables in a given equation

The Order Condition of Identifiability[4]

A necessary (but not sufficient) condition of identification, known as the *order condition*, may be stated in two different but equivalent ways as follows (the necessary as well as sufficient condition of identification will be presented shortly).

Definition 17.1 In a model of M simultaneous equations, in order for an equation to be identified, it must exclude *at least* $M - 1$ variables (endogenous as well as predetermined) appearing in the model. If it excludes exactly $M - 1$ variables, the equation is just identified. If it excludes more than $M - 1$ variables, it is overidentified.

Definition 17.2 In a model of M simultaneous equations, in order for an equation to be identified, the number of predetermined variables excluded from the equation must not be less than the number of endogenous variables included in that equation less 1; that is,

$$K - k \geq m - 1 \qquad (17.3.1)$$

If $K - k = m - 1$, the equation is just identified; but if $K - k > m - 1$, it is overidentified.

In Exercise 17.1 the reader is asked to prove that the preceding two definitions of identification are equivalent.

To illustrate the order condition, let us revert to our previous examples.

Example 17.1

$$\text{Demand function} \quad Q_t = \alpha_0 + \alpha_1 P_t + u_{1t} \qquad (16.2.1)$$

$$\text{Supply function} \quad Q_t = \beta_0 + \beta_1 P_t + u_{2t} \qquad (16.2.2)$$

---

[4] The term *order* refers to the order of a matrix, that is, the number of rows and columns present in a matrix.

This model has two endogeneous variables P and Q and no predetermined variables. To be identified, each of these equations must exclude at least $M - 1 = 1$ variable. Since this is not the case, neither equation is identified.

Example 17.2

$$Demand\ function \quad Q_t = \alpha_0 + \alpha_1 P_t + \alpha_2 I_t + u_{1t} \qquad (17.2.12)$$

$$Supply\ function \quad Q_t = \beta_0 + \beta_1 P_t + u_{2t} \qquad (17.2.13)$$

In this model Q and P are endogenous and I is exogenous. Applying the order condition given in (17.3.1), we see that the demand function is unidentified. On the other hand, the supply function is just identified because it excludes exactly $M - 1 = 1$ variable I_t.

Example 17.3

$$Demand\ function \quad Q_t = \alpha_0 + \alpha_1 P_t + \alpha_2 I_t + u_{1t} \qquad (17.2.12)$$

$$Supply\ function \quad Q_t = \beta_0 + \beta_1 P_t + \beta_2 P_{t-1} + u_{2t} \qquad (17.2.22)$$

Given that P_t and Q_t are endogenous and I_t and P_{t-1} are predetermined, equation (17.2.12) excludes exactly one variable P_{t-1} and equation (17.2.22) also excludes exactly one variable I_t. Hence each equation is identified by the order condition. Therefore, the model as a whole is identified.

Example 17.4

$$Demand\ function \quad Q_t = \alpha_0 + \alpha_1 P_t + \alpha_2 I_t + \alpha_3 R_t + u_{1t} \qquad (17.2.28)$$

$$Supply\ function \quad Q_t = \beta_0 + \beta_1 P_t + \beta_2 P_{t-1} + u_{2t} \qquad (17.2.22)$$

In this model P_t and Q_t are endogenous and I_t, R_t, and P_{t-1} are predetermined. The demand function excludes exactly one variable P_{t-1}, and hence by the order condition it is exactly identified. But the supply function excludes two variables I_t and R_t, and hence it is overidentified. As noted before, in this case there are two ways of estimating β_1, the coefficient of the price variable.

Notice a slight complication here. By the order condition the demand function is identified. But if we try to estimate the parameters of this equation from the reduced-form coefficients given in (17.2.31), the estimates will not be unique because β_1, which enters into the computations, takes two values and we shall have to decide which of these values is appropriate. But this is a complication that can be obviated because it is shown in Chap. 18 that in cases of overidentification the method of indirect least squares is not appropriate and should be discarded in favor of other methods. One such method is two-stage least squares, which we shall discuss fully in Chap. 18.

As the previous examples show, identification of an equation in a model of simultaneous equations may be secured if that equation excludes one or more variables which are present elsewhere in the model. This is known as the *exclusion* (of variables) *criterion,* or *zero restrictions criterion* (the coefficients of variables not appearing in an equation are assumed to have zero values). This criterion is by far the most commonly used method of securing or determining identification of an equation. But notice that the zero restrictions criterion is based on a priori or theoretical expectations that certain variables do not appear in a given equation. And it is up to the researcher to spell out clearly why he or she does expect certain variables to appear in some equations and not in others.

The Rank Condition of Identifiability[5]

The order condition discussed previously is a *necessary but not sufficient* condition for identification; that is, even if it is satisfied, it may happen that an equation is not identified. Thus, in Example 17.2, the supply equation was identified by the order condition because it excluded the income variable I_t, which appeared in the demand function. But this is so only if α_2, the coefficient of I_t in the demand function, is not zero, that is, if the income variable, not only probably, but actually does enter the demand function.

More generally, even if the order condition $K - k \geq m - 1$ is satisfied by an equation, it may be unidentified because the predetermined variables excluded from this equation but present in the model may not all be independent so that there may not be one-to-one correspondence between the structural coefficients (the β's) and the reduced-form coefficients (the Π's). That is, we may not be able to estimate the structural parameters from the reduced-form coefficients, as we shall show shortly. Therefore, we need both a necessary and sufficient condition for identification. This is provided by the *rank condition* of identification, which may be stated as follows:

> **Rank condition of identification** In a model containing M equations in M endogenous variables, an equation is identified if and only if *at least* one nonzero determinant of order $(M - 1)(M - 1)$ can be constructed from the coefficients of the variables (both endogenous and predetermined) excluded from that particular equation but included in the other equations of the model.

[5] The term *rank* refers to the rank of a matrix and is given by the largest-order square matrix (contained in the given matrix) whose determinant is nonzero. Alternatively, the rank of a matrix is the largest number of linearly independent rows or columns of that matrix.

Table 17.1

Equation no.	1	Y_1	Y_2	Y_3	Y_4	X_1	X_2	X_3
(17.3.2)	$-\beta_{10}$	1	$-\beta_{12}$	$-\beta_{13}$	0	$-\gamma_{11}$	0	0
(17.3.3)	$-\beta_{20}$	0	1	$-\beta_{23}$	0	$-\gamma_{21}$	$-\gamma_{22}$	0
(17.3.4)	$-\beta_{30}$	$-\beta_{31}$	0	1	0	$-\gamma_{31}$	$-\gamma_{32}$	0
(17.3.5)	$-\beta_{40}$	$-\beta_{41}$	$-\beta_{42}$	0	1	0	0	$-\gamma_{43}$

As an illustration of the rank condition of identification, consider the following hypothetical system of simultaneous equations in which the Y variables are endogenous and the X variables are predetermined:[6]

$$Y_{1t} - \beta_{10} \qquad - \beta_{12} Y_{2t} - \beta_{13} Y_{3t} - \gamma_{11} X_{1t} \qquad\qquad\qquad = u_{1t} \quad (17.3.2)$$

$$Y_{2t} - \beta_{20} \qquad\qquad - \beta_{23} Y_{3t} - \gamma_{21} X_{1t} - \gamma_{22} X_{2t} \qquad\quad = u_{2t} \quad (17.3.3)$$

$$Y_{3t} - \beta_{30} - \beta_{31} Y_{1t} \qquad\qquad - \gamma_{31} X_{1t} - \gamma_{32} X_{2t} \qquad\quad = u_{3t} \quad (17.3.4)$$

$$Y_{4t} - \beta_{40} - \beta_{41} Y_{1t} - \beta_{42} Y_{2t} \qquad\qquad\qquad\qquad - \gamma_{43} X_{3t} = u_{4t} \quad (17.3.5)$$

To facilitate identification, let us write the preceding system in Table 17.1, which is self-explanatory.

Let us first apply the order condition of identification, as shown in Table 17.2. By the order condition each equation is identified. Let us recheck with the rank condition. Consider the first equation, which excludes variables Y_4, X_2, and X_3 (this is represented by zeros in the first row of Table 17.1). For this equation to be identified, we must obtain at least one nonzero determinant of order 3×3 from the coefficients of the variables excluded from this equation but included in other equations. To obtain the determinant we first obtain the relevant matrix of coefficients of variables Y_4, X_2, and X_3 included in the other equations. In the present case there is only one such matrix, call it **A**, defined as follows:

$$\mathbf{A} = \begin{bmatrix} 0 & -\gamma_{22} & 0 \\ 0 & -\gamma_{32} & 0 \\ 1 & 0 & -\gamma_{43} \end{bmatrix} \qquad (17.3.6)$$

It can be seen that the determinant of this matrix is zero:

$$|\mathbf{A}| = \begin{vmatrix} 0 & -\gamma_{22} & 0 \\ 0 & -\gamma_{32} & 0 \\ 1 & 0 & -\gamma_{43} \end{vmatrix} = 0 \qquad (17.3.7)$$

Since the determinant is zero, the rank of the matrix (17.3.6), denoted by $\rho(\mathbf{A})$, is less than 3. Therefore, equation (17.3.2) does not satisfy the rank condition and hence is not identified.

---

[6] The simultaneous-equations system presented in (17.1.1) may be shown in the following alternative form, which may be convenient for matrix manipulations.

Table 17.2

Equation no.	No. of predetermined variables excluded $(K - k)$	No. of endogenous variables included less one $(m - 1)$	Identified?
(17.3.2)	2	2	Exactly
(17.3.3)	1	1	Exactly
(17.3.4)	1	1	Exactly
(17.3.5)	2	2	Exactly

As noted, the rank condition is both a necessary and sufficient condition for identification. Therefore, although the order condition shows that equation (17.3.2) is identified, the rank condition shows that it is not. Apparently, the columns or rows of the matrix $\mathbf{A}$ given in (17.3.6) are not (linearly) independent, meaning that there is some relationship between the variables Y_4, X_2, and X_3. As a result, we may not have enough information to estimate the parameters of equation (17.3.2); the reduced-form equations for the preceding model will show that it is not possible to obtain the structural coefficients of that equation from the reduced-form coefficients. The reader should verify that by the rank condition equations (17.3.3) and (17.3.4) are also unidentified but equation (17.3.5) is identified.

To apply the rank condition one may proceed as follows:

1. Write down the system in a tabular form, as shown in Table 17.1.
2. Strike out the coefficients of the row in which the equation under consideration appears.
3. Also strike out the columns corresponding to those coefficients in 2 which are nonzero.
4. The entries left in the table will then give only the coefficients of the variables included in the system but not in the equation under consideration. From these entries form all possible matrices, like $\mathbf{A}$, of order $M - 1$ and obtain the corresponding determinants. If at least one nonvanishing or nonzero determinant can be found, the equation in question is (just or over) identified. The rank of the matrix, say, $\mathbf{A}$, in this case is exactly equal to $M - 1$. If all the possible $(M - 1)(M - 1)$ determinants are zero, the rank of the matrix $\mathbf{A}$ is less than $M - 1$ and the equation under investigation is not identified.

Our discussion of the order and rank conditions of identification leads to the following general principles of identifiability of a structural equation in a system of M simultaneous equations.

1. If $K - k > m - 1$ and the rank of the $\mathbf{A}$ matrix is $M - 1$, the equation is overidentified.
2. If $K - k = m - 1$ and the rank of the matrix $\mathbf{A}$ is $M - 1$, the equation is exactly identified.
3. If $K - k \geq m - 1$ and the rank of the matrix $\mathbf{A}$ is less than $M - 1$, the equation is underidentified.
4. If $K - k < m - 1$, the structural equation is unidentified. The rank of the $\mathbf{A}$ matrix in this case is bound to be less than $M - 1$. (Why?)

Henceforth when we talk about identification we mean exact identification, or overidentification. There is no point in considering unidentified, or underidentified, equations because no matter how extensive the data, the structural parameters cannot be estimated. However, as shown in Chap. 18, parameters of overidentified as well as just identified equations can be estimated.

17.4 SUMMARY AND CONCLUSIONS

In this chapter we considered the problem of identification, a problem that is logically prior to estimation. By the identification problem we mean whether numerical estimates of the structural coefficients can be obtained from the estimated reduced-form coefficients. If this can be done, we say that an equation in a system of simultaneous equations is identified. If this is not possible, then we say that the equation is underidentified, or unidentified. An identified equation can be either just identified or overidentified. In the former case, unique values of the structural coefficients exist; whereas in the latter case, there may be more than one value of one or more structural parameters.

The problem of identification arises because the same set of data may be compatible with different sets of structural coefficients, that is, different models. Thus in the regression of price on quantity only, we may not know whether it is the demand or the supply function that we are estimating because the price and quantity enter into both these functions.

To assess the identifiability of a structural equation, one may apply the technique of reduced-form equations, but this time-consuming procedure can be avoided by resorting either to the order or the rank condition of identification. Although the order condition is easy to apply, it provides only a necessary condition for identification. On the other hand, the rank condition is both a necessary and sufficient condition for identification. If the rank condition is satisfied, the order condition is satisfied, too, although the converse is not true.

In Chap. 18 we shall show how numerical estimates of just identified and overidentified equations can be obtained.

EXERCISES

17.1 Show that the two definitions of the order condition of identification are equivalent.

17.2 Deduce the structural coefficients from the reduced-form coefficients given in (17.2.25) and (17.2.27).

17.3 Obtain the reduced form of the following models and determine in each case whether the structural equations are unidentified, just identified, or overidentified:
  (a) Chap. 16, Example 16.2.
  (b) Chap. 16, Example 16.3.
  (c) Chap. 16, Example 16.5.

17.4 Check the identifiability of the models of Exercise 17.3 by applying both the order and rank conditions of identification.

17.5 In the model (17.2.22) and (17.2.28) of the text it was shown that the supply equation was overidentified. What restrictions, if any, on the structural parameters will make this equation just identified? Justify the restrictions you impose.

17.6 From the model

$$Y_{1t} = \beta_{10} + \beta_{12} Y_{2t} + \gamma_{11} X_{1t} + u_{1t}$$

$$Y_{2t} = \beta_{20} + \beta_{21} Y_{1t} + \gamma_{22} X_{2t} + u_{2t}$$

the following reduced-form equations are obtained:

$$Y_{1t} = \Pi_{10} + \Pi_{11} X_{1t} + \Pi_{12} X_{2t} + w_t$$

$$Y_{2t} = \Pi_{20} + \Pi_{21} X_{1t} + \Pi_{22} X_{2t} + v_t$$

(a) Are the structural equations identified?

(b) What happens to identification if it is known a priori that $\gamma_{11} = 0$?

17.7 Refer to Exercise 17.6. The estimated reduced-form equations are as follows:

$$Y_{1t} = 4 + 3X_{1t} + 8X_{2t}$$

$$Y_{2t} = 2 + 6X_{1t} + 10X_{2t}$$

(a) Obtain the values of the structural parameters.

(b) How would you test the null hypothesis that $\gamma_{11} = 0$?

17.8 The model

$$Y_{1t} = \beta_{10} + \beta_{12} Y_{2t} + \gamma_{11} X_{1t} + u_{1t}$$

$$Y_{2t} = \beta_{20} + \beta_{21} Y_{1t} + u_{2t}$$

produces the following reduced-form equations:

$$Y_{1t} = 4 + 8X_{1t}$$

$$Y_{2t} = 2 + 12X_{1t}$$

(a) Which structural coefficients, if any, can be estimated from the reduced-form coefficients? Demonstrate your contention.

(b) How does the answer to (a) change if it is known a priori that (i) $\beta_{12} = 0$ and (ii) $\beta_{10} = 0$?

17.9 Determine whether the structural equations of the model given in Exercise 16.4 are identified.

17.10 Refer to Exercise 16.8 and find out which structural equations can be identified?

17.11 The following is a model in five equations with five endogenous variables Y and four exogenous variables X:

Equation no.	Y_1	Y_2	Y_3	Y_4	Y_5	X_1	X_2	X_3	X_4
1	1	β_{12}	0	β_{14}	0	γ_{11}	0	0	γ_{14}
2	0	1	β_{23}	β_{24}	0	0	γ_{22}	γ_{23}	0
3	β_{31}	0	1	β_{34}	β_{35}	0	0	γ_{33}	γ_{34}
4	0	β_{42}	0	1	0	γ_{41}	0	γ_{43}	0
5	β_{51}	0	0	β_{54}	1	0	γ_{52}	γ_{53}	0

Determine the identifiability of each equation with the aid of the order and rank conditions of identification.

17.12 Consider the following system:

$$Y_{1t} = \beta_{10} + \gamma_{11} X_{1t} + \gamma_{12} X_{2t} + u_{1t}$$

$$Y_{2t} = \beta_{20} + \beta_{21} Y_{1t} + \gamma_{21} X_{1t} + \gamma_{22} X_{2t} + u_{2t}$$

$$Y_{3t} = \beta_{30} + \beta_{31} Y_{1t} + \beta_{32} Y_{2t} + \gamma_{31} X_{1t} + \gamma_{32} X_{2t} + u_{3t}$$

where $E(u_{1t}, u_{2t}) = E(u_{2t}, u_{3t}) = E(u_{1t}, u_{3t}) = 0$. Can the method of least squares be applied to each equation individually? Why or why not?

Note: The preceding system is known as a *recursive system*, which is discussed more fully in Chap. 18.

EIGHTEEN

SIMULTANEOUS-EQUATIONS METHODS

Having discussed the nature of the simultaneous-equations models in the previous two chapters, in this chapter we turn to the problem of estimation of the parameters of such models. At the outset it may be noted that the estimation problem is rather complex because there are a variety of estimation techniques with varying statistical properties. In view of the introductory nature of this text, we shall consider only a few of these techniques. Our discussion will be simple and often heuristic, the finer points being left to the references.

18.1 APPROACHES TO ESTIMATION

If we consider the general M equations model in M endogenous variables given in (17.1.1), we may adopt two approaches to estimate the structural equations, namely, single-equation methods, also known as *limited information methods*, and system methods, also known as *full information methods*. In the single-equation methods to be considered shortly, we estimate each equation in the system (of simultaneous equations) individually taking into account any restrictions placed on that equation (such as exclusion of some variables) without worrying about the restrictions on the other equations in the system,[1] hence the name *limited information methods*. In the system methods, on the other hand, we estimate all the

---

[1] For the purpose of identification, however, information provided by other equations will have to be taken into account. But as noted in Chap. 17, estimation is possible only in the case of (fully or over) identified equations. In this chapter we assume that the identification problem is solved using the techniques of Chap. 17.

equations in the model simultaneously, taking due account of all restrictions on such equations by the omission or absence of some variables (recall that for identification such restrictions are essential), hence the name *full information methods*.

As an example, consider the following four-equations model:

$$
\begin{aligned}
Y_{1t} &= \beta_{10} + && + \beta_{12} Y_{2t} + \beta_{13} Y_{3t} + && + \gamma_{11} X_{1t} + && + u_{1t} \\
Y_{2t} &= \beta_{20} + && + \beta_{23} Y_{3t} && + \gamma_{21} X_{1t} + \gamma_{22} X_{2t} && + u_{2t} \\
Y_{3t} &= \beta_{30} + \beta_{31} Y_{1t} + && + \beta_{34} Y_{4t} + \gamma_{31} X_{1t} + \gamma_{32} X_{2t} + && + u_{3t} \\
Y_{4t} &= \beta_{40} + && + \beta_{42} Y_{2t} && + \gamma_{43} X_{3t} + u_{4t}
\end{aligned}
\tag{18.1.1}
$$

where the Y's are the endogenous variables and the X's are the exogenous variables. If we are interested in estimating, say, the third equation, the single-equation methods will consider this equation only, noting that variables Y_2 and X_3 are excluded from it. In the systems methods, on the other hand, we try to estimate all four equations simultaneously, taking into account all the restrictions imposed on the various equations of the system.

To preserve the spirit of simultaneous-equations models, ideally one should use the systems method, such as the *full information maximum-likelihood method* (FIML).[2] In practice, however, such methods are not commonly used for a variety of reasons. First, the computational burden is enormous. For example, the comparatively small (20 equations) 1955 Klein-Goldberger model of the United States economy had 151 nonzero coefficients, of which the authors estimated only 51 coefficients using the time-series data. The Brookings–Social Science Research Council (SSRC) econometric model of the United States economy published in 1965 initially had 150 equations.[3] Although such elaborate models may furnish finer details of the various sectors of the economy, computationally it is a stupendous task even in these days of high-speed computers, not to mention the cost involved. Second, the systems methods, such as FIML, lead to solutions which are highly nonlinear in the parameters and are therefore often difficult to determine. Third, if there is a specification error (say, a wrong functional form or exclusion of relevant variables) in one or more equations of the system, that error is transmitted to the rest of the system. As a result, the systems methods become very sensitive to specification errors.

In practice, therefore, single-equation methods are often used. As Klein puts it,

> Single equation methods, in the context of a simultaneous system may be less sensitive to specification error in the sense that those parts of the system that are correctly specified may not be affected appreciably by errors in specification in another part.[4]

---

[2] For a simple discussion of this method, see Carl F. Christ, *Econometric Models and Methods*, John Wiley & Sons, Inc., New York, 1966, pp. 395–401.

[3] James S. Duesenberry, Gary Fromm, Lawrence R. Klein, and Edwin Kuh, eds., *A Quarterly Model of the United States Economy*, Rand McNally & Company, Chicago, 1965.

[4] Lawrence R. Klein, *A Textbook of Econometrics*, 2d ed., Prentice-Hall, Inc., Englewood Cliffs, N.J., 1974, p. 150.

In the rest of the chapter we shall deal with single-equation methods only. Specifically, we shall discuss the following single-equation methods:

1. Ordinary least squares (OLS)
2. Indirect least squares (ILS)
3. Two-stage least squares (2SLS)

18.2 RECURSIVE MODELS AND ORDINARY LEAST SQUARES

We saw in Chap. 16 that because of the interdependence between the stochastic disturbance term and the endogenous explanatory variable(s), the OLS method is inappropriate for the estimation of an equation in a system of simultaneous equations. If applied erroneously, then, as we saw in Sec. 16.3, the estimators are not only biased (in small samples) but also inconsistent; that is, the bias does not disappear no matter how large the sample size. There is, however, one situation where OLS can be applied appropriately even in the context of simultaneous equations. This is the case of the *recursive, triangular,* or *causal* models. To see the nature of these models, consider the following three-equation system:

$$
\begin{aligned}
Y_{1t} &= \beta_{10} & &+ \gamma_{11} X_{1t} + \gamma_{12} X_{2t} + u_{1t} \\
Y_{2t} &= \beta_{20} + \beta_{21} Y_{1t} & &+ \gamma_{21} X_{1t} + \gamma_{22} X_{2t} + u_{2t} \qquad (18.2.1) \\
Y_{3t} &= \beta_{30} + \beta_{31} Y_{1t} + \beta_{32} Y_{2t} + \gamma_{31} X_{1t} + \gamma_{32} X_{2t} + u_{3t}
\end{aligned}
$$

where, as usual, the Y's and the X's are, respectively, the endogenous and exogenous variables. The disturbances are such that

$$ E(u_{1t}, u_{2t}) = E(u_{1t}, u_{3t}) = E(u_{2t}, u_{3t}) = 0 $$

that is, the same period disturbances in different equations are uncorrelated (technically, this is the assumption of zero contemporaneous correlation).

Now consider the first equation of (18.2.1). Since it contains only the exogenous variables on the right-hand side and since by assumption they are uncorrelated with the disturbance term u_1, this equation satisfies the critical assumption of the classical OLS, namely, uncorrelatedness between the explanatory variables and the stochastic disturbances. Hence OLS can be applied straightforwardly to this equation. Next consider the second equation of (18.2.1), which contains the endogenous variable Y_1 as an explanatory variable along with the nonstochastic X's. Now OLS can also be applied to this equation, provided Y_{1t} and u_{2t} are uncorrelated. Is this so? The answer is yes because u_1 which affects Y_1 is by assumption uncorrelated with u_2. Therefore, for all practical purposes, Y_1 is a predetermined variable insofar as Y_2 is concerned. Hence one can proceed with OLS estimation of this equation. Carrying this argument a step further, OLS can also be applied to the third equation in (18.2.1) because both Y_1 and Y_2 are uncorrelated with u_3.

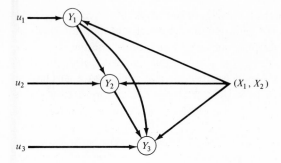

Figure 18.1 Recursive model.

Thus in the recursive system OLS can be applied to each equation separately. Actually, we do not have a simultaneous-equations problem in this situation. From the structure of such systems, it is clear that there is no interdependence among the endogenous variables. Thus, Y_1 affects Y_2, but Y_2 does not affect Y_1. Similarly, Y_1 and Y_2 influence Y_3 without, in turn, being influenced by Y_3. In other words, each equation exhibits a unilateral causal dependence, hence the name causal models.[5] Schematically, we have Fig. 18.1.

As an example of a recursive system, one may postulate the following model of wage and price determination:

Price equation $\dot{P}_t = \beta_{10} + \beta_{11}\dot{W}_{t-1} + \beta_{12}\dot{R}_t + \beta_{13}\dot{M}_t + \beta_{14}\dot{L}_t + u_{1t}$

Wage equation $\dot{W}_t = \beta_{20} + \beta_{21}UN_t + \beta_{32}\dot{P}_t + u_{2t}$ (18.2.2)

where $\dot{P}$ = rate of change of price per unit of output
$\dot{W}$ = rate of change of wages per employee
$\dot{R}$ = rate of change of price of capital
$\dot{M}$ = rate of change of import prices
$\dot{L}$ = rate of change of labor productivity
UN = unemployment rate, %[6]

---

[5] The alternative name *triangular* stems from the fact that if we form the matrix of the coefficients of the endogenous variables given in (18.2.1), we obtain the following triangular matrix:

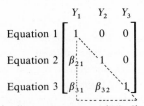

$$
\begin{array}{c}
\text{Equation 1} \\
\text{Equation 2} \\
\text{Equation 3}
\end{array}
\begin{bmatrix}
1 & 0 & 0 \\
\beta_{21} & 1 & 0 \\
\beta_{31} & \beta_{32} & 1
\end{bmatrix}
\quad
\begin{array}{ccc}
Y_1 & Y_2 & Y_3
\end{array}
$$

Note that the entries above the main diagonal are zeros. (Why?)

[6] *Note:* The dotted symbol means "time derivative." For example, $\dot{P} = dP/dt$. For discrete time series, dP/dt is sometimes approximated by $\Delta P/\Delta t$, where the symbol Δ is the first difference operator, which was originally introduced in Chap. 11.

The price equation postulates that the rate of change of price in current period is a function of the rates of change in the prices of capital and of raw material, rate of change in labor productivity, and rate of change in wages in the previous period. The wage equation shows that the rate of change in wages in the current period is determined by the current period rate of change in price and the unemployment rate. It is clear that the causal chain runs from $\dot{W}_{t-1} \to \dot{P}_t \to \dot{W}_t$, and hence OLS may be applied to estimate the parameters of the two equations individually.

Although recursive models have proved to be useful, most simultaneous-equations models do not exhibit such unilateral cause-and-effect relationship. Therefore, OLS, in general, is inappropriate to estimate a single equation in the context of a simultaneous-equation model.

There are some who argue that although OLS is generally inapplicable to simultaneous-equations models, one can use it, if only as a standard or norm of comparison. That is, one can estimate a structural equation by OLS, with the resulting properties of biasedness, inconsistency, etc. Then the same equation may be estimated by other methods especially designed to handle the simultaneity problem and the results of the two methods compared, at least qualitatively. In many applications it may happen that the results of the inappropriately applied OLS do not differ very much from those obtained by more sophisticated methods, as we shall see later. In principle, one should not have much objection to the production of the results based on OLS as long as estimates based on alternative methods devised for simultaneous-equations models are also given. In fact, this might give us some idea about how badly OLS does in situations when it is applied inappropriately.

18.3 ESTIMATION OF A JUST IDENTIFIED EQUATION: THE METHOD OF INDIRECT LEAST SQUARES (ILS)

For a just or exactly identified structural equation, the method of obtaining the estimates of the structural coefficients from the OLS estimates of the reduced-form coefficients is known as the *method of indirect least squares* (ILS), and the estimates thus obtained are known as the *indirect least squares estimates*. ILS involves the following three steps:

Step 1 We first obtain the reduced-form equations. As noted in Chap. 17, these reduced-form equations are obtained from the structural equations in such a manner that the dependent variable in each equation is the only endogenous variable and is a function solely of the predetermined (exogenous or lagged endogenous) variables and the stochastic error term(s).

Step 2 We apply OLS to the reduced-form equations individually. This is permissible since the explanatory variables in these equations are predetermined and hence uncorrelated with the stochastic disturbances. The estimates thus obtained are consistent.[7]

Step 3 We obtain estimates of the original structural coefficients from the estimated reduced-form coefficients obtained in step 2. As noted in Chap. 17, if an equation is exactly identified, there is a one-to-one correspondence between the structural and reduced-form coefficients; that is, one can derive unique estimates of the former from the latter.

As this three-step procedure indicates, the name ILS derives from the fact that structural coefficients (the object of primary enquiry in most cases) are obtained indirectly from the OLS estimates of the reduced-form coefficients.

An Illustrative Example

Consider the demand-and-supply model introduced in Chap. 17, Sec. 17.2, which for convenience is given below with a slight change in notation:

Demand function	$Q_t = \alpha_0 + \alpha_1 P_t + \beta_2 X_t + u_{1t}$	(18.3.1)
Supply function	$Q_t = \beta_0 + \beta_1 P_t + u_{2t}$	(18.3.2)

where Q = quantity
$\quad\quad P$ = price
$\quad\quad X$ = income

Assume that X is exogenous. As noted previously, the supply function is exactly identified whereas the demand function is not identified.

The reduced-form equations corresponding to the preceding structural equations are

$$P_t = \Pi_0 + \Pi_1 X_t + w_t \tag{18.3.3}$$

$$Q_t = \Pi_2 + \Pi_3 X_t + v_t \tag{18.3.4}$$

where the Π's are the reduced-form coefficients and are (nonlinear) combinations of the structural coefficients, as shown in equations (17.2.16) and (17.2.18), and where w and v are linear combinations of the structural disturbances u_1 and u_2.

Notice that each reduced-form equation contains only one endogenous variable, which is the dependent variable and which is a function solely of the exogenous variable X (income) and the stochastic disturbances. Hence, the parameters of the preceding reduced-form equations may be estimated by OLS.

---

[7] In addition to being consistent, the estimates "may be best unbiased and/or asymptotically efficient, depending respectively upon whether (i) the z's [$= X$'s] are exogenous and not merely predetermined and/or (ii) the distribution of the disturbances is normal." (W. C. Hood and Tjalling C. Koopmans, *Studies in Econometric Method*, John Wiley & Sons, Inc., New York, 1953, p. 133.)

These estimates are:

$$\hat{\Pi}_1 = \frac{\sum p_t x_t}{\sum x_t^2} \tag{18.3.5}$$

$$\hat{\Pi}_0 = \bar{P} - \hat{\Pi}_1 \bar{X} \tag{18.3.6}$$

$$\hat{\Pi}_3 = \frac{\sum q_t x_t}{\sum x_t^2} \tag{18.3.7}$$

$$\hat{\Pi}_2 = \bar{Q} - \hat{\Pi}_3 \bar{X} \tag{18.3.8}$$

where the lowercase letters, as usual, denote deviations from sample means and where $\bar{Q}$ and $\bar{P}$ are the sample mean values of Q and P. As noted previously, the $\hat{\Pi}_i$'s are consistent estimators and under appropriate assumptions are also minimum variance unbiased or asymptotically efficient (see fn. 7).

Since our primary objective is to determine the structural coefficients, let us see if we can estimate them from the reduced-form coefficients. Now as shown in Chap. 17, Sec. 17.2, the supply function is exactly identified. Therefore its parameters can be estimated uniquely from the reduced-form coefficients as follows:

$$\beta_0 = \Pi_2 - \beta_1 \Pi_0 \quad \text{and} \quad \beta_1 = \frac{\Pi_3}{\Pi_1}$$

Hence the estimates of these parameters can be obtained from the estimates of the reduced-form coefficients as

$$\hat{\beta}_0 = \hat{\Pi}_2 - \hat{\beta}_1 \hat{\Pi}_0 \tag{18.3.9}$$

$$\hat{\beta}_1 = \frac{\hat{\Pi}_3}{\hat{\Pi}_1} \tag{18.3.10}$$

which are the ILS estimators. Note that the parameters of the demand function cannot be thus estimated.

To give some numerical results, we obtain the data in Table 18.1. First we estimate the reduced-form equations, regressing separately price and quantity on per capita real consumption expenditure. The results are as follows:

$$\hat{P}_t = -9.4283 + 0.0520X_t$$
$$(0.0202) \quad r^2 = 0.3376 \tag{18.3.11}$$
$$t = (2.5750)$$

$$\hat{Q}_t = 47.2196 + 0.0228X_t$$
$$(0.0025) \quad r^2 = 0.8668 \tag{18.3.12}$$
$$t = (9.1740)$$

Using (18.3.9) and (18.3.10), we now obtain ILS estimates:

$$\hat{\beta}_0 = 51.2907 \tag{18.3.13}$$

$$\hat{\beta}_1 = 0.4318 \tag{18.3.14}$$

Table 18.1 Crop production, crop prices, and consumer expenditure, United States, 1960–1974

Year	Index of crop production (1967 = 100), Q	Index of prices (1967 = 100), P	Per capital real consumer expenditure (1958 dollars), X
1960	93	99	1883
1961	92	100	1909
1962	92	103	1969
1963	96	106	2015
1964	93	106	2126
1965	99	103	2239
1966	95	105	2335
1967	100	100	2403
1968	103	101	2486
1969	104	97	2534
1970	101	100	2610
1971	112	107	2683
1972	113	115	2779
1973	119	164	2945
1974	110	212	2846

Source: Economic Report of the President, tables C-84, C-86, and C-18, February 1975.

Therefore, the estimated ILS regression is

$$\hat{Q}_t = 51.2907 + 0.4318 P_t \qquad (18.3.15)[8]$$

Note that the coefficient of P is positive, which should be the case since we are estimating the supply function.

For comparison, we give the results of the inappropriately applied OLS regression of Q on P:

$$\hat{Q}_t = 83.5064 + \;\; 0.1568 P_t$$
$$(0.0621) \qquad r^2 = 0.3295 \qquad (18.3.16)$$
$$t = (2.5270)$$

The results show how OLS can distort the "true" picture when it is applied in inappropriate situations.

---

[8] We have not presented the standard errors of the estimated structural coefficients because, as noted previously, these coefficients are generally nonlinear functions of the reduced-form coefficients and there is no simple method of estimating their standard errors from the standard errors of the reduced-form coefficients. For large sample size, however, standard errors of the structural coefficients can be obtained approximately. For details, see Jan Kmenta, *Elements of Econometrics*, The Macmillan Company, New York, 1971, p. 444.

Properties of ILS Estimators

We have seen that the estimators of the reduced-form coefficients are consistent and under appropriate assumptions also best unbiased or asymptotically efficient (see fn. 7). Do these properties carry over to the ILS estimators? It can be shown that the ILS estimators inherit all the asymptotic properties of the reduced-form estimators, such as consistency and asymptotic efficiency. But (the small sample) properties such as unbiasedness do not generally hold true. It is shown in App. 18A, Sec. 18A.1, that the ILS estimators $\hat{\beta}_0$ and $\hat{\beta}_1$ of the supply function given previously are biased but the bias disappears as the sample size increases indefinitely (that is, the estimators are consistent).[9]

18.4 ESTIMATION OF AN OVERIDENTIFIED EQUATION: THE METHOD OF TWO-STAGE LEAST SQUARES (2SLS)

Consider the following model:

Income function
$$Y_{1t} = \beta_{10} + \quad + \beta_{11} Y_{2t} + \gamma_{11} X_{1t} + \gamma_{12} X_{2t} + u_{1t}$$

$$(18.4.1)$$

Money-supply function $\quad Y_{2t} = \beta_{20} + \beta_{21} Y_{1t} \qquad \qquad + u_{2t}$

$$(18.4.2)$$

where Y_1 = income
$\quad\quad Y_2$ = stock of money
$\quad\quad X_1$ = investment expenditure
$\quad\quad X_2$ = government expenditure on goods and services
The variables X_1 and X_2 are exogenous.

The income equation, a hybrid of quantity-theory–keynesian approaches to income determination, states that income is determined by money supply, investment expenditure, and government expenditure. The *money-supply function* postulates that the stock of money is determined (by the Federal Reserve System) on the basis of the level of income. Obviously, we have a simultaneous-equations problem.

Applying the order condition of identification, it can be seen that the income equation is underidentified whereas the money-supply equation is overidentified. There is not much that can be done about the income equation short of changing the model specification. The overidentified money-supply function may not be

---

[9] Intuitively this can be seen as follows: $E(\hat{\beta}_1) = \beta_1$ if $E(\hat{\Pi}_3/\hat{\Pi}_1) = (\Pi_3/\Pi_1)$. Now even if $E(\hat{\Pi}_3) = \Pi_3$ and $E(\hat{\Pi}_1) = \Pi_1$, it can be shown that $E(\hat{\Pi}_3/\hat{\Pi}_1) \neq E(\hat{\Pi}_3)/E(\hat{\Pi}_1)$; that is, the expectation of the ratio of two variables is not equal to the ratio of the expectations of the two variables. However, as shown in App. 18A.1, plim $(\hat{\Pi}_3/\hat{\Pi}_1) = $ plim $(\hat{\Pi}_3)/$plim $(\hat{\Pi}_1) = \Pi_3/\Pi_1$ since $\hat{\Pi}_3$ and $\hat{\Pi}_1$ are consistent estimators.

estimated by ILS because there are two estimates of β_{21} (the reader should verify this via the reduced-form coefficients).

As a matter of practice, one may apply OLS to the money-supply equation, but the estimates thus obtained will be inconsistent in view of the likely correlation between the stochastic explanatory variable Y_1 and the stochastic disturbance term u_2. Suppose, however, we find a "proxy" for the stochastic explanatory variable Y_1 such that while "resembling" Y_1 (in the sense that it is highly correlated with Y_1) it is uncorrelated with u_2. Such a proxy is also known as an *instrumental variable* (see Chap. 12). If one can find such a proxy, OLS can be used straightforwardly to estimate the money-supply function. But how does one obtain such an instrumental variable? One answer is provided by the *two-stage least squares* (2SLS), developed independently by Henri Theil[10] and Robert Basmann.[11] As the name indicates, the method involves two successive applications of OLS. The process is as follows.

Stage 1 To get rid of the likely correlation between Y_1 and u_2, regress first Y_1 on all the predetermined variables in the *whole system*, not just that equation. In the present case, this means regressing Y_1 on X_1 and X_2 as follows:

$$Y_{1t} = \hat{\Pi}_0 + \hat{\Pi}_1 X_{1t} + \hat{\Pi}_2 X_{2t} + e_t \tag{18.4.3}$$

where e_t are the usual OLS residuals. From equation (18.4.3) we obtain

$$\hat{Y}_{1t} = \hat{\Pi}_0 + \hat{\Pi}_1 X_{1t} + \hat{\Pi}_2 X_{2t} \tag{18.4.4}$$

where $\hat{Y}_{1t}$ is an estimate of the mean value of Y conditional upon the fixed X's. Note that (18.4.3) is nothing but a reduced-form regression because only the exogenous or predetermined variables appear on the right-hand side.

Equation (18.4.3) can now be expressed as

$$Y_{1t} = \hat{Y}_{1t} + e_t \tag{18.4.5}$$

which shows that the stochastic Y_1 consists of two parts: $\hat{Y}_{1t}$, which is a linear combination of the nonstochastic X's, and a random component e_t. Following the OLS theory, $\hat{Y}_{1t}$ and e_t are uncorrelated. (Why?)

Stage 2 The overidentified money-supply equation can now be written as

$$Y_{2t} = \beta_{20} + \beta_{21}(\hat{Y}_{1t} + e_t) + u_{2t}$$
$$= \beta_{20} + \beta_{21}\hat{Y}_{1t} + (u_{2t} + \beta_{21}e_t)$$
$$= \beta_{20} + \beta_{21}\hat{Y}_{1t} + u_t^* \tag{18.4.6}$$

where $u_t^* = u_{2t} + \beta_{21}e_t$.

[10] Henri Theil, "Repeated Least-Squares Applied to Complete Equation Systems," The Hague: The Central Planning Bureau, The Netherlands, 1953 (mimeographed).

[11] Robert L. Basmann, "A Generalized Classical Method of Linear Estimation of Coefficients in a Structural Equation," *Econometrica*, vol. 25, pp. 77–83, 1957.

Comparing (18.4.6) with (18.4.2), we see that they are very similar in appearance, the only difference being that Y_1 is replaced by $\hat{Y}_1$. What is the advantage of (18.4.6)? It can be shown that although Y_1 in the original money-supply equation is correlated or likely to be correlated with the disturbance term u_2 (hence rendering OLS inappropriate), $\hat{Y}_{1t}$ in (18.4.6) is uncorrelated with u_t^* asymptotically, that is, in the large sample (or more accurately, as the sample size increases indefinitely). As a result, OLS can be applied to (18.4.6), which will give consistent estimates of the parameters of the money-supply function.[12]

As this two-stage procedure indicates, the basic idea behind 2SLS is to "purify" the stochastic explanatory variable Y_1 of the influence of the stochastic disturbance u_2. This is accomplished by the reduced-form regression of Y_1 on all the predetermined variables in the system (stage I), obtaining the estimates $\hat{Y}_{1t}$ and replacing Y_{1t} in the original equation by the estimated $\hat{Y}_{1t}$ and then applying OLS to the equation thus transformed (stage 2). The estimators thus obtained are consistent; that is, they converge to their true values as the sample size increases indefinitely.

To illustrate 2SLS further, let us modify the income–money-supply model as follows:

$$Y_{1t} = \beta_{10} + \beta_{12} Y_{2t} + \gamma_{11} X_{1t} + \gamma_{12} X_{2t} \qquad\qquad\qquad + u_{1t} \qquad (18.4.7)$$

$$Y_{2t} = \beta_{20} + \beta_{21} Y_{1t} \qquad\qquad\qquad + \gamma_{23} X_{3t} + \gamma_{24} X_{4t} + u_{2t} \qquad (18.4.8)$$

where, in addition to the variables already defined, $X_3 =$ income in the previous time period and $X_4 =$ money supply in the previous period. Both X_3 and X_4 are predetermined.

It can be readily verified that both equations (18.4.7) and (18.4.8) are over-identified. To apply 2SLS, we proceed as follows: In stage 1 we regress the endogenous variables on *all* the predetermined variables in the system. Thus,

$$Y_{1t} = \hat{\Pi}_{10} + \hat{\Pi}_{11} X_{1t} + \hat{\Pi}_{12} X_{2t} + \hat{\Pi}_{13} X_{3t} + \hat{\Pi}_{14} X_{4t} + e_{1t} \qquad (18.4.9)$$

$$Y_{2t} = \hat{\Pi}_{20} + \hat{\Pi}_{21} X_{1t} + \hat{\Pi}_{22} X_{2t} + \hat{\Pi}_{23} X_{3t} + \hat{\Pi}_{24} X_{4t} + e_{2t} \qquad (18.4.10)$$

In stage 2 we replace Y_1 and Y_2 in the original (structural) equations by their estimated values from the preceding two regressions and then run the OLS regressions as follows:

---

[12] But note that in small samples $\hat{Y}_{1t}$ is likely to be correlated with u_t^*. The reason is as follows: From (18.4.4) we see that $\hat{Y}_{1t}$ is a weighted linear combination of the predetermined X's, with $\hat{\Pi}$'s as the weights. Now even if the predetermined variables are truly nonstochastic, the $\hat{\Pi}$'s, being estimators, are stochastic. Therefore, $\hat{Y}_{1t}$ is stochastic, too. Now from our discussion of the reduced-form equations and indirect least-squares estimation, it is clear that the reduced-form coefficients, the $\hat{\Pi}$'s, are functions of the stochastic disturbances, such as u_2. And since $\hat{Y}_{1t}$ depends on the $\hat{\Pi}$'s, it is likely to be correlated with u_2, which is a component of u_t^*. As a result, $\hat{Y}_{1t}$ is expected to be correlated with u_t^*. But as noted previously, this correlation disappears as the sample size tends to infinity. The upshot of all this is that in small samples the 2SLS-procedure may lead to biased estimation.

$$Y_{1t} = \beta_{10} + \beta_{12} \hat{Y}_{2t} + \gamma_{11} X_{1t} + \gamma_{12} X_{2t} + u_{1t}^* \qquad (18.4.11)$$

$$Y_{2t} = \beta_{20} + \beta_{21} \hat{Y}_{1t} + \gamma_{23} X_{3t} + \gamma_{24} X_{4t} + u_{2t}^* \qquad (18.4.12)$$

where $u_{1t}^* = u_{1t} + \beta_{12} e_{2t}$ and $u_{2t}^* = u_{2t} + \beta_{21} e_{1t}$. The estimates thus obtained will be consistent.

Salient Features of 2SLS

Note the following features of 2SLS:

1. It can be applied to an individual equation in the system without directly taking into account any other equation(s) in the system. Hence for solving econometric models involving a large number of equations, 2SLS offers an economical method. It is for this reason that this method has been used extensively in practice.

2. Unlike ILS, which provides multiple estimates of parameters in the overidentified equations, 2SLS provides only one estimate per parameter.

3. It is easy to apply because all one needs to know is the total number of exogenous or predetermined variables in the system without knowing any other variables in the system.

4. Although specially designed to handle overidentified equations, the method can also be applied to exactly identified equations. But then ILS and 2SLS will give identical estimates. (Why?)

5. If the R^2 values in the reduced-form regressions (that is, stage 1 regressions) are very high, say, in excess of 0.8, the classical OLS estimates and 2SLS estimates will be very close. But this should not be surprising because if the R^2 value in the first stage is very high, it means that the estimated values of the endogenous variables are very close to their actual values, and hence the latter are less likely to correlated with the stochastic disturbances in the original structural equations. (Why?)[13] If, however, the R^2's in the first-stage regressions are very low, the 2SLS estimates will be practically meaningless because we shall be replacing the original Y's in the second-stage regression by the estimated $\hat{Y}$'s from the first-stage regressions which will essentially represent the disturbances in the first-stage regressions. In other words, in this case, the $\hat{Y}$'s will be very poor proxies for the original Y's.

6. Notice that in reporting the ILS regressions in (18.3.15) we did not state the standard errors of the estimated coefficients (for reasons explained in fn. 8). But this can be done for the 2SLS estimates because the structural coefficients are directly estimated from the second-stage (OLS) regressions. There is, however, a caution to be exercised. The estimated standard errors in the second-stage regressions need to be modified because, as can be seen from equation (18.4.6), the error term u_t^* is, in fact, the original error term u_{2t} plus $\beta_{21} e_t$. Hence the variance of u_t^* is not exactly equal to the variance of the original u_{2t}. However, the modification required can be easily effected by the formula given in App. 18A.2.

---

[13] In the extreme case if $R^2 = 1$ in the first-stage regression, the endogenous explanatory variable in the original (overidentified) equation will be practically nonstochastic. (Why?)

Table 18.2 Gross National Product, money stock, gross private domestic investment, and government expenditure on goods and services, United States, 1960–1974 (billions of dollars)

Year	GNP, Y_1	Money stock, Y_2	Investment, X_1	Government expenditure, X_2
1960	503.7	144.2	74.8	53.5
1961	520.1	148.7	71.7	57.4
1962	560.3	150.9	83.0	63.4
1963	590.5	156.5	87.1	64.2
1964	632.4	163.7	94.0	65.2
1965	684.9	171.3	108.1	66.9
1966	749.9	175.4	121.4	77.8
1967	793.9	186.9	116.6	90.7
1968	864.2	201.7	126.0	98.8
1969	930.3	208.7	139.0	98.8
1970	977.1	221.4	136.3	96.2
1971	1054.9	235.3	153.7	97.6
1972	1158.0	255.8	179.3	104.9
1973	1294.9	271.5	209.4	106.6
1974	1396.7	283.8	208.9	116.4

Note: The money stock refers to currency plus demand deposits.
Source: Economic Report of the President, tables C-1 and C-52, February 1975.

A numerical example To illustrate the 2SLS method, consider the income–money-supply model given previously in equations (18.4.1) and (18.4.2). As shown, the money-supply equation is overidentified. To estimate the parameters of this equation we resort to the two-stage least-squares method. The data required for analysis are given in Table 18.2.

Stage 1 regression We first regress the stochastic explanatory variable income Y_1, represented by GNP, on the predetermined variables private investment X_1 and government expenditure X_2, obtaining the following results:

$$\hat{Y}_{1t} = -44.7925 + 4.9322X_{1t} + 3.1521X_{2t} \qquad R^2 = 0.9896$$
$$(0.4785) \qquad (1.0391) \qquad \text{df} = 12 \qquad (18.4.13)$$
$$t = (10.3083) \qquad (3.0336)$$

Stage 2 regression We now estimate the money-supply function (18.4.2) replacing the endogenous Y_1 by $\hat{Y}_1$ estimated from (18.4.13). The results are as follows:

$$Y_{2t} = 60.7887 + 0.1624\hat{Y}_{1t} \qquad R^2 = 0.9781$$
$$(0.0034) \qquad \text{df} = 13 \qquad (18.4.14)$$
$$t = (47.7647)$$

Note: The estimated standard error has been found by the correction method given in App. 18A, Sec. 18A.2.

OLS regression For comparision, we give the regression of money stock on income as shown in (18.4.2) without "purging" the stochastic Y_1 of the influence of the stochastic disturbance term.

$$Y_{2t} = 60.3646 + 0.1629Y_{1t} \qquad R^2 = 0.9944$$
$$(0.0034) \qquad df = 13 \qquad (18.4.15)$$
$$t = (48.2817)$$

Comparing the "inappropriate" OLS results with the stage 2 regression, we see that the two regressions are virtually the same. Does this mean that the 2SLS procedure is worthless? Not at all. The fact that in the present situation the two results are practically identical should not be surprising because, as noted previously, the R^2 value in the first stage is very high, thus making the estimated $\hat{Y}_{1t}$ virtually identical with the actual Y_{1t}. Therefore, in this case the OLS and second-stage regressions will be more or less similar. But there is no guarantee that this will happen in every application. An implication, then, is that in overidentified equations one should not accept the classical OLS procedure without checking the second-stage regression(s).

18.5 SUMMARY AND CONCLUSIONS

Assuming that an equation in a simultaneous-equations model is identified (either over or exactly), there are several methods to estimate it. These methods fall into two broad categories: single-equation methods and systems methods. For reasons of economy, specification errors, etc., the single-equation methods are by far the most popular. A unique feature of these methods is that one can estimate a single equation in a multiequation model without worrying too much about other equations in the model.

In this chapter we considered three commonly used single-equation methods, namely, OLS, ILS, and 2SLS. Although OLS is, in general, inappropriate in the context of simultaneous-equations models, it can be applied to the so-called recursive models where there is a definite but unidirectional cause-and-effect relationship among the endogenous variables. The method of ILS is suited for just or exactly identified equations. In this method OLS is applied to the reduced-form equations, and it is from the reduced-form coefficients that one estimates the original structural coefficients. The method of 2SLS is specially designed for over-identified equations, although it can also be applied to the exactly identified equations. But then the results of ILS and 2SLS are identical. The basic idea behind 2SLS is to replace the stochastic endogenous explanatory variable by a linear combination of the (nonstochastic) predetermined variables in the model and use this combination as the explanatory variable in lieu of the original variable.

A unique feature of both ILS and 2SLS is that the estimates obtained thereof are consistent, that is, as the sample increases indefinitely the estimates tend to their true population values. The estimates may not satisfy small sample properties such as unbiasedness and minimum variance. Therefore, the results obtained by applying these methods to small samples should be interpreted with due caution.

Although OLS is generally not applicable to simultaneous-equations models, the results based on such applications are often given for comparative purposes. In some situations OLS does as well as 2SLS, but the reader is warned against the indiscriminate use of OLS in situations where a priori one expects the endogenous explanatory variables in a structural equation to be correlated with the stochastic disturbance term of that equation.

EXERCISES

18.1 Refer to Exercise 16.1. For the two-equation system there obtain the reduced-form equations and estimate their parameters. Estimate the indirect least-squares regression of consumption on income and compare your results with the OLS regression.

18.2 Why is it unnecessary to apply the two-stage least-squares method to exactly identified equations?

18.3 Consider the following modified keynesian model of income determination:

$$C_t = \beta_{10} + \beta_{11} Y_t + u_{1t}$$

$$I_t = \beta_{20} + \beta_{21} Y_t + \beta_{22} Y_{t-1} + u_{2t}$$

$$Y_t = C_t + I_t + G_t$$

where C = consumption expenditure
I = investment expenditure
Y = income
G = government expenditure
G_t and Y_{t-1} are assumed predetermined.

(a) Obtain the reduced-form equations and determine which of the preceding equations are identified (either just or over).

(b) Which method will you use to estimate the parameters of the overidentified equation and of the exactly identified equation? Justify your answer.

18.4 Consider the following results:[14]

$$\text{OLS: } \dot{W}_t = 0.276 + 0.258\dot{P}_t + 0.046\dot{P}_{t-1} + 4.959V_t \qquad\qquad R^2 = 0.924$$

$$\text{OLS: } \dot{P}_t = 2.693 + 0.232\dot{W}_t - 0.544\dot{X}_t + 0.247\dot{M}_t + 0.064\dot{M}_{t-1} \qquad R^2 = 0.982$$

$$\text{2SLS: } \dot{W}_t = 0.272 + 0.257\dot{P}_t + 0.046\dot{P}_{t-1} + 4.966V_t \qquad\qquad R^2 = 0.920$$

$$\text{2SLS: } \dot{P}_t = 2.686 + 0.233\dot{W}_t - 0.544\dot{X}_t + 0.246\dot{M}_t + 0.046\dot{M}_{t-1} \qquad R^2 = 0.981$$

where $\dot{W}_t$, $\dot{P}_t$, $\dot{M}_t$, and $\dot{X}_t$ are percentage changes in earnings, prices, import prices, and labor produc-

---

[14] *Source:* *Prices and Earnings in 1951–1969: An Econometric Assessment*, Department of Employment, U.K., Her Majesty's Stationery Office, 1971, p. 30.

tivity (all percentage changes are over the previous year) and where V_t represents unfilled job vacancies (percentage of total number of employees).

"Since the OLS and 2SLS results are practically identical, 2SLS is meaningless." Comment.

*18.5 Assume that production is characterized by the Cobb-Douglas production function

$$Q_i = A K_i^\alpha L_i^\beta$$

where Q = output
$\quad\quad\quad K$ = capital input
$\quad\quad\quad L$ = labor input
A, α and β = parameters
$\quad\quad\quad i$ = ith firm

Given the price of final output P, the price of labor W, and the price of capital R and assuming profit maximization, we obtain the following empirical model of production:

Production function: $\ln Q_i = \ln A + \alpha \ln K_i + \beta \ln L_i + \ln u_{1i}$ (1)

Marginal product of labor function:

$$\ln Q_i = -\ln \beta + \ln L_i + \ln \frac{W}{P} + \ln u_{2i}$$ (2)

Marginal product of capital function:

$$\ln Q_i = -\ln \alpha + \ln K_i + \ln \frac{R}{P} + \ln u_{3i}$$ (3)

where u_1, u_2, and u_3 are stochastic disturbances.

In the preceding model there are three equations in three endogenous variables Q, L, and K. P, R, and W are exogenous.

(a) What problems do you encounter in estimating the model if $\alpha + \beta = 1$, that is, when there are constant returns to scale?

(b) Even if $\alpha + \beta \neq 1$, can you estimate the equations? Answer by considering the identifiability of the system.

(c) If the system is not identified, what can be done to make it identifiable?

Note: Equations (2) and (3) are obtained by differentiating Q with respect to labor and capital, respectively, setting them equal to W/P and R/P, transforming the resulting expressions into logarithms, and adding (the logarithm of) the disturbance terms.

18.6 Consider the following demand-and-supply model for money:

Demand for money $M_t^d = \beta_0 + \beta_1 Y_t + \beta_2 R_t + \beta_3 P_t + u_{1t}$

Supply of money $M_t^s = \alpha_0 + \alpha_1 Y_t + u_{2t}$

where M = money
$\quad\quad\quad Y$ = income
$\quad\quad\quad R$ = rate of interest
$\quad\quad\quad P$ = price
Assume that R and P are predetermined.

(a) Is the demand function identified?

(b) Is the supply function identified?

(c) Which method would you use to estimate the parameters of the identified equation(s)? Why?

(d) Suppose we modify the supply function by adding the explanatory variables Y_{t-1} and M_{t-1}.

* Optional.

What happens to the identification problem? Would you still use the method you used in (c)? Why or why not?

18.7 Consider the following data.

Gross National Product Y, money supply M, gross domestic private investment I, government expenditure on goods and services G, and interest rates on 3 to 5 years government securities R (billions of dollars)

Year	Y	M	I	G	R, %
1960	503.7	144.2	74.8	53.5	3.99
1961	520.1	148.7	71.7	57.4	3.60
1962	560.3	150.9	83.0	63.4	3.57
1963	590.5	156.5	87.1	64.2	3.72
1964	632.4	163.7	94.0	65.2	4.06
1965	684.9	171.3	108.1	66.9	4.22
1966	749.9	175.4	121.4	77.8	5.16
1967	793.9	186.9	116.6	90.7	5.07
1968	864.2	201.7	126.0	98.8	5.59
1969	930.3	208.7	139.0	98.8	6.85
1970	977.1	221.4	136.3	96.2	7.37
1971	1054.9	235.9	153.7	97.6	5.77
1972	1158.0	255.8	179.3	104.9	5.85
1973	1294.9	271.5	209.4	106.6	6.92
1974	1396.7	283.8	208.9	116.4	7.81

Source: Economic Report of the President, February 1975.

Consider the following model:

$$R_t = \beta_0 + \beta_1 M_t + \beta_2 Y_t + u_{1t}$$

$$Y_t = \alpha_0 + \alpha_1 R_t + u_{2t}$$

where M_t is determined exogenously.

(a) How would you justify the model?

(b) Are the equations identified?

(c) Using the preceding data; estimate the parameters of the identified equation(s). Justify the method(s) you use.

18.8 Suppose we change the model in Exercise 18.7 as follows:

$$R_t = \beta_0 + \beta_1 M_t + \beta_2 Y_t + \beta_3 Y_{t-1} + u_{1t}$$

$$Y_t = \alpha_0 + \alpha_1 R_t + u_{2t}$$

(a) Find out if the system is identified.

(b) Using the data given in Exercise 18.7, estimate the parameters of the identified equation(s).

18.9 Consider the following model:

$$R_t = \beta_0 + \beta_1 M_t + \beta_2 Y_t + u_{1t}$$

$$Y_t = \alpha_0 + \alpha_1 R_t + \alpha_2 I_t + u_{2t}$$

where the variables are as defined in Exercise 18.7. Treating I and M exogenously, determine the identification of the system. Using the data of Exercise 18.7, estimate the parameters of the identified equation(s).

18.10 Suppose we change the model of Exercise 18.9 as follows:

$$R_t = \beta_0 + \beta_1 M_t + \beta_2 Y_t + u_{1t}$$

$$Y_t = \alpha_0 + \alpha_1 R_t + \alpha_2 I_t + u_{2t}$$

$$I_t = \gamma_0 + \gamma_1 R_t + u_{3t}$$

Assume that M is determined exogenously.

(*a*) Find out which of the equations are identified.

(*b*) Estimate the parameters of the identified equation(s) using the data given in Exercise 18.7. Justify your method(s).

APPENDIX 18A

18A.1 BIAS IN THE INDIRECT LEAST-SQUARES ESTIMATORS

To show that the ILS estimators, although consistent, are biased, we use the demand-and-supply model given in equations (18.3.1) and (18.3.2). From (18.3.10) we obtain

$$\hat{\beta}_1 = \frac{\hat{\Pi}_3}{\hat{\Pi}_1}$$

Now

$$\hat{\Pi}_3 = \frac{\sum q_t x_t}{\sum x_t^2} \qquad \text{using (18.3.7)}$$

and

$$\hat{\Pi}_1 = \frac{\sum p_t x_t}{\sum x_t^2} \qquad \text{using (18.3.5)}$$

Therefore, on substitution, we obtain

$$\hat{\beta}_1 = \frac{\sum q_t x_t}{\sum p_t x_t} \tag{1}$$

Using (18.3.3) and (18.3.4), we obtain

$$p_t = \Pi_1 x_t + (w_t - \bar{w}) \tag{2}$$

$$q_t = \Pi_3 x_t + (v_t - \bar{v}) \tag{3}$$

where $\bar{w}$ and $\bar{v}$ are the mean values of w_t and v_t, respectively.

Substituting (2) and (3) into (1), we obtain

$$\hat{\beta}_1 = \frac{\Pi_3 \sum x_t^2 + \sum (v_t - \bar{v})x_t}{\Pi_1 \sum x_t^2 + \sum (w_t - \bar{w})x_t}$$

$$= \frac{\Pi_3 + \sum (v_t - \bar{v})x_t / \sum x_t^2}{\Pi_1 + \sum (w_t - \bar{w})x_t / \sum x_t^2} \tag{4}$$

Since the expectation operator $\mathbf{E}$ is a linear operator, we cannot take the expectation of (4), although it is clear that $\hat{\beta}_1 \neq (\Pi_3/\Pi_1)$ generally. (Why?)

But as the sample size tends to infinity, we can obtain

$$\text{plim } (\hat{\beta}_1) = \frac{\text{plim } \Pi_3 + \text{plim } \sum (v_t - \bar{v})x_t/\sum x_t^2}{\text{plim } \Pi_1 + \text{plim } \sum (w_t - \bar{w})x_t/\sum x_t^2} \tag{5}$$

where use is made of the properties of plim, namely, that

$$\text{plim } (A + B) = \text{plim } A + \text{plim } B \text{ and plim } \left(\frac{A}{B}\right) = \frac{\text{plim } A}{\text{plim } B}$$

Now as the sample size is increased indefinitely, the second term in both the denominator and the numerator of (5) tends to zero (why?), yielding

$$\text{plim } (\hat{\beta}_1) = \frac{\Pi_3}{\Pi_1} \tag{6}$$

showing that although biased, $\hat{\beta}_1$ is a consistent estimator of β_1.

18A.2 ESTIMATION OF STANDARD ERRORS OF 2SLS ESTIMATES

The purpose of this section is to show that the standard errors of the estimates obtained from the second-stage regression of the 2SLS procedure, using the formula applicable in OLS estimation, are not the "proper" estimates of the "true" standard errors. To see this, we use the income–money-supply model given in (18.4.1) and (18.4.2). We estimate the parameters of the overidentified money-supply function from the second-stage regression as

$$Y_{2t} = \beta_{20} + \beta_{21}\hat{Y}_{1t} + u_t^* \tag{18.4.6}$$

where
$$u_t^* = u_{2t} + \beta_{21}e_t \tag{7}$$

Now when we run regression (18.4.6), the standard error of, say $\hat{\beta}_{21}$ is obtained from the following expression:

$$\text{var } (\hat{\beta}_{21}) = \frac{\hat{\sigma}_{u*}^2}{\sum \hat{y}_{1t}^2} \tag{8}$$

where
$$\hat{\sigma}_{u*}^2 = \frac{\sum (\hat{u}_t^*)^2}{N-2} = \frac{\sum (Y_{2t} - \hat{\beta}_{20} - \hat{\beta}_{21}\hat{Y}_{1t})^2}{N-2} \tag{9}$$

But $\hat{\sigma}_{u*}^2$ is not the same thing as $\hat{\sigma}_{u_2}^2$, where the latter is an unbiased estimate of the true variance of u_2. This can be readily verified from (7). To obtain the true (as defined previously) $\hat{\sigma}_{u_2}^2$, we proceed as follows:

$$\hat{u}_{2t} = Y_{2t} - \hat{\beta}_{20} - \hat{\beta}_{21}Y_{1t}$$

where $\hat{\beta}_{20}$ and $\hat{\beta}_{21}$ are the estimates from the second-stage regression. Hence,

$$\hat{\sigma}_{u_2}^2 = \frac{\sum (Y_{2t} - \hat{\beta}_{20} - \hat{\beta}_{21} Y_{1t})^2}{N - 2} \tag{10}$$

Note the difference between (9) and (10): In (10) we use actual Y_1 rather than the estimated Y_1 from the first-stage regression.

Having estimated (10), the easiest way to correct the standard errors of coefficients estimated in the second-stage regression is to multiply each one of them by $\hat{\sigma}_{u_2}/\hat{\sigma}_{u*}$. Note that if Y_{1t} and $\hat{Y}_{1t}$ are very close, that is, the R^2 in the first-stage regression is very high, the correction factor $\hat{\sigma}_{u_2}/\sigma*$ will be close to 1, in which case the estimated standard errors in the second-stage regression may be taken as the true estimates. But in other situations, we shall have to use the preceding correction factor.

A REVIEW OF SOME STATISTICAL CONCEPTS

This appendix provides a very sketchy introduction to some of the statistical concepts encountered in the text. The discussion is nonrigorous, and no proofs are given because there are several excellent books in statistics which do that job very well. Some of these books are listed in Sec. A.8.

A.1 SAMPLE SPACE, SAMPLE POINTS, AND EVENTS

The set of all possible outcomes of a random, or chance, experiment is called the *sample space*, and each member of this sample space is called a *sample point*. Thus, in the experiment of tossing two coins, the sample space consists of these four possible outcomes: *HH*, *HT*, *TH*, and *TT*, where *HH* means a head on the first toss and also a head on the second toss, *HT* means a head on the first toss and a tail on the second toss, and so on. Each of the preceding occurrences constitutes a sample point.

An *event* is a subset of the sample space. Thus, if we let A denote the occurrence of one head and one tail, then, of the preceding possible outcomes, only two belong to A, namely, *HT* and *TH*. In this case A constitutes an event. Similarly, the occurrence of two heads in a toss of two coins is an event. Events are said to be *mutually exclusive* if the occurrence of one event precludes the occurrence of another event. If in the preceding example *HH* occurs, it rules out the occurrence of the event *HT* at the same time. Events are said to be (collectively) *exhaustive* if they exhaust all the possible outcomes of an experiment. Thus, in the example, the events two heads, two tails and one tail, one head exhaust all the outcomes; hence they are (collectively) exhaustive events.

A.2 PROBABILITY AND RANDOM VARIABLES

Probability

Let A be an event in a sample space. By $P(A)$, the probability of the event A, we mean the proportion of times the event A will occur in repeated trials of an experiment. Alternatively, in a total of n possible equally likely outcomes of an experiment, if m of them are favorable to the occurrence of the event A, we define the ratio m/n as the relative frequency of A. For large values of n, this relative frequency will provide a very good approximation of the probability of A.

Properties of probability $P(A)$ is a real-valued function and has these properties:

1. $0 \leq P(A) \leq 1$ for every A.
2. If A, B, C, ..., are an exhaustive set of events, then $P(A + B + C + \cdots) = 1$, where $A + B + C$ means A or B or C, and so forth.
3. If A, B, C, ..., are mutually exclusive events, then

$$P(A + B + C + \cdots) = P(A) + P(B) + P(C) + \cdots$$

Random Variables

A variable whose value is determined by the outcome of a chance experiment is called a *random variable* (rv). Random variables are usually denoted by the capital letters X, Y, Z, and so on, and the values taken by them are denoted by small letters x, y, z, and so on.

A random variable may be either *discrete* or *continuous*. A discrete rv takes on only a finite (or countably infinite) number of values.[1] Thus, in throwing two dice each numbered 1 to 6, if we define the random variable X as the sum of the numbers showing on the dice, then X will take one of these values: 2, 3, 4, 5, 6, 7, 8, 9, 10, 11, and 12. Hence it is a discrete random variable. A continuous rv, on the other hand, is one that can take on any value in some interval of values.

A.3 PROBABILITY DENSITY FUNCTION (PDF)

Probability Density Function of a Discrete Random Variable

Let X be a discrete rv taking distinct values $x_1, x_2, \ldots, x_n, \ldots$. Then the function

$$\begin{aligned} f(x) &= P(X = x_i) &&\text{for } i = 1, 2, \ldots, n, \ldots \\ &= 0 &&\text{for } x \neq x_i \end{aligned}$$

---

[1] For a simple discussion of the notion of countably infinite sets, see R. G. D. Allen, *Basic Mathematics*, Macmillan Company, London, 1964, p. 104.

is called the *discrete probability density function* (*PDF*) of X, where $P(X = x_i)$ means the probability that the discrete rv X takes the value of x_i.

Example As noted previously, in a throw of two dice, the random variable X, the sum of the numbers shown on the two dice, can take one of the 11 values shown. The PDF of this variable can be shown to be as follows:

$$x = \quad 2 \quad 3 \quad 4 \quad 5 \quad 6 \quad 7 \quad 8 \quad 9 \quad 10 \quad 11 \quad 12$$

$$f(x) = (\tfrac{1}{36})(\tfrac{2}{36})(\tfrac{3}{36})(\tfrac{4}{36})(\tfrac{5}{36})(\tfrac{6}{36})(\tfrac{5}{36})(\tfrac{4}{36})(\tfrac{3}{36})(\tfrac{2}{36})(\tfrac{1}{36})$$

The preceding probabilities can be verified easily. In all there are 36 possible outcomes of which one is favorable to number 2, two are favorable to number 3 (since the sum 3 can occur either as 1 on the first die and 2 on the second die or 2 on the first die and 1 on the second die), and so on.

Probability Density Function of a Continuous Random Variable

Let X be a continuous rv. Then, $f(x)$ is said to be the PDF of X if the following conditions are satisfied:

$$f(x) \geq 0$$

$$\int_{-\infty}^{\infty} f(x)\, dx = 1$$

and

$$\int_{a}^{b} f(x)\, dx = P(a < x \leq b)$$

where $f(x)\, dx$ is known as the *probability element* (the probability associated with a small interval of a continuous variable) and where $P(a < x \leq b)$ means the probability that X lies in the interval a to b. Geometrically, we have Fig. A.1.

For a continuous rv, in contrast with a discrete rv, the probability that X takes a specific value is zero; probability for such a variable is measurable only over a given range or interval, such as (a, b) shown in Fig. A.1.

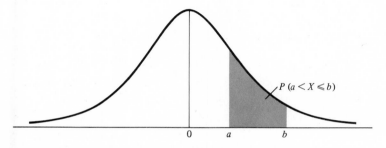

Figure A.1 Density function of a continuous random variable.

Joint Probability Density Functions

Discrete joint PDF Let X and Y be two discrete random variables. Then the function

$$f(x, y) = P(X = x \text{ and } Y = y)$$

$$= 0 \quad \text{when } X \neq x \text{ and } Y \neq y$$

is known as the *discrete joint probability density function* and gives the (joint) probability that X takes the value of x and Y takes the value of y.

In relation to $f(x, y)$, $f(x)$ and $f(y)$ are called *individual*, or *marginal*, probability density functions. These marginal PDFs are derived as follows:

$$f(x) = \sum_y f(x, y) \qquad \text{marginal PDF of } X$$

$$f(y) = \sum_x f(x, y) \qquad \text{marginal PDF of } Y$$

where, for example, $\sum_y$ means the sum over all values of Y.

Conditional PDF As noted in Chap. 2, in regression analysis we are often interested in studying the behavior of one variable conditional upon the values of another variable(s). This can be done by considering the conditional PDF. The function

$$f(x \mid y) = P(X = x \mid Y = y)$$

is known as the *conditional PDF of X*; it gives the probability that X takes on the value of x given that Y has assumed the value y. Similarly,

$$f(y \mid x) = P(Y = y \mid X = x)$$

which gives the *conditional PDF of Y*.

The conditional PDFs may be obtained as follows:

$$f(x \mid y) = \frac{f(x, y)}{f(y)} \qquad \text{conditional PDF of } X$$

$$f(y \mid x) = \frac{f(x, y)}{f(x)} \qquad \text{conditional PDF of } Y$$

As the preceding expressions show, the conditional PDF of one variable can be expressed as the ratio of the joint PDF to the marginal PDF of another variable.

Continuous joint PDF The PDF $f(x, y)$ of two continuous variables X and Y is such that

$$f(x, y) \geq 0$$

$$\int_{-\infty}^{\infty} \int_{-\infty}^{\infty} f(x, y) \, dx \, dy = 1$$

$$\int_c^d \int_a^b f(x, y) \, dx \, dy = P(a < x \leq b, c < y \leq d)$$

The marginal PDF of X and Y can be obtained as

$$f(x) = \int_{-\infty}^{\infty} f(x, y)\, dy \qquad \text{marginal PDF of } X$$

$$f(y) = \int_{-\infty}^{\infty} f(x, y)\, dx \qquad \text{marginal PDF of } Y$$

Statistical Independence

Two random variables X and Y are statistically independent if and only if

$$f(x, y) = f(x)f(y)$$

that is, if the joint PDF can be expressed as the product of the marginal PDFs.

A.4 CHARACTERISTICS OF PROBABILITY DISTRIBUTIONS

A probability distribution can often be summarized in terms of a few of its characteristics, known as the *moments* of the distribution. Two of the most widely used moments are the *mean*, or *expected value*, and the *variance*.

Expected Value

The expected value of a discrete rv X, denoted by $E(X)$, is defined as follows:

$$E(X) = \sum_{x} xf(x)$$

where $\sum_{x}$ means the sum over all values of X and where $f(x)$ is the (discrete) PDF of X.

> **Example A.1** Consider the probability distribution of the sum of two numbers in a throw of two dice given previously. Multiplying the various X values given there by their probabilities and summing over all the observations, we obtain $E(X) = 7$, which is the average value of the sum of numbers observed in a throw of two dice.

The expected value of continuous rv is defined as

$$E(X) = \int_{-\infty}^{\infty} xf(x)\, dx$$

The only difference between this case and the expected value of a discrete rv is that we replace the summation symbol by the integral symbol.

Properties of Expectations

1. The expected value of a constant is the constant itself. Thus, if b is a constant, $E(b) = b$.
2. If a and b are constants,

$$E(aX + b) = aE(X) + b$$

This can be generalized. If $X_1, X_2, \ldots, X_N$ are N random variables and $a_1, a_2, \ldots, a_N$ and b are constants, then

$$E(a_1 X_1 + a_2 X_2 + \cdots + a_N X_N + b)$$
$$= a_1 E(X_1) + a_2 E(X_2) + \cdots + a_N E(X_N) + b$$

3. If X and Y are independent random variables, then

$$E(XY) = E(X)E(Y)$$

that is, the expectation of the product XY is the product of the (individual) expectations of X and Y.

Variance

Let X be a random variable and let $E(X) = \mu$. The distribution, or spread, of the X values around the expected value can be measured by the variance, which is defined as

$$\text{var}(X) = \sigma_X^2 = E(X - \mu)^2$$

The positive square root of σ_X^2, σ_X is defined as the standard deviation of X. The variance or standard deviation gives an indication of how closely or widely the individual X values are spread around their mean value.

The variance defined previously is computed as follows:

$$\text{var}(X) = \sum_x (X - \mu)^2 f(x) \qquad \text{if } X \text{ is a discrete rv}$$

$$= \int_{-\infty}^{\infty} (X - \mu)^2 f(x)\, dx \qquad \text{if } X \text{ is a coninuous rv}$$

Properties of Variance

1. $E(X - \mu)^2 = E(X^2) - \mu^2$.
2. The variance of a constant is zero.
3. If a and b are constants, then

$$\text{var}(aX + b) = a^2 \, \text{var}(X)$$

4. If X and Y are independent random variables, then

$$\text{var}(X + Y) = \text{var}(X) + \text{var}(Y)$$

This can be generalized to more than two variables.

5. If X and Y are independent rvs and a and b are constants, then

$$\text{var} (aX + bY) = a^2 \text{ var} (X) + b^2 \text{ var} (Y)$$

Covariance

Let X and Y be two rvs with means μ_x and μ_y, respectively. Then, the covariance between the two variables is defined as

$$\text{cov} (X, Y) = E\{(X - \mu_x)(Y - \mu_y)\}$$

It can be readily seen that the variance of a variable is the covariance of that variable with itself.

The covariance is computed as follows:

$$\text{cov} (X, Y) = \sum_y \sum_x (X - \mu_x)(Y - \mu_y) f(x, y)$$

if X and Y are discrete random variables

and

$$\text{cov} (X, Y) = \int_{-\infty}^{\infty} \int_{-\infty}^{\infty} (X - \mu_x)(Y - \mu_y) f(x, y) \, dx \, dy$$

if X and Y are continuous random variables

In passing, note that if the rvs X and Y are independent, cov $(X, Y) = 0$.

Correlation Coefficient

The (population) correlation coefficient ρ (rho) is defined as

$$\rho = \frac{\text{cov} (X, Y)}{\sqrt{\{\text{var} (X) \text{ var} (Y)\}}} = \frac{\text{cov} (X, Y)}{\sigma_x \sigma_y}$$

ρ thus defined is a measure of *linear* association between two variables and lies between -1 and $+1$, -1 indicating perfect negative association and $+1$ indicating perfect positive association.

Variances of correlated variables Let X and Y be two rvs. Then,

$$\text{var} (X + Y) = \text{var} (X) + \text{var} (Y) + 2 \text{ cov} (X, Y)$$
$$= \text{var} (X) + \text{var} (Y) + 2\rho\sigma_x\sigma_y$$

and

$$\text{var} (X - Y) = \text{var} (X) + \text{var} (Y) - 2 \text{ cov} (X, Y)$$
$$= \text{var} (X) + \text{var} (Y) - 2\rho\sigma_x\sigma_y$$

If, however, X and Y are independent, cov (X, Y) is zero, in which case the var $(X + Y)$ and var $(X - Y)$ are both equal to var $(X) +$ var (Y), as noted previously.

Conditional Expectation and Conditional Variance

Let $f(x, y)$ be the joint PDF of random variables X and Y. The conditional expectation of X, given $Y = y$, is defined as

$$E(X \mid Y = y) = \sum_{x} x f(x \mid Y = y) \qquad \text{if } X \text{ is discrete}$$

$$= \int_{-\infty}^{\infty} x f(x \mid Y = y) \, dx \qquad \text{if } X \text{ is continuous}$$

where $E(X \mid Y = y)$ means the conditional expectation of X given $Y = y$ and where $f(x \mid Y = y)$ is the conditional PDF of X. The conditional expectation of Y, $E(Y \mid X = x)$, is defined similarly. Note that $E(X \mid Y = y)$, although a function of Y, is not a random variable since it is a function of a given value of $Y = y$.

Conditional Variance

The conditional variance of X given $Y = y$ is defined as

$$\text{var } (X \mid Y = y) = E\{[X - E(X \mid Y = y)]^2 \mid Y = y\}$$

$$= \sum_{x} [X - E(X \mid Y = y)]^2 f(x \mid Y = y) \qquad \text{if } X \text{ is discrete}$$

$$= \int_{-\infty}^{\infty} [X - E(X \mid Y = y)]^2 f(x \mid Y = y) \, dx \qquad \text{if } X \text{ is continuous}$$

A.5 SOME IMPORTANT THEORETICAL PROBABILITY DISTRIBUTIONS

In the text extensive use is made of the following probability distributions.

Normal Distribution

The best known of all the theoretical probability distributions is the normal distribution, whose bell-shaped picture is familiar to anyone with a modicum of statistical knowledge.

A (continuous) random variable X is said to be normally distributed if its PDF has the following form:

$$f(x) = \frac{1}{\sigma\sqrt{2\Pi}} \exp\left(-\frac{1}{2} \frac{(x - \mu)^2}{\sigma^2}\right) \qquad -\infty < x < \infty$$

where μ and σ^2, known as the *parameters of the distribution*, are, respectively, the mean and the variance of the distribution. The properties of this distribution are as follows:

1. It is symmetrical around its mean value.
2. Approximately 68 percent of the area under the normal curve lies between the

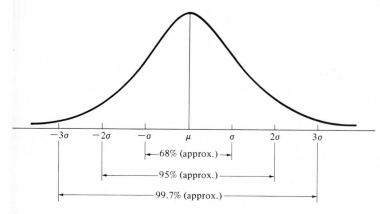

Figure A.2 Areas under the normal curve.

values of $\mu \pm \sigma$, about 95 percent of the area lies between $\mu \pm 2\sigma$, and about 99.7 percent of the area lies between $\mu \pm 3\sigma$, as shown in Fig. A.2.

3. Since the normal distribution depends on the two parameters μ and σ^2, once these are specified one can find out the probabilities of X lying within a certain interval by using the PDF of the normal distribution. But this task can be lightened considerably by referring to Table D.1 of App. D. To use this table, we convert the given normally distributed variable X with mean μ and σ^2 into a standardized normal variable Z by the following transformation:

$$z = \frac{x - \mu}{\sigma}$$

An important property of any standardized variable is that its mean value is zero and its variance is unity. Thus Z has zero mean and unit variance. Substituting z into the normal PDF given previously, we obtain

$$f(z) = \frac{1}{\sqrt{2\Pi}} \exp\left(-\frac{1}{2} z^2\right)$$

which is the PDF of the standardized normal variable. The probabilities given in App. D, Table D.1, are based on this standardized normal variable.

By convention, we denote a normally distributed variable as

$$X \sim N(\mu, \sigma^2)$$

where $\sim$ means "distributed as," N stands for the normal distribution, and the quantities in the parentheses are the two parameters of the normal distribution, namely, the mean and the variance. Following this convention,

$$X \sim N(0, 1)$$

means X is a normally distributed variable with zero mean and unit variance. In other words, it is a standardized normal variable Z.

The χ^2 Distribution

Let $Z_1, Z_2, \ldots, Z_k$ be independent standardized normal variables (i.e., normal variables with zero mean and unit variance). Then, the quantity

$$Z = \sum_{i=1}^{k} Z_i^2$$

is said to possess the χ^2 distribution with k degrees of freedom (df), where the term df means the number of independent quantities in the previous sum. A chi-squared-distributed variable is denoted by χ_k^2, where the subscript k indicates the df. Geometrically, the chi-square distribution appears in Fig. A.3.

Properties of the χ^2 distribution

1. As Fig. A.3 shows, the χ^2 distribution is a skewed distribution, the degree of skewness depending on the df. For comparatively few df, the distribution is highly skewed to the right; but as the df increase, the distribution becomes increasing symmetrical. As a matter of fact, for df in excess of 100, the variable

$$\sqrt{2\chi^2} - \sqrt{(2k-1)}$$

can be treated as a standardized normal variable, where k is the df.
2. The mean of the chi-square distribution is k, and its variance is $2k$, where k is the df.
3. If Z_1 and Z_2 are two independent chi-square variables with k_1 and k_2 df, then, the sum $Z_1 + Z_2$ is also a chi-square variable with df $= k_1 + k_2$.

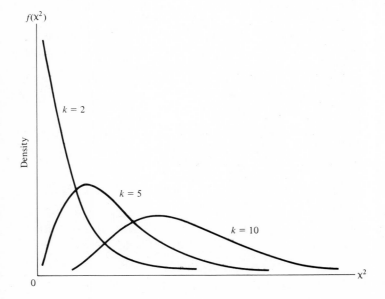

Figure A.3 Density function of the χ^2 variable.

Student's t Distribution

If Z_1 is a standardized normal variable [that is, $Z_1 \sim N(0, 1)$] and another variable Z_2 follows the chi-square distribution with k df and is distributed independently of Z_1, then the variable defined as

$$t = \frac{Z_1}{\sqrt{(Z_2/k)}}$$

$$= \frac{Z_1\sqrt{k}}{\sqrt{Z_2}}$$

follows Student's t distribution with k df. A t-distributed variable is often designated as t_k, where the subscript k denotes the df. Geometrically, the t distribution is shown in Fig. A.4.

Properties of the t distribution

1. As Fig. A.4 shows, the t distribution, like the normal distribution, is symmetrical but flatter than the normal distribution. But as the df increase, the t distribution approximates the normal distribution.
2. The mean of the t distribution is zero, and its variance is $k/(k - 2)$.

The t distribution is tabulated in Table D.2, App. D.

The F Distribution

If Z_1 and Z_2 are independently distributed chi-square variables with k_1 and k_2 df, respectively, the variable

$$F = \frac{Z_1/k_1}{Z_2/k_2}$$

follows (Fisher's) F distribution with k_1 and k_2 df. An F-distributed variable is denoted by F_{k_1, k_2} where the subscripts indicate the df associated with the two Z

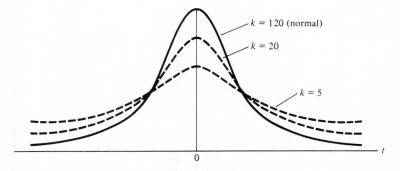

$k = 120$ (normal)

$k = 20$

$k = 5$

Figure A.4 t distribution for selected degrees of freedom.

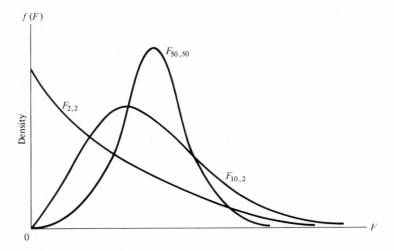

Figure A.5 F distribution for various degrees of freedom.

variables, k_1 being called the *numerator df* and k_2 the *denominator df*. Geometrically, the F distribution is shown in Fig. A.5.

Properties of the F distribution

1. Like the chi-square distribution, the F distribution is also skewed to the right. But it can be shown that as k_1 and k_2 become large, the F distribution approaches the normal distribution.
2. The mean value of an F-distributed variable is $k_2/(k_2 - 2)$, which is defined for $k_2 > 2$, and its variance is

$$\frac{2k_2^2(k_1 + k_2 - 2)}{k_1(k_2 - 2)^2(k_2 - 4)}$$

which is defined for $k_2 > 4$.
3. The square of a t-distributed random variable with k df has an F distribution with 1 and k df. Symbolically,

$$t_k^2 = F_{1,k}$$

In passing, note that since for large df, the t, chi-square, and F distributions approach the normal distribution, these three distributions are known as the *distributions related to the normal distribution*.

A.6 STATISTICAL INFERENCE: ESTIMATION

In Sec. A.5 we considered several theoretical probability distributions. Very often we know or are willing to assume that a random variable X follows a particular probability distribution but do not know the value(s) of a (the) parameter(s) of the distribution. For example, if X follows the normal distribution, we may want to know the values of its two parameters, namely, the mean and the variance. To estimate the unknowns, the usual procedure is to assume that we have a random sample of size N from the known probability distribution and use the sample data to estimate the unknown parameters.[2] This is known as the *problem of estimation*. In this section, we take a closer look at this problem. The problem of estimation can be broken down into two categories: point estimation and interval estimation.

Point Estimation

To fix the ideas, let X be a rv with PDF $f(x; \theta)$, where θ is the parameter of the distribution (for simplicity of discussion only, we are assuming that there is only one unknown parameter; our discussion can be readily generalized). Assume that we know the functional form, that is, we know the theoretical PDF, such as the t distribution, but do not know the value of θ. Therefore, we draw a random sample of size N from this known PDF and then develop a function of the sample values such that

$$\hat{\theta} = f(x_1, x_2, \ldots, x_N)$$

provides us an estimate of the true θ. $\hat{\theta}$ is known as a *statistic*, or an *estimator*, and a particular numerical value taken by the estimator is known as an *estimate*. Note that $\hat{\theta}$ can be treated as a random variable because it is a function of the sample data. $\hat{\theta}$ provides us with a rule, or formula, that tells us how we may estimate the true θ. Thus, if we let

$$\hat{\theta} = \frac{1}{N}(x_1 + x_2 + \cdots + x_N) = \bar{X}$$

where $\bar{X}$ is the sample mean, then $\bar{X}$ is an estimator of the true mean value, say, μ. If in a specific case $\bar{X} = 50$, then this provides an estimate of μ. The estimator $\hat{\theta}$ obtained previously is known as a *point estimator* because it provides only a single (point) estimate of θ.

Interval Estimation

Instead of obtaining only a single estimate of θ, suppose we obtain two estimates of θ by constructing two estimators $\hat{\theta}_1(x_1, x_2, \ldots, x_N)$ and $\hat{\theta}_2(x_1, x_2, \ldots, x_N)$, and say with some confidence (i.e., probability) that the interval between $\hat{\theta}_1$ and $\hat{\theta}_2$

---

[2] Let $X_1, X_2, \ldots, X_N$ be N random variables with joint PDF $f(x_1, x_2, \ldots, x_N)$. If we can write

$$f(x_1, x_2, \ldots, x_N) = f(x_1)f(x_2) \cdots f(x_N)$$

where $f(x_i)$ is the common PDF of each X, then $x_1, x_2, \ldots, x_N$ is said to constitute a random sample of size N from a population with PDF $f(x_i)$.

includes the true θ. Thus, in interval estimation, in contrast with point estimation, we provide a range of possible values within which the true θ may lie.

The key concept underlying interval estimation is the notion of the *sampling,* or *probability distribution, of an estimator.* For example it can be shown that if a variable X is normally distributed, then, the sample mean $\bar{X}$ is also normally distributed with mean $= \mu$ (the true mean) and variance $= \sigma^2/N$, where N is the sample size. In other words, the sampling or probability distribution of the estimator $\bar{X}$ is: $\bar{X} \sim N(\mu, \sigma^2/N)$. As a result, if we construct the interval

$$\bar{X} \pm 2 \frac{\sigma}{\sqrt{N}}$$

and say that the probability is approximately 0.95 or 95 percent that intervals like it will include true μ, we are, in fact, constructing an interval estimator for μ. Note that the interval given previously is random since it is based on $\bar{X}$, which will vary from sample to sample.

More generally, in interval estimation, we construct two estimators $\hat{\theta}_1$ and $\hat{\theta}_2$, both function of the sample X values, such that

$$\Pr\left(\hat{\theta}_1 \leq \theta \leq \hat{\theta}_2\right) = 1 - \alpha \qquad 0 < \alpha < 1$$

that is, we can state that the probability is $1 - \alpha$ that the interval from $\hat{\theta}_1$ to $\hat{\theta}_2$ contains the true θ. This interval is known as a *confidence interval* of size $1 - \alpha$ for θ, $1 - \alpha$ being known as the *confidence coefficient.* If $\alpha = 0.05$, then $1 - \alpha = 0.95$, meaning that if we construct a confidence interval with a confidence coefficient of 0.95, then in repeated such constructions resulting from repeated sampling we shall be right in 95 out of 100 cases if we maintain that the interval contains the true θ. When the confidence coefficient is 0.95, we often say that we have a 95 percent confidence interval. In general, if the confidence coefficient is $1 - \alpha$, we say that we have a $100(1 - \alpha)$ percent confidence interval.

There are several methods of obtaining point estimators, the best known being the methods of maximum likelihood (ML) and least squares. We have discussed the method of least squares in depth in the text and alluded to the method of ML. Both these methods possess several desirable statistical properties, which we consider next.

Properties of Point Estimators

The desirable statistical properties fall into two categories: small-sample, or finite-sample, properties and large-sample, or asymptotic, properties. Underlying both these sets of properties is the notion that an estimator has a sampling, or probability, distribution.

Small-sample properties

1. *Unbiasedness.* An estimator $\hat{\theta}$ is said to be an unbiased estimator of θ if the expected value of $\hat{\theta}$ is equal to the true θ; that is,

$$E(\hat{\theta}) = \theta$$

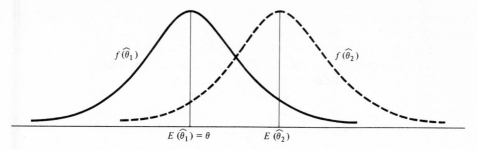

Figure A.6 Biased and unbiased estimators.

If this equality does not hold, then the estimator is said to be biased. Geometrically, we have Fig. A.6, which shows two estimators of θ (obtained by two different methods). It is clear that $\hat{\theta}_1$ is unbiased, whereas $\hat{\theta}_2$ is a biased estimator because its mean or expected value is not equal to true θ.

In passing, note that unbiasedness is a property of repeated sampling, not of any given sample: Keeping the sample size fixed, we draw several samples, each time obtaining an estimate of the unknown parameter. The average value of these estimates is expected to be equal to the true value if the estimator is to be unbiased.

2. *Minimum variance.* $\hat{\theta}_1$ is said to be a minimum-variance estimator of θ if the variance of $\hat{\theta}_1$ is smaller than or at most equal to the variance of $\hat{\theta}_2$, which is any other estimator of θ. Geometrically, we have Fig. A.7, which shows three estimators of θ, namely, $\hat{\theta}_1$, $\hat{\theta}_2$, and $\hat{\theta}_3$ and their probability distributions. As shown, the variance of $\hat{\theta}_3$ is smaller than that of either $\hat{\theta}_1$ or $\hat{\theta}_2$. Hence, assuming only the three possible estimators, in this case $\hat{\theta}_3$ is a minimum-variance estimator. But note that $\hat{\theta}_3$ is a biased estimator.

3. *Efficiency.* If $\hat{\theta}_1$ and $\hat{\theta}_2$ are two *unbiased* estimators of θ, and the variance of $\hat{\theta}_1$ is smaller than or at most equal to the variance of $\hat{\theta}_2$, then $\hat{\theta}_1$ is said to be a

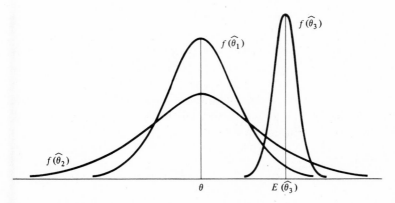

Figure A.7 Distribution of three estimators of θ.

minimum-variance unbiased, or *efficient*, estimator. Thus in Fig. A.7, of the two unbiased estimators $\hat{\theta}_1$ and $\hat{\theta}_2$, $\hat{\theta}_1$ is an efficient estimator.

4. *Linearity*. An estimator $\hat{\theta}$ is said to be a linear estimator of θ if it is a linear function of the sample observations. Thus, the sample mean defined as

$$\bar{X} = \frac{1}{N} \sum X_i = \frac{1}{N}(x_1 + x_2 + \cdots + x_N)$$

is a linear estimator because it is a linear function of the X values.

5. *Best linear unbiased estimator (BLUE)*. If $\hat{\theta}$ is linear, is unbiased and has minimum variance in the class of all linear unbiased estimators of θ, then it is called a *best linear unbiased estimator*, or BLUE for short.

Large-sample properties Often it happens that an estimator does not satisfy one or more of the desirable statistical properties in small samples. But as the sample size increases indefinitely, the estimator possesses several desirable statistical properties. These properties are known as the *large sample*, or *asymptotic*, *properties*.

1. *Asymptotic unbiasedness*. An estimator $\hat{\theta}$ is said to be an asymptotically unbiased estimator of θ if

$$\lim_{N \to \infty} E(\hat{\theta}) = \theta$$

where lim means limit and where N denotes the sample size. In words, $\hat{\theta}$ is an asymptotically unbiased estimator of θ if its expected, or mean, value approaches the true value as the sample size gets larger and larger. As an example, consider the following measure of the sample variance of a random variable X:

$$S^2 = \frac{\sum (X_i - \bar{X})^2}{N}$$

Now it can be shown that

$$E(S^2) = \sigma^2 \left(1 - \frac{1}{N}\right)$$

where σ^2 is the true variance. It is obvious that in a small sample S^2 is biased, but as N increases indefinitely, $E(S^2)$ approaches true σ^2; hence it is asymptotically unbiased.

2. *Consistency*. $\hat{\theta}$ is said to be a consistent estimator if it approaches the true value θ as the sample size gets larger and larger. Geometrically, we have Fig. A.8, which gives the sampling distribution of $\hat{\theta}$ based on varying sample sizes. It shows that as the sample size increases, the variance of $\hat{\theta}$ becomes progressively smaller. If in the limit (i.e., when the sample size increases indefinitely) the distribution of $\hat{\theta}$ collapses to the single point θ, that is, if the distribution of $\hat{\theta}$ has zero spread, or variance, we say that $\hat{\theta}$ is a *consistent estimator* θ.

More formally, an estimator $\hat{\theta}$ is said to be a consistent estimator of θ if the probability of the absolute value of the difference between $\hat{\theta}$ and θ being less than

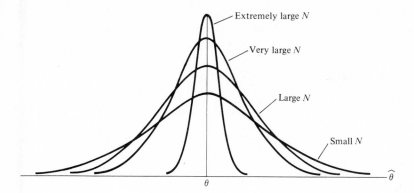

Figure A.8 Property of consistency.

δ (an arbitrarily small positive quantity) approaches unity. Symbolically,

$$\lim_{N \to \infty} P\{|\hat{\theta} - \theta| < \delta\} = 1 \qquad \delta > 0$$

where P stands for probability. This is often expressed as

$$\operatorname*{plim}_{N \to \infty} \hat{\theta} = \theta$$

where plim means probability limit.

Note that the properties of unbiasedness and consistency are conceptually very much different. The property of unbiasedness can hold for any sample size, whereas consistency is strictly a large-sample property.

To find out whether an estimator is consistent, the sufficient conditions are that

$$\lim_{N \to \infty} E(\hat{\theta}) = \theta$$

and

$$\lim_{N \to \infty} \operatorname{var}(\hat{\theta}) = 0$$

That is, $\hat{\theta}$ is asymptotically unbiased, and as N increases indefinitely, the variance of $\hat{\theta}$ approaches 0. In other words, the distribution of $\hat{\theta}$ becomes increasingly concentrated on true θ as N increases indefinitely.

The following rules about probability limits are noteworthy.

(a) *Invariance (Slutsky property)*. If $\hat{\theta}$ is a consistent estimator of θ and if $h(\hat{\theta})$ is any continuous function of $\hat{\theta}$, then

$$\operatorname*{plim}_{N \to \infty} h(\hat{\theta}) = h(\theta)$$

What this means is that if $\hat{\theta}$ is a consistent estimator of θ, then $1/\hat{\theta}$ is also a consistent estimator of $1/\theta$ or that $\log(\hat{\theta})$ is also a consistent estimator of $\log(\theta)$. Note that this property does not hold true of the expectation operator E; that is, if $\hat{\theta}$ is an unbiased estimator of θ [that is, $E(\hat{\theta}) = \theta$], it is *not true* that $1/\hat{\theta}$ is an unbiased estimator of $1/\theta$, that is, $E(1/\hat{\theta}) \neq 1/E(\hat{\theta}) \neq 1/\theta$.

(b) If b is a constant, then

$$\underset{N \to \infty}{\text{plim}} \, b = b$$

that is, the probability limit of a constant is the same constant.

(c) If $\hat{\theta}_1$ and $\hat{\theta}_2$ are consistent estimators, then

$$\text{plim} \, (\hat{\theta}_1 + \hat{\theta}_2) = \text{plim} \, \hat{\theta}_1 + \text{plim} \, \hat{\theta}_2$$

$$\text{plim} \, (\hat{\theta}_1 \hat{\theta}_2) = \text{plim} \, \hat{\theta}_1 \, \text{plim} \, \hat{\theta}_2$$

$$\text{plim} \left(\frac{\hat{\theta}_1}{\hat{\theta}_2} \right) = \frac{\text{plim} \, \hat{\theta}_1}{\text{plim} \, \hat{\theta}_2}$$

The last two properties, in general, do not hold true of the expectation operator E. Thus, $E(\hat{\theta}_1 / \hat{\theta}_2) \neq E(\hat{\theta}_1)/E(\hat{\theta}_2)$. Similarly, $E(\hat{\theta}_1 \hat{\theta}_2) \neq E(\hat{\theta}_1)E(\hat{\theta}_2)$. If, however, $\hat{\theta}_1$ and $\hat{\theta}_2$ are independently distributed, $E(\hat{\theta}_1 \hat{\theta}_2) = E(\hat{\theta}_1)E(\hat{\theta}_2)$, as noted previously.

3. *Asymptotic normality.* An estimator $\hat{\theta}$ is said to be asymptotically normally distributed if its sampling distribution tends to approach the normal distribution as the sample size N increases indefinitely. For example, it can be shown that if $X_1, X_2, \ldots, X_N$ are independent random variables all having the same PDF (not necessarily normal) with mean μ and variance σ^2, then the sample mean $\bar{X}$ is asymptotically normally distributed with mean μ and variance σ^2/N. This is one form in which the celebrated *central limit theorem* of statistics is often stated. Incidentally, note that if the X_i are normally and independently distributed with mean μ and variance σ^2, the sample mean $\bar{X}$ is normally distributed with the same mean and variance σ^2/N in small as well as large samples.

A.7 STATISTICAL INFERENCE: HYPOTHESIS TESTING

Estimation and hypothesis testing constitute the twin branches of classical statistical inference. Having examined the problem of estimation, we briefly look at the problem of testing statistical hypothesis.

The problem of hypothesis testing may be stated as follows: Assume that we have a rv X with a known PDF $f(x; \theta)$, where θ is the parameter of the distribution. Having obtained a random sample of size N, we obtain the point estimator $\hat{\theta}$. Since the true θ is rarely known, we raise the question: Is the estimated $\hat{\theta}$ " compatible" with some hypothesized value of θ, say, $\theta = \theta^*$, where θ^* is a specific numerical value of θ? In other words, could our sample have come from the PDF $f(x; \theta = \theta^*)$? In the language of hypothesis testing $\theta = \theta^*$ is called the *null* (or maintained) *hypothesis* and is generally denoted by H_0. The null hypothesis is tested against an *alternative hypothesis*, denoted by H_1, which, for example, may state that $\theta \neq \theta^*$. (*Note:* In some textbooks, H_0 and H_1 are designated by H_1 and H_2, respectively.)

The null hypothesis as well as the alternative hypothesis can be *simple* or *composite*. A hypothesis is called *simple* if it specifies the value(s) of the parameter(s) of the distribution; otherwise it is called a *composite* hypothesis. Thus, if $X \sim N(\mu, \sigma^2)$ and we state that

$$H_0: \quad \mu = 15 \quad \text{and} \quad \sigma = 2$$

it is a simple hypothesis, whereas if we state that

$$H_0: \quad \mu = 15 \quad \text{and} \quad \sigma > 2$$

it is a composite hypothesis because here the value of σ is not specified.

To test the null hypothesis (i.e., to test its validity), we use the sample information to obtain what is known as the *test statistic*. Very often this test statistic turns out to be the point estimator of the unknown parameter. To illustrate, let $X \sim N(\mu, 1)$; that is, X is normally distributed with mean μ (which is unknown) and variance 1 (which is known in advance). Now suppose we posit that

$$H_0: \quad \mu = \mu^*$$

and

$$H_1: \quad \mu \neq \mu^*$$

where μ^* is a specific numerical value of the mean μ.

To test the null hypothesis, suppose we obtain a random sample of size N and compute the sample mean $\bar{X}$ and use it as a test statistic. Intuitively, we might accept the null hypothesis that $\mu = \mu^*$ if $\bar{X}$ is "sufficiently close" to μ^*; otherwise we may reject it in favor of the alternative hypothesis. How do we decide if $\bar{X}$ is sufficiently close to μ^*? Recall that the sample mean $\bar{X}$ follows the normal distribution with mean $= \mu$ and variance $\sigma^2/N = 1/N$ since in the present example $\sigma^2 = 1$. (Note that since X follows the normal distribution, so does $\bar{X}$ in small as well as large samples.) Therefore, if H_0 is true, the interval

$$\mu^* \pm 1.96 \frac{1}{\sqrt{N}}$$

has a 95 percent chance of including $\bar{X}$. Diagramatically, we have Fig. A.9.

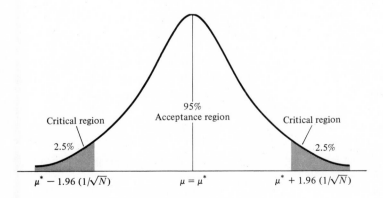

Figure A.9 Acceptance and critical regions.

Therefore, if the sample mean $\bar{X}$ falls within the preceding interval, we may accept the null hypothesis that our sample comes from a population with mean $= \mu^*$ and variance $= 1$. In the language of hypothesis testing, the preceding interval is called the (95 percent) *acceptance region* and the area(s) outside the acceptance region is (are) called the *critical region(s)*, or the *region(s) of rejection* of the null hypothesis. If the test statistic falls in the acceptance region, one may accept the null hypothesis; whereas if it falls in the critical region(s), one may reject the null hypothesis.

It should be noted that in deciding to accept or reject H_0, we are likely to commit two types of errors: (1) We may reject H_0 when it is, in fact, true; this is called *type I error*. In this case $\bar{X}$ lies in the critical region although the X values observed in the sample did, in fact, come from the population with mean $\mu = \mu^*$. (2) We may accept H_0 when it is, in fact, false; this is called *type II error*. In this case $\bar{X}$ lies in the acceptance region although the sample of X values did come from a population whose mean value was different from μ^*. Therefore, a hypothesis test does not establish the value of true μ. It merely provides a means of deciding whether we may act as if $\mu = \mu^*$.

Ideally, we would like to minimize both type I and type II errors. But unfortunately, for any given sample size, it is not possible to minimize both the errors simultaneously. The classical approach to this problem, embodied in the work of Neyman and Pearson, is to assume that a type I error is likely to be more serious in practice than a type II error. Therefore, one should try to keep the probability of committing a type I error at a fairly low level, such as 0.01 or 0.05, and then try to minimize the type II error as much as possible.

In the literature the probability of type I error is designated as α and is called the *level of significance*, and the probability of type II error is designated as β. The probability of not committing type II error, $1 - \beta$, is called the *power of the test*. The classical approach to hypothesis testing is to fix α at levels such as 0.01 or 0.05 and then try to maximize the power of the test; that is, minimize β. How this is actually accomplished is somewhat involved, and we leave the subject for the references. Suffice it to note here that in practice the classical approach simply specifies the value of α without worrying too much about β.

A.8 REFERENCES

For the details of the material covered in this appendix, the reader may consult the following references:

Hoel, Paul G.: *Introduction to Mathematical Statistics*, 4th ed., John Wiley & Sons, Inc., New York, 1974. This book provides a fairly simple introduction to various aspects of mathematical statistics.

Mood, Alexander M., Franklin A. Graybill, and Duane C. Boes: *Introduction to the Theory of Statistics*, 3d ed., McGraw-Hill Book Company, New York, 1974. This is a comprehensive yet very readable introduction to the theory of statistics, and it can also be used as a reference book.

RUDIMENTS OF MATRIX ALGEBRA

This appendix offers the essentials of matrix algebra required to understand Chap. 8 and some of the material in Chap. 17. The discussion is nonrigorous, and no proofs are given. For proofs and further details, the reader may consult Sec. B.7.

B.1 DEFINITIONS

Matrix

A matrix is a rectangular array of numbers or elements arranged in rows and columns. More precisely, a matrix of *order*, or *dimension*, M by N (written as $M \times N$) is a set of $M \times N$ elements arranged in M rows and N columns. Thus, letting the boldface letters denote matrices, an $(M \times N)$ matrix $\mathbf{A}$ may be expressed as

$$
\mathbf{A} = [a_{ij}] = \begin{bmatrix} a_{11} & a_{12} & a_{13} & \cdots & a_{1N} \\ a_{21} & a_{22} & a_{23} & \cdots & a_{2N} \\ \cdots\cdots\cdots\cdots\cdots\cdots\cdots\cdots\cdots\cdots \\ a_{M1} & a_{M2} & a_{M3} & \cdots & a_{MN} \end{bmatrix}
$$

where a_{ij} is the element appearing in the ith row and the jth column of $\mathbf{A}$ and where $[a_{ij}]$ is a shorthand expression for the matrix $\mathbf{A}$ whose typical element is a_{ij}. The order, or dimension, of a matrix, that is, the number of rows and columns, is often written underneath the matrix for easy reference.

Examples

$$\underset{2 \times 3}{A} = \begin{bmatrix} 2 & 3 & 5 \\ 6 & 1 & 3 \end{bmatrix} \qquad \underset{3 \times 3}{B} = \begin{bmatrix} 1 & 5 & 7 \\ -1 & 0 & 4 \\ 8 & 9 & 11 \end{bmatrix}$$

Scalar

A scalar is a single (real) number. Alternatively, a scalar is a 1×1 matrix.

Column Vector

A matrix consisting of M rows and only one column is called a column vector. Letting the boldface lowercase letters denote vectors, an example of a column vector is

$$\underset{4 \times 1}{x} = \begin{bmatrix} 3 \\ 4 \\ 5 \\ 9 \end{bmatrix}$$

Row Vector

A matrix consisting of only one row and N columns is called a row vector.

Examples

$$\underset{1 \times 4}{x} = \begin{bmatrix} 1 & 2 & 5 & -4 \end{bmatrix} \qquad \underset{1 \times 5}{y} = \begin{bmatrix} 0 & 5 & -9 & 6 & 10 \end{bmatrix}$$

Transposition

The transpose of an $M \times N$ matrix A, denoted by A' (read as A prime or A transpose) is an $N \times M$ matrix obtained by interchanging the rows and columns of A; that is, the ith row of A becomes the ith column of A'.

Example

$$\underset{3 \times 2}{A} = \begin{bmatrix} 4 & 5 \\ 3 & 1 \\ 5 & 0 \end{bmatrix} \qquad \underset{2 \times 3}{A'} = \begin{bmatrix} 4 & 3 & 5 \\ 5 & 1 & 0 \end{bmatrix}$$

Since vectors are a special type of matrices, the transpose of a row vector is a column vector and the transpose of a column vector is a row vector. Thus

$$x = \begin{bmatrix} 4 \\ 5 \\ 6 \end{bmatrix} \qquad \text{and} \qquad x' = \begin{bmatrix} 4 & 5 & 6 \end{bmatrix}$$

We shall follow the convention of indicating the row vectors by primes.

Submatrix

Given any $M \times N$ matrix **A**, if all but r rows and s columns of **A** are deleted, the resulting matrix of order $r \times s$ is called a submatrix of **A**. Thus, if

$$\underset{3 \times 3}{\mathbf{A}} = \begin{bmatrix} 3 & 5 & 7 \\ 8 & 2 & 1 \\ 3 & 2 & 1 \end{bmatrix}$$

and if we delete the third row and the third column of the preceding matrix, we obtain

$$\underset{2 \times 2}{\mathbf{B}} = \begin{bmatrix} 3 & 5 \\ 8 & 2 \end{bmatrix}$$

which is a submatrix of **A** whose order is 2×2.

B.2 TYPES OF MATRICES

Square Matrix

A matrix which has the same number of rows as columns is called a square matrix.
   Examples

$$\mathbf{A} = \begin{bmatrix} 3 & 4 \\ 5 & 6 \end{bmatrix} \qquad \mathbf{B} = \begin{bmatrix} 3 & 5 & 8 \\ 7 & 3 & 1 \\ 4 & 5 & 0 \end{bmatrix}$$

Diagonal Matrix

A square matrix with at least one nonzero element on the main diagonal (running from the upper-left-hand corner to the lower-right-hand corner) and zeros elsewhere is called a diagonal matrix.

   Example

$$\underset{2 \times 2}{\mathbf{A}} = \begin{bmatrix} 2 & 0 \\ 0 & 3 \end{bmatrix} \qquad \underset{3 \times 3}{\mathbf{B}} = \begin{bmatrix} -2 & 0 & 0 \\ 0 & 5 & 0 \\ 0 & 0 & 1 \end{bmatrix}$$

Scalar Matrix

A diagonal matrix whose diagonal elements are all equal is called a scalar matrix. An example is the variance-covariance matrix of the population disturbance of the classical linear regression model given in equation (8.2.5), namely,

$$\text{var-cov}(\mathbf{u}) = \begin{bmatrix} \sigma^2 & 0 & 0 & 0 & 0 \\ 0 & \sigma^2 & 0 & 0 & 0 \\ 0 & 0 & \sigma^2 & 0 & 0 \\ 0 & 0 & 0 & \sigma^2 & 0 \\ 0 & 0 & 0 & 0 & \sigma^2 \end{bmatrix}$$

Identity, or Unit, Matrix

A diagonal matrix whose diagonal elements are all unity is called an identity or unit matrix and is denoted by **I**. It is a special kind of scalar matrix whose diagonal elements are all 1s.

Examples

$$\mathbf{I}_{3 \times 3} = \begin{bmatrix} 1 & 0 & 0 \\ 0 & 1 & 0 \\ 0 & 0 & 1 \end{bmatrix} \qquad \mathbf{I}_{4 \times 4} = \begin{bmatrix} 1 & 0 & 0 & 0 \\ 0 & 1 & 0 & 0 \\ 0 & 0 & 1 & 0 \\ 0 & 0 & 0 & 1 \end{bmatrix}$$

Symmetric Matrix

A square matrix whose elements above the main diagonal are mirror images of the elements below the main diagonal is called a symmetric matrix. Alternatively, a symmetric matrix is such that its transpose is equal to itself; that is, $\mathbf{A} = \mathbf{A}'$. That is, the elements a_{ij} of $\mathbf{A}$ is equal to the element a_{ji} of $\mathbf{A}'$. An example is the variance-covariance matrix given in equation (8.2.4). Another example is the correlation matrix given in (8.8.1).

Null Matrix

A matrix whose elements are all zero is called a null matrix and is denoted by **0**.

Null Vector

A row or column vector whose elements are all zero is called a null vector and is also denoted by **0**.

Equal Matrices

Two matrices **A** and **B** are said to be equal if they are of the same order and their corresponding elements are equal; that is, $a_{ij} = b_{ij}$ for all i and j.

Example If

$$\mathbf{A}_{3 \times 3} = \begin{bmatrix} 3 & 4 & 5 \\ 0 & -1 & 2 \\ 5 & 1 & 3 \end{bmatrix} \qquad \text{and} \qquad \mathbf{B}_{3 \times 3} = \begin{bmatrix} 3 & 4 & 5 \\ 0 & -1 & 2 \\ 5 & 1 & 3 \end{bmatrix}$$

then $\mathbf{A} = \mathbf{B}$.

B.3 MATRIX OPERATIONS

Matrix Addition

Let $A = [a_{ij}]$ and $B = [b_{ij}]$. If A and B are of the same order, we define matrix addition as

$$A + B = C$$

where C is of the same order as A and B and is obtained as $c_{ij} = a_{ij} + b_{ij}$ for all i and j; that is, C is obtained by adding the corresponding elements of A and B. If such addition can be effected, A and B are said to be *conformable* for addition.

Example If

$$A = \begin{bmatrix} 2 & 3 & 4 & 5 \\ 6 & 7 & 8 & 9 \end{bmatrix} \quad \text{and} \quad B = \begin{bmatrix} 1 & 0 & -1 & 3 \\ -2 & 0 & 1 & 5 \end{bmatrix}$$

then

$$C = \begin{bmatrix} 3 & 3 & 3 & 8 \\ 4 & 7 & 9 & 14 \end{bmatrix}$$

Matrix Subtraction

Matrix subtraction follows the same principle as matrix addition except that $C = A - B$; that is, we subtract the elements of B from the corresponding elements of A to obtain C, provided A and B are of the same order.

Scalar Multiplication

To multiply a matrix A by a scalar λ (a real number), we multiply each element of the matrix by λ:

$$\lambda A = [\lambda a_{ij}]$$

Example If $\lambda = 2$ and $A = \begin{bmatrix} -3 & 5 \\ 8 & 7 \end{bmatrix}$, then

$$\lambda A = \begin{bmatrix} -6 & 10 \\ 16 & 14 \end{bmatrix}$$

Matrix Multiplication

Let A be $M \times N$ and B be $N \times P$. Then the product AB (in that order) is defined to be a new matrix C of order $M \times P$ such that

$$c_{ij} = \sum_{k=1}^{N} a_{ik} b_{kj} \qquad \begin{aligned} i &= 1, 2, \ldots, M \\ j &= 1, 2, \ldots, P \end{aligned}$$

that is, the element in the ith row and the jth column of C is obtained by multiplying the elements of the ith row of A by the corresponding elements of the jth column of **B** and summing over all terms; this is known as the *row by column* rule of multiplication. Thus, to obtain c_{11}, the element in the first row and the first column of **C**, we multiply the elements in the first row of **A** by the corresponding elements in the first column of **B** and sum over all terms. Similarly, to obtain c_{12}, we multiply the elements in the first row of **A** by the corresponding elements in the second column of **B** and sum over all terms, and so on.

Note that for multiplication to exist, matrices **A** and **B** must be conformable with respect to multiplication; that is, the number of columns in **A** must be equal to the number of rows in **B**.

Examples If

$$\underset{2 \times 3}{\mathbf{A}} = \begin{bmatrix} 3 & 4 & 7 \\ 5 & 6 & 1 \end{bmatrix} \quad \text{and} \quad \underset{3 \times 2}{\mathbf{B}} = \begin{bmatrix} 2 & 1 \\ 3 & 5 \\ 6 & 2 \end{bmatrix}$$

then $\mathbf{C} = \mathbf{AB} = \begin{bmatrix} (3 \times 2) + (4 \times 3) + (7 \times 6) & (3 \times 1) + (4 \times 5) + (7 \times 2) \\ (5 \times 2) + (6 \times 3) + (1 \times 6) & (5 \times 1) + (6 \times 5) + (1 \times 2) \end{bmatrix}$

$$= \begin{bmatrix} 60 & 37 \\ 34 & 37 \end{bmatrix}$$

But if

$$\underset{2 \times 3}{\mathbf{A}} = \begin{bmatrix} 3 & 4 & 7 \\ 5 & 6 & 1 \end{bmatrix} \quad \text{and} \quad \underset{2 \times 2}{\mathbf{B}} = \begin{bmatrix} 2 & 3 \\ 5 & 6 \end{bmatrix}$$

the product **AB** is not defined since **A** and **B** are not conformable with respect to multiplication.

Properties of Matrix Multiplication

1. Matrix multiplication is not necessarily *commutative;* that is, in general, **AB** $\neq$ **BA**. Therefore, the order in which the matrices are multiplied is very important. **AB** means that **A** is *postmultiplied* by **B** or **B** is *premultiplied* by **A**.
2. Even if **AB** and **BA** exist, the resulting matrices may not be of the same order. Thus, if **A** is $M \times N$ and **B** is $N \times M$, **AB** is $M \times M$ whereas **BA** is $N \times N$, hence of different order.
3. Even if **A** and **B** are both square matrices, so that **AB** and **BA** are both defined, the resulting matrices will not be necessarily equal.

Example If

$$\mathbf{A} = \begin{bmatrix} 4 & 7 \\ 3 & 2 \end{bmatrix} \quad \text{and} \quad \mathbf{B} = \begin{bmatrix} 1 & 5 \\ 6 & 8 \end{bmatrix}$$

then, $\quad \mathbf{AB} = \begin{bmatrix} 46 & 76 \\ 15 & 31 \end{bmatrix} \quad \text{and} \quad \mathbf{BA} = \begin{bmatrix} 19 & 17 \\ 48 & 58 \end{bmatrix}$

Thus, $\mathbf{AB} \neq \mathbf{BA}$. An example of $\mathbf{AB} = \mathbf{BA}$ is when both $\mathbf{A}$ and $\mathbf{B}$ are square and are identity matrices.

4. A row vector postmultiplied by a column vector is a scalar. Thus, consider the ordinary least-squares residuals $e_1, e_2, \ldots, e_N$. Letting $\mathbf{e}$ be a column vector and $\mathbf{e}'$ be a row vector, we have

$$
\mathbf{e}'\mathbf{e} = [e_1 e_2 e_3 \cdots e_N]\begin{bmatrix} e_1 \\ e_2 \\ e_3 \\ \vdots \\ e_N \end{bmatrix}
$$

$$
= e_1^2 + e_2^2 + e_3^2 + \cdots + e_N^2
$$

$$
= \sum e_i^2 \qquad \text{a scalar [see equation (8.3.5)]}
$$

5. A column vector postmultiplied by a row vector is a matrix. As an example, consider the population disturbances of the classical linear regression model, namely, $u_1, u_2, \ldots, u_N$. Letting $\mathbf{u}$ be a column vector and $\mathbf{u}'$ be a row vector, we obtain

$$
\mathbf{uu}' = \begin{bmatrix} u_1 \\ u_2 \\ u_3 \\ \vdots \\ u_N \end{bmatrix}[u_1 u_2 u_3 \cdots u_N]
$$

$$
= \begin{bmatrix} u_1^2 & u_1 u_2 & u_1 u_3 & \cdots & u_1 u_N \\ u_2 u_1 & u_2^2 & u_2 u_3 & \cdots & u_2 u_N \\ \multicolumn{5}{c}{\dotfill} \\ u_N u_1 & u_N u_2 & u_N u_3 & \cdots & u_N^2 \end{bmatrix}
$$

which is a matrix of order $N \times N$. Note that the preceding matrix is symmetrical.

6. A matrix postmultiplied by a column vector is a column vector.
7. A row vector postmultiplied by a matrix is a row vector.
8. Matrix multiplication is associative; that is, $(\mathbf{AB})\mathbf{C} = \mathbf{A}(\mathbf{BC})$, where $\mathbf{A}$ is $M \times N$, $\mathbf{B}$ is $N \times P$, and $\mathbf{C}$ is $P \times K$.
9. Matrix multiplication is distributive with respect to addition; that is, $\mathbf{A}(\mathbf{B} + \mathbf{C}) = \mathbf{AB} + \mathbf{AC}$ and $(\mathbf{B} + \mathbf{C})\mathbf{A} = \mathbf{BA} + \mathbf{CA}$.

Matrix Transposition

We have already defined the process of matrix transposition as interchanging the rows and the columns of a matrix (or a vector). We now state some of the properties of transposition.

1. The transpose of a transposed matrix is the original matrix itself. Thus, $(\mathbf{A}')' = \mathbf{A}$.

2. If **A** and **B** are conformable for addition, then **C** = **A** + **B** and **C'** = (**A** + **B**)' = **A'** + **B'**. That is, the transpose of the sum of two matrices is the sum of their transposes.
3. If **AB** is defined, then (**AB**)' = **B'A'**. That is, the transpose of the product of two matrices is the product of their transposes in the reverse order. This can be generalized: (**ABCD**)' = **D'C'B'A'**.
4. The transpose of an identity matrix **I** is the identity matrix itself; that is, **I'** = **I**.
5. The transpose of a scalar is the scalar itself. Thus, if λ is a scalar, $\lambda' = \lambda$.
6. The transpose of $(\lambda \mathbf{A})'$ is $\lambda \mathbf{A}'$ where λ is a scalar. [*Note:* $(\lambda \mathbf{A})' = \mathbf{A}'\lambda' = \mathbf{A}'\lambda = \lambda \mathbf{A}'$.]
7. If **A** is a square matrix such that **A** = **A'**, then **A** is a symmetric matrix. (Cf. the definition of symmetric matrix given previously.)

Matrix Inversion

An inverse of a square matrix **A**, denoted by $\mathbf{A}^{-1}$ (read *A* inverse), if it exists, is a unique square matrix such that

$$\mathbf{A}\mathbf{A}^{-1} = \mathbf{A}^{-1}\mathbf{A} = \mathbf{I}$$

where *I* is an identity matrix whose order is the same as that of **A**.

Example If

$$\mathbf{A} = \begin{bmatrix} 2 & 4 \\ 6 & 8 \end{bmatrix}$$

then

$$\mathbf{A}^{-1} = \begin{bmatrix} -1 & \frac{1}{2} \\ \frac{6}{8} & -\frac{1}{4} \end{bmatrix}$$

for

$$\mathbf{A}\mathbf{A}^{-1} = \begin{bmatrix} 1 & 0 \\ 0 & 1 \end{bmatrix} = I$$

We shall see how $\mathbf{A}^{-1}$ is computed after we study the topic of determinants. In the meantime note these properties of the inverse.

1. $(\mathbf{AB})^{-1} = \mathbf{B}^{-1}\mathbf{A}^{-1}$; that is, the inverse of the product of two matrices is the product of their inverses in the reverse order.
2. $(\mathbf{A}^{-1})' = (\mathbf{A}')^{-1}$; that is, the transpose of **A** inverse is the inverse of **A** transpose.

B.4 DETERMINANTS

To every square matrix **A**, there corresponds a number (scalar) known as the determinant of the matrix, which is denoted by det **A** or by the symbol $|\mathbf{A}|$, where $|\ \ |$ means "the determinant of." Note that a matrix per se has no numerical value but the determinant of a matrix is a number.

Example If

$$A = \begin{bmatrix} 1 & 3 & -7 \\ 2 & 5 & 0 \\ 3 & 8 & 6 \end{bmatrix}$$

then

$$|A| = \begin{vmatrix} 1 & 3 & -7 \\ 2 & 5 & 0 \\ 3 & 8 & 6 \end{vmatrix}$$

The $|A|$ in this example is called a determinant of order 3 because it is associated with a matrix of order 3×3.

Evaluation of a Determinant

The process of finding the value of a determinant is known as the *evaluation*, *expansion*, or *reduction* of the determinant. This is done by manipulating the entries of the matrix in a well-defined manner.

Evaluation of a 2 × 2 determinant If

$$A = \begin{vmatrix} a_{11} & a_{12} \\ a_{21} & a_{22} \end{vmatrix}$$

its determinant is evaluated as follows:

$$|A| = \begin{vmatrix} a_{11} & a_{12} \\ a_{21} & a_{22} \end{vmatrix} = a_{11}a_{22} - a_{12}a_{21}$$

which is obtained by cross multiplying the elements on the main diagonal and subtracting from it the cross multiplication of the elements on the other diagonal of matrix A, as indicated by the arrows.

Evaluation of a 3 × 3 determinant If

$$A = \begin{bmatrix} a_{11} & a_{12} & a_{13} \\ a_{21} & a_{22} & a_{23} \\ a_{31} & a_{32} & a_{33} \end{bmatrix}$$

Then

$$|A| = a_{11}a_{22}a_{33} - a_{11}a_{23}a_{32}$$
$$+ a_{12}a_{23}a_{31} - a_{12}a_{21}a_{33} + a_{13}a_{21}a_{32} - a_{13}a_{22}a_{31}$$

A careful examination of the evaluation of a 3×3 determinant shows:

1. Each term in the expansion of the determinant contains one and only one element from each row and each column.
2. The number of elements in each term is the same as the number of rows (or columns) in the matrix. Thus, a 2×2 determinant has two elements in each

term of its expansion, a 3×3 determinant has three elements in each term of its expansion, and so on.

3. The terms in the expansion alternate in sign from $+$ to $-$.
4. A 2×2 determinant has two terms in its expansion, and a 3×3 determinant has six terms in its expansion. The general rule is: The determinant of order $N \times N$ has $N! = N(N-1)(N-2) \cdots 3 \cdot 2 \cdot 1$ terms in its expansion, where $N!$ means "N factorial." Following this rule, a determinant of order 5×5 will have $5 \cdot 4 \cdot 3 \cdot 2 \cdot 1 = 120$ terms in its expansion.[1]

Properties of Determinants

1. A matrix whose determinantal value is zero is called a *singular matrix*, whereas a matrix with a nonzero determinant is called a *nonsingular matrix*. The inverse of a matrix as defined before does not exist for a singular matrix.
2. If all the elements of any row of $\mathbf{A}$ are zero, its determinant is zero. Thus,

$$|\mathbf{A}| = \begin{vmatrix} 0 & 0 & 0 \\ 3 & 4 & 5 \\ 6 & 7 & 8 \end{vmatrix} = 0$$

3. $|\mathbf{A}'| = |\mathbf{A}|$; that is, the determinant of $\mathbf{A}$ and $\mathbf{A}$ transpose are the same.
4. Interchanging any two rows or any two columns of a matrix $\mathbf{A}$ changes the sign of $|\mathbf{A}|$.

Example If

$$\mathbf{A} = \begin{bmatrix} 6 & 9 \\ -1 & 4 \end{bmatrix} \quad \text{and} \quad \mathbf{B} = \begin{bmatrix} -1 & 4 \\ 6 & 9 \end{bmatrix}$$

where $\mathbf{B}$ is obtained by interchanging the rows of $\mathbf{A}$, then

$$|\mathbf{A}| = 24 - (-9) \quad \text{and} \quad |\mathbf{B}| = -9 - (24)$$
$$= 33 \qquad\qquad\qquad = -33$$

5. If every element of a row or a column of $\mathbf{A}$ is multiplied by a scalar λ, then $|\mathbf{A}|$ is multiplied by λ.

Example If

$$\lambda = 5 \quad \text{and} \quad \mathbf{A} = \begin{bmatrix} 5 & -8 \\ 2 & 4 \end{bmatrix}$$

and we multiply the first row of $\mathbf{A}$ by 5 to obtain

$$\mathbf{B} = \begin{bmatrix} 25 & -40 \\ 2 & 4 \end{bmatrix}$$

it can be seen that $|\mathbf{A}| = 36$ and $|\mathbf{B}| = 180$, which is $5|\mathbf{A}|$.

---

[1] To evaluate the determinant of an $N \times N$ matrix $\mathbf{A}$, see the references.

6. If two rows or two columns of a matrix are identical, its determinant is zero.

7. If one row or a column of a matrix is a multiple of another row or column of that matrix, its determinant is zero. Thus, if

$$\mathbf{A} = \begin{bmatrix} 4 & 8 \\ 2 & 4 \end{bmatrix}$$

where the first row of $\mathbf{A}$ is twice its second row, $|\mathbf{A}| = 0$. More generally, if any row (column) of a matrix is a linear combination of other rows (columns), it's determinant is zero.

8. $|\mathbf{AB}| = |\mathbf{A}| \, |\mathbf{B}|$; that is, the determinant of the product of two matrices is the product of their (individual) determinants.

Rank of a Matrix

The rank of a matrix is the order of the largest square submatrix whose determinant is not zero.

Example

$$\mathbf{A} = \begin{bmatrix} 3 & 6 & 6 \\ 0 & 4 & 5 \\ 3 & 2 & 1 \end{bmatrix}$$

It can be seen that $|\mathbf{A}| = 0$. In other words, $\mathbf{A}$ is a singular matrix. Hence although its order is 3×3, its rank is less than 3. Actually, it is 2, because we can find a 2×2 submatrix whose determinant is not zero. For example, if we delete the first row and the first column of $\mathbf{A}$, we obtain

$$\mathbf{B} = \begin{bmatrix} 4 & 5 \\ 2 & 1 \end{bmatrix}$$

whose determinant is -6, which is nonzero. Hence the rank of $\mathbf{A}$ is 2. As noted previously, the inverse of a singular matrix does not exist. Therefore, for an $N \times N$ matrix $\mathbf{A}$, its rank must be N for its inverse to exist: if it is less than N, $\mathbf{A}$ is singular.

Minor

If the ith row and jth column of an $N \times N$ matrix $\mathbf{A}$ are deleted, the determinant of the resulting submatrix is called the minor of the element a_{ij} (the element at the intersection of the ith row and the jth column) and is denoted by $|\mathbf{M}_{ij}|$.

Example

$$\mathbf{A} = \begin{bmatrix} a_{11} & a_{12} & a_{13} \\ a_{21} & a_{22} & a_{23} \\ a_{31} & a_{32} & a_{33} \end{bmatrix}$$

The minor of a_{11} is

$$|\mathbf{M_{11}}| = \begin{vmatrix} a_{22} & a_{23} \\ a_{32} & a_{33} \end{vmatrix} = a_{22}a_{33} - a_{23}a_{32}$$

Similarly, the minor of a_{21} is

$$|\mathbf{M_{21}}| = \begin{vmatrix} a_{12} & a_{13} \\ a_{32} & a_{33} \end{vmatrix} = a_{12}a_{33} - a_{13}a_{32}$$

The minors of other elements of $\mathbf{A}$ can be found similarly.

Cofactor

The cofactor of the element a_{ij} of an $N \times N$ matrix $\mathbf{A}$, denoted by c_{ij}, is defined as

$$c_{ij} = (-1)^{i+j}|\mathbf{M_{ij}}|$$

In other words, a cofactor is a signed minor, the sign being positive if $i + j$ is even and being negative if $i + j$ is odd. Thus, the cofactor of the element a_{11} of the 3×3 matrix $\mathbf{A}$ given previously is $a_{22}a_{33} - a_{23}a_{32}$, whereas the cofactor of the element a_{21} is $-(a_{12}a_{33} - a_{13}a_{32})$ since the sum of the subscripts 2 and 1 is 3, which is an odd number.

Cofactor Matrix

Replacing the elements a_{ij} of a matrix $\mathbf{A}$ by their cofactors we obtain a matrix known as the cofactor matrix of $\mathbf{A}$, denoted by (cof $\mathbf{A}$).

Adjoint Matrix

The adjoint matrix, written as (adj $\mathbf{A}$), is the transpose of the cofactor matrix; that is, (adj $\mathbf{A}$) = (cof $\mathbf{A}$)'.

B.5 FINDING THE INVERSE OF A SQUARE MATRIX

If $\mathbf{A}$ is square and nonsingular (that is, $|\mathbf{A}| \neq 0$), its inverse $\mathbf{A}^{-1}$ can be found as follows:

$$\mathbf{A}^{-1} = \frac{1}{|\mathbf{A}|} \text{(adj } \mathbf{A})$$

The steps involved in the computation are as follows:

1. Find the determinant of $\mathbf{A}$. If it is nonzero, then proceed to step 2.
2. Replace each element a_{ij} of $\mathbf{A}$ by its cofactor to obtain the cofactor matrix.

3. Transpose the cofactor matrix to obtain the adjoint matrix.
4. Divide each element of the adjoint matrix by $|A|$.

Example Suppose we want to find the inverse of the matrix

$$A = \begin{bmatrix} 1 & 2 & 3 \\ 5 & 7 & 4 \\ 2 & 1 & 3 \end{bmatrix}$$

Step 1 We first find the determinant of the matrix. Applying the rules of expanding a 3×3 determinant given previously, it can be seen that

$$|A| = -24$$

Step 2 We now obtain the cofactor matrix, say, **C**.

$$C = \begin{bmatrix} \begin{vmatrix} 7 & 4 \\ 1 & 3 \end{vmatrix} & -\begin{vmatrix} 5 & 4 \\ 2 & 3 \end{vmatrix} & \begin{vmatrix} 5 & 7 \\ 2 & 1 \end{vmatrix} \\ -\begin{vmatrix} 2 & 3 \\ 1 & 3 \end{vmatrix} & \begin{vmatrix} 1 & 3 \\ 2 & 3 \end{vmatrix} & -\begin{vmatrix} 1 & 2 \\ 2 & 1 \end{vmatrix} \\ \begin{vmatrix} 2 & 3 \\ 7 & 4 \end{vmatrix} & -\begin{vmatrix} 1 & 3 \\ 5 & 4 \end{vmatrix} & \begin{vmatrix} 1 & 2 \\ 5 & 7 \end{vmatrix} \end{bmatrix}$$

$$= \begin{bmatrix} 17 & -7 & -9 \\ -3 & -3 & 3 \\ -13 & 11 & -3 \end{bmatrix}$$

Step 3 Transposing the preceding cofactor matrix, we obtain the following adjoint matrix:

$$(\text{adj } A) = \begin{bmatrix} 17 & -3 & -13 \\ -7 & -3 & 11 \\ -9 & 3 & -3 \end{bmatrix}$$

Step 4 We now divide the elements of (adj **A**) by the determinantal value of -24 to obtain

$$A^{-1} = -\tfrac{1}{24}\begin{bmatrix} 17 & -3 & -13 \\ -7 & -3 & 11 \\ -9 & 3 & -3 \end{bmatrix}$$

$$= \begin{bmatrix} -\frac{17}{24} & \frac{3}{24} & \frac{13}{24} \\ \frac{7}{24} & \frac{3}{24} & -\frac{11}{24} \\ \frac{9}{24} & -\frac{3}{24} & \frac{3}{24} \end{bmatrix}$$

It can readily verified that

$$AA^{-1} = \begin{bmatrix} 1 & 0 & 0 \\ 0 & 1 & 0 \\ 0 & 0 & 1 \end{bmatrix}$$

which is an identity matrix. The reader should verify that for the illustrative example given in Chap. 8 the inverse of the $X'X$ matrix is as shown in equation (8.9.5).

B.6 MATRIX DIFFERENTIATION

To follow the material in App. 8A, Sec. 8A.2, we need some rules regarding matrix differentiation.

Rule 1 If $a' = [a_1 a_2 \cdots a_n]$ is a row vector of numbers, and

$$x = \begin{bmatrix} x_1 \\ x_2 \\ \vdots \\ x_n \end{bmatrix}$$

is a column vector of the variables $x_1, x_2, \ldots, x_n$, then

$$\frac{\partial(a'x)}{\partial x} = a = \begin{bmatrix} a_1 \\ a_2 \\ \vdots \\ a_n \end{bmatrix}$$

Consider the matrix $x'Ax$ such that

$$x'Ax = [x_1 x_2 \cdots x_n] \begin{bmatrix} a_{11} & a_{12} & \cdots & a_{1n} \\ a_{21} & a_{22} & \cdots & a_{2n} \\ \multicolumn{4}{c}{\cdots\cdots\cdots\cdots\cdots} \\ a_{n1} & a_{n2} & & a_{nn} \end{bmatrix} \begin{bmatrix} x_1 \\ x_2 \\ \vdots \\ x_n \end{bmatrix}$$

Then,

$$\frac{\partial(x'Ax)}{\partial x} = 2Ax$$

which is a column vector of n elements, or

$$\frac{\partial(x'Ax)}{\partial x} = 2x'A$$

which is a row vector of n elements.

B.7 REFERENCES

Chiang, Alpha C.: *Fundamental Methods of Mathematical Economics*, 2d ed., McGraw-Hill Book Company, New York, 1974, chaps. 4 and 5. This is an elementary discussion.

Hadley, G.: *Linear Algebra*, Addison-Wesley Publishing Company, Inc., Reading, Mass., 1961. This is an advanced discussion.

APPENDIX
C

A LIST OF SOME PACKAGED COMPUTER PROGRAMS

I. Name of program: *BMD Biomedical Computer Programs*
   Author: W. J. Dixon (ed.)
   Publisher: University of California Press, Berkeley, Calif.
   Which machine: IBM 360/370
   Machine language: Fortran IV
   Programs: *A. Multivariate Analysis*
   1. Principal component analysis
   2. Regression on principal components
   3. Discriminant analysis for two groups
   4. Discriminant analysis for several groups
   5. Stepwise discriminant analysis
   6. Factor analysis
   7. Canonical correlation analysis
   8. Identification of outliers

   B. Regression Analysis
   1. Simple regression analysis
   2. Stepwise regression
   3. Multiple regression with case combinations
   4. Periodic regression and harmonic analysis
   5. Polynomial regression
   6. Asymptotic regression
   7. Nonlinear least squares

   C. Variance Analysis
   1. Analysis of variance for one-way design
   2. Analysis of variance for factorial design
   3. Analysis of covariance for factorial design
   4. Analysis of variance with multiple covariates
   5. General linear hypothesis
   6. General linear hypothesis with contrasts
   7. Multiple-range tests
   8. Analysis of variance
   9. Analysis of covariance
   10. General linear hypothesis (no. 2)
   11. Multivariate general linear hypothesis
   12. Multivariate analysis of variance and covariance

II. Name of program: *Statistical Package for the Social Sciences (SPSS)*
   Authors: Norman H. Nie, Dale H. Bent, and C. Hadlai Hull
   Publisher: McGraw-Hill Book Company, New York
   Which machine: IBM 7090, 360
   Machine language: Fortran IV
   Programs:

1. Bivariate correlation analysis: Pearson and rank order
2. Partial correlation
3. Multiple regression analysis
4. Factor analysis

III. Name of program: *Econometric Software Package (ESP)*
   Author: J. Phillip Cooper
   Publisher: Graduate School of Business Administration, University of Chicago, Chicago, Ill., 60637
   Which machine: IBM 360/370
   Machine language: Fortran IV
   Programs: ESP is computer language for the statistical analysis of time-series data by the methods of ordinary least squares and two-stage least squares and can do the following routines:

1. Simple and multiple regression
2. Regression with first-order serially correlated errors (iterative Cochrane-Orcutt procedure and scanning technique)
3. Principal components
4. Time-series plot
5. Comparison of actual and predicted time series
6. Statistical groups: means, correlations, etc.
7. Seasonal adjustment
8. Two-stage least squares with first-order serially correlated errors
9. Random coefficient regressions
10. Box-Jenkins time-series analysis
11. Three-stage least squares
12. Almon-polynomial-distributed lags

IV. Name of program: *Regression Analysis Program for Economists (RAPE)*
   Author: Harvard Institute of Economic Research
   Publisher: Harvard University Press, Cambridge, Mass.
   Which machine: IBM 360/370
   Machine language: Fortran IV
   Programs: **Essentially the same as** *Econometric Software Package (ESP)*

V. Name of program: *The Modified Auto-Econ Regression Program*
   Author: Walter D. Davis
   Publisher: Division of Research and Statistics, **Board of Governors of the Federal Reserve System, Washington, D.C.**
   Which machine: IBM 360/370

Machine language:	Fortran IV
Programs:	In addition to the least-squares estimation of an equation, the program can be used to estimate a first-order and second-order autoregressive scheme of the error term. Two methods of autoregressive transformation are available:

1. Cochrane-Orcutt iterative technique for first-order serial correlation
2. Scanning technique for first- and second-order serial correlation

In addition, the program can estimate Almon lags for time-series data. It has an option to store control and label cards, which allows the user to run the same regressions on many sets of data without duplicating these cards.

As noted elsewhere, the preceding programs cover almost all the techniques discussed in this text. For a brief discussion of some of the specialized computer programs in the area of multivariate analysis the reader may refer to S. James Press, *Applied Multivariate Analysis*, Holt, Rinehart & Winston, Inc., New York, 1972, app. A, pp. 423–455.

STATISTICAL TABLES

Table D.1 Areas under the standardized normal distribution

Example

$$\Pr (0 \leq z \leq 1.96) = 0.4750$$

$$\Pr (z \geq 1.96) = 0.5 - 0.4750 = 0.025$$

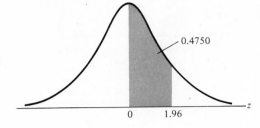

z	.00	.01	.02	.03	.04	.05	.06	.07	.08	.09
0.0	.0000	.0040	.0080	.0120	.0160	.0199	.0239	.0279	.0319	.0359
0.1	.0398	.0438	.0478	.0517	.0557	.0596	.0636	.0675	.0714	.0753
0.2	.0793	.0832	.0871	.0910	.0948	.0987	.1026	.1064	.1103	.1141
0.3	.1179	.1217	.1255	.1293	.1331	.1368	.1406	.1443	.1480	.1517
0.4	.1554	.1591	.1628	.1664	.1700	.1736	.1772	.1808	.1844	.1879
0.5	.1915	.1950	.1985	.2019	.2054	.2088	.2123	.2157	.2190	.2224
0.6	.2257	.2291	.2324	.2357	.2389	.2422	.2454	.2486	.2517	.2549
0.7	.2580	.2611	.2642	.2673	.2704	.2734	.2764	.2794	.2823	.2852
0.8	.2881	.2910	.2939	.2967	.2995	.3023	.3051	.3078	.3106	.3133
0.9	.3159	.3186	.3212	.3238	.3264	.3289	.3315	.3340	.3365	.3389
1.0	.3413	.3438	.3461	.3485	.3508	.3531	.3554	.3577	.3599	.3621
1.1	.3643	.3665	.3686	.3708	.3729	.3749	.3770	.3790	.3810	.3830
1.2	.3849	.3869	.3888	.3907	.3925	.3944	.3962	.3980	.3997	.4015
1.3	.4032	.4049	.4066	.4082	.4099	.4115	.4131	.4147	.4162	.4177
1.4	.4192	.4207	.4222	.4236	.4251	.4265	.4279	.4292	.4306	.4319
1.5	.4332	.4345	.4357	.4370	.4382	.4394	.4406	.4418	.4429	.4441
1.6	.4452	.4463	.4474	.4484	.4495	.4505	.4515	.4525	.4535	.4545
1.7	.4554	.4564	.4573	.4582	.4591	.4599	.4608	.4616	.4625	.4633
1.8	.4641	.4649	.4656	.4664	.4671	.4678	.4686	.4693	.4699	.4706
1.9	.4713	.4719	.4726	.4732	.4738	.4744	.4750	.4756	.4761	.4767
2.0	.4772	.4778	.4783	.4788	.4793	.4798	.4803	.4808	.4812	.4817
2.1	.4821	.4826	.4830	.4834	.4838	.4842	.4846	.4850	.4854	.4857
2.2	.4861	.4864	.4868	.4871	.4875	.4878	.4881	.4884	.4887	.4890
2.3	.4893	.4896	.4898	.4901	.4904	.4906	.4909	.4911	.4913	.4916
2.4	.4918	.4920	.4922	.4925	.4927	.4929	.4931	.4932	.4934	.4936
2.5	.4938	.4940	.4941	.4943	.4945	.4946	.4948	.4949	.4951	.4952
2.6	.4953	.4955	.4956	.4957	.4959	.4960	.4961	.4962	.4963	.4964
2.7	.4965	.4966	.4967	.4968	.4969	.4970	.4971	.4972	.4973	.4974
2.8	.4974	.4975	.4976	.4977	.4977	.4978	.4979	.4979	.4980	.4981
2.9	.4981	.4982	.4982	.4983	.4984	.4984	.4985	.4985	.4986	.4986
3.0	.4987	.4987	.4987	.4988	.4988	.4989	.4989	.4989	.4990	.4990

Table D.2 Percentage points of the t distribution

Example

Pr $(t > 2.086) = 0.025$

Pr $(t > 1.725) = 0.05$ for df $= 20$

Pr $(|t| > 1.725) = 0.10$

Pr df	0.25 0.50	0.10 0.20	0.05 0.10	0.025 0.05	0.01 0.02	0.005 0.010	0.001 0.002
1	1.000	3.078	6.314	12.706	31.821	63.657	318.31
2	0.816	1.886	2.920	4.303	6.965	9.925	22.327
3	0.765	1.638	2.353	3.182	4.541	5.841	10.214
4	0.741	1.533	2.132	2.776	3.747	4.604	7.173
5	0.727	1.476	2.015	2.571	3.365	4.032	5.893
6	0.718	1.440	1.943	2.447	3.143	3.707	5.208
7	0.711	1.415	1.895	2.365	2.998	3.499	4.785
8	0.706	1.397	1.860	2.306	2.896	3.355	4.501
9	0.703	1.383	1.833	2.262	2.821	3.250	4.297
10	0.700	1.372	1.812	2.228	2.764	3.169	4.144
11	0.697	1.363	1.796	2.201	2.718	3.106	4.025
12	0.695	1.356	1.782	2.179	2.681	3.055	3.930
13	0.694	1.350	1.771	2.160	2.650	3.012	3.852
14	0.692	1.345	1.761	2.145	2.624	2.977	3.787
15	0.691	1.341	1.753	2.131	2.602	2.947	3.733
16	0.690	1.337	1.746	2.120	2.583	2.921	3.686
17	0.689	1.333	1.740	2.110	2.567	2.898	3.646
18	0.688	1.330	1.734	2.101	2.552	2.878	3.610
19	0.688	1.328	1.729	2.093	2.539	2.861	3.579
20	0.687	1.325	1.725	2.086	2.528	2.845	3.552
21	0.686	1.323	1.721	2.080	2.518	2.831	3.527
22	0.686	1.321	1.717	2.074	2.508	2.819	3.505
23	0.685	1.319	1.714	2.069	2.500	2.807	3.485
24	0.685	1.318	1.711	2.064	2.492	2.797	3.467
25	0.684	1.316	1.708	2.060	2.485	2.787	3.450
26	0.684	1.315	1.706	2.056	2.479	2.779	3.435
27	0.684	1.314	1.703	2.052	2.473	2.771	3.421
28	0.683	1.313	1.701	2.048	2.467	2.763	3.408
29	0.683	1.311	1.699	2.045	2.462	2.756	3.396
30	0.683	1.310	1.697	2.042	2.457	2.750	3.385
40	0.681	1.303	1.684	2.021	2.423	2.704	3.307
60	0.679	1.296	1.671	2.000	2.390	2.660	3.232
120	0.677	1.289	1.658	1.980	2.358	2.167	3.160
∞	0.674	1.282	1.645	1.960	2.326	2.576	3.090

Note: The smaller probability shown at the head of each column is the area in one tail; the larger probability is the area in both tails.

Source: From E. S. Pearson and H. O. Hartley, eds., *Biometrika Tables for Statisticians*, vol. 1, 3d ed., table 12, Cambridge University Press, New York, 1966. Reproduced by permission of the editors and trustees of *Biometrika*.

Table D.3 Upper percentage points of the F distribution

Example

$\Pr(F > 1.59) = 0.25$
$\Pr(F > 2.42) = 0.10$ for df $N_1 = 10$
$\Pr(F > 3.14) = 0.05$ and $N_2 = 9$
$\Pr(F > 5.26) = 0.01$

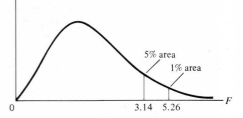

df for denom- inator N_2	Pr	\multicolumn{12}{c}{df for numerator N_1}
		1	2	3	4	5	6	7	8	9	10	11	12
---	---	---	---	---	---	---	---	---	---	---	---	---	---
1	.25	5.83	7.50	8.20	8.58	8.82	8.98	9.10	9.19	9.26	9.32	9.36	9.41
	.10	39.9	49.5	53.6	55.8	57.2	58.2	58.9	59.4	59.9	60.2	60.5	60.7
	.05	161	200	216	225	230	234	237	239	241	242	243	244
2	.25	2.57	3.00	3.15	3.23	3.28	3.31	3.34	3.35	3.37	3.38	3.39	3.39
	.10	8.53	9.00	9.16	9.24	9.29	9.33	9.35	9.37	9.38	9.39	9.40	9.41
	.05	18.5	19.0	19.2	19.2	19.3	19.3	19.4	19.4	19.4	19.4	19.4	19.4
	.01	98.5	99.0	99.2	99.2	99.3	99.3	99.4	99.4	99.4	99.4	99.4	99.4
3	.25	2.02	2.28	2.36	2.39	2.41	2.42	2.43	2.44	2.44	2.44	2.45	2.45
	.10	5.54	5.46	5.39	5.34	5.31	5.28	5.27	5.25	5.24	5.23	5.22	5.22
	.05	10.1	9.55	9.28	9.12	9.01	8.94	8.89	8.85	8.81	8.79	8.76	8.74
	.01	34.1	30.8	29.5	28.7	28.2	27.9	27.7	27.5	27.3	27.2	27.1	27.1
4	.25	1.81	2.00	2.05	2.06	2.07	2.08	2.08	2.08	2.08	2.08	2.08	2.08
	.10	4.54	4.32	4.19	4.11	4.05	4.01	3.98	3.95	3.94	3.92	3.91	3.90
	.05	7.71	6.94	6.59	6.39	6.26	6.16	6.09	6.04	6.00	5.96	5.94	5.91
	.01	21.2	18.0	16.7	16.0	15.5	15.2	15.0	14.8	14.7	14.5	14.4	14.4
5	.25	1.69	1.85	1.88	1.89	1.89	1.89	1.89	1.89	1.89	1.89	1.89	1.89
	.10	4.06	3.78	3.62	3.52	3.45	3.40	3.37	3.34	3.32	3.30	3.28	3.27
	.05	6.61	5.79	5.41	5.19	5.05	4.95	4.88	4.82	4.77	4.74	4.71	4.68
	.01	16.3	13.3	12.1	11.4	11.0	10.7	10.5	10.3	10.2	10.1	9.96	9.89
6	.25	1.62	1.76	1.78	1.79	1.79	1.78	1.78	1.78	1.77	1.77	1.77	1.77
	.10	3.78	3.46	3.29	3.18	3.11	3.05	3.01	2.98	2.96	2.94	2.92	2.90
	.05	5.99	5.14	4.76	4.53	4.39	4.28	4.21	4.15	4.10	4.06	4.03	4.00
	.01	13.7	10.9	9.78	9.15	8.75	8.47	8.26	8.10	7.98	7.87	7.79	7.72
7	.25	1.57	1.70	1.72	1.72	1.71	1.71	1.70	1.70	1.69	1.69	1.69	1.68
	.10	3.59	3.26	3.07	2.96	2.88	2.83	2.78	2.75	2.72	2.70	2.68	2.67
	.05	5.59	4.74	4.35	4.12	3.97	3.87	3.79	3.73	3.68	3.64	3.60	3.57
	.01	12.2	9.55	8.45	7.85	7.46	7.19	6.99	6.84	6.72	6.62	6.54	6.47
8	.25	1.54	1.66	1.67	1.66	1.66	1.65	1.64	1.64	1.63	1.63	1.63	1.62
	.10	3.46	3.11	2.92	2.81	2.73	2.67	2.62	2.59	2.56	2.54	2.52	2.50
	.05	5.32	4.46	4.07	3.84	3.69	3.58	3.50	3.44	3.39	3.35	3.31	3.28
	.01	11.3	8.65	7.59	7.01	6.63	6.37	6.18	6.03	5.91	5.81	5.73	5.67
9	.25	1.51	1.62	1.63	1.63	1.62	1.61	1.60	1.60	1.59	1.59	1.58	1.58
	.10	3.36	3.01	2.81	2.69	2.61	2.55	2.51	2.47	2.44	2.42	2.40	2.38
	.05	5.12	4.26	3.86	3.63	3.48	3.37	3.29	3.23	3.18	3.14	3.10	3.07
	.01	10.6	8.02	6.99	6.42	6.06	5.80	5.61	5.47	5.35	5.26	5.18	5.11

				df for numerator N_1										df for denominator N_2
15	20	24	30	40	50	60	100	120	200	500	∞	Pr	
9.49	9.58	9.63	9.67	9.71	9.74	9.76	9.78	9.80	9.82	9.84	9.85	.25	
61.2	61.7	62.0	62.3	62.5	62.7	62.8	63.0	63.1	63.2	63.3	63.3	.10	1
246	248	249	250	251	252	252	253	253	254	254	254	.05	
3.41	3.43	3.43	3.44	3.45	3.45	3.46	3.47	3.47	3.48	3.48	3.48	.25	
9.42	9.44	9.45	9.46	9.47	9.47	9.47	9.48	9.48	9.49	9.49	9.49	.10	2
19.4	19.4	19.5	19.5	19.5	19.5	19.5	19.5	19.5	19.5	19.5	19.5	.05	
99.4	99.4	99.5	99.5	99.5	99.5	99.5	99.5	99.5	99.5	99.5	99.5	.01	
2.46	2.46	2.46	2.47	2.47	2.47	2.47	2.47	2.47	2.47	2.47	2.47	.25	
5.20	5.18	5.18	5.17	5.16	5.15	5.15	5.14	5.14	5.14	5.14	5.13	.10	3
8.70	8.66	8.64	8.62	8.59	8.58	8.57	8.55	8.55	8.54	8.53	8.53	.05	
26.9	26.7	26.6	26.5	26.4	26.4	26.3	26.2	26.2	26.2	26.1	26.1	.01	
2.08	2.08	2.08	2.08	2.08	2.08	2.08	2.08	2.08	2.08	2.08	2.08	.25	
3.87	3.84	3.83	3.82	3.80	3.80	3.79	3.78	3.78	3.77	3.76	3.76	.10	4
5.86	5.80	5.77	5.75	5.72	5.70	5.69	5.66	5.66	5.65	5.64	5.63	.05	
14.2	14.0	13.9	13.8	13.7	13.7	13.7	13.6	13.6	13.5	13.5	13.5	.01	
1.89	1.88	1.88	1.88	1.88	1.88	1.87	1.87	1.87	1.87	1.87	1.87	.25	
3.24	3.21	3.19	3.17	3.16	3.15	3.14	3.13	3.12	3.12	3.11	3.10	.10	5
4.62	4.56	4.53	4.50	4.46	4.44	4.43	4.41	4.40	4.39	4.37	4.36	.05	
9.72	9.55	9.47	9.38	9.29	9.24	9.20	9.13	9.11	9.08	9.04	9.02	.01	
1.76	1.76	1.75	1.75	1.75	1.75	1.74	1.74	1.74	1.74	1.74	1.74	.25	
2.87	2.84	2.82	2.80	2.78	2.77	2.76	2.75	2.74	2.73	2.73	2.72	.10	6
3.94	3.87	3.84	3.81	3.77	3.75	3.74	3.71	3.70	3.69	3.68	3.67	.05	
7.56	7.40	7.31	7.23	7.14	7.09	7.06	6.99	6.97	6.93	6.90	6.88	.01	
1.68	1.67	1.67	1.66	1.66	1.66	1.65	1.65	1.65	1.65	1.65	1.65	.25	
2.63	2.59	2.58	2.56	2.54	2.52	2.51	2.50	2.49	2.48	2.48	2.47	.10	7
3.51	3.44	3.41	3.38	3.34	3.32	3.30	3.27	3.27	3.25	3.24	3.23	.05	
6.31	6.16	6.07	5.99	5.91	5.86	5.82	5.75	5.74	5.70	5.67	5.65	.10	
1.62	1.61	1.60	1.60	1.59	1.59	1.59	1.58	1.58	1.58	1.58	1.58	.25	
2.46	2.42	2.40	2.38	2.36	2.35	2.34	2.32	2.32	2.31	2.30	2.29	.10	8
3.22	3.15	3.12	3.08	3.04	2.02	3.01	2.97	2.97	2.95	2.94	2.93	.05	
5.52	5.36	5.28	5.20	5.12	5.07	5.03	4.96	4.95	4.91	4.88	4.86	.01	
1.57	1.56	1.56	1.55	1.55	1.54	1.54	1.53	1.53	1.53	1.53	1.53	.25	
2.34	2.30	2.28	2.25	2.23	2.22	2.21	2.19	2.18	2.17	2.17	2.16	.10	9
3.01	2.94	2.90	2.86	2.83	2.80	2.79	2.76	2.75	2.73	2.72	2.71	.05	
4.96	4.81	4.73	4.65	4.57	4.52	4.48	4.42	4.40	4.36	4.33	4.31	.01	

Table D.3 Upper percentage points of the F distribution (*continued*)

df for denom-inator N_2	Pr	1	2	3	4	5	6	7	8	9	10	11	12
						df for numerator N_1							
10	.25	1.49	1.60	1.60	1.59	1.59	1.58	1.57	1.56	1.56	1.55	1.55	1.54
	.10	3.29	2.92	2.73	2.61	2.52	2.46	2.41	2.38	2.35	2.32	2.30	2.28
	.05	4.96	4.10	3.71	3.48	3.33	3.22	3.14	3.07	3.02	2.98	2.94	2.91
	.01	10.0	7.56	6.55	5.99	5.64	5.39	5.20	5.06	4.94	4.85	4.77	4.71
11	.25	1.47	1.58	1.58	1.57	1.56	1.55	1.54	1.53	1.53	1.52	1.52	1.51
	.10	3.23	2.86	2.66	2.54	2.45	2.39	2.34	2.30	2.27	2.25	2.23	2.21
	.05	4.84	3.98	3.59	3.36	3.20	3.09	3.01	2.95	2.90	2.85	2.82	2.79
	.01	9.65	7.21	6.22	5.67	5.32	5.07	4.89	4.74	4.63	4.54	4.46	4.40
12	.25	1.46	1.56	1.56	1.55	1.54	1.53	1.52	1.51	1.51	1.50	1.50	1.49
	.10	3.18	2.81	2.61	2.48	2.39	2.33	2.28	2.24	2.21	2.19	2.17	2.15
	.05	4.75	3.89	3.49	3.26	3.11	3.00	2.91	2.85	2.80	2.75	2.72	2.69
	.01	9.33	6.93	5.95	5.41	5.06	4.82	4.64	4.50	4.39	4.30	4.22	4.16
13	.25	1.45	1.55	1.55	1.53	1.52	1.51	1.50	1.49	1.49	1.48	1.47	1.47
	.10	3.14	2.76	2.56	2.43	2.35	2.28	2.23	2.20	2.16	2.14	2.12	2.10
	.05	4.67	3.81	3.41	3.18	3.03	2.92	2.83	2.77	2.71	2.67	2.63	2.60
	.01	9.07	6.70	5.74	5.21	4.86	4.62	4.44	4.30	4.19	4.10	4.02	3.96
14	.25	1.44	1.53	1.53	1.52	1.51	1.50	1.49	1.48	1.47	1.46	1.46	1.45
	.10	3.10	2.73	2.52	2.39	2.31	2.24	2.19	2.15	2.12	2.10	2.08	2.05
	.05	4.60	3.74	3.34	3.11	2.96	2.85	2.76	2.70	2.65	2.60	2.57	2.53
	.01	8.86	6.51	5.56	5.04	4.69	4.46	4.28	4.14	4.03	3.94	3.86	3.80
15	.25	1.43	1.52	1.52	1.51	1.49	1.48	1.47	1.46	1.46	1.45	1.44	1.44
	.10	3.07	2.70	2.49	2.36	2.27	2.21	2.16	2.12	2.09	2.06	2.04	2.02
	.05	4.54	3.68	3.29	3.06	2.90	2.79	2.71	2.64	2.59	2.54	2.51	2.48
	.01	8.68	6.36	5.42	4.89	4.56	4.32	4.14	4.00	3.89	3.80	3.73	3.67
16	.25	1.42	1.51	1.51	1.50	1.48	1.47	1.46	1.45	1.44	1.44	1.44	1.43
	.10	3.05	2.67	2.46	2.33	2.24	2.18	2.13	2.09	2.06	2.03	2.01	1.99
	.05	4.49	3.63	3.24	3.01	2.85	2.74	2.66	2.59	2.54	2.49	2.46	2.42
	.01	8.53	6.23	5.29	4.77	4.44	4.20	4.03	3.89	3.78	3.69	3.62	3.55
17	.25	1.42	1.51	1.50	1.49	1.47	1.46	1.45	1.44	1.43	1.43	1.42	1.41
	.10	3.03	2.64	2.44	2.31	2.22	2.15	2.10	2.06	2.03	2.00	1.98	1.96
	.05	4.45	3.59	3.20	2.96	2.81	2.70	2.61	2.55	2.49	2.45	2.41	2.38
	.01	8.40	6.11	5.18	4.67	4.34	4.10	3.93	3.79	3.68	3.59	3.52	3.46
18	.25	1.41	1.50	1.49	1.48	1.46	1.45	1.44	1.43	1.42	1.42	1.41	1.40
	.10	3.01	2.62	2.42	2.29	2.20	2.13	2.08	2.04	2.00	1.98	1.96	1.93
	.05	4.41	3.55	3.16	2.93	2.77	2.66	2.58	2.51	2.46	2.41	2.37	2.34
	.01	8.29	6.01	5.09	4.58	4.25	4.01	3.84	3.71	3.60	3.51	3.43	3.37
19	.25	1.41	1.49	1.49	1.47	1.46	1.44	1.43	1.42	1.41	1.41	1.40	1.40
	.10	2.99	2.61	2.40	2.27	2.18	2.11	2.06	2.02	1.98	1.96	1.94	1.91
	.05	4.38	3.52	3.13	2.90	2.74	2.63	2.54	2.48	2.42	2.38	2.34	2.31
	.01	8.18	5.93	5.01	4.50	4.17	3.94	3.77	3.63	3.52	3.43	3.36	3.30
20	.25	1.40	1.49	1.48	1.46	1.45	1.44	1.43	1.42	1.41	1.40	1.39	1.39
	.10	2.97	2.59	2.38	2.25	2.16	2.09	2.04	2.00	1.96	1.94	1.92	1.89
	.05	4.35	3.49	3.10	2.87	2.71	2.60	2.51	2.45	2.39	2.35	2.31	2.28
	.01	8.10	5.85	4.94	4.43	4.10	3.87	3.70	3.56	3.46	3.37	3.29	3.23

15	20	24	30	40	50	60	100	120	200	500	∞	Pr	df for denominator N_2

df for numerator N_1

15	20	24	30	40	50	60	100	120	200	500	∞	Pr	N_2
1.53	1.52	1.52	1.51	1.51	1.50	1.50	1.49	1.49	1.49	1.48	1.48	.25	
2.24	2.20	2.18	2.16	2.13	2.12	2.11	2.09	2.08	2.07	2.06	2.06	.10	10
2.85	2.77	2.74	2.70	2.66	2.64	2.62	2.59	2.58	2.56	2.55	2.54	.05	
4.56	4.41	4.33	4.25	4.17	4.12	4.08	4.01	4.00	3.96	3.93	3.91	.01	
1.50	1.49	1.49	1.48	1.47	1.47	1.47	1.46	1.46	1.46	1.45	1.45	.25	
2.17	2.12	2.10	2.08	2.05	2.04	2.03	2.00	2.00	1.99	1.98	1.97	.10	11
2.72	2.65	2.61	2.57	2.53	2.51	2.49	2.46	2.45	2.43	2.42	2.40	.05	
4.25	4.10	4.02	3.94	3.86	3.81	3.78	3.71	3.69	3.66	3.62	3.60	.01	
1.48	1.47	1.46	1.45	1.45	1.44	1.44	1.43	1.43	1.43	1.42	1.42	.25	
2.10	2.06	2.04	2.01	1.99	1.97	1.96	1.94	1.93	1.92	1.91	1.90	.10	12
2.62	2.54	2.51	2.47	2.43	2.40	2.38	2.35	2.34	2.32	2.31	2.30	.05	
4.01	3.86	3.78	3.70	3.62	3.57	3.54	3.47	3.45	3.41	3.38	3.36	.01	
1.46	1.45	1.44	1.43	1.42	1.42	1.42	1.41	1.41	1.40	1.40	1.40	.25	
2.05	2.01	1.98	1.96	1.93	1.92	1.90	1.88	1.88	1.86	1.85	1.85	.10	13
2.53	2.46	2.42	2.38	2.34	2.31	2.30	2.26	2.25	2.23	2.22	2.21	.05	
3.82	3.66	3.59	3.51	3.43	3.38	3.34	3.27	3.25	3.22	3.19	3.17	.01	
1.44	1.43	1.42	1.41	1.41	1.40	1.40	1.39	1.39	1.39	1.38	1.38	.25	
2.01	1.96	1.94	1.91	1.89	1.87	1.86	1.83	1.83	1.82	1.80	1.80	.10	14
2.46	2.39	2.35	2.31	2.27	2.24	2.22	2.19	2.18	2.16	2.14	2.13	.05	
3.66	3.51	3.43	3.35	3.27	3.22	3.18	3.11	3.09	3.06	3.03	3.00	.01	
1.43	1.41	1.41	1.40	1.39	1.39	1.38	1.38	1.37	1.37	1.36	1.36	.25	
1.97	1.92	1.90	1.87	1.85	1.83	1.82	1.79	1.79	1.77	1.76	1.76	.10	15
2.40	2.33	2.29	2.25	2.20	2.18	2.16	2.12	2.11	2.10	2.08	2.07	.05	
3.52	3.37	3.29	3.21	3.13	3.08	3.05	2.98	2.96	2.92	2.89	2.87	.01	
1.41	1.40	1.39	1.38	1.37	1.37	1.36	1.36	1.35	1.35	1.34	1.34	.25	
1.94	1.89	1.87	1.84	1.81	1.79	1.78	1.76	1.75	1.74	1.73	1.72	.10	16
2.35	2.28	2.24	2.19	2.15	2.12	2.11	2.07	2.06	2.04	2.02	2.01	.05	
3.41	3.26	3.18	3.10	3.02	2.97	2.93	2.86	2.84	2.81	2.78	2.75	.01	
1.40	1.39	1.38	1.37	1.36	1.35	1.35	1.34	1.34	1.34	1.33	1.33	.25	
1.91	1.86	1.84	1.81	1.78	1.76	1.75	1.73	1.72	1.71	1.69	1.69	.10	17
2.31	2.23	2.19	2.15	2.10	2.08	2.06	2.02	2.01	1.99	1.97	1.96	.05	
3.31	3.16	3.08	3.00	2.92	2.87	2.83	2.76	2.75	2.71	2.68	2.65	.01	
1.39	1.38	1.37	1.36	1.35	1.34	1.34	1.33	1.33	1.32	1.32	1.32	.25	
1.89	1.84	1.81	1.78	1.75	1.74	1.72	1.70	1.69	1.68	1.67	1.66	.10	18
2.27	2.19	2.15	2.11	2.06	2.04	2.02	1.98	1.97	1.95	1.93	1.92	.05	
3.23	3.08	3.00	2.92	2.84	2.78	2.75	2.68	2.66	2.62	2.59	2.57	.01	
1.38	1.37	1.36	1.35	1.34	1.33	1.33	1.32	1.32	1.31	1.31	1.30	.25	
1.86	1.81	1.79	1.76	1.73	1.71	1.70	1.67	1.67	1.65	1.64	1.63	.10	19
2.23	2.16	2.11	2.07	2.03	2.00	1.98	1.94	1.93	1.91	1.89	1.88	.05	
3.15	3.00	2.92	2.84	2.76	2.71	2.67	2.60	2.58	2.55	2.51	2.49	.01	
1.37	1.36	1.35	1.34	1.33	1.33	1.32	1.31	1.31	1.30	1.30	1.29	.25	
1.84	1.79	1.77	1.74	1.71	1.69	1.68	1.65	1.64	1.63	1.62	1.61	.10	20
2.20	2.12	2.08	2.04	1.99	1.97	1.95	1.91	1.90	1.88	1.86	1.84	.05	
3.09	2.94	2.86	2.78	2.69	2.64	2.61	2.54	2.52	2.48	2.44	2.42	.01	

Table D.3 Upper percentage points of the F distribution (continued)

df for denominator N_2	Pr	\multicolumn{12}{c}{df for numerator N_1}											
		1	2	3	4	5	6	7	8	9	10	11	12
22	.25	1.40	1.48	1.47	1.45	1.44	1.42	1.41	1.40	1.39	1.39	1.38	1.37
	.10	2.95	2.56	2.35	2.22	2.13	2.06	2.01	1.97	1.93	1.90	1.88	1.86
	.05	4.30	3.44	3.05	2.82	2.66	2.55	2.46	2.40	2.34	2.30	2.26	2.23
	.01	7.95	5.72	4.82	4.31	3.99	3.76	3.59	3.45	3.35	3.26	3.18	3.12
24	.25	1.39	1.47	1.46	1.44	1.43	1.41	1.40	1.39	1.38	1.38	1.37	1.36
	.10	2.93	2.54	2.33	2.19	2.10	2.04	1.98	1.94	1.91	1.88	1.85	1.83
	.05	4.26	3.40	3.01	2.78	2.62	2.51	2.42	2.36	2.30	2.25	2.21	2.18
	.01	7.82	5.61	4.72	4.22	3.90	3.67	3.50	3.36	3.26	3.17	3.09	3.03
26	.25	1.38	1.46	1.45	1.44	1.42	1.41	1.39	1.38	1.37	1.37	1.36	1.35
	.10	2.91	2.52	2.31	2.17	2.08	2.01	1.96	1.92	1.88	1.86	1.84	1.81
	.05	4.23	3.37	2.98	2.74	2.59	2.47	2.39	2.32	2.27	2.22	2.18	2.15
	.01	7.72	5.53	4.64	4.14	3.82	3.59	3.42	3.29	3.18	3.09	3.02	2.96
28	.25	1.38	1.46	1.45	1.43	1.41	1.40	1.39	1.38	1.37	1.36	1.35	1.34
	.10	2.89	2.50	2.29	2.16	2.06	2.00	1.94	1.90	1.87	1.84	1.81	1.79
	.05	4.20	3.34	2.95	2.71	2.56	2.45	2.36	2.29	2.24	2.19	2.15	2.12
	.01	7.64	5.45	4.57	4.07	3.75	3.53	3.36	3.23	3.12	3.03	2.96	2.90
30	.25	1.38	1.45	1.44	1.42	1.41	1.39	1.38	1.37	1.36	1.35	1.35	1.34
	.10	2.88	2.49	2.28	2.14	2.05	1.98	1.93	1.88	1.85	1.82	1.79	1.77
	.05	4.17	3.32	2.92	2.69	2.53	2.42	2.33	2.27	2.21	2.16	2.13	2.09
	.01	7.56	5.39	4.51	4.02	3.70	3.47	3.30	3.17	3.07	2.98	2.91	2.84
40	.25	1.36	1.44	1.42	1.40	1.39	1.37	1.36	1.35	1.34	1.33	1.32	1.31
	.10	2.84	2.44	2.23	2.09	2.00	1.93	1.87	1.83	1.79	1.76	1.73	1.71
	.05	4.08	3.23	2.84	2.61	2.45	2.34	2.25	2.18	2.12	2.08	2.04	2.00
	.01	7.31	5.18	4.31	3.83	3.51	3.29	3.12	2.99	2.89	2.80	2.73	2.66
60	.25	1.35	1.42	1.41	1.38	1.37	1.35	1.33	1.32	1.31	1.30	1.29	1.29
	.10	2.79	2.39	2.18	2.04	1.95	1.87	1.82	1.77	1.74	1.71	1.68	1.66
	.05	4.00	3.15	2.76	2.53	2.37	2.25	2.17	2.10	2.04	1.99	1.95	1.92
	.01	7.08	4.98	4.13	3.65	3.34	3.12	2.95	2.82	2.72	2.63	2.56	2.50
120	.25	1.34	1.40	1.39	1.37	1.35	1.33	1.31	1.30	1.29	1.28	1.27	1.26
	.10	2.75	2.35	2.13	1.99	1.90	1.82	1.77	1.72	1.68	1.65	1.62	1.60
	.05	3.92	3.07	2.68	2.45	2.29	2.17	2.09	2.02	1.96	1.91	1.87	1.83
	.01	6.85	4.79	3.95	3.48	3.17	2.96	2.79	2.66	2.56	2.47	2.40	2.34
200	.25	1.33	1.39	1.38	1.36	1.34	1.32	1.31	1.29	1.28	1.27	1.26	1.25
	.10	2.73	2.33	2.11	1.97	1.88	1.80	1.75	1.70	1.66	1.63	1.60	1.57
	.05	3.89	3.04	2.65	2.42	2.26	2.14	2.06	1.98	1.93	1.88	1.84	1.80
	.01	6.76	4.71	3.88	3.41	3.11	2.89	2.73	2.60	2.50	2.41	2.34	2.27
∞	.25	1.32	1.39	1.37	1.35	1.33	1.31	1.29	1.28	1.27	1.25	1.24	1.24
	.10	2.71	2.30	2.08	1.94	1.85	1.77	1.72	1.67	1.63	1.60	1.57	1.55
	.05	3.84	3.00	2.60	2.37	2.21	2.10	2.01	1.94	1.88	1.83	1.79	1.75
	.01	6.63	4.61	3.78	3.32	3.02	2.80	2.64	2.51	2.41	2.32	2.25	2.18

				df for numerator N_1										df for denominator
15	20	24	30	40	50	60	100	120	200	500	∞	Pr	N_2
1.36	1.34	1.33	1.32	1.31	1.31	1.30	1.30	1.30	1.29	1.29	1.28	.25	
1.81	1.76	1.73	1.70	1.67	1.65	1.64	1.61	1.60	1.59	1.58	1.57	.10	22
2.15	2.07	2.03	1.98	1.94	1.91	1.89	1.85	1.84	1.82	1.80	1.78	.05	
2.98	2.83	2.75	2.67	2.58	2.53	2.50	2.42	2.40	2.36	2.33	2.31	.01	
1.35	1.33	1.32	1.31	1.30	1.29	1.29	1.28	1.28	1.27	1.27	1.26	.25	
1.78	1.73	1.70	1.67	1.64	1.62	1.61	1.58	1.57	1.56	1.54	1.53	.10	24
2.11	2.03	1.98	1.94	1.89	1.86	1.84	1.80	1.79	1.77	1.75	1.73	.05	
2.89	2.74	2.66	2.58	2.49	2.44	2.40	2.33	2.31	2.27	2.24	2.21	.01	
1.34	1.32	1.31	1.30	1.29	1.28	1.28	1.26	1.26	1.26	1.25	1.25	.25	
1.76	1.71	1.68	1.65	1.61	1.59	1.58	1.55	1.54	1.53	1.51	1.50	.10	26
2.07	1.99	1.95	1.90	1.85	1.82	1.80	1.76	1.75	1.73	1.71	1.69	.05	
2.81	2.66	2.58	2.50	2.42	2.36	2.33	2.25	2.23	2.19	2.16	2.13	.01	
1.33	1.31	1.30	1.29	1.28	1.27	1.27	1.26	1.25	1.25	1.24	1.24	.25	
1.74	1.69	1.66	1.63	1.59	1.57	1.56	1.53	1.52	1.50	1.49	1.48	.10	28
2.04	1.96	1.91	1.87	1.82	1.79	1.77	1.73	1.71	1.69	1.67	1.65	.05	
2.75	2.60	2.52	2.44	2.35	2.30	2.26	2.19	2.17	2.13	2.09	2.06	.01	
1.32	1.30	1.29	1.28	1.27	1.26	1.26	1.25	1.24	1.24	1.23	1.23	.25	
1.72	1.67	1.64	1.61	1.57	1.55	1.54	1.51	1.50	1.48	1.47	1.46	.10	30
2.01	1.93	1.89	1.84	1.79	1.76	1.74	1.70	1.68	1.66	1.64	1.62	.05	
2.70	2.55	2.47	2.39	2.30	2.25	2.21	2.13	2.11	2.07	2.03	2.01	.01	
1.30	1.28	1.26	1.25	1.24	1.23	1.22	1.21	1.21	1.20	1.19	1.19	.25	
1.66	1.61	1.57	1.54	1.51	1.48	1.47	1.43	1.42	1.41	1.39	1.38	.10	40
1.92	1.84	1.79	1.74	1.69	1.66	1.64	1.59	1.58	1.55	1.53	1.51	.05	
2.52	2.37	2.29	2.20	2.11	2.06	2.02	1.94	1.92	1.87	1.83	1.80	.01	
1.27	1.25	1.24	1.22	1.21	1.20	1.19	1.17	1.17	1.16	1.15	1.15	.25	
1.60	1.54	1.51	1.48	1.44	1.41	1.40	1.36	1.35	1.33	1.31	1.29	.10	60
1.84	1.75	1.70	1.65	1.59	1.56	1.53	1.48	1.47	1.44	1.41	1.39	.05	
2.35	2.20	2.12	2.03	1.94	1.88	1.84	1.75	1.73	1.68	1.63	1.60	.01	
1.24	1.22	1.21	1.19	1.18	1.17	1.16	1.14	1.13	1.12	1.11	1.10	.25	
1.55	1.48	1.45	1.41	1.37	1.34	1.32	1.27	1.26	1.24	1.21	1.19	.10	120
1.75	1.66	1.61	1.55	1.50	1.46	1.43	1.37	1.35	1.32	1.28	1.25	.05	
2.19	2.03	1.95	1.86	1.76	1.70	1.66	1.56	1.53	1.48	1.42	1.38	.01	
1.23	1.21	1.20	1.18	1.16	1.14	1.12	1.11	1.10	1.09	1.08	1.06	.25	
1.52	1.46	1.42	1.38	1.34	1.31	1.28	1.24	1.22	1.20	1.17	1.14	.10	200
1.72	1.62	1.57	1.52	1.46	1.41	1.39	1.32	1.29	1.26	1.22	1.19	.05	
2.13	1.97	1.89	1.79	1.69	1.63	1.58	1.48	1.44	1.39	1.33	1.28	.01	
1.22	1.19	1.18	1.16	1.14	1.13	1.12	1.09	1.08	1.07	1.04	1.00	.25	
1.49	1.42	1.38	1.34	1.30	1.26	1.24	1.18	1.17	1.13	1.08	1.00	.10	∞
1.67	1.57	1.52	1.46	1.39	1.35	1.32	1.24	1.22	1.17	1.11	1.00	.05	
2.04	1.88	1.79	1.70	1.59	1.52	1.47	1.36	1.32	1.25	1.15	1.00	.01	

Table D.4 Upper percentage points of the χ^2 distribution

Example

$$\Pr\left(\chi^2 > 23.8277\right) = 0.25$$
$$\Pr\left(\chi^2 > 31.4104\right) = 0.05 \qquad \text{for df} = 20$$
$$\Pr\left(\chi^2 > 37.5662\right) = 0.01$$

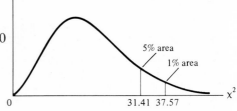

df \ Pr	0.250	0.100	0.050	0.025	0.010	0.005	0.001
1	1.32330	2.70554	3.84146	5.02389	6.63490	7.87944	10.828
2	2.77259	4.60517	5.99146	7.37776	9.21034	10.5966	13.816
3	4.10834	6.25139	7.81473	9.34840	11.3449	12.8382	16.266
4	5.38527	7.77944	9.48773	11.1433	13.2767	14.8603	18.467
5	6.62568	9.23636	11.0705	12.8325	15.0863	16.7496	20.515
6	7.84080	10.6446	12.5916	14.4494	16.8119	18.5476	22.458
7	9.03715	12.0170	14.0671	16.0128	18.4753	20.2777	24.322
8	10.2189	13.3616	15.5073	17.5345	20.0902	21.9550	26.125
9	11.3888	14.6837	16.9190	19.0228	21.6660	23.5894	27.877
10	12.5489	15.9872	18.3070	20.4832	23.2093	25.1882	29.588
11	13.7007	17.2750	19.6751	21.9200	24.7250	26.7568	31.264
12	14.8454	18.5493	21.0261	23.3367	26.2170	28.2995	32.909
13	15.9839	19.8119	22.3620	24.7356	27.6882	29.8195	34.528
14	17.1169	21.0641	23.6848	26.1189	29.1412	31.3194	36.123
15	18.2451	22.3071	24.9958	27.4884	30.5779	32.8013	37.697
16	19.3689	23.5418	26.2962	28.8454	31.9999	34.2672	39.252
17	20.4887	24.7690	27.5871	30.1910	33.4087	35.7185	40.790
18	21.6049	25.9894	28.8693	31.5264	34.8053	37.1565	42.312
19	22.7178	27.2036	30.1435	32.8523	36.1909	38.5823	43.820

† For df greater than 100, the expression

$$\sqrt{2\chi^2} - \sqrt{(2k-1)} = Z$$

follows the standardized normal distribution, where k represents the degrees of freedom.

Source: From E. S. Pearson and H. O. Hartley, eds., *Biometrika Tables for Statisticians*, vol. 1, 3d ed., table 8, Cambridge University Press, New York, 1966. Reproduced by permission of the editors and trustees of *Biometrika*.

df \ Pr	0.250	0.100	0.050	0.025	0.010	0.005	0.001
20	23.8277	28.4120	31.4104	34.1696	37.5662	39.9968	45.315
21	24.9348	29.6151	32.6706	35.4789	38.9322	41.4011	46.797
22	26.0393	30.8133	33.9244	36.7807	40.2894	42.7957	48.268
23	27.1413	32.0069	35.1725	38.0756	41.6384	44.1813	49.728
24	28.2412	33.1962	36.4150	39.3641	42.9798	45.5585	51.179
25	29.3389	34.3816	37.6525	40.6465	44.3141	46.9279	52.618
26	30.4346	35.5632	38.8851	41.9232	45.6417	48.2899	54.052
27	31.5284	36.7412	40.1133	43.1945	46.9629	49.6449	55.476
28	32.6205	37.9159	41.3371	44.4608	48.2782	50.9934	56.892
29	33.7109	39.0875	42.5570	45.7223	49.5879	52.3356	58.301
30	34.7997	40.2560	43.7730	46.9792	50.8922	53.6720	59.703
40	45.6160	51.8051	55.7585	59.3417	63.6907	66.7660	73.402
50	56.3336	63.1671	67.5048	71.4202	76.1539	79.4900	86.661
60	66.9815	74.3970	79.0819	83.2977	88.3794	91.9517	99.607
70	77.5767	85.5270	90.5312	95.0232	100.425	104.215	112.317
80	88.1303	96.5782	101.879	106.629	112.329	116.321	124.839
90	98.6499	107.565	113.145	118.136	124.116	128.299	137.208
100	109.141	118.498	124.342	129.561	135.807	140.169	149.449
Z†	+0.6745	+1.2816	+1.6449	+1.9600	+2.3263	+2.5758	+3.0902

Table D.5*a* Durbin-Watson *d* statistic: Significance points of d_L and d_U at 0.05 level of significance

	$k' = 1$		$k' = 2$		$k' = 3$		$k' = 4$		$k' = 5$	
n	d_L	d_U	d_L	d_U	d_L	d_U	d_L	d_U	d_L	d_U
15	1.08	1.36	0.95	1.54	0.82	1.75	0.69	1.97	0.56	2.21
16	1.10	1.37	0.98	1.54	0.86	1.73	0.74	1.93	0.62	2.15
17	1.13	1.38	1.02	1.54	0.90	1.71	0.78	1.90	0.67	2.10
18	1.16	1.39	1.05	1.53	0.93	1.69	0.82	1.87	0.71	2.06
19	1.18	1.40	1.08	1.53	0.97	1.68	0.86	1.85	0.75	2.02
20	1.20	1.41	1.10	1.54	1.00	1.68	0.90	1.83	0.79	1.99
21	1.22	1.42	1.13	1.54	1.03	1.67	0.93	1.81	0.83	1.96
22	1.24	1.43	1.15	1.54	1.05	1.66	0.96	1.80	0.86	1.94
23	1.26	1.44	1.17	1.54	1.08	1.66	0.99	1.79	0.90	1.92
24	1.27	1.45	1.19	1.55	1.10	1.66	1.01	1.78	0.93	1.90
25	1.29	1.45	1.21	1.55	1.12	1.66	1.04	1.77	0.95	1.89
26	1.30	1.46	1.22	1.55	1.14	1.65	1.06	1.76	0.98	1.88
27	1.32	1.47	1.24	1.56	1.16	1.65	1.08	1.76	1.01	1.86
28	1.33	1.48	1.26	1.56	1.18	1.65	1.10	1.75	1.03	1.85
29	1.34	1.48	1.27	1.56	1.20	1.65	1.12	1.74	1.05	1.84
30	1.35	1.49	1.28	1.57	1.21	1.65	1.14	1.74	1.07	1.83
31	1.36	1.50	1.30	1.57	1.23	1.65	1.16	1.74	1.09	1.83
32	1.37	1.50	1.31	1.57	1.24	1.65	1.18	1.73	1.11	1.82
33	1.38	1.51	1.32	1.58	1.26	1.65	1.19	1.73	1.13	1.81
34	1.39	1.51	1.33	1.58	1.27	1.65	1.21	1.73	1.15	1.81
35	1.40	1.52	1.34	1.58	1.28	1.65	1.22	1.73	1.16	1.80
36	1.41	1.52	1.35	1.59	1.29	1.65	1.24	1.73	1.18	1.80
37	1.42	1.53	1.36	1.59	1.31	1.66	1.25	1.72	1.19	1.80
38	1.43	1.54	1.37	1.59	1.32	1.66	1.26	1.72	1.21	1.79
39	1.43	1.54	1.38	1.60	1.33	1.66	1.27	1.72	1.22	1.79
40	1.44	1.54	1.39	1.60	1.34	1.66	1.29	1.72	1.23	1.79
45	1.48	1.57	1.43	1.62	1.38	1.67	1.34	1.72	1.29	1.78
50	1.50	1.59	1.46	1.63	1.42	1.67	1.38	1.72	1.34	1.77
55	1.53	1.60	1.49	1.64	1.45	1.68	1.41	1.72	1.38	1.77
60	1.55	1.62	1.51	1.65	1.48	1.69	1.44	1.73	1.41	1.77
65	1.57	1.63	1.54	1.66	1.50	1.70	1.47	1.73	1.44	1.77
70	1.58	1.64	1.55	1.67	1.52	1.70	1.49	1.74	1.46	1.77
75	1.60	1.65	1.57	1.68	1.54	1.71	1.51	1.74	1.49	1.77
80	1.61	1.66	1.59	1.69	1.56	1.72	1.53	1.74	1.51	1.77
85	1.62	1.67	1.60	1.70	1.57	1.72	1.55	1.75	1.52	1.77
90	1.63	1.68	1.61	1.70	1.59	1.73	1.57	1.75	1.54	1.78
95	1.64	1.69	1.62	1.71	1.60	1.73	1.58	1.75	1.56	1.78
100	1.65	1.69	1.63	1.72	1.61	1.74	1.59	1.76	1.57	1.78

Note: n = number of observations

k' = number of explanatory variables excluding the constant term

Source: J. Durbin and G. S. Watson, "Testing for Serial Correlation in Least Squares Regression," *Biometrika*, vol. 38, pp. 159–177, 1951. Reprinted with the permission of the authors and the *Biometrika* trustees.

Table D.5b Durbin-Watson d statistic: Significance points of d_L and d_U at 0.01 level of significance

	$k' = 1$		$k' = 2$		$k' = 3$		$k' = 4$		$k' = 5$	
n	d_L	d_U	d_L	d_U	d_L	d_U	d_L	d_U	d_L	d_U
15	0.81	1.07	0.70	1.25	0.59	1.46	0.49	1.70	0.39	1.96
16	0.84	1.09	0.74	1.25	0.63	1.44	0.53	1.66	0.44	1.90
17	0.87	1.10	0.77	1.25	0.67	1.43	0.57	1.63	0.48	1.85
18	0.90	1.12	0.80	1.26	0.71	1.42	0.61	1.60	0.52	1.80
19	0.93	1.13	0.83	1.26	0.74	1.41	0.65	1.58	0.56	1.77
20	0.95	1.15	0.86	1.27	0.77	1.41	0.68	1.57	0.60	1.74
21	0.97	1.16	0.89	1.27	0.80	1.41	0.72	1.55	0.63	1.71
22	1.00	1.17	0.91	1.28	0.83	1.40	0.75	1.54	0.66	1.69
23	1.02	1.19	0.94	1.29	0.86	1.40	0.77	1.53	0.70	1.67
24	1.04	1.20	0.96	1.30	0.88	1.41	0.80	1.53	0.72	1.66
25	1.05	1.21	0.98	1.30	0.90	1.41	0.83	1.52	0.75	1.65
26	1.07	1.22	1.00	1.31	0.93	1.41	0.85	1.52	0.78	1.64
27	1.09	1.23	1.02	1.32	0.95	1.41	0.88	1.51	0.81	1.63
28	1.10	1.24	1.04	1.32	0.97	1.41	0.90	1.51	0.83	1.62
29	1.12	1.25	1.05	1.33	0.99	1.42	0.92	1.51	0.85	1.61
30	1.13	1.26	1.07	1.34	1.01	1.42	0.94	1.51	0.88	1.61
31	1.15	1.27	1.08	1.34	1.02	1.42	0.96	1.51	0.90	1.60
32	1.16	1.28	1.10	1.35	1.04	1.43	0.98	1.51	0.92	1.60
33	1.17	1.29	1.11	1.36	1.05	1.43	1.00	1.51	0.94	1.59
34	1.18	1.30	1.13	1.36	1.07	1.43	1.01	1.51	0.95	1.59
35	1.19	1.31	1.14	1.37	1.08	1.44	1.03	1.51	0.97	1.59
36	1.21	1.32	1.15	1.38	1.10	1.44	1.04	1.51	0.99	1.59
37	1.22	1.32	1.16	1.38	1.11	1.45	1.06	1.51	1.00	1.59
38	1.23	1.33	1.18	1.39	1.12	1.45	1.07	1.52	1.02	1.58
39	1.24	1.34	1.19	1.39	1.14	1.45	1.09	1.52	1.03	1.58
40	1.25	1.34	1.20	1.40	1.15	1.46	1.10	1.52	1.05	1.58
45	1.29	1.38	1.24	1.42	1.20	1.48	1.16	1.53	1.11	1.58
50	1.32	1.40	1.28	1.45	1.24	1.49	1.20	1.54	1.16	1.59
55	1.36	1.43	1.32	1.47	1.28	1.51	1.25	1.55	1.21	1.59
60	1.38	1.45	1.35	1.48	1.32	1.52	1.28	1.56	1.25	1.60
65	1.41	1.47	1.38	1.50	1.35	1.53	1.31	1.57	1.28	1.61
70	1.43	1.49	1.40	1.52	1.37	1.55	1.34	1.58	1.31	1.61
75	1.45	1.50	1.42	1.53	1.39	1.56	1.37	1.59	1.34	1.62
80	1.47	1.52	1.44	1.54	1.42	1.57	1.39	1.60	1.36	1.62
85	1.48	1.53	1.46	1.55	1.43	1.58	1.41	1.60	1.39	1.63
90	1.50	1.54	1.47	1.56	1.45	1.59	1.43	1.61	1.41	1.64
95	1.51	1.55	1.49	1.57	1.47	1.60	1.45	1.62	1.42	1.64
100	1.52	1.56	1.50	1.58	1.48	1.60	1.46	1.63	1.44	1.65

Note: n = number of observations
k' = number of explanatory variables excluding the constant term
Source: J. Durbin and G. S. Watson, "Testing for Serial Correlation in Least Squares Regression," *Biometrika*, vol. 38, pp. 159–177, 1951. Reprinted with the permission of the authors and the *Biometrika* trustees.

Table D.6a Critical values of runs in the run test

											N_2								
N_1	2	3	4	5	6	7	8	9	10	11	12	13	14	15	16	17	18	19	20
2											2	2	2	2	2	2	2	2	2
3					2	2	2	2	2	2	2	2	2	3	3	3	3	3	3
4			2	2	2	2	3	3	3	3	3	3	3	3	4	4	4	4	4
5		2	2	3	3	3	3	3	4	4	4	4	4	4	4	4	5	5	5
6		2	2	3	3	3	3	4	4	4	4	5	5	5	5	5	5	6	6
7		2	2	3	3	3	4	4	5	5	5	5	5	6	6	6	6	6	6
8		2	3	3	3	4	4	5	5	5	6	6	6	6	6	7	7	7	7
9		2	3	3	4	4	5	5	5	6	6	6	7	7	7	7	8	8	8
10		2	3	3	4	5	5	5	6	6	7	7	7	7	8	8	8	8	9
11		2	3	4	4	5	5	6	6	7	7	7	8	8	8	9	9	9	9
12	2	2	3	4	4	5	6	6	7	7	7	8	8	8	9	9	9	10	10
13	2	2	3	4	5	5	6	6	7	7	8	8	9	9	9	10	10	10	10
14	2	2	3	4	5	5	6	7	7	8	8	9	9	9	10	10	10	11	11
15	2	3	3	4	5	6	6	7	7	8	8	9	9	10	10	11	11	11	12
16	2	3	4	4	5	6	6	7	8	8	9	9	10	10	11	11	11	12	12
17	2	3	4	4	5	6	7	7	8	9	9	10	10	11	11	11	12	12	13
18	2	3	4	5	5	6	7	8	8	9	9	10	10	11	11	12	12	13	13
19	2	3	4	5	6	6	7	8	8	9	10	10	11	11	12	12	13	13	13
20	2	3	4	5	6	6	7	8	9	9	10	10	11	12	12	13	13	13	14

Note: Tables D.6a and D.6b give the critical values of runs n for various values of N_1(+ symbol) and N_2(− symbol). For the one-sample runs test, any value of n which is equal to or smaller than that shown in Table D.6a or equal to or larger than that shown in Table D.6b is significant at the 0.05 level.

Source: Sidney Siegel, *Nonparametric Statistics for the Behavioral Sciences*, McGraw-Hill Book Company, New York, 1956, table F, pp. 252–253. The tables have been adapted by Siegel from the original source: Frieda S. Swed and C. Eisenhart, "Tables for Testing Randomness of Grouping in a Sequence of Alternatives," *Annals of Mathematical Statistics*, vol. 14, 1943. Used by permission of McGraw-Hill Book Company and *Annals of Mathematical Statistics*.

Table D.6b Critical values of runs in the run test

N_1	\(N_2\) 2	3	4	5	6	7	8	9	10	11	12	13	14	15	16	17	18	19	20
2																			
3																			
4				9	9														
5			9	10	10	11	11												
6			9	10	11	12	12	13	13	13	13								
7				11	12	13	13	14	14	14	14	15	15	15					
8				11	12	13	14	14	15	15	16	16	16	16	17	17	17	17	17
9					13	14	14	15	16	16	16	17	17	18	18	18	18	18	18
10					13	14	15	16	16	17	17	18	18	18	19	19	19	20	20
11					13	14	15	16	17	17	18	19	19	19	20	20	20	21	21
12					13	14	16	16	17	18	19	19	20	20	21	21	21	22	22
13						15	16	17	18	19	19	20	20	21	21	22	22	23	23
14						15	16	17	18	19	20	20	21	22	22	23	23	23	24
15						15	16	18	18	19	20	21	22	22	23	23	24	24	25
16							17	18	19	20	21	21	22	23	23	24	25	25	25
17							17	18	19	20	21	22	23	23	24	25	25	26	26
18							17	18	19	20	21	22	23	24	25	25	26	26	27
19							17	18	20	21	22	23	23	24	25	26	26	27	27
20							17	18	20	21	22	23	24	25	25	26	27	27	28

Example In a sequence of 30 observations consisting of 20 + signs $(= N_1)$ and 10 − signs $(= N_2)$, the critical values of runs at the 0.05 level of significance are 9 and 20, as shown by Tables D.6a and D.6b, respectively. Therefore, if in an application it is found that the number of runs is equal to or less than 9 or equal to or greater than 20, one can reject (at the 0.05 level of significance) the hypothesis that the observed sequence is random.

ANSWERS AND HINTS TO SOLUTIONS OF SELECTED EXERCISES*

2.2 (*a*)

X	$E(Y\,|\,X)$	Y	$E(X\,|\,Y)$
20	26.67	20	20.00
30	32.67	30	29.29
40	41.43	40	38.00
50	51.10	50	48.00
60	60.00	60	60.00
70	65.00	70	66.67

(*b*) The scattergram will show a strong positive relationship between the two variables.

(*c*) The scattergram will show that the conditional means do lie approximately on straight lines.

2.7 Models (1) to (3) are linear regression models, whereas models (5) to (7) are nonlinear regression models. If we let $\alpha = \ln \beta_0$ in model (4), then it is a linear regression model, linear in the parameters α and β_1.

3.3 Write the Cauchy-Schwarz inequality as $[E(XY)]^2 / E(X^2)E(Y^2) \le 1$ and recall the definition of ρ, the population correlation coefficient, given in App. A.

3.6 The rank correlation coefficient is 0.84, which indicates a high degree of positive association between the ranks on the midterm and final examinations.

3.9 (*b*) The estimated regression is

$$\hat{Y}_i = 4.6103 + 0.7574X_i \qquad r^2 = 0.5868$$
$$(0.5476) \quad (0.1500)$$

(*c*) Common stocks are a hedge against inflation but not perfect. Our sample shows that on the average a 1 percent increase in the consumer prices is accompanied by less than 1 percent increase in stock prices.

---

* Unless stated otherwise, we have used 0.05 level of significance in answering the questions. The figures in parentheses underneath the regression coefficients are the estimated standard errors.

3.14 The estimated regression is as follows:

$$\widehat{\ln Y_t} = 6.9484 + 0.0217X_t \qquad r^2 = 0.9840$$
$$(0.0068)$$

β_1 measures the quarterly rate of growth in GNP, which is about 2.2 percent. The corresponding annual rate is about 8.9 percent.

3.15 Letting Y = consumer price index and X = money supply, the scattergram will reveal that Y is linearly related to X as follows:

$$\hat{Y}_i = -80.9 + 0.00575X_i \qquad r^2 = 0.9963$$
$$(0.00038)$$

The intercept term has little economic meaning. The slope coefficient of 0.00575 means that a rise of 1 (billion Yen) in the money supply will raise the consumer price index by 0.00575 units on the average.

3.19 (a) True; (b) false; (c) true.

5.1 (a) $\text{se}(\hat{\beta}_0) = 0.5476$; $\text{se}(\hat{\beta}_1) = 0.1500$; $\hat{\sigma}^2 = 11.4988$.

(b) The 95 percent confidence intervals for β_0, β_1, and σ^2 are, respectively, (3.46 to 5.76), (0.4418 to 1.072), and (6.5645 to 25.1490).

(c) (i) $t = 5.0520$ and (ii) 8.4191. The critical t value is 2.101. Therefore, individually we can reject the null hypotheses.

(d) The predicted value is 9.1547 with the standard error of 0.7665.

(e) The predicted value is 9.1547 with the standard error of 3.4839

(f) The F value is 25.518, which is about equal to $t^2 = (5.0520)^2$ obtained in (c)(i).

5.7 The estimated regression is

$$\hat{E}_i = 5.8808 + 0.4571\sigma_i \qquad r^2 = 0.9139$$
$$(0.0494)$$

Since the estimated slope coefficient is highly significant, we can conclude that the data support the theory.

5.9 (a) The regression results are as follows:

$$\widehat{\text{GNP}_t} = -541.9148 + 7.0043M_t \qquad r^2 = 0.998$$
$$(0.1380)$$

$$\widehat{\ln \text{GNP}_t} = -0.7522 + 1.4216 \ln M_t \qquad r^2 = 0.998$$
$$(0.0278)$$

Both models give excellent fit, as judged by the r^2, t ratios, and the expected positive relationship between GNP and money supply.

(b) The two r^2 values cannot be compared directly for reasons given in Sec. 6.7. The two models may be compared on the basis of the slope coefficients and whether they meet some a priori expectations.

(c) In model I, the slope coefficient measures the (average) rate of change in GNP following a unit (say, $1) change in M, whereas in model II, it measures the elasticity of GNP with respect to M, that is, the percentage change in GNP following a 1 percent change in the money supply.

(d) There are two ways of looking at the problem: Run the regression $\text{GNP}_t = \alpha + \beta M_t$ and see if the estimated α is statistically equal to zero. Alternatively, run the regression $(\text{GNP}/M)_t = \beta_0 + \beta_1 t$, where t is time, and see if the estimated β_1 is statistically insignificant.

6.1 The estimated regressions are

$$\hat{Y}_i = -31074.5898 + 2.4406X_{2i} + 0.3354X_{3i} \qquad r^2 = 0.9905$$
$$(6.1253) \qquad (0.0402)$$

$$\widehat{\ln Y_i} = -8.0498 + 0.7068 \ln X_{2i} + 1.1353 \ln X_{3i} \qquad r^2 = 0.9839$$
$$(0.1538) \qquad (0.2965)$$

Although the R^2 values of both models are very high, the labor coefficient is statistically significant in the second model but insignificant in the first model. Therefore, model II may be preferable. For model II the required elasticities are given directly by the slope coefficients. For model I, however, these elasticities may be computed at the mean values of output, labor, and capital inputs. To compare the R^2 of model II with that of model I, we compute r^2 between antilog $(\widehat{\ln Y})$ and Y, which is 0.9900.

6.10 It follows at once from (6.9.7). This is the coefficient of partial determination and may be interpreted as giving the proportion of the variation in Y not explained by X_3 that has been explained by the addition of the variable X_2.

6.13 Use, for example, formula (6.8.2) and see if the computed $r_{12.3}$ lies between the limits of -1 and $+1$.

6.19 Use the relation $R^2 = (r_{12}^2 + r_{13}^2 - 2r_{12}r_{13}r_{23})/(1 - r_{23}^2)$.

6.20 In the four-variable case there are 6 zero-order correlations and 12 first-order correlations. In the n-variable case, there are $n!/2!(n - 2)!$ zero-order correlations and $n!/2!(n - 3)!$ first-order correlations, where $n!$, read "n factorial," means $n(n - 1)(n - 2) \cdots 3 \cdot 2 \cdot 1$.

7.3 (a) Real income and real interest rate elasticities are 1.6987 and -0.6146, respectively.

    (b) The interest elasticity is not significant $(t = -1.4082)$, but the income elasticity is $(t = 4.8867)$.

    (c) The estimated F value is 66.286, which is significant at the 0.05 level of significance.

    (d) $t = (1.6987 - 1.0)/0.3476 = 2.01$, which is significant at 0.05 level (one-tail test). Hence one can conclude that the income elasticity is different from unity.

    (e) Since the absolute t value of the interest rate coefficient is greater than unity, it may be retained in the model.

7.6 The zero-order correlations are $r_{13} = 0.9885$, $r_{12} = 0.9985$, and $r_{23} = 0.9839$. Using these values, we obtain $r_{13.2} = 0.6786$, $r_{23.1} = -0.4930$, and $r_{12.3} = 0.9705$. The t values for these partial correlations are, respectively, 3.20, 1.9630, and 13.9498. On the basis of one-tail test, each of these t values is statistically significant at 0.05 level of significance.

8.4 $r_{12.3} = 0.5766$, $r_{14.3} = -0.1899$, and $r_{24.3} = -0.3450$. Therefore,

$$r_{12.34} = (r_{12.3} - r_{14.3}r_{24.3})/\sqrt{(1 - r_{14.3}^2)}\sqrt{(1 - r_{24.3}^2)} = 0.5545.$$

$r_{15.34}$ and $r_{25.34}$ can be computed similarly. Then, by substitution $r_{12.345}$ and similar coefficients can be computed from the reduction formula.

8.10 (a) The estimated regression is as follows:

$$\hat{Y}_i = -36.0275 + 0.02035X_{2i} + 15.66734X_{3i} + 0.85497X_{4i} \qquad R^2 = 0.2758$$
$$\phantom{\hat{Y}_i = -36.0275} (49.8344) \quad (0.01912) \qquad (9.52935) \qquad (1.9114)$$

$$t = (-0.7229) \quad (1.0640\ ) \qquad (\ 1.6444\ ) \qquad (0.4473)$$

As can be seen, the model fits the data poorly.

    (b) A priori, β_3 is expected to be positive. β_2 can be positive or negative, depending on the nature of the income and substitution effects. β_4 can be positive (added worker hypothesis) or negative (discouraged worker hypothesis).

    (c) The t ratio of the unemployment-rate coefficient is only 0.4473, indicating that the unemployment rate has no effect on labor-force participation.

    (d) Since the t ratio of the unemployment-rate coefficient is less than unity in absolute value, it may be dropped from the model.

    (e) Some other variables that may be considered are the level of education, unemployment benefits, and other public assistance benefits.

*8.12 The likelihood function (LF) is

$$(2\pi\sigma^2)^{-N/2} \exp\left[-\frac{1}{2\sigma^2}(\mathbf{y} - \mathbf{X}\boldsymbol{\beta})'(\mathbf{y} - \mathbf{X}\boldsymbol{\beta}) \right]$$

Therefore,

$$\ln LF = -\frac{N}{2} \ln (2\pi\sigma^2) - \frac{1}{2\sigma^2} (\mathbf{y} - \mathbf{X}\boldsymbol{\beta})'(\mathbf{y} - \mathbf{X}\boldsymbol{\beta})$$

Differentiate ln LF with respect to $\boldsymbol{\beta}$ and show that the ML and OLS estimators of $\boldsymbol{\beta}$ are identical.

9.1 If one X variable is an exact linear combination of the other X's, we have, in fact, $k - 1$ equations in k unknowns; that is, there are more unknowns than the equations to estimate them. Hence unique solutions are not possible.

*9.4 If $|\mathbf{R}|$ is zero, there is perfect multicollinearity. If $|\mathbf{R}|$ is small, it will indicate less than perfect collinearity. If, however, $|\mathbf{R}| = 1$, the X's are uncorrelated.

9.8 $r_{12.3} = r_{13.2} = r_{23.1} = \pm 1$ and $R^2_{1.23} = 1$.

9.11 The answer can be obtained from Exercise 9.10.

9.13 (a) Yes; the answer is obvious from the formulas to estimate $\beta_{12.3}$ and $\beta_{13.2}$ when cov (X_2, X_3) is zero.

(b) $\hat{\beta}_1 = \hat{\alpha}_1 + \hat{\gamma}_1 - \bar{Y}$.

(c) The variance of $\hat{\beta}_2$ is not equal to the variance of $\hat{\alpha}_2$ nor is the variance of $\hat{\gamma}_3$ equal to the variance of $\hat{\beta}_3$.

10.2 $A = 7.2774$ and $B = 1.0417$; therefore, $\chi^2 = A/B = 6.9897$. The 0.05 level critical χ^2 value for 8 df is 15.51; therefore, the estimated χ^2 value is not significant.

10.3 No because the models are nonlinear in the parameters. For some estimating techniques, see Chap. 15.

10.5 (b) The estimated regression is

$$\hat{Y}_i = -4664.3640 + 0.9168X_i \qquad r^2 = 0.6664$$
$$(0.2451)$$
$$t = (3.7398)$$

(c) It seems that the standard deviation of productivity increases linearly with average productivity, which itself generally increases with the employment size. Therefore, in a regression of average compensation on average productivity one may expect heteroscedasticity.

10.9 (a) The regression equation is

$$\hat{Y}_i = 1999.0466 + 0.2323X_i \qquad r^2 = 0.4356$$
$$(0.1000)$$

(b) $e_i = -2350.3179 + 0.5647Y_i \qquad r^2 = 0.5640$
$$(0.1870)$$
$$t = (3.013)$$

As the regression shows, e_i and Y_i are positively correlated. Perhaps heteroscedasticity is suspected.

(c) $\ln e_i^2 = 35.9010 - 2.8099 \ln X_i \qquad r^2 = 0.0595$
$$(\ \ 4.2160)$$
$$t = (-0.6670)$$

(d) $|e_i| = 409.2041 - 0.0205X_i \qquad r^2 = 0.0130$
$$(0.0680)$$

$$|e_i| = 578.7556 - 3.7411\sqrt{X_i} \qquad r^2 = 0.0112$$
$$(13.3220)$$

In neither case is $|e_i|$ systematically related to X_i or $\sqrt{X_i}$.

(e) The rank correlation coefficient is -0.5167, which is statistically insignificant.

11.3 (a) Compute the von Neumann ratio. Using the formulas for the mean and the variance of the ratio, find out from the normal distribution table how many σ units does the estimated ratio lie from the mean value. If it lies, say, more than 2σ units from the mean, one may accept the hypothesis of serial correlation.

(b) $\delta^2/s^2 = (N/N - 1)\, d.$

(c) When $d = 0$, $\delta^2/s^2 = 0$

$$d = 4,\ \delta^2/s^2 = 4N/(N - 1)$$
$$d = 2,\ \delta^2/s^2 = 2N/(N - 1)$$

(d) Even if the population disturbances u_t are randomly and normally distributed, it is unlikely that the (sample) residuals are themselves likely to be so distributed, especially in small samples. But note that OLS does not require the assumption of normality. Moreover, even if the residuals are nonrandom, the OLS estimators of the classical linear model are still unbiased.

(e) Mean $= 2.02$; variance $= 0.0399$. From the normal distribution table we see that $2.02 \pm 3(0.1999) = (1.4203, 2.6197)$ covers about 99.7 percent of the area under the normal curve. Hence we can reject the hypothesis of no serial correlation.

11.8 (b) Yes $(d_L = 1.08$ and $d_U = 1.36$ for $k' = 1$, $N = 15$, and $\alpha = 0.05)$.

(c) The Theil-Nagar and Cochrane-Orcutt estimates are 0.8250 and 0.6640, respectively.

(d) The Theil-Nagar transformation gives the following results:

$$\hat{Y}_t = 14.2112 + 29.6871X_t, \qquad r^2 = 0.6061$$
$$(\ 9.9402)\ \ (\ 6.6378) \qquad\qquad d = 0.7765$$

(e) Since the d value obtained in (d) still shows positive autocorrelation, one can repeat the Theil-Nagar procedure one or more times. Alternatively, the Cochrane-Orcutt procedure may be used. This latter method gives the following equation:

$$\hat{Y}_t = 0.9303 + 34.7899X_t, \qquad r^2 = 0.9859$$
$$(2.1464)\ \ (\ 1.3531) \qquad\qquad d = 1.7378$$

As can be seen, one may now accept the hypothesis of no positive autocorrelation in the residuals because the estimated d is sufficiently close to 2.

11.13 $\qquad \ln{(HWI)}_t = 0.5441 - 0.9411\ \ln{U_t} + 0.6958\ \ln{U_{t-1}} + 0.8249\ \ln{(HWI)}_{t-1}$
$$(0.9270)\ (0.4794) \qquad (0.3194) \qquad\qquad (0.2920)$$
$$R^2 = 0.9634$$

Therefore, $\hat{\rho} = 0.8249$. Other estimates of ρ are 0.7393 and 0.7763. The Theil-Nagar estimate is 0.5598. Since the Durbin two-step estimate of ρ differs from the Theil-Nagar estimate, the results based on transforming the data using the Durbin estimate are expected to be different from those given in the text.

11.15 If the X's are mutually uncorrelated, (11.2.4) reduces to var $(\beta_1^*) = \sigma^2/\sum x_t^2$, which is identical to the usual OLS variance of $\hat{\beta}_1$. But note that the var (β_1^*) is still not optimum for reasons explained in the text.

11.19 Cost $= 166.4666 + 19.9333$ (output) $\qquad r^2 = 0.8409$
$$(\ 3.060) \qquad\qquad\qquad d = 0.716$$

Since the number of observations is less than 15, we cannot use the Durbin-Watson tables. However, the estimated d is rather low, perhaps suggesting autocorrelation. But Exercise 8.9 will show that X^2 and X^3 terms are individually statistically significant. Therefore, the observed low value of d may very well reflect specification bias, the bias resulting from omitting X^2 and X^3.

11.23 Since the Durbin-Watson d is inappropriate to test for serial correlation in autoregressive models, one cannot tell much about it from the estimated d. However, the so-called Durbin h statistic (see Chap. 12) may be used, provided the number of observations is large.

11.25 Since $\hat{\beta}_0(1 - \hat{\rho}) = 1.4091$ (where $\hat{\rho} = 0.5598$),

$$\hat{\beta}_0 = \frac{1.4091}{1 - \hat{\rho}}$$

which is a nonlinear function of $\hat{\rho}$. Therefore, even if $E(\hat{\rho}) = \rho$, we cannot say that $E(\hat{\beta}_0) = \beta_0$ because E is a linear operator.

12.1 The estimated short-run demand function is as follows:

$$\hat{Y}_t = -1.648 + 0.3191X_t + 0.5157Y_{t-1} \qquad R^2 = 0.9428$$
$$(\ 2.320)\ (0.1079) \qquad (0.1819) \qquad\qquad \delta = 0.4843$$

The long-run demand function is as follows:

$$Y_t^* = -\frac{1.648}{0.4843} + \frac{0.3191}{0.4843}X_t$$

$$= -3.4028 + 0.6589X_t$$

12.9 $Y_t = \alpha\ \delta\gamma + \beta\delta\gamma X_t + [(1 - \gamma) + (1 - \delta)]Y_{t-1} - (1 - \delta)(1 - \gamma)Y_{t-2} + [\delta u_t - (1 - \gamma)u_{t-1}]$

12.16 The degree of the polynomial should be at least one more than the number of turning points observed in the series. Follow this rule in deciding the degree of the polynomial.

12.18 Without imposing any restrictions, we obtain the following regression:

$$\hat{Y}_t = -1.0684 + 0.2208X_t + 0.8038X_{t-1} + 0.4242X_{t-2} - 0.9182X_{t-3}$$
$$(0.1982) \qquad (0.2347) \qquad (0.1916) \qquad (\ 0.3256)$$

Imposing the end (zero) restrictions, we obtain

$$\hat{Y}_t = -0.0018 + 0.1230X_t + 0.1844X_{t-1} + 0.1844X_{t-2} + 0.1230X_{t-3}$$
$$(0.0175) \qquad (0.0261) \qquad (0.0261) \qquad (0.0175)$$

The mean lags for the two regressions are -2.0774 and 1.5, respectively. The analysis shows clearly why one may want to impose the (zero) end restrictions.

13.5 Use the t test as follows:

(a) $t = \dfrac{\hat{\alpha}_1 - \hat{\alpha}_2}{\sqrt{[\operatorname{var}(\hat{\alpha}_1) + \operatorname{var}(\hat{\alpha}_2) - 2\operatorname{cov}(\hat{\alpha}_1, \hat{\alpha}_2)]}}$

(b) $t = \dfrac{\hat{\alpha}_1 - \hat{\alpha}_3}{\sqrt{[\operatorname{var}(\hat{\alpha}_1) + \operatorname{var}(\hat{\alpha}_3) - 2\operatorname{cov}(\hat{\alpha}_1, \hat{\alpha}_3)]}}$

(c) Not necessarily. Whether $\alpha_1 = \alpha_2$ can be tested by the t test as $t = (\hat{\alpha}_1 - \hat{\alpha}_2)/\operatorname{se}(\hat{\alpha}_1 - \hat{\alpha}_2)$.

13.8 (a) The regression on the transformed data is

$$\hat{Y}_t = 6525.0 + 0.0393X_t \qquad r^2 = 0.3974$$
$$(1580.0)\ (0.0103)$$

(b) The slope coefficients are virtually identical, which should not be surprising because we are assuming implicitly that the effect of the seasonal, if any, is reflected in the intercept term only.

13.11 (a) $\hat{Y}_t = -1.7502 + 1.4839D + 0.1504X_t - 0.1034(DX)_t \qquad R^2 = 0.9425$
$\qquad\quad (\ 0.3319)\ (0.4707) \quad (0.0163) \qquad (0.0332) \qquad\qquad d = 1.47$

(b) Since the differential intercept and slope coefficients are statistically significant, we can conclude that the two savings-income regressions are statistically different.

(c) The advantages are (i) unlike the Chow test, we need to run a single regression, and (ii) the Chow test will tell whether two regressions differ without identifying the source(s) of the difference. The dummy-variable procedure shows whether the difference is due to the intercept or slope coefficient or both. That is, the dummy technique handles AOV and ACOV problems in just a single regression.

13.12 When $D = 5$ (first period) and when $D = 2$ (second period), the regression results are as follows:

$$\hat{Y}_t = -2.739 + 0.4946Z_t + 0.2194\ X_t - 0.0345(ZX)_t \qquad R^2 = 0.9526$$
$$\qquad\quad (0.5960)\ (0.1568) \qquad (0.0333) \qquad (0.0111) \qquad\qquad d = 1.47$$

When $D = 1$ or 0, the regression is as shown in Exercise 13.11. Comparing the results, we see that the differential intercept and slope dummies are significant in both regressions although their numerical values are different. But this difference is more apparent than real because it can be seen that on the Z scale the values of the differential intercept and slope dummies are $\frac{1}{3}$ the corresponding values on the D scale, which should be the case in view of the postulated relationship between Z and D.

13.15 (a) $\hat{Y}_t = 1526 - 242.50D_1 - 334.67D_2 - 101.67D_3 \qquad R^2 = 0.1787$
$\qquad\quad (\ 123)\ \ (174.10) \qquad (174.10) \qquad (174.10)$

(b) The differential intercepts may represent seasonal effect, if any, associated with the second, third, and fourth quarters.

(c) Only the dummy coefficient associated with the third quarter is statistically significant at the 0.05 level (one-tail test). Therefore, there may very well be some seasonal factor operating in that quarter. To remove this seasonal component, for the third quarter of each year add 334.67 to the sales figures for that quarter; the sales figure thus obtained is now free of the seasonal effect. But note that this procedure is valid only if we assume that the seasonal effect is additive and that the dummy-variable method does indeed identify the seasonal effect.

14.1 (a) The estimated regression is

$$\hat{Y}_i = -0.9457 + 0.1021X_i \qquad r^2 = 0.8046$$
$$\qquad\qquad (0.0082)$$

The equation gives the conditional probability of a family with a given income owning a house.

(b) Substitute the various X values in the preceding equation and obtain the corresponding estimated Y_i. It will be seen that several estimated Y_i are negative or in excess of 1. If $\hat{Y}_i$ is negative, treat it as zero; and if it exceeds 1, treat it as 1. This is a major problem with the linear probability models; the estimated Y_i do not necessarily lie between 0 and 1.

14.5 Given $\bar{R}^2 = 0.1336$, $R^2 = 0.175$, $N = 25,143$, and $k = 27$, it can be seen that $F = 204.8856$, which is highly significant.

15.3
$$\frac{\partial \sum u_i^2}{\partial \alpha} = 2 \sum (Y_i - \alpha X_1^{\beta_1} X_2^{\beta_2})(-X_1^{\beta_1} X_2^{\beta_2}) = 0$$

$$\frac{\partial \sum u_i^2}{\partial \beta_1} = 2 \sum (Y_i - \alpha X_1^{\beta_1} X_2^{\beta_2})\{-\alpha X_2^{\beta_2} X_1^{\beta_1} \ln(X_1)\} = 0$$

$$\frac{\partial \sum u_i^2}{\partial \beta_2} = 2 \sum (Y_i - \alpha X_1^{\beta_1} X_2^{\beta_2})\{-\alpha X_1^{\beta_1} X_2^{\beta_2} \ln(X_2)\} = 0$$

(a) Unlike the usual OLS normal equations, the preceding equations contain the unknowns themselves and are highly nonlinear in the parameters.

(b) As a result, the unknowns cannot be expressed solely in terms of the (observable) sample quantities. Hence they cannot be readily estimated.

(c) Informally, one can resort to a search procedure. For example, one can assign some "initial" values to α, β_1, and β_2 and solve the preceding normal equations. Based on these values, calculate the R^2 value. Change the initial values of α, β_1, and β_2 and see if one obtains a higher R^2, and so on. The search procedure stops when the successive changes in the values assigned to the parameters do not change the value of the estimated R^2 substantially. Formally, one can systematize the preceding search procedure. For details, consult the references.

15.4 The results of the restricted least squares ($\beta_2 + \beta_3 = 1$) are as follows:

$$\ln \frac{\text{output}}{L} = 5.7487 - 0.3629 \ln \frac{K}{L} \qquad r^2 = 0.3057$$
$$(0.1517)$$
$$\sum e_2^2 = 0.236$$

The results of the unrestricted least squares are

$$\ln (\text{output}) = -8.0498 + 0.7068 \ln L + 1.1353 \ln K \qquad R^2 = 0.9839$$
$$(0.1538) \qquad (0.2965) \qquad \sum e_1^2 = 0.072$$

To test whether the restriction $\beta_2 + \beta_3 = 1$ is valid, we use the F test. The resulting F value is 27.3333, which is highly significant. Thus, we can conclude that the restriction is not valid.

15.10 By definition, the unrestricted least squares gives the minimum residual sum of squares $\sum e_i^2$. Therefore, any departure (because of any restrictions) will give a value greater than or at most equal to $\sum e_i^2$.

15.12 As noted in the text, $F_{1,k} = t_k^2$; that is, an F variable with 1 df (in the numerator) and k df (in the denominator) is t^2 with k df.

15.14 (a) $\hat{\gamma} = \text{antilog} (\hat{\beta}_0)$

$$\hat{\delta} = \frac{\hat{\beta}_1}{\hat{\beta}_1 + \hat{\beta}_2}$$

$$\hat{v} = \hat{\beta}_1 + \hat{\beta}_2$$

$$\hat{\rho} = \frac{-2\hat{\beta}_3(\hat{\beta}_1 + \hat{\beta}_2)}{\hat{\beta}_1 \hat{\beta}_2}$$

(b) Generally not, although a large sample approximation can be used (see Chap. 18).

(c)

$$\qquad\qquad \hat{\beta}_0 \qquad\qquad \hat{\beta}_1 \qquad\qquad \hat{\beta}_2 \qquad\qquad \hat{\beta}_3$$

$$\ln (\text{output}) = -30.8056 - 6.9160 \ln L_i + 8.8173 \ln K_i - 0.6578 \left(\ln \frac{K}{L}\right)^2$$
$$(6.9482) \qquad (7.0193) \qquad (0.5988)$$
$$R^2 = 0.9852$$

Using the equation, we obtain

$$\hat{\gamma} = \text{antilog} (-30.8056) \qquad \hat{\delta} = 4.6375 \qquad \hat{v} = 1.9013 \qquad \hat{\rho} = -0.0410$$

Note that although the estimated R^2 is very high, none of the partial slope coefficients is statistically significant. This may be due to collinearity between K and L and or specification bias. Perhaps the Cobb-Douglas production function seems more appropriate than the CES production function in the present case.

16.1 Consumption $= -18.12 + 0.6777$ income $\qquad r^2 = 0.9960$
$$\qquad\qquad\quad (6.90) \ (0.0107)$$

16.3 (a) There is really no simultaneous-equations bias here because each of the equations estimated expresses an endogenous variable solely as a function of predetermined or exogenous variables. Therefore, OLS will provide consistent estimates of the parameters.

(b) Note that all variables are measured in the first difference form. R^2 values are generally lower for such regressions because the first difference transformation often removes the trend which is generally the cause of high R^2 values.

17.2

$$\hat{\beta}_0 = \hat{\Pi}_3 - \hat{\beta}_1 \hat{\Pi}_0 \qquad \hat{\beta}_1 = \frac{\hat{\Pi}_4}{\hat{\Pi}_1} \qquad \hat{\beta}_2 = \hat{\Pi}_5 - \frac{\hat{\Pi}_2 \hat{\Pi}_4}{\hat{\Pi}_1}$$

$$\hat{\alpha}_0 = \hat{\Pi}_3 - \hat{\alpha}_1 \hat{\Pi}_0 \qquad \hat{\alpha}_1 = \frac{\hat{\Pi}_5}{\hat{\Pi}_2} \qquad \hat{\alpha}_2 = \hat{\Pi}_4 - \frac{\hat{\Pi}_1 \hat{\Pi}_5}{\hat{\Pi}_2}$$

17.6 (a) By the order condition of identification, it can be readily checked that both the equations are identified; the first equation excludes X_1, and the second equation excludes X_2.

(b) If $\gamma_{11} = 0$, the model becomes

$$Y_{1t} = \beta_{10} + \beta_{12} Y_{2t} + u_{1t}$$
$$Y_{2t} = \beta_{20} + \beta_{21} Y_{1t} + \gamma_{22} X_{2t} + u_{2t}$$

In this situation, the first equation is identified but the second is not.

17.9 The endogenous variables are Y, I, C, and Q, and the predetermined variables are Y_{t-1}, C_{t-1}, P_t, Q_{t-1}, and R_t. Applying the order condition, it can be seen that all four structural equations are overidentified.

17.12 For recursive models OLS can be applied to each equation individually. For details, see Chap. 18.

18.1 The ILS regression of consumption on income is

$$\hat{C}_t = 11.8318 + 0.5994 Y_t$$

whereas the corresponding OLS regression is (see Exercise 16.1)

$$\hat{C}_t = -18.12 + 0.6777 Y_t$$

18.4 As noted in the text, if the R^2 value is high in the first-stage regressions, 2SLS does no better than OLS. But this does not mean 2SLS is useless in such cases. The reasons are spelled out in the text.

18.6 (a) The demand function is unidentified.

(b) The supply function is overidentified.

(c) 2SLS may be used to estimate the parameters of the overidentified supply function.

(d) Both the functions are now overidentified. 2SLS may still be used to estimate their parameters.

18.8 (a) The first equation is underidentified, and the second is overidentified.

(b) To estimate the second equation, we use 2SLS as follows:

First-stage regression

$$\hat{R}_t = 5.7074 - 0.0834 M_t + 0.0205 Y_{t-1} \qquad R^2 = 0.8842$$
$$\phantom{\hat{R}_t = 5.7074 - }(0.0345) \qquad (0.0063)$$

Second-stage regression

$$\hat{Y}_t = -176.0757 + 194.1922 \hat{R}_t \qquad R^2 = 0.9106$$
$$\phantom{\hat{Y}_t = -176.0757 + }(17.5670)$$

18.9 Both equations are now identified; therefore, they can be estimated by ILS. The reduced-form regressions are

$$\hat{R}_t = -0.6203 + 0.0345 M_t - 0.0072 I_t \qquad R^2 = 0.7878$$
$$\phantom{\hat{R}_t = -0.6203 + }(0.0244) \qquad (0.0252)$$
$$\hat{Y}_t = -253.5516 + 4.4057 M_t + 1.7818 I_t \qquad R^2 = 0.9968$$
$$\phantom{\hat{Y}_t = -253.5516 + }(0.5940) \qquad (0.6141)$$

From the preceding reduced-form regressions, the following ILS regressions can be obtained:

$$\hat{R}_t = -1.6345 + 0.0167 M_t - 0.0040 Y_t$$
$$\hat{Y}_t = -332.7648 + 127.7014 R_t + 0.8623 I_t$$

SELECTED BIBLIOGRAPHY

BOOKS

Introductory

Frank, C. R., Jr.: *Statistics and Econometrics*, Holt, Rinehart and Winston, Inc., New York, 1971.
Hu, Teh-Wei: *Econometrics: An Introductory Analysis*, University Park Press, Baltimore, 1973.
Klein, Lawrence R.: *An Introduction to Econometrics*, Prentice-Hall, Inc., Englewood Cliffs, N.J., 1962.
Walters, A. A.: *An Introduction to Econometrics*, Macmillan & Co., Ltd., London, 1968.

Intermediate

Aigner, D. J.: *Basic Econometrics*, Prentice-Hall, Inc., Englewood Cliffs, N.J., 1971.
Draper, N. R., and H. Smith: *Applied Regression Analysis*, John Wiley & Sons, Inc., New York, 1967.
Dutta, M.: *Econometric Methods*, South-Western Publishing Company, Incorporated, Cincinnati, 1975.
Goldberger, A. S.: *Topics in Regression Analysis*, The Macmillan Company, New York, 1968.
Huang, D. S.: *Regression and Econometric Methods*, John Wiley & Sons, Inc., New York, 1970.
Kelejian, H. A., and W. E. Oates: *Introduction to Econometrics: Principles and Applications*, Harper & Row, Publishers, Incorporated, New York, 1974.
Koutsoyiannis, A.: *Theory of Econometrics*, Harper & Row, Publishers, Incorporated, New York, 1973.
Murphy, James L.: *Introductory Econometrics*, Richard D. Irwin, Inc., Homewood, Ill., 1973.
Netter, J., and W. Wasserman: *Applied Linear Statistical Models*, Richard D. Irwin, Inc., Homewood, Ill., 1974.
Pindyck, R. S., and D. L. Rubinfeld: *Econometric Models and Econometric Forecasts*, McGraw-Hill Book Company, New York, 1976.
Sprent, Peter: *Models in Regression and Related Topics*, Methuen & Co., Ltd., London, 1969.
Tintner, Gerhard: *Econometrics*, John Wiley & Sons, Inc., (science ed.), New York, 1965.
Valavanis, Stefan: *Econometrics: An Introduction to Maximum-Likelihood Methods*, McGraw-Hill Book Company, New York, 1959.
Wallis, K. F.: *Introductory Econometrics*, Aldine Publishing Company, Chicago, 1972.
Wonnacott, R. J., and T. H. Wonnacott: *Econometrics*, John Wiley & Sons, Inc., New York, 1970.

451

Advanced

Christ, C. F.: *Econometric Models and Methods*, John Wiley & Sons, Inc., New York, 1966.
Dhrymes, P. J.: *Econometrics: Statistical Foundations and Applications*, Harper & Row, Publishers, Incorporated, New York, 1970.
Goldberger, A. S.: *Econometric Theory*, John Wiley & Sons, Inc., New York, 1964.
Johnston, J.: *Econometric Methods*, 2d ed., McGraw-Hill Book Company, New York, 1972.
Klein, Lawrence R.: *A Textbook of Econometrics*, 2d ed., Prentice-Hall, Inc., Englewood Cliffs, N.J., 1974.
Kmenta, Jan: *Elements of Econometrics*, The Macmillan Company, New York, 1971.
Madansky, A.: *Foundations of Econometrics*, North-Holland Publishing Company, Amsterdam, 1976.
Maddala, G. S.: *Econometrics*, McGraw-Hill Book Company, New York, 1977.
Malinvaud, E.: *Statistical Methods of Econometrics*, 2d ed., North-Holland Publishing Company, Amsterdam, 1976.
Theil, Henry: *Principles of Econometrics*, John Wiley & Sons, Inc., New York, 1971.

Specialized

Dhrymes, P. J.: *Distributed Lags: Problems of Estimation and Formulation*, Holden-Day, Inc., Publisher, San Francisco, 1971.
Goldfeld, S. M., and R. E. Quandt: *Nonlinear Methods in Econometrics*, North-Holland Publishing Company, Amsterdam, 1972.
Graybill, F. A.: *An Introduction to Linear Statistical Models, vol. 1*, McGraw-Hill Book Company, New York, 1961.
Rao, C. R.: *Linear Statistical Inference and Its Applications*, 2d ed., John Wiley & Sons, New York, 1975.
Zellner, A.: *An Introduction to Bayesian Inference in Econometrics*, John Wiley & Sons, Inc., New York, 1971.

Applied

Bridge, J. I.: *Applied Econometrics*, North-Holland Publishing Company, Amsterdam, 1971.
Cramer, J. S.: *Empirical Econometrics*, North-Holland Publishing Company, Amsterdam, 1969.
Desai, Meghnad: *Applied Econometrics*, McGraw-Hill Book Company, New York, 1976.
Leser, C. E. V.: *Econometric Techniques and Problems*, 2d ed., Hafner Publishing Company, Inc., 1974.
Rao, Potluri, and Roger LeRoy Miller: *Applied Econometrics*, Wadsworth Publishing Company, Inc., Belmont, Calif., 1971.

ARTICLES

Multicollinearity

Farrar, D. E., and R. R. Glauber: "Multicollinearity in Regression Analysis: The Problem Revisited," *Review of Economics and Statistics*, vol. 49, pp. 92–107, 1967.
Geary, R. C.: "Some Results about Relations between Stochastic Variables: A Discussion Document," *Review of International Statistical Institute*, vol. 31, pp. 163–181, 1963.
Silvey, S. D.: "Multicollinearity and Imprecise Estimation," *Journal of the Royal Statistical Society*, ser. B, vol. 31, pp. 539–552, 1969.

Heteroscedasticity

Glejser, H.: "A New Test for Heteroscedasticity," *Journal of the American Statistical Association*, vol. 64, pp. 316–323, 1969.
Goldfeld, S. M., and R. E. Quandt: "Some Tests for Homoscedasticity," *Journal of the American Statistical Association*, vol. 60, pp. 539–547, 1965.

Lancaster, T.: "Grouping Estimators on Heteroscedastic Data," *Journal of the American Statistical Association*, vol. 63, pp. 182–191, 1968.

Park, R. E.: "Estimation with Heteroscedastic Error Terms," *Econometrica*, vol. 34, no. 4, p. 888, October 1966.

Autocorrelation

Cochrane, D., and G. H. Orcutt: "Application of Least-Squares Regressions to Relationships Containing Autocorrelated Error Terms," *Journal of the American Statistical Association*, vol. 44, pp. 32–61, 1949.

Durbin, J.: "Testing for Serial Correlation in Least-Squares Regression When Some of the Regressors Are Lagged Dependent Variables," *Econometrica*, vol. 38, pp. 410–421, 1970.

Durbin, J., and G. S. Watson: "Testing for Serial Correlation in Least-Squares Regression," *Biometrika*, vol. 27, pp. 409–428, and vol. 38, pp. 159–178, 1951.

Griliches, Z.: "A Note on the Serial Correlation Bias in Estimates of Distributed Lags," *Econometrica*, vol. 29, pp. 65–73, 1961.

Henshaw, R. C.: "Testing Single-Equation Least-Squares Regression Models for Autocorrelated Disturbances," *Econometrica*, vol. 34, pp. 646–660, 1966.

Kadiyala, K. R.: "A Transformation Used to Circumvent the Problem of Autocorrelation," *Econometrica*, vol. 36, pp. 1227–1236, 1968.

Sargent, T. J.: "Some Evidence on the Small-Sample Properties of Distributed Lag Estimators in the Presence of Autocorrelated Disturbances," *Review of Economics and Statistics*, vol. 50, pp. 87–95, 1968.

Theil, H., and A. L. Nagar: "Testing the Independence of Regression Disturbances," *Journal of the American Statistical Association*, vol. 56, pp. 793–906, 1961.

Autoregressive and distributed-lag models

Almon, S.: "Lags Between Investment Decisions and Their Causes," *Review of Economics and Statistics*, vol. 50, pp. 193–206, 1968.

DeLeeuw, F.: "The Demand for Capital Goods by Manufacturers: A Study of Quarterly Time Series," *Econometrica*, vol. 30, pp. 407–423, 1962.

Griliches, Z.: "Distributed Lags, A Survey," *Econometrica*, vol. 35, pp. 16–49, 1967.

Jorgenson, D.: "Rational Distributed Lag Functions," *Econometrica*, vol. 34, pp. 135–149, 1966.

Solow, R. M.: "On a Family of Lag Distributions," *Econometrica*, vol. 28, pp. 393–406, 1960 (errata on p. 375).

Tinsley, P. A.: "An Application of Variable Weight Distributed Lags," *Journal of the American Statistical Association*, vol. 62, pp. 1277–1289, 1967.

Dummy variables

Chow, Gregory C.: "Tests of Equality Between Sets of Coefficients in Two Linear Regressions," *Econometrica*, vol. 28, no. 3, pp. 591–605, 1960.

Fisher, Franklin M.: "Tests of Equality Between Sets of Coefficients in Two Linear Regressions: An Expository Note," *Econometrica*, vol. 38, pp. 361–366, 1970.

Gujarati, Damodar: "Use of Dummy Variables in Testing for Equality Between Sets of Coefficients in Two Linear Regressions: A Note," *The American Statistician*, vol. 24, no. 1, pp. 50–52, 1970.

Gujarati, Damodar: "Use of Dummy Variables in Testing for Equality Between Sets of Coefficients in Linear Regressions: A Generalization," *The American Statistician*, vol. 24, no. 5, pp. 18–21, 1970.

Lovell, Michael C.: "Seasonal Adjustment of Economic Time Series and Multiple Regression Analysis," *Journal of the American Statistical Association*, vol. 58, pp. 993–1010, 1963.

Suits, Daniel B.: "Use of Dummy Variables in Regression Equations," *Journal of the American Statistical Association*, vol. 52, pp. 548–551, 1957.

Errors in variables

Bartlett, M. S.: "Fitting a Straight Line When Both Variables Are Subject to Error," *Biometrika*, vol. 5, pp. 207–212, 1949.

Durbin, J.: "Errors in Variables," *Review of the International Statistical Institute*, vol. 26, pp. 37–47, 1958.

Griliches, Z.: "Errors in Variables and Other Unobservables," *Econometrica*, vol. 42, pp. 971–998, 1974.

Halperin, M.: "Fitting of Straight Lines and Prediction When Both Variables Are Subject to Error," *Journal of the American Statistical Association*, vol. 56, pp. 657–669, 1961.

Hooper, J. W., and H. Theil: "The Extension of Wald's Method of Fitting Straight Lines to Multiple Regression," *Review of the International Statistical Institute*, vol. 26, pp. 37–47, 1958.

Wald, A.: "The Fitting of Straight Lines If Both Variables Are Subject to Error," *Annals of Mathematics and Statistics*, vol. 11, pp. 284–300, 1940.

Specification bias

Ramsey, James B.: "Tests for Specification Errors in Classical Linear Least-Squares Regression Analysis," *Journal of the Royal Statistical Society*, ser. B, vol. 31, pp. 350–371, 1969.

Theil, Henry, "Specification Errors and the Estimation of Economic Relationships," *Review of the International Statistical Institute*, vol. 25, pp. 41–51, 1957.

Restricted least squares

Judge, L. G., and T. Takayama: "Inequality Restrictions in Regression Analysis," *Journal of the American Statistical Association*, vol. 61, pp. 166–181, March 1966.

Theil, H., and A. S. Goldberger: "On Pure and Mixed Statistical Estimation in Econometrics," *International Economic Review*, vol. 2, pp. 65–78, 1961.

Nonlinear (in parameters) regression

Marquardt, D. W.: "An Algorithm for Least-squares Estimation of Nonlinear Parameters," *Journal of the Society of Industrial and Applied Mathematics*, vol. 2, pp. 431–441, 1963.

Simultaneous-equations models

THE IDENTIFICATION PROBLEM

Koopmans, T. C.: "Identification Problems in Economic Model Construction," *Econometrica*, vol. 17, pp. 125–144, 1949.

Working, E. J.: "What Do Statistical 'Demand Curves' Show?" *Quarterly Journal of Economics*, vol. 41, pp. 212–235, 1927.

Working, H.: "The Statistical Determination of Demand Curves," *Quarterly Journal of Economics*, vol. 39, pp. 503–543, 1925.

ESTIMATING METHODS

Anderson, T. W., and H. Rubin: "Estimation of the Parameters of a Single Equation in a Complete System of Stochastic Equations," *Annals of Mathematics and Statistics*, vol. 20, pp. 46–63, 1949.

Chow, G.: "A Comparison of Alternative Estimators for Simultaneous Equations," *Econometrica*, vol. 32, pp. 532–553, 1964.

Cragg, J.: "On the Relative Small Sample Properties of Several Structural Equation Estimators: The Results of Some Monte Carlo Experiments," *Econometrica*, vol. 35, pp. 89–110, 1967.

Koopmans, T. C.: "The Estimation of Simultaneous Linear Economic Relationships," in W. C. Hood and T. C. Koopmans, eds., *Studies in Econometric Method*, John Wiley & Sons, Inc., New York, 1953, pp. 112–199.

Sargan, J. D.: "The Estimation of Economic Relationships Using Instrumental Variables," *Econometrica*, vol. 32, pp. 393–415, 1964.

Sargan, J. D.: " The Three-Stage Least-Squares and Full Maximum Likelihood Estimates," *Econometrica*, vol. 32, pp. 77–81, 1964.

Zellner, A., and H. Theil: "Three-Stage Least-Squares: Simultaneous Estimation of Simultaneous Equations," *Econometrica*, vol. 30, pp. 54–78, 1962.

APPLICATIONS

Adleman, I., and F. L. Adleman: "The Dynamic Properties of the Klien-Goldberger Model," *Econometrica*, vol. 27, pp. 596–625, 1959.

Christ, C. F.: "Aggregate Econometric Models: A Review Article," *American Economic Review*, vol. 46, pp. 385–408, 1956.

Suits, D. B.: "Forecasting and Analysis with an Econometric Model," *American Economic Review*, vol. 52, pp. 104–132, 1962.

SUBJECT INDEX